(A) truly brilliant biography.

—John Kenneth Galbraith
THE CHICAGO TRIBUNE

(A) rousingly entertaining, marvelously well-written biography.

—William E. Leuchtenburg
THE NEW REPUBLIC

Beatty's book is a delight—rich, witty, flowing, and full of insight about the nature of political corruption.

—Constance Casey
LOS ANGELES TIMES

(A) panoramic, exquisitely incisive biography that illuminates the triumphs, debacles, and personal sorrows of the irrepressible man known as Boston's "Mayor of the Poor."

—Judy Bass
BOSTON HERALD

A thoughtful, colorful biography of the ultimate Irish-American pol.

—Robert Wilson
USA TODAY

To learn (how cities work as political organisms) it helps to turn to the history books, and Jack Beatty's The Rascal King *is a splendid place to start.*

—Timothy Noah
WALL STREET JOURNAL

This beautifully written, richly detailed, vibrant biography of James Michael Curley, should, if there is any justice, win a Pulitzer Prize.

—Robert Sherrill
CHICAGO SUN-TIMES

❖   ❖   ❖   ❖

Curley had charm, and even some virtues, and Jack Beatty's biography is alive to them all.
—Richard Brookhiser
THE NEW YORKER

As history, Jack Beatty's The Rascal King *compares well with such classics as Richard J. Whallen's* Founding Father: The Story of Joseph P. Kennedy *and William V. Shannon's* American Irish.
—Kevin Phillips
THE NEW YORK TIMES BOOK REVIEW

In The Rascal King, *Curley comes alive again, from his gilded speeches to his fist fights with rivals, to his bottomless bags of dirty tricks.*
—Timothy Dwyer
PHILADELPHIA INQUIRER

As Beatty so wonderfully observes in this wonderful book, here was "a hero to break your heart."
—Murray Kempton
THE NEW YORK REVIEW OF BOOKS

Beatty's graceful and deft writing, his gift for spinning stories, his intuitive grasp of politics, his feel for Curley's milieu, and his grasp of Curley's place in our public history make The Rascal King *an impressive literary and analytical achievement.*
—Mark Leccese
THE BOSTON PHOENIX

The Rascal King *is an exemplary political biography. It is thorough, balanced, reflective, and gracefully written.*
—Jonathan Yardley
THE HOUSTON POST

An enthralling new biography. . . . A gripping, often hilarious argument for campaign reform.
—Mary McGrory
THE WASHINGTON POST

Beatty's biography is a gripping narration of an important episode in American political history. . . . If you love politics, read this book this year if you read no other.
    —Lawrence J. Goodrich
    THE CHRISTIAN SCIENCE MONITOR

An eloquent and even-handed biography.
    —Janice Harayda
    CLEVELAND PLAIN DEALER

A bio that is as brilliant as it is bruising, as compelling as it is disturbing. Beatty's book should be short-listed for the big prizes.
    —Maureen Connelly
    IRISH ECHO

A finely honed depiction. . . . A work that will delight and astound the body politic.
    —Genevieve Stuttaford
    PUBLISHERS WEEKLY

Beatty relates this appalling and entertaining story well, with great sympathy for Curley's milieu and a good eye for telling detail and social nuance.
    —Rhoda Koenig
    NEW YORK

The Rascal King (is) a definitive account of the greatest of Boston's Irish-American political bosses. Beatty writes with a pre-postmodern devotion to narrative and factual accuracy.
    —Fred Siegel
    THE AMERICAN SPECTATOR

(A) hugely entertaining book.
    —Eugene Kennedy
    THE BOSTON SUNDAY GLOBE

The Rascal

KING

❖   ❖   ❖   ❖

*The town of Boston has a history. It is not an
accident, not a windmill, or a railroad station, or
cross-roads tavern, or an army barracks grown up
by time and luck to be a place of wealth; but a seat
of humanity, of men of principle, obeying sentiment
and marching loyally whither that should lead them;
so that its annals are great historical lines,
inextricably national. . . .*

RALPH WALDO EMERSON

*The first time I sat down with Ronald Reagan in the
White House, the President wanted to hear all about
James Michael Curley. . . . The same was true of
Jimmy Carter—and just about every other politician
I've ever known.*

THOMAS P. ("TIP") O'NEILL, JR.

*The three things that a Tammany leader most
dreaded were, in ascending order of repulsiveness,
the penitentiary, honest industry, and biography.*

EDWIN L. GODKIN

The Rascal

KING

The Life and Times of

JAMES MICHAEL CURLEY

1874–1958

❖   ❖   ❖   ❖

JACK BEATTY

DA CAPO PRESS

A CIP catalog record for this book is available from the Library of Congress.
ISBN 0-306-81002-6

First Da Capo Press Edition 2000

Grateful acknowledgment is made to the following for permission to reprint previously published material:

Macmillan Publishing Company: excerpts from "A Model for the Laureate" and "Cuchulain's Fight with the Sea" by William Butler Yeats. Copyright © 1940 by Georgie Yeats, renewed 1968, 1983 by Bertha Georgie Yeats, Michael Butler Yeats, and Anne Yeats. Reprinted from *The Poems of W.B. Yeats: A New Edition*, edited by Richard J. Finneran. By permission of Macmillan Publishing Company.

Interior photographs courtesy of the Rare Books Department, Dinand Library, The College of The Holy Cross, Worcester, Massachusetts.

Published by Da Capo Press
A Member of the Perseus Books Group
http://www.dacapopress.com

3 4 5 6 7 8 9 10——04

The Rascal

KING

The Life and Times of

JAMES MICHAEL CURLEY

1874–1958

❖　　❖　　❖　　❖

JACK BEATTY

DA CAPO PRESS

Copyright © 1992 by Jack Beatty

A CIP catalog record for this book is available from the Library of Congress.
ISBN 0-306-81002-6

First Da Capo Press Edition 2000

Grateful acknowledgment is made to the following for permission to reprint previously published material:

Macmillan Publishing Company: excerpts from "A Model for the Laureate" and "Cuchulain's Fight with the Sea" by William Butler Yeats. Copyright © 1940 by Georgie Yeats, renewed 1968, 1983 by Bertha Georgie Yeats, Michael Butler Yeats, and Anne Yeats. Reprinted from *The Poems of W.B. Yeats: A New Edition*, edited by Richard J. Finneran. By permission of Macmillan Publishing Company.

Interior photographs courtesy of the Rare Books Department, Dinand Library, The College of The Holy Cross, Worcester, Massachusetts.

Published by Da Capo Press
A Member of the Perseus Books Group
http://www.dacapopress.com

3   4   5   6   7   8   9   10——04

To the memory of my father, John J. Beatty,
1893–1982, of South Boston

and to my son, Aaron David Beatty

Contents

❖   ❖   ❖   ❖

Acknowledgments

❖   ❖   ❖   ❖

Two people first: William Whitworth, the editor in chief of the *Atlantic Monthly*, generously gave me time to research and write *The Rascal King*; but more, he offered me a daily example of the morality of the word, the belief that nothing matters more than to write clearly and truthfully, and without fear of the consequences. This is a better book for his example, as I am a better man.

Francis X. Curley, who died while *The Rascal King* was in production, started to write a life of his father some years ago, but lost his manuscript in a fire. His book would have been very special. Mr. Curley was a storyteller of rare gifts who possessed great humanistic learning in several languages and as many fields—literature, music, philosophy, theology, history. The past lived in him, and its memories were by no means all happy ones. His mother, Mary Emelda Curley, died when he was six; his older brothers and sisters fell away from him in cruel increments, two of them dying on the same day. Yet the sadness of the story he carried within him, the tragic history of the doomed house of Curley, made him seek relief in wit, and all who knew him relished his mordant merriment. In many hours of conversation, he provided me with details about his father that I could get nowhere else. In addition, he gave me the benefit of his insights into his father's character. He knew he would not agree with everything I wrote, but he wanted his father's story told inside and out, and he was willing to take a chance on me and my intention to render a true portrait. I could not have written this book without Frank Curley's cooperation. He became my friend, and how I wish he were still alive to give me one of his patented candid judgments on the fruits of his trust.

I would also like to thank the John Simon Guggenheim Memorial Foundation for providing me with a fellowship to complete my research. I was honored to receive the patronage of this distinguished institution. For helping me obtain that patronage, I warmly thank Thomas Winship, the gifted former editor of the *Boston Globe*, and chairman of the Center for Foreign Journalists; Christopher Lydon, of WGBH television in Boston, whose lamented "Ten O'Clock News" was a nightly triumph of imagination; Maureen Murphy, my editor at the *Los Angeles Times*, who helped to improve my style and refine my judgments of American politics; and Professor Thomas Brown, of the University of Massachusetts at Boston, whose wise counsel helped me, as it has better-known authors, see my subject in deeper perspective.

The dedicated staff at Holy Cross College, where the nearly six hundred volumes of the Curley scrapbooks can be found, assisted me in all sorts of ways—even by coming in on Sundays to let me into the archives. Mr. James Mahoney, the curator of the rare books collection and my office-mate for two years, by his infectious wit and high spirits lightened my burden immeasurably.

Jane Isay, former editorial director at Addison-Wesley, helped launch this project, bracing its author at shaky moments in its gestation. Thanks, Jane. William Patrick saw the book and author through to the end. An accomplished writer as well as an editor, Bill improved virtually every page of the manuscript. What he left undone, the copy editor, Rachel Parks (my mother's maiden name), completed with impressive skill. Special thanks, too, to John Fuller, Senior Production Coordinator at Addison-Wesley, who handled the challenge presented by my muddled habits with reassuring professionalism.

For their critical reading of the manuscript, I should also like to thank Thomas Mulvoy, Managing Editor for News Operations at the *Boston Globe*, who saved me from an embarrassing number of factual gaffes; David M. Kennedy, Chairman of the History Department at Stanford University and the author of *Over Here: The First World War and American Society*, among other books; Doris Kearns Goodwin, the author and historian whose book on the wartime lives of Franklin and Eleanor Roosevelt the reading world eagerly awaits; and James Carroll, the novelist, and a man of marked moral intelligence.

The notion that I should write a book at all originated with my wife, Lois Masor Beatty. When I did not believe in myself she believed in me, and for that, as well as for lending her artist's sensibility and fine editorial judgment—first to my thoughts, then to my sentences, and finally to my book—I have incurred a debt which I look forward to repaying throughout the rest of our lives.

Some boast of beggar-kings and kings
Of rascals black and white
That rule because a strong right arm
Puts all men in a fright.
W.B. YEATS, "A MODEL FOR THE LAUREATE"

❖ ❖ ❖ ❖

November 1958

❖   ❖   ❖   ❖

The true story of his contribution to the state will be known only when it is written in the light of the future.

GOVERNOR FOSTER FURCOLO
IN HIS PUBLIC STATEMENT ON THE DEATH OF JAMES M. CURLEY

A whole city marches past Trotsky's bier: the great die differently from the small.

GEORGE STEINER

❖   ❖   ❖   ❖

I t was the biggest wake the old city had ever seen: one hundred thousand mourners filed past the catafalque in the Hall of Flags in the State House. They came all through the day and into the night, and the tide of them lapped over to the next day. The biggest wake was followed by the biggest funeral. A crowd of one million, in the impeachable estimates of the police, lined the sidewalks to watch the hearse carrying James Michael Curley pass through the streets of the city he had led and to which he had given life and laughter, sorrow and scandal, for over fifty years. He had been their mayor four times, but he was more than that to them, more than the sum of his other offices, whether alderman or congressman or governor. For the Irish Americans among them, especially, he was a political and cultural hero, an axial figure in their annals. He had lived for them ("His triumph was their triumph," the *Boston Herald* noted in its obituary); he had been a cynosure of their hopes and fears, and now in a sense, he had died for them, freeing them for a new era, with new horizons and new heroes.[1]

The span of his life stretched from a time when the Boston Irish had been a rapidly multiplying but rejected minority to a time when one of them (technically: in reality, Senator John F. Kennedy was more Brookline than Boston and more Bronxville than either) was being introduced on local radio stations as "our next president." James Michael Curley had lived grandiloquently. The massive public funeral suited his style no less than his significance.

In the months before his final illness, the newspapers had kept up a death watch on Curley's house. Sightings of a florist in the vicinity would prompt bluntly inquisitive calls from reporters.

Without salutation, without greeting, the old man would pick up the phone, growl in his unmistakable baritone, "Yes, I'm still alive," and hang up. News of his hospitalization, surgery, recovery, brief convalescence, and swift decline occupied the front pages for a week. His death and funeral captured and held the headlines for four more days. Only the Kennedy assassination, five Novembers later, would surpass that record.[2]

Boston's heroes and Boston's martyrs, Curley and Kennedy and their star-crossed families, enacted a cautionary parable about the price of fame, the levy of fate on good fortune. The Catholic faith accustoms its adherents to frame experience in such parables—which are in their way political, in as much as contemplating the sufferings of the rich reconciles the poor to their poverty—and to see afflictions as tests of faith. James Michael Curley had suffered faith-challenging afflictions in the deaths of his first wife and seven of his nine children. And he had suffered them in public, where flinching can be seen, despair witnessed. Yet, in a proof of the power of faith that amounted to a kind of existential service to his constituents—a municipal cleanup campaign in the higher numbered wards of the spirit—he had not despaired. He died believing in a Catholic God Who had tried him sorely. That he could still believe tended to vindicate belief. The thousands filing past his casket and lining the streets for a final look at James Michael Curley were thus responding to impulses as much spiritual as political in kind. His death was an event in the civil religion of Boston just as John F. Kennedy's was to be in that of the United States.

But this was the end of an old pol, the last of the big-city bosses, not the murder of a young president, and for days the papers printed anecdotes testifying to Curley's roguery and wit.

There was the one about the time he ushered a young man in to see Governor Paul Dever.

"Governor, this young man is the son of an old and very dear friend of mine, now deceased. I promised him on his deathbed that I would look out for the boy. He needs a job, and I would appreciate it if you could find a place for him in the state service."

Dever replied that he would do what he could, depending on the young man's abilities.

"What's his name?" he asked.

"Young man," Curley inquired, "what is your name?"

There was the ritual of the cigars. "Frank, get the cigars," Curley would tell his secretary when he had a visitor in his office he wanted to impress. Frank would go over to his desk, reach into the bottom left-hand drawer, remove a box of cigars and ceremoniously pass it to the guest. "No, no, Frank," Curley would say, "the good ones, Frank, the good ones." Frank would feign embarrassment. "I'm sorry, Governor, I forgot." He would then close the box of cigars, return to his desk, and take out another box which was, of course, identical to the first one.

There was his quip following the collapse of an approach ramp to an overpass built by one of his pet contractors: the ramp was, he said, composed of an "injudicious mixture of sand and cement."

There was the one about his plan to rid Boston of the British.

During the First World War a wounded British officer was sent to these shores on a recruiting drive. Arrived in Boston, he asked the greenest mayor in America permission to sign up a battalion of soldiers from among persons of British nationality living in the city.

"Go ahead, Colonel," Curley replied, beaming. "Take every damn one of them."

There was the one of more recent vintage that caught his endearing remoteness from mid-twentieth-century fads.

Riding with his chauffeur through the South End in one of his last campaigns, he looked at the signs that seemed to be everywhere. "Who is this fellow 'Pizza'?" he asked. Properly informed, Curley remarked, "Oh, I thought he was like Howard Johnson. I figured we might get a contribution out of him."

There was his comeback to a man, not known to be among his supporters, who had congratulated him ("I think you'll be a great Governor") on his greatest victory. "Very nice of you to say that, Bill," he replied. "Do say it behind my back someday."

And surely his one-liner on Herbert Hoover belongs in *Bartlett's*: "If we have another era of Hoover, Gandhi will be the best-dressed man in America."

"As of now," the *Boston Globe* noted in its obituary, "it is difficult to imagine a time when Boston will cease recalling stories about him." That time has not yet come.[3]

James Michael Curley is preserved in set-piece stories that float free of context and history, and often plausibility, the way yarns about "characters" often do. In fact Curley had achieved the status of a fictional "character" two years before his death: Mayor Frank Skeffington in Edwin O'Connor's best-selling novel *The Last Hurrah*, which gave a cliché to a still-grateful world, was widely taken to have been based on Curley. When the *Globe*, in an inspired whimsy, sent the novel to Curley for review, he returned it with a note hinting that he was considering a libel action against O'Connor. As O'Connor later described the episode to his friend Arthur Schlesinger, Jr., for some weeks "threats of lawsuits were coming regularly from the house on the Jamaicaway, all filtered through a succession of middlemen whose appearance, to put it mildly, did not inspire trust." Leaving the Parker House (site today of a bar called, inevitably, The Last Hurrah) a month after the book's publication, O'Connor spotted Curley getting into a cab. Tempted to brave the old man's wrath, he stuck his head in the window and introduced himself. There was a pause; then Curley laughed and held out his hand.

"Well, well. Nice to see you. You've written quite a book. I like that book."

O'Connor allowed as how that was a surprise to him, given the threats of litigation that had lately filled the air.

"No, no," Curley said, dismissing all such talk with a wave. "That's a fine book. I enjoyed it. Do you know the part I enjoyed the most?"

"No," O'Connor said.

"The part where I die," Curley replied.[4]

The part where he died, even as he died, was bringing tears to the eyes of the audience at the Loew's Orpheum Theater, where the film version of *The Last Hurrah* was being held over for a fourth week. IT COULD HAPPEN ANYWHERE, read the teaser in the newspaper ads below the illustration of Spencer Tracy as Skeffington, INCLUDING OUR FAIR CITY OF BOSTON. The ad's coyness was a tactic on the part of Columbia Pictures, the maker of the film, a poke in the community ribs meant to play off a recent controversy. Refusing to attend an advance private showing, Curley had sought an injunction to prevent *The Last Hurrah* from opening. It was, he charged, an invasion of his privacy. It tended (clearly he had not seen the film, a sentimental hagiography) to degrade and ridicule him. Finally, he had valuable property rights, presumably the spoor of his reputation, in it. Skeffington, he maintained, was "a pale and distorted carbon copy of myself."

Columbia countered that it had paid Curley $25,000 for signing a release before the movie was filmed, producing a document to prove it. Curley insisted that the signature was a forgery. Before that question could be adjudicated, the two sides reached an out-of-court settlement, which is to say that Columbia paid Curley another $15,000. Had Curley pocketed the $25,000, or had someone claiming to act for him forged his signature on the release and made off with the money? Curley's version has the transparency of a story concocted to save face. What was another $15,000 to a big Hollywood studio? At the last minute, with the picture about to have its world premiere in his own city, the eighty-three-year-old Curley had apparently decided to do to Columbia what he had done to Boston contractors for generations—squeeze them for a little something extra. He would be dead in two months. This was his last hurrah.[5]

❖   ❖   ❖

Black bunting hung on City Hall for the first time in fifty-three years: in 1905 Patrick Collins, President Cleveland's former envoy to Great Britain and Boston's second Irish-born mayor, had been accorded the same funerary honors. The years 1905 and 1958 bracketed an epoch: the death of Mayor Collins had begun the era of ethnic politics in Boston; now, with Curley's death, that era was finally over, though its knell had clearly sounded in 1949, when Curley was voted out of office for the last time. Collins had practiced a politics of coalition with the city's then-powerful Yankee Protestant Democrats. Forged a decade and more before by Patrick Maguire, Boston's only true Democratic "boss," this alliance was sometimes spoken of as one between "Harvard College and the slums," and through the 1880s and part of the 1890s it worked. Boston elected mainly Democratic mayors, and the ethnic issue between Irish Catholics and Yankee Protestants remained dormant, a fact of class and culture but not yet of politics.[6]

In 1876 Patrick Collins, then the first Irishman ever elected to the Massachusetts state Senate, gave memorable utterance to his views about the place of ethnic and religious differences in politics. Speaking on behalf of the gubernatorial candidacy of the Brahmin grandee Charles Francis Adams, he said: "I denounce any man or body of men who seek to perpetuate divisions of races or religions in our midst. . . . I love the land of my birth but in American politics I know neither race, nor color, nor creed. Let me say that there are no Irish voters among us. There are Irish-born citizens . . . but the moment the seal of the court was impressed on our papers we ceased to be foreigners and became Americans."

Patrick Collins had lived as nobly as he spoke; no scandal ever tarnished his name. President Eliot of Harvard led the movement to raise a statue to him. Yet it was said that he died an unhappy man, seeing in the activities of a young alderman from Roxbury a vision of the future of Boston politics that left him heartsick. What he had sensed in the rhetoric and public conduct of Alderman James Michael Curley was the death of his coalition politics, the breakup of the alliance between Harvard and the slums, the end of harmony between the two leading ethnic groups in Boston and the birth of a politics of ethnic and religious polarization led by a man who would strain the comity of the city to forward his ambitions.[7]

Patrick Collins was far from the minds of those who walked past City Hall on November 12, 1958, the day Curley died. Yet Collins's spirit was invoked in a candid editorial comment on the career as opposed to the unanimously beloved "personality" of James Michael Curley. "For many years," the *Christian Science Monitor* wrote, "Mr. Curley was one of the most controversial political figures in the United States. Even his most bitter opponents recognized that he was a man of exceptional political ability. . . . On the other hand, it was often said that, had he used his abilities in other ways, he might have made a far greater contribution to American life." Those abilities included rare oratorical gifts. ("His voice," Nat Hentoff, an authority on jazz who heard Curley up close, writes, "was a continuous astonishment. It was a vintage pipe organ and, like Buddy Bolden's horn, could call in the voters from all the wards.") He had a capacity to project an infectious enjoyment of the fun and fakery of politics, a penchant for warming the abstract workings of government such that ordinary people felt it was on their side, and a habit of being indomitable—of not giving up in the face of political defeats and personal desolations. Could he have "made a far greater contribution to American life" with these endowments of talent, intellect, and character? His contemporaries raised that question about him at every stage of his fifty-year career. This was a tribute to his abilities; but it was also a reflection on the gap between them and his accomplishments. His wake and funeral—"a spectacle unparalleled in the Bay State's 300 year history," the *Monitor* noted—proved beyond cavil that he had done at least one extraordinary thing with them: he had won the hearts of thousands, had become the object of the easy, incurious affection accorded those aged symbolic figures who inherit the authority of the past stripped of their responsibility for it. Though he had wrought this achievement through politics, it was in a sense beyond politics. The politician had become a legend; the man had become a myth.

Governor Foster Furcolo honored the legend by turning the State House into a funeral parlor for James Michael Curley. In the general election just the week before, the Massachusetts Democracy had swept every state constitutional office ("We're one ahead now," Curley had remarked as he cast a physical disability ballot from his hospital bed). For the first time in history, both houses of the legislature were in Democratic hands. Curley may have been the state's most controversial governor; his term, 1935–37, may have been a disaster mitigated only by moments of farce. He may have been compared to Caligula, Nero, James II, George III, Huey Long, Mussolini, even Hitler. But it would have taken a churlish Republican indeed to bring any of that up now. He would in any case have been ignored. Politically dominant, the Democrats would honor their old battler in their own way. Throughout his later career, if you wanted to get James Michael Curley's attention you called him "Governor," even if he was mayor of Boston at the time. It was the title he preferred. In waking him at the State House, not at City Hall, the party was respecting his preference.[8]

Just off the Hall of Flags at the State House, where the body was to lie in state, were the offices of John F. Kennedy. In a thoughtful gesture, Kennedy made these available to the Curley family as a place to rest from the rigors of greeting half the city. Having just received 1,137,569 votes in his reelection bid, Kennedy had reason to be in a generous mood. Four years earlier he had been an obscure stockroom clerk. Since then, having withstood a primary challenge from a John M. Kennedy in 1956, he had parlayed the nimbus surrounding his name into the Commonwealth's fourth highest office—Treasurer and Receiver General. There was even talk of his running for governor in 1960; Senator John F. Kennedy, should he be at the top of the ticket, might just pull his namesake in.

Curley, who had once shared a state ticket with a Charles F., a Charles M., and a Joseph L. Hurley, must have taken wry satisfaction from Treasurer Kennedy's rise on the zephyr of his name. Respectful of individuals, Curley had a low opinion of voters. He well

understood the forces—fear, prejudice, the struggle for existence
in a competitive economy—that kept the personal goodness of individual men and women from being reflected in a good society.
Something happened to that personal goodness in the medium—
politics—connecting the individual with society. There was a conflict of essence between the personal and the political. He lived it
out himself. A faithful husband, a caring father, a practicing Catholic: by any measure he had been a "good" man. But from first to
last, crimes and scandals had marked his life in politics. He was not
the only politician in American history to have been reelected from
jail, but he was surely alone in having twice been in jail while in
office, at either end of his career, a parenthesis of disgrace. Politics
brought out the worst in him just as it brought out the worst in the
people. Otherwise intelligent and personally upright men and
women too often voted their ignorance—when, that is, they did
not vote their resentment.[9]

This general proposition about politics had special application
to the brand practiced in Boston and Massachusetts. Boston was
home to the most influential upper class in American history, the
Brahmins of Beacon Hill and the Back Bay. These "sifted few," in
Oliver Wendell Holmes's phrase, had power over city and state out
of all proportion to their numbers. Long after they ceased to count
politically, they weighed on the psyche of aspirant groups, making
the hope of rising seem futile and intimidating the rare instances of
immigrant wealth with the scepter of good taste. They controlled
the citadels of culture—to the Irish, as Upton Sinclair wrote in his
novel *Boston*, "a far-off mysterious thing, but awe-inspiring, like
the power of a voodoo magician." They manned the redoubts of
finance. And their wealth and position made them passionately resented not only by the Irish, who from the 1880s on were the majority in Boston, but also by enterprising Yankee merchants like
William Dean Howells's Silas Lapham, who could buy a house on
Beacon Street but not the neighborhood's gentility. It wasn't for
sale. "When are the nice people of Boston going to accept us?"
Rose Kennedy once asked a well-born Harvard friend of her sons'.
The answer was only after her son had trumped social snobbery
with political achievement.[10]

The democracy of the dollar could not bring down the
Brahmins. Neither could the democracy of the ballot. They were
an unassailable caste; hence the appellation "Brahmin." Curley

might mock their ancestors as slave traders and pirates, and so many of them were. But however they got their power, however many crimes lay at the bottom of their family trusts, the fact of it was maddening, and it fed political anger with the fury of impotence. Looking back on the nineteenth century, Henry Adams wrote, "Politics, as a practice, whatever its professions, had always been the systematic organization of hatreds, and Massachusetts politics had been as harsh as the climate." In the twentieth century, as James Michael Curley's career was to prove, the passions of Massachusetts politics would not be spent."

Short of outright hatred, upper-class Protestants were divided from working-class Irish Catholics by fundamentally different conceptions of the ends of politics. The former saw politics, to quote Richard Hofstadter, as "an arena for the realization of moral principles of broad application—and even, as in the case of temperance and vice crusades—for the correction of private habits." To them the role of Government was to set neutral standards of justice and procedure in its pursuit of the general interest. The latter believed in what the historian Thomas H. O'Connor calls "the personal politics of help and succor." To them government was about jobs, and neutral justice be damned.¹²

An archetypal Boston story illustrates the resulting clash of political cultures.

A Beacon Hill lady once went ringing doorbells in Irish South Boston on behalf of a high-minded candidate for the School Committee. At one house, an Irish housewife listened politely to the lady's pitch for her paladin, and then asked, "But doesn't he have a sister who works for the schools or who has something to do with the school system?" The Beacon Hill lady was shocked at what she took to be a suggestion of patronage. "I assure you, madam," she replied, "he is not the kind of man who would ever use his position to advance the interests of his sister!" To which the South Boston housewife responded, "Well, if the son-of-a-bitch won't help his own sister, why should I vote for him?" There spoke a Curley voter.¹³

The Beacon Hill lady, though, may have had the last laugh. Through their ideological and financial sway over the Boston press, her sort set the terms of political discussion. They did not regard the Irish view of politics as a rival legitimate ideal, but as a formula for boodle, and denied it and those who espoused it any claim to legitimacy. Curley was to make his stormy way against a fearful tide of respectability.

❖   ❖   ❖

At the State House on that November day, the first person in line to view the body was a Republican, Vincent J. Celeste, of East Boston. Celeste had a redoubtable distinction. The week before he had been the Republican nominee for the U. S. Senate seat held by the other John F. Kennedy, and had lost by over eight hundred thousand votes, a record drubbing ("We didn't reach the housewife, the man in the street," he explained). As for the senator himself, he was in Los Angeles to attend the christening of little Victoria Frances Lawford, the daughter of his sister Patricia and the actor Peter Lawford. For longer than John Kennedy had been alive, his family had been locked in a feud with James Michael Curley. His grandfather, John F. Fitzgerald, and his mother, Rose Kennedy, both knew Curley as a man who would stop at nothing to get what he wanted, including political blackmail over Fitzgerald's dalliance with a young woman his daughter's age. When his time came, John Fitzgerald Kennedy upheld his family's part in what amounted to a vendetta between Boston's two most prominent Irish families.

Behind Celeste came the governor and the members of the Governor's Council, two hundred members of the state legislature, and the mayor of Boston, John B. Hynes. Curley's former secretary and the man who ended his career by defeating him three times for mayor, Hynes would weep openly at Curley's funeral Mass at the Cathedral of the Holy Cross. But from 1:00 P.M., when the body went on view, these notables were overwhelmed in the line by ordinary people. "None was young," one reporter noted.

As the afternoon drew on, their numbers increased, the lines first extending down the long steps of the State House, then down Beacon Street, pushing in one direction toward School Street and City Hall and in another toward the residential district of Beacon Hill, whose mostly wealthy Protestant inhabitants had always regarded Mayor Curley as a civic embarrassment, a revenge inflicted on them by the Irish for the cruelty and callousness and reproductive funk of their ancestors. Watching the people from Curley's Boston, not the red-brick Protestant city of Beacon Hill and the

Back Bay but the wooden three-decker Catholic city that lay beyond, in Roxbury and Brighton and South Boston and Dorchester, villages that had been annexed by the old seaport in the nineteenth century and that had changed its political destiny—watching people from these distant neighborhoods waiting patiently in the November twilight, a television cameraman, a New Yorker, was heard to speak cynically of how Curley had gulled the Boston Irish for fifty years and grown rich off their credulity. A prominent local lawyer confronted the cameraman. "Have you ever been hungry?" he asked. "Have you ever really wanted for anything? Of course not. Well, until you experience hunger or want, and someone willingly helps you, you'll never understand why these people are here."

"He was a saint and a sinner," a businessman in the line remarked. "He got me my first job," said a red-faced man. Approaching Curley's body, a man in a shiny blue suit murmured, "I'm sorry, Jim, so sorry." A tiny old woman handed one of Curley's surviving sons a bouquet of five white carnations in a water-filled milk bottle. "I knew your father when I was young," she said, and then moved past the catafalque, through the Hall of Flags, and back into the Boston night.

Looming above the throng outside was the floodlit golden dome of the State House. Once the highest point in Boston and still among the most arresting features of the city's skyline, the great dome had received its coat of gilt in 1874—the year of James Michael Curley's birth. The threads of his life were all drawing together there under the golden dome.

His mother Sarah was there in the seamed faces of the State House scrubwomen, who came by in a body at 2:45 A.M. to say tearful prayers over "Jim." Lincoln freed the slaves; Curley got the scrubwomen off their knees. It was his defining humanitarian gesture: before Curley was mayor, the cleaning women had had to scrub the marble floors of City Hall on their knees. Declaring that a woman should go down on her knees only when praying to God, Curley got them long-handled mops. And not only that. According to one of the matrons seeing him off under the golden dome that night, "It was him who did away with calling us scrubwomen, getting us called matrons and cleaners and putting us on the civil service," laying a proper emphasis on Curley's understanding of the gain in dignity represented by the change in titles.

The emancipation of the scrubwomen left no trace on the public record. No headlines proclaimed, CURLEY SAYS "LET THERE BE MOPS." Yet, though Bostonians still remember scores of "Curley stories," this is the sole act of his still alive in common memory. His mother had been a scrubwoman—had scuttled like a crab over the implacable floors of the Immaculate Conception Church in the South End, her knees growing callused from the grind. James Michael Curley never forgot her rough knees; in delirium just before his death, he was overheard chastising the old priest at Immaculate Conception for them. He could not raise his mother off her knees when he was a child. But when he had the power he remembered her, and he got those women off their knees.

That was the main thread in Curley's public life: doing little things for little people who repaid him in votes and gratitude, and who as the years went by and they tasted something of the world's indifference, magnified manifold the value of the little thing Curley had done for them, their parents, or their friends until it became a big thing—the stern lecture that made a husband swear off drink, the job that saved a family, the gift of a turkey with all the trimmings that brought joy to a dreary Christmas. But there were also other threads in the human tapestry coming together under the golden dome.

A man from Curley's nineteenth-century childhood in Roxbury was there; he and Curley used to fetch buckets of water together from the pump in the local park (the Curley house had no bathtub). The aged Dr. Delbert Moyer Staley, the founder of the Staley College of the Spoken Word, was there. Staley had helped transform Curley from a rough bravo of the ward who had left school after the ninth grade into a compelling public speaker capable of turning a hostile audience, and of moving grown men and women to wonder and tears.

A deputation from the locally famous L Street Brownies was there. This year-round South Boston swimming club still used the handsome bathhouse Curley had built on Carson Beach in his third term, as so many residents of the city's neighborhoods still used the parks, playgrounds, schools, and other public buildings he had built for them, and from which, as everyone knew, he had derived a fortune in kickbacks from contractors.

The legendary John ("Up-Up") Kelly was there. As Governor Curley's barker, it was his job to urge audiences to their feet just as the governor arrived. "Up, up, for the governor," he would shout.

"Up, up, for the governor!" Once the governor had accepted an invitation to speak, via a sign language interpreter, to a deaf audience. But no one had told Up-Up.

"All up for the governor!" he commanded. They didn't move.

"What's the matter with these people?" he asked Curley. "Are they all deaf?"

"Yes, John," replied Curley, "they are."

Of course, the second Mrs. Curley, Gertrude Casey Dennis Curley, was there. She and James had been married on his last day as governor. Massachusetts tradition called for the retiring governor to walk alone down the steps of the State House, cross Beacon Street, and in a poignant symbol of democracy, merge with the milling crowd on Boston Common. Curley would have none of this merging—he was *from* the people, not of them. He left the State House in his wedding clothes and, instead of making the lonely walk across the Common, went no farther than Beacon Street, where his glamorous bride was waiting for him in a new green limousine. Amid shouts and cheers, they set off on their honeymoon.

His daughter Mary's ex-husband was there. Mary had been a public figure in her own right—the first lady of Massachusetts during the governor's term, when he was still a widower. Her wedding to a dashing, handsome, and wealthy military aide-de-camp of her father's was a lavish affair. The newspapers had relished every detail, from the tons of lobster thermidor served up to the two thousand guests to the mahogany bookends sent by President and Mrs. Roosevelt. The glittering wedding, however, was cruelly at variance with the subsequent marriage. The couple had no children and were divorced within a few years.

After the collapse of her marriage, Mary talked seriously about running for office. Charming, intelligent, well spoken, the family liberal, she would have made a good congresswoman. But her father, who after losing races for senator, governor, and mayor had finally won a seat in Congress himself, would have none of it; he feared being shown up in debate by his own daughter, whose forensic lash he had felt too often around the dinner table. Thereafter, Mary turned to drink. In February 1950, while talking on the phone in the bedroom of her Beacon Street apartment, she suffered a cerebral hemorrhage and died on the spot. She was forty-one. Later that same day, talking from the same phone in the same room, her brother Leo also had a cerebral hemorrhage. He died in the same spot. He was thirty-four. Their deaths bonded the city in grief to James Michael Curley, who stood for fourteen hours in the great hall of his house greeting each one of the thousands who came to pray over the bodies of his children and to offer him such comfort as words could give.

The threads of his life, and those of his second life, in fiction, too. For Edwin O'Connor was also there under the golden dome. The next day the local Hearst tabloid featured a front-page picture of him looking at the dead man in the catafalque. EPILOGUE TO LAST HURRAH, reads the headline. Already the literary version of Curley was eclipsing the Curley who belonged to history.

The photograph shows a shocking lot of Curley; it's rare to see the face of a well-known corpse blown up across the front page of a newspaper. He looks dead but also, as one of O'Connor's wake-going old women might say, younger than his years. His hair is thick: silver on top, dark on the sides. His features—the flaring nose, the trumpet ears, the strong jaw—are senatorial. In looks he recalls W. C. Fields and Lionel Barrymore, whom he sounded like, and Sidney Greenstreet, whom he was shaped like. He was a big man, six feet and well over two hundred pounds, before illness gaunted him, and the photograph manages to suggest his bulk in the days when he decked a three-hundred-pound man in the Parker House bar. He is wearing a formal cutaway coat, a gray striped tie, and a diamond stickpin; this friend of the common man always dressed like a squire. Pinned to his chest are three decorations he received in the First World War, way back in his first term, when he was one of the youngest mayors in Boston's history; they were awarded him by the French, Italian, and Serbian governments for the work his leathern lungs performed for the Allied cause. The photograph doesn't show it, but wrapped around the fingers of his left hand is a set of rosary beads. The scores of political opponents he had slandered, vilified, blackmailed, bribed, and bullied over the years would not have believed it, but Curley said his prayers on his knees beside his bed every night, with the simple piety of a child. And, a final thread joining the ends of his life, he is wearing his father's wedding ring.[14]

The Shin
of a
Sparrow

✦   ✦   ✦   ✦

Of those who resort to cities to better their condition but a very few succeed in obtaining wealth or other reputable distinction. Most of them . . . very soon sink down under the weight of care, labor and misfortune, and perish and are forgotten.

JESSE CHICKERING,
IN A CITY OF BOSTON
STATISTICAL REPORT, 1851

Anyhow I was received with open arms that sometimes ended in a clinch. I was afraid I wasn't goin to assimilate with the airlyer pilgrim fathers, but before I was here a month I felt enough like a native born American to burn a witch.

MR. DOOLEY

Grievance is too heavy a burden to bear. You have to turn around and look back to pick it up. And then, when you're carrying it, you can't go forward.

JESSE JACKSON

❖   ❖   ❖   ❖

Michael Curley came to America at age fourteen; he married at twenty-one; he died at thirty-four. "No obituary marked his death," one historian writes, "and not even a death notice appeared in the Boston newspapers. Michael Curley had arrived in Boston unnoticed, worked in Boston unnoticed, died in Boston unnoticed." He bequeathed to his son a wedding ring and, in his unseasonal death, the shared privation of the leading Irish-American politicians of his era. For Martin Lomasney, the longtime boss of Boston's West End; John F. Fitzgerald, Boston's mayor and John F. Kennedy's grandfather; David I. Walsh, Massachusetts' first Catholic governor and senator; Al Smith, the New York governor and Democratic presidential candidate; and the slightly younger John W. McCormack, the Boston congressman and Speaker of the House—all these men, each of whom would figure centrally in the different chapters of Curley's life, lost their fathers when they were between the ages of ten (Curley) and fourteen (Fitzgerald). Their fathers worked themselves to death; they died from the way they were obliged to live.[1]

Michael Curley was born on a small family farm in County Galway in the west of Ireland in 1850, a year too late for the Great Potato Famine of 1845–49. But of the thirty-two counties of Ireland, Galway had the second highest excess death rate through those years—"in the west whole families walled themselves into their cabins and died"—and the memory of what many Irish regard as the first genocide in modern times must have been passed on to him with his mother's milk.

That memory was one of cosmic insecurity. The Irish had depended on the potato for everything. ("It enabled subsistence on a tiny holding," one authority writes, "providing food for nine months of the year; it sustained early and fecund marriages. It was also miraculously prolific and nutritious: the only single cheap food that can support life as a sole diet, according to recent nutritive research.") And the potato, fungus-struck, had failed the Irish utterly. For children of the Famine like Michael Curley, the scale of life contracted fearfully. There was no thought of "getting ahead," even if there had been the possibility. Eating regularly filled the horizon of desire. Eighty and more years later, Irish-American fathers, before saying grace at the evening meal, would declare to the bewilderment of their youngest children, "So long as there's meat on the shin of a sparrow, we'll eat in this house." This would be said with a wink at the wife, but the Famine joke would serve to introduce the Famine measure as the children pondered the quantity of meat to be found on a sparrow's shin.[2]

Besides insecurity, the Famine imbued those who fled it to come to America with a bone-deep distrust of the free-market economy and its justifying doctrine. Ireland's British rulers had not caused the Famine, but, as a consequence of their laissez-faire ideology, they did little to relieve the distress it brought, fearing that the moral fiber of the eight million starving Irish would be destroyed if Her Majesty's government bestirred itself to feed them. The idea was to let them die morally intact, so to speak. "Demands from some localities for a 'dole' to keep people working on their farms were defined by Sir Charles Trevelyan"—who oversaw Irish relief during the Famine—as "the masterpiece of that system of social economy according to which the machine of society should be worked backwards, and the government should be made to support the people, instead of the people the government." In America, the Irish would stand Trevelyan on his head. That the government—through works, not welfare—"should be made to support the people, instead of the people the government" would be not only their credo but their gift to American public policy. Michael Curley need never have spoken of politics to his son for the boy to have learned this lesson; it was the reflection in political theory of what the Irish had suffered in political fact.[3]

In the late 1840s, when as many as fifteen thousand Irish came to America in a single year, hunger drove the emigration. By the 1860s, the motive had changed. Now what made younger sons like Michael Curley uproot themselves from their country was the need to preserve the family farm as a viable economic unit. The Irish smallholders had long since adopted the "stem family" system of inheritance, under which the oldest son stood to inherit the whole of the property while his younger siblings were urged to emigrate as they came of age. Having just emerged from a "Malthusian apocalypse," the Irish harbored few illusions about the land's capacity to support a surplus population. The land was not divided; the family was.[4]

Michael, along with his two half-brothers Daniel and Patrick, arrived in Boston in 1864, in the midst of the Civil War. If Michael had been older, he might have enlisted in the Union army (immigrants were generally not liable for conscription) or hired himself out as a substitute to take the place of a native draftee. Because he was small, about five feet five inches tall, faking his age was out of the question. Until he could make his own way he would board with friends in Roxbury, then not yet part of Boston, where a colony of Galway émigrés had settled just beyond the mud flats of the South Bay.[5]

Michael could not have known it, but the Civil War was changing the social contract of Boston. In place of the open conflict of the forties and fifties, his generation of Irish immigrants would experience a new relationship with the Protestant establishment of Boston. One scholar calls it "deference democracy," a system under which Irish voters elected Yankee mayors and received tokenist patronage in return. To enjoy even these meager benefits of cooperation, however, the Irish had to forget a good· deal of fresh history—and not just the odd convent burning by liquored-up Protestant mobs, but official government persecution. Social amnesia cannot long be willed, however, and there would come a time when the Irish would remember. The instrument of their remembrance would be James Michael Curley, who would reach back beyond his father's generation to reclaim for politics the ethnic bitterness stemming from the events of the fifties that had been kept out of politics for decades. The bitterness would be preserved in the political unconscious of the Boston Irish. It would be what lent them the sullen psychology of an aggrieved minority long after they had become a majority. It would be the burden of grievance that Curley's generation, under his leadership, would, in Jesse Jackson's words, "look back to pick up," and that would prevent them from going forward.[6]

The Irish did not flourish in Boston. For the longest time they did not show the kind of economic advance, from one generation to the next, that most Americans took for granted, until a host of factors—the relative economic decline of America, the new division of labor wrought by the international economy, the decline in union membership, the high cost of housing, the favor-the-rich tax policies pursued by Republican presidents and Democratic Congresses in the 1980s—dashed that social hope, making the experience of historically anomalous groups like the Boston Irish seem resonant, perhaps, of a politics to come in America. Trapped in a declining economy, the Boston Irish needed scapegoats. And they would have them: James Michael Curley would see to that.*

Michael Curley was born too late for the Famine. He arrived in Massachusetts too late for the anti-Irish upsurge of the 1850s. Yet these events in the anteroom of his life, particularly the latter events, would profoundly shape the character and career of his son. The charismatic leader sculpts in the passionate clay of collective emotion. To know the leader, we must first know something of the led.

✦   ✦   ✦

Prior to the Civil War, the Irish had been a lump—"undigested, indigestible," in Oscar Handlin's words—in the throat of a city that had not asked them to come, and that regarded them as the human equivalent of locusts. Boston had been a clean and salubrious place before the arrival of the "Famine Irish"; now it was dirty and noisome. Boston had been a unified moral community; now it was divided. Boston had stood for progress in religion and politics; now it was home to a reactionary religion whose official organ, *The Pilot*, called the sacred cause of abolition "niggerology" and Lincoln a "boob."[7]

It was the suddenness of their coming as much as the sheer engulfing fact of it that so upset the social equilibrium. During the

---

* In *The Other Bostonians: Poverty and Progress in the American Metropolis, 1880-1970* (Cambridge, Mass., 1973); a quantitative study debunking the Horatio Alger version of success in America, Stephan Thernstrom notes: "The dramatic tendency of Catholic youths who had begun their careers in nonmanual jobs was to lose those jobs and to end their lives wearing a blue rather than a white collar, with all that this shift implied for wage levels, employment security, and social prestige." He goes on to speak of "the Catholic propensity for high downward mobility," and to demonstrate that thesis with heart-breaking demographic statistics (p. 152).

entire year of 1840 fewer than 4,000 Irish arrived in Boston, whereas on the single day April 10, 1847, more than 1,000 debarked. By 1850 the number of Irish had risen to 35,000 in a total population of 136,900. On arriving in Boston earlier immigrants, Germans and Scandinavians, had been warned: "Go farther west; not until you reach Koshknonong (Wisconsin) will you find America." America was land and space. Boston had neither. Pinched by the sea on one side, girded by a broad river on the other, it was a tiny enclave of a few square miles. Boston was not America in another respect: it lacked opportunity. Boston's capital typically built great industries in distant locations, not at home. So why did the Irish come to such an unpromising place? And, having come, why did they remain?[8]

They came because in 1841 Her Majesty's government decided that the best way to get mail to Canada was through the port of Boston. Cunard Lines, which was subsidized by the British government to maintain contact with the colonies, was asked to set up a terminal there in 1842. Other British lines followed. Thus the link had already been made when the Famine terribly forced the pace of Irish emigration.[9]

The mail kept going; the people stopped in Boston, Canada not being a politically acceptable destination for the Irish. "The native Irishman had become convinced," Cecil Woodham Smith writes, "that no justice or opportunity could exist for him under the Union Jack, and he shrank from the British North American colonies." As for the United States, it was far more to the Irish than the end of the line. "The Irishman looks upon America," wrote Thomas Grattan, the Irish statesman, "as the refuge of his race, the home of his kindred, the heritage of his children and their children. . . . The shores of England are farther off in his heart's geography than those of Massachusetts or New York."[10]

Happenstance and hope, then, conspired to land the Irish in Boston. They stayed because they could not afford to move on, having come with nothing but their lives. "Unable to find employment or transportation elsewhere," an 1848 report for the Benevolent Fraternity of Churches found, "without one penny in store, the question, how should they live, was more easily put than solved." Piled up in "rookeries" along the Boston waterfront, the Irish bred children who, a census taker wrote, were "literally born to die." They also bred disease. Smallpox, eradicated from the city years before, returned, as did cholera; and tuberculosis thrived.[11]

They looked about them. Much in this new city was not in their heart's geography.

It was a city where proper aunts policed the family library, blacking out the erotic lines in Byron and Shelley. It was a city of formidable literacy; in 1848 Boston published no fewer than 120 periodicals with a total circulation of over half a million. It was a city of sages venerated throughout the country. William Dean Howells liked to tell a story that illustrates the reach of their fame. Returning from Boston to his native Ohio in the mid-1860s, Howells stopped overnight in the small town of Hiram, where he met Congressman James A. Garfield and began to talk of his friends among the immortals of Boston, Cambridge, and Concord. Before he could fairly get under way, Garfield interrupted him. "He ran down the grassy space," Howells remembered, "first to one fence and then to the other at the sides, and waved a wild arm of invitation to the neighbors who were sitting on their back porches. 'Come over here!' he shouted. 'He's telling of Holmes and Longfellow and Lowell and Whittier!' and at his bidding dim forms began to mount the fences and follow him up to the veranda." Boston was a city run by and for graduates of Harvard—"the seminary and academy for the inner circle of Bostonians," as George Santayana labeled it years later. In 1850 nearly half of its richest residents, half of its lawyers, a third of the directors of its major financial institutions, and 95 percent of the doctors at its leading hospital were all Harvard men. Conservative in politics, a Whig stronghold, Boston was liberal in religion. Two-thirds of the wealthiest Bostonians in 1850 were subscribers to the pallid mysteries of Unitarianism. The "Boston religion," as it was often called, was too refined to make much of a fuss over theology. In years to come, James Michael Curley might mock its adherents as "a curious sect who seem to believe that our Lord Jesus was a young man with whiskers who went around in his underwear," but who could doubt that the Unitarian God was a Bostonian?[12]

The Irish shared a language with these people, but little else. To keep them docile their British rulers had enforced illiteracy through the Penal Laws, which denied Catholics the right to attend school. So the newcomers could not sup the feast of Boston's culture, even if necessity had permitted them the leisure, which it did not. Boston was a center of agitation for temperance, women's rights, and abolition. To the Irish, pessimists by history and religion alike, such meliorism was impious, a prideful tinkering with a Creation that it was the task of humankind to accept, not to set right. Accordingly, though they inveighed against the evils of drunkenness, their priests opposed state efforts to legislate temperance, derided the women's rights movement as "Bloomerism," and castigated abolitionists as "hypocrites" oozing false concern over the lot of "pickaninnies" in Alabama but indifferent to an evil right under their noses—the exploitation of immigrant labor in the factories of Massachusetts. Fearful of the economic consequences of abolition, Oscar Handlin writes, in words that span the epochs, the Irish valued "the security that came from the existence in the country of at least one social class beneath them."[13]

At first the political response to the Celtic flood was mild. There were even public expressions of sympathy for Ireland's catastrophe. Edward Everett, the president of Harvard, led a meeting at Faneuil Hall "to consider what Boston should do for Ireland." The city merchants petitioned Congress to use the *Jamestown*, a sloop lying idle at Charlestown Navy Yard, to send food and supplies to the starving people of Ireland. At the death of Bishop Fenwick, Boston's first Roman Catholic prelate, Mayor Josiah Quincy ordered tanbark strewn on the streets around Holy Cross Cathedral to keep the noise of passing traffic from disturbing the mourners inside.[14]

But the Irish were not the only people who valued "the security that came from the existence in the country of at least one class beneath them." To the Yankee factory operatives and laborers and artisans of Massachusetts, the Irish were the class beneath and they feared to let the Irish rise. "Our lower people hate the Irish," the preacher Lyman Beecher declaimed, "because they keep their wages lower, are good at a fight, and they despise them for their ignorance, poverty, and superstition." Economic competitors for the native-born workingman, the Irish were also a burden on the native-born taxpayer. Poor relief in Boston rose from $43,700 in 1845 to $137,000 in 1851, and over the same period the number of foreign-born paupers tripled, from four to twelve thousand. Moralists worried over the proliferation of "groggeries"—numbering 1,200 by 1849—where whiskey sold for twenty-eight cents a gallon. Drunkenness brought crime: between 1843 and 1848 "attempts to kill," to use the language of the clerk of the Boston Police Court, went up by an unbelievable 1,700 percent; "assaults on police officers," by 400 percent; "aggravated assaults" with weapons ranging from pistols to bricks, by 465 percent. Nativists were alarmed at the 200 percent surge in the Irish population between 1850 and 1855, compared with the feeble 15 percent blip in the non-Irish population. If the number of living Irishmen and women stirred anxiety, the number of dead Irish babies affronted the conscience; in a census of the newcomers, Dr. Lemuel Shattuck found that 62 percent of those who had died over the five-year period 1850–55 were under five years of age. Boston had never known such poverty. Summing up the changes wrought by the Irish in the "once orderly and peaceful city of the Pilgrims," Ephraim Peabody judged that they were "about equivalent to a social revolution."[15]

Revolutions beget counterrevolutions. One was now brewing in Massachusetts.

It began in a secret society that spread rapidly through the Commonwealth in the early 1850s. Divided into lodges, linked by passwords and special handshakes, the secret society took its name from the answer its members gave to queries about its purpose: "I know nothing about it." Officially, the Know-Nothings would be called the American party, but in the months before it surfaced in the election of 1854 the secret society was identified by its members only by a code name, Sam. Membership in Sam was reserved for native-born Americans, Protestants "born of Protestant parents, reared under Protestant influence, and not united in marriage with a Roman Catholic." These were not strenuous criteria in Massachusetts; virtually every nonimmigrant resident could meet them. Consequently, the Know-Nothings quickly became a mass, albeit still clandestine, movement.[16]

Some later historians have been at pains to bring out the good points of the Know-Nothings, citing their championing of the ten-hour day for factory workers, their opposition to slavery, and their support of temperance and women's rights. They wanted the little man to get a better break in a state long dominated by Whig businessmen. But he had to be the right sort of little man. He could be neither Catholic nor Irish. Prejudice was the invigorating principle of the Know-Nothings. Persecution was their aim.

The Know-Nothing irruption came first in the municipal elections held in the spring. Running on "Citizen" tickets, Know-Nothing candidates swept such Whig strongholds as Salem, Cambridge, and Roxbury. In Boston a Know-Nothing, J. V. C. Smith, won the largest vote ever cast for mayor. The state elections in the fall brought an even more dramatic example of the secret party's mass following. Heavy rain fell as the polls opened and, one reporter wrote, "it poured water and Know-Nothings all day." In the greatest triumph for a single party in the tumultuous history of Massachusetts politics, the Know-Nothings swept every state constitutional office, including governor; they won all forty state Senate races; they carried every U.S. Congressional District; and out of 381 seats in the state House of Representatives, they won 379. Henry J. Gardner, the Know-Nothing gubernatorial candidate, carried every city in the Commonwealth and all but twenty of its three-hundred-odd towns. In his inaugural address, Governor Gardner pointed to the Irish Catholic influx as the chief problem facing the Commonwealth of Massachusetts, and in the name of the native workingman and the native taxpayer he vowed to lead a crusade to "Americanize America." Toward that end, he called for constitutional amendments that would exclude naturalized citizens from public office and impose on them a strict literacy test and a twenty-one-year residency requirement before they would be allowed to vote.[17]

The Know-Nothing legislature enacted laws requiring the reading of the King James, or Protestant, Bible in the public schools, banning the teaching of foreign languages, disbanding Irish militia units, and forcing the Irish off the state payroll. Several proposed constitutional amendments that were equally persecutory sailed through, including one forbidding Roman Catholics from holding public office in Massachusetts. Under a "pauper removal law" more than thirteen hundred Irish paupers in the state almshouses and unfortunates in its asylums were forcibly collected and shipped back to Liverpool. The Know-Nothing party press jubilated that "these leeches upon our taxpayers" were beyond the sea, "where they belong."[18]

The Know-Nothing government did not fail to overlook the nuns—a prurient interest in convents being a mark of the anti-Catholic bigot. A "Joint Special Committee on the Inspection of Nunneries and Convents" was established by unanimous vote. It held hearings and heard petitions. Their purport was that something dark and depraved was going on in the Catholic convents. Action swiftly followed.

It took the form of raids on convents and boarding schools. On one, in Curley's Roxbury, a swarm of state inspectors terrified the children, chased a nun from her prayers in the chapel, and subjected the body of a sick girl to careful scrutiny to make sure that she was not a kidnaped boy. One of the men on the Roxbury raid, the Grand Worshipful Instructor of the Know-Nothing lodges, who was also a state representative, made "suggestive remarks" to two nuns. He later went too far in that direction while on a nunnery inspection tour in Lowell. Not only did he charge the Commonwealth for his meals, lodging, wine, gin, and cigars; he added a bill for a prostitute. The ensuing uproar in the press brought a halt to the convent raids.[19]

While they were persecuting Irish Catholics, the Know-Nothings were also pushing the cause of "reform." They made vaccination for school children compulsory, required youths working in factories to attend school a minimum of twelve weeks a year, passed a brace of laws aimed at making wives more equal partners with husbands, and issued the first racial desegregation law in the nation.

Know-Nothing government gave "reform" a bad name among the Irish. Generations later, James Michael Curley would wake the ghost of the 1850s by exploiting the enduring and periodically renewed local association of reform with anti-Irish bigotry. "The Lord knows I never want to pose as a reformer," he said in a typical animadversion on the floor of a City Council meeting in 1910. "I like to associate with people who have some sense of common decency, instead of a parcel of crooks who pose as reformers and whom it wouldn't be safe to leave with an umbrella or a pair of rubbers." Reformers would, of course, return his enmity. But their opposition never worried him; in Irish Catholic Boston, after the reign of Sam, there would always be votes in it.[20]

Too ideologically diffuse to last beyond a season, the Know-Nothing coalition of antislavery and antialien groups was more a spasm than a movement. Writing to the abolitionist Owen Lovejoy in 1855, Abraham Lincoln noted the central contradiction: "I do not perceive how anyone sensitive to the wrongs of the Negro can join in a league to degrade a class of white men." With sectional differences over slavery sharpening, the politics of ethnic and religious difference began to seem irrelevant. By 1858 the Know-Nothings had been swept from power by a new party, one that spoke to the urgent issues of the hour. Yet partly because it absorbed remnants of the Know-Nothings, for generations this new party, the Republican, would have about as much claim on Irish Catholic affections as reform. The party of the native farmer, small-town businessman, and skilled tradesman was not one in which the immigrant, urban, wage-earning, unskilled laborer could feel at home.

The grammar of Massachusetts politics was being laid down in the 1850s. Galvanic national issues like the debate over slavery, Populism, and the New Deal would not change the terms of the decree by which the Irish voted Democratic, the native Yankee Protestants Republican. Only the increasing suburbanization of the Boston Irish in the late 1960s would weaken the Irish bond with the Democratic party. By then, however, the Democrats would themselves have become a party of "reform," championing late-twentieth-century versions of the causes espoused by the Know-Nothings, notably civil rights for blacks and abortion rights for women. Thus in leaving their party, along with their city, the "Boston" Irish would be paying ironic tribute to the enduring power of the events that had wedded them to that party in the first place.

Powerful enough to echo in ethnic voting behavior a century later, the Know-Nothing attack of the mid-1850s, paradoxically, failed to elicit a strong response from those who were its first targets. The election of 1854 saw violence between immigrants and nativists in Baltimore, New Orleans, St. Louis, and Louisville that left fifty dead and a hundred wounded. But in Boston, which in the judgment of one historian "could have exploded into open warfare at any given moment," violence was averted. The bishop of Boston, John Fitzpatrick, deserves much of the credit. "Faced with religious bigotry, political rejection, and social discrimination on all sides," his biographer writes,

> he consistently urged tolerance, respect for the law, and recourse to the courts and the Constitution as the immigrants' only hope for ultimate acceptance as American citizens. His successful efforts to hold the excitable passions of his people in check, to prevent confrontation, and to prohibit retaliation helped undermine the Know-Nothing cause in Boston by depriving it of those combustible ingredients so necessary to fuel its flames of hatred and violence.

Fearing to provide just such an ingredient himself, Bishop Fitzpatrick refused the honor of being made an archbishop. His sometime friend, the intellectual Orestes Brownson, a Catholic by conversion, counseled him that the Irish must act as "guests" in someone else's home. If the Know-Nothings had lost sight of true Americanism, the Irish would show them by being more American than the Americans. Such was Fitzpatrick's calming message to his flock.[21]

They listened, they obeyed, but in few places at few times in America had a white minority been subject to such official maltreatment, and the scars went deep. The 1860 election campaign brought stark evidence of the continuing political cleavage between Boston's two communities. At a rally in Irish Fort Hill, Stephen A. Douglas drew a crowd of ten thousand cheering people. That November, while Douglas carried the two predominantly Irish wards, Abraham Lincoln won all the other wards in the city by big margins. As war approached in the weeks after Lincoln's election, Boston appeared to be two cities—one Protestant, the other Catholic; one antislavery, the other proslavery; one loyal to the new Republican administration, the other opposed to it. Yet with the bombardment of Fort Sumter, there could be no doubt where the Boston Irish stood. Slavery was no longer the issue; the survival of the Union had replaced it.

"We Catholics have only one course to follow," *The Pilot* announced: "stand by the Union; fight for the Union; die by the Union." If before Sumter the abolitionists had talked revolution, threatening to dissolve the political order to realize their reform agenda, the southern secessionists had now gone beyond talk to light the blaze itself. For this generation of Irish, with its immigrants' reverence for established authority, that was enough to put the South irrevocably in the wrong.[22]

Drawn by the lure of the soldier's bonus, but also by a sudden fervor of patriotism, two regiments of Boston Irishmen rapidly signed up with Meagher's famed Irish Brigade. Banned by the Know-Nothings, the Columbian Artillery, an Irish marching group, formed the backbone of the Ninth Massachusetts regiment, whose green battle flag would hang closest to the catafalque containing what was mortal of James Michael Curley on the night of his great wake. Known as a fighting people, a quarter of the city's population, the Irish were at last wanted in Boston. At Malvern Hill and Antietam, Fredericksburg and Gettysburg, the Wilderness and

Spotsylvania Courthouse, among other placenames that once made men's spines stiffen with emotion, the Irish would die their way into the esteem of the native community.[23]

With the continuation of Bishop Fitzpatrick's policy of social and political accommodation under his successor Bishop John Williams, with the slackening of Irish immigration after 1860, and under the emollient leadership of politicians like Patrick Maguire and Patrick Collins, the Boston Irish entered the postwar era as a tolerated minority in Boston. This was the tenor of the city when Michael Curley arrived. Opportunity was still limited; hard work still led only to poverty. But political and religious persecution seemed a thing of the past.

❖   ❖   ❖

If the account in his son's autobiography is correct, Michael Curley owed his livelihood in Boston to an act of political intervention in the free market for labor. The intervenor was P. James ("Pea-Jacket") Maguire—tailor, member of the Boston Common Council, and boss of the ward. For the green immigrant, Maguire was the man to see to find work. Maguire (no relation to Patrick J. Maguire, the leader of the Democratic party in the city) secured Michael a job as a hod carrier, first with a friendly contractor and then with the city's paving division. Michael could have a life in America, could marry and raise a family, because a powerful man had exerted influence on his behalf. Since James Michael Curley's career would in essential respects be a footnote to what Pea-Jacket Maguire had done for his father, the anatomy of the patronage relationship is worth a glance.

Pea-Jacket's power wore the mask of beneficence. He was doing a favor for young Michael. In return, when he came of age, Michael would do something for Pea-Jacket—he would vote for him, work the ward for him, "go through" for him on election day, and perhaps kick a little of his salary back to him. But this was not too much to ask, considering what the job meant to Michael. Giving more than he got—or appearing to—the ward boss always occupied the higher moral ground. Here was a form of power that the touchy Irish Catholic conscience could not only approve but pursue. James Michael Curley would be reckoned a thief and scoundrel in many people's books, but he would rarely betray a bad conscience. Rather, as Pea-Jacket Maguire could do vis-à-vis Michael Curley, he would usually comport himself like a man in moral surplus, if a little in arrears legally.

In 1870 Michael married tiny nineteen-year-old Sarah Clancy, who had made the journey from Galway to Roxbury with her mother and father and two sisters in the same year Michael did. They rented a cold-water flat on the third floor of a wood frame house on Northampton Street, across from the Roxbury Canal, a finger of foul water protruding from Boston's South Bay, a block distant. Their first child, John, was born two years later; James (who as a gesture to the memory of his father, would take Michael as a middle name at his Confirmation), arrived two years later. A third son, Michael, born in 1879, could not squeeze through the gates of death that Dr. Lemuel Shattuck had seen closing on so many immigrant children; Michael died at two and a half, of what cause is not known. In his ghostwritten autobiography, *I'd Do It Again*, produced to cash in on the new interest raised by *The Last Hurrah*, as well as in scattered newspaper interviews, Curley had barely more to say about Michael Curley than he did about his father's tiny namesake. He described Mike Curley as "a grand man with humour, compassion, and an understanding heart" whose "one thought was for the home." Chiefly, though, he remembered him for punishing feats of labor—for working eleven hours a day, for walking several miles each way to a job site in remote Brighton, and for manhandling huge stones on his job with the city's paving division.

There are 104 Curleys listed in the Boston City Directory for 1884; of these 85 percent are identified as day laborers—"a classification not of their function but of their lack of function." In the year James was born, the superintendent of the U.S. Census Bureau described Michael Curley's occupation with zoological finality: "In respect of their industrial occupations, the foreigners among us may be divided as those who are where they are because they are doing what they are doing; and those who are doing what they are doing because they are where they are. In the former case, occupation has determined location; in the latter, location has determined occupation." Location would also determine James Michael's occupation. But he would exploit his location, not succumb to it; Boston would be his opportunity, not his fate. And, as if to compensate for Michael's anonymous life, he would early achieve the auxiliary selfhood of fame, eventually taking to describing himself in the third person, an admiring chronicler of that marvel, "Curley."[24]

For the Curley family, sorrow followed hard upon sorrow. Three years after the death of Michael Jr., his father lifted a heavy curbstone or timber (accounts differ) from the ground to the tail board of a tipcart, and burst a blood vessel in the act. He lingered for three days in a coma, long enough for his sons, John, twelve, and James, ten, to torture themselves with vain hopes of his recovery; long enough, as well, for Sarah Curley to secure a plot for him near that of her infant son in Old Calvary Cemetery, where Boston's Irish immigrants buried their dead, and close by where James Michael Curley would bury his wife and children as he lost them through the years.[25]

"Throughout Curley's career," the historian Charles Trout writes, "he reserved a special place for prominent men who had either lost their fathers at an early age, or for men whose fathers had been so greatly reduced in circumstances that they could not protect their sons. Abraham Lincoln, not surprisingly, exemplified the former, while William Shakespeare was frequently used to illustrate the latter." Of Shakespeare, for example, Curley would say, "The lad from Stratford had no academic training. He never was within the halls of a university. In boyhood he had, like Charles Dickens, to go through the most terrible experience which a sensitive child can suffer, that of seeing his father wrecked and ruined. . . ."[26]

Trout's phrasing—"fathers . . . that . . . could not protect their sons"—is provocative. James Michael Curley was to be in the business of protecting people from illness, hunger, homelessness, and unemployment. Especially in his later terms as mayor, he was a true city father, one who cared about the troubles of ordinary people, who promised to do something to help and tried to deliver on the promise. Yet there was a tragic irony in his career as protector: Curley did for strangers what his father could not do for him, and what he was unable to do for his own children. He could not protect them from death any more than Michael Curley could protect him from loss. He could perhaps turn the pain of that loss inside out by acting the protective father to generations of his constituents. But his power stopped at his own doorstep. That much he would always share with his father.

Both in his autobiography and in an authorized ("I told him that if he'd tell me the story of his life, I would write it as he told it") 1949 biography by Joseph F. Dinneen, a veteran reporter for the *Boston Globe*, Curley daubed rouge on the impersonal facts of his father's death. Michael Curley's character, in this telling, sealed his destiny. Still tragic, his death was less absurd.

"Michael Curley," Dinneen writes, "had a reputation as a neighborhood strong man. He boasted that he could lift almost anything. . . .

"One day a man on a construction job looked speculatively at a huge stone that had to be moved. 'Can you lift that, Mike?' he asked."

Bets were taken on either side of the question.

Curley told his son Francis that Michael did manage to lift the stone—and that he was buried with the money won in the bet that killed him.[27]

The
Boy from
Home

❖   ❖   ❖   ❖

*Neighborhoods like individuals carry stigmata which
tell their story plainer than any statistical
accounting could possibly do. Ward 17 impresses the
observer as does a man who has lost confidence
in himself.*

ALBERT J. KENNEDY,
A SETTLEMENT HOUSE WORKER, 1905

❖   ❖   ❖   ❖

The problem was serious enough for the new mayor to mention in his inaugural address. "The owners of real estate in the district lying between Northampton Street and Eustis Street," Mayor Samuel Cobb said on taking office in January 1874, "have been notified to fill their land to the grade of twelve feet above mean low water, in order to abate and prevent nuisances . . . caused by bad drainage." The "nuisances" Mayor Cobb referred to were overflowing outhouses; the land still had its feet in the sea—the houses and factories, the lumber and brickyards all about had been built on tidal flats. At high water outhouses and basements would flood over, and to the ambient tide reek would be added a stench fouler still. The elevation of one's house mattered greatly in a district like this, for "there seemed to be a correlation between the altitude at which one lived and the death rate (even a difference of six to eight feet above sea level could make a remarkable difference). . . ." The lower the house, the higher the incidence of consumption and pneumonia, the prime killers of Irish children. The Curleys' section of Northampton Street was so close to the water that "bowsprits raked windows"; and the house where James Curley was born on November 20, 1874, number 28, was among the lowest houses on the lowest street in a notably low neighborhood.[1]

By inner-city standards, it was not a densely populated neighborhood. The district that between 1895 and 1915 would be designated as Ward 17, (it began a few blocks from the Curley home on Northampton Street, which actually defined the farthest reach of the South End's Ward 9, and stretched back a mile to include most of lower Roxbury) had a population density of 59.2 people per acre.

By contrast, Ward 8, in the cramped West End, where so many immigrants of all kinds got their foothold in the New World, had 173.6 people per acre; Ward 9, in the South End, had 132.2; and even the adjoining Roxbury Ward 18, in the years of Curley's youth, was nearly twice as crowded as Ward 17. To an extent not shared by these other wards, however, Ward 17 was stippled with large-scale industrial enterprises, among them factories operated by the New England Piano Company (where Curley would briefly work), the Putnam Nail Works, and the E. Howard Watch and Clock Company, which made fine clocks for the railway stations, churches, and town halls of late-nineteenth-century America. The ward, in short, was far from being a bosky dell. And what was true of the ward was even truer of the immediate neighborhood. There was a soap works nearly adjacent to Curley's house, a lumberyard just across the dusty track of Northampton Street, a brickyard hard by that, and several gas works close enough to see—and impossible not to smell. In the state census taken in 1905, only 29 percent of the ward's 24,313 residents were listed as American born and these were mostly of Irish descent; 58 percent of the foreign-born residents were Irish-born, 18 percent were Canadians, 8 percent English or Scotish, and there was an ecumenical sprinkling of Russian Jews and Italians.[2]

The bulk of the Irish had settled in the neighborhood in the 1870s and 1880s, although the local church, St. Patrick's, just down Northampton Street from the Curley house, dated from the 1830s. When St. Patrick's was being built, the men of the parish had had to patrol the construction site carrying muskets with fixed bayonets to discourage raids by Protestant mobs. On St. Patrick's fiftieth anniversary, in 1885, a neighborhood paper recalled that "nearly every man of the parish took his night in turn to perform the work of the literal soldier of the cross." Curley would thus have been reminded of the ordeal of his faith and people in Boston every time he entered St. Patrick's. It was one of the two symbolic buildings in his daily line of sight. The other was the Boston City Hospital, diagonally across the Roxbury Canal and the great thoroughfare of East Chester Park from 28 Northampton. Established in the 1860s to combat a cholera outbreak among the city's poor, the hospital really stood for Yankee benefaction—it was begun with funds from the estate of Elisha Goodnow, an old-time Boston merchant—but that is not what it would mean to James Michael Curley, nor what it has meant to generations of Bostonians. Throughout his four terms as mayor, Curley added wards, departments, and buildings to the City Hospital in such number and of such quality that its origins were forgotten, and it is thought of simply as the hospital he built, a monument to "The Mayor of the Poor." Fittingly, he would die there, in a building put up during one of his terms, within sight of the house where he was born.[3]

In talking of his boyhood, Curley often heaped gloom on what was unquestionably a hard life—telling of scrambling with his brother John for bits of coal in the local dump, of walking barefoot because the family had no money for shoes, and of sometimes being close to hunger. These stories were political gold, a warrant of legitimacy for his constituents, and it is hard to sift the truth in them from the blarney. Yet sometimes when he described his childhood an impulse of authenticity would break through. Consider this comment from a 1930 interview, for example: "In the winter . . . the winters were pretty bad. Work was lost in the winter, and the poor man was not likely to turn down odd jobs and chances to shovel snow." That catch in the throat at the mention of "winter" hints at memories too painful for chat, and is far more eloquent than dubious Dickensian anecdotes. Another fragment from that time has the same ring. Walking down an unpaved alley near his home with one of his uncles, he kicked a stone, and suddenly a handful of silver coins appeared in the dust. Startled, he bent down to pick up this treasure when his uncle kneed him in the groin, pushed him out of the way, and made off with the coins himself. Money would have an outsize importance for James Curley. He would forfeit his reputation to get as much of it as he could and to spend as much as he got. The memory of need drove this getting and spending. He was making things up to himself, repairing the hurt left by incidents like this, fashioning for himself and his family a world where such things could not happen.[4]

Still, life was by no means all grim. Michael Curley took his boys to the great parade of 1880, and like generations of Boston children since, they rode the swan boats in the Boston Public Garden. From the money earned on their paper routes, they bought jelly rolls and soda pop. In season there was coasting and skating. They played Duck-on-the-Rock and Relievo in the alleys back of Northampton Street; launched punts in the Roxbury Canal; and on hot summer days swam in the nude in the ship channel of the South

Bay and dove off the docks. Seagulls screeched in the air; frogs croaked at night. "We had our hands full," John Curley remembered, "but we were happy."[5]

The credit for that achievement must go to Sarah Clancy Curley. There is a photograph of her taken when James first entered school—he is in a Buster Brown suit in the foreground; she is sitting behind him, backing him up in art as she did in life. With her scanty dark hair parted in the middle and pulled down tight against her skull, her large ears fully exposed, and a hint of beard in the shadow cast upon her jaw, she might easily be mistaken for a man. Yet the impression of severity would not be wholly true to the little we know of her character. "I can't remember that she ever had to raise her hand to either of us," John once said of her. This was a woman who told Irish fairy tales to the local children, and who shared whatever she had with her neighbors. John Curley's daughters knew her as children in her last years, and recall a person without grandmotherly warmth who seemed to exude disapproval of them and their generation; a dour, stout, forbidding old woman, given to heroic squeezing of her rosary beads. But that was the Sarah Curley of 1918. Forty years earlier, before she was widowed, and before her purgatorial labors on the floors of the Immaculate Conception Church and sundry downtown office buildings, she had warmth enough to love her sons enough so that they could go on to love as men. John married at thirty-five and raised a large family. James would forge deeply romantic marriages to two women, one in his youth, the other in his middle and old age. "The Irish widow exercised an emotional hegemony rarely equaled in other American families," the late William V. Shannon writes in his magisterial social history, *The American Irish*. "Her sufferings and sacrifices were crucial in keeping the home together in the critical years after the father's death. Those sacrifices earned from her children obedience and respect for her opinions on every important subject." This points to the secret of Sarah's noncoercive discipline: her sons respected her sacrifices too much to give her trouble.[6]

No doubt there can be better maternal influences on a man's character. But clearly there can be worse. James respected his wives' opinions; he also felt and expressed strong love for them both. This is the essential gift, surely, the key to adult happiness, and he owed it to his primal connection to Sarah. "You will understand that it is not easy for a man to speak of his mother," he once said. "A man's love for his mother goes beyond words." He was a politician, not a poet: words were tools of mystification, not candor. So he was probably speaking the truth. What he felt for her, what he owed to her, he could not put into the distorting medium of words.[7]

Sarah prepared him for his successful emotional commitments; did she do the same for his political success?

In an edifying speech given in his first term as mayor, Curley lay a revealing stress on the role Thomas Jefferson's mother had played in the formation of Jefferson's egalitarianism. Jefferson was fourteen, "a lad of delicate health," and his mother was "a confirmed invalid" when his father died. "Stunned by the loss of his father and at the thoughts of his mother," Curley stated, Jefferson was afflicted with "an impediment in his speech which remained with him through a lifetime." Yet as Charles Trout, whose insight this is, writes "Jefferson's mother, although unable to furnish physical protection, provided her son with spiritual and intellectual inspiration." According to Curley, "the presence . . . of the word equality" in that "immortal document," the Declaration of Independence, could "undeniably be traced to his mother, who during his lifetime served both as counsel and inspirer to her gifted son."[8]

Curley built his public life on two contradictory props: his ability to express powerful collective rancors and his capacity to care "even for people who really didn't deserve it," as his son Francis put it. Whence did this latter quality come if not from the example of Sarah, and not only of her need but of her nature?[9]

We know something of her generosity. When James was a congressman, she once borrowed $50 from him on a Friday, only to ask for more the next week. What had she done with the money he had given her the week before, he gently inquired. She replied that she had gone to the store and bought food for some neighbors who needed it—which silenced him. That was the template of his own generosity. Beneath all his Barnumism, beneath the calculation and brutality of his nature, and beyond what was required politically, he always cared.[10]

A policeman assigned to act as his chauffeur remembers a defining instance that happened during his first week on the job. Having finished work in his City Hall office one Saturday noon, Curley, instead of starting for his car, which was parked behind the building, walked around to the front entrance, on School Street. He stood there, alone, for fifteen minutes, until a drunk he had been expecting rounded the corner of Tremont and started down School Street in his direction. Recognizing his man, Curley boomed out, "Hello there, young fellow!" and then, to protect the man's dignity, "Here's that money I owe you," as he passed him a five-dollar bill. This weekly ritual went beyond the call of political duty. Curley would not go home for lunch before he had given that unfortunate man money to buy oblivion for the weekend. Caring like this, "even for people who really didn't deserve it," approximates one ideal of maternal love; an unsifted love, without regard for the quality of its object, or for the possibility of requital.¹¹

From his earliest days in politics, James Michael Curley had the name of a caring man. And that reputation, in a time and place when caring was not to be had in other quarters, made his career.

❖   ❖   ❖

Michael Curley must have been losing ground in Boston because, in 1880, the family moved to an even smaller apartment on Fellows Court, a dead-end alley behind 28 Northampton. For James, it would have been a short walk from his new home to the Yeoman Primary School, about a block away. There, as well as at the slightly more distant Dearborn Grammar School, he encountered a disparity in status that was to be found throughout the city, and from which he would later wring every possible vote: "While the Yeoman and Dearborn School janitors were exclusively Irish," Trout has found, "only two of the twenty-seven faculty and staff had recognizably Irish names." Classes were large—fifty, sixty, or even seventy pupils might be crowded into one room at the Dearborn—yet young Curley stood out from the crowd. "Curley was not the outstanding student in the school," a former teacher said of him, "but he was a good student, particularily in English, and he was eager to learn."¹²

Alanson H. Mayers had come to the Dearborn after graduating from Harvard as a Greek and Latin scholar in the class of 1881. "I liked him the first time he came to school," Mayers reminisced on the occasion of Curley's election as governor. "It wasn't long before I saw in him the innate qualities that have made him famous. Even then, when we had our regular Friday afternoon speaking of pieces, he was a good orator, the best in the school. We didn't have any of these foolish fickle things you hear on radio nowadays; no, they were good, solid, historical selections from Daniel Webster and Lincoln and Shakespeare." Curley looked forward to these school assemblies, and the teachers were proud of his performances. Interestingly, this hellion of a man had been a tractable boy, for Mayers also remarked, as if it was unusual, "I never had to give him a whipping."[13]

Following the death of his father, Curley was obliged to combine his studies at the Dearborn with work. He began as a newspaper boy. After school he would ride the green Roxbury horse car of the West End Street Railway downtown to the offices of the *Boston Globe* on Newspaper Row, pick up a bundle of papers, and return to his stand near the corner of Northampton and Washington streets. Saturdays brought a change of venue: a job as a delivery boy at the Washington Market on East Lenox Street. Pay was three cents for every basket of groceries delivered. He worked until all the orders were dispatched, which could take sixteen hours. He was eleven years old.[14]

His next job lasted two weeks. One Saturday—it must have been during summer vacation—his brother John was hired as a delivery boy by C. S. Johnson, a large Roxbury grocer, and told to start work on the following Monday. But on Sunday a spider bit him on the face, and the resulting swelling closed one eye tight. He could not possibly report for work. "It was a worrisome time we had figuring the matter out," Curley recalled forty years later. "John had to keep the job, for we needed the money. There was nothing for it but that Jimmie Curley must go round on Monday morning and see if he could manage to substitute." Donning a pair of homemade overalls, he set out for Johnson's just before the 6:00 A.M. starting time. "Well, I got away with it. I started into work and no questions were asked. It was taken for granted that I was John Curley." He worked there for two weeks, until his brother had recovered and could replace him. "However, although I had succeeded in substituting for John, and nobody the wiser, John was detected immediately."

Behind its mist of charm, this anecdote is paradigmatic of the fortunes of the two brothers: James was able to keep up the deception, whereas John could not. That would pretty much be the story of John's life. James outpaced him from the start. James appointed him to a succession of jobs in his administrations, and he invariably served competently, if sometimes controversially. With James's help, John founded an insurance agency and made a success of it. But he was always in James's shadow. Years later, a visitor intruded on Mayor Curley just as he was finishing dressing his brother down. No Lyndon Johnson, Curley was characteristically respectful of the feelings of those who worked for him, so perhaps this incident was atypical. John's children remember their father as drawing the line at certain of James's practices, of trying to dissuade his brother from taking politically or ethically risky steps. James's senior counselor: that may indeed have been John's role. But that would have been behind the scenes. In public he was "the mayor's brother," a slighting identification. Only a protracted miracle of tact on James's part could have kept their relationship free from strain.[15]

At twelve James took a job as a boy-of-all-work at Stephen Gale's drugstore, at the corner of Washington and Chester Square. (later Massachusetts Avenue). "I went on the job at seven in the morning," Curley told an interviewer, "and worked till half-past eight, when I started for the Dearborn School. I got there when the first bell rang at five minutes to nine." The Dearborn being almost a mile away, he must have hurried. At noon he ran home for lunch; John Curley, back from his own job, would usually prepare it for him, since Sarah was out at work herself. He and John would take turns scrubbing the floors and doing the rest of the housework, but very soon it would be time to be off for the drugstore until half-past one, then back to school again, and once more to the drugstore between half-past four and six o'clock. "I had three-quarters of an hour to get home, get my supper, and get back to work," he recalled, "and I stayed in the drugstore till ten at night. I had one Sunday afternoon off one week, and one Saturday afternoon the next." For what often would be a fifty-seven-hour week, he received the sum of $2.50—and, he later said, "I earned every penny of it."[16]

He paid a price for this crammed regimen: a submaster at the Dearborn recalled that he did not play with the other boys at recess or after school. "I really never learned to play baseball or football or any of the other athletic games that are usually enjoyed by boys in this period of their lives," Curley wrote. His father's death cost him his youth.[17]

At Stephen Gale's, Curley tended the soda fountain, delivered prescriptions, swept the floor, and—"a regular Pinafore chap"—

polished up the handle of the big front door. "Mr. Gale had a mania for cleanliness. He was strict . . . but just. . . . And in the course of the time I worked for him I had a thorough course in social hygiene and deportment." He stayed at Gale's for four years, and what with sprinting back and forth to school and walking the streets of Boston carrying prescriptions, he acquired a physical stamina that would serve him in good stead throughout his life. No opponent would ever outcampaign him.[18]

He acquired something else, too. "Supreme egotism and utter seriousness are necessary for the greatest accomplishment," William Shannon writes, "and these the Irish find hard to sustain; at some point, the instinct to see life in a comic light becomes irresistible, and ambition falls before it." James Michael Curley would not be deficient in the ethnic endowment of wit. Indeed, he is remembered today for his one-liners, his comic stunts, his general air of ironic merriment, and his retinue of retainers with their Runyonesque nicknames, their omnipresent cigars, and their funny fedora hats. Forgotten is his drive, his hunger, his "utter seriousness" of purpose. Many poor boys of his time and class and people suffered like or worse deprivations as children; what made him unusual was that childhood poverty did not leave him poor in spirit. He suffered his losses; he did not perpetuate them in depression. Moreover, luck or psychic destiny led him to choose a profession in which he always had an enemy, someone on whom he could take out his bitterness for his blighted childhood, displace his grief, and project his anger.[19]

Although Curley would always be able to laugh at himself, his ambition never fell before the corrosive self-deprecation so habitual among the American Irish. Only a serious, earnest boy could keep to the schedule he set for himself between school and work. A nurse at the City Hospital remembered seeing him sitting in the doorway of his Northampton Street house—reading a book, alone, while other neighborhood boys played together nearby.[20]

From an early age he began to validate himself against his own standards and dreams, not those of the gang. His gregariousness was always tactical. He never built a "machine"; such organizations as he put together were no more than temporary platforms to assist his climb. Coming to maturity in what has been called "the last age of heroes"—the age of Theodore Roosevelt, William Jennings Bryan, Robert La Follette, Woodrow Wilson, and Eugene V.

Debs—he lived out the essentially aristocratic vision of the political hero, the "man in the arena" who accepts the scorn of the timid as the price of daring and doing boldly. Once when asked the secret of his political success, he replied, "You've always got to stay ahead of the mob."[21]

"The mob": did the aristocrat Franklin Roosevelt ever call his voters that? Probably not. But aside from his character-molding struggle with polio, he did not have to make himself from the ground up as Curley did. Roosevelt's class position could do for him what only his own will could do for Curley. And heroes of the will are not known for their democratic sympathies.

At Stephen Gale's, then, Curley was banking away the self-discipline, the ability to act as well as to be on his own, that would keep this man of the people well ahead of them—more, that would make him contemptuous of them. Among the least attractive qualities of the mature Curley was a certain self-infatuation, along with a related tendency to discount the admittedly flickering wisdom of the voters, as if he could not respect them because he knew how often he had fooled them.

❖   ❖   ❖

We cannot leave the drugstore without mentioning the Temptation of James Michael Curley, which is recounted in his autobiography—a book that sometimes soars above the facts of his life, the better to print his legend. The story goes that a wealthy matron, a regular customer of Gale's, admired young Curley's speaking voice so much that she made him a perfidious proposition. She would support his mother and send him to college, but in return he must agree to become a Methodist missionary. Told of this offer, Sarah Curley replied: "I don't care if she pays me fifty dollars a week and pays all your expenses while you're getting a college education. Nobody is going to make a Protestant out of you, so we'll talk about it no more." Catholics of the pre-ecumenical age had an obsessive fear of being seduced from the one true faith by improbable sirens of Protestantism.[22]

At fifteen, instead of going on to high school after completing the ninth grade at the Dearborn, he left Gale's for a better-paying job at the New England Piano Company, on the Roxbury end of Tremont Street. The company was hiring because there was a na-

tional craze for cheap pianos, and the New England was able to
turn out twenty-five in a day. Curley was put to work on the spiral
screw machine, affixing piano plates to action boards. The New
England was his blacking factory. The temperature in the building
had to be kept artificially high to prevent the green wood from
shrinking until it was put in place in the instruments. "I weighed
135 pounds when I started there," Curley recalled. "After nine
months my weight was down to 85 pounds." The work was as haz-
ardous as it was hot. "I remember a ghastly thing that happened
with a circular saw. They put a green man to work on it, a man who
had no training in the handling of such a saw. . . . I saw him wave
his hand at a friend. His hand passed against the saw, and it took off
four fingers. He didn't even know he had lost them till he saw the
blood." After the eighth month he was put on piecework. "The
first week I earned $14.00 [as against $7.50 a week at the hourly
rate] then $15, then $16. It was far too much money for a laboring
man to earn. 'Beginning Monday,' I was told one day, 'you go back
on day work.' 'I do not,' I replied, 'you can't work a trick like that
on me. I'm through right now.' . . . Those were brutal days."[23]

Next he sought work with a tinsmith in the South End. "One
day, with a rope tied around my waist as a 'safety belt,' I crawled
onto the dome of a building to repair a leak, and my mother, who
happened to be passing by, was horrified when she saw me." So
much for that job. Finally he was hired back by his old though brief
employer of five years before, C. S. Johnson. His job was to deliver
groceries not only in Roxbury, but in the Back Bay, Dorchester,
and distant Hyde Park. He drove a wagon pulled by "an old grey
horse who couldn't run faster than a walk if an electric battery
were attached to him." He stayed at Johnson's for eight years, from
age sixteen to twenty-four.[24]

The job had its uses. Through it he met the voters of his ward;
but he also saw something of the other Boston, the Protestant city
of fine brick houses, smart carriages, and fashionable people. Combined with John's earnings, the income from James's new job allowed Sarah to get off her knees. Still far from prosperous, the
family was at last out of crisis.

Driving alone on cross-city deliveries, moreover, must have
given James time to think. Did he want to follow his father's path,
and perhaps share his father's fate? Manning the open wagon in all
weather was already beginning to sap his vitality. He came down

with a severe case of sciatica, and was confined to home for five months. The young men of the neighborhood would meet to pitch quoits on a patch of cinder sidewalk near the Curley house. One of them, on his way to meet friends after the game, later remembered looking up at the window of a building he had to pass and frequently catching sight of a teenager all wrapped up in blankets staring out on the darkening street. "I'd play my game of quoits, and as I started for home I'd look back over my shoulder. The lights would be on but still that lad would be sitting in his chair, wrapped in the blanket." It is a lonely image. It was a lonely life.[25]

Bent on improving himself, James enrolled in the Boston Evening High School and for two years spent two nights a week there, working toward his high school diploma. "About that time I began to feel that I would study, read, and work hard over my books and absorb knowledge from men of ability and learning in the community that I might be able to better my condition," Curley recalled. "I suppose I may date the beginnings of my ambition to amount to something more than the ordinary man . . . from the moment that I got that idea into my head." The self-evaluation "something more than the ordinary man" is revealing. Contemporary politicians are usually at pains to emphasize what ordinary men they really are, as if that wasn't clear.[26]

His first ambition was to prepare for the civil service examination for the Fire Department, which he then took and passed, receiving one of the "top scores." He could not have known it at the time, but what failed to happen next changed the course of his life: he did not become a fireman; he was, it turned out, too young to be eligible. He would have to stick with C. S. Johnson's—where, though he had risen to chief order clerk, salesman, and collector, his salary was only $11 a week—until he reached the right age or until some other calling should tempt him.[27]

❖   ❖   ❖

In the wider city beyond his window, new prospects were opening for the likes of the young man wrapped in the blanket. The first Irish member of the city's legislature, the Common Council, had been elected in 1857, the first alderman in 1870, the first congressman in 1880. Progress was tenuous—Mayor Frederick O. Prince was turned out of office in 1878 for appointing Irishmen to

the police force—but steady. Irish Catholics were elected mayor of Scranton, Pennsylvania, in 1878, New York City in 1880, Lawrence, Massachusetts, in 1881, and, finally, in 1884, Boston. One historian of the period writes, "Where their fathers and grandfathers had generally turned inward before a hostile environment, the generation of the 1880s, now reasonably well-established, held their heads high and fought back." The battle for the city was on. The issue would remain undecided through the 1890s, yet in the end immigrant numbers would tell.[28]

For the native Protestant elite, that seeming demographic certainty raised anew the fears of the 1850s. "The Roman Catholic vote is more or less perfectly controlled by the priests," Josiah Strong noted, expressing a broadly shared political fear. "That means the Pope can dictate some hundreds of thousands of votes in the U.S." Signaling a new direction for public policy, the nativist Robert Dequincy Howe declared, "All the great problems, the liquor question, the public school question . . . are tied up with the one great problem of foreign immigration." The logic of this position was clear, if harsh. In 1894, such eminent Brahmins as Leverett Saltonstall, Henry Parkman, Robert DeC. Ward, and Robert Treat Paine, Jr., a descendant of a signer of the Declaration of Independence, the founder of Associated Charities of Boston, and a large property owner in Curley's neighborhood, founded the Immigration Restriction League. Based in Boston, its aim was to lobby Congress to pass legislation drastically limiting foreign immigration. The battle for the city might yet be won at the water's edge.[29]

James Michael Curley is on record as saying that he first took part in politics in 1896, when he was twenty-two. But even before that, the rituals and rites of politics—the parades, the pole raisings, the displays of "red fire," the marching bands, the street corner speeches—must have shown as vivid against the drabness of the ward. For Curley was born into the age of popular politics when turnout in presidential elections in the North reached 83 percent. Political interest and excitement ran so high in 1876 that the *Boston Herald* printed 223,000 copies of its postelection edition—at the time, the largest edition ever put out by an American newspaper. In the presidential election of 1880 (Garfield versus Hancock), more than a fifth of northern voters played an active role in the campaign organizations of the candidates. To break the story of Garfield's assassination, in 1881, the *Boston Globe* published a special midnight edition; from 1:00 to 3:00 A.M., shouting newsboys wakened the people of Boston to the shocking news. Curley might not have remembered their shouts, but the fervor surrounding politics and public affairs in those days certainly would have impressed itself on him.[30]

"The ritual of partisan display captivated young men in the nineteenth century and bonded them to a party and to politics," a modern student of late-nineteenth-century electoral enthusiasm writes. The bands, the speeches, the parades made for an "enveloping experience" from which susceptible imaginations never recovered. "In the long run, the most important impact of electoral pageantry may not have been on men already old enough to vote, but on those boys and young men . . . still too young to cast a ballot. Later generations would not receive such an intense initiation into politics."[31]

James Michael Curley would carry an increasingly unfashionable nineteenth-century relish for electioneering halfway into the twentieth century, the age of the "vanishing voter." Politics always seemed fresh to him—a theater of the streets. From brass bands to television, from mass participation to voter alienation, his lifetime encompassed a significant rise and fall. Ironically, as a charismatic leader who practiced a politics of personal appeal, with little regard for "issues" or ideology, he hastened the fall.

This may seem paradoxical; with our pallid politicians, we tend to think that compelling personalities on the ballot would increase turnout. In fact, in their classic article "The Vanishing Voter," published in 1924, Arthur M. Schlesinger and Erik M. Eriksson found an inverse relationship between "personality" and voter participation in presidential elections between 1880 and 1920. Their findings, they realized, confuted "the common assumption that the average American is more interested in magnetic or spectacular personalities than in basic principles."[32]

Aside from their effect on turnout, which may show a temporary increase in any given election, candidates who make themselves the issue distract voters from the real issues. They render politics at once interesting and empty. Thus while Curley would perpetuate the nineteenth-century forms of campaigning, his type of politician paved the way for the issueless desert of today's television campaigns, which have depressed turnout more than thirty points below its late-nineteenth-century highs. In *The Last Hurrah*,

Edwin O'Connor sets Skeffington's ineffably noble personal politics against the phony TV ads of his opponent, but that is a projection of nostalgia, for the two modes of politics were equally lacking in ideological or issue-based substance. We need to remember this, to take the measure of Skeffington's model.

If the heated atmosphere of popular politics introduced Curley to the poetry of campaigning, his work for the local parish baptized him into the prose of governance—organization, administration, the discipline of running things. In 1895 the twenty-one-year-old Curley approached Father Phillip J. G. O'Donnell, the pastor of St. Patrick's, to volunteer his services in running the parish. "Young as Jim was," a journalist who interviewed surviving members of the parish wrote, "the pastor took him on practically as lieutenant and counselor, and he presided over church meetings." With his brother John, he also became a church usher; he spent five years as superintendent of the church Sunday school; he served as floor director for dances, parties, and parish reunions; and he organized outings, picnics, and minstrel shows. Father O'Donnell gave him much of the credit for the establishing of St. Philip's, near the corner of Northampton and Harrison, a new parish that replaced the relocated St. Patrick's.[33]

Joseph Dinneen depicts him as a kind of drudge, "a worker so little concerned with fun that he could be depended upon to sell tickets, schedule entertainment, hire bands and attend to all details and chores." This may be accurate, although faith in Dinneen's assertions—"he did not dance"—weakens when he gets the name of the parish wrong. Yet Dinneen also concedes that as a result of his behind-the-scenes work for the parish, Curley's "name was printed on programs and he got rising votes of thanks at the next meeting—all glory and no personal enjoyment, unless glory be personal enjoyment." Those "rising votes of thanks" must have been a tonic to the spirits of the young teamster. Thus keened, his appetite for glory would not easily be sated.[34]

As if his work for the parish was not enough to fill his evenings and weekends, Curley also threw himself into the philanthropic activities of the Hamden Street division of the Ancient Order of Hibernians, ultimately rising to a countywide leadership position in the fraternal order, whose officers were among the most prominent and successful of the Boston Irish. The A.O.H. gave him opportunities to make himself known not only to people in distress—the sick and needy of the ward—but also to important people, who would someday help him move beyond the ward to conquer the city.

The A.O.H. pulled out all the stops for the city's many parades, including—a new tradition—one on St. Patrick's Day. Here Curley's capacity for single-minded work found real scope: a fellow who could fight his way clear of self-deprecation and the snare of conviviality long enough to get things done was invaluable in putting on a parade.

One St. Patrick's Day, Curley, as an officer of the A.O.H., was made a parade marshal. Mounted on a big horse, wearing a morning coat and a silk hat topped by a green plume, he cut an impressive figure. But the Irish "instinct to see life in a comic light" never has far to seek for occasions to express itself. One such occasion arose for those watching the parade at the main intersection in Irish South Boston when the horse bearing the dashing parade marshal from Roxbury stopped in its tracks, bringing the parade to a halt. The young marshal cursed and kicked, but the horse would not budge. Finally, as some of the watchers urged him to "set its tail on fire," the young man got off the horse, crouched down in front of it, and commenced pleading with it to move. The horse caught sight of the fine green plume on his tall silk hat and, thinking it "at least a second cousin to grass," proceeded to chomp it off. As the crowd whooped and roared, the horse, now replete, at last started to move. The young marshal "nearly killed himself laughing," witnesses remembered. The drudge was an Irishman after all.[35]

It says something both about the economic distress in the ward and Curley's eye for wresting advantage from others' need that he could glimpse opportunities for patronage in a one-day event like a parade. Jim Kenney, the head of the Musicians Protective Association, remembers Curley at about this time, the middle nineties, or perhaps slightly later. "It was the Sunday before Labor Day, about eleven at night," he told an interviewer decades afterward, "and it was raining—raining pitchforks, and, if you like, spades, rakes, hoes—and if you want to add McCormick Harvesters I won't be the one to deny it." Suddenly there was a ring at the door of Kenney's Roxbury home. Standing outside in the deluge of farm implements was a young man in a rubber coat and big rubber boots.

"Does Mr. Kenney live here?" he asked.

Kenney replied that he was himself.

"You've got charge of all the bands in the parade tomorrow, haven't you?"

"I'm music marshal."

"Well sir," the young man made bold to say, "I want you to put some men to work."

Kenney said that was out of the question—all the musicians were already hired. "That should have stumped him," Kenney said.

But the young man pressed on. "How much do you pay the man who carries the big drum?"

"He gets three dollars," Kenney replied.

"How long does he have to work?"

"Oh, two or three hours."

"And how many bands will there be, Mr. Kenney?" asked the young man.

"Ten."

"Mr Kenney," the young man concluded, "I've got ten men that money will be a godsend to. Can you put them on?"

"And that gives you a faint idea of the way Jim Curley was hustling in those days," Kenney remembered. "He was out to help all he could help and the dirtiest night you could remember would not keep him from an errand that would help others. Did I give those men the job? You can bet your last dollar that I did. And from that day to this I've sworn by James M. Curley."[36]

Even allowing for Kenney's expansiveness, this is a remarkable portrait of a young man as a proto-politician. And if Kenney thereafter swore by Curley, the men he had gotten a day's pay for did not soon forget him either. Such men were Curley's opportunity, and in Ward 17, in the last years of the century, their number was increasing.

❖   ❖   ❖

Between 1895 and 1900 more than ten factories employing a total of nearly fifteen hundred workers closed down in the ward. The business depression of 1898–1900 caused some of these plant closings; behind others lay the unchecked national movement toward the formation of trusts, combines of corporations that tended to suppress competition. The Cordage Works was closed after being taken over by the Cordage Trust; the Nail Works was absorbed by the U.S. Steel Trust. Feeling the pinch of the industrial depression of the late 1890s, the E. Howard Watch Company shut down its operations; soon thereafter, so did the New England Piano Company. This latter closing, noted two settlement house workers in their report on the ward, was an "especially bitter blow," an assessment with which even a disgruntled former employee like Curley would have agreed. "In the summer the older school boys found jobs in its processes and prepared themselves for regular work," Robert A. Woods and Albert J. Kennedy wrote in *The Zone of Emergence*. "Many young men started their industrial careers in the factory, and were paying for their homes on the strength of the future. When the blow came many lost all their savings and had to seek work of another character. A proportion of forepeople and skilled workers went to pieces morally and never recovered." In a sign of the times, a failed leather factory in the ward was converted into a Salvation Army barracks.[37]

There were forty-four saloons in Ward 17, and they did not want for customers. A settlement house worker saw thirteen men walk out of one saloon in five minutes, and during an hour's walk through the ward on a Saturday night counted 391 men drinking in twenty-seven establishments. The family man shambling from bar to bar—this was a common sight. Economic distress was also adding an energy of desperation to the people's attachment to the therapeutic sacrament of their faith. In one month in 1898 a priest at St. Patrick's heard 1,728 confessions; in a single evening he heard the sins of 128 troubled men.[38]

Though laughable by the standards of that neighborhood today, a poor black area hard hit by drugs and violent crime, juvenile delinquency was fast becoming a serious problem in the ward, and policemen went there only in pairs. Industrial expansion and its promise of jobs had drawn a flood of new arrivals from the North and West ends; the neighborhood's flimsy buildings were put up so fast that it was said "a man might contract for a three family tenement on his way to work in the morning, and find his family moving in on his return at night." Apartments were built over stores; wooden tenements filled in the spaces between factories. Now, in the late 1890s, the unregulated boom had given way to an unregulated bust. The instability of economic life altered the facades of streets and the look of neighborhoods, with single-family houses being converted into two-families, and two-families into three as homeowners divided their nests to keep up with their mortgage payments. Woods and Kennedy summed up the dreariness: "In this neighborhood, the streets are still unpaved, the back alleys damp and unwholesome and the whole atmosphere one of depression."[39]

American politics has one constant law: blame for hard economic times falls on those in power. The Democratic ward organization in Ward 17 was failing its constituents: their needs were both too serious in kind and too great in number to be met by any prewelfare state political entity. To make matters worse, one of the leading political figures in the ward, Timothy J. Connolly, a member of the Common Council, was a slum lord, the builder of "some of the worst tenement property in the district . . . , so badly planned and constructed that it argues a special dispensation from the building department . . . for its erection." In the saloons, in the cramped living rooms of the jerry-built houses, amid the swelling ranks of the unemployed, a reaction was building against the local political establishment. It developed slowly, and for those who would seek to exploit it, timing would be crucial. James Michael Curley, launching his career with a try for a seat on the seventy-five-member Common Council, at first ran ahead of the mounting anger, and that cost him. But distress creates charismatic leaders; their personal qualities are enlarged by their followers' projected longing for deliverance. And the circle of distress was expanding. Ward 17 was typical of the "zone of emergence" into which thousands of immigrants and first-generation Americans had migrated from the inner city wards, their dreams of a better life in conflict with the pitiless imperatives of economic decline. Hopes had been raised in the zone—in Roxbury, South Boston, Charlestown, East Boston, Dorchester, and Brighton—only to be dashed. The zone—the "great Irish belt of the city," according to Woods and Kennedy—would deliver Curley's pluralities for forty years. Ward 17 was a microcosm of the zone, as the zone was a microcosm of the changing city. A leader who could win the ward could win the zone in his bid for the mayoralty. Within five years of his entry into ward politics, within three years of his first electoral victory, Curley, as the voice of its economic distress, would seize control of the ward himself. He would then have a municipally resonant political base.[40]

A later Massachusetts politician, Congressman Barney Frank, defines the importance of a base succinctly: "Your base in politics is made up of the people who are with you even when you are wrong." After his conquest of the ward, Curley would have a clutch of people like that behind him, people who would be with him even when he was wrong, a base from which to strike out for higher office.[41]

In his autobiography—"He didn't change a word," his ghost-writer says—Curley claimed that he made his debut as a political worker in the 1896 mayoral contest between the Democrat Owen Galvin and the Republican Thomas Hart. But there was no mayoral election that year; in 1895, with the election of Josiah Quincy, the mayoral term had been extended from one to two years. Galvin did run against Hart, but in 1889, not 1896. Possibly Curley worked in the Galvin campaign in the earlier year, but he would have been only fifteen, and, between the Dearborn School and Stephen Gale's, would have had little time and less energy for campaigning. Curley claimed that he boomed Galvin to his customers at C. S. Johnson's and "rang every doorbell in the neighborhood" after work. It was all to no avail, for Galvin lost. But according to Curley, his work on Galvin's behalf so impressed local politicians that they urged him to run for a seat on the Common Council two years later, in 1898.[42]

"Some forgotten Warwick who frequented Peter Whalen's cigar store," Curley told Joseph Dinneen, "was the first to suggest that I stand for office.

" 'Why don't you go out for the common council?' he asked.

" 'I haven't the money to make a campaign,' I objected.

"But Whalen dipped his good hand [he was One-Arm Peter Whalen] into his pocket and came up with $10. Tom Donnellon, a city health inspector, and his brother, Mark, contributed $15 more. I made the fight on that $25 and a few dollars of my own."

The boys at Peter Whalen's could not have been impressed by Curley's campaigning for Galvin in a year when Galvin did not run. Curley made his first try for the Council in 1897, not 1898. And the nondescript Peter Whalen mentioned in an interview with Curley in 1914 had lost an arm by this telling to Dinneen in 1948. But the doubtful facts should not divert us from the underlying truth. Curley doubtless got his start in politics in some such way as this.

The Common Council did not pay much—$300 a year; nor did it have much power. But it met only one night a week, and at its public hearings the "gripes of the electorate"—the aspiring politician's opportunity—were aired. It would do as a start. With his stake from Whalen's, Curley said, he bought a cutaway coat and a natty brown checked vest at Max Keezer's, a second-hand clothing store in Cambridge that specialized in the leavings of Harvard students, and plunged into the first of his thirty-two election campaigns. Beginning with a seat on the Common Council, he would run for state representative, for alderman, for the U.S. Congress (five times), for mayor (ten times), for governor (three times), and for the U.S. Senate. Nor would his hunger for office stop there. At the 1936 Democratic national convention in Philadelphia, he would march in his own welcoming parade under a banner that read,

Governor
JAMES M. CURLEY
of Massachusetts
"Man of Destiny"
WATCH 1940

Since he was then, in June of 1936, a candidate for election to the U.S. Senate and the term of the seat for which he was running would not be up until 1942, what voters were to watch in 1940 was a bid for the presidency.[43]

He worked hard in that first campaign, carrying a bucket of paste through the ward and putting up his own posters, but he was running as an outsider, unaffiliated with either of the ward's two rival Democratic factions, and the caucus system was hard on outsiders. Each party held its own caucus at city-owned ward rooms, with the Republican and Democratic candidates nominated at these caucuses facing off in the general election. Since Ward 17 was heavily Democratic, the outcome of the general election was not in doubt. The key was to win at the caucus. In the 1897 caucus, 362 of Curley's neighbors voted for him, which placed him a respectable fourth in a field of eleven. However, since each of the city's twenty-five wards could send only three representatives to the Common Council, fourth was not good enough. He tried again in 1898 and again he placed fourth, this time with 423 votes to the third-place finisher's 526. Curley would later claim that he really won his first two races—the first by 200 votes, the second by 500— but that he was counted out in the ward room by the ward committee. "Since such thefts of elections in Boston commonly occurred;

his charge deserves some credence," a recent researcher writes. "But it is impossible to tell whether Curley had any real basis for his allegations." More likely, Curley lost because, as an outsider, he could not use party ward rooms and assembly halls for rallies and had to get his votes "retail" in a painstaking canvass, house to house and face to face.[44]

According to Dinneen, Curley was heckled during the 1898 campaign for not serving in the war with Spain: "He explained in later years that he had tried to enlist and was turned down for hemorrhoids." Aside from this vulnerability, Curley had another unexpected liability: as a neophyte, he was an awkward stump speaker. To improve, between elections he went to the library to study the orations of Gladstone, Disraeli, Burke, Lincoln, and Daniel Webster.[45]

.   Words were his way up. Asked near the end of his life to estimate what his speaking ability had meant to him, he replied that it was ."the most important thing—without it there wouldn't have been a career—there would have been nothing." A correspondent for the *New York Times* once described Curley's speech this way: "The words roll off his tongue with a precision of diction, a clarity of expression, and an occasional vivid phrase which makes him a man well worth hearing, even on casual subjects." If the conversational Curley was impressive, the oratorical Curley could be overwhelming. His voice was smooth and rich and it had extraordinary range; in a single sentence, he could shift from baritone to tenor to countertenor. Elliot Norton, the dean of Boston's drama critics, knew of only three performers over his long career who could throw their voices in this manner—Tallulah Bankhead, Laurence Olivier, and Curley.[46]

So ardently did one Beacon Hill lady admire his voice, Curley once told his son Francis, that she made him a familiar offer—to underwrite his education, this time as an opera singer. "I can hear an opera singer's voice even when you are simply delivering groceries," she said. He replied that, having decided on a political career, he needed to study oratory. "I will not pay for training as an orator," she said, frowning on politics.

These Lady-Bountiful-as-temptress stories should be seen as political parables about the price of independence: the boy must renounce a safe route to power under the wing of an alien people in order to pursue his own destiny. The movement parallels what the Boston Irish were to do in the municipal realm, where under leaders who could not be co-opted they would make a clean break with the politics of deference.

Another customer, glimpsing theatrical possibilities in his voice, once gave Curley a ticket to see a performance of *Richard III*. He fell under the spell of Shakespeare that night. From then on, Curley would use him as a kind of political consultant, summoning quotations from memory to garnish his speeches or to put opponents in their place with a barb from the Bard. The language, the plot, the portrait of a ruthless man's rise to power—this first encounter with Shakespeare in *Richard III* was intoxicating. In his unpublished memoirs Curley re-created the scene: "I was seated well down front, the lights turned down low, when Richard was speaking, making a dramatic appearance with his misshapen body and his hands folded over each other, when John's wife spoke up and said, 'Why did you murder my husband?' Richard, replying, stated, 'In order that in me you might find a better one.' Frankly, I could not restrain myself and I shouted to the top of my voice, 'You are a son of a bitch!' The audience roared out but I succeeded in getting out of my seat and the theatre before the lights went on. I was completely carried away, so to speak."[47]

Such was the power of words. Curley admired U.S. attorney Owen Galvin, whose base was in a neighboring South End ward, because he was "a fine talker." Indeed he was, thanks in part to his memory. Galvin's obituary notes of this "sturdy Democrat," an appointee of Grover Cleveland, that "he carried more law in his head than the average lawyer does in his library." The carrying in his head would have impressed Curley, who himself rarely spoke from a finished text in political campaigns. Disraeli, his model among politicians of the past, had the same mnemonic gift.[48]

Disraeli's plumage also appealed to the young Curley. "Father admired the way he would use deliberate ostentation to provoke the opposition," Francis Curley recalled. The trip to Max Keezer's for the stylish clothes suggests that he also had an intuitive Disraeli-like appreciation for the symbolic uses of appearance. He never dressed—or talked—down to his constituents. Neither did Huey Long. Both politicians appreciated the vicarious element in their sartorial no less than in their rhetorical appeals. T. Harry Williams writes of Long, "He understood the social forces that made his success possible and . . . he respected those forces." One of these, propelling the ascent of both Curley and Long, was an identification upward, an envy cut by awe. Long had seen the "Great White Chief" of Mississippi, James K. Vardaman, campaigning in the piney-woods towns dressed in white from his hat to his shoes and conveyed in a wagon pulled by two white oxen—he had seen poor dirt farmers mesmerized by Vardaman's immaculacy, and their reaction, Williams writes, taught him a counterintuitive lesson: "The masses were more likely to follow one of their own if that man showed that in some ways he was better than they were."

That insight would not only be at the root of Curley's affectations of high culture but also of his unashamed pursuit of high living. His vocal accent would often be called "Oxonian." His diction and syntax were deliberately rococo. He would live in a mansion, summer at the shore, be waited on by servants and ferried around in limousines. During the worst years of the Depression he deployed a household staff consisting of a parlor maid, a cook, a gardener, an upstairs maid, an outside twice-a-week woman to do the cleaning, a chauffeur, a governess for his son Francis, and a social secretary for his daughter Mary. He collected expensive Orientalia procured through Gumps of San Francisco. His wine cellar, hidden in his basement behind a large photograph of Calvin Coolidge, boasted the rarest vintages. In this way, and not forgetting the winter sojourns in Palm Beach, Sea Island, Georgia, Bermuda, and Cuba; the extensive European travel, with long stays in first-class hotels; the big tips, lavish parties, and Havana-Havanas; the daily purchases of fresh flowers, the private schools for the children; the yachts and diamonds—in this way he spent hundreds of thousands of dollars, much of which he did not earn but took, indirectly, from the working- and lower-middle-class taxpayers of Boston. Yet he said that the title he cherished most was "the Mayor of the Poor," and the poor venerated him. Political affection is a strange one-way emotional exchange—too impersonal to be love, yet just as blind.[49]

In his second try at winning nomination to the Common Council at the ward caucus, Curley employed a trick that throws light on the roots of political affection, the tie between leader and led that scholars of leadership refer to as the "charismatic bond." To cast their ballots, voters had to run a gantlet past the candidates standing in the ward room, who were lined up at a rail separating them from the ballot box. The candidates would urge on the voters, sometimes challenging them, sometimes even reaching over and buttonholing them for a last-minute pep talk. It was the kind of spontaneous politics that greatly exercised upper-middle-class reformers, who passed regulations banning the practice and forbidding candidates or their agents from communicating their wishes to the voters. But Curley circumvented these regulations with an ethnic ruse. "I had learned to talk some Gaelic from my parents in the early days . . . ," he later recalled, "and as each voter came along I addressed them in the Gaelic tongue." His opponent on the rail was puzzled. "What's Curley saying?" he asked a bystander who, as the Irish say, "had the tongue." The fellow clapped his hands and laughed. "He's saying, 'Don't forget the boy from home.'" Unable to understand what Curley was saying, the Yankee police sergeant on duty in the ward room could not rightly stop him. The "boy from home" had found a way past the law and into voters' hearts.[50]

Sometime during 1897 or 1898 Curley left C. S. Johnson's; his hectic electioneering had apparently annoyed Mr. Johnson. His new job, as a traveling salesman for a Boston bakery supply house, was not without a political application. His route lay in northern Massachusetts and southern New Hampshire. Sales were slow, so he worked up a stratagem in the psychology of suggestion. To convince customers that his wares were desirable, he filled his order book with the names and addresses of phony customers. He would thumb through this bogus list as he made his pitch, the while displaying a stubby pencil, worn down, he would truthfully say, from writing out orders.[51]

"I had no time for girl friends," he later said of this period. Sarah was still the only woman in his life. If he was out late with a friend, he would stay over rather than risk waking his mother from her hard-won sleep. One Christmas Eve he embarked on a search for a shawl for Sarah in the stores downtown. Not finding just the right one, he made his way from store to store, from downtown all the way back to Roxbury, where at last he found a shawl worthy of her sainted shoulders. The fine gift left her more embarrassed than pleased. "Take it back, Jimmie," he remembered her saying. "Sure it's not for the likes of me."[52]

Here is another clue to the Irish widow's emotional hegemony: sacrifice, self-denial—this was all she knew. For her children it was an ambiguous legacy. They revered her goodness, which was the very model of that of the saints they heard about in church. But her inability to ask for anything for herself gave them a twisted idea of desire, the motive for most human achievement. "Hasn't Curley had enough?" one of his opponents later asked about him. The answer was no—Curley never had enough. Driven by the polar logic of the psyche, he was as unbalanced in his immoderation as his mother had been in her abnegation. Raised by a saint, he became a sinner.

For the rest, he continued to be active in the affairs of the fledgling St. Philip's Church, the parish he had helped organize. He primed his speaking skills at A.O.H. meetings. He pored over classic orations and tried them on his own tongue. He had run for office twice and lost twice, but defeat would never daunt him. He would run again in 1899.

In his autobiography Curley depicted himself as an antiestablishment candidate in 1899, using the two elections that were stolen from him as a winning issue against the local machine. It makes a delicious irony: James Michael Curley beginning his career as a reformer inveighing against "crooked" politicians. But the truth is precisely the opposite. Rather than run against the ward establishment, he ran as its chosen candidate.[53]

Ward 17 was then in the midst of what the *Boston Globe* characterized as "the most bitter and stubborn fight in the history of the ward." Charles Ignatius Quirk, a governor's councilor and a leading figure in the Boston Democracy, led one faction; a coming politician, twenty-eight-year-old Timothy E. McCarthy, led the other. In 1899 the election machinery in the ward was under the control of the Quirk faction, which, in view of his claims of electoral fraud, gave Curley a clinching reason to join forces with Quirk. The ward room in Ward 17 was the former Vine Street Church on Dudley Street, which had been built by Congregational Trinitarians in 1857, when no one could have imagined that within forty years it would be the haunt of Irish politicians. The caucus held there on the afternoon and evening of November 14, 1899, was said by a reporter on the scene to be "very quiet." Lieutenant Rich and Sergeant Eagan of the Boston Police Department were on hand to see that it stayed that way, and they had twenty policemen with them, a figure that argues the expectation of trouble.

There was, however, only a wisp of it. When Charles Quirk challenged the credentials of one man, who was accompanied by three others, all four fled—they were either nonresidents or "repeaters," hirelings who would vote several times under different names in different locations, perhaps in the pay of the McCarthy faction. Aside from that incident, however, "the largest caucus ever held in the ward," according to the *Globe,* passed harmoniously. Nine candidates were in the running for the three council nominations. When the ballots were counted, three Quirk-controlled councilmen had won: George A. Flynn with 984 votes, James M. Curley with 927, and Timothy J. Connolly with 704. In the general election held a few weeks later, all three Democratic nominees easily beat their Republican opponents, Byram W. Hatch, William N. Humphreys, and Alfred Mitchell—Flynn winning 2,183 votes, Curley 2,134, and Connolly 1,981. "It proved to be the beginning of a new era in the ward," Curley later said, in a rare foray into understatement.[54]

The Crouching Tiger

❖   ❖   ❖   ❖

He had an instinctive and impulsive sympathy for anybody who was deprived of something, and he liked the feeling of power that came to him when he could help such a person.

T. HARRY WILLIAMS,
HUEY LONG

It twists my heart when I see poverty, and unemployment, and hunger, and can do little with my own poor efforts to help out.

JAMES MICHAEL CURLEY

❖   ❖   ❖   ❖

There were seventy-five members in the Common Council that began its term in January 1900. Only one of them ever climbed to the top of the greasy pole of Boston politics; only one is remembered today. Why? That question does not admit of a brisk answer. But among the factors in Curley's rise one stands out: publicity, the sheer getting of his name in circulation in the first place, at the dawn of the era of mass journalism, and the reasons it was in circulation in the second. Between 1900 and 1914, Curley bred unprecedented tumult in Boston politics. He was de- nounced from pulpits and excoriated by editorialists. Headlines made his name synonymous with scandal. His "image," as we would call his reputation today, would never be cleansed of this early taint. And yet without it his political ascent would not have been possible. For every enemy bad publicity made him, it made him two friends. It did so by transforming him into a martyr for things he never openly championed because they could not be avowed. Economic frustration and class hatred, wounded pride and ethnic resentment, thwarted hope and strangled aspiration—these were the mute causes that found their tribune in James Michael Curley. Boston was in decline, the Boston Irish were caught in a spiral of downward mobility, throughout the first half of the twentieth century. Curley rose as Boston fell.

Sometime after the 1899 election, Curley's boss at the bakery supply house called him into his office to tell him he was through. "Mr. Curley," Curley later remembered him saying, "you have done fine work for us, but it seems that lately your interest has been divided, and that you are not heart and soul in the bakery business." These organs were occupied elsewhere.

Curley had won his seat on the council by allying himself with a divided and failing ward organization. His first political challenge, therefore, was to ensure that he did not go down with it. Toward that end, he compiled a creditable progressive record in the Common Council session of 1900. His first official act was to request that the Republican mayor—the same Thomas N. Hart who had defeated Owen Galvin eleven years before—instruct his department heads to observe the new eight-hour-workday law for city employees. He introduced measures to give city employees a half-holiday on Saturdays, to replace the outhouses behind school buildings with indoor plumbing, and to build a hospital for consumptives. He protested Mayor Hart's dismissal of city workers "for no other reason than that they are politically allied with the Democratic party," and he came out for the annual publication of a list of all city employees in order to expose payroll padding. He might almost have been mistaken for a reformer.

He also dealt feelingly with constituents who were in distress. After his autobiography was published, in 1957, Curley received a letter from a Mrs. Harriet M. Brennan of Glide, Oregon. "Because I have always admired you there is one incident of many years ago when you were a member of the Common Council that you may have forgotten, but I shall always remember," Mrs. Brennan wrote. "I was a member of the Union Church on Columbus Ave. at the time. A Miss Robinson who was a secretary there was severely injured when a Fire Engine went over the sidewalk on Mass Ave. The Council turned down any aid for her—but you went to the City Hospital—visited her—and gave her a box of candy. She discovered $5.00 in it after you left. To me it was a wonderful thing— your kindness."[1] He was a born master of the politics of gesture.

Within the ward, meanwhile, Curley broke ranks with Charles Quirk to join forces with Timothy McCarthy, who, in the roundabout of the factions, controlled the election machinery for the caucuses held in November 1900. The McCarthy slate won the caucus "hands down," according to the *Boston Globe*, but not without a dash of chicane. To distract the attention of the police lieutenant on duty at the Vine Street Church, a fistfight was staged on the sidewalk. While the lieutenant was outside separating the combatants, the McCarthy people inside, to use Curley's euphemism, "properly decorated" the ballot box.[2]

In the romance of American politics, politicians may habitually betray the electorate, but they always keep their word to each other, guild loyalty being their supreme—some would say solitary—virtue. Curley never succumbed to that romance. He was loyal only to his ambition, to "amount to something more than the ordinary man." Throughout his career he would attach himself first to one political figure, then when he had gotten as far as he could go battened on that man, leap to another. From Quirk to McCarthy, from Champ Clark to Al Smith to Franklin Roosevelt—for Curley, the restless barnacle, early and late it was all one pattern.

"It's the safest thing to have an anchor to windward if you are in politics," Curley said of this period, meaning a source of outside income. Soon after his election to the council, he threw out his anchor: he and his brother John became agents for the New York Life Insurance Company, establishing themselves in an office downtown. He devoted four days a week to the job, reserving the fifth day for Common Council business and political maneuver. He did well—he claimed to have made $12,000 in one year (equivalent to $100,000 today)—and the family moved to a larger apartment on Albany Street. There was a new security in his life, a margin for ease. Curley had his anchor to windward, and he held his first public office; all he needed now was a base from which to run for others.[3]

In the Common Council session of 1901, he showed particular solicitude for the problems of the most hard-pressed of his constituents, urging in one debate that persons put into institutions for the destitute not be called "paupers," because "of the odium which is cast around anybody who is regarded as a pauper," and requesting in another that some disused buildings near the City Hospital be turned into a facility for the treatment of delirium tremens. "It seems inhumane," he said in his remarks, "to oblige unfortunates who are addicted to the habit of drink—which physicians tell us is a disease in itself—it seems rather inhumane to confine these people to a station house for anywhere from twelve to fifteen hours, then put them on trucks or aboard boats to carry them to Deer Island, having to put them in strait jackets and deprive them of medical attendance until such time as they reach the island. . . ." Paupers, drunks, truant boys: such were the casualties of industrial contraction, of market failure, in Ward 17.[4]

Curley did not run for a third term in the Common Council in the fall elections; instead he sought and won a seat in the lower house of the Massachusetts state legislature. He told Joseph Dinneen that he went to the legislature "to add another qualification to his record" for future higher office. In the same campaign, he strongly backed Timothy McCarthy for a seat on the thirteen-member Board of Aldermen. He had become McCarthy's chief lieutenant in the ward and, with McCarthy's help, had been elected chairman of the powerful ward committee. But McCarthy—young, well connected with the Boston Democratic party, and with more political experience than Curley—was an obvious rival, and Curley was scheming with other members of the local Democratic organization, known as the Jackson Club after its meeting place, to stage a coup against him and seize control of the ward. When the ward committee met at the Jackson Club to pick its new chairman just after the election, Curley and a group of dissidents launched their revolt. They spoke against McCarthy's leadership, and nominated Curley for another term as ward chairman. "We won by about seven votes," he later said, in another familiar refrain—to hear him tell it, the only honest elections he ever entered were those he won—"but we were counted out by the opposition." Flanked by eight of the dissidents, Curley walked boldly out of the Jackson Club. Outside, the night air was bracing. He would never be part of another man's organization again.[5]

A few weeks after the walkout, Tom McCann, a friend who had been one of the dissidents, went looking for Curley. He found him at home, lounging on a couch. He was taking his self-imposed banishment from the Jackson Club hard.

Under McCann's prompting, Curley shook off his melancholy torpor, and the two men set out to look for a clubhouse of their own. Crossing a nearby park, they met another of the dissidents, Johnny McCarthy, who joined them. At the corner of Hampden and George streets, the three men stopped abruptly; the two-story triangular-shaped wooden building in front of them had caught their collective eye.

"I see that the Temperance Society sign is down," said McCann, pointing to the vacant top floor.

"Let's go and have a look at it," Curley said.

They peered into the dappled room. Before them was a large meeting hall, with windows on either side, and offices at the further end.

"It's the ideal place," Curley pronounced.[6]

The rent was $25 a month. When the McCarthy people discovered that Curley was about to start a rival club, they offered the landlord $15 more to rent the space. But they were too late. The Tammany Club was born.

The name bristled with affront. New York City's Tammany Hall, the storied Democratic organization, had just been through a decade of scandal and official investigations. Under Richard Croker, an Irish immigrant who had once been tried for murder (the jury split, six to six), the Hall had recovered from the Tweed Ring exposures of the late 1860s and early 1870s, and regained its hold on New York. Beginning in the mid-nineties, however, Croker's luck turned. The Tammany system depended on vice—prostitution, gambling, illegal liquor—which was protected by the police in return for a fee to the Hall. From the proceeds, Croker had accrued a fortune of $8,000,000, with which he bought a house on Park Avenue, a huge diamond stickpin, and his own Pullman railroad car.

The basis of this lucrative graft was threatened when Dr. Charles Parkhurst, pastor of the Madison Square Presbyterian Church, mounted his famous crusade against the fleshpots. With the help of a private detective, who later wrote a sensational book about their escapades, Dr. Parkhurst, under cover as a "gay boy from the West," toured the city's brothels. At an establishment run by a certain Hattie Adams he was treated to a "dance of nature," in which five naked young women danced the can-can for his edification. A game of leapfrog followed, with his detective-guide playing the frog while one by one the naked dancers nimbled over him. Parkhurst's sermons describing these and like revels raised a storm against Tammany, and an outraged public swept into office a reform mayor pledged to clean up the city.

Fearing indictment, Croker fled to his English estate, where he took especial delight in feeding the pigs, "to each of whom he gave the name of a New York politician." But, in a way typical of New York politics, reform soon outstayed its welcome, and Croker returned to the city in 1897. His candidate for district attorney that year—running on the brazen slogan "To Hell with Reform!"—won, as did his man in the mayoral race. This was an indignity past endurance for the Republican-controlled state legislature, which began a series of investigations against Tammany that culminated in the exposure of the "ice trust," a conspiracy of leading businessmen and politicians (including the mayor) to reap high profits from the city's purchase of ice. With the tide of reform once more about to come in, Croker resigned his leadership of Tammany Hall and returned to his native Ireland, this time for good, to raise Derby-winning horses on his estate.[7]

Boston was not New York—it prided itself on that comparative felicity. There had never been municipal corruption in Boston on anything like the sordid scale of New York (and there never would be). In naming his club after Tammany Hall, Curley was flying in the face of respectable opinion.

To his constituents in the ward, however, the name Tammany had a different connotation. "The Ward 17 Tammany Club," he once told an interviewer, "was organized to do here in Boston what the decent side of the New York Tammany Club did there." On another occasion he said of it: "Tammany was peculiarly acceptable to us as an organization because of the humane and brotherly character of the work necessary at that time in that place." The "decent side" of Tammany meant jobs, a bag of coal for the grate, a set of teeth for an old man down to his gums. In that pre–New Deal world, it meant a measure of protection against what the economist Joseph Schumpeter called "the gales of creative destruction" unleashed by the unmitigated capitalism of the day. This was the tradition of help to which the Tammany Nine—Curley, his brother John, Thomas F. Curley (no relation), Jeremiah J. Good, George H. Norton, William Dolan, Anthony J. McNealey, Ernest Cummings, and Tom McCann—appealed in naming their club.[8]

The club was set up in February 1902, but its official opening came on the Fourth of July. The celebration started the night before the Fourth and stretched through the day. Drawn by the promise of oratory and lemonade (apparently the spirit of the Temperance Society lived on), a crowd of curious people filled the club's rooms, jammed the stairway, and spilled over into the street. The highlight of the festivities was a welcoming speech by the club's acting president, Representative Curley, in which he explained its purposes and then, to signify that the occasion was a real "open house," threw the key out the window. "After the gala opening," one historian writes, "attracted by the dynamic personality of young Jim Curley, many of the members of the Jackson Club migrated into the Tammany ranks."[9]

That dynamic personality united charm with doggedness. And sometimes the doggedness itself was charming, as in this anecdote from a recipient of the Curley persuasion.

"What stands between you and me?" he once asked a diffident fellow on the way home from a meeting of the Ancient Order of Hibernians.

"Nothing that I know of," was the unpromising reply.

"What have I ever done to you?"

"Nothing."

"Why don't you be with me then?"

"I don't like you."

Curley thought that one over. "Well," he sighed, "I can't help that."

The fellow allowed as how that was true, and yet he found himself smiling at this beguiling candor, and soon was liking Curley, and soon *was* with him.[10]

A more straightforwardly endearing manifestation was Curley's way of telegraphing a laugh before he got to it. "The Curley smile would prepare you for the laugh to come," a witness remembers. Even if the joke was not equal to the buildup—which was often the case, since much of Curley's humor was of the "you had to be there" variety—his auditors would enjoy the pleasure of expectancy. And sometimes the arrival would live up to the journey. At one dance, after the piano player had been banging away unmercifully at the keyboard, Curley took the stage to make an announcement. He then paused, cracked his editorial smile, and said, "The village blacksmith will now resume."

He had the sense of timing of an accomplished performer. One man who saw him in action in his middle to late years remembers: "He was like Bob Hope in the way he could deliberately race ahead of his audience, wait for them to catch up with a humorous remark, and then, just as the laughter or applause began, he would embellish his first phrase with another crack and, at the right split second when the audience caught up with that one, he would be off and running again." It took years to become so adroit, but even in bud this talent was uncommon.

Curley was also exceptionally deft at political jujitsu: the use of an opponent's strength or charge against him, a maneuver that often climaxes in a percussive burst of laughter. One of his enemies had been getting a hand by punctuating his speeches with the question "Where is this coward Curley?" Curley turned the line against him at a meeting in the Vine Street Church. He knew that the speaker could work only from a prepared text, that he was fixated on his barbed question, and that he would stumble if it should misfire. Curley put on a big hat, raised the collar of his overcoat as high as it would go, and entered the church, managing to worm his way into the front rows. The speaker was just reaching his crescendo.

"Where is this coward Curley?"

Curley shouted up at him, "Here I am, Tom! Right here."

Having come to boo Curley, the audience stayed to laugh at Tom."

To publicize the club's activities and attract new members, the Tammany Nine posted handbills throughout the ward. Anthony McNealey, the only member who owned a horse, would drive a wagon laden with posters and buckets of paste, with Curley sitting in the back and Tom McCann walking ahead of them. McCann's assignment was to engage passing policemen in conversation while Curley shinnied up lampposts or climbed walls, putting up his posters in the choice spots with the signs that read, POST NO BILLS. One night this stalling tactic did not work; and Curley was splayed on a lamppost when a policeman happened by.

"Who's that up there?" he shouted.

"Have a heart. It's Jim, officer," McCann replied.

"Well, get down and beat it, Jim, before I recognize you," the policeman said.

On other occasions, when the policeman was unknown to them, Curley, smeared with incriminating quantities of paste, would have to scramble off the pole and sprint for the wagon. McNealey would put the lash to the horse, and with the police whistle blowing behind them, they would be off at a gallop through the echoing streets.[12]

To raise money, the club began the practice of holding "powwows" at the end of every summer. The site for the first one, held in 1903, was the Caledonian Grove on the banks of the Charles River in suburban West Roxbury, a nickel fare from the Dudley Station terminal of the elevated street railway in Roxbury. These all-day picnics featured such novel attractions as greased pig snatches and balloon ascensions. Before the first powwow, Curley sent this droll note to club members: "All committee members are hereby asked to bring axes to the powwow—but not to use them on each other." Axes? For ten cents a whack, contestants could have at a beat-up piano, with the one who did the most damage winning a prize of $5.

The powwows offered Punch and Judy shows for the children, as well as foot races, tug-of-war competitions, and baseball games for both sexes. There was also a beauty contest (which Curley supplemented with a contest for ugliest man) and a certified freak—a fellow who could drink a pailful of water and, twisting his ear like the crank of a pump, expel it in a revolting flood.

Oratory was also on the bill. Curley recruited a roster of speakers for each powwow, including some national figures. One year John L. Sullivan, the Roxbury Strong Boy, a former heavyweight champion of the world and a close Curley ally, gave an address on temperance.° At the 1903 powwow the featured speaker was the Honorable Gerald O'Keefe of New York's Tammany Hall. "You are adopting the machine methods as well as can be done in a town like this," he said with the invariable New York condescension toward Boston yokels, "but you must keep the good work up. Every one of you here should get out and hustle. Get after the voters and find out where they stand. . . . None of you are in politics for your health; you are all looking for something. Well, get out and hustle for it; work for the party and the party will be compelled to look after you."[13]

Curley needed no imported advice to hustle. He not only worked on current voters; he targeted their children—future voters. Starting in 1903, Tammany gave an annual Christmas party for the poorest families in the ward. The club furnished Christmas dinners with all the trimmings and put on a special stereopticon show. Each child went home with a bag of candy and a pair of woolen mittens. Working in shifts, Tammany feted seven hundred children on Christmas Day 1906.

For the adults of the ward, for the homeless, the unemployed, the people no level of government in those pre–New Deal days would or could protect, the Tammany Club was the only place to turn for help. An anonymous letter to the editor of the *Boston Post* suggests why with graphic sympathy:

> practically everything is against them. If they seek a position in some factory, the union is against them; if they seek a position in the

---

° "If a man comes home to his wife after filling up with a lot of that stuff and eating Limburger cheese and pig's feet," Sullivan told the rapt crowd, "and says, 'If you love me, kiss me,' do you think she is going to kiss that?"

government, the civil service bars them; if they want to open a little store, the trust is against them. The only person whom they can approach is the politician.[14]

They were in luck if that politician was James Curley. Two years after the founding of the Tammany Club, a newspaperman asked Curley to account for its success. "Why has the Tammany Club, under my leadership, been successful? Briefly put, the reason is that for many years the interests of Ward 17 people have been neglected by those elected as their servants." That answer vindicated Curley's judgment in breaking with the established ward leadership after using it to get himself elected. "The Tammany Club has worked faithfully to assist the needy," Curley added, "help the unfortunate, encourage those who merit encouragement, and at all times stands ready to give a helping hand to any resident of Ward 17." Curley claimed that he and the other club officers had "secured and provided employment for over 700 men," and with justifiable pride he went on to tell how they did it.

> Each morning we have, on an average, seven new applications for work. Mr. Good, Mr. Thomas Curley, and myself sort out the applications. Then we take three different routes. From the builders we secure employment for men who can be useful in the building trades. From contractors we secure work for laboring men. From corporations we secure work of a varied nature for men who must earn money.
>
> The common supposition is that our field is confined to city patronage. It is the smallest portion. We have tramped Atlantic Avenue and the waterfront, appealing for work. Men who made pianos have become longshoremen. Watchmakers have taken to driving trucks. So it goes on. We assisted in securing employment in New Hampshire for 50 men.

That category of persons from a meaner day, the "truly needy," also got a boost from this neighborhood antipoverty agency. "Then there are the destitute," Curley concluded, "who need shelter and good food. For these we do our utmost. If our own pocketbooks cannot afford the necessary money, we find someone who can. Our headquarters are open the year round. There is always heat and comfort for the homeless man. . . . Summing it all up, we do our very best to help everyone."

The welfare check, food stamps, the medicaid mill: nothing in the impersonal, dependency-inducing system of contemporary social policy can equal what the self-interested politicians at the Tammany Club did for the poor. "Get me a job and I will give you my vote": in taking the politics out of welfare, we have broken a contract beneficial to the whole of society. The political boss, David Riesman observed when a few specimens of the species still flourished, is "soaked in a gravy which we can well afford."[15]

Curley kept a book listing every favor he did, and, according to his fellow Tammanyite Jeremiah Good, he tried to do "at least fifty favors a week." That book, Good told a reporter, was "a handy thing to have"—especially on election day. "Curley's method of providing help was intensely personal," one scholar observes. "He once wrote that 'he did not appoint captains or lieutenants, since this practice might have promoted jealousy'; but he probably also favored this 'hands-on' approach to providing assistance because recipients would know that their help had come from Jim Curley." Remarkably, Curley got other club members to let his be the fingerprints that showed on their collegial favors. Money might have bought their loyalty, but it could not have kept it. "Time and again," Tom McCann testified, "I've seen men go through real discomfort for Jim Curley." He bound them to him by the promise of his energy. He was well launched in politics. As he climbed higher, so would they.[16]

In October 1902, Curley put his fingerprints all over a favor that would nearly derail his career. Running for reelection, he needed campaign workers to help him. On the evening of October 15, two potential volunteers came into the Tammany Club seeking help. James Hughes and Bartholomew Fahey were known to Curley, as well as to Thomas F. Curley (no relation), the other top figure in the Tammany Club, who was also on the premises that night. Hughes, thirty-eight, a native of County Meath in Ireland, was a conductor on the elevated street railway. He lived in Roxbury, but in Ward 21, not Ward 17. Fahey, twenty-six, born in Galway, was a store clerk from Cambridge. The men wanted to take the upcoming civil service examination for the position of letter carrier, but doubted their ability to pass it. Hughes had taken the exam twice before, in 1900 and 1901, and had scored 48.55 percent the first time, 49.40 percent the second. He "couldn't spell Constantinople," Curley once quipped, "but he had wonderful feet for a letter carrier." He needed help, and a scheme was quickly hatched to provide it.[17]

Tom would impersonate Hughes; James would do Fahey. On December 4, the Curleys showed up at the examining room at the Federal Building in downtown Boston. On their way in, Tom Curley boldly stopped to pass the time of day with Commissioner Stebbins, the head of the U.S. Civil Service Commission in Boston, to see if Stebbins recognized him—which he did not. Tom Curley and James Curley not only took the exam fraudulently, they also cheated on it, making no fewer than twelve duplicated blunders. For example, both placed Fort Smith in Illinois, then both changed it, correctly, to Arkansas. Still, they passed. They left the examining room confident that they had pulled a fast one. In fact they had been recognized.[18]

Back in the ward, meanwhile, Curley was going from strength to strength. In the Massachusetts legislature he supported bills favorable to his constituents, introducing one measure limiting the amount of consecutive time firemen had to stay on the job, and helping pass another that permitted truant children to be released from the reform school on the death or illness of either parent. The defection of Jackson Club members to Tammany, coupled with Curley's use of his legislative office to attract yet more recruits, so alarmed Timothy McCarthy that he formed an alliance of convenience with his former enemy Charles Quirk. Their common objective became the defeat of Tammany in the fall elections of 1902. Feelings were running high in the ward, and on the night before the filing deadline for caucus nominations they came to a head.[19]

To ensure that Tammany-backed candidates got the top places on the ballot—which, since immigrants were thought to vote for the first name they saw, could mean a great deal—Curley and two of his fellow club members, big Tom McCann and Tom Reedy, the club janitor, went downtown to the Democratic City Committee headquarters on the eve of the day nomination papers were due. Knowing that "first come, first served" was the rule in getting names on the ballot, they waited in the committee offices until the police ordered them to leave at 7:00 P.M., then retreated to the steps outside. They intended to stand guard until morning, when they would be first in line. In the middle of the night, a gang of McCarthy-Quirk men showed up and promptly set about clearing the three Tammanyites off the stairs. They grabbed Curley's legs and started to pull in one direction, while McCann hooked his arm around Curley's neck and pulled in the other. "If it had gone on much longer," Curley later remarked, "I'd have been seven feet tall."

In extremis, he gasped, "The window! The window!" McCann, seeing what he meant, dropped his end of Curley, then picked up the slender Reedy and held him aloft, shouting to him to break the small window overhead. Reedy kicked it in, and, as Curley had hoped, the noise alerted the policeman on the beat. A whistle sounded; the McCarthy men let go of Curley and took off. The next morning, Curley was first in line to file nomination papers, and the names of Tammany's candidates crowned the ballot.[20]

In the state primary caucus, Curley and Good easily won the Democratic nominations for the ward's two seats in the state legislature. The municipal caucus later that fall saw Tammany win a "clear majority" of the seats on the ward committee. The combined forces of McCarthy and Quirk had been defeated; James Michael Curley was the undisputed boss of what would now rapidly become known as the Tammany ward, with its dual associations of scandal and social work.[21]

There remained the problem of McCarthy's incumbency as the alderman of Ward 17, a possible beachhead from which he might retake the ward. In the party caucus Thomas Curley had tried to win the nomination for alderman away from McCarthy. "If McCarthy had gone on to win the regular election," one scholar writes, "he might well have . . . blocked, or at least delayed, Curley's rise to power." But McCarthy lost his seat in the general election to the Republican candidate. As unemployment increased in the ward, support for Socialist candidates also went up—from 3 percent in the state election of 1901 to nearly 12 percent in 1902. Enough Democratic crossover voters cast ballots for the Socialist candidate for alderman to defeat McCarthy, who of course got no support from the Tammany Club within Ward 17. He was through in ward politics.

Twisting the knife (magnanimity would never be his strong suit), on New Year's Day 1903 Curley sent him the following note:

"Honorable"? T. E. McCarthy,

Dear Sir—
When I last saw you in the Aldermanic Chambers you promised faithfully to pay the $10.00 which you hold belonging to me the following day, although a considerable time has elapsed you have not yet done

so. If you keep your word as well to your constituents as you do to me I am not in the least surprised that the district is this year represented by a republican. The people probably prefer a promise-keeping republican to a democrat who does not possess that virtue.

Whom the gods would destroy, they first make arrogant. The two Curleys had been seen taking the civil service exam by allies of the Honorable T. E. McCarthy.[22]

The story broke on February 11, 1903. The headline across the front page of the *Boston Herald* read, PROMINENT WARD 17 DEMOCRATIC POLITICIANS SUSPECTED OF FRAUD BY FEDERAL OFFICERS. According to the text, some of the ninety-odd men in the examining room on December 4th had recognized the Curleys and inquired of the government official on the scene whether their names were on the list of those signed up to take the exam. The official checked the list; no, neither Curley's name was there. The handwriting on the two examinations, subsequent investigation revealed, bore no resemblance to that on the applications filled out by Fahey and Hughes.

Rumors about the Curleys had been circulating in political circles for two months. The wider public got its first whiff of the scandal in late January, when Tom Curley, who had been named deputy collector of the city by the incoming mayor, the redoubtable Patrick Collins, was told not to report for work. Collins had heard enough of the rumors not to want Tom Curley in his administration. On February 26, a front-page headline in the *Boston Globe* asked, WERE POLITICIANS EXAMINED FOR CIVIL SERVICE? The story, which was illustrated by blown-up photographs of the two Curleys, related the circumstances leading to the "surrender" of Tom and James Curley, Fahey, and Hughes to the U.S. marshal at noon on the previous day. Bail was set at $2,500. It was the first time a member of the Massachusetts state legislature had ever been submitted to criminal arrest.[23]

The charge, "combining, conspiring, confederating and agreeing together to defraud the United States," sounded grave.

The trial opened in federal district court on September 23, 1903, and closed the next day. Presiding was Judge Francis Cabot Lowell. That the judge at the trial of James Michael Curley should bear the two Brahmin names preserved for facetiousness in the ditty that includes the line, "And the Cabots speak only to the Lowells / And the Lowells speak only to God"—that fate should

These boys would grow up to vote for Curley in the 1930s and 1940s.
His career straddled decades; he was in politics for life.

(Above) With what look like Russian sailors. As an Irish American, Curley warmed to the "British war" slowly but soon saw its political uses.

(Right) War mayor with warrior—Marshal Joffre.

(Right) With an obscenely happy Andrew J. Peters. If only Dan Coakley, Curley's Mephisto, had known of Peters's seduction of an eleven-year-old girl.

(Below) With James Jr., and Mary at an army camp. James was to be Curley's political heir.

(Above) With navy officers and Mrs. Curley. Curley let interned German sailors celebrate the kaiser's birthday on the Common, and once the war broke out he protected the rights of German Americans and dissenters.

(Left) The tigerish grin belongs to Theodore Roosevelt; Calvin Coolidge is two to Roosevelt's left. It was an age of heroes, when politicians embodied great social and cultural forces.

At the North Bridge in Concord with Calvin Coolidge (extreme right).

The yin and the yang of Massachusetts politics: Calvin Coolidge and James M. Curley. The police strike made Coolidge president. Could it have done the same for Curley?

A wartime parade honoring Premier Viviani.

(Left) With James Jr.

(Below) The most notorious house in Boston: 350 the Jamaicaway.

The congressman's wife. Mary became fast friends with Nellie Taft, the president's wife.

Mary Emelda Curley. Curley forged deeply romantic marriages to two women: one in his youth, the other in his middle and old age.

have arranged matters in this ethnically polarized way, was to prove a boon for Curley.

The prosecution easily showed that Fahey was at his job on December 4, 1902, the day he was supposed to have taken the civil service exam. The handwriting, the duplicated blunders, Commissioner Stebbins's testimony that Tom Curley had spoken to him before entering the room—against such damning evidence the defense's contention that the two witnesses who saw the Curleys take the exam were politically biased showed as pathetic stuff indeed. One of those witnesses testified that he had been offered $100 to say that he had not seen the Curleys—a revelation that did nothing to help their cause. The other witness, twenty-nine-year-old William J. O. Meara, had fled Boston in panic after hearing rumors of a coming attempt, as one paper put it, to "do him in."

After being out for ninety minutes, the jury—made up of people with Yankee names like Turner, Otis, Abbott, and Holmes—filed back into the courtroom. While waiting for the jurors to return, Tom Curley had seemed indifferent, but James's anxiety had been palpable. The courtroom rapidly filled up as the jurors took their seats. "Are the defendants here?" the Clerk of Courts called. From the rear of the courtroom Tom Curley and James Curley answered. Fahey and Hughes being absent, the judge delayed the reading of the verdict until they could be found.

"An intense silence seemed to fall upon the court while it awaited the return of the missing men," a reporter noted. James Curley twitched nervously in his seat as he scanned the faces of the jurors for some clue to his fate. After a twenty-minute interval the U.S. attorney, Henry P. Moulton, rose and addressed Judge Lowell: "I ask that the court declare the defendants Fahey and Hughes defaulted and that it proceed with the verdict." The judge gave the order. Both defendants stood to hear the verdict as the clerk addressed the jury:

"What say you, Mr. Foreman and gentleman: are the defendants guilty or not guilty?"

"Guilty," returned the foreman as each name was read.

When he heard his name, James Michael Curley shuddered. He had not anticipated the verdict. He later claimed that he and Tom Curley "had looked up the matter beforehand, and could not find anything to show that this was a breach of the law, although we knew it was a breach of the rules." To be sent to jail for breaking "the rules" seemed a punishment out of proportion to the crime. He had worked so hard to get where he was, and now the way was clear for him to slide back to the bottom, there to rejoin the company of ordinary men.

The moment came—and passed. He had faced the worst, and ever after that knowledge would level future dangers, lessening his fear of them, sometimes calamitously beneath the threshold of caution.

Since the maximum penalty was two years in jail and a $10,000 fine, Judge Lowell was lenient in sentencing the four men to only two months at the Charles Street Jail. Pending an appeal of the jury's verdict, they were released on bail.[24]

Their lawyers appealed their conviction on the grounds that the charge of fraud could apply only to circumstances in which the government was knowingly deprived of money or property. In short, what happened on December 4, 1902, was not a crime covered by the statute that the defendants had been found guilty of violating. The case was sent on to the U.S. Circuit Court of Appeals.

"We paid our counsel . . . $2,000 as a retaining fee, and he demanded another $1,500 before the case went to court," Curley wrote in his autobiography. "The Tammany Club came to our rescue, raising funds at a minstrel show and at other social functions." Some of the entertainment at that minstrel show was provided by the Creole Belles, a singing group of young women from Curley's neighborhood. Among them was a tall, slim nineteen-year-old with angular features, dark hair, and coal-bright eyes. Mae Herlihy thus entered the life of her future husband in the aspect of his rescuer. Her talents were at his service. They always would be.[25]

❖   ❖   ❖

Politicians cannot afford too much dignity; shamelessness is as necessary to their profession as money. Brass, gall—call it what you will, successful politicians have it exceedingly. That is why they are so widely disliked. They succeed as politicians only by failing as men and women. Machiavelli held that a man must choose: either he can be a good Christian, or he can enter public life, a realm in which Christian scruples do not and cannot apply. Max Weber had the same thought: public figures must practice an "ethic of responsibility," their only loyalty not to abstract standards of morality, not to notions of personal honor, decency, or dignity, but to what works.

At twenty-nine, James Michael Curley was about to make a discovery in the surprisingly broad field of what works. Instead of retiring in shame from public office—after all, he was the only legislator in the history of the Commonwealth of Massachusetts to have been placed under arrest, and he had subsequently been found guilty of a federal crime—instead of retiring, or at least trimming his political ambitions by falling back on his stronghold in the ward, Curley did what he would always do in such circumstances. "I have never been afraid to make the bold move," he confided to a friend late in life. "I think that is why my life has been such an adventure." In this case, the bold move was to declare his intention to run for a seat on the Board of Aldermen, the upper house of Boston's bicameral legislature. To make the move even bolder, he would be running in the first at-large aldermanic election in the city's history. He could not win with support just from his own district but would have to pick up votes from across the city.[26]

Here was a man with a criminal conviction hanging over him running for higher office, and the monitors of Boston's political morality were livid. When Curley won the primary, becoming one of eight Democratic nominees for alderman, many saw it as a portent. "I would not vote for such a man to manage my cow barn," the Reverend Herbert B. Johnson, pastor of the Warren Avenue Baptist Church in the South End, declared from his pulpit; "yet he succeeded in getting the nomination for alderman, his vote exceeding that of his most formidable opponent by more than 1000. The present condition of politics in this city is a call from God to all good citizens to rally to the support of the city, which is in danger of being ruled by its worst elements." The Good Government Association, a new citizens' group swept into being on the wave of indignation the Curley case had roused, which was funded by the Chamber of Commerce, the Merchants' Association, the Associated Board of Trade, the Fruit and Produce Association, and the Bar Association, bluntly said of Curley, "His record should make his election impossible." The Reform Club condemned the voters of Ward 17 for wanting to be represented by the likes of Curley: "A community that would do this is unfit—certainly as unfit as the Filipinos—to govern itself." One member, W. R. Thayer of Cambridge, said that "if she had many more Curley cases," Massachusetts might become a second Pennsylvania—a shocking thought. "Resolved," the members declared, "that this Club is disgusted."[27]

Curley fought back. "Curley knew full well that Boston's Mayors, including the third Josiah Quincy, had shoehorned their favorites onto the municipal payroll by inventing special job categories not covered by civil service regulations," Charles Trout writes. "The Water Department, for instance, boasted a 'ship-caulker,' 'miners,' and 'expert swimmers'—stroke unspecified. Because of this ethos, Curley could not believe that he had done anything so dreadfully wrong. . . . When the Good Government Association . . . , heavy with Bostonians who were no strangers to anti-Irish causes, came into being . . . in part to block Curley's election to the Board of Aldermen, James Michael was apoplectic." His personal anger, however, would have been politically nugatory if many among the Boston Irish did not resent the whole institution of the civil service.[28]

❖   ❖   ❖

"To the victors belong the spoils": such was the motto of the Jacksonian Democrats who swept the old Federalists out of office in 1828. Party government meant that party men must be appointed to office to carry out the party's mandate. This was the accepted way of American politics down through the Civil War—when Lincoln broomed out 1,457 of 1,639 federal employees—and beyond. "What are we here for," asked a bluff fellow at the Republican convention in 1880, "if not for the offices?" To the men of the mid-nineteenth century, the spoils system seemed a fact of nature, one that helped explain the intense partisanship of the era—and much else besides. Artemus Ward blamed the rout of the Union Army at Bull Run on a rumor of three vacancies in the New York Custom House.[29]

The modern practice of appointment by merit developed slowly. In 1864 senator Charles Sumner of Massachusetts introduced the first in a twenty-year series of bills aimed at replacing patronage with a system modeled on the British civil service. Cynics derided the idea as the "snivel service," and nothing came of it until the scandals of the Grant administration, the era when, as Henry Demarest Lloyd remarked, "Standard Oil did everything to the Pennsylvania legislature except refine it." For reformers, writes one authority, the spoilsmen of the Grant era, "representing a new aristocracy of plunder and patronage, replaced the slaveholder as the new jinni of evil."

No element of the political culture felt this sentiment with such huffy sincerity as did a group of independent Republicans who became known as the Mugwumps.[30]

With their "mugs" on one side of the fence and their "wumps" on the other, the Mugwumps agonized over whether to remain in the party of the tainted Republican presidential candidate of 1884, James G. Blaine, or bolt to the reform Democrat Grover Cleveland. Massachusetts was the Mugwump base. The Massachusetts Mugwumps wanted to make politics safe for gentlemen. They had little interest in substantive social or economic reform. The boom-and-bust cycles of capitalism that beat like fury against so many lives, the growing power of trusts and cartels over the prices of basic commodities, the harrowing conditions in the immigrant slums of northern cities—to these and other problems of the day they were indifferent. "They were deeply disturbed about people, not things." For them, the whole science of government came down to appointing "good" men to office. By "good" they meant incorruptible, money-honest; that Cleveland had fathered an illegitimate child did not bother them.[31]

In 1881 President Garfield had been shot dead by a disappointed office seeker, and overnight an assassin's bullet transformed civil service reform from a coterie cause to a public demand. A Puck cartoon pictured the assassin pointing a pistol at Garfield and carrying a note saying, AN OFFICE OR YOUR LIFE! A bill to adopt a civil service system on the British model, introduced in Congress the year before, had languished; after the assassination, it sped through. The full title of the Senate committee that devised the civil service conveys some idea of why Curley's subversion of its rules would help, not hurt, his reputation among the Boston Irish. The title: "Senate Committee on Civil Service and Retrenchment." Not only would jobs be handed out according to "merit," but fewer jobs would be handed out.

In the years immediately after the adoption of the Pendleton Act (for the Ohio senator who sponsored it), more and more federal workers fell under the protection of the civil service. By Cleveland's second term (1892–96), nearly half of the 190,000 federal workers had come in through the civil service. The 75,000 postal workers still remained outside, but by an executive order of

November 1901, 9,000 postal positions (for rural free delivery) were brought under the civil service. Presumably these were the jobs that James Hughes and Bartholomew Fahey hoped to win with the help of the two Curleys the next year.[32]

Civil service reform was one of the rare passions of the Boston Protestant elite, and Curley's likely voters knew that. Some of them remembered and others had heard the story of how Patrick Collins had been denied the cabinet post of secretary of war under President Cleveland because of pressure from the Massachusetts Mugwumps, who would accept any Yankee Democrat in the cabinet but no Irish immigrant. These were things that Curley, in his citywide race for alderman, did not need to say. Publicity had cast him in the role of an enemy of the civil service—of "reform," with all its ethnically specific reverberations. That was enough for the Irish. Certainly there were plenty among them, like James Hughes, who could not spell "Constantinople," but who had the feet to be letter carriers. What was the purpose of the civil service tests, anyway, if not to keep immigrants off the federal payroll?[33]

Attacked by the press, abandoned by the city's leading Democrats—Patrick Collins, Martin Lomasney, the powerful boss of Ward 8 who delivered the votes not only of the living but of the dead, and John F. Fitzgerald all refused to endorse him—Curley had at least one influential supporter. He was Henry S. Pritchett, president of the Institute of Technology (later M.I.T.). In a controversial address to the Twentieth Century Club shortly after Curley's nomination for alderman, Pritchett scandalized the Mugwumps in his audience when he said that "goodness is only one of the essential characteristics of politics." He continued in an even more inflammatory vein:

> when we speak of men of high ideals and character, I wish to mention one who is a leader that it would be well worthy of every leader in the city to follow—James Curley. He has had more to do with clean politics than any other politician in the municipality. He will succeed because he is a young man, a local leader who knows his own business and minds it all the time, who is a man of his word. He has studied the political problem thoroughly and does all in his power to help everyone in his ward. It would be well for every young aspirant for political position to study the methods of James Curley and follow in his footsteps.

Pritchett, who had lately come to Boston from Missouri, "may have found it easier to make a balanced judgment about Curley than did the Yankees who had grown to adulthood surrounded by anti-Irish biases," notes Joan Tonn, the biographer of Mary Parker Follett.

A political thinker and social theorist, Follett for some years operated the Highland Union, a settlement house in Ward 17. Institute of Technology students volunteered to work with Follett; some of them even tried to set up their own settlement house in the ward. But what was known as Tech House closed down after a few years because its leader was convinced that Curley's Tammany Club, along with Follett's Highland Union, provided all the social work Ward 17 needed. Pritchett had gone too far in hailing Curley as a model of clean politics—Tammany routinely hired repeaters, for example, at a dollar a vote, to vote early and often for its slate. But he spoke out of a much richer imagination of the social problem and of the need for substantive reform than the genteel "reformers" who applied their gentleman's code to Curley, found him wanting, and closed the book on him.[34]

At all events, and whether because of the stigma of his conviction or in spite of it, Curley won election as alderman, placing fifth out of the thirteen winning candidates. Tom Curley, running for James's House seat, also won his race. And the three Tammany Club candidates for the Common Council swamped their rivals by three-to-one margins. The Tammany sweep, noted one paper, "meant that for the first time since the ward lines were drawn one faction controlled everything and held every elective office." Talking to a reporter in the President's Room of the Tammany Club, Curley characterized the campaign as "a complete and convincing vindication."

The reporter surveyed his surroundings. With its potbellied stove and fans on its high ceilings, the big meeting room was warm and welcoming. Over a score of men were waiting there, on benches and chairs, seeking help in finding work. Dominating the room from within the proscenium of a picture frame with the single word TAMMANY above it was a large crouching tiger.[35]

❖   ❖   ❖

The shudder that had passed over Curley in Judge Lowell's courtroom had not been the harbinger of any lasting mood. Nor had it been an accurate presentiment: Curley easily won both his citywide election and control of the ward. Thus as he waited to hear the verdict of the appellate court he could be fairly confident that his political career would weather what his indictment termed "an offense against the peace and dignity of the United States."[36]

In its case against the Curleys, the government had contended, to quote from the court record, that "the word 'defraud' not only signifies pecuniary fraud, but has the broad meaning of depriving another of a right by deception or artifice." The government had a right to determine the fitness of its employees. Tom and James had deprived it of that right. They had, in that sense, committed a fraud against it. Accepting the government's interpretation of the law, the appellate court upheld the Curleys' conviction. Their lawyers quickly appealed to the Supreme Court (one wonders why, given the voters' verdict), which, on October 17, 1904, refused to hear the case. Their appeals exhausted, they were ordered to appear before Judge Lowell on November 7, 1904, for sentencing.

The Tammany Club gave them a morale-boosting send-off the night before that fateful day. The meeting room was packed so tight with supporters that they were unable to lift their hands to applaud and had to bellow their sentiments. With the picture of the crouching tiger behind him, James Curley spoke to them from atop a settee that raised him slightly above his hearers.

> What we are going to serve time for is not more serious than if one got drunk or broke a pane of glass. And we did it without the slightest criminal intent, or the least desire to hurt or injure the community or nation. Two of our followers, two neighbors who wished to better their condition—in our effort to assist them to obtain the necessaries of life . . . we took the examination for them. That is what we are going to that stone house for, to face two months of monotony, to be separated from our families, friends, and all that we hold dear.

He was shouting now, his voice was hoarse.

> Fellow Tammanyites! Fellow Tammanyites! Let not the gloom of this unhappy ordeal offset the bright promise of future victory. Let us close this wonderful meeting by singing . . . "America."

The men doffed their caps; they plucked clay pipes and cigars from their mouths. His face pale from intensity of emotion, his eyes flashing, Curley led them in song. Afterward, the window panes rattled.

with hurrahs and "tigers," the Tammany roar. As he left the club a crowd followed, buoying him home with volleys of cheers.[37]

"Have they shown any appreciation of the crime they committed, or any remorse?" Judge Lowell, next day, asked one of the Curleys' character witnesses, Salem D. Charles, the street commissioner of Boston. "Yes," he replied. "They have been very sorry." That was not good enough for the judge. He had made up his mind.

He knew that Alderman Curley, claiming that he "did it for a friend," had used his conviction to win sympathy votes in the 1903 election; he was now employing the same tactic in his current drive for reelection. And as for Thomas Curley, far from being "humiliated" by the conviction, as Commissioner Charles had maintained, he had run for and won a seat in the Massachusetts legislature. These were signs more of defiance than remorse. Speaking to the defendants through their counsel, Judge Lowell's was the voice of the outraged civic conscience. "On account of the effrontery of their conduct since the election," he declared, "if I saw any legal way to sentence them to the maximum penalty for this offense, I should certainly overrule my former sentence in this case." After the clerk read the names of all four men—Fahey and Hughes were included—and with each name repeated the sentence each was to serve, the judge directed the federal marshals to take the prisoners away. Shouts of "Goodbye, Jim," "Goodbye, Tom" trailed them down the corridor. "We'll get you out!" "We'll get a petition! The Tammany Club won't go back on you." The prisoners were put into a carriage, and as it pulled away from the courthouse the men of Tammany let out a cheer.

The next day, while the two Curleys were beginning their sentence, the voters of Ward 17 reelected Tom Curley to the House. A few weeks later, James Curley easily won renomination as the Democratic candidate for alderman from the district comprised of Wards 12 and 17. His showing in the subsequent citywide general election was even more striking; with his Tammany surrogates fanning out across Boston to deliver speeches he had composed in jail, Curley finished third in a field of twenty-six, winning more votes than he had the year before, and more than he would win in his four future campaigns for alderman. Within Ward 17, he won 2,107 votes to his Republican opponent's 786, and the Republican presidential candidate's (Theodore Roosevelt) 859.

With help like this from their friends, the Curleys could be at their ease in jail. They were leading Democratic politicians; Sheriff Fred H. Seavey, in charge of the jail, was also a Democratic politician. He gave them cells twice the size of the regular cells and allowed them to see numerous visitors each week, though jail rules limited ordinary prisoners to just one. They took saltwater baths every morning, sent out for baskets of fruit, exercised, wrote letters and speeches, and read lots of books. "One of the best chances I ever had to read," Curley recalled, "was the time I went to jail. . . . I read fourteen hours a day, every book in the jail library, and I made a lot of new friends among the authors. I never should have got to know some of them if we had not met in just that way. . . ." Visiting for Thanksgiving dinner, friends found the prisoners "light-hearted and gay." Altogether, aside from the barred windows and the rude clang as the bolt shot into the lock separating them from the outside world, jail was an unexpected lark.[38]

The notes of a ragtime tune played by one of the faithful on the piano were just dying out when James Curley walked into the smoke-filled meeting room of the Tammany Club on the evening of January 6, 1905. Shouts of surprise greeted him. Smiling, waving to friends, shaking hands, he made his way to his platform on the settee. Every chair and table was full, with some men standing up for a better look. He had been released from jail that morning, and after a day at home ("The meeting between Alderman Curley and his mother was affecting," the *Boston Post* noted) had come to the club to receive a hero's welcome. He was joined at the settee by Tom Curley, whom he introduced as his "fellow boarder and bedfellow for the past two months." This brought laughter and shouts of "You're all right, Jim!" He was overwhelmed by their devotion, he told the members. He wished he could express his gratitude; but they "must imagine it all." On one subject he would speak to them, however.

"I might express to you my opinion on the civil service that it is right in principle but cannot be used when there are two parties struggling for mastery." Everybody knew, he said, that "if an influential man has a friend who stands tenth in an examination and an enemy who stands first, the poorest man will get the job." In other words, if you failed a civil service exam, it wasn't because you had shorn a syllable off "Constantinople"; it was because the fix was in. Democrats, especially Irish Democrats, could not get federal jobs with a Republican in the White House. That 58 of the 90 persons who had taken the exam on December 4 were of Irish descent, that 75 percent of the 1,126 persons who had taken exams for letter carrier that fall were also of Irish descent, and that 69 percent of all those on the eligible list had either been born in Ireland or were of Irish descent—of these impediments to his anger at the political and ethnic bias of the civil service he said nothing. He admitted that he and Tom Curley had done wrong "in not respecting a law of whose existence we did not know," but their motive was unassailable: "We were doing nothing more than trying to help a friend." He spoke for half an hour. "Your loyalty to us," he stirringly concluded, "is only equalled by our loyalty to you, and we will go as far as justice will permit and good sense allow in doing all that we can for you."[39]

Tom Curley had just been expelled by the Massachusetts legislature—his colleagues would not serve with a man who had been in jail—but in answer to a question from the floor, James said that he was not worried about how he would be received by his fellow aldermen. In general, his confidence was borne out by events.

❖ ❖ ❖

He had been in jail when the twelve other aldermen were sworn in, however, and embarrassing references to that awkward circumstance were unavoidable. Three weeks into the session, he responded to complaints of Alderman Frank J. Linehan about irregularities in the granting of liquor licenses with the suggestion that he should take his grievance to the district attorney. Linehan would have none of it. He rose to state that "the gentleman on my right should be the last man in the world to advise me to appear before the District Attorney." (Linehan was a fine one to take a high moral line: within two years he would be in jail himself for stealing city property.)

Curley had been having innocent fun with Linehan, and out of the blue had come this gratuitous thrust. Thereafter, he would have to tread carefully in debate. He could not have known it at the time and could not have stopped it if he had, but something was beginning here, something that would never let up for him. The publicity surrounding his incarceration was a two-edged sword: it catapulted him into prominence, but it also left him with a wound that his enemies could reopen at any time. Invariably there would be a Linehan around to bring it all back. In time, unable to escape it, he would repeat the past. A new gravity entered his life now, and a new bitterness. The lark was over.[40]

Seven months later, Curley again made the front pages, and again the occasion was a sensational scandal.

A few weeks short of his death, Mayor Collins vetoed an aldermanic order authorizing an East Boston shipping firm, the National Dock and Storage Warehouse Company, to lay track on the city's streets for the purpose of shunting boxcars from one loading dock to another. Alderman Curley had led the fight to accommodate the company, citing Boston's declining status as a commercial seaport (it had slipped from second to sixth place, behind Philadelphia, since the 1880s) and its need to modernize its docking facilities, and stipulating in detail the steps the company would take to en- sure the safety of East Boston residents. A majority of his col- leagues accepted these arguments, but not Mayor Collins, who felt strongly that any economic gain to be had from this improvement would be outweighed by the congestion and danger the tracks would bring to already crowded streets and by the noise passing locomotives would inflict on the neighborhood. Late one August afternoon the board took up the mayor's veto and, by a margin of one vote, failed of the two-thirds majority needed to override.

Some minutes later, however, that one vote, in the person of Alderman Patrick Bowen, appeared in the aldermanic chambers. Springing to his feet, Curley demanded a second vote. When on exceedingly technical grounds the chairman, Daniel Whelton, turned down Curley's request, according to one witness, Curley "stormed and raved. He defied the Chair. . . . In fact he defied the whole Board," refusing to yield the floor until the chairman agreed to order the clerk to call the roll a second time. At this point, one of the three votes for the mayor, none other than Alderman Linehan, made a dramatic announcement.

He declared that he had been offered a bribe to change his vote from anti- to pro-National Dock and its plans to lay track on the streets of East Boston, and pointing to each alderman in turn made unprecedented accusations. "Mr. Chairman, an auction has taken place in which the member from Ward 9 (pointing to Alder- man Bowen) was bought and bought cheap." Shouts of "Lies" came from Bowen. "You Mr. Alderman (pointing to Alderman

Frank J. O'Toole) were bought and bought cheap." Curley inter-
jected: "The only thing I can say is that the asylums must be over-
crowded. That is where he belongs." Paying no attention, Linehan
continued his list of those who had been bought, changing his refrain slightly to fit Curley. "The gentleman from Ward 17 was also
bought, but not so cheap. You received twice as much because you
handled the matter." Charges like this had "never before in the
history of municipal government," according to the *Boston Herald*,
been leveled by a member of the city government. The ensuing
vote to override the mayor's veto was anticlimactic. Alderman Linehan's *j'accuse* stole the headlines.

A grand jury was empaneled. An investigation was opened.
The accused aldermen were summoned to testify.

Among them was Alderman Frothingham of the Back Bay and
several others who had been endorsed by the Good Government
Association. Lawrence Minot, its head, told the press that he could
not believe that any of its endorsees would stoop to a bribe. Such
people could not do such a thing—innocence by association was
helping Curley and his less-favored colleagues. Whether because it
found the idea that a Frothingham could take a bribe inconceivable,
or whether because it found no basis for Alderman Linehan's
charges, the grand jury refused to indict. Still, the weeks of publicity had hurt. In a speech in the aldermanic chambers after the grand
jury's announcement, Curley made reference to the aldermen who
had been accused: "Every member of this Board realizes that these
men take the same view of their good name that Othello did." In a
lament for what the scandals of 1905 had cost him, he then quoted
lines that he would cite through the years over and over again:[41]

> *Who steals my purse steals trash; 'tis something, nothing;*
> *'Twas mine, 'tis his, and has been slave to thousands;*
> *But he that filches from me my good name*
> *Robs me of that which not enriches him,*
> *And makes me poor indeed.*

"He did it for a friend": such was Curley's campaign slogan.
On the contrary, the *Boston Herald*, an organ of the Republican
party, charged in late 1905 that he did it for a fee. Curley exploded.
Speaking before the Board of Aldermen, he attacked the reporter
who had written the story in terms so raw that the board voted, as

another paper put it, "to blot out Curley's ravings." In his story the next day, a reporter for the *Boston Traveler*, the *Herald*'s evening paper, described a man that rage had driven past reason. "Flushed . . . , white at the lips, and shaking with the intense excitement he was laboring under, Curley lost complete control of himself as he retailed gossip, scandal, and libel. . . ."

Plainly the *Herald* story had touched a nerve. Now the *Traveler*'s report of the speech renewed Curley's wrath. Fearing, as he later said, that he would "punch his face" if he complained about the story to the *Traveler* reporter directly, he wrote a foolish letter to the paper's editor. The headline across the top of the front page for November 28, 1905, broadcast his folly to the world. CURLEY ATTEMPTS BLACKMAIL, it said, in bold type. Beneath the headline was published a photostatic copy of his handwritten letter.

> If those articles continue I shall be obliged to protect myself. In view of the indebtedness of the city I am convinced that a move in the interests of economy that would appeal to taxpayers would be the abolition of the publication of the minutes of the city council, the cost of which is $8500 per year.
>
> As I am a member of the committee on printing such an order, if presented by a member of that committee, would unquestionably be adopted. I have no desire to take this action and trust I shall not be obliged to.
>
> Sincerely Yours
>
> Jas. M. Curley
> Alderman

"I authorized the letter," Curley claimed in an accompanying interview, "but it was written by Good." This statement was as false as it was ignoble: the handwriting was unmistakably Curley's. "Who says I wrote such a letter?" Jeremiah Good asked the reporters who tracked him down at the Tammany Club. Told that it was Curley he seemed, understandably, at a loss for words. When he found his tongue, he was blunt: "Now the newspapers have got to let him alone. We're goin' after them if they don't." He warned that there were "at least a dozen huskies" in the Tammany Club who were eager to "pound the face off" the editor of the *Herald*. Curley had only to say the word.[42]

Violence was the "indecent side" of the other Tammany, violence masking graft. At one Tammany meeting, when a new member asked how the proceeds from the latest powwow were to be spent, he was bodily removed from the hall. "Why shouldn't he ask?" a puzzled interviewer queried another club member, years after the event. "He was a member, wasn't he?" The response was sinisterly Leninist. "Sure, he was a member," the fellow replied. "That's the point. What right had a member of the club to ask about powwow profits? That was the business of the executive committee"—that is, the business of James Michael Curley and his hand-picked cronies who made up the committee. In its internal procedures at any rate, the Tammany Club was closer in spirit to the "democratic centralism" of the early Bolsheviks than it was to a real democracy.

Intimidation was an intermittent feature not only of Tammany's internal operations but also of its political struggles against other factions. Timothy Connolly challenged Curley for his aldermanic seat in the municipal primary held that fall. With a four-car caravan led by a bandwagon carrying a full complement of musicians, Connolly staged an evening rally near the borders between Wards 12 and 17. He had just begun speaking when contractors' wagons carrying James Curley, Thomas Curley, and a number of torch-bearing followers rounded the corner. Standing up on his wagon on one side of the street, James Curley shouted, "Connolly, you're a grafter," across a crowd of mixed Connolly and Curley supporters estimated at two thousand. From the opposite side of the street, Connolly roared back, "You, sir, are owned, body and soul, by the Dock Trust." The pleasantries continued, the language deteriorating. To drown out the noise, the band, as one witness put it, "commenced a selection of discords." At this insult to their musical taste, Curley's toughs leaped from their wagons and began beating Connolly's men with torch sticks and jabbing lighted torches at their faces. Connolly himself was scorched by a torch, and another man was hit with a brick. The toughs also assaulted the Connolly bandwagon, first ripping the signs and banners from its side and then driving the musicians off and using their chairs to smash the instruments they had left behind. Only the hoop rods were left of the big brass drum. It took police officers from two divisions to quell the riot, but not before Connolly had been chased from the scene. Curley went on to beat Connolly by two to one in the primary, but in the general election he dropped six places from his third-place finish of the year before. Apparently the brass-knuckle tactics that enacted the frustrations of Ward 17 were somewhat less popular in the city at large.[43]

The year 1906 brought more violence, as James Curley and Tom Curley burst into an opposition meeting at the Vine Street Church and disrupted it by repeated heckling. They tried to storm the platform, but the police ejected them.

The alliance between James and Tom Curley was the occasion for violence a year later.[44]

It was an alliance doomed by ambiguity. There was no room in Boston politics for two politicians from the same ward with the same name and the same ambitions. Also, James Michael Curley could not then or later share power. He was in politics for gold and glory, not to build an impersonal machine that could grind on without him. His mania for control, his need always to be the man in charge, would in later years complicate his basically good relationships with his children. But in politics it helped. New York's Tammany Hall was run by interchangeable Irishmen in derby hats. Roxbury's Tammany Club was the den of a charismatic leader, and it had room for only one tiger.

After losing his seat in the Massachusetts House, Tom Curley had gone on to win a seat in the state Senate. Running against a primary opponent in 1906, he won easily. In the general election two months later, however, he was defeated by the candidate of the Independence League, former congressman Michael J. McEttrick, who carried Ward 17 1,817 to 1,647. Tom blamed his defeat on James: the Tammany Club had failed to mount an all-out drive for him. When the election for city offices came in December, ten days after his defeat, Tom Curley endorsed Theodore Glynn, of whom we will hear more, as candidate for alderman against James Curley. The Tammany Club was on the verge of civil war.

At a meeting of the club called by James Curley to discuss their differences, a special platform was set up for Tom and his closest allies. Places of honor had been arranged for them. Peace appeared to be at hand. As soon as they were seated, however, James shouted "Lock the doors!" and proceeded to read the "traitors" out of the club. Finishing, he yelled, "This meeting is adjourned! Put out the lights!" It was the signal for an all-out brawl to begin. In the program notes for the Tammany Club's Sixth Annual

Ball, James wrote: "Entering upon the seventh year of its existence, the organization, purged of certain barnacles, whose conceit, arrogance, and false sense of superiority have been a
detriment, sees the future as bright." Note the Bolshevik verb,
"purged."[45]

Each campaigning season now brought renewed brawling between the former friends. In 1908 James encountered Tom Curley,
head of the new Jefferson Club just two doors down Hampden
Street from the Tammany Club, in the corridor outside the office of
the Democratic City Committee. A donnybrook ensued. In 1909,
during a street confrontation between forces from the rival clubs,
James leaped off the stone wall he had been speaking from,
plunged into a crowd of six thousand, muscled his way across it
toward a rival speaker who was holding forth from atop a barrel,
and reached up and pushed the fellow off. In 1910 Curley was approached at the bar of the Parker House, the watering hole for
Boston's politicians, by six-foot-plus, three-hundred-pound Big Bill
Kelliher, the brother of a Boston congressman whom the Tammany
Club had heckled off the stage in a recent campaign appearance. "I
suppose I shall have to chastise you publicly," Big Bill said to Curley, then knocked him to the floor. Most men would have stayed
there; Curley got up swinging. They traded punches at the bar, but
Curley landed the heavier blows, and the brute went down.

Unlike Huey Long, a notorious physical coward who let his
brother Earl do his fighting for him, James Michael Curley was
good with his fists. In his autobiography, he tells a brutal anecdote
about inviting a heckler up to a platform ("make a path for the
gentleman") and when he reached the top step giving him "a
wicked uppercut." Some might call that a sucker punch and feel a
twinge of shame about it. Not Curley; there was no Marquis of
Queensberry nonsense about him. The sucker punch, the knee in
the groin—his fighting was along these Darwinian lines. He was a
tough man in a tough country. Kipling's reputation in America had
suffered when, a decade before, he had refused to fight with a man
who blocked his way on a Vermont road. On the day in 1917 when
Congress declared war on Germany, Senator Henry Cabot Lodge,
age sixty-seven, was accosted outside his office by a momentarily
backsliding pacifist; Lodge slugged him in the jaw. Politicians did
their fighting directly in those days, not through the medium of
foreign policy.[46]

Moreover, fighting was the one clear comparative advantage the Boston Irish enjoyed over the other, older Bostonians. It was the heyday of the Irish boxer; boys struck John L. Sullivan poses and brayed out Sullivan's boast, "I can lick any man . . . !" Curley's generation of Irishmen was fighting back, striking the (sometimes literal) blows their fathers and grandfathers had forgone.

For Curley, the show of brawn had another function as well. Being handy with his fists gave him sexual cover to espouse a generous politics—to be what we would call a liberal. "Real men" in those days thought that the tariff and immigration restriction exhausted the topics of politics and the tasks of public policy alike. What government chiefly did for ordinary people was to punish them; thirteen-year-old boys in Ward 17, for example, were routinely arrested and, if they could not post bail, sent to the Charles Street Jail for the crime of throwing stones in the street. At the Tammany Club Curley was pioneering a new public agenda, one less abstract and more caring.

From her vantage point at the Highland Union settlement house in Ward 17, Mary Follett could set what she in her sphere and Curley in his were doing against the official politics of the day. "When the political questions were chiefly the tariff, the trust, the currency," she wrote in 1918, "closely as these questions affected the lives of people, there was so little general knowledge in regard to them that most of us could contribute little to their solution." Crime, poverty, unemployment, illness—the subjects of politics in both clubhouse and settlement house—were by contrast things "which we all know a great deal about." She looked ahead to the time when "our daily needs [would] become the basis of politics." That day has not yet come. Real men still mostly talk of the contemporary equivalents of the tariff and the currency. But neither Curley's brawling nor his habit of autocracy should blind us to the continuing relevance of the politics of daily needs he practiced in Ward 17.[47]

Ironically, as mayor of Boston Curley would centralize in distant City Hall the functions he performed as ward boss and thus render obsolete the form of neighborhood government he had helped to perfect. The New Deal further centralized those functions in remote Washington, rendering city bosses like Curley obsolete. This change should not be confused with progress. The experience of local self-government, even if it is not "good" government, seems to be necessary to make social policy work. Curley had to treat people as potentially powerful: otherwise they might withhold their votes from him. They were citizens, and the benefits they derived were contingent on their political participation.

How different things are today. The objects of a niggardly—$60 a month is the food stamp allotment for a single person—bureaucratic pity, our dependent poor are not citizens; they get their benefits by formula, not according to their behavior. They have "rights" to these "entitlements," but no responsibilities. Few of them even vote; while 78 percent of all professionals cast ballots in the presidential election of 1988, only 39 percent of the unemployed did so. In Curley's terms, it is as if only the Back Bays of the nation participate in the political process today; the Ward 17s inhabit a prepolitical wilderness outside the system. The voguish notion of "empowerment"—of devolving power and money and responsibility from Washington to neighborhood institutions—marks a return to a model that once made citizens out of immigrants from foreign lands. It might help do the same thing for the internal immigrants who filled our cities while the nation was busy fighting the cold war—those who are forgotten until they riot, and who have been rendered politically quiescent by welfare, drugs, and fear of each other.

❖ ❖ ❖

To his daughter Mary, Curley once described the political vocation as a "picket fence existence," with highs following lows and lows, highs. That pattern is writ large in this narrative of Curley's life. Having saluted Curley the social worker, we now turn to Curley the grafter.

1 SENATOR, 2 ALDERMEN INDICTED! read the headline in the October 1, 1907, issue of the *Boston American*. Curley, whose photograph ran from the bottom of the fold to the top, was one of the aldermen. They were charged with using their offices to pressure the publicly-regulated New England Telephone and Telegraph Company into hiring "phantom workers" who never showed up for their jobs yet received a full week's pay. This pay, as one editorial asserted, "was a thin disguise for the distribution of corruption funds"—bribes to politicians. Over a six-month period the company had spent $92,000 in this way. Substantial houses cost $3,000 in Boston in those days, so the sum should be magnified accordingly. Perhaps Curley used

his cut to throw Christmas parties at the Tammany Club, and to help the widows and orphans of Ward 17. But much of it went right into his own pocket. For if Curley occasionally did good, he always did well.

Though telephone company officials had previously agreed to plead guilty to the charges of bribery, the district attorney, John B. Moran, who had been elected as a member of William Randolph Hearst's Independence League on the slogan "The Man Who Dares," had a change of heart just as the case was about to go to trial. In a meeting with lawyers for both the phone company and the politicians, Moran was told that if he went ahead with his prosecution he would be asked to testify about "frequent visits" he had made to the hotel room of a member of the grand jury that had brought the indictments. The implication—cryptic stories leaked to the press—was that Moran had engaged in jury tampering. Faced with this threat to his reputation, the Man Who Dares decided to "nol pros" (*nolle prosequi*) the case—to exercise the district attorney's power to desist from further prosecution of a case even after a grand jury has handed down an indictment.

The chief lawyer for the defendants was Daniel H. Coakley, a boyish-looking man with a big voice who had been a streetcar driver for the local transit company until he was fired for leading a strike. He then worked for some years as a sports reporter for the *New York Sun* and the *Boston Herald*, and finally wound up as a trial lawyer known for winning large settlements in personal injury cases, especially against the Boston Elevated Railway Company, which had made a capital mistake in firing him. His legal specialty, blackmail, was how he got the indictments dropped against Curley, the two other politicians, and the phone company. Curley was now in his debt—and he will figure later in Curley's story. Indeed, in time he came to fill the role of Curley's Mephisto: a wicked man who brought Curley close to real criminality.[48]

Thus for the third time in two years Curley had figured prominently in the juiciest kind of news. "In San Francisco, New Orleans, or, for that matter, in London," an editorial noted, "when Boston is mentioned, it is an even chance that instead of talking of the genius of our fair city," people talked about the political rogue and former jailbird seeking to become chairman of the Board of Aldermen— potentially the acting mayor of Boston. Curley did want to be chairman and by 1909 was the senior member on the board, but every year the outcry over that prospect from press and pulpit killed his chances. "His election as an Alderman is an insult to this city," the *Boston Traveler* thundered, "but his selection as Chairman of its highest legislative body and next in line to become Mayor if any accident should happen to the chief executive would be a calamity." The editorial went on to note that Curley had been winning reelection for years "on the manufactured sentiment that he was being made a martyr of, when as a matter of fact he was convicted of a crime that . . . struck at the very foundation of principles of fair play."

In a speech before the Board of Aldermen that must have taken more than an hour to deliver, Curley attacked not only the editorial, but the editor.

> Mr. Chairman, if my deed struck at the very foundation principles of fair play, or in other words, the principles of American government, what did McSweeney's deed as immigration inspector of the port of New York strike at? . . . What shall we say of a character charged as he was charged in the indictment—not only with stealing naturalization papers, but with being a procurer?

Whatever this last calumny referred to, stealing naturalization papers was a charge calculated to resonate among a city electorate in which immigrants or first-generation Americans bulked large. Curley then leveled a second charge that would resonate among another large group, the city's Roman Catholics.

Making play with the *Traveler*'s motto, "Fit for the Home," he appealed to prurient interest.

> A clean sheet, fit to go into the home? . . . I refer Mr. McSweeney to Page No. 3, the bottom of the first column, and ask him if he feels that that is a fit ad, to take into the home of a decent, respectable family— the illuminated ad of an article intended to destroy life, to prevent children coming into the world? . . . I stand prepared, Mr. Chairman, to compare my citizenship with Mr. McSweeney's, and his position in relation to that illuminated ad and to this editorial places me standing on the curbstone and McSweeney standing in his proper place—in the gutter.

The ad was for the "wonderful Marvel Whirling Spray . . . the best—safest—most convenient, it cleans instantly . . . new vaginal syringe"—an appliance, to judge from the illustration, modeled on the bellows of a Bessemer furnace. Birth control was both a moral and political lapse for Irish Catholics. It meant sex not for procreation but for pleasure, which was as bad as sin got. And, as Curley went on to say, it also meant "race suicide": fewer Irish babies today equaled fewer Irish voters tomorrow. Curley knew what he was doing in becoming embroiled over the religiously charged issue of birth control with a leading Republican newspaper. There were votes in the right kind of bad publicity, and this was it.[49]

❖ ❖ ❖

A skillful politician uses his enemies to make friends. Curley was rapidly mastering the politics of ethnic and religious polarization. And Boston was ripe for that politics.

Sometimes the largest turnings in a culture, the moment when the balance of forces making up a given social order shift to one side over the other, can be glimpsed in what Lionel Trilling once called the whir and buzz of implication—when people begin to take certain things for granted and come to affirm them indirectly, perhaps in a nod, a wink, or a laugh. Such a moment came on July 12, 1909. It was a small moment, but through it we can see the outlines of big changes.

On that day James Michael Curley gave a droll speech before his colleagues on the Board of Aldermen. The issue at hand could not have been more trivial: should dogs on Boston Common, like their kind elsewhere in the city, be leashed? The Committee on Public Improvements had said no, not on the Common. Curley rose to protest. He wanted the phrase "except dogs on Boston Common" struck from the ordinance drawn up by the committee. "Mr. Chairman," he said,

> I trust that the motion to recommit will not prevail. This matter has been on the calender for two months, and during that time the number of squirrels . . . that have been destroyed by bull dogs coming from Ward 10 [the Back Bay] has been very great. I recognize that the product of Ward 10 should have some place in which to recreate, and since they do not produce children in large numbers in Ward 10, and do produce bull dogs, it might perhaps be proper to permit them to recreate on the Common. But the Common is a place of recreation for squirrels that . . . were there in large numbers some years ago,

and of late years have almost been wiped out because of the existence
of the bull dogs. The squirrel is a very beautiful animal. It compares
very favorably with the bull dog, in everything but viciousness, and
while perhaps it is not as lovable as a household pet in Ward 10 as the
natural product of Ward 10—bull dogs—it still affords amusement
and considerable pleasure to the children who occasionally are permitted to pass through the Common.[50]

Bulldogs, not children, were the "natural product" of Yankee Protestant Ward 10. One sees the drift.

In his successful mayoral campaign later that year, John Fitzgerald posed for political ads with his six children: a symbol, as the legend underneath read, of MANHOOD, against the MONEY of the Yankee
patrician-banker James Jackson Storrow. The Irish were not only becoming aware of their natal advantages over the local Protestants;
they were crowing over them. It was to be a constant strophe in
ethnic and racial politics from then on. "Follow me, brothers and
sisters," Louis Farrakhan told an auditorium full of black politicians,
intellectuals, and organizers in a speech in New Orleans in 1989.
"According to demographers, if the plummeting birth rate of white
people in America continues, in a few years it will reach zero population growth. As for blacks, Hispanics, and Native Americans, . . .
by the year 2080 [they] will conceivably be 50% or more of the
United States population. . . . If things continue just birthwise, we
could control the Congress, we could control the Supreme Court,
we could control state legislatures, and then 'Run, Jesse, run,' or
'Run Jesse Junior, run,' or 'Run, Jesse the Third, run.'"

In Boston this theme was all mixed up with religion. The politicians were following the priests. Curley's rise cannot be understood without a brief divagation on the transformation in the mood
of Boston Catholicism that took place in these years.[51]

Bishop Fitzpatrick's successor, Archbishop John J. Williams,
who ran the archdiocese from 1866 to 1907, followed in Fitzpatrick's accommodative footsteps. "We want no aggressive Catholics
in Boston," he said, and he refused a cardinal's red hat because he
feared it might provoke Protestants. For the same reason ("they
might disturb the peace and good will of our Yankee friends") he
opposed the construction of parochial schools. Williams's successor, however, set a markedly different tone for Boston Catholics
in the twentieth century. In a speech marking the one hundredth

anniversary of the Boston Archdiocese the year before Curley's ramble on the bulldogs of Ward 10, William Henry O'Connell struck an invigoratingly new note. Capturing a sea change in political demography in an epigram, he said, "the Puritan has passed; the Catholic remains." "The city where a century ago he came unwanted he has made his own. . . . The child of the immigrant is called in to fill the place which the Puritan has left." This development was not to everybody's liking ("Poor Boston," Henry Adams confided to a friend, "has run up against it in the form of its particular Irish maggot, rather lower than the Jew, but with more or less the same appetite for cheese"), but it had already happened at the level of population, and O'Connell set out to make it happen at the level of culture. He wanted Catholics to be proud of their faith, conscious of its history and traditions, eager to display it, and quick to defend it. "The time has come when every Catholic must stand up and be counted for the faith or against it," he wrote in 1915. "It is time for Catholic manhood to stand erect, square its shoulders, look the world in the eye and say, 'I am a Roman Catholic citizen; What about it?'"

The eleventh child born to immigrant parents in Lowell, O'Connell had lived and studied in Rome for years; and, knowing Dante and Thomas Aquinas, he was not subdued into reverence by "Mr. Emerson" and William James. Dubbed *sua Pomsita*—"His Pomposity"—for his finish of old-world pretension, he took with him to Portland, Maine, where he was made bishop prior to coming to Boston, a domestic establishment fit for a Roman noble—a valet named Peppino, along with his wife and children, a coachman, and a private "music master," "Count" Pio de Luca. When in 1911 he was given the red hat of Cardinal from the Vatican, far from shrinking to accept it as Archbishop Williams had done, he requested that the governor of the Commonwealth send the Ninth Massachusetts regiment to meet him at the dock on his return from Rome. His view of parochial schools was also the opposite of his predecessor's. "There is, as you know, just one point of view and that is, Catholic children should attend Catholic schools," he wrote in a pastoral letter of 1913. During his reign (1908–44) the number of Catholic colleges in the Boston area increased from 1 to 3; private academies and prep schools went from 10 to 24; the number of parochial elementary schools doubled, from 75 to 158; and the enrollment in parish high schools burgeoned from 792 to 10,567.

Authoritarian in temper, medieval in outlook, Cardinal O'Connell sought to remake Boston's Catholics as soldiers of a modern-day Counter-Reformation, keen to win back ground from a now decadent Protestantism. O'Connell construed decadence intimately, taking the same line as Curley on the frigidity of the Protestant bed next to the carnival of (procreative) sexuality to be found in the Catholic. In a review of Charles Francis Adams's autobiography, he was taunting: "The wonder is psychological and physiological that there were ever any children at all in Puritan homes."[52]

Reluctantly he plunged the church into politics, especially on issues touching the family, morality, and sexuality. "When I ask you to do anything, trust me and do it," he told his flock, and they obeyed. In 1924 his opposition killed a proposed constitutional amendment banning child labor. "It is Socialistic as it puts the State above the Parents," said one of his pastors. The initiative containing the amendment was defeated in Catholic Boston by a margin of almost four to one. Similarly, a mere hint of displeasure from His Eminence in 1935 was enough to stampede a majority of state legislators into switching their votes from for to against the adoption of a state lottery. In 1942 O'Connell led a campaign against an initiative petition liberalizing the sale of contraceptives in the Commonwealth; with majorities of three and four to one against it in the heavily Catholic cities, the measure went down to defeat. O'Connell's successor, Richard Cushing, led a drive to defeat a similar ballot initiative in 1948. This campaign against the "birth frustrators of Massachusetts" featured radio ads in the form of a question-and-answer quiz in which contestants were asked to identify famous people (Marie Curie, Harriet Beecher Stowe, Thomas Gainsborough, and Benjamin Franklin) who had come from big families. Stigmatized as an "anti-baby" bill, the initiative petition was defeated by 278,000 votes.°[53]

Beyond these discrete political interventions, a wholesale Catholicizing of Boston institutions and attitudes took place in the

---

° Cushing later carried the habit of intervention beyond the borders of Massachusetts. "I'll tell you who elected Jack Kennedy," he told Hubert Humphrey in 1966. "It was his father, Joe, and me, right here in this room." He had helped to pick which Protestant ministers should receive $100 to $500 "contributions" from the Kennedys in their decisive West Virginia primary fight against Humphrey in 1960. "It's good for the Lord. It's good for the church. It's good for the preacher, and it's good for the candidate," he explained.

O'Connell years. By 1930, for example, there were seventy-eight Sullivans, fifty Murphys, thirty-seven O'Briens, twenty-five Kellys, and twenty-four Lynches teaching in the Boston public schools. "Indeed," the church historian James W. Sanders writes, "every tenth teacher possessed one of only sixteen Celtic surnames, and many others possessed a variety of similar surnames." At least half the principals in the Boston schools in 1930 were Catholics; and fully 27 percent were graduates of Boston College, the Jesuit school. (The sister of the Jesuit in charge of teacher training at Boston College was in charge of teacher development in the Boston public schools.) Whether staffed by lay Catholics or members of religious orders, both public and parochial systems taught a similar curriculum and instilled similar moral values.

The chief difference between the systems, aside from the explicitly religious content of the Catholic school curriculum, was, increasingly, one of class. The more affluent the parents, the less likely they were to send their children to parochial schools. One scholar has found "strong evidence that the Catholic Church in Boston, including its schools, tended to preach a gospel that diminished or at least set limits to ambition"—which accounts for much of the class skew in using the parochial system.

This attitude came right from the top. The mouthpiece of the archdiocese, the *Sacred Heart Review*, approvingly quoted Booker T. Washington's advice to blacks "to quit taking five dollar buggy rides on six dollars a week" and not to "put a five dollar hat on a five cent head." Such lessons, the *Review* noted, might be taken to heart "by races other than the Negro." The political ramifications of this negative view of ambition and success were profound. Not only did it do all that ideas could do to increase economic frustration; it also sanctioned failure, and lent a permanent color of envy to local politics.

The matter was more complex yet. O'Connell, a believer in the "gospel of wealth," taught that the "complete abolition of poverty is a futile dream . . . there will always be rich and poor." To those reformers who wanted to lessen inequality, he said, "Can't you see that the poverty of some is infinitely more beautiful than the guilty wealth of others?" The fortune of the banker-financier J. P. Morgan had his benediction: "There is no vulgarity in wealth like this."

The potentially progressive energy in the Boston Catholic resurgence ran up hard against this principled conservatism. On the one hand, O'Connell taught, have pride in your religion; bring children into the world; and through the weight of numbers in a democratic polity assume your rightful place in politics and government. On the other hand, Catholics were not to challenge the economic power of the Protestant elite. The message was, "Be proud but submissive, assertive but resigned." This teaching acted as an ideological brake on local politics. It meant that progressive impulses had to be cloaked in the rhetoric of ethnic and religious chauvinism. I have used the word "liberal" to describe James Michael Curley, but that was only to place him on our impoverished ideological map. He was really an urban populist; no liberal could have flourished in an archdiocese presided over by William Henry O'Connell.[54]

The new assertive mood in the church closely paralleled the new ethnic politics. The former was the cultural and psychic ground of the latter. James Michael Curley's outraging of the minions of respectability—his naming his club after Tammany Hall, his subversion of the civil service, his two-fisted control of Ward 17, his threatening of major newspapers, his implication in scandals, whether the charges were true or false—would either have had no result or a hurtful result politically if it had not fitted in to this larger cultural pattern. The milieu made possible the emergence of the man.

❖   ❖   ❖

Late one blustery winter night in 1906, Tom McCann and James Curley were walking home after an evening's work at the Tammany Club. "Come spend the night with me," Tom said. "We'll have a talk before turning in." Curley said he thought he'd go right home. Pausing at the corner of Hampden and George, the chill wind cutting through them, Tom hinted at what it was he wanted to talk about: his bachelor days might soon be over. "Well," James replied, "I expect I'll be married pretty soon myself." "Is it Mae Herlihy?" Tom guessed.

It was not exactly a wild surmise. Just a few weeks before, Mae had been James's partner at the annual Tammany Grand Ball. He had become aware of her at a minstrel show given for the benefit of St. Philip's at the Dudley Street Opera House that past September. She was one of the end girls in the Florodora Sextet. Tall, dark, slender she displayed "a gaiety that was a joy to see." Politics had been all that mattered to Curley in life; now politics had a rival.

Mary Emelda Herlihy was born on Thanksgiving Day 1884, the second of the eleven children of Ellen McCarthy Herlihy and Dennis Herlihy, a Boston schoolteacher who had settled in Roxbury after leaving Dublin in the 1860s. Ellen Herlihy died in 1902 and Mary's elder sister soon after, so Mary, after graduating from the Hyde Grammar School, had to cut short her education to keep house for her father and look after the younger children. She loved to waltz, and those who heard her sing were struck by the sweetness of her voice.[55]

James's schedule did not leave him much time to observe the punctilio of courtship. Typically, his day started at 8:00 A.M., with a breakfast meeting among a half dozen or so of his constituents at the Albany Street apartment he shared with his mother. Next he went to the Tammany Club, where he might write a letter of recommendation for one man, make a telephone call for another, and give a handful of cash to a third. Around eleven he would travel downtown to City Hall, where he tended to aldermanic business and saw constituents. Then he would walk the few blocks to his brother's real estate and insurance firm, where between spots of business he conferred with his political allies and saw more constituents. Late in the afternoon he took a break from his benefactions, but at seven o'clock he would return to the Tammany Club to see yet more constituents. Last call for favors was around eight or nine, after which he might attend a wake or a dance or a meeting at the church. The day ended with a late-night round of cards and talk at the Tammany Club.

It sounds exhausting; in fact it was sustaining. He gave much of himself, but got back more than he gave. Of Huey Long's similar drive to display his sympathy "for anybody who was deprived of something," T. Harry Williams remarks that "he liked the feeling of power that came to him when he could help such a person." That feeling of power was something special, something that the ruck of men do not have in their lives; but the ruck of men do have love, and Curley wanted that too.[56]

James and Mae's first date may have been a trip, by horse and buggy, to the Brockton Fair. It was growing dark when they set out for home. The horse was not used to automobiles, and the noise and the bright intrusion of the headlights made it rear and once even start to bolt. But Curley held the reins fast: the lonely years driving the team for C. S. Johnson's had been good for something after all.

On another occasion they took a trip to see the foliage in the Berkshire Hills of western Massachusetts. They caught the 7:30 A.M. train out of North Station and did not come back until 8:00 that night.[37]

Would marriage interfere with his career? Curley may have felt some uneasiness on that score. He needn't have. "It has always been the woman's part to create the atmosphere in which politics flourish," Mary remarked years later. "Politics materialize in drawing rooms and at the dining table. I love being responsible for stage settings that are pleasant and inspiring." If she offered a preview of that attitude on the trip to the Berkshires, it must have put his mind at ease.[58]

The circumstances surrounding their wedding were peculiar. For several years John Curley had been seeing a woman named Margaret Gargan; they had become engaged, and had planned to marry that June. But they would have to wait. James Curley and Mary Herlihy, their love ripening fast, had also picked that month for their wedding. There was an Irish superstition against having two weddings in the same year; having two in the same month might have brought the Famine back for an encore. So John and Margaret put their wedding off until June 1907. Had James, his passion too urgent to brook delay, worked this business out with John? Had he known about the superstition before setting the date for his own wedding? Had he cared?[59]

This odd note was soon matched by another. Curley told his friends, members of the Tammany Club, his fellow aldermen, and anyone else who would listen that his wedding would take place on June 28. Yet he and Mary actually planned to have a small private ceremony, and he tricked them all by getting married the day before. Once again, as with shouldering John out of his wedding plans, the last word that one would use to describe this behavior is straightforward.

The ceremony took place late in the afternoon of a blistering day, the temperature in the upper eighties, at St. Francis de Sales Church, the Herlihys' home parish, in Roxbury. The Reverend Cornelius Herlihy, Mary's first cousin, performed the service. Mary wore what was described as a "traveling costume of gray,"

James a tall hat, Prince Albert coat, striped pants, and white bow tie. George Norton, one of the original Tammany Nine, was his best man. Only the two families and a few friends attended. Afterward the Herlihys hosted a small reception in honor of the couple.

That evening the Curleys had dinner at the Essex House downtown, then headed for North Station, the gateway to their honeymoon. There they were surprised by the rattles, war whoops, and tiger growls of a brace of Tammany braves who, learning of the wedding, had come to the station to see them off in style. This demonstration held the couple up, and in the end they had to dash for the train. As it pulled away from the platform, they could hear the chant dying out behind them, "Tam-man-y—Tam-man-y—Tam-man-y!"[60]

❖　　　❖　　　❖　　　❖

To Washington and Back

❖ ❖ ❖ ❖

CONGRESSMAN *(to Champ Clark, Speaker of the
House): I hear the burglar is in town.*
SPEAKER CLARK: *Well, you may call him a burglar in
Boston, but if I were President I'd put him in
my Cabinet.*

❖　　　❖　　　❖　　　❖

James and Mary Curley spent the Fourth of July 1906 in Montreal, paid the obligatory postnuptial visit to Niagara Falls, and then toured the resorts of upstate New York. After a stop at Saratoga Springs to attend the annual convention of the Ancient Order of Hibernians, they returned to Boston. Their new home, a five-room wood frame gothic cottage on a quiet Roxbury street, awaited them. "We didn't have a pile of money," Curley remembered. "But we had faith in each other."[1]

And soon they had more than each other: they had a son, James Michael Jr., in 1907; a daughter, Mary, in 1908; and another daughter, Dorothea, in 1910. On the subject of children, of hearth and home generally, Curley could be treacly. "It may be that I am a little different from many other men," he once told an interviewer. "To me marriage and birth have always been holy sacraments. For two days before and two days after the birth of every child of mine, I never left the house. When they wanted to find me, they always knew where I might be found. I would be outside her door, kneeling down and saying the rosary." Curley on his knees saying the rosary is one of his Dickensian touches; he could not resist the extra, the too improbable detail. He was tireless about the business of magnifying himself, as if, like many people smitten by language, what he actually did seemed paltry next to what he could say he did.[2]

The house at 114 Mount Pleasant Avenue became a "Mecca for everyone in need"—some more colorful than others. Take the distinguished old party who came by one night seeking a free meal. When he asked how he could repay the Curleys' hospitality, Curley came up with one of his signature schemes. He had a round of political rallies to make that night, he said; the old man could attend each one and, at a propitious moment, and with the aid of a cane Curley plucked out of his umbrella stand, shuffle up to the platform and deliver this speech: "I desire, sir, to make a statement on behalf of my associates of the Grand Army of the Republic who fought under General Grant in the Battle of the Wilderness. It is my pleasure, sir, to present you with a cane cut from a cottonwood tree during this conflict in appreciation of your work for the Grand Army of the Republic." (When he was a member of the state legislature, Curley had sponsored a bill raising the salaries of GAR veterans employed at the State House.) The old man agreed to the plan, and the touching scene was repeated at rally after rally that evening. Finally, at a stop in Roxbury, Walter Ballantyne, a candidate who had made the circuit with Curley, had had enough of the ersatz veteran. "This is the fourth time I've seen that cane presented tonight. If it is presented again, I will expose it." To which Curley replied: "My dear Ballantyne, I regret you are mistaken as to the number of times—this is the fifth time and will be the last time it will be presented this evening."[3]

In 1909 Curley won a seat on the just-constituted City Council, a nine-member body that, under the terms of the new City Charter, replaced both the Board of Aldermen and the Common Council. Curley's term ran for two years, which meant that in November 1910 he could run for a higher office without giving up his council incumbency. In politics that is known as being in the catbird seat.

The office Curley sought was that of U.S. congressman. In March 1910 he announced his intention to run for the Tenth Congressional District seat held by Joseph O'Connell, a two-term incumbent from Boston's Dorchester section. O'Connell, he implied, should resign. Otherwise: "If he announces his candidacy I will then direct an attack on him and I will keep firing until he retires from the fight or until he is defeated at the polls."

Since both men were Democrats, Curley needed an issue of party principle to use against O'Connell. Here he was in luck: O'Connell had been on the wrong side of what Curley termed "the greatest Democratic measure of the generation." This was the drive mounted by insurgent Republicans and reform Democrats in 1909–10 against the Republican Speaker of the House, the grizzled Joseph G. ("Uncle Joe") Cannon. It was the high noon of Progressivism; through his dictatorial control of the House, especially his power to select the members (including himself) of the Rules Committee, which decided whether and when legislation would come to the floor Cannon had frustrated efforts to lower the tariff and in general had set himself up as an obstacle in the path of all forward-looking legislation. "I am goddamned tired of listening to all this babble of reform," he gruffed in a characteristic utterance. "America is a hell of a success." He was a "stand-patter," a symbol of reaction in an age of reform. In 1909, with the help of President Taft, he had beaten back a direct challenge to his Speakership. But in March 1910, in a parliamentary coup, Congressman George W. Norris (R-Neb.) got onto the House floor a proposal to democratize the rules by dethroning the Speaker as chairman of the Rules Committee, and stripping him of the power to appoint its members. The Norris amendment was debated around the clock for three days. In the end, with the support of forty-six Republicans and every Democrat on the floor it passed.[4]

Joseph O'Connell, in South Boston to attend the annual St. Patrick's Day parade, was not one of those Democrats. He had failed to vote on "the greatest Democratic measure of the generation." Speculation in political circles was that his absence had been a return favor to Cannon. In 1908 O'Connell had beaten his Republican opponent, J. Mitchell Galvin, by four votes. Galvin lodged a protest against the election, but nothing came of it. Had Cannon made a deal with O'Connell to let him take his seat in return for his support against the insurgents? Such was the damaging talk. The label "Cannon Democrat" was stuck fast to O'Connell.

O'Connell had an additional problem. With a population of 32,000 (to Ward 17's 25,000), his home Ward 20 was easily the biggest prize in the Tenth District, which included three wards in Roxbury, two in Dorchester, and two in South Boston, as well as the city of Quincy and the town of Milton, both on Boston's southern border. If O'Connell had been as sure of his Dorchester base as Curley was of Ward 17, he would have been unbeatable. But Ward 20 was split between a faction loyal to him and one pledged to Curley. O'Connell would have to get replacement votes in wards where Curley, in his aldermanic races, had run well for years. Curley looked like a surefire winner.

But there was a chafing complication: the entry into the race of a third candidate, former congressman William S. McNary of South Boston. Originally McNary had been in Curley's corner; indeed,

Curley later told Joseph Dinneen that, in a chance meeting in a downtown barbershop, McNary had come up with the idea of his running against O'Connell in the first place. However that might be, McNary clearly hoped that Curley and O'Connell would split the Roxbury and Dorchester vote between them, allowing him to win the primary on a heavy vote from South Boston. Somehow, Curley had either to steal or to neutralize McNary's base. His chosen tactic was what he later called "the deadly and dreaded weapon of humor." After McNary put up billboards across South Boston emblazoned with SEND A BIG MAN TO DO A BIG JOB, Curley's operatives used the cover of night to paste small Curley posters over the billboards: ELECT A HUMBLE MAN, the legend read—JAMES MICHAEL CURLEY. When at campaign rallies McNary dilated on his honesty ("The indelicate implication," in Curley's words, "was that William was honest, but that James and Joseph were not"), Curley hired a layabout, dressed him in a construably Attic costume, gave him a lantern, and pinned a sign on his back reading, I AM DIOGENES SEEKING THE HONEST MAN, MCNARY. He set this "perambulating billboard" loose on the streets of South Boston. The mirth was at McNary's expense.[5]

The two candidates next exchanged literary fusillades, with Curley comparing McNary to Micawber and McNary firing back in kind. "In a recent speech in this ward," McNary said in South Boston, "he compared Congressman O'Connell to Oliver Twist and myself to Micawber. Mr. Curley should have read deeper in his Dickens and he would have found his prototype in the man who was always protesting, like Mr. Curley, that he was humble, Uriah Heep, the humble man, the greatest hypocrite in literature." McNary further charged that Curley was unversed on "the great question of the day, the tariff." Curley's "measure" was "that of the ward politician, and his horizon that of city politics."

A few days before the primary, Curley took McNary's measure. Imagine the effect of hearing this malediction delivered live, in Curley's Mosaic baritone: "You have hidden in your political life behind a smirking mask," he said, addressing the missing McNary.

> False to the Democratic candidates in every campaign for Mayor in the last twelve years, you have, like a Brutus, triumphed upon the body of a dead Caesar and then, like the vulture, fed upon the very vitals. I say to you tonight, look you well into your own tremendous

past, read its stern lesson in the manifest teachings of the present hour, and as you approach nearer the abyss of your own political destruction, look down and see the rent garments and the whitened bones which show that other men have trod upon your road and way and met a civic death.[6]

Toward O'Connell, Curley was nearly as sulphuric, "Will you deny," he asked in one speech, "upon your solemn oath to the people of the 10th District that you have not been the recipient of the bounty of Armour Sulzberger Company and Swift, the notorious beef packers of the country?" The hapless O'Connell rose to this Do-you-still-beat-your-wife bait by taking a notarized oath denying that the packers had given him money. Curley's intent was to connect in the voter's mind O'Connell, Speaker Cannon, the tariff (along with the meat and other trusts it sheltered from foreign competition), and the high cost of living. "With the return to Congress of such a man as O'Connell, the ardent champion of Cannonism," he charged in one South Boston speech, "there is no opportunity to properly secure a diminution or reduction of the tariff, because he is pledged to the trusts." And, to complete the logic, if the tariff on imported goods remained high, so would the cost of living. In South Boston, home to many Galway émigrés, Curley used a more provincial issue against O'Connell, who had roots in County Cork. "Who is the better man," he asked at rally after rally, "a man from Cork or a man from Galway?"

Perhaps sensing defeat, O'Connell mounted a tepid campaign, sedulously denying that he was a Cannon ally, and setting few pulses tingling with oratory long on formulations like this: "The nation should cooperate with the state in dredging the waters and widening the channels." In the event, Curley won the primary with 6,844 votes to O'Connell's 5,659 and McNary's 3,868. Whereas Curley got a 1,584 vote plurality in Ward 17, capturing 80 percent of the vote, O'Connell won by only 547 votes in Ward 20, where he got just 50 percent of the vote. Curley's hold over his base had put him over.

His Republican opponent in the general election was J. Mitchell Galvin, who, as we have seen, had come within four votes of unseating O'Connell in 1908. But by depicting Galvin as a friend of Senator Henry Cabot Lodge, who was no friend of the immigrant, Curley won easily, 20,345 to 15,783.[7]

Nineteen ten was a Democratic year. The Democrats elected twenty-six of the forty-six governors, among them Woodrow Wilson of New Jersey, who was already being touted as a presidential candidate in 1912. Though the Senate still had a Republican majority, it was controlled by a Democratic–insurgent Republican bloc. As for the House of Representatives, for the first time in sixteen years it had a Democratic majority. The new Democratic Speaker of the House was also said to have presidential ambitions. He was James Beauchamp ("Champ") Clark of Missouri, and before Congress convened James Curley made a special trip to Washington to seek him out.

Curley needed a favor, ever the coin of political fraternity. Refusing to go gently to his civic death, William McNary had reportedly been lobbying old friends in the Massachusetts congressional delegation to deny Curley his seat because he had violated a federal law. Clark had the power to check this effort. When Curley showed up at his office, still carrying his traveling bag, Clark was just leaving for New York to attend memorial exercises for Mark Twain. Curley turned on his heel and went with him. During the five-hour train trip, Curley told Clark about his problem, and on the anvil of mutual advantage a friendship between the two men was forged.[8]

His rival Woodrow Wilson once lampooned the six-foot, 225-pound Clark as "a sort of elephantine smart aleck." His sobriquet has not helped Clark to be taken any more seriously by later historians, who have referred to "Champ" Clark as a "rural clown" and "the statesman from Pike County." This is unfair. Clark was a man of parts.

Born in Lawrenceburg, Kentucky, in 1850, educated at Bethany College in West Virginia and Kentucky University (from which he was expelled for firing a revolver at a fellow student who had hit him with an iron), as a young man Clark moved to Missouri, where he worked first as a lawyer and later as county prosecutor, then became a college president and finally a newspaper editor before entering Congress in 1892. A free-trader and an enemy of the civil service, Clark was an old-fashioned country Democrat; indeed, with his black slouch hat, white vest, and long black coat, he was an old-fashioned man. In photographs he looks like a better-barbered Carl Sandburg. The craggy visage suggests character, and the suggestion was accurate: Clark proved it in the debate over the annexation of Hawaii in 1898. Asked by Speaker Tom Reed, a Republican but a close friend, to forgo a seat on the Ways and Means Committee for one on Foreign Affairs where Reed needed Clark's help in the battle against the United States' emulating the imperialist powers of Europe, Clark agreed. "I'll stand by you," he replied, much affected by this call to honor. Barbara Tuchman writes, "He agreed to sacrifice the place he had long coveted to help his party's most uncompromising opponent."[9]

In 1911 Champ Clark was looking ahead to the approaching presidential election. A stranger to New England, he needed allies there, and on the ride to New York he found one.

Claiming that he wanted to spare the city the expense of calling a special election to fill his council seat before the expiry of his term, Curley would serve Boston in 1911 as both congressman and city councilor, an arrangement without precedent in city history.* Staying on the council was a way of signaling that his ambition remained fixed on the city. In 1911 he missed sixteen council meetings (mostly in the spring and late fall) out of forty-four. His colleagues obliged him by not assigning him to the more time-consuming committees. It was as if the political establishment were clearing obstacles from his way in expectation of his next move. Under the terms of the new City Charter, John F. Fitzgerald had been elected to a four-year term in 1910 (beating the banker James Jackson Storrow by a nail-biting sixteen hundred votes). He would be eligible to run for re-election in 1914. Whether Curley would challenge him then was the all-absorbing question of Boston politics.[10]

Besides his family, Curley took with him to Washington as the political equivalent of a gentleman's gentleman, his secretary Standish Willcox. The name conjures·up the image of the man: an urbane, vaguely English fellow with a taste for formal clothes—ascot, bat-wing collar, cutaway coat; a wide culture, courtly manner, and precise elegant diction. Born in Fairhaven, Massachusetts, about 1880, Willcox, who seems to have deliberately kept much about his life mysterious, managed to become an authority on horses and horse racing, both in the United States and in Europe. He parlayed this expertise into a turf column for the *Boston American*, a Hearst tabloid, eventually becoming executive editor of the paper.

---

* Curley made such double-dipping a habit: briefly in 1914 and throughout 1945, he served as both congressman and mayor, and if he had won his gubernatorial race in 1924 he might have served as mayor and governor.

In 1910 Curley's campaign headquarters was in the basement of his Mount Pleasant Avenue home. "In walked a dignified gentlemanly fellow one night, carrying a green baize bag," Curley recalled of their first meeting. "He talked but did not look exactly like a poet. He spoke laconically his conclusion that Curley was the best man in the field, ought to win, would win—said he wanted to help on the publicity, expected no pay." Every evening thereafter Willcox would come by with several pages of typewritten copy containing "some of the most wonderful speeches on the high cost of living that I have ever read and every newspaper in Boston to which they were submitted printed them verbatim." Shortly before the primary Curley made a disconcerting discovery. "In substance, those glittering speeches . . . had all been delivered by statesmen and politicians in the campaign of 1876, when high-cost-of-living had been the issue—but Stan had polished them off with current facts and figures." Angry, he took Willcox to task. "There is no fear of an exposé," Willcox complacently assured him, citing his source for the speeches; "while many people get the *Congressional Record* few, if any, ever read it." Clearly he was an invaluable man.

Once elected, Curley asked Willcox to go with him to Washington as his secretary. Willcox demurred. He was a Protestant with the first name of a legendary Puritan; a district as overwhelmingly Irish as the Tenth should be served by a Catholic. But Curley, a bulldog in persuasion, wore him down. They would be together for the next twenty-two years.

The Willcox influence soon began to register in the expanded range of Curley's literary reference. Dr. Johnson shows up in Curley's speeches—sometimes passing himself off as Curley—and Dickens and Shakespeare recede to make way for cameo appearances by an exotic cast led by Petrarch, Tasso, Ariosto, Tourneur, Milton, Keats, Byron, and Shelley. Willcox also won a name among congressional staffers for what Curley called the "Chesterfeldian" letters he sent out under Curley's name to Tenth District constituents. Years later, an unemployed man walked into Mayor Curley's office carrying one of these missives and asked for immediate and substantial help. "The man had simply cast a vote for me twenty years before. But Stan's formula for thanking him was couched in such lofty diction that the man got the idea I owed him my right eye."[11]

Willcox was hard of hearing, and this infirmity spawned many stories about him. "You could yell something right in his ear," Curley recalled, "and he would reply, 'That's right, beastly weather.'

But if you stood at his office door and whispered, 'Stan, I'll buy you a drink,' he would leap for his hat." Of such endearing peculiarities are lasting friendships made.

In Washington, the Curleys rented a house on Massachusetts Avenue, near Dupont Circle, opposite the McLean mansion. "We had a splendid time," Curley remembered. "Under Taft, Washington was a magnificent social centre. There were dinners given by foreign ambassadors, and affairs at the White House, and the Pan-American building had just been completed, so that the dignitaries from South America were cutting a wide swath. We were on the go constantly." A fragment written in 1912 from a diary kept by Mary Emelda proves that this was no exaggeration:

> Attended reception of President and Mrs. Taft at W. H. at 10 P.M. Home at 12
> Attended dinner given by Mr. Mrs Murray Crane (the Massachusetts Senator) at their home at 1500 K Street. Motorcar
> Att reception to Sec. of Navy and Mrs. von Meyer at their home
> Went to Capital at 5 P.M. Very strong debate on tariff. Had the pleasure of listening to Father at 11:40. Made a good speech.
> Dinner in honor of Sec of State & Mrs Knox at Pan. Amer. Bldg. Sat out to Italian Embassy
> To Capitol at 12:30   Met Mayor & Mrs Fitz. Lunch at House Rest. She & I attended theatre in P.M. Dinner at Willard.
> Brought Jas to Capitol & Father had him meet Champ Clark . . . Champ gave him a quarter.
> Father had b-fast with President Taft & I dined alone.

A man who knew the Curleys in Washington later paid tribute to Mary's social skill. "You can imagine the sudden changes in the surroundings of the wife of a Boston alderman from her comparatively humble Roxbury neighborhood to Washington, where she was called on to meet, almost daily, the wives of ambassadors and ministers, of cabinet officers, of senators and of the most eminent personages in the land. Mrs. Curley was equal to the situation, with a native aptitude . . . that made her one of the most popular hostesses at the capitol. The Curleys took the old Portuguese legation on Dupont Circle and for years it was thronged by the elite of Washington society."

Mary made an instant hit with Nellie Taft, the president's wife. At the first White House reception the Curleys attended Mrs. Taft "was fascinated with the grace and charm shown by the wife of an unknown Boston congressman, and asked her to remain until the·

reception was over and make a good old-fashioned visit." Mrs. Taft must have been taken with Mary's conversation, for the two of them quickly became "firm friends," and phone calls between the White House and the Curley residence were "frequently exchanged."

In a story headed WOMAN OF MANY SIDES, a society reporter for a Boston paper described Mary as "exceptionally handsome and cordial" and said that she had been among the most popular of the newly-arrived congressional hostesses. James and Mary both loved music, and the house on Massachusetts Avenue often echoed with the sounds of Verdi, Puccini, Mascagni, and other composers sung by one of their talented new friends, a Signore La Cellini, an Italian diplomat and a vocalist of renown. He gave the Curleys gramophone recordings of his songs, which they played for guests on their Victrola. When La Cellini himself would come by and alternate live performances of vocal pieces with phonographic reproductions, "it used to be a common saying in Washington that to be invited to the Curley mansion on these occasions was a greater privilege than to hear grand opera itself in the opera house."[12]

Mary's heaping schedule argues happiness. And why not? As a congressman James had position without the burdens of power, status without responsibility. She had time and appetite for everything because he had time for her.

❖ ❖ ❖

Champ Clark had assigned the freshman congressman a seat on the prestigious Foreign Affairs Committee—hence the embassy and State Department receptions noted in Mary's diary. The Great War was still three years away, American entry into the war six. By current globe-girdling standards, the United States of that day had no foreign policy at all. "Foreign relations were composed of incidents, not policies," one historian of the period explains. "The national government treated foreign relations much as it did the rest of its business. In almost all cases the initiative lay elsewhere—with private citizens or foreign countries—and unless some event touched the political needs of the responsible officials, they usually did not react."[13]

What was true of government officials was even truer for congressmen. They selected international issues with a view toward winning the favor of domestic constituencies. Curley's issues were the tariff (he wanted it lower, to reduce his constituents' cost of living), the abrogation of U.S. commercial treaties with Czarist Russia (Boston's population, by 1910, was 12 percent Jewish, and the Jews were being persecuted in Russia), the building of more battleships for the fleet (Boston had a U. S. Navy yard, and Quincy, part of his district, a naval shipyard), and continued unrestricted immigration to the United States (Boston was a city of immigrants).

Only with the last of these issues—the debate over imposing a literacy test on new immigrants as a condition of their admittance to the United States—would Curley make any big stir. That would come in 1913. Meanwhile, he won applause from the floor of the House for flourishes like this, from a speech on lowering the tariff: "The economic system places the burden upon the many for the benefit of the few, for without the present extravagant tariff there never could have been the vast accumulation of wealth by the trusts of the country." He castigated the czarist government: "The bestiality of the Russian crown has repelled the civilized nations, and the rule of fire and sword and brutal assassination has appalled the world." And he had the honor of serving as Speaker pro tem when the bill canceling commercial treaties with Russia passed the House. He bucked his party to push for an American navy second to none. He lobbied for a federal child labor act, advocated judicial recall, and favored the compulsory arbitration of labor disputes. Nor did he neglect constituent service. To jump a year ahead, for a mother in South Boston, for example, who was prostrate with grief because her son had enlisted in the navy, he interceded with Assistant Secretary Franklin D. Roosevelt. Though he had claimed to be twenty on his application, the boy was really seventeen. Curley produced his birth certificate, and Roosevelt agreed to discharge him.[14]

In addition, he looked after his political future by attaching himself to the presidential campaign of Champ Clark.

❖   ❖   ❖

Woodrow Wilson's biographer, Arthur Link, has called Clark "the major political phenomenon of 1912." With the strong support of his party caucus, Clark stayed in the Speaker's chair and let his congressmen campaign for him in the state primaries. Beyond the House, Clark had a powerful ally in William Randolph Hearst. Avid to play kingmaker if he could not himself be king, in

.1911 Hearst had made overtures to Woodrow Wilson. "Tell Mr. Hearst to go to hell," Wilson had responded. So Hearst fixed on Clark.

On January 29, 1912, Hearst opened a national drive for Clark with editorials in his newspapers in New York, Atlanta, San Francisco, Los Angeles, Chicago, and Boston. The papers made much of some regrettable passages of prose that Wilson had written when he was a college professor. In his *History of the American People*, published in 1902, Wilson displayed "a profound contempt for the Farmers' Alliance, the Populists, greenbackers, bi-metallists, trade unions, small office seekers, Italians, Poles, Hungarians, pensioners, strikers, armies of the unemployed," in the words of George Fred Williams, one of Clark's Massachusetts supporters. Hearst wasted no time reproducing sentences like this:

> but now there came multitudes of men of the lowest class from the south of Italy and men of the meaner sort out of Hungary and Poland, men out of the ranks where there was neither skill nor energy nor any initiative of quick intelligence, and they came in numbers which increased from year to year, as if the countries of the south of Europe were disburdening themselves of the more sordid and hapless elements of their population. . . . [15]

This view of the so-called New Immigration was hardly calculated to endear Wilson to naturalized citizens from these places, who, however sordid and hapless, could read and vote and were Democrats. Wilson was in trouble with the base of his party.

In February Clark swept the primaries in his home state. In March he won the Kansas state convention and half the delegates from Oklahoma, both states where Wilson was supposed to do well. After beating Wilson by two to one in the Illinois primary on April 9, Clark was cheered on the House floor as "the next President." The Massachusetts primary was to be held on April 29. Running Wilson's campaign there was former congressman William McNary. Running Clark's campaign, with George Fred Williams, was James Michael Curley.

Four days before the primary Wilson came to Boston and made a tough speech attacking Hearst. But he was up against a political dervish in Curley, who canvassed Massachusetts for Clark, won him the support of the state Democratic machine, and persuaded Eugene Victor Foss, the Democratic governor, not to make a favorite-son appeal for delegates. With Foss off the ballot, Clark captured nearly every delegate in the state, winning the popular vote 34,500 to Wilson's 15,000. Clark had scored a signal victory, and he owed the best part of it to Curley.[16]

Distributing CLARK FOR PRESIDENT buttons with the title of Clark's risible campaign song—YOU GOTTA QUIT KICKIN' MY DAWG AROUND—printed on the bottom, Curley, along with Representatives Joseph Robinson of Arkansas and Scott Ferris of Oklahoma, next took the Clark campaign into Rhode Island, where they won, and to the Democratic state convention in New Hampshire, where Curley wowed the delegates with a speech comparing Clark to Jefferson, Jackson, and, for good measure, Lincoln.[17]

"Clark was running like a prairie fire," one Wilson campaign operative later said of that spring of 1912. But although he might win the nomination, could Champ Clark of Pike County be elected president of the United States? Theodore Roosevelt, then in the midst of his comeback drive to oust his erstwhile friend William Howard Taft from the White House, did not think so. "Pop is pray-ing for the nomination of Champ Clark," Theodore's son Kermit wrote to his cousin Franklin Roosevelt. This view was tenable right up to the Republican convention in mid-June—it was one of the Wilson campaign's main arguments for their man—but not after, with Roosevelt bolting from the Republican party to run as a third-party candidate against Taft and a yet-to-be-named Democrat. The Republican vote would be split between Taft and Roosevelt, so any Democrat who could hold on to the party's vote would win. Sum-ming up the prospects for Taft and Roosevelt after the Republican convention, Chauncey Depew, the former New York senator, was mordant: "The only question now is which corpse gets the most flowers."[18]

At the opening of the Democratic convention, held in Balti-more in late June, Clark had 436 delegates to Wilson's 248. A total of 545 votes was needed for a majority, and 224 of these were con-trolled by the sort of urban bosses whom Governor Wilson had won a national reputation for defying in New Jersey. "Just between you and me," Wilson wrote to a friend, as the delegates converged on Baltimore, "I have not the least idea of being nominated." In pro-ceedings that one participant remembers as "an indescribable tur-bulent chaos, a cacophony of howls, groans, and yells punctuated by futile attempts to obtain some sort of order," Clark did in fact gain a majority on the tenth ballot. Since the 1840s, however, the party had required its presidential nominee to win two-thirds of the delegates. A simple majority was not enough.

Working the floor for Clark in Baltimore in 1912, Curley would see all this happen again in 1932, when the two-thirds rule would give his candidate, Franklin D. Roosevelt, some tense moments. And at the Democratic convention of 1936, Governor Curley would have the pleasure of watching Champ Clark's son, Senator Bennett Champ Clark, lead the successful fight against the two-thirds rule, saying, "My father would have been elected in 1912 . . . this country would not have gone into the World War" if only a simple majority had been enough to win the nomination in 1912.

The Clark forces had their moment of elation. When Clark passed the false summit of a majority, they marched on the speaker's platform, triggering an hour-long demonstration. Just as it was about to subside, an elderly southerner appeared on the platform with a hunting horn and tooted "Off Hounds." Pandemonium broke out all over again. The convention was surging to Clark. From his summer home at Sea Girt, New Jersey, Woodrow Wilson, losing his nerve, sent a message to his floor manager directing him to release his delegates. At the Speaker's office in Washington, Champ Clark prepared a telegram accepting the nomination. But it was not to be. William Jennings Bryan, the three-time Democratic presidential nominee, would not let it be.[19]

The votes of New York's Tammany Hall had put Clark over the 545 majority threshold, and Bryan, fanning his rufous neck with a palmetto fan from his seat in the Nebraska delegation, seized on this as a way to deadlock the convention and perhaps emerge himself as the party's choice in a year when the party could not lose. He had been neutral in the battle between Wilson and Clark, but now, in a dramatic speech on the eleventh ballot, he announced that he could not vote for any candidate supported by that symbol of corruption, Tammany Hall. Bryan's residual moral influence over many of the delegates, along with a complicated series of switches from lesser candidates to Wilson (whose floor manager had wisely refrained from acting on his instructions) braked Clark's momentum.

Curley was among a group of advisers who met with Clark— who had by this time arrived in Baltimore—in his hotel room. He was especially bitter toward Bryan, Clark told Curley, because when Bryan had first run for president in 1896 he had worked hard for his election and contributed thousands to his campaign. On hearing this, Curley, with others, urged Clark to give Bryan a pasting before the convention. But a second group of advisers counseled him to remain silent. "There were people who knew what kind of language Clark could use under great provocation," a witness on the scene remembered, "and they seemed to feel that if he spoke from the convention platform grave consequences might result." Clark took their advice rather than that of the Curley group. He would not rebut Bryan's charge—that he had made a deal with Tammany Hall—before the delegates. "Locked in a Baltimore hotel room," the most recent chronicler of the convention writes, "Clark watched his chances die."

It took days, but on the forty-sixth ballot the Democrats nominated Woodrow Wilson. A reporter who was there left this description of Bryan during the triumphant Wilson demonstration. "Beyond rising [Bryan] did not participate in the demonstration. His face seemed to have frozen and apparently he had aged ten years. . . . Many who studied his expression in the closing minutes believe they saw there the emotions of hope lost and a lifetime ambition again defeated." A grateful Wilson would appoint him secretary of state.[20]

What was the significance of Wilson's victory for the thirty-seven-year-old congressman from the Tenth Congressional District of Massachusetts? Curley dropped a hint in his autobiography. A congressman speaking to Clark once referred to Curley, then mayor of Boston, by saying that "the burglar is in town." Clark replied, "Well, you may call him a burglar in Boston, but if I were President I'd put him in my Cabinet."

Clark's defeat meant that there would be no cabinet or sub-cabinet appointment for Curley. He would remain a provincial figure, never to mount the national stage like those appointed to high office by the winner in Baltimore. William Gibbs McAdoo, Wilson's secretary of the treasury, was to be a presidential candidate and Senator from California. Newton D. Baker, Wilson's secretary of war, was spoken of as presidential timber throughout the 1920s and ran as a dark-horse candidate at the 1932 Democratic convention. Herbert Hoover, appointed food administrator in Wilson's second term, was later secretary of commerce under Harding and Coolidge before ascending to the presidency in 1928. The secretary of the

navy under Wilson, Josephus Daniels, was too old to exploit his
prominence in the post-Wilson era, but his assistant secretary,
Franklin D. Roosevelt, was the Democratic vice presidential nominee in 1920 and was elected governor of New York in 1928 and president in 1932. Even minor figures in the Wilson ambit, like George
Creel and A. Mitchell Palmer and Carter Glass, at intervals in coming years cast long shadows in national politics.

If Champ Clark had been nominated in Baltimore, in all likelihood he would have beaten the Taft-Roosevelt hydra and been
elected twenty-eighth president of the United States. He would
have appointed different men to his administration, and they
would have carried out different policies from those adopted by
the men Wilson appointed. But they would have been the
McAdoos, Bakers, Hoovers, and Roosevelts of the Clark era, for it
was their prominence in the eight-year Wilson government that
either made or solidified the national reputations of these men.
The Capitoline geese, whose quacking warned the night watch of
approaching danger, saved Rome, according to Thomas Hobbes,
not because they were they but because they were there. Curley
would have been there under President Champ Clark, and who
knows where being there might have taken him?

Champ Clark's defeat in Baltimore meant something else to
Curley as well. The taint of Tammany Hall had cost Clark the nomination. This raised a question that would split the Democratic
party in the 1920s: was there room in the same party for both urban
ethnic machines and the southern and western followers of William Jennings Bryan? To ask the question in another way, was there
room for Roman Catholics in a party increasingly dominated by
fundamentalist Protestants? Could the party of reform, which
would ultimately come to mean Prohibition, also accommodate
antireformers like Charles Murphy, the sachem of Tammany Hall,
and James Michael Curley of the Tammany Club? The fault lines of
the 1920s were visible for all to see in 1912. Feeling alien in their
national party, urban Democrats like Curley and Al Smith, later
governor of New York and presidential candidate, would in coming
decades practice a "politics of provincialism," holding defensively
to the symbols and rhetoric of their differentness.

In 1928 Al Smith, the first Catholic to run for president, went
out of his way to kiss the ring on a bishop's finger; and nothing
would make him take off his brown derby, say "work" instead of

"woik," or subdue his cigar. His world, wrote H. L. Mencken, "begins at Coney Island and ends at Buffalo." When reporters on the campaign trail asked him what he would do to help states west of the Mississippi, he was culpably quick with the quip: "What states are west of the Mississippi?"

The sense of grievance, of exclusion, of marginality felt by urban politicians in the Wilson and especially in the post-Wilson Democratic party would bite even more deeply among their constituents. For the Boston Irish, the Puritan might have passed, but the southern bigot remained.° His emergence on the national scene in the 1920s helped prolong the political career of James Michael Curley, a clarion of ethnic defensiveness, long past the point it would have reached if propelled solely by the flagging local dynamics of Irish versus Yankee. The saliency of the religious issue in Al Smith's loss in 1928 rankled Boston Catholics, whose attachment to Smith bordered on hysteria, for more than a generation, and it contributed to their embrace of Curley's shamrock politics. Only in 1960, with the election of John F. Kennedy, a Boston Catholic, did the hurt of 1928 begin to heal. But even as late as 1960, it is sobering to realize, Kennedy's Catholicism, though it gained him an estimated 1.6 percent of the vote outside the South, cost him 16.5 percent of the vote in the South and 2.2 percent of the overall vote. If E. Digby Baltzell, the ethnographer of the Protestant aristocracy, is right, the rejection of Kennedy by those in the genteel denominations had more to do with Kennedy's being a *Boston* Catholic than with his being simply a Catholic. He cites this opinion of Lucius Beebe, an "old-stock American," writing in a San Francisco newspaper in 1960, as "the extreme caste view" of Kennedy. Beebe wrote: "A good many people are fed up with both parties for not having nominated somebody of gentility, good breeding and manners for the First Citizen of the Republic. Hostility to Nixon on these grounds has an evasive quality. . . . Prejudice against Kennedy is much easier to pinpoint: it is [his] lace curtain Irish background in a political pigsty so liberally befouled by the late Mayor of Boston and jailbird, James M. Curley, that honest Democrats elsewhere in the land are appalled by it."[21]

° Dr. Mordecai Ham of the First Baptist Church of Oklahoma City warned his congregants in 1928, "If you vote for Al Smith, you are voting against Christ, and you'll all be damned."

Clark's defeat, finally, had a personal significance for Curley. He would not be able to make the next move in his career by attaching himself to an upward-moving politician. He was on his own. After easily winning reelection to Congress in November 1912 (he had retired from the City Council in February), Curley found the issue that, a little over a year later, would help to elect him mayor of Boston. That issue was immigration.

❖   ❖   ❖

The American tradition, from the Civil War to the end of the nineteenth century, was well expressed by Oliver Wendell Holmes's boast that Americans were "the Romans of the modern world, the great assimilating people." Unrestricted by law, immigration increased year by year in the era of expansion, rising to a peak of 1,000,000 in 1907 and leveling off thereafter to somewhat above 650,000 people annually up to the outbreak of the First World War. To be sure, the nativism of the 1850s, flaring up repeatedly during the period, had found expression in efforts to restrict immigration. In 1882 Congress enacted the first federal immigration acts in U.S. history—laws barring lunatics, idiots, convicts and those likely to become public charges. Bowing to nativist pressure from the West Coast later that year, Congress passed the Chinese Exclusion Act. Still, given the country's manifest need for quantities of cheap labor, the economic argument for continued unrestricted immigration, at any rate from the white peoples of Europe, continued to carry the day. The historian David M. Kennedy sums up the national faith: "The melting pot, Americans believed, would fuse the various foreign elements into an acceptably homogeneous national amalgam."[22]

Immigrant radicalism in the late 1880s, the changing character of the immigration, from northern Europe to "the strange and suspect lands southeast of the Alps and beyond the Danube and the Vistula," and the official closing of the frontier in 1890 brought a new claustral mood. Its herald was Henry Cabot Lodge.

James Michael Curley and Henry Cabot Lodge: the names bracket the duality of Massachusetts' polarized political culture. The conflict of these two men in the debate over restricting immigration was a clash of symbols. Lodge embodied the old Massachusetts; Plymouth Rock was somehow implicated in the weathered features of his aristocratic face. Fleeing the slave rebellion in Haiti, his ancestor John Ellerton Lodge had come to Boston in 1791, but the Cabots, who had been in Boston from the days of its first settlement, had always stood high in the city and played no small role in the affairs of the young country. John Ellerton Lodge's son, Henry Cabot Lodge, who as a child had hidden under the sideboard to spy on George Washington eating breakfast, was still alive in 1850 when his namesake was born.

While growing up, young Lodge had had to contend with gangs of tough Irish boys from the North End, who would fight over prized sections of the Boston Common, sometimes using stones concealed in snowballs, with the tamer Yankee boys from Beacon Hill. "What was more serious," Lodge wrote in *Early Memories*, "the ever-increasing numbers of our opponents gradually by sheer weight pushed us, and still more our successors, from the Common hills and the Frog Pond to seek coasting and skating in the country." The experience recorded in that sentence would echo down the years in Lodge's politics.

Lodge went to the Boston Latin School and then on to Harvard, where he was eventually awarded a doctorate in history for his thesis on Anglo-Saxon land law (he was a lifelong Anglophile). After marrying a descendant of John Alden, he settled down to the life of a Harvard professor. He was a less than inspiring teacher, however—his manner was described as "repellently cold" and the sound of his voice likened to "the tearing of a bedsheet"—and after one of his classes dwindled from fifty students to three, Lodge decided to go into politics.

It was an unlikely choice of profession. A spare, fastidious man with an every-hair-must-do-its-duty crew cut and an elegant Vandyke beard, Henry Cabot Lodge was far from the back-slapping type of politician. Daily at his oceanfront summer home in Nahant, a promontory on the North Shore of Boston, he would plunge into the icy waters of the Atlantic, an invigorating austerity that summed up his character. Yet by power of intellect—he was a steady producer of both popular and scholarly histories and biographies—and by a sometimes controversial gift for compromise, Lodge got on in politics, rising from the Massachusetts legislature to the U.S. House to the Senate.

One of Lodge's compromises came in the area of his opinions. Early in his career, when he did not know that he would someday

need their votes, he had written that the Irish were "a very unde-
sirable addition," "a hard drinking, idle, quarrelsome and disorderly class" of people "always at odds with the government." By
1909, partly from research on what the Irish had already contributed to America, and partly because numbers of them had since
proved their good sense by voting for him, Lodge's views had
changed. He could tell the Boston City Club that "the Irish presented no difficulties of assimilation, and they adopted and sustained our system as easily as the peoples of earlier settlement."

The Irish may have had his revised approval, but Lodge feared
for the racial and cultural survival of the country if unlettered Jews
and Italians, Poles and Hungarians were allowed to come by the
thousands. Displacement, being forced off the hills of the Common
by gangs of Irish boys, had been among his earliest experiences with
immigrants. What had happened to him as a child would happen to
people like him and to the republic their ancestors had built if the
great immigrant tide ran unchecked into the American future.[23]

Appropriately for a man known as "the scholar in politics," his
instrument for checking the tide was a test of literacy: he would
refuse entry to those immigrants who could neither read nor write
in their native language. Legislation embodying this aim passed
both the Senate and the House in early 1897, but it was vetoed by
President Cleveland just weeks before he left office on the grounds
that it broke with the American tradition. Another sixteen years
went by before Lodge was again able to get his literacy test
through both houses of Congress. In February 1913 it was on President Taft's desk, waiting for his signature. Taft was undecided on
the bill, and to help him make up his mind he called a hearing
at the White House to air the arguments on both sides. A member
of the Committee on Immigration and Naturalization, Curley was
among the leaders of the fight against Lodge's literacy test. He
would head the delegation speaking against the bill.

It was an extraordinary assemblage. With the help of the National Liberal Immigration League, Curley and Willcox brought
together a large delegation representing the variegated contribution made to the country by unlettered immigrants. The president
had intended to hold the meeting in his White House office, but
confronted with a crowd of about 250 persons, he switched the
venue to the East Room. He presided, judgelike, with a gavel,
while Curley summoned witnesses to testify against the literacy

test. "One was a Polish lawyer, who, after entering this country as an illiterate peasant at the age of eleven, had become an Assistant Attorney General of Illinois," he later recalled. "Another star witness was Chief Justice Olsen of the Wisconsin Supreme Court. A third was a prominent New York importer, an Italian, who could neither read nor write when he came to these shores. I also presented Julius Rosenwald of Chicago and other distinguished Jews who were in the same category." The spokesman for the other side was Frank M. Morrison, secretary of the American Federation of Labor—which had obvious economic reasons for wanting to restrict immigration. According to Curley, Taft—who could easily doze off under the burden of his weight—showed great interest in the hearing.[24]

After calling his witnesses, Curley made a speech himself, probably a reprise of a stem-winder he had delivered on the floor of the House when the bill was under consideration. On that occasion he pointed out that the forebears of several signers of the Declaration of Independence had been illiterate, detailed the role played by American Jews in the Revolutionary War, and confronted those who held that the Italians coming into America were unassimilable with this review of the Italian pantheon: "How strange, Mr. Chairman, is this flaunt of prejudice in the faces of Dante and Tasso and Petrarch, of Raphael and Michael Angelo and Canova, of Verdi and Rossini, Bellini and Donizetti, of Ristori and Duse and Salvini and Rossi, of Alfieri and Gidcometti, of Cavour and Mazzini . . . (Applause)." When a member from Ohio asked if the immigrants now coming to America were the "worthy successors of the distinguished men whom the gentleman from Massachusetts has named," why would he object to requiring them to read and write? Curley replied: "I will answer by saying that if the restriction that is proposed in this bill had been in operation a hundred years ago undoubtedly the gentleman from Ohio would not be here now, and certainly I would not." Which was the point: the doctrine embodied in the bill, that literacy was a sovereign predictor of achievement, had been refuted by common American experience. Curley's parade of witnesses before President Taft capped that argument with human proof. "They were a group that any nation would have been proud to claim, and when they said, 'Our parents could neither read nor write,' it was pretty strong evidence."[25]

Impressed by what he heard and saw, Taft, with only weeks left in his term, vetoed the bill. (Curley asked for and received the pen Taft used to do it.) In his message to Congress the president maintained that while he favored portions of the bill, he could not accept a literacy test for the reasons stated in an attached letter written by his secretary of commerce and labor, Charles Nagel, a German-American lawyer from St. Louis. "The census returns show conclusively," Nagel wrote, "that the importance of illiteracy among aliens is overestimated, and that these people are prompt after their arrival to avail themselves of the opportunities which this country affords"—free public schools first among them. Unswayed by Nagel's arguments, the Senate, with Lodge bringing the motion, promptly overrode Taft's veto, seventy-two to eighteen. Now the scene shifted to the House.[26]

As the congressmen filed into the House chamber, their desks were strewn with yellow-and-red envelopes containing telegrams urging some to sustain and others to override the president's veto. Henry Cabot Lodge had come over to the House floor from the Senate side to witness this historic vote and to cheer on his son-in-law, Congressman Augustus P. Gardner (R-Mass.), to whom he had in recent years passed the torch of the restrictionist cause, and who led the forces seeking an override. In the course of the debate Gardner cited statistics provided to him by a county prosecutor in New Jersey that seemed to correlate every crime known to villainy with immigrant illiteracy. Curley couldn't resist poking fun at this overkill. He asked to be recognized by the Speaker. "I was going to ask the gentleman how many illiterates had been arrested for forgery"—one crime an illiterate would be unlikely to commit. "How many teeth has a hen?" Gardner shot back, and a further thrust and parry ensued.

As one of the leaders of the fight to sustain the veto, Curley was deliberately stalling for time. From the first gavel, it had become apparent that seven members on the president's side were absent. Champ Clark, in the Speaker's chair, directed that the entire bill be read aloud to the House. The opposing side quickly motioned to dispense with the reading, which brought Curley and another congressman to their feet to protest. The Speaker assured them that he had directed the bill to be read aloud, and it would be. While the long reading went on, messengers scurried through the Capitol rousting laggard members from barbershops and smoking rooms. When the final vote was taken, enough of them had been found to sustain the president's veto, 114 to 213. The effort to override had fallen short of the necessary two-thirds by five votes.

Before the final vote was cast, counting the missing members as they filed onto the floor, Henry Cabot Lodge left the chamber.

"It is a stinging rebuke to those men in public life who have substituted prejudice for judgement," said Curley, who was being hailed as one of the heroes of the hour by pro-immigration groups. "My heartiest congratulations on the action of the House in sustaining the President's veto," Edward Lauterbach, the president of the National Liberal Immigration League, wired him. "To you, on whom we all relied for leadership against this un-American measure, I acknowledge our vast indebtedness." Curley, generously giving most of the credit to President Taft, said this in his formal statement to the press: "The liberal spirit of America in its broadest sense was manifested by the House of Representatives today in its vote to sustain the President's veto upon the immigration bill."[27]

That liberal spirit would not long endure. In January 1915 President Wilson vetoed yet another bill to require a literacy test and used his patronage powers to pressure Congress to sustain it. But in February 1917, a mood of xenophobia brought on by the approach of war swept through Congress, and more than twenty years after he had first introduced it, Senator Lodge's literacy test at last became law. America was closing the golden door. The Immigration Act of 1921 was aimed squarely at excluding Jews from Eastern Europe. (Appended to the House bill were characterizations of Jews from American consuls overseas, such as, "filthy, un-American, and dangerous in their habits.") The 1924 act banned all immigrants from Asia. Discrimination, once considered un-American, was codified in American law.[28]

Class tells, even from beyond the grave. To Henry Cabot Lodge, who was among the most narrowly partisan senators of his day and, with Speaker Cannon, a symbol of reaction to most of his contemporaries, posterity, if not history, has accorded the name and reputation of a statesman, whereas James Michael Curley— ethnic, urban, a Democrat—tends to be thought of as a cross between a clown and a crook. Thus in the immigration debate, Senator Lodge and Congressman Gardner appear to be standing on the ground of disinterested principle, however offensive to contemporary sensibility, while Curley's position seems dictated strictly by votes. But Lodge had powerful interests behind him too; notably (and paradoxically for so conservative a lawmaker) big labor. In any case, it is a strange sort of retrospective approval that regards only the form of a political act and ignores its substance. Curley had received help from the National Liberal Immigration League in his 1912 reelection campaign, and he knew that his position on the literacy test would not hurt him among Boston's Italians, Poles, and Jews. But he also believed in it. Curley's parents had been illiterate when they came to America; he had only to look at his own life to know that Lodge was wrong.

❖   ❖   ❖

Mayor John F. Fitzgerald had gone to bed early. He had been injured, nearly killed, two weeks before, when he fell down a long flight of stairs while inspecting a Washington Street boarding house. The day before his fall, on December 3, 1913, he was among the first to enter the charred hulk of another rooming house, this one destroyed by a fire in which twenty-eight people were killed. The stench, the sight of the bodies laid out on the sidewalk, the guilty knowledge that the rooming house had not been properly inspected by the government of which he was chief executive—all this had left him in shock. And just two days before that, he had experienced another kind of shock. On that day a black-bordered letter addressed to Josephine Fitzgerald was delivered to his Dorchester home. It told of a lubricious relationship between her husband and a twenty-three-year-old cigarette girl with an unambiguous nickname—"Toodles." The scandal would be made public, the letter said, if Fitzgerald did not withdraw from the mayoral race forthwith. Plump, smiling John Fitzgerald had opened his door that evening to find his wife and his eldest daughter, Rose (who, like Toodles, was twenty-three), waiting for him in the hallway. He later told a friend that it was the worst moment of his life. Josephine had insisted that he comply with the letter's demand. But he had dithered, and then came his fall. Now he was home, confined to his bed, trying to get some needed rest.[29]

Shouts of "Oh you, Jim!" and "Curley!" were faintly audible through his window. A Curley rally was in progress outside the school just down the street.

Fitzgerald had been rushed to the hospital after his accident, and while he was convalescing the other candidates running against him, with one exception, suspended their campaigns until he recovered. The exception was James Michael Curley. "I have been asked to stop campaigning because one of my opponents is ill," Curley told the press. "It would be just as reasonable for Jordan Marsh to ask Filene's to close because the owner of Jordan's has a bellyache."

Fitzgerald raised himself from his pillow to listen, but either the wind had shifted or the rally was over for he could hear nothing. "Huh, guess it's only a nightmare," he said, falling back on his pillow. Suddenly, loud and clear, a boy's shout filled the room: "Good night, Mayor Curley!" John Fitzgerald sighed deeply.[30]

In a sense it *was* a nightmare. Curley was taunting him publicly—"You're an old man. Get your slippers and pipe and stretch out in your hammock and read the *Ladies' Home Journal*," he had been quoted as saying—and tormenting him privately. The black-bordered letter to Mrs. Fitzgerald came from his campaign. Now Curley began to make good on its threat by announcing a series of public lectures on such themes as "Great Lovers in History: From Cleopatra to Toodles" and "Libertines in History from Henry the Eighth to the Present Day." Lying in his bed that night, John Fitzgerald knew what he must do. He must head off the Toodles lecture—the happiness of his family was at stake. The next day, saying that he was acting on his doctor's orders, he announced his withdrawal from the race. The *Boston American* ascribed his decision to pressure from the "petticoat element" in his family; fearing for his health if he persisted in his campaign, his wife and his eldest daughter Rose had put their feet down.[31]

Doris Kearns Goodwin has recounted the story of Elizabeth ("Toodles") Ryan and John Fitzgerald in masterly fashion. She has told how it was Daniel Coakley who approached Curley with the information about Ryan, a "triumphantly beautiful young woman" from a big family in rural Connecticut who had been corrupted by the wicked city; how her job at the Ferncroft Inn, a suburban roadhouse outside Boston, had been to lure men from the restaurant to a gambling den upstairs; how she had met Fitzgerald at the inn; and how he had flirted with her openly, danced with her held tight against his chest, and ardently, repeatedly, and in front of witnesses, lavished her with kisses. Coakley's motive was vengeance:

years earlier Fitzgerald had given damaging testimony against a client and friend of his, a former official in Fitzgerald's first administration (1905–1907). Curley's motive had in it no such tincture of justice. Fitzgerald was simply in his way, an impediment to his ambition.[32]

Blackmail was low, true, but Curley was hardly the first Bay State politician to stoop to it. In 1905 the scholar in politics, Henry Cabot Lodge, along with his Republican colleague in the Senate Winthrop Murray Crane, induced the Democratic governor of the Commonwealth, William L. Douglas, not to run for reelection by threatening to publicize the fact that he had not, as he claimed, served in the Civil War, but had hired a substitute and secured a fraudulent discharge for himself. Blackmail was low, but so was any sexual congress in the vicinity of adultery to the maritally righteous Curley. Faithful to his wife because he loved her, he had no tolerance for the peccadilloes of men who were less fortunate in their marriages than he. Besides, to his strict Irish Catholic conscience, sins of the flesh were damnable.

He also felt betrayed by Fitzgerald. Earlier in the year, on more than one occasion—Curley named the dates—Fitzgerald had hinted that he would not be a candidate for reelection.° Fitzgerald's sights were set on running for the Senate seat held by Henry Cabot Lodge in 1916, the first year in which senators, previously elected by state legislatures, were to stand for direct election by the voters. In the meantime, Fitzgerald did not want a reprise of his bloody mayoral race of 1910 against James J. Storrow. He had pinned his hopes on being appointed collector of the Port of Boston, which would give him a prestigious office from which to launch his race against Lodge. In October 1913, however, President Wilson appointed someone else to the job. When twenty-four of the twenty-six ward chairmen on the Democratic City Committee formally urged him to run for reelection, arguing that Curley would retire once he saw the phalanx arrayed against him, Fitzgerald came around. "I am led to believe by the petitions that have come to me from innumerable sources that I owe it to Boston to run again," he said in his announcement of November 28. He

---

° Curley conveniently forgot a matching list of his own explicit endorsements of Fitzgerald's reelection: "I am with Mayor Fitzgerald against all comers," he had declared in March 1913.

would serve only two years of his term, he went on, hinting that if Curley withdrew from the race he could count on the support of that Gibraltar of constancy, John F. Fitzgerald, in the *next* mayoral election. Curley, however, would not withdraw: "My velour is in the center of the circle, there to remain until my opponent succeeds in accomplishing the impossible mathematical problem of squaring that circle. . . . Fitzgerald wants a licking, and he will get it." But Toodles had since made that unnecessary.

Politics is about more than who gets what, more than is dreamt of in the philosophy enshrined in that storied admonition, "The economy, stupid." To borrow a distinction from psychoanalysis, these rational formulae cover only the manifest content of politics. But politics also has a latent content, the realm of the passions as opposed to the interests, and over it James Michael Curley exerted a rare mastery. In its latent content, he knew, politics was the sublimination of fear, envy, and revenge. He understood that a politician has to show the electorate that he is a fit vehicle for their hopes, yes, but also for their fears and prejudices. Ruthlessness is a time-tested way of convincing them. It takes a man who will stop at nothing, seemingly, to represent the dark forces of the political unconscious. The Dwight Eisenhowers and Ronald Reagans, who remain above the battle, suggest there is wind in that generalization. But they weigh in the balance against the John and Robert Kennedys, the Lyndon Johnsons, and the Richard Nixons. What Curley did with the information Daniel Coakley had given him was despicable. And if he had not done it—and, what is more, if a decisive slice of the Boston electorate did not think him capable of doing things like it—he would probably not have become mayor of Boston.

With Fitzgerald out of the race, Curley was confident of beating the remaining candidates. These were: a former state legislator from Charlestown named John R. Murphy; a former congressman from the South End, John A. Kelliher; a Republican city councilor, Ernest Smith; and the president of the City Council, Thomas J. Kenny of South Boston. Fitzgerald withdrew on December 18; under peculiar circumstances, John Murphy followed suit four days later. Murphy's campaign manager, Francis A. McLaughlin, met Curley in front of City Hall on the final day on which candidates could withdraw their names. "By five o'clock this afternoon," Curley told him, "Murphy will withdraw and Governor Walsh will name him to the Finance Commission." Dumbfounded, McLaughlin hurried over to Murphy's office. Murphy was all assurance. "Nothing will take me out," he said. Yet at just before five, as Curley had predicted, Murphy withdrew. Also as Curley had predicted, Murphy was later made chairman of the Finance Commission by the Democratic governor, David I. Walsh, but whether the promise of that job was the reason he withdrew from the race or whether Curley used some other form of persuasion remains a mystery.

Unable to make headway, Kelliher also withdrew. As for Smith, there were reports that Curley was helping him get enough signatures to put his name on the ballot in hopes of drawing Good Government Association votes away from the only serious candidate left in the race, Thomas Kenny.[33]

The Good Government Association and its political arm, the Citizens' Municipal League, had learned a lesson from the Fitzgerald-Storrow election of 1910. In Boston a Yankee politician, of however high a luster, could no longer defeat an Irish politician, of however low a repute. They therefore decided to back an Irish American for mayor themselves. Their choice, Kenny, was a quiet, dignified lawyer who had first won office in 1898, when he had been elected to the School Committee, where he served for eight years, becoming chairman of the committee on supplies and making a name for probity and frugality. In his last School Committee race he received more votes than had ever before been cast for that office—65,794, twice as many as Curley received in either his city council or his congressional races, and more than enough to elect Kenny mayor. In 1910 he won a seat on the City Council; two years later, after his reelection, his colleagues elected him president of the council. "Tom reminds me of electricity," a friend said of him. "Electricity makes no fuss on the wires between the power plant and the light. It shoots along silently until its services are needed." The metaphor was a concession to a Kenny liability: he made a somnolent candidate. One of his Good Government Association backers described Kenny campaigning this way: "Kenny arrived at halfpast nine and had a loyal welcome. But his speech did not measure up to the occasion. He is not majestic, but on the contrary cold and austere. He will make a good Mayor, if he can get in, but he's a poor hand in getting." Curley called him "a lawyer who would have made a brilliant accountant."[34]

Kenny's platform breathed the spirit of business efficiency. He pledged to spend to repair the city streets, but otherwise his emphasis was on cutting taxes and spending and obtaining "100 cents of value for every dollar spent." The aura of soundness surrounding both his platform and his person, coupled with the standard journalistic hostility to Curley, won Kenny the unqualified support of eight of Boston's nine newspapers. "The business welfare of the community in a large degree depends on the forthcoming decision of the voters," the *Boston Herald* said in a typical endorsement. The Good Government Association promised that Kenny would run Boston "as a corporation." The association's leaders knew what they were talking about; several of its officers, both past and present, were leading corporation lawyers. Here was Kenny's vulnerable point.[35]

"Save me from my friends" is the politician's immemorial lament. Kenny's friends included people like Richard Olney, who, as President Cleveland's attorney general, had sworn in thirty-four hundred deputies to break the Pullman strike. A proven friend of the railroads, Olney was a former director of the Boston & Maine and a counselor to the New Haven railways. Another of Kenny's friends was Lawrence Minot, one of the founders of the Good Government Association. Minot had been a director of the New Haven Railroad, and his realty company still performed development work for the corporation. The complicated mergers by which the New Haven had absorbed other local lines several years earlier had brought disgrace on the Massachusetts political establishment. "In this sordid affair," one historian writes, "the principles of the old Commonwealth gave way before the claims of commercial need and in-group loyalty." Throughout the month of December 1913 and into January 1914, the height of the mayoral election campaign, legislative hearings were daily publicizing the bribes, campaign contributions, fees, and retainers by which the New Haven had its way with state government. "If the Railroad was engaged in illegal and improper practices," Herbert M. Zolot observes, "then the men associated with it who were so closely affiliated with the Good Government Association, the Citizens' Municipal League, and Kenny's candidacy could not with moral consistency call for scrupulously clean municipal government."

As we have seen with Senator Lodge, history has a selective memory. Everybody knows that Mayor Curley took money from contractors who did business with the city. But that Charles H.

Innes, the Republican boss of the Back Bay, accepted $40,000 from the New Haven Railroad for offering legal opinions whose nature he had trouble recalling in testimony before the legislative committee looking into the railway's lobbying practices—this common knowledge among Boston newspaper readers in 1914 has been washed away by time. "These Republicans say that we are a machine," the veteran Chicago Congressman Frank Annunzio once remarked during a campaign. "What the hell do you think they are, a knitting society, a sewing circle?" To understand why Bostonians in 1914 elected as mayor a man with James Curley's baggage, Annunzio's observation must be kept in mind. Curley was not running against a knitting society.[36]

To distract attention from the issue of his friends and what they meant when they said he would run the city like a corporation, Kenny did what any contemporary political consultant would have advised him to do. He went negative. "There has never been a man in my experience in the city government . . . whose record in public life is more questionable than that of Mr. Curley," he said in his stump speech. "Curley has been absolutely unscrupulous as a public servant . . . he is one of the most dangerous men to the public interest that has ever misrepresented the citizenship of Boston." The newspapers echoed this charge on their editorial pages. Over the breakfast table the *Boston Post* offered its lower-middle-class readers the choice of "Kenny or Curley, honest and scrupulously clean government or the ways and means of Tammany." Over the tea stand the *Boston Evening Transcript* told its upper-class readers: "It is no exaggeration to say that the present campaign is the most important ever to have been conducted in our city," for Curley "was as clear an embodiment of civic evil as ever paraded before the electorate." His election "would be the most humiliating experience in the history of the city." Curley's record, the *Boston Herald* fulminated, "is seething with disgrace."[37]

Kenny's friends were James Michael Curley's ideal enemies. Ernest Smith, the Republican councilor, had failed to get enough signatures to remain on the ballot; it was now a two-man race. Curley knew he needed to look like a winner to sway critical ward bosses and their heelers his way. "I'll beat Mr. Kenny in his own ward by 5 to 1," he said in a classic effusion of bravado. "I'll carry wards 13 and 14 in his own district by 4 to 1. I'll beat him in his own precinct, in his own street, and if he lived in a six-tenement house

I'd beat him in his own house 5 to 1." John Fitzgerald had been expected to endorse Kenny, but he held off, and other key city Democrats followed his lead. They did not want to be with a loser, and Curley's vaunt of victory made them think he had something up his sleeve.[38]

He did. Beyond hanging Kenny's friends around his neck ("I ask every God-fearing citizen to save Boston from the banks and railroads"); beyond matching Kenny's platform promises to cut taxes and provide "an economical and honest administration of city business"; beyond pledging to develop the port, attract new industry, widen the streets, install new sewers, and build a parkway along the South Boston peninsula—beyond the boilerplate, Curley had two other issues working for him.

One was Kenny's mediocrity. "I have charged that Mr. Kenny as a member of the City Council displayed mediocre ability, lack of initiative and an absolute failure to comprehend the importance attached to his membership in the City Council. Mr. Kenny has annually introduced orders that bells be hung up on holidays, that streets be roped off and closed during parades and that sidewalks be repaired in the vicinity of his South Boston home." If Kenny had not stepped up to the challenge of being a councilor, occupying himself with trivialities, how on earth would he rise to the much sterner challenge of being mayor? Though Curley may have had the reputation of being unscrupulous, few could question his energy or ability. When he offered to debate, Kenny refused. When he offered to print Kenny's public record at his own expense if Kenny would return the compliment, Kenny ignored him. "My record in public office," Curley said, "would take about sixteen newspaper columns. My opponents would not take a half of a column." This boast happened to be true.[39]

Curley's second issue was immigration. His part in the defeat of the restriction bill in Congress had received heavy publicity in Boston. Jewish organizations had given him testimonial dinners. Other groups had presented him with awards. Though all but one of the Boston dailies printed in English opposed his candidacy (and that one, the *Globe*, did not run editorial endorsements), all the city's nearly forty foreign-language papers endorsed him. Days before the election Curley, using his congressional frank, mailed thousands of copies of his major speech against immigration restriction to residents of selected neighborhoods in Boston. Reporters thereafter noted a "Curley current" running among the Jewish voters in Ward 8, the domain of boss Martin Lomasney. On the Sunday before the election, going with the current, Lomasney endorsed Curley for mayor. (Curley would not forget his Jewish supporters: in his first term, the number of Jews on the city payroll increased from 200 to 538.)[40]

Meanwhile Curley's Tammany braves were busy behind the scenes, sabotaging Kenny's campaign with a dirty trick in the same family as the one that had neutralized Fitzgerald. Each of the wives of Kenny's campaign workers was called and told that her husband was not out campaigning, but instead keeping tryst with a woman at a "notorious Columbus Avenue boarding house." The wives would be given the address; and some of them, going to investigate, showed photographs of their husbands to the building custodian, who, as the Curley people had paid him to do, would identify the men as frequent visitors to the building. "It's been an open boast by certain Tammany leaders that any man who runs against Curley will have to take it for granted that he will have a family row on his hands within a week," a reporter noted long after the campaign. In addition, seemingly wherever Kenny spoke, there was trouble in the audience. At a rally at Faneuil Hall two carloads of Curley toughs drove women out of their seats by spouting "lurid profanity." Kenny was jeered in Charlestown, harassed on Curley's home turf of Roxbury. In the closing days of the campaign he seemed tired. Curley was on fire.

Two days before the election, Curley raided Kenny's home ground, South Boston's Ward 14, and in a rally in front of St. Augustine's Church entered Boston folklore. He conducted his campaign from the back seat of an open touring car, garbing himself against the Boston winter in a voluminous fur coat. When he quit the car to climb the church steps he left his coat behind, the better to keep his gestures unencumbered. "There never was a time when a South Boston citizen came to me for assistance that he didn't find a true and sincere friend in James Michael Curley," he told the chilled crowd. Responding to some now forgotten statement made by his opponent, he continued, "I am reminded by Brother Kenny of those beautiful words in that beautiful prayer, 'Give us this day our daily bread and forgive us our trespasses—'" then, glimpsing a hand reaching into the open back seat to snatch his coat, he shouted to one of his aides, "Get that sonuvabitch, he's stealing my coat!"—and resumed his sonorous recital right where he had left off: "'as we forgive those who trespass against us. . . .'"

It is the single most recounted Curley story. Told and retold over the years, its locus has shifted from South Boston to the Common to East Boston to Charlestown to the North End to Roxbury—each neighborhood making the story its own, a local marvel. What people seem to relish in it is something essential to Curley. He was, in every sense, a man of two voices: above the people in his flights of rhetorical unction, yet of the people in his angry curse at a sneak thief.[41]

The evening before the voting Curley's twelve-car caravan covered every ward in the city—driving over 150 miles in a five-and-a-half-hour closing rush that saw Curley, in his fur coat and derby, speak before an estimated twenty thousand people. He wound up at a rally in his own ward. A large and enthusiastic crowd, ringing cowbells, escorted him home.

That night temperatures plummeted from the twenties to below zero. By noon the thermometer was reading $-4°$. It was the coldest election day in Boston's history—Curley weather. "If the Republicans and Protestants turn out," George Nutter, a Good Government Association member, noted in his diary, "Kenny can get in. Otherwise this wretched Curley, the worse yet, will be Mayor." But the bitter day daunted Kenny's voters. Curley's supporters, many of whom worked for the city and feared what Kenny's promise of running it like a corporation might mean to them, were voting for their jobs. Cold would not keep them home. Amid reports of cases of frostbite among voters waiting in line, the balloting went on. When it was over the results showed that Curley had failed to carry Kenny's house, street, precinct, or ward; but he had beaten him in the other two wards in his district and, by 5,720 votes, he had won the election—43,362 to Kenny's 37,542. "A deep humiliating disgrace!" Nutter confided to posterity. "The worst depth to which this unfortunate city has sunk."

On its front page that frigid morning the *Boston Herald* featured a large editorial cartoon. It showed a snarling tiger emerging from its den, its awful eye trained on a pile of neatly stacked bags labelled CITY TREASURY. Above the cartoon was the headline, THE LOOT AND THE TIGER. Was this prophecy or prejudice?[42]

The Metamorphistical Mayor

❖　　　❖　　　❖　　　❖

*It is not the salary of any place that did make a man
rich, but the opportunities of getting money while he
is in the place.*

SAMUEL PEPYS

*The Mayor brought a lot of trouble on his shoulders
when he built that wonderful residence in Jamaica
Plain. Politically it was the worst mistake he has
made in his entire term.*

BOSTON JOURNAL.

President Wilson's congratulatory telegram arrived early, before the Curleys left for the short trip downtown. By the time they arrived at the Parker House, the Boston political hotel steps from City Hall at the corner of School and Tremont streets, the crowd gathered in front of Tremont Temple, the site of the inauguration next door to the hotel, filled the sidewalk. Invitations had been sent to five thousand people, and to judge by the size of the crowd, all of them had come and some of them had brought along a friend. By ten-fifteen the three-thousand-odd seats in the Temple, a Baptist meeting hall selected by some genius of incongruity because it had the largest room in the area, were taken, and the aisles had begun to fill up. A crowd nearly equal to that in the Temple would have to wait outside in the bright winter sun until, the ceremony over, the new mayor would emerge and greet them on his way to City Hall.

It had been the "custom of years" for the outgoing mayor to be at the center of the preinaugural observances. But the animosity James Curley had displayed toward John Fitzgerald ruled that out this year, so Fitzgerald was relegated to the sidelines, where he would remain for the rest of his life. Although he was only fifty-one, he would never hold elected public office again. On this, his final morning as Boston's chief executive, he seemed unusually chipper, whistling a tune as he walked out of the mayor's corner office for the last time.[1]

"What might have been can, of course, never be known," Doris Kearns Goodwin writes. "But if Fitzgerald had stood his ground and accepted the risk to his reputation, it is possible that he rather than Curley would have emerged the victor; and had he continued his successful career, it is possible that he, rather than Curley, would have been immortalized as the hero of Edwin O'Connor's *The Last Hurrah*." She adds that if Fitzgerald had beaten Curley he would have been in a much stronger position as mayor of Boston to take on and defeat Senator Henry Cabot Lodge in 1916, when Fitzgerald came within thirty-three thousand votes of victory. "And if Fitzgerald had become the Senator from Massachusetts in 1916 instead of Lodge, the history of the country and indeed the history of the entire world might have been different, for it was from his Senate seat that Lodge played his decisive role in the crushing defeat of the Covenant of the League of Nations, the defeat that, in President Woodrow Wilson's words, 'broke the heart of the world.'" But, to venture further into the realm of what might have been, Lodge might not have been able to play his "decisive role" as chairman of the Senate Foreign Relations Committee if the Republicans had not won control of the Senate in the 1918 elections, which would not have happened if eight Democratic senators had not died during the Sixty-fifth Congress. Indeed, if only one of these senators, Wisconsin's Paul O. Husting, had not been killed in a duck-hunting accident, the Democrats would have retained control of the Senate. Truly, as David M. Kennedy has written, "The very fates seemed arrayed against the President's party," and so against U.S. entry into the League of Nations.[2]

Still, the fates had one lion of an instrument in Henry Cabot Lodge, and in that sense Goodwin's point holds. Her fascinating historical surmise invites us to see James Michael Curley's inauguration in a bizarre and unexpected light—as an event in world history, a small link in the long chain of fatality leading to the Second World War. The angel of history who, in Walter Benjamin's image, flies backward with her face frozen in a look of appalled regret was outside Tremont Temple that February morning, beating her wings in silent protest.

No sooner had Fitzgerald walked out of the mayor's office than messengers and delivery boys began to shuttle in, filling the room with two hundred floral tributes for its new occupant—including one sent by the Pro Bono Publico Club, the sanitized name Curley had given to the Tammany Club during the mayoral campaign. A white streamer across it read SUCCESS, and inscribed with red and white roses in the middle were the dates 1914–1922. The boys at the club were counting on a second term.

At the Parker House, Curley had been having a sort of peace meeting with Thomas Kenny. At just before ten-thirty this broke up and Curley waded through the crowd to Tremont Temple, where the fleeting sight of him, as he passed into an anteroom just off the platform, raised a cheer. He was half an hour late for the traditional preinaugural meeting of the new mayor with the surviving former mayors of Boston and the current heads of the city departments. Tension pervaded the room: everyone was waiting to see how Curley would greet John Fitzgerald. On encountering him in Young's Hotel the night of his election victory, angry at the secret role Fitzgerald had allegedly played in the Kenny campaign, Curley spurned Fitzgerald's proffered hand, and a fistfight had nearly broken out between the two men. Now, as the new mayor entered the anteroom, he shook hands with virtually everybody there except Fitzgerald, though he was among those nearest the door. Conversation in the room died as Curley finally deigned to notice him. "How are you, Mr. Mayor?" he said, extending what one eyewitness called a "cold grasp of the hand." "Good morning" was the best the abashed Fitzgerald could manage. A photograph of the group taken moments later shows John Fitzgerald appearing to be fighting back tears and Curley, his mouth open in a mocking half-smile, looking like a boy about to relieve a butterfly of its wings.

He was sworn in and then, tersely, the senior member of the City Council, Walter Ballantyne, introduced the assembly to "His Honor, James M. Curley." The audience rose as one, the women waving their handkerchiefs, the men applauding. Someone in the balcony shouted, "Three cheers for James M. Curley!" and they were given, with feeling. As Curley stood at the podium, "his face bore a tense expression," according to one reporter, as if, perhaps, just as he was about to speak for the first time as mayor of Boston, he felt a tug of self-doubt.

"For all his bravado," Charles Trout writes, "James Michael Curley lacked the requisite assuredness." In a compelling portrait, Trout sees Curley as driven by a lifelong, "absolutely desperate" search for "legitimacy," by which he means acceptance by the city elite Curley affected to despise. Curley, in short, was a notable casualty of "the hidden injuries of class and caste in Boston."[3]

These injuries may have haunted him in just the way Trout describes. They may even have made him a "self-crippled giant on a provincial stage," to quote William V. Shannon's lapidary judgment on Curley. But on that stage he *was* a giant. The most resourceful, eloquent, energetic, durable political personality of his time and place, he thwarted the ambitions of the generations of politicians who had the bad luck to come of age in the long Curley era. His personal qualities aside, he filled in those years a political space—urban populist—which fitted what pluralities and sometimes majorities of Bostonians wanted from their mayor. In point of experience alone, he was better prepared for the job than any mayor in Boston's history. Through the Tammany Club he had dealt in miniature and on an intimate level with problems akin to those he would confront on a larger scale as mayor. His years on the City Council and in Washington had made him aware of the citywide and national contexts of those problems. In his oratory, finally, he had the capacity to speak for the city with a voice, manner, and diction made for leadership—something lacking at nearly every level of office in these ineloquent times. If what he experienced as he prepared to speak that morning in Tremont Temple was self-doubt, it was misplaced.

In any case, his difficulties always flowed from the apparent opposite of self-doubt—an imperious self-confidence, an arrogance of power, a belief written in conduct that he was not subject to the same limits as ordinary men. His Tammany years as a dictator of benevolence had reinforced his native willfulness, his drive to have everything his own way and on his own terms. If he was "self-crippled," pride and the blindness that protects it did the crippling, not self-doubt. This autocrat by disposition and experience was about to assume an office invested with such power by the new City Charter adopted in 1909 as to make the mayor what one journalist of the time called "a municipal monarch."

Curley had grown somewhat stout during his Washington years. Norman, the political cartoonist for the *Boston Post*, began to draw him with a vestful of belly showing beneath his big chest and broad shoulders. George Nutter, who met him for the first time shortly after the inauguration, described him as "a dark smooth fellow, about forty, of the type whose beard grows out quickly, so that he looks unshorn." At thirty-nine, he was not the youngest man to be elected mayor of Boston, but with former mayors, including John Fitzgerald, sitting just behind him, he was plainly the youngest man on the stage at Tremont Temple, and some in the audience must have hoped that this energetic new mayor would lead the city in a new direction, away from the ethnic bickering and corruption of the Fitzgerald years.

His speech must have been a great disappointment to them. Although it called for some sensible, with-the-times measures—the abolition of the city reform school for truant boys, the establishment of a central purchasing agency for all city departments, and the beginning of something like city planning to take Boston into the twentieth century—it was strangely devoid of eloquence and vision. Worse, from the second sentence—"The old order, which I trust is happily ended, is largely responsible for our present tax rate and debt"—it became a tediously and tendentiously documented attack on the Fitzgerald administration. Sitting in the first row of dignitaries on the flower-rimmed platform behind the speaker, Fitzgerald was visibly uneasy. As Curley's indictment unfolded, his hands fidgeted, the corners of his mouth drooped, and an impeaching blush spread across his face.

"It is not my purpose to criticize my predecessor in the office of Mayor," Curley said at one point, "but it is my determination that the policy of discharging political debts through the mediumship of the city treasury shall cease." This was too much for Fitzgerald. "Hm, Ned, did you hear that?" he asked the city messenger, who was sitting next to him, in a stage whisper that filled the silence opened by a Curley pause. "Give it to him, Jim!" someone shouted from the crowd as if to punish him for interrupting. Gamely, John Fitzgerald joined in the ensuing applause.

When the speech was over, Fitzgerald was among the first to shake Curley's hand. "You're wrong in your figures, Jim," he was heard to say, referring to the mathematical burlesque Curley had performed on his administration. "Oh I guess not," Curley replied flippantly, with a satirical twist of his lip. Fitzgerald quickly left the stage, returned to the anteroom to get his hat and coat, and then shouldered his way through the crowd surging to the front of the hall to congratulate the new mayor.

It took a squad of police to get Mary Curley, her daughter Mary and son James, along with Sarah Curley, from their box to the side of the stage over to the center, where James was waiting for them. When Mary reached him, someone noticed that "her eyes glistened with happy tears." As for Sarah, her son's rise was so far beyond anything the mean circumstances of her life had led her to expect that she simply couldn't comprehend it. There was magic in it, or grace.[4]

He shook so many hands so vigorously in the next hour that a flap of flesh wore off one of his fingers. Emerging from Tremont Temple he was greeted by the cheers and tigers of the Pro Bono Publico (née Tammany) Club. His progress to City Hall was "a series of ovations." Arrived there at twelve-thirty, he fired the first of many Fitzgerald appointees who were to fall under his ax at twelve thirty-five. This was Arthur C. Everett, the head of the Building Department; by removing him as his first official act Curley was reminding the city of the Fitzgerald administration's share of responsibility for the tragic boarding house fire of six weeks before. Next, he ordered the building inspectors to take a careful look at the plant of the *Boston American,* a newspaper that had gotten under his skin during the campaign. It had the look of a "fire trap" to him, and he wanted no harm to come to those who worked there. His first two executive decisions behind him, he took time to admire (and no doubt see who had sent) the floral arrangements in his office, which, along with the plants and flowers from the City Green House on the stage at Tremont Temple, he ordered to be distributed among the patients in the city's hospitals. With the help of Edward Moore, John Fitzgerald's secretary (and the man for whom Senator Edward Moore Kennedy is named), he began to learn to navigate the Niagara of the mayoral paper flow. He posed for pictures; gave a luncheon for the City Council; refused the offer of a local cigar maker to endorse an official "Administration cigar." And at five-thirty, in the day's symbolic keystone, he sent for the City Hall scrubwomen. Eight women, their sleeves rolled up to the elbows and wearing burlap aprons, appeared in his office. He shook hands with each one; in turn, and in chorus, they wished the blessing of God on his administration. Was this the day he got them off their knees? The record is mute. "My time, energy and brains belong to the city," he told a reporter as he left City Hall that night, "and I want the opportunity to use all of them in the interests of all of the people all of the time."

Full of vengeance and solicitude and the abstract promise of his energy, his first day on the job had in it all the abiding Curley elements.

❖ ❖ ❖

What sort of administration would it be, Bostonians asked themselves, reform or, to use the crude designation of the day, "gang"? If Curley's past made the latter seem inevitable, the rhetoric of his inaugural suggested the former. Even before then, Curley had been giving some unmistakable "reform" signals. Just days after the election, he had offered the job of city auditor to Louis D. Brandeis, the famed Boston lawyer and reformer who was in Washington as special counsel to the Interstate Commerce Commission. "I only ask you to serve six months," Curley wrote in his letter to Brandeis, asserting that he could completely revamp the city's auditing methods in that time.

The offer was rich in irony. Brandeis, a founder of the Good Government Association, had branded Curley a corrupt politician. As recently as the year before, Curley had gotten his own back when Brandeis was being talked up for a cabinet post in the new Wilson administration. The New England Democrats, complaining that Brandeis was a registered Republican, protested his rumored appointment to President Wilson. Leaving their caucus, Congressman Curley told the press that Brandeis had been "knocked hard and plenty" inside the room. Yet here was the same Curley who had helped to keep Brandeis out of the cabinet offering him a job. It was an obvious publicity stunt, though Brandeis did not treat it like one. Instead, pleading business in Washington, he respectfully declined the mayor's offer, while pledging to cooperate with him "in any way possible."

A year later that way was found: at Curley's invitation, Brandeis delivered Boston's Fourth of July oration, the first Jew ever accorded that honor. Interestingly, Brandeis's speech touched on the dominant theme of Curley's political career.

> The new nationalism adopted by America proclaims that each race or people, like each individual, has the right and duty to develop, and that only through such differentiated development will high civilization be attained. Not until these principles of nationalism, like those of democracy, are generally accepted will liberty be fully attained and minorities secure in their rights.

With the end of deference democracy, the Boston Irish were engaged in just such a process of "differentiated development." Like peoples emerging from colonialism around the world, *who* governed them would be more important to their group pride than *how* they were governed. The maxim informing their electoral behavior might be summed up as "self-government is fundamental, good government is incidental."[5]

The Brandeis nod in the direction of reform was quickly sur-
passed by Curley's appointment of John A. Sullivan, an indubitable
reformer, as the city's corporation counsel. The former chairman
of the state-appointed Finance Commission, which was charged
with overseeing how Boston's mayors spent the taxpayers' money,
Sullivan had been a torment to Fitzgerald, exposing corruption in
both his administrations with an uncompromising vigor that led
President Eliot of Harvard to hail him as "the last of the Romans."
This last of the Romans lived in America, however, and he was not
above the kind of self-protective calculation that often does duty
for intelligence among American politicians. While secretly writing Kenny's platform, he had lent tacit support to Curley—a
shrewd piece of political insurance that Curley would have been
the first to appreciate. "His appointment means that the man who
has worked most ably and fearlessly for municipal economy during
the last four years," the *Herald* exulted, "is to be placed where his
counsel will be most effective." The editors of the *Boston Journal*
could not believe their eyes. "Today Boston has a reform government of which the Finance Commission has sometimes dreamed,
but nobody else did except in a nightmare."[6]

Indeed, a visitor who had left Boston in January and returned
in March would have received a shock to his verities on reading
and hearing the prevailing appraisals of Curley's first month in
office. "He has proved himself an attentive student of municipal
affairs, eager to do his duty as he saw it in the troublous condition
in which he has fallen," the *Herald* was saying. "For this attitude
of mind he deserves a very large measure of credit. It is time the
good citizens of Boston realized this, and told him so"—this of the
same man that the same paper had depicted as a ravening tiger
bent on plundering the city treasury just two months before. More
astounding yet, the Good Government Association, after a meeting with the new mayor described as a "love feast," declared he
was "entitled to the highest praise." And what in the name of mu-
tability, our visitor might have asked with widening incredulity,
was the meaning of the man-bites-dog headline REFORMERS ENDORSE
CURLEY?[7]

"My idea is to put the city on a business basis," Curley was
saying, quite as if he had been transformed into Thomas Kenny. He
slashed the salaries of city employees and opposed a bill granting
them an annual two-week vacation, quite as if their votes had not

elected him. In an impious economy, he even decreed a shortening in the length of the St. Patrick's Day parade. He would not run for reelection, he declared, making the one promise all reformers love to hear. "I'm making enemies by the score," he said. "But I can't help it, and to speak frankly, I don't care. I'm working for Boston, and I don't care a rap whether I hold public office again or not." He was hissed at the Bunker Hill Day Parade in Irish Charlestown, and when someone in the crowd called for three cheers for the new mayor, none were given. "Curley has been stung by the good government bug and he's dead without knowing it," said Diamond Jim Timilty, a leading Democratic chieftain. Marking the change from Curley past to Curley present, one former state legislator dubbed him "the Metamorphistical Mayor."[8]

These judgments were touchingly premature. Politics drives policy—it clears the mind of cant to make that baseline assumption about American government—and a political motive for Curley's early reform emphasis is not hard to seek. Curley wanted his administration to be seen as the antidote to Fitzgerald's "gang" administration, so it had to wear the mask of reform. He also wanted Fitzgerald as his opponent in 1917. Otherwise, his nettling of Fitzgerald, which was a constant feature of his whole first term, makes little political sense—though it does make psychological sense as the driven behavior of a man with a bad conscience. He may have hoped to provoke Fitzgerald into running against him, may have anticipated that Fitzgerald would use his influence with the other city bosses to be his lone challenger, and if he had gotten that far in savoring the possibilities, may even have hoped that, when it was too late for any last-minute entrant to make a strong run, he could once more play the Toodles card and with it drive Fitzgerald from the race. If Fitzgerald was his future gang opponent, his only real challenge could come from a reform candidate, who might win on a split vote. Thus it was prudent to try to co-opt the reform claque, to forestall its fielding such a candidate against him. It isn't only generals who fight the last war. Toodles had worked her magic once ("A whiskey glass and Toodles' ass made a horse's ass out of Honey-Fitz," went a ribaldry of the day); surely she could work it again.

Whatever their motive, the facts are clear. He fired outright many of Fitzgerald's appointees, accepted with pointed alacrity the resignations of yet others (of that of Fitzgerald's park commissioner, Daniel Coakley, Curley said that he "rendered the city a

real service by resigning and relieving me of the necessity of removing him"), slashed the salary increases Fitzgerald had given
still other high employees, canceled alleged "sweetheart" contracts let by Fitzgerald, forbade the city printing department from
publishing a laudatory history of the Fitzgerald administration, and
made a great show of blocking a deal whereby the city was to buy
land from a relative of Fitzgerald's for a firehouse in a neighborhood that already had one.⁹

On the day of the inaugural, Fitzgerald strode angrily out of
Tremont Temple and, determined to defend his record from Curley's calumny, hurried over to the office of the *Republic*, the political weekly he owned and from which he commenced to return
Curley's fire. One salvo, after Kipling's "Danny Deever," took the
form of a lament from a voter of Ward 17:

> *Oh, what's the news from City Hall?*
> *The guileless voter said;*
> *He's kicked away his ladder:*
> *I guess he's lost his head.*
>
> *He's sent his orders to "the gang"—*
> *We used to be "the boys"—*
> *To know our place and keep it,*
> *And to quit our blooming noise.*
>
> *He's chummin' with the Charter Guards,*
> *He'd please the G.G.A.*
> *For they pet him and they praise him*
> *When they cut the poor devil's pay.*¹⁰

The ballad got it wrong. Curley cut the pay of the higher officers of the police and fire departments, but approved raises for
police patrolmen and privates. He cut the salaries of school doctors, but not of school custodians. In all, while six thousand of the
city's nearly fifteen thousand employees had their salaries reduced, few lost their jobs.¹¹

Seeking authority to cut police salaries, Curley testified before
a committee of the state Senate. He was clear about his priorities:
"I have no desire and do not propose and will not remove a single
laborer or mechanic."

"Why not?" asked the Senate president, who was none other than Calvin Coolidge.

"Because I believe their services are necessary to the protection of the public safety and the public welfare," Curley replied. "It isn't the laborer or mechanic who is responsible for the present fiscal situation in Boston. . . ."

"But the Pennsylvania Railroad has to do the same thing," Coolidge, taking the private sector as his model for the public, put in. "They found they had to."

"I don't know anything about the Pennsylvania road, but I am endeavoring to strike at those who are best able to meet a cut in salary or suffer a removal." In other words, in his decisions Curley was employing a principle alien to the private sector. He was trying to be just.[12]

He was also being canny. An iron political arithmetic governed his decisions about city employees. "Here's the way I figure it," he explained during his first week in office. "The population of Boston is about 740,000 and there are 14,700 people on the payrolls." He calculated an average of five family members and friends for each employee; in addition, there were 6,000 people, from contractors and vendors to lawyers, who had a direct interest in city business, for a total of 103,500 people who had "a personal interest in the payroll or expenditure of the city." "Deduct this number from 740,000 and you have left 636,500 people who are only interested in the honest and efficient conduct of the city. No man need fear for his political future with the confidence of the 636,500. And in my administration I propose to give a square deal to both" the 103,500 and the 636,500.[13]

All mayors have to walk a tightrope between the often conflicting interests of these two voting blocs. Mayors are usually not held as responsible for economic downturns, as governors, unfairly, are. Mayors get into political trouble, characteristically, by playing too aggressively to the interests of the 103,500, in which case they bring on themselves tax revolts from the 636,500 who are paying for their largesse. Under special circumstances, however— when, for example, the property-owning minority who pay the bulk of the taxes do not belong to the same ethnic group as those who receive the taxes as wages—high taxes on property do not necessarily lead to term-ending tax revolts. To use a contemporary example, in Washington, D.C., in 1989, the penultimate year of

Mayor Marion Barry's administration, the District of Columbia government employed one worker for every thirteen residents, for a total of fifty thousand workers—compared with one for every sixty in Chicago and Newark and one for every twenty-two in New York City. The district's $3.2 billion budget came to $5,095 per Washingtonian, and its per capita tax burden was a staggering 50 percent higher than the national average for combined state and local taxes. Yet since this tax burden was mainly carried by surging downtown businesses and affluent but numerically insignificant white property holders, Barry, a black mayor of a city with a black majority, was immune to a tax revolt. It took indefeasible proof of wrongdoing to bring him down—which is the second way mayors get into political trouble.[14]

In general, and especially in his later terms, Curley governed as if the city was the sum of its employees and their dependents, gambling that their votes would be enough to elect him. Moreover, in the absence of a strong independently employed Irish middle class, he possessed something of the ethnic immunity so long enjoyed by Marion Barry. In his first term, however, he ran into a fatal mix of political troubles—corruption, plus disaffection among major elements of both the 103,500 and the 636,500, the tax-eaters and the taxpayers. In a prescient analysis, the *Herald* spotted the emerging problem early on. The mayor, it observed, seemed in danger of "falling between two stools": "He has forfeited the affections of those who elected him to office, nor does he yet enjoy the full confidence of the solid citizens of the town. And he must have one or the other."[15]

That defined the political dilemma of his first term. He ran afoul of the city employees—"those who elected him"—less by purging them or cutting their pay than by seeking to bully them into a politically pliant cadre. Public Works Department workers who refused to support Curley candidates in City Council races were summarily dismissed. Numbered tickets to the annual Tammany Ball ("Pro Bono Publico" was never heard of again after the election) were sent to the homes of city employees, and secret "instructional rallies" were held in their departments. In a Boston first, policemen were all but obliged to tithe for their jobs; those who refused to buy two tickets to the Tammany Ball were requested to return them with their names and addresses on the back. Curley used the Fire Department as a patronage dumping ground, transferring district chiefs suspected of being anti-Curley to less desirable berths and promoting tractable but less qualified captains to the rank of chief; and he played fast and loose with the civil service regulations. There were mitigations: Curley fought for one day off in three for the firemen, and, after discovering that loan sharks had ensnared over three thousand city employees, he established a credit union, where they could borrow money at low interest rates. "Nevertheless," Charles Trout writes, "he increasingly came to view municipal workers as 'his' employees, not as 'city' employees." And the dominant reality for them was the climate of intimidation.

As for the "solid citizens of the town," despite their early approbation, Curley enjoyed their confidence only transiently. They wanted many fewer city employees as a means to the end of lowering taxes on their commercial and residential property. They wanted Curley to be another Seth Low, who, as reform mayor of New York, had cut city spending while coddling big property owners. But Low's reforms were so unpopular with city employees and New York's poor that he was voted out of office after one term. Curley did not intend to suffer that fate. He could work the political arithmetic.[16]

Curley had pledged to cut four hundred workers from the city payroll; in fact the number of employees rose slightly during his first year in office. By April expenditures were running ahead of those of the Fitzgerald administration in April of 1913. By late summer they were $500,000 over the figure for 1913. By November, Curley had spent $700,000 more than Fitzgerald had the year before, during the "epoch of extravagance." This was not what the votaries of good government who had embraced him in March had been led to expect by the tenor of his rhetoric, or by his appointment of John Sullivan as corporation counsel. They were also unhappy with other appointments he had made—notably that of his brother John as head of the Collecting Department. When, in January 1915, the mayor restored many of the salary cuts he had announced the year before, the solid citizens of the town retaliated by withdrawing legal business from Sullivan's firm. By the end of his first year in office, Curley had fallen off one of the *Herald*'s two stools.[17]

Expenditures were rising partly in response to the deteriorating local economy. Running for his fourth term, in 1945, Curley characterized his earlier incumbencies as "terms of adversity, of crisis." His third term began a few months after the stock market crash of 1929 signaled the advent of the Great Depression. His second coincided with the post–World War I economic slump. His first was only six months old when war broke out in Europe. By the fall of 1914, the threat of German U-boats had greatly slowed transatlantic commerce. In Boston longshoremen and other workers along the affected economic chain were thrown out of work. Lines of the jobless gathered at City Hall. Now began what the *Boston Evening Transcript* scornfully called "the spectacle of the corridors."

A Curley operative recalls the scene: "His secretary would go through the line every day, interview them on what they wanted, then do the preliminary weeding out. Then Curley would call them in, 12 or 15 at a time, and ask, individually, 'What do "*you*" want? What do "you" want? What do "you" want?' And if he could give it to them, he gave it to them, and if he couldn't, he didn't. When he stood up, that was the sign for everybody to leave." Chicago mayor Richard J. Daley is reputed to have told his staff, "I won't see nobody, nobody sent." Curley saw everybody. His philosophy of help was simple: "People don't want charity—they want work. . . ." He had a moral detestation of welfare; during the Depression he boasted that Boston had no bread lines, and he even tried to stop a suburban minister from distributing free sandwiches to the unemployed on Boston Common. To some of the men in the corridors he gave temporary city jobs—shoveling snow and working on new parks and playgrounds—and sent others to department heads carrying notes like the following: "The bearer, Mr. O'Brien of Roxbury, who is the father of a large family, is very much in need of some sort of work to provide for them. Will you use your good offices with some one of the contractors doing work for the city who might be able to put him to work as a watchman?" Still others went directly onto the payrolls of public utilities. As these were not philanthropic enterprises, they expected something from Curley in return.[18]

Curley could talk like one of the urban liberal "reform bosses" of the Progressive Era—the Tom Johnsons, Hazen Pingrees, and Brand Whitlocks—who were champions of the rate payer against the utilities, the municipal equivalent of trust busters. "I have a great interest in the prosperity of the Edison Company," he said in a March 1914 speech to executives of the Edison Illuminating Light Company of Boston, "because it will need its prosperity to offset the 25% reduction in the new lighting contract with the city, and I am going to try real hard to secure that reduction."

In the contract Curley negotiated with Edison, however, streetlights that cost Detroit $45 and Philadelphia $70 a year to keep lighted would have cost Boston $87. Under pressure from the City Council, Curley attached conditions to the original ten-year contract that lowered its cost. Still, Edison got a deal that could have left it with as much as $1 million more than its sister utility in Philadelphia received for providing the same service. Aside from any direct kickbacks the grateful utility may have given him, Curley got what one careful scholar calls "considerable patronage." He could provide jobs to the men in the corridors and perhaps also boost his salary (the rumor was that he got 5 percent off the top of contracts), and the taxpayers—property holders who would probably never vote for Curley anyway—would pay for the lot. Those corridors were rarely empty: Curley estimated that he saw two hundred people a day; and the men given jobs would owe Curley votes. Indeed, decades after, they and their families and some of their close friends would support Curley no matter what he was accused of doing, just as their predecessors in Ward 17 had done before them. Thus Curley was steadily accumulating an electoral reserve—enough to sway a close race—against the day when his graft would come to light. "Curleyism," as this formula for perpetual incumbency soon came to be known, was born.[19]

For the next forty years people asked, "How could Curley get away with it?" This is how.

By "Tammanizing" City Hall, by becoming Boston's ward boss, Curley undermined the waning power of the city's remaining ward bosses. The Democratic City Committee had not supported Curley in the mayoral campaign. Once he was elected mayor, Curley ignored the committee, and tried to end the career of its chairman, Diamond Jim Timilty, the powerful state senator from Roxbury, by maneuvering to run a candidate against him in the 1914 primary election. The attempt failed, and thereafter Curley sought a rapprochement with Timilty, whose Central Construction Company won more than its share of city contracts, and restored relations with the Democratic committee. Curley followed a similar pattern with Martin Lomasney, the boss of the West End, first trying to weaken him, then granting him City Hall patronage, including the appointment of his brother, Joseph, to the School Building Commission. Curley even indulged in fitful gestures of reconciliation with John Fitzgerald, though the heavens proclaimed their cynicism. The point is that, largely for tactical reasons—to help him withstand increasingly sharp attacks from the city's reformers—Curley had to back off his early antiboss rhetoric. As his term wore on, he would need the Democratic bosses in his corner. Whether they would stay there, of course, was another question.[20]

Beyond the impromptu spending required to keep up with the lines in the corridors, Curley's positive program for Boston, while impressive, fell as short of some of the extravagant claims made for it as truth stubbornly does of legend. Running for reelection in 1917, Curley cited as his greatest accomplishments the beginnings of an $11 million expansion of the Boston City Hospital and of the Strandway, a beach-lined motor parkway set along the Dorchester Bay side of the South Boston peninsula. He rightly took credit for abolishing the nineteenth-century Parental School, to which the courts often sentenced truant boys for terms of up to two years. "There were 110 boys committed a year to the parental school for playing hookey before I took office," he said in an interview surveying his accomplishments at the end of his term. "Most of these youngsters were not vicious, they were just redblooded and full of life." Such boys were thereafter sent to supervised day programs within the school system; they would never be treated as criminals again. Curley was also proud of promoting prevocational education in the Boston Trade School, of increasing the number of maternity beds in the City Hospital from 30 to 150, of establishing special hospitals for the care of the diseases of children, and of increasing spending on medical care generally by 50 percent.

Curley raised the salaries of lower-paid workers. The City Hall scrubwomen not only achieved the nirvana of long-handled mops; they also got a raise of $10 a week. He improved living conditions for the destitute residents of the city's homeless shelter at Long Island, restricted the areas in which dangerous three-decker houses could be built, and secured legislation outlawing apartments beneath street level. He also took credit for laying new streets, constructing new playgrounds and municipal buildings, motorizing the fire department, and extending the subway and sewer systems. But as Herbert Zolot has observed, "He failed to show what unique part he had played in implementing these projects," which were the kind of infrastructure improvements that "would have taken place in due course without Curley's presence in city government."[21]

Accused by the Good Government Association of providing bad government, Curley, according to Charles Trout, "was at many points talking about a wholly '*different*' government—one that would spend; one that would not be slavishly devoted to balanced budgets, especially during slumps in the economy; one that would protect the worker; one that would provide municipal services in all areas of the city rather than in the silk-stocking wards alone; one that would be active, energetic, elastic and by all means personal." Yet partly because the Republican-controlled state legislature limited the taxing power of Boston's mayors, and partly because the Good Government–dominated City Council checked many of his plans, Curley actually ran a fairly frugal government.

The real estate tax in his first year in office, for example, was $17.50 per $1,000 of assessed valuation; it was only $17.70 per $1,000 when he left office, though it rose sharply the year after. There were 14,516 city employees in February 1914; four years later there were only 1,200 more, hardly evidence of payroll padding. Nor had Boston borrowed to fund Curley's projects. Thanks to a pay-as-you-go policy, the city debt actually went down during his term. Indeed, over the thirty years 1902 to 1932, which include nearly three of Curley's terms, per capita outlays in Boston went from $35 to $44, a rise of only 25.7 percent. By contrast, in New York, Jersey City, and Albany, cities dominated by Irish machines, per capita outlays soared by 111.8 percent. In Philadelphia and Pittsburgh, cities led by Republican machines, outlays rose by 75 percent; while in Chicago and San Francisco, cities neither dominantly Irish nor ruled by machines, spending per citizen increased by 93 percent, nearly four times the Boston rate. Clearly, in this period at least, "Curleyism" was not a recipe for ruin through public spending.[22]

What made Curley's first term memorable to his contemporaries and what makes it remarkable in retrospect was not the size or kind of Curley's spending, then, nor his espousal of any new idea of city government. It was the pugnacious dash with which he did everything. It was his histrionic ethnic baiting. It was his serio-comic reign as Boston's chief censor. It was the mansion—mysteriously financed, luxuriously appointed—that he built. It was the labyrinthine ingenuity of his graft.

❖   ❖   ❖

Curley was "a man of wonderful force, but without scruple," one city councilor remarked, in a comment typical of the way Curley's fierce will-to-do impressed even hostile observers. Right after his election the papers were full of accounts of the mayor-elect's aggressive lobbying of Assistant Secretary Franklin Roosevelt to have the Navy Department award a contract for a new supply ship to the Boston Naval Shipyard. Shortly after their meeting, the navy yard got the contract. Next, Curley lobbied Treasury Secretary McAdoo to locate a new bank of the just-created Federal Reserve system in Boston. An announcement soon followed that Boston would get the bank. The man got things done.[23]

In his inaugural he called for the creation of a fund to which substantial private citizens would subscribe to "boom Boston"—that is, to attract new businesses through publicity. When a leading banker refused to contribute, Curley threatened to withdraw the city's deposits from his bank. Like many of his efforts to run over people, this one backfired, but it put the city on notice that its new mayor would use irregular means to achieve his ends. When James J. Storrow, the city councilor from Beacon Hill, held up a measure of Curley's, the mayor told a reporter that he "very much feared" the lights might go out along Beacon Street, the garbage go uncollected, and the sewers plug up, backing so much water into Storrow's basement that he would need a canoe to navigate it—unless, of course, the councilor saw things Curley's way. "We do not expect tyrants of the Russian or Asiatic type in our American cities," one newspaper observed, while noting that Boston appeared to have the makings of one in Mayor Curley.

He began his workday a well-advertised hour before John Fitzgerald had begun his, and, to sustain his energy through the afternoon, frequently dipped into a box of choice candies he kept in his rolltop mahogany desk. Though he was home for dinner every evening, he often took a secretary, a chief clerk, and sometimes a stenographer along with him, turning the Mount Pleasant Avenue house into a virtual annex of City Hall at night. Whether exhausting a photographer walking with him from Mount Pleasant to City Hall with the breathless mayoral gait, or leading officials on an 11:00 P.M. to 2:00 A.M. tour of the city's most sordid lodging houses, or taking part in a raid on a Chinatown gambling den, or winning a horse race at Franklin Field, or dispatching two toughs who had set upon an old man on Boston Common, or snuffing out the flame of a match with a single pistol shot while taking some target practice in his office, or leaping onto the field during a Braves-Giants game to demand that the umpire eject a Giant who had thumbed his nose at

the fans—Mayor Curley seemed to be everywhere, doing everything. Two years of this pace was enough for his chauffeur; having
put over 125,000 miles on the mayor's imposing black machine,
Tammany Tess, he quit to spend more time with his family.[24]

You can't get people excited about a sewer, Fiorello La Guardia
once said, capturing a problem of municipal politics (and politicians)
in a quip. The problem is the meager claim the stuff of city government makes on the imagination. People don't get excited about
street repairs or subway extensions, and fire trucks leave them cold.
Nor does city government engage ideological passion. There is no
"liberal" or "conservative" way to pick up the trash. Mayors have to
find some other way to make what they do interesting.[25]

Curley made his government interesting by acting out the impulses of his core constituency. He knew that each one of those
thousands of fans wanted personally to tell the umpire to eject that
contumelious Giant, so he did it for them. Similarly, he knew his
constituents wanted to voice their clotted resentments against Boston's Protestant elite; and, with an appetite for the work, he did it
for them.

✤   ✤   ✤

It was an outrageous proposition: meant as a joke, it showed reckless judgment; meant seriously, it argued lunacy. Such was the
instant consensus about the mayor-elect's wantonly casual suggestion to sell the Boston Public Garden for $10 million and use the
proceeds to retire the city debt and establish a new garden away
from the city's downtown and out where the people lived—in the
neighborhoods. While not so sacred to history as the adjoining Boston Common, the twenty-four-acre Public Garden, with its flower
beds and immaculate lawns and great ancient trees (Curley was
unimpressed: "Those along Beacon Street look more like hatracks
than trees"), was a Brahmin shrine. Curley, who had dropped this
bombshell in Washington (he delayed resigning his congressional
seat until after he had been sworn in as mayor, and quit then only
under Republican pressure), rapidly had to retreat. But the publicity depicting him as the scourge of Brahmin Boston was tonic to his
followers in the outer wards.

More followed. Seeking to rest up from the campaign and
to prepare his inaugural address, he and Mrs. Curley traveled

incognito to the Berkshires, where the press tracked them down in a Pittsfield hotel. And, once again, he bore down hard on the city's parks. "Too much has been devoted in the past to the aesthetic side," he told reporters. "Look at the expenditure of $30 million in 10 years for the parks, recreational grounds and the like, and the paltry sum of $3,000,000 for the development of the waterfront. I propose to change all that." Under Curley, jobs came before beauty.

He could not let the revered turf alone. After he was sworn in as mayor, he came out for the building of a high-pressure pumping station under the Common. Why stop there? an incredulous former governor, Curtis Guild, asked. Why didn't the mayor plump to adorn the Common with "a gasometer or a soap-boiling establishment for the reduction of offal" while he was at it? Under Curley, nevertheless, public safety—a pumping station would put water in the hoses of the city's firefighters—came before beauty.

Relishing the symbolism, he also ignored the protests of the Art Commission and backed a Parks and Recreation Department proposal to install a comfort station on the Common. Under Curley, it seemed, even the bladder came before beauty.[26]

These were the opening shots in a thirty-year Kulturkampf.

One of Curley's favorite tactics in this war was to insist that there was an Irishman at the bottom of everything American. He made himself something of a one-eyed expert on colonial America, and what that eye saw was the hitherto hidden contribution that the Irish had made to that history. Myles Standish, in Curley's telling, was really an Irish soldier of fortune "whom the Pilgrim fathers secured to do their fighting for them." The Boston Tea Party was really a beer party: Sam Adams's Indians had fortified themselves against the night air by getting a snout full of ale at a waterfront saloon run by an Irishman. The "shot heard 'round the world" was not fired at the North Bridge in Concord after all. The American Revolution had really begun months earlier, when a raiding party captured British munitions stored at Fort William in Portsmouth, New Hampshire. The raiding party was led by—who else?—an Irishman.

Curley's historical contributions, tossed off in speeches or offered as ruminations to reporters, elicited countercontributions from members of the Protestant elite, who resented Curley's attempts to adulterate their roots. One South End pastor, trumping Curley in audacity, went so far as to claim that St. Patrick was really a Scot.[27]

Much of this revisionism was offered in good spirits. But there was something permanently bitter in the ethnic cup, and Curley was the man to stir it to the top. In January 1916, at a particularly low point in his administration, the Lord delivered John Farwell Moors into his hands.

Moors was a banker, a member of the Finance Committee, an Anglo-Saxon Protestant grandee, and one of the charter members of the Immigration Restriction League—in short, an ideal foil for Curley. One afternoon, speaking to the New England Woman's Department of the National Civic Federation gathered at the Back Bay home of Mrs. Frederick L. Ames, Moors made what he thought were some anodyne remarks about the failure in recent years of the "highly educated portions" of the Boston community—code for its Anglo-Saxon Protestant members—to run for public office. "Not a rich man's son under forty years of age today is taking an important part in the political life of this city." He urged them to do so. And then he turned to the community that was politically ascendant. The passage is worth quoting in full because it prompted a gorgeously purple burst from Curley. "Boston," Moors told the women gathered in Mrs. Ames's parlor,

> became a city nearly two hundred years ago. . . . A generation later the potato famine in Ireland drove hither for a refuge thousands of suffering people, mostly peasants. The third generation of famine-stricken people is now dominant in the city.
>
> Their ancestors were united by English oppression and absentee landlordism into a compact mass of antagonism to all things Anglo-Saxon. We Anglo-Saxons gave them a refuge here, but . . . the welcome was not of a kind to break the mass into individual units. When they became numerically supreme, as in time they did, they became also politically supreme, to our exclusion.
>
> The one great need for years has been this, that the different races which make up our cosmopolitan city, should not remain distinct and antagonistic, but should work together, as, in truth, fellow citizens. . . .

Not a warm passage, certainly. Its bland face does not hide the speaker's resentment at being politically displaced, like the youthful Henry Cabot Lodge from the hills of the Common, by the Irish horde. And that plea for ethnic harmony at the end has the look of a sop. Still, the passage would not seem to supply much tinder for offense.

The mayor was attending a dinner at the Boston City Club in honor of the eighty-seven-year-old former mayor of Boston Thomas N. Hart when he was asked his reaction to Moors's speech. Earlier in the evening he had shaken the hand of John F. Fitzgerald, and in that singular gesture exhausted his quota of charitable feeling. "I shall spend two hours getting the facts together," he said. "A thing like that merits two hours spent in preparation."

He prepared a written reply. Assailing Moors as "a pathetic figure of a perishing people who seek by dollars and denunciations to evade the inexorable and inevitable law of the survival of the fittest," he called for his resignation from the Finance Committee. In saying that the Famine had forced the Irish to come to America, Curley implied, Moors had committed an ethnic slur—though in truth if Moors had said that the Irish had come for the waters Curley would have found some other equally gossamer pretext on which to hang his attack. For he was after bigger game than Moors.

"A strange and stupid race, the Anglo-Saxon," he went on. "Beaten in a fair, stand-up fight, he seeks by political chicanery and hypocrisy to gain the ends he lost in battle, and this temperamental peculiarity he calls fair play." He heaped sarcasm on Moors's political theory. "'And,' adds Mr. Moors, sadly, 'When the Irish became numerically supreme they became politically dominant'! How absurdly American this was, the majority daring to rule the minority; but that is one of the peculiarities of the American system, so different from the Anglo-Saxon system of the man doffing his hat and pulling his forelock to his masters and betters." And he launched into his patented recital on the perfidious colonial past, "the halcyon days when the traders in rum, salt cod and slaves were . . . engaged with the New England Genealogical Society in fabricating family histories." Quoting Cardinal O'Connell's very words of nine years before, he concluded, "The Puritan is passed; the Anglo-Saxon is a joke; a newer and better America is here. . . . No country is ever ruined by a virile, intelligent, God-fearing, patriotic people like the Irish, and no land was ever saved by clubs of female faddists, old gentlemen with disordered livers, or pessimists croaking over imaginary good old days and ignoring the sunlit present. . . . What we need in this part of the world is men and mothers of men, not gabbing spinsters and dog-raising matrons in federation assembled"—a hit at the ladies in Moors's audience.

Moors replied that he did not recognize "either what I said or the spirit in which I said it" in Curley's jeremiad. He was partially right there, and right all through that the mayor's aim was "to stir up ill will on the part of the citizenship of Boston." The attack was an arrant piece of demagogy. But only those insensible to the charm of invective will wholly regret it.

The following Sunday Curley was denounced by some of Boston's leading Protestant ministers. From the pulpit of the Warren Avenue Baptist Church, the Reverend Frederick E. Heath put to a missing Curley a series of rhetorical questions. "Mr. Curley, did you ever hear of Charles Sumner? Mr. Curley, did you ever hear of a man named Webster? Was he a 'clod'? Were Lloyd Garrison, Channing, Longfellow, scores of others all 'clods'? Were the Puritans all clods? Who founded Massachusetts? The Celtic people, I suppose you say." If the mayor could traffic in personalities, so could the minister. "Where did he go on one occasion?" he asked the audience, which laughed at this tickle of the jail issue. "I'll not say it. You have fully answered for me."

From the pulpit of the Clarendon Street Church, the Reverend Madison C. Peters retailed a ranker brand of bigotry. In whatever cities in whatever states the Irish had achieved political dominance, he said, they had been "a hiss and a byword, violating every law of God and man, increasing taxes, depreciating property and disgracing the city." Sixty years after the reign of "Sam," Boston was still two cities.[28]

The controversy simmered for weeks, providing newspaper readers with comic relief from the ghastly news of the European war. And yet the diversion was dearly bought. In a pluralist society there is always plenty of intergroup tension to go around. When politicians exploit that tension or inflame it they poison the common well. Who knows how many relationships between Irish and Yankee Bostonians were strained, how many intimacies choked off, how much spontaneous feeling curdled by Curley's tirade and the polarization of opinion it created? Blacks and whites in New York City must have gone through something similar during the mayoralty of Ed Koch, with many whites cheering his blunt comments about black leaders and issues, while most blacks winced at them. BRING US TOGETHER: so read the famous sign Richard Nixon glimpsed in Ohio during the 1968 presidential campaign. That is what people say they want from politicians, but they so rarely get it and so rarely punish the politicians who don't give it to them that it may be a mere piety, something they say to throw pollsters off the scent of their resentments.

❖   ❖   ❖

As mayor of Boston, Curley had broad powers to regulate public entertainment. No reader who has gotten this far will be surprised to learn that he was not shy about exercising them. He had pronounced views about cultural matters: cross those of Cotton Mather with those of Cardinal O'Connell and you have them. Reinforcing his views was the politics of his views. He knew where the votes lay, and in Catholic Boston they were not on the side of those favoring free artistic expression.

While still mayor-elect, Curley stated that he considered public morals "perhaps the most important problem of all." He promised that he would be guided in his "course of action by recognized authority on moral questions, [subscribing] to the views so timely and ably expressed by His Eminence, Cardinal O'Connell." Since the cardinal, by all reports, considered the mayor an embarassment to the Catholic faith, Curley's pledge of fealty must have scalded him. And in equal degree it must have disturbed those who feared that Curley would extend Irish majoritarianism from politics to culture. Would the arch baiter of the Puritan theocracy sponsor a Catholic version of what he condemned?[29]

Indeed he would. The phrase "banned in Boston," that infallible booster of sales for theatrical producer and publisher alike, entered the language in the Curley years. As he suffered his texts' "bitch" and "bastard" genteeled to "dame" and "buzzard," the playwright Ben Hecht would wash his hands of Boston. Even as late as 1939, *Life with Father*, in which New Yorkers could hear "Oh, God," was considered too daring for Bostonians, whose ears would be offended by anything stronger than "Oh, Gad." In 1927, during a Curley interregnum, Boston banned sixty-eight books, including works by H. G. Wells, Ernest Hemingway, John Dos Passos, Sinclair Lewis, and Sherwood Anderson.[30]

Even without Curley, Boston would not have been a center of cultural modernism. "I say that Boston commits the scholastic error and tries to remember too much," wrote H. G. Wells after a visit in 1905, "and has refined and studied and collected herself into a state of hopeless intellectual and aesthetic repletion. . . .

The capacity of Boston, it would seem, was just sufficient but no more than sufficient, to comprehend the whole achievement of the human intellect up, let us say, to the year 1875 A.D. Then an equilibrium was established. At or about that year Boston filled up." Boston's impermeable self-content echoes in the old joke about the Beacon Hill lady who, chided for never traveling, replies, "Why should I travel when I am already here?"[31]

Nor was Curley a pioneer in local censorship. Since 1878 Boston's morals had been monitored by the Watch and Ward Society, which described itself as a "quasi-governmental law enforcement agency" dedicated to "the protection of family life in New England." It had succeeded in banning *Leaves of Grass* in the year of its founding, and through the influence of the Lowells, Peabodys, and Cabots who were its officers, this WASP bastion, to quote Cleveland Amory, "maintained a militant inhospitality to sex stimula of all sorts" right up to 1945, when it banned Kathleen Winsor's *Forever Amber* into bestsellerdom. Curley's Puritanism, in short, was as much in the Boston tradition as bad restaurants serving inedible sticky buns.[32]

What Curley did was to apply this tradition with his characteristic sweep—sometimes giving it a twist of ethnic politics. Thus early in his term he sought to ban the late-night dances held at the Copley-Plaza Hotel by S. Hooper Hooper, the leader of the Boston cotillion. Curley's case was both moral° and political. If sailors and marines could not cavort all night in the dance halls of Charlestown, he argued, why should Back Bay debutantes be granted the privilege? Hooper, who prided himself on running irreproachable dances—he had kept the Bunny Hug and the Turkey Trot on a year's probation in Boston when they were all the rage across the country—fought back, telling the mayor there was no question of the dances' legality. When Curley's corporation counsel, John Sullivan, ruled that the dances were strictly private affairs—it would have been a bold sailor who dared to crash one—Curley had to relent.[33]

He could and did ban the tango at Franklin Park, however. Somehow it ran afoul of the moral code he drew up under which

---

° "There have been more young girls ruined in Boston through the medium of all-night dancing," he declared, "than by any other force in the community."

bare feet, suggestive jokes, impersonations of effeminate persons, depictions of drug fiends, disrobing scenes, Salome dances, and plays teaching lessons in immorality were banned in Boston. Perhaps the tango dancers were shoeless.

Isadora Duncan wore shoes, but Curley banned her interpretive Grecian dances anyway because she showed her bare legs. He had similar scrapes with Pavlova and Ruth St. Denis. Mary Curley had him pull down the curtain in the middle of Mary Garden's performance of *Thaïs*, according to Francis Curley. As Garden peeled off the fourth veil in her Salome dance, Mary, sitting up front next to her husband, grew agitated. "James"—a mark of her displeasure; in good weather he was "Father"—"I want this show stopped. It's nothing but burley." He objected. She persisted. He complied.

Curley shut down the war drama *Across the Border* because it contained "curses and oaths." When the theater management urged the realism of such language, Curley was unmoved; maybe that was how soldiers died on the western front, but more was expected of them in Boston. The play reopened, minus the oaths. David Belasco's play *Marie O'Dile* may have run for a year in New York, Chicago, and Philadelphia, but the Knights of Columbus had condemned it, and that was all Curley needed to warn it away from Boston. Eugène Brieux may have been a member of the French Academy, but his *Maternity* touched on the subject of abortion, making it impossible for the play to be presented in Boston. On receiving the report of John Casey, his "morality censor"—a man described by a contemporary newspaper as the "brigadier general of the municipalities' purity brigade"—Curley stopped the Boston run of *The Hypocrites*, a film in which a nymph representing the allegorical figure of Truth flitted across the screen "wearing so few garments that Venus by comparison looked like a little woman in a big fur coat."[34]

Given the mayor's zeal to ban even bare feet in public, Bostonians were shocked to discover, in September 1916, that Curley not only allowed a movie condemned by the American Federation of Catholic Societies to open in Boston, but he had also lobbied a leading Pennsylvania politician to get the film past the Philadelphia censors, one of whom had characterized it as "unspeakably vile." *Where Are My Children?* was promoted in ad copy like this: "Do you believe in birth control? There are realistic reasons pictured for and against it in that daring photoplay 'Where Are My Children?' . . . Why do not the censors stop this film?" The answer to that question, in Boston at any rate, was simple; the mayor seemed to have a financial interest in it. "I merely helped a friend, who had money invested in the project. I did it for a friend . . . ," the mayor said, repairing to a tested locution, when reporters asked him why he had gone to Washington to lobby Senator Boise Penrose, the Republican boss of Pennsylvania, to get the film shown in his state. But even as he was giving that interview in his second-floor office, the shouts of newsboys flogging the evening editions on the narrow street outside could be heard in the room: "Curley exposed! Curley exposed! Read all about it! Just out!" For Penrose, in an interview quoted in those editions, was saying that Curley had told him that he did have a financial interest in the film.[35]

The situation was irresistibly ironic. "Mayor James M. Curley, the man who saw a menace to our morals in the twinkling toes of Pavlova," the *Boston Journal* noted, "a demoralizing danger in the dreamy dances of the diaphanous Duncan, and a calamity in the bare-legged prancing of the brown-stained St. Denis, has lobbied in Washington on behalf of a movie based on birth-control." And "birth-control" was a euphemism: *Where Are My Children?* is about young women who receive abortions without, to quote someone who has seen it, "undergoing any dire consequences."[36]

The episode exposes a hard truth about our subject: he would sometimes allow shameless vistas to open between his principles and his practices. Money, then and later, was the root of his hypocrisy.

As czar of Boston culture, finally, Curley entered the history of the civil rights movement, among the last places one would expect to find him. He was mayor when D. W. Griffith's tribute to the Ku Klux Klan, *The Birth of a Nation,* was released. Ohio had banned the film; St. Louis and Chicago would not allow it to be shown. "It hurt me, Mr. David, to see what you do to my people," Griffith's black maid told him after seeing it. No black person could watch it without sharing her pain. For Curley, so sensitive to slights to his own people, the issue presented by the film would not seem to offer much of a challenge. He had carried the black vote in the mayoral election, and he was the reverse of a civil libertarian—a civil authoritarian, the harshest censor in Boston's history. Moreover, he was willing to censor expression on other than moral grounds. Early in his term, he had announced that he was sending his chief clerk to a Socialist meeting held at the Franklin Union; if any of the speakers dared to "indulge in any defamation of the country, the President or the flag," he warned, he would pressure the trustees of the union to prevent the Socialists from holding future meetings there. All this made many in Boston's black community of fifteen thousand hopeful that Curley would ban *The Birth of a Nation*.[37]

The leader in the fight over *The Birth of a Nation* was William Monroe Trotter, a forty-three-year-old Boston editor and political activist. Trotter was born in suburban Hyde Park, the only son of a veteran of the all-black Fifty-fifth Massachusetts, the sister regiment to the Fifty-fourth Massachusetts whose heroism in the Civil War is commemorated in St. Gauden's bas-relief sculpture across the street from the Massachusetts State House, in Robert Lowell's poem "For the Union Dead," and in the film *Glory*. James Trotter, a post office clerk who became a leading black Democratic appointee under President Cleveland, raised his son to take pride in his race. The Trotters lived in a prosperous white neighborhood, and William was told that if a white boy beat him in a fight he would face another beating at home. Few white boys did—they weren't fighting for their race.

From the time he was five, Trotter recalled, he dedicated himself to "work for race equality." He considered entering the ministry, but his father, arguing that a black minister would inevitably serve a segregated congregation, dissuaded him. In 1891, after working as a shipping clerk for a year, he entered Harvard College, where he studied under George Santayana and William James, where his lowest mark was a B in freshman English, where he became the first black ever elected to the college's chapter of Phi Beta Kappa. After graduating magna cum laude is 1895 he turned down an attractive offer of a teaching job in Washington, D.C., on the principled ground that the school was a segregated one. With his Harvard connections and a $20,000 inheritance from his father, he could have gone on to enjoy a comfortable upper-middle-class life as an insurance agent and mortgage negotiator. After marrying in 1899, however, he and his wife, a Boston woman whose uncle had been one of the leaders in the struggle to integrate the city's schools under the Know-Nothings, started a radical newspaper. *The Guardian* changed the course of their lives. In order to run a paper dedicated to the cause of "race equality," they put any thought of a comfortable life behind them.[38]

What made *The Guardian* radical was its contempt for the nation's most famous Negro, the confidant of President Theodore Roosevelt and the darling of white editors, Booker T. Washington. From his position as president of the Tuskegee Institute, Washington assured white southerners that blacks would not agitate for political or social equality if in return white businessmen would hire native blacks rather than "those of foreign birth and strange tongue and habits" for their lowliest jobs. At a time when the condition of blacks in the Jim Crow South was the worst it had been since emancipation, Washington's accommodationist approach outlined in his Atlanta Compromise speech of 1895 was a formula for racial subservience, and as such *The Guardian* denounced it. "The policy of compromise has failed," Trotter wrote. "The policy of resistance and aggression deserves a trial."

Trotter even went so far as to disrupt a lecture Washington was delivering in a South End church by rising from the audience with a list of questions ("Are the rope and the torch all the race is to get under your leadership?") calculated to embarrass the Sage of Tuskegee. Amid shouts of "Throw Trotter out the window!" the police hauled him from the church and arrested him and some of his associates for instigating what became known and deplored as the "Boston riot." "If the Boston negro is not capable of understanding so able a representative of his race," the *St. Louis Post-Dispatch* marveled, "what is to be expected of other Afro-Americans?" Trotter was sentenced to thirty days in Charles Street Jail. It was 1903, the year before James Michael Curley's sojourn in the same place.[39]

Through *The Guardian* and two pressure groups he founded, the New England Suffrage League and the National Association for Equal Rights, Trotter advocated a militance in the fight for equal rights that looked ahead to the civil rights movement of the 1960s. He also briefly pioneered another movement that would come to fruition only in the 1960s, the realignment of black voters from the party of Lincoln to the Democracy.

In 1912 *The Guardian* endorsed Woodrow Wilson in the hope that he would prove a better friend to the Negro than either Taft or Roosevelt had been. That hope seemed misplaced when Wilson appointed five southern white men to his cabinet, including a Texan, Albert Burleson, to head the U.S. Post Office, a substantial employer of blacks. At an early cabinet meeting, when Burleson proposed separating the Washington postal clerks by race, Wilson gave his permission. Two other southern cabinet members, Josephus Daniels at the Navy Department and William McAdoo at Treasury, followed suit, ordering the resegregation of their departments. The president, who was said by a fellow Princeton alumnus to be "the best narrator of darky stories that I have ever heard in my life," thereafter sent a racial signal of his own by naming a white southerner as minister to the republic of Haiti, a post that had customarily gone to blacks. Many northern Democrats protested, Congressman James M. Curley (who also protested the resegregation of the departments) among them, but Wilson would not reverse his decision.[40]

In November 1914, Trotter led a delegation to the White House to protest the president's wandering so far from his campaign pledge for "absolute fair dealing" toward black Americans. The year before, Trotter had met with Wilson and asked him to look into halting the resegregation of federal departments. Wilson agreed to do so, and now in answer to Trotter's question told him that his cabinet officers had ordered the move because of "friction between colored and white clerks." Wilson continued: "Segregation is not humiliating but a benefit, and ought to be so regarded by you gentlemen." Trotter had heard enough. "For fifty years white and colored clerks have been working together in peace and harmony and friendliness," he said, setting the president straight, "doing so even through two Democratic administrations. Soon after your inauguration, segregation was drastically introduced."

Wilson interrupted. "If this organization is ever to have another hearing before me it must have another spokesman. Your manner offends me."

"In what way?" Trotter asked.

"Your tone, with its background of passion."

"But I have no passion in me, Mr. President, you are entirely mistaken; you misinterpret earnestness for passion."

The meeting went on like that for forty-five minutes, with the two men repeatedly interrupting each other—until Wilson bluntly told Trotter that he was the one to do the interrupting. Outside the president's office, an angry Trotter told reporters what he had said inside, calling Wilson's explanation of the resegregation "entirely disappointing." The episode made national news. "The Tucker darkey who tried to 'sass' the President," wrote a Texas newspaper, getting Trotter's name wrong, "is not a Booker T. Washington type of colored man. He is merely a nigger."[41]

To use the publicity to build his organization, Trotter embarked on a speaking tour, describing his interview with Wilson to audiences that must have been amazed at his boldness. While on tour he got word that *The Birth of a Nation* was about to open in Boston. Nine years earlier he had persuaded Mayor Fitzgerald to ban *The Clansman*, the play on which *The Birth of a Nation* was based. Hoping that Mayor Curley would prove as helpful as his predecessor and more grateful for black support than President Wilson, Trotter hurried back.

Trotter may have come away empty-handed from his meeting with the president, but Thomas Dixon was luckier. The author of *The Clansman*, a best-selling novel before he turned it into a play, Dixon had been a classmate of Wilson's at the Johns Hopkins Graduate School. He too had protested what the cabinet members were doing in their departments, but what bothered him was the news that Wilson, as a transitional stage of resegregation, had put a black man in charge of the Registry Division of the Treasury. "I am heartsick," he wrote Wilson, "over the announcement that you have appointed a negro to boss white girls as Registrar of the Treasury. Please let me as one of your best friends utter my passionate protest." Dixon was a clinical racist; the dread possibility of sex between the races haunted his imagination, as it haunts *The Birth of a Nation*.

A little over a year later he wrote his friend again, asking for a half-hour appointment. He wanted Wilson to see a new film that demonstrated movies could be "a new process of reasoning by which will could be overwhelmed with conviction." Wilson, for whom Dixon had once done a favor—arranging for Professor Wilson to receive an honorary degree from Wake Forest College—agreed. "I want you to know, Tom, that I am pleased to be able to do this little thing for you." Because he was still in mourning over the death of his first wife, he asked if the film could be shown at the White House, something that had never been done before; and on February 18, 1915, before the cabinet, the president, his daughters, Dixon, and Griffith, it was. Wilson's verdict on what he saw must have exceeded Dixon's wildest hopes. "It is like writing history with lightning," Wilson said, making the most famous endorsement in film history. "And my only regret is that it is all so terribly true." This of a film version of Reconstruction in which the black freedmen are the lascivious villains and the hooded riders of the Klan are the heroes, "a complete inversion of the historical truth," in the words of a reviewer of the day less swayed by sectional feeling and race prejudice than the Virginia-born, Georgia-bred Wilson.[42]

The film—longer, lusher, and technically more advanced than anything seen up until that time—opened to generally ecstatic notices in New York in March. The Tremont Theatre began to take ads in the Boston papers to publicize its opening there in April. Bowing to the mounting public pressure, Curley decided to hold a hearing before the opening to consider the arguments of both sides. He had already heard by letter from one high-minded supporter of the film, the Reverend Charles H. Parkhurst of New York, whose highly publicized tour of Manhattan's brothels nearly twenty years before had brought the wrath of the voters down on Tammany Hall. "The criticism that [*The Birth of a Nation*] exhibits the Negro in an unfortunate light . . . ," he wrote Curley, "is fully met by the consideration that it represents the Negro not as he now is at all, but as he was in the days when he had just had the chains broken from him and when he was rioting in the deliciousness of a liberty so new and untried. . . ." This was to accept lurid fantasy as history and to ignore the effect this bad history, seen by twenty-five million people on its first release, might have on living blacks, seventy-nine of whom would be lynched in 1915. Two days before *The Birth of a Nation* opened in Atlanta, an itinerant Methodist minister named William Joseph Simmons received a charter from the state of Georgia to revive a Ku Klux Klan to which David Griffith and Thomas Dixon had given a sheen of glamour. It was the birth of a new era of bigotry.[43]

Held in the old aldermanic chambers of City Hall, the hearing before Mayor Curley was packed; several hundred mostly "negro-citizens of Boston" stood against the walls, sat on the windowsills, and filled the corridors. Trotter and a delegation from the fledgling NAACP were to speak for one side; Griffith and a lawyer for the film company for the other. Curley began by reading aloud the statute under which he exercised his censorship powers. It applied only to works that were "indecent, immoral" or that tended "to corrupt public morals." Was *The Birth of a Nation* such a work? That question, which was by no means easily answered within the letter of the law, hung over the proceedings.

Curley's beginning could not have pleased the NAACP delegation, who had judged him to be a "democratic and very kindly Irishman." Their dismay grew as Curley turned his inquisitorial powers on the first hostile witness called, Mary White Ovington, a New York settlement house worker—just the sort of apostle of pity and progress Curley could not abide. She reported that as she left a New York showing of the film she had heard someone in the audience say, "I would like to kill every nigger. I would like to sweep every nigger off the earth." She added, shocked, "Why, the colored women in the picture are shown in low gowns, and drinking champagne."

"Did you ever see anything like this in high society?" Curley asked.

She replied that she had never been in high society, but that the expressions on the faces of the black women in the movie were "awful," meaning lewd.

"Do you know your Shakespeare?" Curley shot back. "You have seen, then, that when Lady Macbeth commits murder . . . was there not an awful expression on her face at the time?" He warmed to his theme. "Don't you think the Jews have as much right to protest the playing of 'The Merchant of Venice' as you have to oppose the moving picture of the Negro? Was not the expression on Shylock's face more horrible than the face of 'Gus' in the movie?"

A witness objected to the scene near the end of the film showing a white father about to bash in the head of his daughter with a gun butt rather than let her fall into the hands of the black soldiers besieging the cabin where the whites have sought refuge. The mayor, who had seen the picture at an advance showing, explained that the father merely wanted to protect his daughter from immorality—death, as everyone knows, being preferable to sin. When another witness said that the movie showed a Negro being flogged, Curley replied that men were still flogged in the state of Delaware, some for petty crimes.

Finally, when Moorfield Storey, the NAACP's first (and white) national president, argued that the effect of the film would be to "discredit the Negro race all over the country," Curley interposed that on those grounds the English could protest the showing of

Shakespeare's *Henry VIII.* Storey, angry, complained that the mayor was representing "the other side." A great friend of the Negro, Storey, in the manner of the Know-Nothings, saw immigration as the downfall of American democracy. "The immigration of every year adds to the mass of poverty and ignorance in our country," he wrote in 1889. Immigrants were unfit "to take part in our political contests, yet in a few years they become citizens and their votes in the ballot box count as much as our own." The gravamen of his complaint against immigrants was their propensity to elect "bosses" like Curley. A man with these known views should not have pled the case against the film before Curley; events might have taken a different turn if the opponents of *The Birth of a Nation* had not been such palpable reformers.

Curley was noticeably kinder to the lawyer for the Epoch Producing Company and Griffith. When the former, John F. Cusick, read President Wilson's endorsement aloud, the audience hissed Wilson's name. Curley rapped his gavel for order. "To think that this would happen in the good old Democratic city of Boston," Cusick commented. Curley, enjoying the badinage, laughed: "Yes, and with a non-partisan Mayor in the chair." Griffith—whose father, an officer in the Confederate First Kentucky Cavalry, could have met Trotter's father in battle—made a high-toned presentation, arguing his constitutional rights, and reading a letter from a Catholic priest urging the children of America to see his edifying film. Just a few days before, meeting with a Boston religious editor a few doors up Beacon Street, Thomas Dixon had been less lofty. His intention with *The Birth of a Nation,* he confided, was "to create a feeling of abhorrence in white people, especially white women, against colored men."[44]

Trotter, who had suffered the forensics in silence, brought the meeting back to politics. He reminded the mayor of the black support he had received in the past; future support would depend on what he did about *The Birth of a Nation.* Votes for favors: that was Curley's way. He had gotten the votes; now he had to pay for them. It was not the most admirable political code, but Curley would have come out right in the eyes of posterity if he had just stuck with it now.

But the mayor who had kept "damn" off the Boston stage could not see his way clear to ban an artful piece of racist propaganda. At the close of the hearing he said he would suppress the film if he had the power—"Bosh!" someone in the audience shouted—but that the law did not give him that power for this film. The best he could do was to ask Griffith to cut some of the "immoral" scenes.

This Griffith agreed to do. At Curley's request he excised the scene in which the mulatto lieutenant governor of South Carolina tries to force marriage on the bound and gagged daughter (Lillian Gish) of a radical Republican senator; the famous chase sequence, in which a white actor in blackface, playing the brutish Gus—his mouth literally foaming with lust thanks to the hydrogen peroxide Griffith had him ingest—pursues the innocent Little Sister (Mae Marsh) through the forest; the scene in which the senator and his mulatto mistress, alone, exchange unambiguously erotic looks; the depiction of the black South Carolina legislators whooping with carnal joy over the passage of a law "providing for racial intermarriage"; and a shot of several leering blacks. These cuts made, the film opened as scheduled.

A week later, on a Saturday night, Trotter led a crowd of demonstrators to the theater. When the management shut the ticket window in their faces, while still admitting whites, Trotter vehemently protested. Just then, police with billy clubs moved in to clear the lobby. One of them struck Trotter, who was placed under arrest. A street brawl now erupted between the black protesters and two hundred white policemen. In the melee, a few blacks managed to sneak into the theater. At the moment when Little Sister leaps off the cliff rather than submit to Gus, one of them threw a "very ancient egg" right at the middle of the screen. Shouts of "Hit the nigger!" and "Look out for razors!" filled the theater. When the movie ended more fighting broke out, this time between whites spilling out into the street and the few blacks still waiting outside. "It is a rebel play, an incentive to great racial hatred here in Boston," Trotter, free on bail, told reporters as he left the police station. "It will make white women afraid of Negroes and will have white men all stirred up on their account. If there is any lynching here in Boston, Mayor Curley will be responsible."

One historian judges the demonstration "the most ominous racial incident in Boston . . . since the Civil War era."

The next afternoon, an "indignation meeting" at Faneuil Hall jeered, booed, and hissed any mention of the mayor who had caused it. "Don't hiss," Trotter told them. "The Mayor has yet a chance to stop the play. We have asked him to lay aside the technicalities of the law in this case and request that the play be stopped. He has stopped other plays without invoking the law. . . . We claim that any production which represents the men of one race assaulting the women of another should be forbidden in a country where all must live together. Unless this play is stopped," he added, wistfully, "Boston will never be as Boston of old to the colored people who live here. . . .

"Where is the valiant Jim Curley of old?" he asked, and was answered by shouts of "He's bought up! He's sold out! He's afraid of the money class." "The friend of the people," Trotter continued, "—lovable Jim Curley, whom we colored people supported for the mayoralty against the advice of some of our white friends? . . . If this was an attack on the Irish race he would find a way pretty quick to stop it." Surely Trotter was right there: without giving a thought to the legal niceties, and acting consistently with his public character, Curley would have banned any play or picture that did to the Irish what *The Birth of a Nation* did to blacks.[45]

Transferring ethnic sympathy in just the way Trotter had expected of Curley, David I. Walsh, the Commonwealth's first Irish Catholic governor, told a Trotter-led demonstration of two thousand people outside the State House the following day that he would work to broaden the censorship laws to keep works offensive to any race out of the state. "I sympathize with you tremendously. If there is anything tending to destroy or undermine American institutions and American liberty," he told them, in words one wishes had come from Curley, "it is race and religious prejudice."[46]

Walsh was as good as his word. A month later the legislature passed a bill establishing a three-man board of censors in Boston, made up of the mayor, the police commissioner, and the chief justice of the municipal court, with greatly augmented powers. Trotter immediately demanded action from the new board. Curley had said he would ban *The Birth of a Nation* if he had the power. He had it now—but he was not as good as his word. In a unanimous ruling, the new board refused to stop the showing of *The Birth of a Nation*, which went on to have a six-and-a-half-month, 360-performance Boston run.[47]

Curley tried to make it up to Boston's blacks. In the midst of the controversy over *Birth*, he was lobbying the secretary of war to allow a deceased local man, an army veteran, to be the first black buried in Arlington National Cemetery; later he issued a proclamation honoring the hundredth anniversary of the birth of Frederick Douglass and appointed blacks to high posts in his administration. He even submitted an anti-lynching bill to Senator Henry Cabot Lodge ("G-r-r-r eat!" the *Boston Journal* commented. "It almost makes the community forget that Curley is the Mayor who, despite his promises, sanctioned 'Birth of a Nation.' . . .") Still, nothing he did later could quite efface what he had failed to do then. By his third term (1930–34) he had recovered his former popularity among blacks through, among other things, appointing the first black registrar in the history of the city, the first black secretary to the mayor, and—at a time when there were only thirty-eight black lawyers in the state—two black lawyers to the office of the corporation counsel, "the first time in the history of any American municipality," according to a black newspaper, "that colored citizens were so honored." But, although it is a history with many more turnings, Trotter's prediction, that "Boston will never be as Boston of old" to her black citizens if *The Birth of a Nation* played there, came true. Reading reviews of the film like the one in the *Boston Globe*—"As a work of art it is so wonderful and so beautiful that it robs one of the power of criticism"—jarred Boston's blacks out of their complacency about living in the capital of abolition, the city of Garrison and Sumner, and into an awareness of the racial chasm separating them from Boston's whites. The current isolation of Boston's African-American citizens—only 20 percent of the city's black students attend integrated schools—has manifold roots, but a thick knot of them extend back to an April evening in 1915.[48]

Why did Curley fail to honor his own code? He may have recognized the power of film as an electioneering tool (he used films about himself as propaganda in both his 1917 reelection bid and his 1921 campaign against John R. Murphy) and did not want to alienate theater owners over an issue, unlike the dreaded "immorality," to which he was not committed as a matter of right. As we have seen, money, too, could play him false. Before rendering his final verdict on the film, he held a private conference with one of the directors of the Epoch Producing Company, Martin W. Littleton, a former colleague from the House of Representatives. Perhaps it was just a friendly lobby, but who knows? Louis B. Mayer, then an obscure theater owner in Haverhill, Massachusetts, later boasted that he personally made $500,000 from the New England rights to *The Birth of a Nation*, a profit the film historian Richard Schickel calls "crucial to his rise in the motion picture industry." Curley was not money-honest—there is no getting around that fact. With such sums at stake, anything was possible.[49]

❖   ❖   ❖

A merican history textbooks treat political corruption as if it was a phase, a developmental stage the Republic went through in the bad old days when "bosses" like Curley and their "machines" ruled our great cities. This progressive schema lulls the innocent student into thinking that politics was dirtier and politicians less honest in the past than it is or they are today. Yes, things are different today. In the past politicians took bribes, but the practice was illegal, so the standard of political virtue was preserved. Now, thanks to the campaign reform acts of the 1970s, it is legal to take bribes so long as they are "declared." Congressmen and senators spend much of their time cadging declared bribes from groups that have an interest in legislation. In this way they annually collect hundreds of thousands of dollars meant to finance their reelection campaigns. The congressmen are not corrupt; the system is.

That conclusion, however, is not alarming enough. In an exhaustive survey of congressional spending for the 1990 election, the *Los Angeles Times* found that 65 percent of the $445 million spent by congressmen and senators to get themselves reelected went for "items that have little or nothing to do with winning the support of ordinary voters." What did they do with the money? One congressman spent $200,000 on an election in which he had no opponent. Four others used campaign donations to pay their mortgages. Another spent $100,000 for meals, travel, and salaries for his staff; he, too, was unopposed. Others used campaign money to buy a Lincoln Continental (Rep. C. W. ["Bill"] Young, [R-Fla.]), to commission a portrait of a parent (Rep. Carroll Hubbard, Jr., [D-Ky.]), and to pay nearly $60,000 for rent and home improvements (Rep. Stephen L. Neal, [D-N.C.]). In sum, congressmen themselves routinely corrupt the already rotten system of campaign finance. As former congressman Tony L. Coelho, who should know, puts it, "the process buys you out." This is the age not of the Keating Five but of the Keating 535.[50]

It is an age when Dan Rostenkowski (D-Ill.) can legally raise over three-quarters of a million dollars from corporations and unions to finance a "party" to mark the two hundredth anniversary of the House Ways and Means Committee, of which he is chairman. "I thought it was a good way to study our past, celebrate our history, and think about our future," he said, in words that make one wish H. L. Mencken still walked this earth. It is an age, to quote the *National Journal*, when Congress can exempt itself from a federal criminal law banning executive branch employees from "taking actions that benefit their own financial interests or their spouses"—and when over a score of congressional spouses take advantage of this exemption by serving as lobbyists, fixers, consultants, and go-betweens of several sorts. It is an age when a headline like FORMER CONGRESSMAN GIVES HIMSELF $345,000 in the *New York Times* does not stir an outcry, for what just-retiring congressman Gene Taylor of Missouri did in pocketing the money he had left over in his campaign finance fund was "perfectly legal." Congressmen elected before 1980—there were 191 of them still in Congress in 1989, with cash reserves totaling $39 million— can keep the money they cadged from interest groups before that year for their personal use, if they retire before 1993. Several members, including Chairman Rostenkowski, have accumulated over $1 million through this grandfather clause. It is an age when 163 of the 346 members of Congress listed as "retired" in 1989, thanks to benefits they created for themselves while in office, can expect to collect upwards of $1 million in pension benefits; more than a third already receive more money in their pension checks than they received as their congressional salaries. It is an age when a president can appoint and the Senate approve as secretary of education a man who, partly while still governor of Tennessee, to quote the *Wall Street Journal*, "earned a $569,000 profit without investing a cent, or much of his own time" in stock transactions and other large sums in other deals, some with companies that did business with the state. It is an age when an aide to the president can use a White House limousine to take him to New York to attend a rare-stamp auction, then fly back to Washington on a jet owned by a company that has an interest in federal legislation— and his use of the corporate jet can be considered by the White House legal counsel an ethical improvement over the aide's former practice of taking air force planes to visit his dentist or go

.skiing. In this age of tumescent corruption, American politics is its own Mencken. It satirizes itself.

In the past, political alienation comported with lack of interest in or information about politics and government. Today, according to an intensive study of voters' attitudes, falling participation in politics "flows as much from *informed frustration* as from lack of interest"—specifically from the view that campaign contributions, not voting, "determine political outcomes." To Arthur Schlesinger, Jr., advocates of term-limitation legislation assume that "the democratic process itself is the enemy of the public interest." When the "democratic process" of elections is so lavishly financed by private economic interests, are they mistaken?⁵¹

Things are indeed different today: in our "informed frustration," we accept the unacceptable, tolerate the intolerable. The borders of our indignation retreat daily before the scale of contemporary political corruption. Numbed, we teach our children values honored only in the breach in Washington, D.C.

Put Curley's peculations into this age and they would show as no worse than the norm in a political system polluted by Big Money. We need to keep that in mind as we return to his age to expound the crookedness of this "crooked" mayor.

❖   ❖   ❖

James Curley took "honest graft." The oxymoron comes from George Washington Plunkitt, the sage of Tammany Hall, a New York State senator, and a fellow who would feel right at home in a world where taxes are "revenue enhancements" and liars "misspeak." In "A Series of Very Plain Talks on Very Practical Politics," published in 1905, Plunkitt explained to the journalist William R. Riordon how he had made politics pay. "There's all the difference in the world between the two," he said of honest versus dishonest graft. "Yes, many of our men have grown rich in politics. I have myself. I've made a big fortune out of the game, and I'm gettin' richer every day, but I've not gone in for dishonest graft—blackmailin', gamblers, saloon-keepers, disorderly people, etc.—and neither has any of the men who made big fortunes in politics. There's an honest graft and I'm an example of how it works. I might sum up the whole thing by sayin': 'I seen my opportunities and I took 'em.'" Senator Plunkitt's opportunities came in this form: when the city was about to buy a piece of land, he would get wind of it through friends at City Hall, buy up the land, and sell it to the city at profit. That was "honest" graft. Of course, only by comparison with the organized vice run by Tammany Hall did it merit the epithet.

Curley's opportunities were different from Plunkitt's, but he took them with the same unembarrassed grasp. Having grown up poor, he intended to live rich.

On March 17, 1915, St. Patrick's Day, construction began on a house that would symbolize Curley and "Curleyism" to generations of Bostonians. The house sat on a two-acre rise of land facing a park in the "green necklace" that Frederick Law Olmsted, a poet in landscape, had planted across Boston twenty years before. Between the park and the house was a twisting motor parkway; past the park, visible through its trees, lay a prim pond. Beyond, nestled among the hills of Brookline, were the estates and "farms" of some of the oldest and wealthiest families in Massachusetts. Altogether, the district was as far in ambience as one could go from Ward 17 and still be within the city limits. "It has a pleasing, picturesque, garden-like air," George William Curtis wrote in 1859. "It is the same smooth and comfortable and respectable landscape that strikes the American eye in England." It was, as a recent historian of the area has written, a "gentleman's landscape." And James M. Curley, no gentleman, was building a fine brick house there.[32]

"Where did Curley get it?" press and public alike began to ask almost as soon as the ground was broken. Where did a man with a salary of $10,000 a year and no declared savings get the money to build such a house? That question could not be answered without taking one over into illegality. The land alone cost that much. And just the year before, the mayor had bought a summer home in Hull, a resort town on the South Shore of Boston, worth $10,000. Moreover, as the house took shape over the spring and summer, people could see that there was nothing ordinary about it. Designed by the architect Joseph McGinniss, who did commissioned work for the city, it was a neo-Georgian mansion of twenty-one-plus rooms and over ten thousand square feet, with a thick tile roof, sculptural medallions on its brick cladding, a heated garage, and gracious landscaped grounds. Outside it was impressive enough; inside it was downright opulent. The twenty- by thirty-two-foot oval mahogany-paneled dining room with its crystal chandelier, the baronial forty-by sixty-foot first-floor hall, the twenty-eight carved mahogany doors, the five bathrooms (by now the Curleys had five children), the high ceilings, the Italian marble fireplaces, the gold-plated light fixtures, the massive two-story bronze chandelier in the front hall taken from the Austro-Hungarian embassy in Washington, and the breathtaking three-story spiral staircase that curled around it were the appurtenances of great wealth—in fact, many of them had come from the estate of an owner of Standard Oil. The only sign that a man of the people lived in this palazzo were the shamrocks cut into the thirty white shutters outside.[53]

The house swallowed the Curley administration. It led to graft; graft led to scandal; scandal led to defeat. To pay for the land, Curley had to engage in one kind of graft. The labor took another; the interior Versailles yet another. Besides paying for the house, Curley had to find the money to live up to it, to afford the servants, gardeners, and cooks needed to run it. So the house cost him (to say nothing of the taxpayer) dear. Abandoning the old neighborhood cost him politically, too. In the 1915 state election the Tammany-backed candidate running for state representative in Ward 17 lost to a candidate who predicted that Curley "would lose his head with his sudden rise to power and forget the people who made him what he is politically" when he moved out to the shores of Jamaica Pond. Yet there was vision behind this mansion on a jut of land next to a busy highway where all eyes could see it—or so the years would prove.

To divert attention from the unanswerable question "Where did he get it?" Curley did one of the strangest things in his career. He quoted to the press portions of a letter that a Yankee neighbor of his, Dr. Edmund D. Spears, had sent him. The letter, which complained about the "abomination on the shutters"—the shamrock cutouts—caused a sensation; one didn't have to be the proverbial well-balanced Irishman—a fellow with chips on both shoulders—to take offense at this. But later, when reporters pressed him for a copy of Spears's letter, the mayor said that he had, well, misspoken. Dr. Spears's complaint had really been about the funerary urns set in the brickwork over the front entrance. Curley made no attempt to explain why he had distorted Spears's letter except to imply that it was all somehow a joke. To this day, people remember Curley's libel of Dr. Spears, the "rich Yankee neighbor" offended in his contemptibly narrow heart by the shamrock shutters. It is part of the Curley legend. It was also a lie told by a man trapped in lies about money.[54]

Watergate did not stop the federal government in its lumbering tracks. The Nixon administration continued, with the president feigning unconcern about the "fifth-rate burglary" and its toxic ramifications. Yet the essential story of the Nixon administration can be written as the history of Watergate. In the same way the history of the first Curley administration can be read in the bricks and mortar and, more to the point, the stained glass and gold plate of Curley's house.

Curley got the fancy appointments from a Roxbury junk dealer and former treasurer of the Tammany Club named Marks Angell, who had purchased them from the Fairhaven, Massachusetts, estate of Henry H. Rogers. Marks Angell (né Max Angelovitz) had backed Curley early in his career and had long stood in the sun of Curley's favor. In 1908, while on the Board of Aldermen, Curley helped Angell secure a license to open a kosher slaughterhouse in Ward 17. At the time Thomas M. Joyce, a member of the Common Council who was often embroiled with Curley, charged him with being Angell's secret partner. That charge would be leveled again.[55]

Under Mayor Curley, Angell's Roxbury Iron and Metal Company got a street (Hill Top Street in Dorchester) built solely for its convenience, to give its trucks easier passage; there had been no pressure from the neighborhood for a new street. The city generously paid Angell more in damages for the land-taking than it assessed him in betterments for the improvement. First Angell's son-in-law and then his brother-in-law also got special consideration from the mayor in the bidding to run the refreshment concession at Franklin Park. It took a protest from the Finance Commission to stop their too-high bid from winning the contract. Angell did submit a low bid to demolish the city-owned Probate Building—but alone among the bidders, only Angell knew that the city would not enforce the time limitation in the contract. Because he did not have to remove the debris within the stipulated twenty days, he could bid lower than the competition. Curley had suggested the twenty-day clause to the superintendent of the Buildings Department, as he had suggested to the Transit Commission that it let Angell's junk firm handle its refuse without the bother of bidding for the job. His "suggestions" were, of course, commands to city employees. Finally, Angell was a habitué of the mayor's office, using Curley's telephone and often posing as his special agent on visits to local corporations to solicit their junk business.

In incendiary testimony before the Finance Commission in late 1917, a former city treasurer threw light on why Angell got so much city business and enjoyed the run of City Hall. Curley, he told the startled commissioners, had once let slip in conversation that he had a half interest in the Roxbury Iron and Metal Company. In granting contracts to Angell, Curley was filling his own pocket. This was in direct violation of the City Charter, which prohibited any city official from having a financial interest in firms doing business with the city.[56]

Having workmen perform labor on the mayor's private residence in exchange for city contracts was also a violation of the charter, yet that is how 350 the Jamaicaway got built. The contractors who worked on the house did so on the understanding that city contracts would come their way. Curley paid them either nothing or a fraction of their fees. When the Finance Commission was about to open an investigation of a contractor who had installed some flooring in City Hall after laying the floors at the house, Curley quickly paid his bill to the contractor, whose books carried the notation "NC"—"no charge"—opposite the entry for the Curley job. The whole house was "NC." "Governor, did you pay for that house?" John Henry Cutler, the ghostwriter of *I'd Do It Again*, asked Curley in 1956. "He had the largest brown eyes I've ever seen on a person," Cutler said, "and he gave me a wink as if to say of course he didn't pay."[57]

There remained the land—the $10,000 question. The Finance Commission, in hearings held in the fall of 1917, finally got to the bottom of the land. On September 2, 1913, Francis L. Daly, the co-proprietor of the firm Sullivan & Daly, a plumbing supply house, bought out his partner, Daniel P. Sullivan, for $8,000. The money, he told the Finance Commission, was a gift from his uncle, who had since died, destitute, leaving no record of any loan to his nephew. Daly wrote his check to Sullivan on August 28, the same day that his close friend, Congressman James M. Curley, about to launch his campaign for mayor, had withdrawn $4,100 from one bank and taken a $3,900 loan from another. Testifying under oath before the Finance Commission, the mayor claimed he used this $8,000 to buy stock from a New York wool broker named Nathan Eisman, who, like Daly's uncle, had also since died—leaving no sign of ever

At the front door of the Curley mansion in 1922. Mary's intervention made Curley mayor for the second time.

Curley's 1921 campaign song. The most famous of these songs was the 1945 rendition: "Vote Early and Often for Curley."

Official Curley Campaign Songs

Everybody Sing
With the Curley Serenaders

CHORUS

In the old City Hall, in the old City Hall,
That's the place and we'll send them there,
For we never had such a wonderful Mayor
In the old City Hall, those happy days we recall.
The last election, we know was a frame,
But this time the Goo Goo's won't work that old game,
For Curley will warm up the chair once again
In the old City Hall.

CHORUS

All by themselves they've been scheming,
Trying to pull something new;
They sit alone in their cozy office chairs,
Talking graft affairs, but they must beware;
They think they're fooling the public,
But they are fooling themselves.
For Murphy loves to fall asleep on Lomasney's shoulder,
He hates to grow older, all by himself.

CHORUS

If you want a fighting man, choose Curley.
For he's absolutely square and true,
And you know its Curley's plan to help you when he can
Now you voters show him what you can do.
If you want improvements made, see Curley,
There's a welcome sign upon his door.
Tammany, victory, and Curley for four years more.

JAMES M. CURLEY
The People's Only Candidate for Mayor

If his voice could not "wake the hogs in the next county," like Alben Barkley's, it was only because there were no hogs there to be waked.

Norman, editorial cartoonist for the Boston Post, *conveyed the fragile harmony among the contenders in the mayoral race of 1921.*

(Right) From his cutaway coats to his ice cream suits, Curley was never less than sartorially impressive. Like Huey Long, he grasped the vicarious nature of his appeal.

(Below) During the 1921 campaign. Was this the coat a sneak thief nearly stole from him in 1917?

(Above) "The Place of Rest," Mary Emelda called their home. He would lose that when he lost her.

(Left) Lovely, doomed Dorothea. Mary Emelda never recovered from the almost theological shock of her death.

Mary Emelda's last photograph. It moved Curley deeply when she insisted on going to the polls in 1929 to cast her last vote for him.

At the Vatican to see the pope. Curley badly wanted to be Roosevelt's ambassador to Italy, but his religion proved a barrier.

Putting the memory of Mary's and James's death behind him with travel. Here, a reciprocating visit to Boston, England.

At the dedication of the new federal post office in 1933. James Roosevelt, next to Jim Farley on the left, seems to be imploring the great New Deal in the sky to stop Curley's stem-winder.

Curley the builder, at the opening of the I. J. Fox Building on Washington Street in 1934.

(Above) God's pork barrel. Catholicism hung over Curley's Boston like a thick civic cloud.

(Right) He loved the theater of politics. "It was B. F. Keith's all day long," one crony recalls.

having lived. From this stock deal, Curley said, he realized $12,500, a profit of 166 percent, and with that sum bought the land for what was by then the most notorious house in Massachusetts.

This was almost certainly perjury. During the mayoral campaign Curley had spoken openly of what he had done with the $8,000. "I am a partner in the Daly Plumbing Supply Company," he said in a speech on January 7, 1914, "from which concern I net a sufficient income to render me independent of political office." And in a signed article published in the *Boston Post* on December 13, 1915—which he later disavowed, disingenuously—he said he had bought the land for his house from the proceeds of his half interest in the Daly firm, which on becoming mayor he sold back to Daly. But this too was a lie; he never sold his interest in Daly Plumbing Supply. Daly himself, in headline-making testimony, denied that he had bought out Curley (which was why Curley had to invent Eisman).

At the Finance Commission hearing, Curley was questioned about the *Post* article saying he had bought his house on his share of the Daly business. "Didn't you think it was your duty to correct the impression?" one of the commissioners asked. Curley replied, with revealing scorn, "No, when you consider the kind of cattle it would interest." Asked how the writer of the article (Standish Willcox took the blame) obtained the information in it, the mayor denied that he was the source. "It was merely a matter of current rumor evolved into a statement"—a truly Nixonian formulation in the way it dispensed with human agency.[58]

If the $10,000 did not come from Daly and if Eisman was a phantom, where *did* Curley get it?

In all probability the $10,000 came from two contractors, George M. Stevens, the general manager of Timilty's Central Construction Company, and his brother-in-law, William J. Clark, an officer of another construction firm. Daly met them over lunch. He knew they wanted to do business with the city. They knew he was a close friend of the mayor's. When he suggested they might want to invest $10,000 in a real estate venture of a suspiciously vague character, they agreed. Ostensibly they were buying fifty shares in the Oakmont Land Company, the municipal equivalent of one of those CIA fronts with names like Southern Trading Company. Run by Daly's brother-in-law, Edwin Fitzgerald, Oakmont was supposed to use the money to buy some industrial land in Jamaica Plain. Investigation revealed, however, that Oakmont had already secured

funds for that purchase from a bank. Daly gave Fitzgerald the
$10,000, but he returned it to Daly, who testified that he was not
sure what he had done with it. To quote Gertrude Stein, this was
interesting if true.

The following train of conjecture cannot be far short of the
facts: Clark and Stevens, and their firms, wanted contracts from the
city, and they paid for them. Daly either passed along their $10,000
to Curley, who used it to pay off his note on the land, or kept it to
satisfy a loan for the land that he had made earlier to Curley. For its
part, Central Construction got its bribe back, with interest. It received a steady flow of no-bid jobs, magnanimously charging the
city $2.26 a square yard of paving for work that cost $1.66 a square
yard in New York. The paving contract, wrote the *Boston Journal*,
"is as crooked as a snake in a hurry."[59]

For *his* pains Daley got fat on city contracts. The month before
Curley's inaugural speech ("Special privilege in any form is objec-
tionable and the removal of this cancer from the body politic must
be undertaken at once"), Daly's father-in-law, Peter Fitzgerald, to
quote the arch language of the Finance Commission report, "was
engaged in selling from a cart butter, cheese, and eggs." But six
weeks later he and his son Edwin were in the insurance and bonding business. As exclusive agents for the National Surety Company,
the Fitzgeralds got 80 percent of the city's employee bonding business, which totaled $784,000, in 1914 and 94 percent, totaling
$965,000, in 1915. They also captured 76 percent of the bonds the
city required of contractors, which, in 1915, came to $1,149,000; a
large share of the city's automobile insurance business; and half its
policies covering elevators and boilers.

In addition, the Finance Commission found suggestive irregularities in the Fitzgeralds' accounting practices. "Loans" made to
Francis L. Daly were not paid back. A phantom New York stock-
broker named John J. Cassidy, whom Peter Fitzgerald claimed
lived at the Hotel Knickerbocker (which had never heard of him),
got $4,000. Only the terminally credulous could doubt the real
destination of this money. In his testimony before the Finance
Commission, John Sullivan removed even their doubts when he
said that Curley had spoken several times of his half-interest in the
Daly firm. The corporation counsel had warned Curley either to
sell out or to declare his interest, as the law required. Curley fired
him before he could resign.[60]

Confronted with clear evidence of multiple violations of the City Charter and of perjury, the Finance Commission instructed its special counsel, Henry F. Hurlburt, to present its case against Curley to the district attorney of Suffolk County, Joseph C. Pelletier, for possible prosecution. Unimpressed by Hurlburt's case, Pelletier refused to prosecute. Curley had dodged another bullet, one that would have ended the career of most politicians, though reversals seemed rather to propel Curley. According to Martin Lomasney, "Curley went in to Pelletier, got down almost on his knees, talked of his wife and family, and begged him to stay the execution of the law. 'Hold on, Joe, for God's sake, give me a chance. Think of my wife and family. Think of our party. Think of our people.'" But Curley did not have to beg.[61]

The mayor and the district attorney were firm political friends. Years before, when Curley was on the City Council, Pelletier had refused to prosecute Curley on another set of charges. When Pelletier tried to take the gubernatorial nomination away from the incumbent governor, Eugene Victor Foss, in the 1912 Democratic primary, a grateful Curley delivered his ward for Pelletier—one of only three Boston wards he won. In the person of Daniel Coakley, who had moved from the suburbs of Curley's displeasure in 1914 to become his lawyer in the Finance Commission hearings in 1917, Curley and Pelletier shared a less savory link.[62]

On the evening of March 6, 1917, Paramount Pictures gave a dinner at the Copley-Plaza Hotel for Roscoe ("Fatty") Arbuckle, the comic star of the silent screen. Paramount exhibitors from all over New England came to see Arbuckle and to mingle with the Paramount executives on hand to honor him—among them Adolph Zukor, Hiram Abrams, and Walter Greene, the three owners of Paramount, and Jesse Lasky, its vice president. Arbuckle retired after the dinner, but Abrams had arranged a late-night chicken-and-champagne party for some of the special guests at an establishment called Mishawum Manor in the nearby city of Woburn. Mishawum Manor was presided over by a woman variously known as Brownie Kennedy, Lillian Kingston, Stella Webber, Helen Morse, Lillian Dale, and Stella Kennedy. More than a dozen of the movie men, including Zukor, Greene, and Lasky, arrived at the manor sometime after midnight. While they were enjoying their chicken and champagne, someone started to play the piano in the background and a huge salver was carried into the room. Its cover was removed—and out popped a pulchritudinous young woman wearing only "a few small pieces of parsley and a sprinkling of salad dressing." Fourteen other young women, all naked, now walked in. When news of the affair finally leaked out four years later, the *New York Times* called what happened next a "midnight frolic,"—though "orgy," for once, would have been accurate.[63]

Near dawn, Abrams paid Brownie Kennedy $1,000 for fifty-two bottles of champagne and other favors, and the movie men went on their way.

Two months later, while in Portland, Maine, on business, Abrams received a telephone call from Mayor Curley advising him of a "serious matter likely to arise" in connection with the Woburn revel and urging him to come to Boston at once. He did so. In a meeting at the Hotel Touraine, Curley, accompanied by Coakley, told Abrams that some of the young women at the Mishawum Manor had been under the age of consent, that the husbands of others were bringing alienation of affection suits against the Paramount executives, and that the district attorney of Middlesex County, Nathan Tufts, was investigating the charges. The mayor introduced Coakley as someone who could help them—at a price. Coakley demanded a retainer of $10,000, to which Abrams agreed. With suspicious celerity, Coakley then arranged a conference with Tufts, and soon after Curley, Coakley, Abrams, and his lawyer met with the district attorney in his Cambridge offices.

After calling Abrams and his associates "licentious Jews" and taking a high line on the low ways of Hollywood, Tufts said that he would drop his investigation if the complaining husbands could be persuaded to drop their suits. Coakley estimated that $100,000 would silence the husbands and settle his own fee and those of the husbands' lawyers. Following a conference with his Paramount colleagues, all of whom were married, Abrams sent checks in that amount to Coakley and to other principals he designated in the case. Curley was not one of them, but what other motive than money could he have had for lending his office to this sexual shakedown? If the distinction has any meaning, this was dishonest graft.[64]

Coakley by then was a veteran pander. In addition to furnishing Curley with the Toodles information, he and Tufts and Joseph Pelletier, the chief law enforcement officers of Massachusetts' two most populous counties, had for some years been operating a sexual entrapment racket or "badger game" whose mechanisms were similar to those used in the Mishawum Manor squeeze. A prostitute hired by the trio would lure a rich elderly gentleman to a hotel room. When they were in flagrante delicto, an irate "husband" or "father" of the woman would burst in, or the police would enter and charge the man with fornication or contributing to the delinquency of a minor. The man would be told that an alienation of affection suit could be avoided only by hiring Attorney Daniel H. Coakley, who by a miracle of legal art would persuade either District Attorney Tufts or District Attorney Pelletier, depending on the location of the tryst, to "nol pros" the suit. That was what Pelletier had done with the charges brought against Curley by the Finance Commission; the lawyer who pleaded Curley's case before Pelletier was, of course, Daniel Coakley.

Over a period of years Coakley got $300,000, a vast sum in those days, from one seventy-five-year-old bachelor who had fondled a sixteen-year-old. The love letters of another man were good for $150,000. The sex angle in these crimes drew the attention of Godfrey Lowell Cabot, who as the longtime treasurer of the Watch and Ward Society kept an unblinking eye on Boston's morals. He made it his life's business to stop the blackmailers.[65]

A scion of one of Boston's most distinguished families, Cabot was himself a man of pronounced, if unusual, erotic passion. "I wish that your bladder were full to bursting with urine," he confided to his wife, in German, while away on a business trip, "and that you could save your life only by urinating into my mouth until you had entirely emptied yourself, and I was full to bursting with your urine." A man possessed of such ardors would naturally regard blackmail with horror.

Cabot dedicated himself to exposing the racket, which he had been tracking through private detectives since 1914. In the summer of 1917, he had a bill submitted to the legislature calling for a formal investigation of Pelletier. The district attorney fought back by playing the religious card, charging that the legislator who brought Cabot's bill was a defender of the Birth Control League "who advocated the rights of his clients to teach the public, even young girls, how to use contraceptive devices." When the bill died in the state Senate, Cabot filed a petition for Pelletier's impeachment with the Supreme Judicial Court. Nothing came of the impeachment effort either. But though he had to stay on the case several more years, though he had to resist the charms of a prostitute sent by Coakley and Pelletier to ensnare him, and though he even had to hire a detective to break into Coakley's office, Godfrey Lowell Cabot, whose resolve was such that he made out a will earmarking $30,000 to continue his investigation after his death, would get his men.[66]

There is no evidence that Curley was a party to the Pelletier-Coakley badger game. But he was a party to Coakley, whom he made a trustee of the Boston Public Library, and he had to have been in on the Mishawum Manor caper. Coakley kept turning up in Curley's life. He spoke to the side of Curley that wanted to live in a mansion no matter the cost in reputation. The prospect of disgrace, which serves to keep a man straight long after the sense of honor has atrophied, held no terror for him. He had been disgraced—and had turned disgrace into votes.

❖   ❖   ❖

"I am a candidate for reelection," Curley announced to the Tammany Club in a ninety-minute speech on New Year's Eve 1916, "and I have not the slightest fear of the outcome." He was getting a year's jump on the election because he knew it was not going to be an easy fight. The City Charter of 1909, which increased the mayoral term from two to four years, also provided for a recall election to be held midway in the mayor's term. For Curley, this had come in November 1915. The Good Government Association did not work for his recall, as it had for that of John Fitzgerald in 1912. But the Republican City Committee—"comic opera politicians," Curley called them—did. Also, the "liquor interest," the bar owners and local brewers, fearing, rightly, that women would use the vote to bring in Prohibition, spent money to defeat Curley for endorsing a woman suffrage amendment on the state ballot. "I will vote yes on the suffrage amendment," Curley had said, "because the doctrine of equal rights should mean all that the words imply." Mrs. Curley herself was strong for women's rights; according to her son, she even took part in a suffragist demonstration at City Hall.[67]

It was still risky for an Irish Catholic politician to back woman suffrage. Far from dying out, the old association of women's rights with nativism had gained new life in the late 1880s and 1890s, when a religious war broke out in the Boston public schools over the teaching of history. After the School Committee disciplined a teacher for ridiculing Catholic doctrine on indulgences in a history class, a nativist uproar ensued. Since 1882, Massachusetts women had been allowed to vote in School Committee elections, and in 1888, urged on by Protestant ministers, the Protestant women of Boston turned out in numbers to elect a stoutly nativist School Committee to save the schools from Romish contamination. For Catholics the lesson was clear: woman suffrage (cultural inhibitions kept Catholic women from voting) led to anti-Catholicism.[68]

But time was changing Catholic attitudes. The election of David Walsh in 1913 showed that nativist sentiment had subsided in Massachusetts. Labor backed suffrage, and Catholic women were now active in the cause. Sensing the altered mood, Cardinal O'Connell muted his public opposition. With O'Connell silent and Walsh strongly backing the amendment, Curley felt safe in coming out for woman suffrage in a year when he would be on the ballot himself.[69]

Largely because it was opposed by the Republican establishment led by Henry Cabot Lodge, however, the amendment lost by 133,000 votes statewide, and by almost two to one in Boston. Walsh, hurt by the liquor interest, also lost. On woman suffrage, it appears, Curley had gotten too far ahead of his constituents. Tellingly, his old home ward rejected the amendment, 1,911 to 1,065.[70]

Whether woman suffrage was the issue that hurt him, or whether the voters were signaling their displeasure with the scandal enshrouding the building of his house, forty-seven thousand Bostonians voted for his recall while only thirty-five thousand voted to keep him as mayor—and this without much of an organized campaign against him. The law required the vote of 50 percent of registered voters, not of the total vote cast, to recall a mayor (which would have entailed holding another mayoral election), and though 57 percent of those voting rejected Curley, they represented only 42 percent of registered voters. He had dodged another bullet.

In 1914 46 percent of the voters had rejected him. To these another 11 percent had now been added—and they came from former Curley strongholds like South Boston. At prerecall rallies for the mayor, observers noted, only "The Star-spangled Banner" would get people out of their seats. What tune, they wondered, would avail in his reelection drive in 1917?[71]

His campaign got a power of help from history. James M. Curley was a war mayor in 1917. He warmed to the cause slowly—as late as June, two months after war was declared, he denounced it in a speech in the North End as a "war for commerce," in the *Boston Journal*'s paraphrase, and played on "the ancient prejudices of his hearers by attacking Great Britain, now our ally in a war to the death for democracy." But soon he glimpsed the war's political uses. He did not visit any flag factories, but no parade, flag raising, or troop embarkation was safe from him. He embraced the war in its most Wilsonian aspect, as democracy's crusade against despotism. In his war proclamation to the city, he put it this way: "Truly, God hath said, 'I am tired of kings.'" As an Irish American, he cannot have liked joining an alliance led by a British government that had the blood of Irish patriots—the Dublin rising had been crushed the year before—still dripping from its hands. And President Wilson's failure to protest the hanging of Sir Roger Casement for running German guns to Ireland was a special trial. Even so, the president had carried 80 percent of the vote in Irish South Boston in the November presidential election, putting the lie to aspersions on Irish-American loyalty, while making it easier for Curley to praise Wilson and, with whatever reservations, to support his war.[72]

Curley was a patriot, not a jingo. While he was mayor there were no outrages against German Americans in Boston (Dr. Karl Muck, the German-born director of the Boston Symphony Orchestra, would be arrested under Curley's successor for failing to play "The Star-spangled Banner") and no abridgments of the right to dissent.

The United States' entry into the war released what one historian calls a "brainless fury" against all things German. "Hamburger" and "sauerkraut" disappeared from restaurant menus to be replaced by "liberty sandwich" and "liberty cabbage." In San Rafael, California, a man suspected of disloyalty had his hair cut in the shape of a cross. In Pensacola, Florida, a committee of vigilantes flogged a German American, forced him to shout "To hell with the Kaiser; hurrah for Wilson," and ordered him to leave the state. In New Brunswick, New Jersey, Rutgers students stripped an antiwar protester, coated him with molasses and feathers, and paraded him through the streets as an object lesson for "pro-Germans." The governor of Iowa banned the speaking of German, even over the telephone. In Collinsville, Illinois, a mob of five hundred seized a young German American—who, ironically, had tried to enlist in the navy but had been turned down because he was blind in one eye—bound him in an American flag, dragged him through the streets, and hanged him. A jury acquitted the mob's leaders in twenty-five minutes. By contrast, a New Hampshire jury sentenced a man to prison for three years for calling the conflict "a [J. P.] Morgan war and not a war of the people."

Partly to sway the German-American vote in the 1916 City Council election, Curley had allowed interned German sailors to give a band concert on the Common to mark the kaiser's birthday. Now, in wartime, while President Wilson repeatedly refused to speak out against attacks on German Americans, Curley insisted that the enemy was the German militarists, not the German people, whose liberation from the Prussian clique he spoke of as an Allied war aim. While Wilson was clapping Socialists and dissenters into jail for exercising their constitutional rights, Curley was defending the right of Socialists and peace demonstrators to meet on Boston Common. "The right of free speech is a very sacred one," he said. "In its defense, Mary Dyer, years ago, gave her life on Boston Common, near the very spot where these men will conduct their meeting. These men are asking for the same right—free speech."[73]

Curley later said that the most moving experience of his life was listening to Madame Schumann-Heink, the great Austrian-born opera singer, give a performance on the Common for three thousand departing soldiers and their families. Hearing that she was in town staying with friends, he called to ask if, with only a day's notice, she could sing the boys off to war. He made a special request of a song: "Boy of Mine," an excusably saccharine ballad popular that grim year. She agreed, and mastered the song in an hour. A naturalized American citizen, Madame Schumann-Heink, owing to her two German and one American marriages, had sons fighting in both the U.S. and German armies. Shortly before she was to go to the Parkman bandstand for the concert, she received a cable informing her that her son in the German army had been killed in action. She showed Curley the cable and, overcome with grief, said she could not go on with the show. "You do understand the meaning of the English words, don't you?" Curley gently pressed, meaning the words to "Boy of Mine." Madame Schumann-Heink squared her Wagnerian shoulders. "Ja, I think this is what they want, the mommas and the poppas." She would do it.

He introduced her to the audience as the woman who was famous for singing "Stille Nacht" on Christmas Eve. Families, some of them with their sons for the last time, waited on the grass as the big woman with the cablegram crumpled in her dress pocket made ready to sing. From the first note, tears streamed down her cheeks.

> *Boy of mine*
> *Boy of mine*
> *Although my heart is breaking*
> *I seem to know you'd want to go,*
> *Pride in your manhood waking. . . .*
>
> *But I'll be here waiting, dear*
> *And at the glad dawn's waking*
>
> *I'm here to say I love you so*
> *Dear little boy of mine.*
> *Dear little boy of mine.*

One by one the Allied nations sent missions to Boston. Parades, dinners, flowery toasts: Curley was in his element. Marshal Joffre's visit in May was the grandest of these occasions. In his welcoming speech, Curley predicted that the kaiser would "abdicate through fear" at the prospect of fighting the American soldier, an observation that must have given brittle amusement to the hero of the Marne. Half a million persons cheered the marshal (with the mayor beside him in an open touring car) as the parade in his honor wound through streets lined with schoolchildren waving the tricolor and shouting, "Vive la France!" Mrs. Curley, waiting on the reviewing stand in front of City Hall with Boston's veterans of the Civil War, waved two French flags as a signal for the crowd to pay tribute to Joffre—at which the wizened GAR treasures beside her, grappling with their canes, stood and cheered with such unseasonal vim that the whole place, according to one observer, "went mad." Later, in a ceremony on the Common, nine-year-old Mary Curley, ducking to avoid being kissed by Joffre's great white furry mustachios, presented the marshal with a check for $175,000 for the war orphans of France. She made the presentation in French, and if this wasn't one of the proudest moments in her father's life, then one misreads the width of his smile in the news photographs.[74]

Afterward, over and over in a darkened theater, Mary sat through the newsreel of the presentation. She stayed for just one more showing, and what a shame she did, for as the marshal bent down to buss her on the cheek a lady in the row in front of her remarked to her neighbor, "Who is that ugly little girl?"[75]

❖   ❖   ❖

For his reelection drive, the Metamorphistical Mayor once again changed shape. The process began in earnest after his scare in the 1915 recall election. "It was tiresome work posing as a reformer with public sentiment against him," he was said to have conceded before an executive session of the City Council. "He had started with the best of intentions but had been given no support." Furious at the Back Bay Republicans for opposing him, he told an associate, "If those sons of bitches think I'm not good enough, I'll show them." So he dropped the pose. The *Boston Evening Transcript* noted: "It is an altogether different man in the executive chair than the Curley of three years ago who, standing on the platform of Tremont Temple announced that the old days at City Hall had passed and that a new regime of efficiency had begun." The Democratic "machine"—the city's twenty-six ward committee chairmen whom he had spurned in 1914, after they spurned him in the election campaign—was now behind him "with banners flying and countenances aglow, forgetting the first two years at City Hall, which were starvation years." As the mayor began to pick up early endorsements from the unions representing various city employees, the *Transcript* borrowed a metaphor from the western front to describe the Curley juggernaut: "It is a machine no longer but a veritable tank of modern warfare, as much designed to frighten opponents by its great show of power as it is for use as an offensive weapon against the popular will."[76]

Yet this appearance of strength was deceptive. For one thing, although the heads of city unions might endorse him, Curley could not be sure what the rank and file would do in the privacy of the voting booth. His efforts to compel their loyalty might well backfire. "The only time a city employee dares speak now is in his sleep," a City Hall reporter noted, "and that only after first scanning carefully the black void under the bed."[77]

For another, starting in the summer, the Finance Commission inquiries into the connections between Marks Angell, Frankie Daly, Fitzgerald père and fils, and the mayor began to make headlines and the stories beneath them to sow disenchantment.

Consider this colloquy between special counsel Hurlburt and Francis L. Daly taken from a Finance Commission hearing.

HURLBURT: Isn't it a coincidence that the $10,000 you got from two contracting concerns you can't account for? The Mayor says he got $10,000 out of the Daly Plumbing Supply Company. You say he did not. There is that $10,000 unexplained. Isn't it strange that that $10,000 is unaccounted for and that the Mayor says he got $10,000 from you or the Daly Plumbing Supply Company?

DALY: As a matter of fact, it is just a coincidence, absolutely a coincidence.[78]

For yet another, being mayor during wartime had its pitfalls. Patriotism was running so high in Boston that a traveling display of a life jacket from the *Lusitania* had theater audiences close to tears—and digging deeper into their pockets to buy war bonds. In this context, Curley's penchant for manufactured enthusiasm could lead to grotesque lapses of taste, as when, at a solemn moment during one flag raising, he had a "leather-lunged rummy" howl "Three cheers for Jim Curley!" The incident got wide coverage, and reporters noted that he was "slipping badly" in its wake.[79]

When Curley's defense of free speech for the Socialists brought a sharp response from John Fitzgerald—who, branding Curley a friend of the kaiser, declared, "Boston Common is no place for treason to be perpetuated upon the people of the United States"—it looked as if the former mayor, who had just lost a close race against Senator Henry Cabot Lodge, would challenge Curley in the grudge match for which the city had long been waiting. But Curley, too angry at Fitzgerald to think strategically, immediately ordered Fitzgerald's brother, who had a sinecure at police headquarters, to walk the beat. Then, in a written statement that he handed out to reporters himself, he fired his secret weapon. "The only individual anxious to suppress truth or restrict free speech is the one whose acts, public or private, will not permit of thorough scrutiny or exposure to the world. . . . I am preparing three addresses which, if necessary, I shall deliver in the fall, and which if a certain individual had the right to restrict free speech, I would not be permitted to deliver." The second lecture was to be called "Great Lovers: From Cleopatra to Toodles." Fitzgerald, toodled again, subsided.[80]

The whole episode was painfully typical of Curley. No sooner
did he hit a high note—defending the right of free speech in wartime—than he stooped to Toodles. He would make a stirring patriotic speech one day; the next, under oath on the witness stand, he
would invent a farrago about a wool broker, a stock tip, and a fabulous profit. He needed a Michael Deaver to prune his persona, to
draw the chalk marks of his identity and tell him, "Thus far and no
farther." Habitually, he spoiled his own effects, as if bent on prov-
ing that he was no cardboard politician eager to sacrifice spontaneity to dignity. By his third term he had these words, sent by an
admirer, typed up and placed on his desk:

> WHEN YOU ARE MAD, WHICH IS OFTEN,
>
> THEN STOP TALKING AT THE RISK OF CHRONIC SILENCE.
>
> FOR YOUR MOUTH IS NOT ONLY YOUR GREATEST ASSET,
>
> BUT IT IS ALSO YOUR GREATEST LIABILITY.

Some risk! He never took that advice. Whether what we are describing was authenticity or just garrulity, honesty or blindness, it
was part of his enduring appeal. The mayor who was famous for
winking after making a moving speech mirrored life in its hope-
lessly alloyed state.[81]

The great danger to Curley had always been a simultaneous
challenge from both an Irish candidate minus Fitzgerald's libidi-
nous baggage and a Protestant "reform" candidate. While he and
the other Irish candidate divided the Irish vote, the reform candidate could win merely by holding Kenny's 1914 vote. That danger
now materialized.

The Irish candidate was first in the ring. Congressman James
A. Gallivan was a native of South Boston, graduate of the Boston
Latin School, the city's most prestigious public high school, and a
star first baseman on the Harvard team of 1888. He had served two
terms as state representative and two as state senator, and spent
thirteen years on the Board of Street Commissioners before winning Curley's former congressional seat in 1914. "I'll tear the hide
off him," he said of the mayor in announcing his candidacy.[82]

The city's citadel of reform, the Good Government Association,
one wit noted, "will endorse anybody who runs against Curley,
even if it was a cockeyed, bowlegged Chinaman who wears pajamas
to work and a kimono when he goes to a party." The association did

not have to cast its net so far as that. In March, former congressman Andrew J. Peters resigned his post as Wilson's assistant secretary of the treasury and moved back to Boston. He seemed to be making himself available as a candidate for mayor, though as one association member's diaries reveal, in the end he had to be actively courted.

Like Curley, Peters lived in Jamaica Plain, but in the house where, in 1872, he had been born, and which had been in the Peters family—whose fortune was sturdily built on wholesale lumber and the China trade—since the late eighteenth century. Andrew went to St. Paul's School, Harvard College, and Harvard Law. The family summered in Maine, and Andrew grew to manhood among the improving props of spinnakers and spars. The house in Jamaica Plain, the "cottage" on Vinalhaven Island, the farm in Dover, a rustic Boston suburb—the life that he and his wife, Martha, heiress to the great Phillips estate in Boston, carved out for themselves was the stuff of an upper-class nineteenth-century idyll. After several terms representing Jamaica Plain in the state legislature, Peters won four terms in the House of Representatives from the Eleventh Congressional District, which included eight Boston wards, before Wilson appointed him to the Treasury Department. A member of the Tavern, the Tennis and Racket, the Somerset, the Exchange, the Eastern Yacht, and the New York Harvard clubs—and also of the Country Club, in Brookline—Andrew J. Peters was a man of reputation and standing.[83]

"Yet beneath Peters' brownstone exterior," to quote the late Francis Russell, "lurked a perverse personality known only to a select few." Unfortunately for Curley, Peters's was one of the few perversions in Boston of which Daniel Coakley was unaware.

Sometime in 1917, perhaps as a result of the tensions of the campaign, Peters became morbidly attracted to an eleven-year-old girl who would become known by the plangent name of Starr Faithfull. Her father, a Beacon Hill wastrel, had abandoned Starr, her mother, and her sister. Peters, a distant cousin by marriage, agreed to act as temporary guardian to the girls, who soon became playmates of his five children. He began reading Starr choice bits of Havelock Ellis's *Studies in the Psychology of Sex*. He taught her to use ether. And one day, while she was in a stupor, he raped her. Thereafter, she knew no rest from his "anesthetic advances."

Starr looked much older than she was, and within a few years Peters was taking her with him on out-of-town trips. She kept a diary of their travels. "Spent night AJP Providence. Oh Horror, Horror, Horror!!!" reads one entry.

Starr's mother soon remarried, and her new husband, Stanley Faithfull, on learning his stepdaughter's secret, did just what Daniel Coakley would have done in his shoes: he blackmailed Peters for a large sum of money, perhaps as much as $80,000. Starr had fallen into a world of evil men.

The Faithfulls moved away, to New York; and in 1927, while on an ocean cruise, Starr developed a fearfully intense crush on the ship's doctor, an Englishman. Mistaking his pleasantry for the love she craved, she confessed her feelings to the doctor, and pursued him, unavailingly, for several years. To win his pity, she may even have told him about Peters and what he had done to her. Before jumping to her death from another ship, she left him this note: "I am going (definitely now—I've been thinking of it for a long time) to end my worthless, disorderly bore of an existence—before I ruin anyone else's life as well. . . . I have certainly made a sordid, futureless mess of it." On the morning of June 8, 1931, a Long Island beachcomber found her—a slim young woman wearing a silk dress, black coat, and stockings—washed up on the beach.[84]

Her diaries repeatedly mentioned "AJP," and damaging conjectures about Peters soon appeared in the New York papers. He hired the famed corporate lawyer John W. Davis, who had been the Democratic presidential candidate in 1924, to deny the rumors and to inhibit their recurrence through a show of prestige. Davis issued this statement in his client's name: "The girl was a distant cousin of Mr. Peters' wife. Mr. Peters has told me that never in his life did he have any improper relations with her in any way." That was all Andrew J. Peters—a man the *Transcript* saluted as "full of integrity of personality" in endorsing him for mayor in 1917—ever said publicly about the strange death and stranger life of Starr Faithfull.[85]

❖   ❖   ❖

"Ripping," James Michael Curley replied when reporters asked him what he thought of Peters's candidacy. One reporter misunderstood; did the mayor say "Rip him"? Vexed, Curley corrected him. "Ripping. Don't you know the meaning of ripping? Haven't you heard the word 'bully'?"[86]

The last candidate to enter the race, Congressman Peter F. Tague, was Martin Lomasney's cat's-paw. Lomasney had resolved to drive Curley from office because Curley had done nothing to stop a City Council dominated by members of the Good Government Association from gerrymandering his ward. Lomasney, who finally endorsed Peters two days before the election, hoped Tague would drain Irish votes away from Curley in Charlestown and East Boston, which were both in Tague's congressional district. Like Gallivan, whom John Fitzgerald had persuaded to enter the race, Tague could keep his congressional seat while running for mayor. He had nothing to lose by playing the spoiler.[87]

With Irish South Boston lost to Gallivan, Irish Charlestown seemingly lost to Tague, and Boston's thirty-five thousand registered Republicans sure to turn out heavily for Peters, "Mayor Curley as a potential political factor is gone," a leading Democrat predicted. Day after day now, a kite flew over City Hall with a sign on it saying, PETERS FOR MAYOR. "Many consider it an omen," wrote one reporter. Asked if he planned to come to Boston to stump for Mayor Curley, Curley's old friend Speaker Champ Clark ingenuously replied, "I didn't even know there was a mayoral campaign on in Boston."[88]

Curley had only one card left to play, a journalist observed: "That card is his own driving and magnetic personality on the stump." A month before the opening of the campaign in November, he had already made a staggering 678 public appearances in this red-white-and-blue year. Now, in the last weeks before the election on December 17, he seemed to be trying to surpass that record. He kept shirts of different collar sizes in the drawers of his big chiffonier, and as the sinews of his speaking parts swelled from delivering as many as ten non–acoustically assisted speeches a night, he would go up a collar size—16½ at the beginning of the evening, 17 in the middle, and a turgid 18 inches at the end. He had become his voice, his "magnetic and mellifluent larynx," as the *Boston Journal* labeled it.[89]

There were no arguments he could advance either for himself or against the other candidates that could stand a moment's scrutiny. Gallivan was asking audiences, "Who put the 'plum' in 'plumbing'?" and Curley could hardly pretend that if he were reelected the city would not get "eight years of Marks Angell and Frankie Daly." The most he could say against the "slacker Congressmen" was that, in the hour of national crisis, they belonged in Washington, passing a bill to draft "alien slackers"—foreign nationals who happened to be in the United States when war broke out. In fact, Gallivan and Tague had come out for a bill that would do just that, but, citing the divisive effect it would have on inter-Allied relations, the State Department asked them to drop it. The most Curley could say against "the gentleman from Dover," as he tauntingly called Peters, was that the nation needed him at his former job, "for the first duty of every citizen is to serve his country in whatever capacity will best contribute to a speedy ending of the war. . . . More money is being handled by the Treasury than ever in the history of the country. If Peters wants to serve, the way to do it is to go back to his old job in the Treasury Dept. . . ." As an "issue," this was almost contemporary in its vacuity.[90]

With no case to make, Curley's rhetoric had to substitute for argument. He had to do it all with a phrase. Thus he called the newspapers, which were against him, "wells of information poisoned by subsidy." Thus he said of Peters's head that it "more nearly resembled a complete vacuum than ever before known in the history of Boston," warned of the real Peters campaign "being waged under the cloak of dignity," and unmasked Peters's supporters as "purchasable camp followers." Gallivan was "a desperado of American politics." John R. Murphy, the chairman of the Finance Commission, "had the brains of a caterpillar." Curley waxed biblical on "the floodgates of wrath, envy, malice, vituperation, corruption and debauchery" opened by his opponents, whom he referred to collectively as "this distinguished and motley array of plunderers." In a rally across the street from "that foul sheet," the *Boston Post*, he put all of his frustration and fury into a cascade of Homeric invective. "With the rotten Post against me, with the American against me, with the Herald against me, with the Romanoff of Ward 8 against me, with Peters and his millions, with Tague, with Gallivan and his egotism against me, with every corrupt boss and rotten newspaper against me—with all of these powers of rottenness and corruption against me, they can't beat Jim Curley."[91]

He had two short films made: *Boston Doing Its Bit*, which showed him doing his bit to kill the kaiser with words, and *A Day in the Life of the Mayor of Boston*, which accompanied him, as one reviewer noted, "from the moment he sips his morning coffee until he tucks himself in under his bedclothes at night." And he put the owners of Boston's twenty-six theaters on notice that if they wanted their licenses renewed they had better show his films. Speaking to a Negro audience, Gallivan charged that D. W. Griffith had sneaked back to Boston to wield the camera for his old friend.[92]

Through a surrogate, Curley raised the "race issue" against Peters, whom he often identified as "my only opponent," in hopes of polarizing the contest on ethnic grounds. In *The Hibernian,* edited by a political ally, there appeared a full-page political ad with a cutout of Curley:

RE-ELECT JAMES M. CURLEY, MAYOR.
Do not be deceived by false issues.
The Peters Issue Is—Down with the Irish.
The Good Government Issue Is—Down with the Irish.

The text of the ad continued: "We know that a quiet house-to-house canvass is being made among the Republicans in the interests of Peters, in which it is whispered that the Irish are fighting among themselves and now is the time to elect one of our own, meaning a Yankee." It was a stiff dose of the old poison.[93]

On the Sunday before the election Curley made twenty-eight appearances across the city in eight hours. But such prodigies of energy would not help him now. People had ample doubts about whom he would use that energy for—them, or Marks Angell; Boston, or Jim Curley.

On election day, hundreds of Peters voters in the South End fell victim to a Curley trick: they had been mailed cards bearing Peters's signature directing them to the wrong polling places. A Charlestown drunk was released from the Charles Street Jail after serving only a week of a thirty-day sentence on condition that he vote for Curley. There was a near-riot in Martin Lomasney's West End ward as city officials, challenging voters waiting in line, fought with city employees suspected of planning to vote against Curley. Two fistfights broke out in front of City Hall, where a Negro in a tall hat walked up and down all day carrying a sign that said, SHOP EARLY, KEEP TO THE RIGHT, RE-ELECT CURLEY.

At just before five the newsboys came running down School Street shouting "Peters Elected! Peters Elected!" And then, "Curley Out!" Led by a vagrant hope, perhaps, the mayor dropped by the old aldermanic chambers, where the city clerks were writing

the returns up on blackboards. A glance at th the worst. Peters, barely adding to Kenny's to with 39,924 votes; Gallivan, the real spoiler, nonfactor, 1,694; a Socialist candidate, a few 28,850. He had won only six of Boston's twe lost the Jewish vote (Gallivan had introduce the first Hebrew chaplains in the U.S. arme had withdrawn city deposits from a bank o local Jew after he had endorsed Gallivan); vote (Trotter had urged Boston's Negroes to ish Curley for *The Birth of a Nation,* and they his own Jamaica Plain precinct by three to o the poorest Irish districts, which then and ley" despite Curley. He made a brief state have served four years as Mayor with hon to the city"—and when he finished there

Directly, he left City Hall, passing th remembers as "a group of silent men" on h Just as he emerged, a band carrying a rounded the corner. Spying Curley, th Chopin's Funeral March. In the upper flo nex, one of the mayor's supporters who di of the moment disturbed—and who must say that the life of politics was a picket-fe tin pot down on their heads.[94]

Builder and Demagogue

❖ ❖ ❖ ❖

He is the real American type. Ambitious, alert, mind like a razor, confident and aggressive. A bit cold, perhaps. But the average American who has made success in life is usually a ruthless sort of person.

JOHN BANTRY, SPEAKING OF JAMES M. CURLEY

The capacity to distance the ego from misfortune must rank high among the unheralded mechanisms of sanity. Curley had that gift by nature; as Mary Emelda once said of him, he discarded the day's cares with the day. Eddie Shea, his driver, noted the same quality the night of Curley's defeat, when he and Curley reached 350 the Jamaicaway. "When we got out of the car to go into the house," Shea reported, "Curley started whistling. You'd have thought he was the happiest man alive. The boss is no whiner."[1]

The sources of Curley's self-confidence remained inviolate. His Catholicism gave him a bedrock of surety that whatever happened was the verdict of destiny. Thus *he* didn't lose the election: "It was God's will." He may, in addition, have been one of those people who rise so high, so fast from so low that they come to experience their achieved lives as a kind of dream. In this way they deny misfortune the weight of reality. The sometimes admirable fog that used to surround Ronald Reagan—his ability to quip through an assassination attempt, to face cancer surgery with a smile—had this character. As in Mr. Reagan's case, so in Curley's the fog was a joint production; Mary Emelda saw her job as preparing a bower of bliss for her husband to repair to every night. Discussing her role in his career, she once said, "I will be in my husband's home trying to make it what he always calls it, The Place of Rest. I have no other ambition until my children grow up. Then I want to see them successful, God-fearing Americans worthy of being known as James Michael Curley's children. There is nothing else I ask in life." She kept family troubles from him, the better to ensure his ease in the Place of Rest. No wonder he spent the evening of his defeat there, reading "Plutarch's Lives."[2]

"I am a candidate for Governor of Massachusetts," he told the Tammany Club in his annual New Year's address for 1918. "I will meet all comers. My campaign has begun and I do not fear the outcome." His probable opponent, he thought, would be the lieutenant governor of the Commonwealth, Calvin Coolidge, he of the "blackest record of any before the public." This was mighty bold talk from a man who had just been rejected by the voters of his own city and who was held in even less esteem in the small cities and towns outside Boston than he was within it. But what a prospect: Silent Cal versus James Michael Curley. A clash of archetypes, the yin and yang of Massachusetts politics.[3]

Yet one of the shrewdest political commentators of Curley's early to middle period, Clifton B. Carberry, the managing editor of the *Boston Post*, and, under the pen name John Bantry its leading columnist, once played on the likenesses between these twain in a startling conceit.

> Should some keen historian, after an intelligent inquiry, turn the spotlight on the personalities of some of our Massachusetts notables, there is one man of whom he might write the following:
>
> "He was a solitary and lonely man. He had few close friends. He had scant capacity for comradeship because he did not easily make friends. He lacked the incentive to relax and enjoy himself. His political honors came not from the hands of an army of enthusiastic admirers, but from the public, which, not knowing him intimately, has accepted the legendary ideas that have grown up concerning him."
>
> "Ah," you say, "The answer is easy. It's Calvin Coolidge."
>
> No, it isn't. It is James M. Curley.

John Bantry knew Curley well, and he knew men who knew him even better. He says that, "If you ever were seeking a lively companion to complete a party . . . and had to choose between Curley and Coolidge, by all means take Coolidge." Bantry was not Curley's biographer, although Curley fascinated him as a political phenomenon, and he did not provide the evidence that led him to see Calvin Coolidge, that totem of Yankee parsimony (he must have been weaned on a pickle, said Alice Longworth), as a merrier companion than the robustious Irishman. He merely left us with his unballasted conclusion. What are we to make of it?[4]

We are first of all tempted to throw up our biographical hands. Confident, like Dickens, that the smoke would not indict him, James Curley burned most of his private papers a few years before his death—"The thought of going to jail at age eighty after having gone to jail at seventy did not appeal to him," his son remarked. The teller of his life, therefore, must educe the whole of him from the parts of him on the public record. And going by those parts, we would not be led to Bantry's conclusion. Yet Bantry was not a writer to indulge in willful paradox. We must assume that his characterization of Curley caught a truth of selfhood. We must assume that the ten-year-old who was left all but unprotected in the world by the freakish death of his father, the boy-of-all-work in Stephen Gale's drugstore who had no time for sports, the drudge of St. Philip's parish, the lonely teamster, the tireless retail politician, pacing the streets and pounding the doors of Ward 17—we must assume that this bereft child, this solitary young man, was father to the mature politician. We must read much that we cannot document into these sentences of Bantry's: "You have only to look at Curley's strong face to read the story of his life. The thirst for power is there but underneath you can see the deep lines that tell of his struggles and how much they have cost him." For such a man, we must imagine, holding office was a compensation for what his struggles had cost him, a way, perhaps, of healing himself.[5]

Interesting for the unanticipated light it throws on Curley's character, Bantry's comparison of Curley and Coolidge is historically tantalizing. For Curley did not run for governor against Calvin Coolidge in the fall of 1918. Instead he ran for Congress against James Gallivan, who had spoiled his chance of being reelected mayor; and Gallivan, exploiting the inconvenient fact that Curley did not live in the district he sought to represent, defeated him. As for Calvin Coolidge, he was elected governor of Massachusetts in 1918 and, rather like Peter Sellers's character in the movie *Being There*, somnambulated his way to a moment of national fame a year later by doing little more to end the celebrated Boston police strike than to write a single terse sentence after it was over. But that sentence, "There is no right to strike against the public safety, by anybody, anywhere, anytime," captured the imagination of a public that craved order in a time of social upheaval. In 1920 his party put Coolidge on its presidential ticket with Warren Harding. When Harding died, in 1923, he succeeded to the presidency. His career in politics—from the City Council of Northampton, Massachu-setts, to the Massachusetts House, back to Northampton as mayor, on to the state Senate, and then by way of the offices of lieutenant governor, governor, and vice president to the presidency—was, as one historian has written, "a shining example of what inertia could do for a man of patience."[6]

Suppose Curley had been governor during the police strike; or suppose he, not Andrew Peters, had been mayor of Boston? If the strike made the inert Coolidge president, could it have done the same for the molten Curley? Curley buffs love to speculate about that one, though it has a simple answer—no, and certainly not on the Coolidge timetable. Curley belonged to the wrong party. In 1920 the Republican presidential nominee was an amiable nullity— "The times do not require a first-rater," Senator Penrose said of Harding—and his running mate was a caricature out of America's rural past, a man who, on hearing by telephone that he had unex-pectedly been nominated to the nation's second highest office, could turn to his wife and squeeze past the wall of his silence just one word: "Nominated." Yet these men not merely beat the better-qualified Democrats—three-term governor James Cox of Ohio and his running mate Franklin D. Roosevelt—but crushed them, win-ning a higher percentage of the popular vote than any presidential ticket in nearly a hundred years. Reflecting on the meaning of Har-ding's election victory, its chronicler writes, "The election of 1920 still stands as one of the greatest affronts to the democratic process that the American record affords."[7]

The Boston police strike could make a Republican president, not a Democrat. The Democrats were beyond help from a public-ity miracle like the police strike. The Wilson years had made them so unpopular and their internal divisions between North and South, urban and rural, Catholic and Protestant were so profound that it would take more than a miracle to return them to office. It would take a calamity.

In any case, Curley was on the wrong side of the issue. "These men, loyal and true," he said years later of the one thousand po-licemen out of a force of fifteen hundred who struck to raise their prewar wages to match postwar prices, "believed they were vic-tims of gross injustice. I personally believe they were." He also declared that there never would have been a strike if he had been mayor—implying that he would have negotiated a deal with the policemen, which would have pulled the rug out from under history.[8]

At the time, with mobs looting stores and roaming the streets, Curley played politics with the strike. He had his chauffeur drive him downtown, and at the corner of Bromfield and Washington streets, near City Hall, he spoke to a crowd from the running board of his car. Did he ask the people to return to their homes, urge calm, call for compliance with the law? Perhaps. All the record shows, however, is that he lambasted Mayor Andrew Peters, whose ineffectuality in the strike was exceeded only by that of Governor Coolidge, for sailing in the Gulf of Maine when the strike might have been settled. "Then, as if to underline his contempt for Peters," Francis Russell, the historian of the strike, writes, "he ordered his chauffeur to drive the wrong way down one-way Washington Street."[9]

So James Michael Curley was not governor of Massachusetts when the Boston Police went on strike. He was something more improbable yet—a bank president. In 1914, former congressman Joseph O'Connell, one of the original incorporators of the Hibernia Savings Bank, a small local firm, nominated Curley as one of its trustees. In 1919 the bank's president stepped down; hoping his name would prove a magnet for depositors, the trustees picked Curley over O'Connell as the new president. In this hope they were mistaken. Although in the years he was out of office Curley listed his occupation in the Boston City Directory as banker, he "took little interest in the Bank's business," to quote from its official history. "Even though Curley commanded an army of followers," it continues, "the number of accounts opened had increased by only 700" at the end of his twenty years as president.[10]

The bank had an office hard by City Hall, however, and from it Curley conducted a three-year campaign to take back that Victorian confection, which Ed O'Connor would describe as "a lunatic pile of a building: a great, grim, resolutely ugly dust catcher."

Andrew Peters would not be running for reelection in 1921. In his inaugural address, he had promised to submit a bill to the state legislature barring Boston's mayors from succeeding themselves. Seen as directed against Curley, the bill was quickly passed by the Republican-controlled legislature in 1918. Curley could not build a machine at City Hall; the bill killed any chance of that. From then on all he could do was mount the odd raid on it.

The cry of reform had elected Andrew Peters. Business priorities now dictated city spending. Whereas Curley had not increased the budget of the paving department—good roads were businesses' chief demand—Peters increased it by 56 percent. Curley had added an eighty-bed wing to the City Hospital and sharply increased spending for the poor; Peters stopped all hospital expansion and, in the midst of the postwar recession, cut the number of poor receiving aid by a third. Peters opposed the granting of city pensions, broke the union in the city's printing department, and refused wage increases to the poorly paid library employees. And his mulishness in the face of the reasonable demands of the police led to the disaster of the police strike. Nor did his administration write a lustrous chapter in the history of clean government. Personally honest, Peters was too preoccupied with the pursuit of ancestral leisure (sailing, golf) and debauchery (Starr Faithfull) to monitor his appointees, who sold jobs and promotions as if they owned them. His administration gave reform a bad name.[11]

All this must have greatly encouraged the fledgling bank president casting a covetous eye on City Hall. Hard times also helped him. The postwar slump was especially severe in New England, which was now entering a decades-long crisis of economic decline. By the fall of 1921 there were sixty thousand unemployed in Boston alone, and homeless men had taken nocturnal possession of the benches on the Common. These were just the conditions to give dimension to Curley's essentially charismatic appeal.[12]

The reform candidate in 1921 was Peters's fire commissioner and Curley's old antagonist as head of the Finance Commission, John R. Murphy. In appearance a taller version of Theodore Roosevelt, with his smile full of teeth and his dangling pince-nez, Murphy had first won elected office in 1884—a fact Curley would use against him. There were also two minor candidates, Charles O'Connor, a school committeeman from South Boston, and Charles H. Baxter, a Back Bay Republican, but they were no threat. The threat came from the fifth candidate in the race, District Attorney Pelletier. The presence of this popular veteran politician, the Supreme Advocate of the Knights of Columbus, would split the "gang" vote. Unless either Curley or Pelletier dropped out, the pundits were saying, John Murphy would be the next mayor of Boston.[13]

Curley had two secret weapons in the race, however. One of them was Godfrey Lowell Cabot. The other—in this, the first mayoral election held after the Nineteenth Amendment gave women the right to vote—was Mary Emelda Curley.

Cabot had stayed on Pelletier's trail, and now, several judicial proceedings later, he was within reach of his prey. That fall disbarment proceedings against Coakley and Tufts finally got under way, and the Boston papers were full of stories about their entrapment schemes. Cabot had brought similar charges against Pelletier, who awaited a hearing before the Supreme Judicial Court of Massachusetts on his fitness to continue in office. Presenting himself to the electorate as the innocent victim of an anti-Catholic cabal run out of the Union Club, a haunt of the Protestant establishment, Pelletier, a French Irishman, hoped to use ethnic politics to vindicate himself in the election. Much in the Curley manner, he sought to turn legal trouble into political triumph. Perhaps if he won the election he could somehow escape Cabot's grasp. Only Curley stood in his way.[14]

More than Pelletier's political future depended on getting Curley out of the race. Late one evening, less than two weeks before the election, he sent an emissary known to be friendly to Curley to the big house on the Jamaicaway. Curley was still out campaigning, so the emissary delivered his message to Mrs. Curley.

Curley and Pelletier were competing for the same bloc of votes. They would kill each other off—for Murphy's benefit. If her husband lost the election, it would be his third straight defeat; he'd be finished. So ran the emissary's argument.

"Pardon me," she broke in "are you attempting to suggest to me that Mr. Curley should withdraw?"

The emissary admitted as much.

"Please wait here a moment," she said, leaving the room.

Presently she returned— with six little Curleys in tow. Blinking sleep out of their eyes, they gazed wonderingly at the visitor.

"There is your answer," she said, her voice ringing with emotion. "They, and not Mr. Curley, will make the decision. He is fighting for them and not for himself. He could not face these children with a clear conscience if he should betray them by quitting their cause. I know Mr. Curley better than you do and I tell you he will never, never withdraw."[15]

The report of this dramatic colloquy apparently convinced Pelletier that Curley would not get out. Now the race took an electrifying turn.

As election day neared, the rumors that either Pelletier or Curley would withdraw were becoming so insistent that the papers began to call the candidates' headquarters each night just before midnight to make sure they were both still in the race.

On the evening of November 30, one of Curley's press agents, trying to sound confident of victory, made a bold off-the-cuff proposal to a reporter calling to take the temperature of the campaign. He boasted that Curley was willing "to leave it to anyone in Boston who knows anything about the fight" to pick the stronger anti-Murphy candidate.

"Do you mean to say that Curley proposes to leave this thing to arbitration?" the reporter, scarcely believing his ears, put in.

"Sure."

"Will he issue a statement to that effect?"

"Certainly."

"Will you get hold of him and get his statement?"

"Of course."

The press agent hung up the phone—and faced the enormity of what he had done. In two days, the deadline he had agreed to, and if Pelletier concurred, an outside arbitrator would choose which anti-Murphy candidate should stay in the race. He tried to contact Curley to get his approval for this stupendous proposal. But Curley could not be reached. So he called Mrs. Curley.

Would it be sound political strategy to bet everything on this one roll of the dice? he asked.

It was all up to her. She knew that if both men remained candidates her husband would lose, and she knew how much he needed to win. Nature had not shaped him for a bank president, even one who boasted that he never foreclosed on a mortgage. Public office gave him something that neither she nor the children could provide. Dean Acheson once likened losing office to a second death—and he had never won an office to lose. Perhaps Curley, for all his power of oblivion, had undergone something like that after his defeat by Peters; and perhaps she had sensed it, had wanted to help, had finally seen how only the elixir of power could help. It was all up to her.

"Yes," she said.[16]

Curley got in late that night. The first he knew of what Mary had committed him to was when he saw the headlines in the papers the next morning. He nearly fainted. The whole thing had the look of a Pelletier plot—for, the papers reported, Pelletier had accepted Curley's challenge, and had already named an associate to meet with one of Curley's men to pick the arbitrator who would choose between the candidates. Curley had to go through with it. Quickly he named Theodore A. Glynn, one of his old Tammany Club stalwarts, as his negotiator; but he instructed Glynn to make himself scarce, to hide if need be, to do anything to eat up the clock until the deadline had come and gone.

Now began what the *Post* called "the pursuit of Teddy Glynn" as Glynn tried to do Curley's bidding. But Boston being a small city, and Glynn having flaming red hair, he was soon found.

Meeting with Pelletier's representative, Daniel Gallagher, Glynn sought to sabotage the negotiations by naming John Curley as arbitrator. Gallagher rejected him, but startled Glynn by naming someone thought to be strongly pro-Curley—Frederick Enwright, publisher and editor of the *Boston Telegram*, a new morning paper. Glynn could hardly refuse.

Enwright was summoned to a conference of the candidates and their representatives at the Parker House. Pelletier and Curley signed withdrawal statements and handed them to him (Curley later admitted that he had no idea of withdrawing even as he handed Enwright his pledge to do just that). Enwright then retired to another room to hear the arguments of Glynn and Gallagher. Which candidate had the better chance against Murphy? That was the question Enwright was to decide.

About half an hour later he emerged, and with a clutch of reporters following him, walked down the street to the election commissioner's office at City Hall, where he would make his announcement. In the crowded room, he had trouble making himself heard. "Curley is out!" someone shouted—but he was wrong, for Enwright had picked Curley to stay in. "It appeared to me that Curley was the stronger from the point of view of vote-getting," he explained. Pelletier's withdrawal in these extraordinary circumstances was, according to the *Post*, "the biggest bombshell that has exploded in connection with a Boston political contest in years."[7]

In retrospect, sensing that he was more hurt than helped by Cabot's campaign against him, and knowing from his emissary's discussion with Mrs. Curley that Curley would not budge, it seems clear that Pelletier was looking for a graceful way to pull out—or so his nomination of Enwright as arbitrator strongly suggests. Curley couldn't see that, but Mary did.

As the press pieced together her role in the Pelletier withdrawal, she did not seek to play it down. Curley, she remarked, often called her his "eyes of intuition." And she went on, "Do you know I sometimes believe he is right. I warn him at times when we meet a stranger—warn him of this one and that one, all fair spoken and affable, but down in the woman heart of me is a cold feeling at contact with certain ones. Mr. Curley has forced himself to like some of these persons at certain times," she added pointedly—"always to his regret." Wince if you like at the old-timey man-woman dichotomy between head and heart, but these terms were real to Mary Curley. Down in the woman heart of her, she knew what to do.[18]

❖   ❖   ❖

"He deliberately cheapens himself in a campaign," John Bantry wrote of Curley. It is tantamount to picking the most disappointing Red Sox team ever, but nowhere was this truer than in his brief campaign against John Murphy.[19]

Curley attacked from two directions—he stabbed Murphy in the front, and then stabbed him in the back. In the frontal approach, he dredged up some yellowing history. "I am amazed at the audacity of John R. Murphy seeking the votes of the Democrats of Boston," he declared. "Why, he betrayed Patrick Collins, Boston's greatest Democrat." This was an allusion to the mayoral race of 1900, in which Murphy challenged Collins in a primary, weakening him sufficiently so that a Republican, Thomas Hart, could defeat him in the general election. "He did his utmost to keep the great Bostonian from the office of Mayor," Curley said of Murphy. "Shame on him!"

There was, in fact, shame to go around. For as Bantry, whose memory of Boston politics had no bottom, recalled in one of his columns, when Curley had been a Murphy delegate at the Democratic city convention, he "was one of the most loyal men in the city to the Murphy cause" in the primary, and in the fall campaign his ward gave Collins a culpably narrow margin of victory—why, there were even grounds to suspect that Curley himself had voted for Hart.[20]

That dog would not hunt. So Curley made much of Murphy's age, sixty-five, calling him "that venerable old man" and "that youthful reformer whose proud privilege it was to witness the de-

owners of Boston's twenty-six theaters on notice that if they wanted their licenses renewed they had better show his films. Speaking to a Negro audience, Gallivan charged that D. W. Griffith had sneaked back to Boston to wield the camera for his old friend.[92]

Through a surrogate, Curley raised the "race issue" against Peters, whom he often identified as "my only opponent," in hopes of polarizing the contest on ethnic grounds. In *The Hibernian*, edited by a political ally, there appeared a full-page political ad with a cutout of Curley:

RE-ELECT JAMES M. CURLEY, MAYOR.
Do not be deceived by false issues.
The Peters Issue Is—Down with the Irish.
The Good Government Issue Is—Down with the Irish.

The text of the ad continued: "We know that a quiet house-to-house canvass is being made among the Republicans in the interests of Peters, in which it is whispered that the Irish are fighting among themselves and now is the time to elect one of our own, meaning a Yankee." It was a stiff dose of the old poison.[93]

On the Sunday before the election Curley made twenty-eight appearances across the city in eight hours. But such prodigies of energy would not help him now. People had ample doubts about whom he would use that energy for—them, or Marks Angell; Boston, or Jim Curley.

On election day, hundreds of Peters voters in the South End fell victim to a Curley trick: they had been mailed cards bearing Peters's signature directing them to the wrong polling places. A Charlestown drunk was released from the Charles Street Jail after serving only a week of a thirty-day sentence on condition that he vote for Curley. There was a near-riot in Martin Lomasney's West End ward as city officials, challenging voters waiting in line, fought with city employees suspected of planning to vote against Curley. Two fistfights broke out in front of City Hall, where a Negro in a tall hat walked up and down all day carrying a sign that said, SHOP EARLY, KEEP TO THE RIGHT, RE-ELECT CURLEY.

At just before five the newsboys came running down School Street shouting "Peters Elected! Peters Elected!" And then, "Curley Out!" Led by a vagrant hope, perhaps, the mayor dropped by the old aldermanic chambers, where the city clerks were writing the returns up on blackboards. A glance at the numbers confirmed the worst. Peters, barely adding to Kenny's total in 1914, wound up with 39,924 votes; Gallivan, the real spoiler, got 19,415; Tague, a nonfactor, 1,694; a Socialist candidate, a few hundred; and Curley, 28,850. He had won only six of Boston's twenty-six wards. He had lost the Jewish vote (Gallivan had introduced a bill providing for the first Hebrew chaplains in the U.S. armed forces, and Curley had withdrawn city deposits from a bank owned by a prominent local Jew after he had endorsed Gallivan); he had lost the Negro vote (Trotter had urged Boston's Negroes to vote for Peters to punish Curley for *The Birth of a Nation,* and they had); he had even lost his own Jamaica Plain precinct by three to one. He had carried only the poorest Irish districts, which then and later were "with Curley" despite Curley. He made a brief statement to the clerks—"I have served four years as Mayor with honor to myself and benefit to the city"—and when he finished there was no applause.

Directly, he left City Hall, passing through what one witness remembers as "a group of silent men" on his way out the rear door. Just as he emerged, a band carrying a PETERS FOR MAYOR banner rounded the corner. Spying Curley, the bandsmen struck up Chopin's Funeral March. In the upper floors of the City Hall Annex, one of the mayor's supporters who did not want the solemnity of the moment disturbed—and who must never have heard Curley say that the life of politics was a picket-fence existence—hurled a tin pot down on their heads.[94]

6

Builder
and
Demagogue

parture of Massachusetts soldiers answering the call of Abraham Lincoln at the outbreak of the Civil War." Curley knew no one believed these stories, his longtime friend Dan Gillen once told an interviewer; but people came to his rallies expecting to be entertained, and between the displays of "red fire," the performances of jazz music, the hecklers planted and real, and the sallies at Murphy ("To compare Murphy with Teddy Roosevelt is to compare a cootie with an elephant"), they rarely went home disappointed.[21]

According to Francis Curley, Mary warned Curley to keep his tongue off personalities and stick to the issues. She made it a point to attend as many of his rallies as she could, and if he was on to personalities she would signal her displeasure in unmistakable terms. Sitting on the side of the stage, she would slowly begin to take off her long white twelve-button leather gloves. If that didn't get his attention, she would snap the gloves from hand to hand. One night even that didn't work—Curley must have been milking too many laughs from the infirmities of John Murphy—so she walked across the stage to the podium, slapped him across the face with the gloves, and said, "Stick to the issues, James." She told Francis that when his father recovered himself, he strode over to her seat, took her in his arms, and kissed her—and that the audience loved it.[22]

So much for Murphy's front. Turning to his back, Curley had "poison gas squads" play dirty tricks on him. Rumors were circulated that Murphy was planning to divorce his wife of decades and run off with a sixteen-year-old girl, that he was really a Thirty-third Degree Mason, and that he had been seen eating a steak one Friday noon at the Copley-Plaza. Murphy's former campaign manager, Francis McLaughlin, now with Curley, made damaging insinuations about his erstwhile friend.

"Sir, may I ask you a question?" a plant from the audience would ask McLaughlin at rallies. "We all know you know Murphy better than anyone else. Is it really true he has left our church?"

"Brother," McLaughlin would reply, "it grieves me to have to tell you and all you other wonderful citizens here tonight that this charge is true. John R. Murphy has departed from our midst and has joined the infidel. He has become an Episcopalian." God's frozen people were not much esteemed by the Boston Irish.

Curley supporters in clerical garb walked about the city carrying on loud conversations about Murphy's dietary and other apostasies. In his autobiography, Curley says that one group of young people from his camp, posing as members of the Hawes Baptist Club, canvassed South Boston for Murphy. "And, unfortunately, this 'Baptist' endorsement in many cases proved to be the kiss of death for poor John." He also claims that he slipped $2,000 to "a man active in Ku Klux Klan activities" to influence the pastor of the Park Street Congregational Church to denounce Curley from the pulpit. The idea was to stir up "sympathy votes" from Catholics, who, if they had known he was consorting with a Klansman—one called "the Black Pope," at that—would have abandoned him forever. Like other stories in his autobiography, this one seems too bad to be true. For as we have seen, Protestant ministers did not need financial incentives to attack Curley, who, with a view to boosting sales of his book, may have been trying to make himself out to be worse than he was.[23]

Neither sort of stabbing was as politically effective, however, as Curley's constant identification of Murphy as the "reform candidate" and "the candidate of the reformers." The same forces that backed Peters were behind Murphy—the Good Government Association, the downtown businessmen, the big property owners. From their point of view, he had been a good mayor. But had he been a good mayor for the plain people of Boston? Curley could blame the postwar economic slump on his old antagonist: "Four more years of reform such as we have had," he told a noontime rally downtown, "and citizens of Boston can journey through Pemberton Sq. and observe grass growing up through the granolithic sidewalks." Moreover, "reform" had a malign historical association for the Boston Irish—one that had recently been refreshed.

By 1921 the country was in the second year of a reform forced down the throats, as it were, of urban populations by rural yahoos who, in both religion and rhetoric, were kin to the Know-Nothings. In the 1920 census the city eclipsed the country as the main locus of the American population (as in 1990 the suburb eclipsed the city), but the country had its revenge by fastening on the city the noble experiment of Prohibition, "a ludicrous caricature of the reforming impulse, of the Yankee Protestant notion that it is both possible and desirable to moralize private life through public action," to quote Richard Hofstadter. Labels matter in politics. George Bush defeated Michael Dukakis in 1988 by branding him a "liberal." To many thirsty Bostonians in 1921, "reformer" had just that fatal ring.[24]

Murphy may have been fighting the local zeitgeist, but he had a powerful issue to use against Curley—Curley, "the most brutal, selfish, and arrogant man that was ever chosen Mayor of Boston." Who that had lived through his first term could doubt that? "It is beyond the power of man in one night to take up the shortcomings of Mayor Curley," he told a crowd in his home ward, showing a Curleyesque rhetorical flair. "You would have to go on like the brook forever to do justice to the subject."

In a series of effective speeches, he delineated "two Curleys":

> There is the Curley who gives coffee to firemen fighting fires on the eve of an election. There is the Curley who cuts their salaries after the election.
>
> There is the Curley who says he is the persecutor of the rich and the friend of the poor. And there is the Curley who abandons them, hies himself to fashionable Jamaica Plain and ensconces himself in the $60,000 mansion of the Flemish tapestries and the gorgeous fixings. . . .
>
> There is the Curley who declares himself the friend of the colored people. And there is the Curley who allows their race to be slandered on the screen by "Birth of a Nation," the photoplay conceived in the hatred of Tom Dixon, their most bitter enemy. . . .
>
> What is Curleyism? Curleyism is the desertion of friends, the breaking of promises, and the forming of vicious alliances with scheming contractors and unscrupulous bonding gangs, and which now rears its ugly head again.[25]

Next to Curley's persiflage, this was real substance: Murphy was tearing the mask off Curley and his "ism."

Martin Lomasney, Murphy's longtime champion, was even more scathing. His bitterness toward Curley had been heated past the boil by his brother Joseph's decision to join the Curley campaign. Lomasney was by then a lonely old man. For years he had shared his house—his life—with his brother. Now "conceited, cruel, cowardly Curley" had come between them. In his election eve address to his followers at the Hendricks Club, Lomasney drew out the scene of John Murphy, in his capacity as head of the Finance Commission, pleading with District Attorney Pelletier to indict Curley: "Do your duty. He is no better than the man who steals a can of milk or steals a loaf of bread. Prosecute Curley." But Pelletier only "shook his head," and the "serpent" Curley slithered away.[26]

The hatred between the two camps spilled out into the streets. A mob of Curley toughs shouting "Goo Goo, Goo Goo" drowned out a speech by Murphy in Jamaica Plain, surrounded his car, and tried to assault him. Curley says he had to knock down a man who collared him at an event in Charlestown. At another rally, when a man shouted out, "I'd never vote for you, Curley, because you'd steal the gold out of the teeth of the poor," Curley, so he told his son, was ready for him: "And why not, sir? I put it there in the first place." He had no retort to a heckler at a mass meeting near Calvary Cemetery in Roslindale. When he mentioned that both of his parents were buried there (earlier in the year Sarah had fallen down dead while hanging out the wash in John Curley's backyard) a cruel fellow in the audience broke in, "Yes, and we'll bury you here, too, Jim. Wait for those election returns."[27]

On election night, while the returns were being chalked up on the blackboard in front of City Hall, there were cheers and moans from the crowd as the tight race tilted this way and that. The last precincts to report in were from the Tammany ward (now Ward 12) and Murphy's Ward 4 in Charlestown. Curley won them both—his own base and Murphy's—and that gave him a narrow victory. Murphy got 71,562 votes, Curley 74,260, a plurality of only 2,698 votes. Between them, the two other candidates garnered 15,000 votes, with the Republican Baxter's 4,260 being enough to elect Murphy, who charged that Baxter was a Curley plant. Curley issued a snappy denial—"Murphy said a few days ago that he was about to lose his temper. Now he's lost his mind"—but the charge is eminently plausible.[28]

However Curley had done it, he had won. The *Herald* grudgingly saluted "the greatest upset in the history of the city," one accomplished "without the assistance of a single political leader of either party, and with every machine of recognized standing against him." The *Post* hailed "the greatest personal triumph ever achieved by a man in the history of Boston politics," adding with greater justice, "It was an even greater triumph for one woman— Mrs. James M. Curley."[29]

Thumping conclusions about the temper of Boston cannot be drawn from such a close race. Still, the question is unavoidable: given his mottled record in his first term, why did Curley win a second? This wasn't 1914; the voters were not choosing in the dark. They knew what to expect from Curley. So, why?

Because, for enough voters to make the difference, Curley was a rational choice. Boston derived the chief part of its revenue from property taxes. But Boston was not then—with a home ownership rate of 31 percent, it is not now—a city of property owners. It was a city of renters: by 1929 an estimated four out of five Bostonians lived in rental housing. Aside from the small share of their state income tax that was redirected to Boston as local aid, its citizens were not paying for their municipal government. A minority of property owners, personal and commercial, were. In this respect, Boston was a smaller Louisiana, another venue notorious for the baroque corruption of its politics. Wayne Parent, a political science professor at Louisiana State University, recently told the *New York Times*, "Up until 15 years ago, Louisiana had a government that was funded by the oil companies, not the people of the state. So the government and the politicians could be less accountable. It wasn't Louisiana's money. It was Texaco's money. So what if they were playing around with it?"

The money Curley played around with likewise was not that of the average Bostonian. At the same time, the money he spent on public works projects employed many, and many more used the health and recreation facilities he built and the other facilities he expanded or improved. For voters of a certain income, therefore, Curley was truly a Robin Hood mayor. Once when a reporter called him a "two-fisted thief" to his face, he smiled and said, "I never took a quarter from anyone who couldn't afford it," which if far from the whole truth—rising taxes on commercial property squeezed out jobs, and even the poorest resident paid state income taxes, a portion of which was returned to the mayor to disburse—was at any rate close enough to be an article of faith among many Curley voters.[30]

A cartoon by Norman of the *Post* shows Curley entering City Hall with one eye fixed on the State House, where "The Beacon Hill Vamp" is making eyes at him from the governor's office. Norman has him saying, "I may not serve my term out here—the people will demand that I go up there as Governor!" Norman was depicting Curley's political challenge: the term limitation law would force him either to move up or out at the end of his term. And the casual arrogance Norman imputed to Curley was no exaggeration. At a Knights of Columbus banquet in his honor several days later, when a speaker predicted that he would someday run for governor and senator,

Curley responded, "I have no desire for the office of United States Senator. At the same time, when the proper time comes (about three years from now) if my friends stand by me and my enemies are not too numerous, I will attain the office you have conferred upon me, that of Governor of Mass." Television would have soon ended the career of a politician who spoke of his ambitions ("I will attain . . . ") with such naked Napoleonic hauteur.[31]

During his inauguration, held before a crowd of ten thousand at Mechanics Hall, a phone rang in a booth just offstage. A policeman had to answer it to stop the ringing. "Will you please tell Mayor Curley," a voice at the other end said, "that I voted for him and my wife voted for him and I would like to be appointed—" at which the policeman hung up. Voters like that caller would not be disappointed with the new administration.[32]

While the state under Old Guard Republicans and the country under Harding and Coolidge turned right, Boston under Curley turned left. "My conception of municipal administration, or state administration, or federal administration," he said, "is not the hoarding of money but the expenditure of public dollars in such an economic and efficient manner as results in the greatest measure of health, happiness and prosperity of the people. I appreciate that this is not the most popular doctrine at the present time, but I believe it is sound and will ultimately be so regarded." As Michael Kendall has written, this was "the administrative outlook that a decade later would become the accepted fashion of the New Deal."[33]

Boston's new deal took the form of a building boom. Curley committed the city to an $11 million improvement program for the City Hospital, including funds for the construction of research labs, a gynecological and obstetrics wing, and outpatient facilities. "Partly as a result," Kendall points out, "the city enjoyed its lowest death rates in typhoid, childbirth complications, tuberculosis, and diarrhea" in years. He quotes Curley as saying that he "was always of the opinion that tuberculosis was an economic disease, rather than a medical one."

In school building Curley outspent Peters by $4 million. The new schools enabled the School Department to dispense with portable units, to end double sessions, and to decrease the number of children in the average classroom by one-third. Curley completed the Strandway in South Boston, spent $3 million on the refurbishing of city buildings, razed more than two thousand slum dwellings, opened twelve new parks, added three separate subway extensions, rebuilt bridges, cleared mudflats for beaches and bathhouses, and widened major streets. To provide the muscle to perform this work, he established a Municipal Employment Bureau, which put unemployed ex-soldiers on the city payroll while cutting the relief budget dramatically.

Under Teddy Glynn, the new fire commissioner (he had been a protégé of Mary Parker Follett's at the Highland Union settlement house), Boston adopted the two-platoon system, which allowed firemen to spend more time with their families. This humane note marked the whole administration. Curley reinstituted the unions Peters had abolished, granted pensions to the city's lowest paid workers, and, a decade before Social Security, spoke out for a universal old-age pension: "If the ferocity of the struggle for existence is of such a character that the majority of those who arrive at sixty-five years face the poorhouse, then it is time something was done." And more: "I want to see in my country a new planning board that will see to it that economic justice is done to all men," he said in a speech delivered in 1922. "Economic justice": the phrase was as heretical in the 1920s ("the policy of the Harding administration was to do with alacrity whatever business wanted to have done," writes one historian) as it is would be in the 1980s.[34]

To fund his new deal, Curley borrowed beyond the debt limit and raised the assessed valuations on businesses, especially newspapers. Altogether, valuations went up 13 percent in his term. Making business pay made political sense. But in the long run it was injurious to the Boston economy. Consider the case of Young's Hotel. In 1933 the building formerly occupied by the hotel behind City Hall was assessed at $1.3 million. It was offered to the city for $700,000, but the Finance Commission said it was worth only $200,000. So the owners of a building worth $200,000 had to pay taxes on a valuation six times as high. Many of the other commercial buildings in Boston were owned by family trusts and did not have to pay their way on their rents; the trust would pay any taxes owed whether the buildings earned them or not. Raising assessments on owners under no commercial imperative was a temptation Curley rarely resisted. Property owners had the right to appeal for abatements on their assessments, but they had to pay for them; typically, 30 to 50 percent of any abatement they received would go to a group of political lawyers with the right connections. This "abatement racket," as it would be called by the late 1940s, kept businesses from locating in Boston and stunted the growth of the businesses already there. The time would come, several doses of Curleyism on, when businesses would cut the top floors off their buildings to lower their assessments. Along with the hospitals, parks, playgrounds, beaches and schools, this act of economic cannibalism was one of the legacies of Curleyism.

Curley was right to build, right to pay city employees decent wages, right to put the unemployed to work on Boston's infrastructure, right to champion activist government, right to call for economic justice. But he was wrong to make only one segment of the community pay the bills. He should have had the economic understanding and the political courage to tax all Bostonians to pay for what would benefit all Bostonians.[35]

Forty-eight years old in 1922, Curley was in the high summer of his life. He had thickened considerably, though he had the pigeon breast to carry his weight. His face, under silver-streaked black hair, was the mirror of strength, firmness, will to power. As he ran City Hall, so he held undisputed sway in the Place of Rest. Arriving around six, he would repair to the cozy library off the front hall, where, one by one, the children trooped in to tell him of the day's adventures. As he listened he would slice a gout of Mayo cut plug tobacco from the stock he kept in his humidor and fill the bowl of one of his hand-carved meerschaum pipes. Soon the room would float in the tannic fragrance.

Around six-thirty a maid would bring him a stiff bracer—a double shot of whiskey. He would have his drink, disengage himself from the children (anything is possible with domestic help), and mount his grand staircase to his bedroom for his evening nap. He could sleep at need and in timed intervals: thirty minutes later, he would wake up and descend the stairs, announcing to all old enough to come that dinner was about to be served.

Once at a restaurant, when a waiter put a baby lobster before him, he ordered it to be removed. "Take that away and put it on a Ritz cracker and serve it as a canapé," he said. "I want a four-pounder." He was a trencherman; shrimp cocktails, rich soups, fancy sauces—he wanted the best, and the most. Once a week the family had his favorite dish: curried chicken with Major Grey's chutney. Thick broiled porterhouse steak smothered in anchovies dripping in olive oil was another favorite, as was lobster Newburg. Who could be surprised to learn that Richard Nixon actually liked cottage cheese laced with ketchup? The mean fare expressed the man. Curley's love of the table expressed his delight in his ambition. He wanted to eat his status, dress it, drive it, live in it. John Bantry, with his celebrated comparison of Curley and Coolidge—whose home was a rented apartment in a two-family house right up to the time he became vice president—had never dined at 350 the Jamaicaway.

In Curley's congressional years, fearing for the childrens' health in the sweltering Washington summer, Mary had moved back with them to Boston a little over a year before Curley ran for mayor. He commuted by train on weekends..Ten hours up, ten hours back, he spent the time reading. From that period, as well as from his sixty days in jail, flowed his literary culture. Shakespeare, Victor Hugo, Dickens, Dumas, and Kipling were among his favorite authors. As the children grew older, no dinner was complete without Curley reading from one of these masters, peering over his reading glasses or pausing admonitorily at any sign of inattention or restlessness. *Antony and Cleopatra* was his favorite play, and Cleopatra's line as she puts the asp to her breast—"Husband, I come to thee"—his favorite line, but he had read the whole of Shakespeare, including obscure works like *Troilus and Cressida* and *Timon of Athens,* and he could recite passages from memory without pause and sometimes without pretext or prompting. The family would listen, awestruck or bored, until he subsided.

He read for delight in language, for literary pleasure, not for moral instruction. The Catholic church told him how to live, and what life was for; he did not need to learn that from books.

He was an indulgent parent, within sometimes capricious limits. When he noticed his daughter Mary slumping, he would correct her. "Mary, you are not going to get any shorter than you are. Take advantage of what God has given you. Get rid of those sneakers and start wearing high heels. Pile your hair up in a pompadour and come into a room six feet tall and dominate it." When Leo, perhaps nine or ten, called someone a "louse" at dinner, he was sent to his room. Such language was not tolerated. Besides, as Curley explained to the rest of the children, the word was no metaphor to him. As a boy his mother had had to pick lice out of his hair many times, a memory of shame.

He could be equally strict about the language of his guests—Babe Ruth, for example. During Curley's first term, when Ruth was still a member of the Red Sox, and with Mrs. Curley, Mary, James Jr., and Dorothea seated at the dinner table, Ruth, feeling at his ease, was Ruth. "That's a lot of bullshit, Mr. Mayor," he said of some observation of Curley's. There was a train wreck in the conversation. Curley stood up. "Mr. Ruth, you do not use language like that in my house, and especially in front of the women in my family. You are to leave the house immediately. Now get out!" Family apocrypha? Perhaps. But Curley and Ruth did have a long-standing friendship. In 1935 Governor Curley was instrumental in bringing the Babe back to Boston for his last season, with the Braves. And, along with Ed Sullivan, Walter Winchell, Jack Dempsey, William Bendix, Bobby Jones, Westbrook Pegler, and Thomas E. Dewey, James M. Curley was one of the honorary pallbearers at Ruth's funeral in 1948.

Frank Curley, who was born in 1923, says that his father struck him only once—and that was over Frank's use of a demotic endearment. When Frank was a small boy it was his pleasure to sit at the side entrance to the house and wait for his father's big car to turn up the driveway. On this evening when the car appeared and his father opened the door, Frank burst out with "Hi, Dad!"; and Curley slapped him lightly across the face, knocking him down on the Persian rug. "I am your *father* and don't ever forget it, boy!" he exclaimed, and stepped over Frank's recumbent form on his way to the library.

He emerged about half an hour later. Frank was still crying. His anger abated, Curley gently but without a shadow of contrition explained that a child had to respect his father. He was to be called "Father" as a general is to be called "General." "I will not have a word like 'Dad' introduced into my house." Frank tried to explain. He didn't think there was anything wrong with the word; he had simply picked it up from some of the children at school. "They're shanty Irish," Curley replied, in a tone that indicated this was his last word on the subject. "If they wish to allow such things in their homes, that is their business."[36]

The "shanty Irish," as distinct from the "lace-curtain Irish," the "venetian-blind Irish," and those Celtic Rockefellers, the "two-toilet Irish," were Curley followers to the bone. What would they have made of such snobbery? We begin to see that the Place of Rest was also a House of Dreams, where Curley could escape his past.

The past was a memory of pain and deprivation; and for all that Curley used it politically, he was also ashamed of it. Or so one is led to surmise by his strenuous affectations of gentility. Sometimes, though, the past would out, and he would pronounce a culturally redoubtable name as if—which was very likely—he had never heard it said before. Thus William Butler Yeats might emerge as "Yeets." But quickly Curley would sense the gaffe, and his face would assume a mask of dignity. Self-taught, he lacked cultural patina. That is why he strove assiduously to create and maintain an unassailably proper appearance. Sixty years after he lived among them, Francis Curley could remember the brand names of his father's crystal and plate, which no boy would know unless his parents made much of them, and no parent would do unless having them conferred respectability.

Nor would his conscience sting him in the House of Dreams. Mary could count; she knew he earned $10,000 a year, the official salary of the mayor of Boston, but spent ten times that. She was a good Catholic woman. Yet she lived with a man who habitually took money to which he had no legal or moral right. He once rationalized his graft to his son by saying that if a man who wanted a license to open a bar gave him a few thousand dollars—without being asked to, a casuistical stipulation—he would return the money if he could not do the favor. The money was in payment for services rendered. No services, no money. Where was the harm in that? He did not add that the converse was also true: no money, no services. Or that his salary—exactly twice what my own father earned when he retired from his job in 1961, and with which, by denying himself and my mother every *material* pleasure, he managed to feed and house and educate four children—was supposed to compensate him for his services.

Mary prayed for him. But she also wore the jewelry he bought for her, the diamond pendants and pearl necklaces; she shared his collection of precious jade; she enjoyed their stays in Palm Beach, Bermuda, and Cuba; she walked on the fine rugs he bought; she drank from their exquisite Jensen goblets; and she had the services of cooks and maids and nurses and governesses; thanks to the money he got for the services he rendered.

The point is, the wives of powerful men get pulled along,

get caught up in their husbands' ambitions. They share in what the powerful man achieves, and they share the guilt of what the powerful man must do to achieve it. The process, as Tony Coelho says, "buys you out."[37]

There were six children now—James, Mary, and Dorothea had been joined by Paul in 1913, by Leo in 1915, by George in 1919, and finally by Francis. Twin boys—John and Joseph—had died in infancy in 1922. That dark spot and Sarah's more timely death aside, these were happy years for the Curleys. It would never be this good for them again.

Summers in the twenties the Curleys rented a big sprawling fifteen-room house on the beach in Hull. There was a tennis court for the children. Nearby was Nantasket Beach, with its increasingly fabulous amusement park. Curley came down from the city in his chauffeured limousine on Friday afternoons, and the family would have wonderfully simple Saturday night meals together. Curley would take one or another of the children with him to gather clams on the tidal flats and catch fish in the bay. Mary would crush the leaves of young dandelions to make dandelion wine. And the cook would prepare a clam chowder and fish dinner for them— topped off by the dandelion wine.

Herbert Warren Wind, the distinguished *New Yorker* sports writer, was a neighbor of the Curleys' in Hull, and he presents a different portrait of Curley from the one drawn by John Bantry. He recalls how "Mayor Curley's presence irradiated the monotony of the summer with a helpful splash of glamour." Curley would launch the season with a Fourth of July fireworks display, prepared by City of Boston workers, from his lawn. For their additional entertainment, he would hire a hurdy-gurdy man with a monkey to play not just one or two tunes but on the Curley scale, for one or two hours. Then there were the Jay Gatsby dinners the Curleys would occasionally give. "The guests would arrive in the biggest, sleekest cars of the era," Wind remembers, "and each Marmion or Peerless required long and appreciative study from us and a drawn out consultation with its chauffeur. Sometimes, when someone came in a Rolls-Royce, our loyalty was pushed close to the breaking point, but we always managed to conclude that no car was quite in a class with Mayor Curley's own Pierce-Arrow. . . ."

Most of all, there was the pleasure of the mayor's company and the "zest and ubiquity of his interest—particularly in the world of sport." After dinner, Curley would hold forth for his children and their friends while smoking a big cigar in a comfortable wicker chair on his wide screened-in veranda. He talked of books and movies, but mostly, and most memorably, he talked of sports. As the bugs planged against the screens and the waves broke on the beach, the children would listen to him tell of Louis ("Chief") Sockalexis, the "full-blooded Penobscot Indian who played the outfield for the old Cleveland National League team"; of Heinie Groh and his bottle bat; of Jim Thorpe and his Carlisle Indians and of how they had beaten mighty Harvard by tucking the football beneath one of their player's jerseys; of the gilded exploits of figures with "good mouth-filling" names like Paavo Nurmi or Adolf Luque or Paulino Uzcudun. Curley's favorite name of all, however, was Eppa Jeptha Rixey, a pitcher for the Reds. "'He is a superb control pitcher, this Eppa Jeptha Rixey, and you must tell your father to take you to the ball park when Cincinnati next comes to town, so you can see Eppa . . . Jeptha . . . Rixey'—this last intoned oratorically like a man reading the inscription on an important Roman ruin."[38]

Occasionally someone would bring an accordion and the family would walk out on the beach and build a fire. Sitting around it, they sang and told stories and dreamt against the gathering night of even better times to come.

❖   ❖   ❖

The year 1924 was the worst possible year and Massachusetts the worst state for a politician of Curley's views to run for statewide office. The year belonged to the Republicans—and to Calvin Coolidge.

Coolidge had become president the summer before, following Harding's death in office, in pace with the end of the postwar slump and the beginning of the "Coolidge prosperity"; in 1924 he was running for election in his own right. Respected across the country for the integrity he brought to an administration that looked back to Grant's and ahead to Nixon's for its only rivals in improbity, popular for his reassuring cracker-barrel character, and admired for his pithy conservative views ("the business of America is business"), Coolidge, as his secretary of state, Charles Evans Hughes, said, was the only issue in the presidential election. In Massachusetts, the president's adopted state, the Coolidge name retained such magic that, in the September primaries, his Northampton cobbler won the Republican nomination for state representative on the strength of his celebrity as a Coolidge confidant.[39]

Before the Republican national convention, to be held at Cleveland, Coolidge pushed aside Henry Cabot Lodge, who as chairman of the 1920 convention had made a rankling remark about Coolidge—"No man who lives in a two-family house is going to be President"—and replaced him with an enemy of Lodge's, William M. Butler, a Massachusetts industrialist. Spitefully, Coolidge and Butler then froze the senator out of the convention. He went to Cleveland but, spurned by the Coolidge-controlled Massachusetts delegation, spent the time in his hotel room, reading his favorite green-leather volume of Shakespeare. Accompanying him was his grandson and namesake, Henry Cabot Lodge, Jr., who was covering the convention as a reporter for the *Boston Evening Transcript*. Young Lodge was furious at his grandfather's rejection by the party he had served so long and so stoutly, but the Old Senator, months short of his death, was taking it equably. "I still remember him," the younger Lodge later wrote, "lying calmly in his blue-and-white striped pajamas, smiling and turning back to Shakespeare." He was reading thus when a telegram arrived from Mayor Curley.

Curley had been nearly as angry as young Lodge at the Old Senator's treatment, and he did not let his former antagonism over the issue of immigration impede the flow of his feelings. "My Dear Senator Lodge," he wrote. "Pray do not permit the inhospitality of the Republican bosses at Cleveland to cause you great uneasiness. Your votes in favor of the soldiers' bonus . . . and of salary increases for post office workers merited the approval of patriotic citizens of Boston. At their request, I am forwarding to you a key to the city, under separate cover. Regardless of the attitude of the Republican bosses . . . you will experience neither hostility nor coldness when you reenter the gates of our fair city. . . ."[40]

Up or out: Curley had no choice but to buck the Coolidge tide and run for governor in that inauspicious year for Democrats. To the tune of "Mr. Gallagher and Mr. Shehan," his campaign song projected a soaring confidence:

Oh, Mayor Curley, Mayor Curley,
You are the man the people want on Beacon Hill,

Time has passed for secrecy; you must restore Democracy,
Massachusetts calls you forth in '24.
Oh Governor Curley, Oh Governor Curley,
By that name you will soon win future esteem.
The cost of living has gone so high, that we must turn to you and cry,
Positively, Mr. Curley, you are absolutely commandeered.

Forget Coolidge; forget that his Democratic opponent, John W. Davis, a Wall Street lawyer, was trying to out-Coolidge Coolidge on the stump by calling for even steeper tax cuts for business; and just consider the political demography of the Bay State—you could not flatly declare that Massachusetts was as safely Republican as, with rare interruptions, it had been since the Civil War. For one thing, 94.8 percent of the state's population lived in areas classified as urban; Massachusetts was second in this respect only to Rhode Island. For another, 66.8 percent of its residents were either immigrants or the children of immigrants. The Irish bulked large among them, but there were concentrations of what Curley termed the "newer races"—that is, newer to America—all across the state. There were Poles in the mill towns along the Connecticut River, Greeks around Worcester, Portuguese fishermen and textile operatives in New Bedford and Fall River, French Canadians in Lawrence and Lowell, Italians and Jews, Syrians and Lithuanians in Boston. These groups made up the swing vote in state elections between the Irish Democrats in the cities and the old-stock Yankee Republicans in the towns. In the past intrareligious friction— among French Catholics, Irish Catholics, Italian Catholics—and cultural antipathies had kept these "newer races" from making common cause with the Irish Democracy, but the "100 percent Americanism" of the national Republican party, the rise of the Ku Klux Klan, and the passage of the anti-immigration acts had made them aware of the powerful enemies they shared. Recently they had come together in efforts to keep Catholic schools free from state control and to protest Harvard University's attempts to exclude Jews and blacks. The Democrats hoped they would come together again to reelect Senator David I. Walsh (who had captured the seat in 1918) and to elect James M. Curley as governor.[41]

Wisely, Curley and Walsh ignored Davis, who in any case had conceded the state to Coolidge. Wisely, the Democrats nominated a French Canadian and a Jew for two of the lesser constitutional offices. Even more wisely, Curley's Republican opponent, Alvan T. Fuller, the lieutenant governor of Massachusetts, draped himself in the sacred cause of Coolidge, who, in keeping with the inertia that had carried him so far, stayed in the White House throughout the campaign.

It was Curley's most depressing race, not because he lost— that was a foregone conclusion in 1924—but for his handling of the issues of child labor and the Ku Klux Klan.

The Massachusetts ballot that year contained an "advisory referendum" on a proposed federal constitutional amendment banning child labor. If the citizens of Massachusetts voted yes on the referendum, the state legislature would thereby be instructed to ratify the amendment itself. The Child Labor Amendment had been introduced by Senator Thomas J. Walsh, a Montana Democrat and a Catholic. "Nationwide Catholic opinion on the question was divided," the historian James M. O'Toole writes, "although it generally leaned more in the direction of tighter child labor laws." But in Boston, Cardinal O'Connell was strongly opposed to the amendment. As a child he had once taken a summer job in a Lowell textile mill, and in his autobiography gives a hellish account of his experience: "I began to feel faint from the disgusting smell of the oil, whose vapor filled the atmosphere of the room. I looked around me and saw my boyish companions, who at that moment looked to me like shriveled old men. . . . The stench of ammonia that rose from the chemical room near-by made my eyes run water and almost stifled my breath. I suddenly felt a weakness as if I were about to faint." He quit at noon, and never returned.

In the years since, however, partly through inheritance, partly through the contributions of his flock, O'Connell had become a wealthy man. His great house in Brighton boasted a private golf course; he summered at an oceanside estate in Marblehead, wintered in the Caribbean, and carried a gold-knobbed cane. His social circle was made up of other wealthy men, some of them the owners of great mills, where the law still permitted children who could not quit at noon to sweat their guts out. Besides, he looked with the familiar ingrained ethnic suspicion on reform of any sort, especially one, like the ban on child labor, that would substitute the authority on the state for the authority of the parent. That was Bolshevism.[42]

A month before the election he ordered all pastors in the archdiocese to speak against the amendment from their pulpits. At

Mass on Sunday, October 5, Catholics throughout eastern Massachusetts heard from their priests why they should reject the Child Labor Amendment. On October 8, James Michael Curley, who had advocated child labor laws for years and who was a passionate proponent of the amendment ("I emphatically favor the ratification of the child labor amendment to the United States Constitution by the Legislature of Massachusetts. I consider the employment of children in industry a crime against Christianity, civilization, and humanity"), having avowed his support as recently as the day before, recanted. In a radio address, he denounced the Walsh amendment, which had the support of Calvin Coolidge, as "a Bolshevistic scheme" drafted by "the former Miss Wichnewetski, a professional Socialist, translator for the Archive fur Sozialegestzebung at Berlin." It was the most politically craven act of his career. One trusts he got a lexical thrill from pronouncing "Sozialegestzebung."[43]

In the event, with David Walsh avoiding the issue and Curley heaping exotic syllables upon it, the amendment lost heavily, 697,000 to 241,000, and with significance beyond the Bay State. "The amendment's defeat in what was its only direct electoral contest in 1924," O'Toole notes, "served to kill it nationally."[44]

Curley's manipulation of the Klan issue was nearly as odious.

With the help of the glamour conferred on it by *The Birth of a Nation*, the Ku Klux Klan had enjoyed a renascence. In its second coming, the Klan was more anti-Catholic than antiblack—though with ecumenical impartiality it also incited hatred against not only blacks, but also Jews and generic "foreigners"—and it achieved its most exhuberant growth in the defensively Protestant small towns of the central border states and Far West rather than in the Deep South. Klan literature depicted the pope in Rome (a.k.a. "the Dago on the Tiber") as the head of an international conspiracy working through its domestic agents, the Catholic priesthood, to seize control of America. The Klansmen printed up a phony Knights of Columbus oath hinting not only at treachery but also at "lechery," to quote an authority on the Klan. Lechery was also the specialty of Helen Jackson, a self-described "escaped nun" who hit the lecture circuit for the Klan. The author of *Convent Cruelties*, a work right out of the Know-Nothing 1850s, she would display the "little leather bags"—the means of conveyance used by randy priests and guilty nuns to transport their unwanted progeny to "the convent furnaces."

Among the credulous and cretinous in the American rurality, the Klan made recruits by showing photographs of the Episcopal cathedral then under construction in Washington, D.C., claiming it was the new Vatican. Besides the dim, the Klan enlisted members from among that even more numerous category of persons, the venal, handing out bribes to ill-paid Bible thumpers from Indiana to Arizona. With considerable quiet support from the Protestant rank and file, and seeming to stand for decency or at any rate temperance in the era of the flapper, the bootlegger, and the gangster, the Klan by the mid-twenties may have had as many as five million members.[45]

Feeling its strength, the Klan won control of the Oklahoma legislature and proceeded to impeach the state's anti-Klan governor and remove him from office. In Oregon, the Klan got a ballot initiative passed banning parochial schools. With 350,000 Klansmen in the streets, Indiana was practically under Klan rule. The Klan helped elect sixteen senators, five of whom were Klansmen, and eleven governors, four Klansmen among them. The height of its political influence, however, came at the 1924 Democratic national convention in Madison Square Garden, where a thousand New York City policemen were assigned to keep pro- and anti-Klan delegates from each other's throats. Klan pressure kept the Catholic governor of New York, Alfred E. Smith, from winning the presidential nomination. Klan pressure barely ($543 \, ^3/_{20}$ votes to $542 \, ^7/_{20}$) defeated an anti-Klan plank in the party platform. And Klan resistance forced the convention, after 103 ballots, to choose John W. Davis as a compromise candidate. Davis later condemned the Klan, but Calvin Coolidge, sensing that the Klan vote was already his, said not a single word about it.[46]

In heavily Catholic Massachusetts, the first big Klan demonstration took place in Worcester in 1923, when nearly three thousand Klansmen listened to F. Eugene Farnsworth, King Kleagle of Maine, opine that "the future America is not going to put up with hyphenates" and laud the public schools for producing "the highest type mentality in the world, Protestant mentality." In April and May of 1924 crosses were set afire in over a dozen Massachusetts towns, including Georgetown, near the New Hampshire border, where James M. Curley happened to be speaking. Emerging from the Town Hall with Mrs. Curley, he saw a large cross burning on a nearby hill. He finished shaking hands, then walked up to the cross and kicked it over. In September, a "Klonvocation" at the Worcester fair grounds drew a crowd of fifteen thousand—some of whom were beaten as they departed by irate hyphenates of inferior mentality.[47]

Coolidge's silence, along with the decision of Massachusetts governor Channing Cox to send state police to protect Klan rallies from any repetition of the Worcester violence, gave Curley an issue. He had already banned the Klan from holding meetings in Boston (an unlikely venue in any case) and, when the American Civil Liberties Union protested, replied, "This is a law-abiding community, and it will not be transformed into a Klan-infested province of Texas or Oklahoma or a section of the backlots of Maine without opposition." Now, denouncing "Calvin the Silent" for winking at the Klan, Curley declared that "there will never be happiness in the state until the Ku Klux Klan has been wiped out. Once I am situated on Beacon Hill," he promised, "the Ku Klux Klan will cease to exist in Massachusetts." Thus the civil libertarian who could not bring himself to ban a movie glorifying the Klan would drive the real thing out of the state.[48]

It was not inspired tactics to hit at Coolidge, but he was a better target than Curley's Republican opponent in the governor's race, Alvan Fuller. Mrs. Fuller, as her husband frequently pointed out, was a Catholic, and Fuller, a wealthy car dealer, had often contributed to Catholic charities. Moreover, the Klan had opposed him in the September primaries. Curley could and did hit at Fuller's competence, record, and views:

> Your millions cannot hide your patent mediocrity. Your golden store will not lure the honest men of Massachusetts; they expect something nobler and higher than thrift in the man they elect Governor. . . . They will not send a gilded nonentity to Beacon Hill. One gilded dome there is sufficient; yours would be superfluous.

That was fair game. But Fuller was not credibly assailable on the Klan issue, and in a widely reported speech he "waved" it out of the campaign.[49]

Curley intended to keep it in. Speaking in Worcester, he charged that the Klan had 130,000 members in Massachusetts in "secret alliance with the Republican party." At Pittsfield, Klan members distributed their paper, the *Klankread,* while Curley addressed

244 THE RASCAL KING

a crowd. Handed a Klan pamphlet in Westfield, he pledged that as governor he would "secure a number of cattle cars, fill them with that collection of skunks, coyotes, and muskrats, and send them to the land of the hookworm." At a rally in the central Massachusetts town of Athol, Curley issued a typical dare: "I understand there are Klansmen hereabouts. I would like to announce that after this meeting my secretary and I are traveling alone to Gardner. If any Klansmen wish to meet us on the dark and lonely road and try something, they are welcome to make the attempt." Fiery crosses would erupt on nearby hills as he spoke across the state. Pointing to these blasphemous blazes, Curley would denounce the Klan and castigate the Republicans for their silence on the issue.

At the time the fortuitous conjunction of man and prop aroused some doubts. "There are four million people in Massachusetts and the only one who has ever found a burning cross is James M. Curley," charged Representative Elijah Adlow, a Roxbury Republican. "The only one who wants Ku Kluxers burning crosses in this state is James M. Curley, because he must have an issue to run on and he hasn't any other issue."

Curley fired back at Adlow and at Elihu Stone, an assistant U.S. attorney, who had branded Curley an "inverted klansman," playing up the Klan threat for political gain. Dismissing them as Fuller's "janizzaries," Curley took a swipe at their religion, saying that the only Jews who entered politics were those who lacked the capacity to succeed in business. Had he forgotten that he was supposed to be the friend of the "newer races"?[50]

In his autobiography, Curley admitted what only the most partisan souls had suspected at the time: that the crosses had been lit by his campaign workers. With much of the country in the grip of a recrudescence of Know-Nothingism, with Catholic priests being harassed, nuns slandered, the papacy reviled, and the Democratic party rent by anti-Catholic bigotry, Curley had stooped to theatrical tricks to mine votes from Catholic fears. American politics knows worse manipulations of public sentiment, but you have to look hard for them, and you have to look low—to Senator Joseph R. McCarthy and his blank "list of names"; to the race-baiting campaigns of southern demagogues, from Bilbo to Helms; to George Bush and Willie Horton.[51]

Curley could have run an honorable race. He could have denounced the Klan until his lungs were ruddy and contrasted "Fullerism"—economy in government—with "Curleyism," which he defined as "the application of political energy . . . to the betterment of the public service, a fruitful expenditure of public funds to conserve the health, safety, and economic security of the community." With Coolidge sweeping 350 of the Commonwealth's 351 cities and towns and carrying the Republican party with him, Curley would have lost the race but not his dignity. As it was, Fuller beating him 641,000 to 482,000, he lost both.⁵²

"I'll never be Governor of Massachusetts," he told his friends. It seemed a safe prediction after the 1924 election. Yet ten years from the day of his defeat, he would be governor-elect. The life of politics is a picket-fence existence.

❖ ❖ ❖

A nd so is the life of a family.
     Dorothea Curley, fourteen, was her father's special friend. She even looked like him—she had his round face, as Mary had her mother's angular face and features. Sometimes, on leaving City Hall, he would find her in his car waiting for him. They would ride home together, and on the way would have private talks. Dorothea was a sensitive girl; when Curley took the family on his annual Christmas visit to the homeless shelter on Long Island, the loneliness and misery she saw there brought tears to her eyes. She was a sophomore at the Convent of the Sacred Heart School in the Back Bay. A school chum remembers her as having a "beautiful Irish complexion, pink and white, and dark hair." A shy girl, she was more attractive than her older sister, though Mary adored her. Indeed, all who knew her liked her.

She bade her classmates goodbye one Friday afternoon two months after the election, and never returned. "The rest of the year," one of them remembers, "we'd have to look at that empty seat."

That evening she came down with a fever. Dr. Martin English, the Curley family physician, suspected pneumonia. Two specialists concurred: Dorothea had double lobar pneumonia. What the papers referred to as "a heart affection of long standing" had kept her from vigorous outdoor pursuits—and left her too weak to fight off the lung infection. For days, her father and mother maintained a constant vigil at her bedside. Outside, a premonitory silence reigned: that stretch of the Jamaicaway had been closed to traffic; all was quiet for the sick girl. Finally, early on the following Thursday, after regaining consciousness just long enough to look at and recognize the members of her family, Dorothea Curley died. Curley somehow managed to move his legs downstairs to announce her death to the reporters waiting outside, and then he and Mary Emelda bowed their heads and wept. GRIEF OF MAYOR AND MRS. CURLEY BEYOND WORDS TO DESCRIBE, read one headline that evening.

The funeral Mass was held at the Curleys' home parish, Our Lady of Lourdes, in Jamaica Plain. As the casket piled with pink roses was carried down the center aisle, Dorothea's thirty-six classmates, in black dresses and white veils, "wept pitifully." Stony-faced, white-lipped, sorrowing, the Curleys got through the ceremony. A crowd of five thousand waited outside the church to show their grief to the mayor and to witness his own. It had begun to snow.

Dorothea was buried in Calvary Cemetery, and as her body was lowered into the grave the stillness of the moment was broken by rifle shots from the burial of a soldier nearby.[53]

❖ ❖ ❖

His friend Henry Cabot Lodge said of Theodore Roosevelt that he wanted to be the bride at every wedding and the corpse at every funeral. James Michael Curley wanted to be the candidate in every election. That made the mayoral election of 1925 a special ordeal. Prevented by law from succeeding himself, he was deeply ambivalent about helping any Democrat succeed him. For a time, the Good Government Association listed Mary E. Curley as a potential candidate. She did not run but, expecting his brother's support, John Curley did. Curley's fire commissioner and protégé Teddy Glynn also declared his candidacy. Whom should Curley back? The Boston Globe pronounced it "the most vexatious dilemma that has ever confronted him."

Withholding his endorsement so long that the anti-Curley opposition, both Democratic and Republican, had time to consolidate, he finally came out for Teddy Glynn. His abandonment of his own brother brought on the hyperbole from the by now passionately anti-Curley Frederick Enwright at the Telegram: "Since Cain struck down Abel in the first fight for public favor that history records . . . seldom have men heard of a brother fighting a brother because of political expediency." John Curley, who in this administration as in his brother's last was city treasurer, was said to be hurt by the news. He denied published reports that Mrs. Curley, reacting to family discord, had pressured the mayor to come out for Glynn. Defiantly he vowed to stay in the race even without his brother's support. Some days later, however, he withdrew.[54]

Meanwhile, in his stump speeches for Glynn the mayor was touting his own record, as one reporter observed, "99% of the time," leaving the rest for the merits of his candidate, whom he characterized privately as "fourteen ounces lighter than an old straw hat" and of whom he reportedly said, "I tried to make a man of Teddy, but he is only a hunk of mud." If Curley thought so little of Glynn, observers wondered, why had he endorsed him?[55]

John Fitzgerald briefly declared his candidacy but soon dropped out in favor of Joseph O'Neil, a seventy-year-old former congressman Fitzgerald himself had beaten, way back in 1894, and, upon whom, Methuselah being unavailable, he and Martin Lomasney had fastened as the hope of anti-Curley Democrats. Either O'Neil or Glynn might still have had a chance to defeat the Republican candidate, Malcolm Nichols, a former state legislator and the Harding-appointed collector of internal revenue in Boston, but for the entry into the race of Daniel Coakley. Disbarred, disgraced, but unrepentant, Coakley claimed he was running to vindicate the name of Joseph Pelletier, who in the scandal following his removal from office over his badger game partnership with Coakley, had (many believed) committed suicide. His purpose, Coakley told a rally in his home ward of Brighton, was to "make sure that never again will the bigot and the perjurer and the procurer join leprous hands to attack sons of Irish mothers, because they refuse to forget they are sons of Irish mothers." This was the same exculpatory line that Pelletier himself had taken in his brief mayoral campaign of four years before—the charges of sexual entrapment were a Yankee Protestant plot to bring down the powerful sons of Irish mothers. Interreligious relations were so strained in these Klan years and the Irish lower classes were so fearful of Protestant plots that Coakley could expect to capture a substantial slice of the vote with this paranoid appeal to prejudice.[56]

In his autobiography, Curley charged that Coakley had been put into the race by the Republican "boss" Charles Innes, the Martin Lomasney of the Back Bay, to split off enough Democratic votes to elect Nichols. Some evidence bears that out. John Bantry claimed that Innes financed Coakley's $100,000 campaign, and he noted how closely Coakley's moves were coordinated with the Republicans'. Still, Curley's complaints about a Republican plot to split the Irish vote cannot disguise the fact that he did not want a Democrat to win. A Republican could offer him no serious future competition should he choose to keep running for mayor for the rest of his life; a Democrat could. James M. Curley was not a party man. He was a James M. Curley man.[57]

In the event, with Coakley cutting into Glynn's vote in South Boston, Brighton, and Roxbury, and with the ten candidates in the race splintering the vote every which way, Nichols beat Glynn by just slightly more than the 20,030 votes cast for Coakley, 64,486 to 42,698. When Glynn complained about Curley's tepid support, Curley lapsed into facetiae: "Three of the most famous traitors in history—Judas Iscariot, Benedict Arnold, and Teddy Glynn—had another thing in common—they were all redheads." The Democratic city employees who would now be purged by the Republican Nichols cannot have been amused at this remark. The *Herald*, noting that Curley was "probably relieved" at Nichols's victory, drew sardonic attention to their plight. "And as for the 16,000 municipal employees about whose fate he has mourned, we believe he possesses enough self-control to live down the sorrows which other people's troubles give him."[58]

Thus did the Mayor of the Poor resume his avocation as bank president.

Depression Mayor

❖   ❖   ❖   ❖

James Michael Curley is adept in versatility. He is a successful shifter of shrines.

ROBERT WASHBURN

I gues every State and City is the same while these hard times last untill you are President, then people will see a change. When I wrote this letter to you I did not eat anything for 2 days. I slept on a 10 cent flop where there is 500 men. It is worse than an insane isylum.

UNEMPLOYED BOSTONIAN TO FRANKLIN D. ROOSEVELT

❖   ❖   ❖   ❖

One warm October noon in 1926, James Curley was strid-
ing along Devonshire Street in Boston's financial district, deep in conversation with a friend, when the thick
crowd in his path parted to reveal Frederick Enwright.
Accounts differ as to who said or did what first, but the men exchanged words, and then Curley struck Enwright with a powerful
right uppercut that tumbled him into the gutter. He stayed there
while Curley, trembling with rage, stood over him, daring him to
get up for more of the same. Enwright, a big man, started to do so,
but when Curley swung in his direction ("The second swing was in
the way of a gesture," he later explained) Enwright lay down and
stayed down. Enwright's bodyguard, who had been walking behind him, tried to aid his boss, but Curley straight-armed the fellow in the jaw, and he backed off. Finally, at the prompting of his
companion, Curley moved on, leaving in his wake a bewildered
crowd gawking at the still-prostrate Enwright. "That guy Curley,"
one messenger boy was overheard saying, "certainly has a mean
sock. Did you see the Mayor slap him down? It was just one bang
and then curtains."¹

For arranging that this fracas should occur at nearly the exact
site of the Boston Massacre of 1770, Curley owed thanks to the
great press agent in the sky. By midafternoon, the second Boston
Massacre was the talk of town. In a spirit of mock commemoration,
a wag chalked the outline of Enwright's body on the asphalt pavement and printed within it, THIS MARKS THE SPOT WHERE ENWRIGHT FELL.

Reporters hurried to the offices of the Hibernia Savings Bank
to get Curley's side of the story. "Hello boys," he said, coming out
from behind his desk to greet them. "What can I do for you?"

"Haven't you any news for us today?"

"Why yes," he said, a teasing grin spreading across his face. "It looks like Walsh and Gaston in November, without any question," referring to the Democratic nominees for U.S. senator and governor. "You may quote me as saying that."

"But we heard you were assaulted today."

"Why yes, I was assaulted. But I hope you will not accuse me of an overwhelming conceit if I say that I defended myself creditably."

He had taken offense at an article published in Enwright's paper; the *Telegraph* (Enwright had just changed its name from the *Telegram* and its form from broadsheet to tabloid) reported he had settled a $35,000 lawsuit brought against him by a firm of stockbrokers. For obvious reasons, he hated publicity about his financial ventures. "I simply served notice on Enwright that if he published anything untrue about me or my wife or our family, he would have to answer to me. Of course, I didn't put it quite like that—I said it a little more forcefully. . . . He struck me in the cheek. As a matter of self-defense, I punched him in the jaw. He went down like a dog."

Enwright had been vilifying Curley since 1922, ostensibly for his failure to reinstate the striking Boston policemen after his election as mayor, though Curley said it was because Enwright expected a cash payoff for picking him over Pelletier in 1921. In any case, by 1926 the mayor's animus against Enwright did not need the excuse of a fresh provocation.[2]

For his part, Enwright claimed that Curley, declaring "I am feeling pretty good today, and I can lick half a dozen Enwrights," had struck him from behind, and that four men with Curley had then punched and kicked him unmercifully while he was laid out in the gutter.

"Mr. Enwright was propelled to the pavement," the *Post* concluded, "but the after-battle statements of the participants differ as to how he arrived there."

Enwright fought back by giving over the entire front page of the next day's edition of the *Telegraph* to a cartoon of "Curley the Thug." The drawing shows a convict with a Pinocchio nose and truculent expression sitting in his barred cell, his ankle chained to an iron ball. "James Michael Curley, former mayor, whom the depositors of the Hibernia Savings bank allow with others to have charge of funds," the editorial statement beneath began, "learned to hit from the rear while serving a term in jail for a serious criminal offense." The editorial went on to advise Curley, "Get out of town and get off the booze!" Instead, Curley sued Enwright for publishing a libelous cartoon. With the disputants entering and leaving the courthouse by separate entrances to keep Curley from bashing Enwright anew, the case went to trial; and, in an outcome that gave him a taste for litigious retaliation against the press, Curley won a legal victory almost as sweet as his physical one. Enwright was found guilty, fined, and jailed for eight months. The *Telegram/Telegraph* was finished.³

Harvard's President Lowell said that Curley had a touch of the poet in him, and Lowell was right, given a prolix idea of poetry. But if Curley's words won him a following, so also did his fists—or rather both together did, the words giving the fists dimension, the fists lending the words the authority of the street. Francis Hatch, a Boston advertising man, caught the span of Curley's capacities in his popular song, "Vote Early and Often for Curley." The relevant lines: "He'll talk with his fists in a South Boston bar, / And the very next evening, it's no trick at all, / He'll lecture on Browning at Symphony Hall."⁴

❖   ❖   ❖

Alfred Emanuel Smith: the name once had a resonance. It stood for inclusion, for the victory of assimilation, for the vindication of the sacrifices made by parents and grandparents, for the fulfillment of the dream version of America—a country without bigotry, cleansed of the Klan, your land and *mine*. In defeat Al Smith meant more to more Americans than all but the greatest presidents ever mean in victory.

Reporters who covered Jesse Jackson in 1984, when he first ran for president, movingly conveyed the way ordinary African Americans, whose families had endured slavery and segregation, discrimination and poverty, responded to him. Their fierce pride that one of them should be running for president was prefigured in 1928 in ethnic America's rapturous identification with Al Smith.

"Alfred E. Smith of New York and James M. Curley of Boston," William V. Shannon writes, "were the great political leaders of the Irish community in their generation." And Smith's story,

like Curley's, was the story of that generation—a mirror in which
ordinary men and women could see the enlarged reflection of their
own lives.[5]

Smith was born in 1873 on South Street, in lower Manhattan,
beneath the anchorage towers of the Brooklyn Bridge, which
loomed over his childhood like ugly charms. His father, who fought
with the "Bowery Boys" in the Civil War, was a self-employed
teamster who, between caring for his horse and carting freight to
and from the docks on the East River, worked long hours for low
pay. Al remembered him coming home "grimy with the dust of the
street, wet with streaky sweat, peeling off garment after garment,
plunging his neck, hands, and arms into cold water to cool off."
Alfred Emanuel Smith, Sr., had his son's directness of manner; in a
story very like the one that my own father, the son of an Irish immigrant, would tell, Al Smith told how his father had taught him to
swim—by tying a rope around his waist and giving him a pedagogi-
cal heave into the river. Eventually, work wore Al Smith, Sr., away.
The horse and team had to be sold to pay his medical bills. Because
the family had no savings put by, Al had to pass the hat in the
neighborhood barbershop to raise money to bury his father. He
was twelve years old.[6]

Like Sarah Clancy Curley, Catherine Mulvehill Smith, a
daughter of immigrants, now assumed sole responsibility for Al and
his younger sister, Mary. Within hours of her husband's death, she
paid a call on the forewoman of the umbrella factory where she had
worked before her marriage, and got back her old job assembling
umbrellas. To earn extra money she took work home with her at
night. Her sacrifices enabled Al and Mary to finish the eighth
grade, when they both left school to embark on a character-making
education by hard personal endeavor.[7]

When Al Smith was a young assemblyman in the New York
State legislature, a colleague burst into the chamber shouting that
his alma mater, Cornell, had just won a major boat race.

"I too hold a degree," Smith said, proudly rising from his seat.

"What is your alma mater?" asked the Cornell man.

"I'm an F.F.M.," Smith replied.

"I don't think I've ever heard of such a degree."

Smith, smiling, spelled it out for him: "Fulton Fish Market."[8]

"He once said if you doubt the value of an education, ask the
man who never had one. As governor," William V. Shannon contin-

ues, "he signed the largest school appropriation in history up to that time." For a generation of men and women, many of whom had to leave school to support their families, Smith's comment that aside from *The Life and Battles of John L. Sullivan* he had never read a book from cover to cover ("Life furnishes me with all the thrills") proved his industry. Reading takes leisure, and from the time he started on the steep path toward his F.F.M., Al Smith had little of that.

As an assistant bookkeeper, he worked in the reeking fish market from 4:00 A.M. to 4:00 P.M. for twelve dollars a week and a vital perk—he could take home all the fish he wanted. His other job was to sit up on the market roof with a pair of binoculars and watch for the smacks sailing into the harbor. If the boats were riding high in the water, the catch would be poor, fish would be scarce, and prices could be set higher; if the boats were riding low, the opposite logic applied. Smith was learning the importance of exact information clearly conveyed. Livelihoods, lives, depended on it. "Let's look at the record," he would say as a mature politician; and his constant tendency was to search out the unambiguous facts of an issue or problem and base his decisions on them, unswayed by rhetoric or ideology.[9]

His mother, a devout woman, wanted him to be a priest. His own bent was toward the stage. Politics, it turned out, was a good compromise. He came up through the Fourth Ward Tammany Democratic Club, at first running errands for the ward leader, and eventually landing a job as a subpoena server in the jury commissioner's office. This vocational progress made it possible for him to marry Katie Dunn of the Bronx and to begin their family of five children. In 1903, climbing higher in Tammany, he was sent to the New York State Assembly; ten years later, having mastered the craft of legislation and won the respect of members from all parts of the state, he was elected its Speaker.[10]

If Curley was the lone wolf of Irish-American politics, Smith was the organization man. William Allen White would say of him that he took orders from Tammany Hall until he could give them. Yet experience was broadening his outlook, teaching him that politics could be about more than delivering patronage jobs. It could advance a vision of the Good Society.

As vice chairman of the Factory Commission set up to investigate workplace conditions after the death of 145 women in the

Triangle Shirt Factory disaster, Smith toured sweatshops across the state. He saw evils—five-year-olds shelling peas, machinery that could peel off a woman's scalp—a caring government could stop. Elected in 1918 for the first of four terms as governor, Smith gave New York that kind of government. He courageously championed the Child Labor Amendment, and did not, like Curley, recant under local ecclesiastical pressure. He backed progressive social reforms—making the pay of women teachers equal to that of men, obtaining the forty-eight-hour week for women workers—and took pioneering steps in public power and conservation; and he surrounded himself with a cosmopolitan array of advisers from both sexes and diverse ethnic groups.[11]

Curley's eloquence was beyond him (as his sincerity was beyond Curley); but he was Curley's equal in administrative ability, and perhaps because he always enjoyed the support of Tammany Hall and did not have to make and keep remaking himself in politics, Al Smith was money-honest. What one writer calls the "pitch" of Tammany Hall never rubbed off on him. In a radio speech the night before the 1928 presidential election, Smith could say, "At no time during my long public career in elective office did I ever trade a promise for a vote"—and those who knew the record knew that was the truth. If he rose above the bad in Tammany, Smith could count on the good. When he needed money to run for governor, he resigned his seat in the assembly and Tammany appointed him sheriff of New York County, a lucrative job—the sheriff could legally keep half the fees he collected. After he was elected governor, Charles Murphy, the Tammany leader, told him, "Al, it's a great thing for you, Mrs. Smith, and the children and your mother. I am anxious to see you make good so that we can show the people that a young man who has come from the lower east side and has been closely associated with all phases of party activity, can make good." Curley alone was anxious to see Curley make good. That was his pathos, that defined his challenge, and that magnified his lonely triumphs.[12]

In 1928 the Democratic party nominated Al Smith for president. In late October he made a campaign swing through Massachusetts that enduringly changed its politics, forging the electoral alliance among the Irish, the "newer races," labor, progressive academics, professionals, and intellectuals that would come to be known as the New Deal coalition. The climax of his trip was a triumphant two-day visit to Boston, and at the center of it was James M. Curley.

"Was a Catholic a first class citizen equal in rights with every other American?"—that, in Oscar Handlin's words, was the question before America in 1928. Catholic Boston was aflame to answer yes. Wanting to capture the public eye in the run-up to the 1929 mayoral election, Curley shamelessly exploited what Joseph Dinneen called "the most moving political cause in the history of Massachusetts." He did not leap on the Smith bandwagon; he hijacked it. When the nominal leader of the Massachusetts Democracy, Senator David Walsh, maneuvered him out of the Smith campaign, Curley rented the defunct Young's Hotel on Court Street just behind City Hall and put on two-a-day rallies and speakings from what he christened "The Bull Pen."

A poster hanging in the Bull Pen spoke for the inclusive spirit of the Smith campaign. It depicted the Tomb of the Unknown Soldier and bore the legend, WHAT A TRAGEDY IF WE SHOULD LEARN THAT HE WAS A JEW, CATHOLIC, OR NEGRO. Large crowds would gather at the noon hour in the hotel ballroom and spill out onto the sidewalks and nearby streets to hear speakers like Ellery Sedgwick, the editor of the *Atlantic Monthly*, denounce the "whispering campaign" against Smith ("Oh, the base meanness of it, the renunciation of straightforward Yankee ways!"), which slandered him as a secret tippler; and to witness sublunary marvels like the passing of the olive branch between Curley and John Fitzgerald. "We are going to get together," Fitzgerald declared, "not for this year alone, but for years to come and forever." To put Al Smith over, nothing, it seemed, would be allowed to mar the harmony of the Massachusetts Democracy.[13]

In his campaign stopover in Boston, the Republican presidential nominee, Coolidge's secretary of commerce Herbert Hoover, stayed at Governor Fuller's house on Beacon Street; and whether entering or leaving he had to confront an electric portrait of Al Smith, framed by seven bulbs to signify seven Smith voters, in the front window of the house opposite. At Smith's Boston campaign office—AL SMITH HEADQUARTERS, JAMES M. CURLEY DIRECTOR OF ORGANIZATION, a banner as long as the building informed the world—Curley lashed out at the man who paid Chinese, Japanese, and Mexican laborers a dollar a day to work on his California ranch—"and that is the same Mr. Hoover that came here yesterday and talked of the rights of labor." Buoyed by the ballyhoo emanating from within and by the anticipation of Smith's visit, the electoral thermometer in front of Young's inched up daily as the number of registered voters in Boston grazed Curley's goal of three hundred thousand. Loath to praise Curley, the *Transcript* had to concede that "nothing approaching the cleverness of Mayor Curley's stroke in obtaining the hotel for his rallies has been noted in Boston politics for a generation."[14]

From the time Al Smith arrived at Boston's South Station on the evening of October 24 till he departed the next morning, every eye that turned toward him also beheld James Curley. Hoping to boost his own chances for the mayoralty in 1929, Teddy Glynn may have insinuated himself into Smith's car for the triumphal progress from South Station to Parkman bandstand on the Common, but Curley did him one better. Alone, perched on the tonneau of an open touring car, wearing a brown derby and a raccoon coat, and waving a silk American flag, Curley led the Smith cavalcade through streets thick with wildly cheering people, at one point hurling his derby far out into the crowd to fire its enthusiasm. Curley led the cheers for Smith at the bandstand, arranged the mammoth twelve thousand–strong reception for Smith at Mechanics Hall, where he introduced the candidate, and was on the stage at the Boston Arena with Smith when Smith asked, "What is the country actually in need of?" and from the ecstatic audience came the answering cry, "Al Smith!"[15]

❖   ❖   ❖

SMITH WILL WIN, Curley wrote in a full-page ad he took out the day before the election. "If, that is, he gets the vote of every person interested in maintaining the fundamentals of American government, liberty and equality for all without regard to race, creed, or color. . . ." In a radio address that night Curley summed up the meaning of the election in a way that helps us understand why Smith's defeat would embitter so many: "It is all an acid test of our right to the title of American citizen, and I look with confidence to the ultimate decision, the election of the people's champion and democracy's idol, Alfred E. Smith."[16]

Writing on the same day, H. L. Mencken framed the election in similar terms, as a referendum on rum—Smith was a modified "wet" on Prohibition—and Romanism: "If Al wins tomorrow it will be because the American people have decided at last to vote as they drink, and because a majority of them believe that the Methodist bishops [who had led the attack on religious grounds against Smith] are worse than the Pope. If he loses, it will be because those who fear the Pope outnumber those who are tired of the Anti-Saloon League." In the end six million more Americans were more afraid of the pope; Hoover carried forty states and won the Electoral College 444 to 87 in "the most sweeping political victory since the birth of the Republican Party."[17]

Massachusetts was not among those forty states. Thanks to a ninety-eight-thousand-vote majority in Boston, Smith carried the state, the first Democrat—excepting Wilson in 1912, the year of the Republican split—to do so since before the Civil War. He got 81 percent of the vote in Lomasney's Jewish-Italian Ward 3 and 90 percent in an Irish ward in Charlestown. The Portuguese in New Bedford, the Greeks in Haverhill, the French in Lowell all broke big for Smith. A record 93 percent of those eligible voted, a 40 percent increase over 1924. Smith—and the issue of inclusion he stood for—had pulled out that many more than Coolidge. John Bantry credited this historic achievement to Curley: "Without Curley's work for Smith in Boston it is very doubtful if Gov. Smith would have carried the state."[18]

Putting the best face on things, the Republican *Boston Herald* dipped into its reserves of complacency. "It is inevitable that, with the influences of 1928 at work, a great many persons who have been Republican and who will be Republican again, should have gone for a little outing behind the Democratic donkey. But the holiday will be short, the picknickers will return to their regular home fare, and Massachusetts will stand where she has always stood." In fact the "picknickers" would be away for a generation, and would favor candidates even more alien to the *Herald*'s taste than Al Smith. In turning out the vote for Smith, Curley was not only helping himself in the upcoming election for mayor; he was welding the coalition that would elect him governor.[19]

When Curley met Smith's train at South Station he presented Katie Smith with a bouquet sent by Mary Emelda. "I hope you will accept it upon behalf of the Democratic women voters of Boston," Mary wrote in the attached note, "as a token of good will and a sincere wish for the success and happiness of your brilliant husband, yourself, and your family." Graciously, Mrs. Smith carried Mary's bouquet with her throughout the day.[20]

Mary could not make the presentation herself because she was confined to bed by the cancer that would kill her. When he was not electioneering for Smith, James would sit with her for hours, until she fell asleep; and though he would close the door the sonorous purl of his voice flowed downstairs to the kitchen and along the corridor and upstairs to the children's bedrooms as he read Dickens to his dying wife.[21]

❖   ❖   ❖

Surveying the city for *Harper's* in 1928, Elmer Davis found that "the cardinal fact about Boston" remained the "racial antithesis" between the Yankee Protestant remnant and the Irish Catholic majority. Yet flecks of change were appearing in this primordial feature of the local landscape. Harvard, for example, had begun to discover that "it might be more agreeable to beat Yale with an Irish backfield than to go on winning moral victories with a team of Mayflower descendants." This tentative spirit of innovation, however, was wholly absent from economic life. At the height of the Coolidge prosperity, Davis was struck by the "timidity of New England capital." The famous "spendthrift trusts" devised by the Yankee merchants of the nineteenth century to keep their heirs from improvidence also kept them from entrepreneurship. Much of the stock in the region's shoe and textile mills was held by trustees, "who cannot take a chance. . . . And without taking a chance no region sunk in a slump is likely to get itself out." Culture showed the same stagnation. Noting that before the Civil War Boston produced "all of the literary news" in the country, Davis could only deplore the local censorship that made sixty-five current books unobtainable. "The city which used to write most of American literature was now forbidden by the police to read most of American literature." Davis likened Boston to "an old house, cold and clammy and mildewed, where the furnace will never be lighted again."

Social stasis, economic entropy, cultural decline; yet in Boston's politics Davis glimpsed a potential source of vitality. "The city is at present enjoying a 'reform' administration, headed by a Nordic Protestant graduate of Harvard," Davis wrote of the Nichols regime; "but people who count the merit of an administration by what it accomplishes even if the accomplishments cost money, point to a long list of public improvements put over by Curley. So far as an outsider can discern, . . . with all his faults, Curley saw what Boston needed, and got it done, more successfully than any other Mayor of recent times." "And," Davis concluded, "citizens who used to damn Curley when he was Mayor now want him back."[22]

Curley was about to oblige them. He opened his reelection campaign on St. Patrick's Day, when his car, its wheels painted bright green, followed that of Mayor Nichols in the parade as he sought to follow Nichols in office. That day campaign buttons the size of saucers, the biggest ever seen in Boston, sprouted all over town, on coats, hats, windshields, and radiator fronts paying tribute to BOSTON'S BEST AND BOSTON'S NEXT MAYOR and urging Bostonians to VOTE FOR AL SMITH'S FRIEND.[23]

Just how good a friend he had been to Al Smith became a torrid issue as the fall campaigning season approached. Louis K. Liggett, the Republican national committeeman from Massachusetts, charged that Curley had clandestinely distributed anti-Catholic literature during the Smith campaign, hoping to blame it on Hoover and the Republicans. Liggett called for a grand jury to investigate. Incensed by what he termed one of the worst attacks ever made on his character, Curley sought an indictment for criminal libel against Liggett and the *Boston Herald*, which had printed Liggett's statement. Promising that his testimony before the grand jury would "rock the nation," Curley slyly dropped an incendiary suggestion. "It may be necessary to summon Mr. Hoover," he said, to testify on the Republicans' use of Smith's religion in the 1928 campaign. Fearful of the damage any public vetting of that question might do to his party, Governor Fuller called for Liggett's resignation. Without party support, Liggett retreated. Were his charges true? Curley soon admitted that he did have some anti-Smith cartoons on display in the Bull Pen, but strictly as props that speakers could point to "as showing the kind of underground campaign that was being waged against Smith." That ended the controversy; but those who suspected Curley of hiring simulated Klansmen in 1924 now had warrant to suspect him of circulating anti-Catholic propaganda in 1928.[24]

Blithe about his chances of winning, he sent a telegram to the directors of the American Legion asking them to hold the group's annual convention in Boston in 1930: "As Mayor of Boston in 1930, I promise you every service that lies within my power to make this great convention a banner event. . . ." This was the fall of 1929, when he was not mayor of Boston but simply one of three candidates for the job. He was treating the mayoral election in November as a formality. "I am merely on vacation from the mayor's office," he said. Finding the radio room beneath the Parkman bandstand locked, just when he was supposed to give a speech honoring the birthday of Commodore John Barry, Erin's gift to the Revolutionary War, Curley forced it open with a crowbar. "Tell Park Commissioner Long that the Mayor broke the door down," he told astonished reporters. "I will take the mayoralty like Grant took Richmond," he cockily declared, predicting he would win by seventy thousand votes.[25]

His confidence was the flower of the unprecedented harmony wrought by the Smith campaign in the ranks of the Boston Democracy. John Fitzgerald was singing "Sweet Adeline" at his rallies; Martin Lomasney, Teddy Glynn, Tague, McNary, O'Connor—all his enemies of yesterday were his friends today. Even William Monroe Trotter was with him. Speaking at a Curley rally, Trotter alluded to the differences that Boston's blacks had had with Curley in his first term, but said they had forgiven him by his second, and now were solidly behind him for a third: "The colored people of Boston regard ex-Mayor Curley as a champion of equal rights for their race and as one of the most staunch opponents of race and color prejudice in the country." Forty Curley billboards, in every neighborhood of the city, summed up the overriding sentiment: ALLSTON NEEDS CURLEY, BRIGHTON NEEDS CURLEY, SOUTH BOSTON NEEDS CURLEY, BOSTON NEEDS CURLEY.[26]

A saboteur could not resist the opportunity presented by one of these signs, and the Good Government Association could not resist saluting him for it. "The wag who by the change of a single letter transformed 'needs' to 'feeds' was wiser than he knew." In the acid judgment of the association, Curley's feeding off the city was "the issue of the campaign."

The Good Government Association was backing Frederick W. Mansfield, fifty-two, president of the Massachusetts Bar Association, former attorney for the American Federation of Labor, former Massachusetts state treasurer, and former Democratic candidate for governor. Mansfield was Boston's only hope to "prevent the return of machine rule," the association said in its endorsement. "The most aenemic effusion given to the public in the history of the organization," Curley scoffed, identifying the group as "that select and exclusive body of social bounders in the Back Bay. . . . The Back Bay, where they have kitchenettes, dogs, and no children."[27]

Mansfield's ties to the church could not be dismissed so airily. He was known to be close to Cardinal O'Connell; some years later, O'Connell would make him the archdiocese's lawyer. The cardinal did not openly endorse Mansfield, but "everyone in Boston knew that Mansfield was his agent." Mansfield's candidacy sent a message of growing ecclesiastical displeasure with Curley. In the most Catholic city in the country (73 percent of Bostonians professed the faith in 1929), this must sooner or later hurt him politically.[28]

Tall, dour, ponderous in manner, Mansfield seemed to one reporter "as spectacular as a four-day old codfish and as colorful as a lump of mud." But he clearly disliked Curley—perhaps because, as the son of Irish immigrants himself, he thought Curley's bad example sullied the reputation of the Boston Irish—and it showed in the frankness of his attacks.[29]

In early October, with Curley sitting in the same radio station waiting to speak next, Mansfield directly raised the issue of graft. City expenditures, he predicted, "will have to be inflated in order to provide a margin of graft for those contributors who have so lavishly given to Curley's campaign." Curley was spending far more on his campaign, Mansfield alleged, than the $80,000 in salary he would receive over the four-year term—$80,000, because as one of the last acts of his second term, Curley and the City Council had thoughtfully doubled the mayoral salary, from $10,000 to $20,000. Curley's two "discredited" administrations, Mansfield further argued, had frustrated Boston's repeated efforts to achieve "home rule."[30]

This was a potentially telling issue. Since the Irish had won the battle for the city in the mid-1880s the rural-based, Yankee Republican–dominated state legislature had made one incursion after another on Boston's administrative and fiscal autonomy. The governor had the power to appoint the city's police commissioner and to pick the members of its licensing board, which issued liquor and other permits. Boston was the only community in the Commonwealth thus constrained, and it was the only large city in America whose tax limit was set annually by the state legislature. "Home rule" meant Irish rule, and resentment against 'state restrictions born in bigotry ran high. As Irish rule came to mean Curley rule, moreover, many state legislators grew more rather than less averse to granting Boston greater autonomy, so Mansfield's argument appealed to common sense. By the same token, however, it insulted ethnic pride. Implying that the state restrictions sprang from misconduct on the part of Boston's elected officials, Mansfield was not only getting things wrong historically; he was also according legitimacy to an inequitable and spitefully maintained set of arrangements.[31]

"I think the citizens will resist his supreme arrogance," Mansfield said. "They do not want to see Mr. Curley conducted through the streets of Boston with a sceptre in his hands and a crown upon his head. They do not wish the office of Mayor handed down from any king to any crown prince." This last was a reference to the twenty-two-year-old James Michael Jr., who was widely thought to be interested in taking up a political career. Mansfield ended with his deeply insinuating campaign slogan, one emblazoned on an illuminated billboard at the corner of Massachusetts and Huntington avenues: HASN'T CURLEY HAD ENOUGH?[32]

Curley took notes on Mansfield's speech while listening to it in the studio, but he stuck to his written text in his own speech, stressing that his experience could save the taxpayers hundreds of thousands of dollars and warning that City Hall was no place for "a novice, even though he was honest and well-intentioned." This was a more sophisticated pitch than it might at first appear. By now many Bostonians had recognized that there was no necessary correlation between a mayor's personal honesty and his effectiveness, whereas there did appear to be a link between Curley's dishonesty ("an unquestionably dishonest man," Mansfield charged in a later speech) and his capacity to get things done. The one was a condition of the other; the chance to get rich from public office gave Curley an incentive to deliver on his promises so that he could be returned to office to get richer. Conceding Mansfield's honesty, Curley invited his listeners to ponder the worth of that virtue if it went along with (as it was apt to do) administrative timidity, a quailing before hard choices, a delicacy of scruple indistinguishable, perhaps, from incapacity. He adumbrated the "functionalist" view of "boss rule": graft might be the engine of efficiency.[33]

"How long could I hold down a lawyer's job?" he asked in another speech. "But I do say that I know more about running the business of this city than any other man who ever held the position of Mayor. . . . I want you to stand by Curley"—he now habitually referred to himself in the third person—"not because Curley is a prevaricator, not because Curley is a bedtime story teller, but because Curley is the builder of Boston."[34]

Most commentators thought Curley would win easily, but the race had one wild card—the redoubtable Daniel Coakley. Even before he declared his candidacy in September, he sought to manipulate the election by precipitating another Curley into the field. This was Tom Curley, James's old cellmate from the Charles Street Jail, and there seemed no doubt of his role as a Coakley plant. When a Michael J. Curley, a city laborer from Dorchester, also declared his candidacy, the papers began to speak of 1929 as "The Year of the Three Curleys." In due course two of the three dropped out, but by then Coakley himself was in. He could hurt Curley in two ways: not only by splitting the "gang" vote (for which reason, Curley charged, Mansfield had put him into the race: Curley referred to Coakley as "Matador" Mansfield's "picador"), but by exposing Curley's role in a well-remembered scandal.

Although he had been disbarred, Coakley publicly pleaded with Curley to release him from his oath to preserve his clients' confidences. "Oh, shades of Mishawum!" he taunted in one speech. "Curley won't you release me? Why are you so tender of that old Indian name, Mishawum?" Why, he went on, did Curley seek an injunction against the *Boston Herald* to prevent its "using the name Mishawum in connection with you?" This was dangerous territory. By such threats, Curley had kept his role in the sexual blackmail case hidden. "You testified against me in Cambridge when I was on trial," Coakley said in another speech, "and when I had the right to cross examine you, had I asked you one question, you would never have held your head up in Boston again. . . . I would not break my lawyer's oath when you faced me as a government witness, when my liberty was at stake. . . . Even to be Mayor of Boston, I will not speak. Will you release me? Will you let me tell the truth about you?" That prospect must have vexed Curley's sleep.[35]

Speaking at the Hotel Statler before four thousand members of the Woman's *Better* Government League, a group he had created to improve on the merely *Good* Government Association, Curley pilloried Coakley for claiming that Mrs. Curley would shortly issue a circular urging Boston women to vote for her husband. "Mrs.

Curley has suffered intense agony for fifteen long months. . . . I bitterly resent the remark of Coakley that she will be sending a letter from her sickbed to the women of Boston." But Coakley, as he was quick to point out, had never made such a statement: "Shame on you, Jimmy Curley, for lying about me in order that her . . . widely regretted illness might be turned to political capital." Curley clearly was exploiting Mary's condition to win sympathy votes, and compounding the tastelessness of the act with a lie. As John Bantry had written, "He deliberately cheapens himself in a campaign."[36]

On the Sunday before the election, Curley crossed the threshold of Lomasney's Hendricks Club—named for Grover Cleveland's first vice president, who had been a friend of the Irish—for the first time ever to bury the enmity of a generation and to witness the seventy-year-old "Mahatma," as he was known, whip off his straw leghorn, yank out the knot of his bow tie, and shed his collar in a ninety-minute endorsement of James Michael Curley, not a word of which either man believed. This nauseating triumph of "harmony" convinced even skeptics that Curley would win big. "For the first time in his career," Bantry predicted, "James M. Curley is in 'soft.' "[37]

"I can now say, without egotism, that no one can defeat me except myself," Curley pronounced, with more truth than egotism. For his propensity toward self-destruction had yet to display itself. Later that same Sunday it finally appeared, most inopportunely, on a citywide radio broadcast.[38]

Jennie Loitman Barron, a member of the School Committee and a Mansfield supporter, was in the middle of a speech booming Mansfield at radio station WNAC when Curley, who was to follow her, arrived at the station. Citing Finance Commission reports on irregularities in the construction of school buildings during Curley's two administrations, she argued that Curley saw the schools primarily as a means to reward his pet contractors. Curley, listening in the anteroom just off the studio, began making furious notes on her speech. "There's something coming to you, old girl!" he exclaimed.

So there was—and also to him. He had stuck to his prepared remarks after Mansfield had scored him in the same studio a few weeks before. But now he lost control of himself. "Mrs. Barron has just given you a very interesting but untruthful talk," he began, while Barron was still gathering up her things in the studio, "which

I will reply to right now." The roles reversed, Barron now stopped in the anteroom to listen to Curley.

After briefly defending his record in building schools, Curley got down to character assassination. "A gentleman by the name of Sam Goodwin called at my headquarters three weeks ago," he improvised, "and asked if I wanted the services of Mrs. Barron in this campaign. I said that if she came to volunteer her services I would accept them. He then returned and said she wanted a price and could not be with me because she was getting a price from the Good Government Association, so-called." He went on to imply that Barron had improperly profited from the sale of a disused brewery to the city. "I challenge him!" Barron shouted from the anteroom, outraged. Listening at home, Mary must have been unbuttoning her long white leather gloves.

Just then Daniel Coakley, who was to follow Curley on the air, showed up at the station. "Most outrageous thing I ever heard," he said, after friends told him what Curley had said. Curley was running overtime, so to hasten him off the air the announcer summoned Coakley into the studio. Leaning on a piano in the corner, smiling wickedly at Curley, Coakley watched him as he concluded with a paraphrase of Webster's reply to Hayne: "And now I leave the gentleman [Mansfield]. I leave him in the worst company possible, that of himself"—and he looked directly at Coakley—"and Mr. Coakley."

Snatching up his notes, Curley burst into the anteroom. "Where's Jennie?" he shouted. By now in tears, Mrs. Barron turned her back on him. Her husband, who had been waiting for her throughout, looked daggers at Curley as, thinking better of it, he grabbed his derby and left. What the *Post* called "one of the most dramatic incidents in the whole history of Boston politics" was over.[39]

In his tirade Curley had offered Barron a portion of his own airtime to answer his charges, but that was sheer wind. Not until later in the evening, shortly before midnight, was Barron able to obtain some of Mansfield's scheduled time to reply. "Mr. Sam Goodwin came to my law office about four weeks ago and asked me to support Mr. Curley . . . ," she explained. "When I refused he said he was sorry for me because if I came out for Mr. Mansfield, Mr. Curley would stop at nothing to attempt to destroy me or my reputation." She concluded with a fiery appeal "to all mothers, to the chivalry of American men" to punish Curley for his black-guardly eleventh-hour attack.[40]

Denouncing it as "the vicious utterance . . . of a dying political tyrant," Mansfield predicted that for assaulting the "mother of a family, highly respectable, the only woman member of the school committee, elected by over 71,000 votes" Curley would "receive a stinging rebuke by the voters at the polls tomorrow."[41]

For the first time in years, the Curley house was not the scene of an election-night celebration—Mary needed quiet. Little Francis Curley was obliged to tiptoe downstairs to get the results from the older Curleys: their father had won, but the imbroglio with Jennie Barron severely cut into his vote. He got 117,000, Mansfield 96,000, Coakley less than 3,000. A five-to-one favorite, Curley had won by only 19,000 votes out of 216,000 cast. Mansfield demanded a recount. That gave Curley an opening to turn Mansfield's slogan against him: "Hasn't *Mansfield* had enough?"

At the old-fashioned victory parade that wound up in front of Curley's headquarters on Province Street there were shouts of "Curley for Governor!" and "The White House next, Jim!" Curley was not generous in his victory speech: "You will realize that after this little skirmish—of course, you couldn't really call it a battle—I am happy and tired, and I know you won't be offended if I go home and tell somebody else about it." Although Curley had asked her not to, Mary stayed up to congratulate him. The Place of Rest was a sad place for him now, and that must have been a torment to her. The least she could do was help him celebrate his cheerless victory.[42]

While Curley and "Dapper Dan" Coakley had been trading barbs, the stock market crashed. One pictures tiny figures debating on a miniature outdoor stage while in the offing a huge storm gathers terrible shape. That storm was the Great Depression, which would remain over Curley for the next six years, mocking his sometimes theatrical efforts to resist it, and making his febrile plotting to wrest political advantage from it seem intolerably petty.

❖   ❖   ❖

"She's not with him," people murmured as Curley and his children entered Symphony Hall for his inauguration on January 6, 1930, as the then longest-serving mayor in Boston's history. The seat reserved for Mary stayed eloquently vacant throughout the somber proceedings. Catching the mood, and uncomfortably surfacing it, the orchestra struck up "The Girl I Left Behind Me." Curley's long speech lacked fire. "It was apparent that the tremendous strain which he has suffered with the continued illness of his wife has left its effects," the *Transcript* observed. When the ceremony was over, instead of going to City Hall, he went home to share the day with her.[43]

"His third inaugural dealt practically with instant problems and looks intelligently to the future," the *New York Times* adjudged. Two months after the stock market crash, the main instant problem before the city was steadily increasing unemployment. "Until a sane economic policy is devised," Curley said, "unemployment will continue to exist. In its train come poverty, crime, and disease; and to combat these evils it is necessary to furnish work and wages to those in need of sustenance and employment." A slogan was born. Under the banner of "work and wages," Curley would fight the Depression, dabble in presidential politics, run for governor and senator. He pledged to put the unemployed to work building a municipal golf course, extending subway lines, expanding the airport, constructing branch libraries in the city's neighborhoods, and paving streets. He saw the failure of capitalism—mass unemployment—not simply as a challenge for government but as an opportunity, a chance to build up the city and raise the level of amenity and culture in the lives of its people. At $2 per capita, Boston led the nation in spending on public recreation, and Curley intended to maintain this legacy from his earlier administrations.[44]

The limits of Boston's home rule, however, would severely restrict his ability to carry out this pump-priming experiment.

Looking to the future, he pledged to assemble 350 representatives of "religious, educational, labor, industrial commercial, civic and financial organizations" to work with the City Planning Board to create a fifty-year plan for Boston. Reviving an idea he had advocated since his first term, he also boldly called for the formation of a "Greater Boston," a federation of the forty-three cities and towns within a fifteen-mile radius of City Hall along the lines of the London County Council. Boston, he noted, had already slipped to eighth place in population among American cities; Greater Boston would rise to fourth place with triple the city's population— 2,000,000 versus 770,000. Besides the economies of scale to be realized for the taxpayer through replacing forty-three separate governments with a single central authority, the city would be more attractive to investors the larger it became. Boston was 47 square miles in area, Baltimore 92, Los Angeles 444. This was America. Size connoted prestige.

Reaction to the idea from the forty-three cities and towns ranged from amusement to panic. "Metropolitan Boston," said one Cambridge official, "is Curley gone Napoleon." Yet it was also Curley gone visionary. To appreciate why, we have only to imagine how the establishment of a Greater Boston would have affected the two most contentious political issues of recent decades in Massachusetts: race and taxes.[45]

In 1974 a federal judge ordered the Boston public schools, which had long been racially segregated due in large part to the deliberate policies of the all-white School Committee, to integrate forthwith. The resulting racial violence in the schools, as blacks from Roxbury were bused into white South Boston, was a staining ugliness that the city might have been spared if Curley's 1930 plan had come to fruition. For "Boston" would then have included its suburbs, some of them affluent, to which black students could have been equitably and comparatively painlessly apportioned. The white flight that has since caused the resegregation of the city's schools, this time as black schools, might also have been avoided. A recent survey of ten "cities without suburbs"—cities that annexed or merged with their suburbs earlier in the century—found much less white flight than in cities with suburbs and more equal educational opportunities for minorities. Today the predominantly black Boston schools are an educational disgrace, while the white suburban systems around Boston number among the best in the country. This grotesque inequality in life chances for children of color could have been avoided under Curley's plan.[46]

As for taxes, the savings possible under a Greater Boston—one bureaucracy, not forty-four—might well have headed off the "tax revolt" of 1980 that has severely damaged the quality of life in Massachusetts and intensified the inequities not so much between blacks and whites as among localities. Dependence on a regressive property tax to fund public facilities from schools to police led in 1980 to the passage of a ballot initiative, Proposition 2½, that crimped the ability of cities and towns to raise revenue even to keep up with inflation. To increase spending in any given year by more than 2.5 percent, a referendum of the town's voters must be held. Typically, more affluent towns vote to increase their property taxes to pay for better services—schools first among them—while poorer cities and towns routinely reject new spending, sometimes by margins of nine to one. Teachers have been laid off in the thousands and class sizes have markedly increased; police and fire departments have been cut back to the point where public safety, the preservation of which is the basic justification for civil society, has been put at risk; one city has already declared bankruptcy and others teeter on the edge. As a spillover consequence of the tax revolt, state support of public education in Massachusetts, kindergarten through twelfth grade, ranks forty-ninth out of the fifty states. A Greater Boston would have eased the tax burdens that ignited this self-mutilation and at the same time equalized public services in the metropolitan area. Massachusetts would not today present so stark a picture of class inequality. Geography—sometimes the distance of less than a mile—would not so cruelly shape destiny.[47]

Fears of sacrificing any degree of local autonomy killed Curley's plan in its crib—although, as Curley pointed out, the principle of local autonomy "had not been allowed to prevail in the case of the seven leading cities which today outrank Boston in population," and it "should not be allowed to stand in the way of a movement beneficial to every city and town and the state itself." But there were also fears of Curley. What would he do with a city treasury swollen with the taxes of 1,171,880 new residents? The answer is that he would never have gotten his hands on it because annexation would have promptly ended his political career. Indeed, if the wave of annexations in the late 1860s and early 1870s that brought Curley's own Roxbury as well as Dorchester, Charlestown, Brighton, and West Roxbury into Boston had also included the town of Brookline, Curley would never have been mayor. But Brookline, a pastoral Yankee suburb, rejected annexation by a vote of two to one in 1873, the year before Curley was born. If by reason of its ethnic character and economic status the addition of just that one town to Boston could have blocked Curley's rise, the addition of forty-odd cities and towns would have assured his fall.

His proposal was a rare piece of statesmanship, one that had been in the air for generations but whose time had come in the 1920s, when suburbanization began to take off (while Boston's population grew by only 4 percent in the decade, the suburban population grew by 25 percent). The automobile had created new patterns of settlement to which Curley's Greater Boston was an imaginative governmental response. But, though the idea received support from several of the city's newspapers, as well as, surprisingly, the approbation of the Good Government Association, the Republican-dominated towns through their elected representatives in the state legislature would have none of it. "We'd just be the jackasses carrying Boston's load," said the chairman of the Milton Board of Selectmen in a comment that fairly summed up the suburban reaction.[48]

❖   ❖   ❖

Boston celebrated its tercentenary in 1930, and as one of his first official acts, Curley ordered the commissioning of a bas-relief sculpture commemorating the city's founding. Set in a kind of grotto along the Beacon Street side of the Common, the sculpture depicts Governor John Winthrop and the Reverend John Wilson meeting with the first European settler in Boston, William Blaxton. Curley instructed the sculptor, John Francis Paramino, to give Blaxton his own profile. It was a splendid private joke: symbolically, Curley was now Boston's founding father.[49]

The city he would lead into its three-hundredth year was about to be overwhelmed by the "instant" and, as it would come to seem to many Bostonians, everlasting problem of unemployment. But it had other problems as well. Prohibition had made Boston safe for violence—over fifty gang killings had occurred in recent years—as well as for forms of vice incongruous in a city too pure to let Theodore Dreiser's *An American Tragedy* be sold within its boundaries.

By 1928, Bostonians had spent an estimated $60 million on liquor. They could drink at four thousand speakeasies—four on the same block as the central police station; and an estimated fifteen thousand people worked in the illegal trade. "Boston is literally honeycombed with speakeasies," wrote a correspondent for the magazine *Plain Talk.* Returned home from the celebration of the Tricentenary in 1930, the mayor of Boston, England, told friends that in Boston, Massachusetts, "You can swim in liquor. . . . You can drown yourself in it." The speakeasies had to pay protection to corrupt policemen—Oliver P. Garrett, the officer in charge of the vice squad, made a fortune in this racket. To raise the money, many of them let rooms to prostitutes. Huntington Avenue in the Back

Bay was lined with speakeasies cum bordellos, and streetwalkers elsewhere in the city were a common sight.[50]

Run as it was by a "small clique of professional fixers," City Hall under Mayor Nichols presented no more edifying a prospect. To get the mayor to act, these political prostitutes—three of whom were lawyers—had to be seen first, and they demanded bribes in the shape of fees as the price of their intercession. "The people of Boston," Governor Fuller said, "are being systematically robbed by a group of men masquerading as politicians." He denounced his fellow Republican Nichols as "irresponsible" and labeled his four-man Executive Council of political lawyers and Republican heelers "the four horsemen of the apocalypse." The mayor who had held Boston up to national ridicule by banning Eugene O'Neill's *Strange Interlude* presided over an increasingly crapulous city and, if not dishonest himself, delayed action on, for example, the land takings for a subway tunnel across the harbor to East Boston long enough to give his cronies time to buy up the land and so help themselves to a choice bit of "honest graft."[51]

The prevailing tawdriness reached a garish apotheosis on Beacon Hill. There, within a hundred yards of the golden dome of Charles Bulfinch's State House, a huge red-and-gold electric sign proclaimed in multicolor the virtues of Chevrolets. Across the Common was another sign, endlessly blinking back the name of the dishwater sold as legal "near-beer" by Anheuser-Busch. The palpable deterioration under Nichols fed the appetite Davis noted for Curley.[52]

He began his term with his characteristic vow to avoid the mistakes of his predecessor. Pounding on his desk, he read the riot act to the contractors who had been living high on graft under Nichols. He pledged to fire dishonest inspectors and to relax the censorship that he more than anyone else had linked with the name of Boston. He said of Prohibition that "it has proven an ignoble experiment in the incubating of crime and criminals. It has enriched Canada, impoverished America, corrupted law-enforcement officials, made respect for lawfully-constituted authority a mockery and overnight through alcoholic substitutes has elevated humble undertakers to lordly morticians." And he made his personal views unmistakably clear by fixing his car horn to sound out the first notes of "How Dry I Am" and handing out keys to the city with a corkscrew and bottle opener attached. For the rest, he and the city with him turned the

.page on the 1920s. The problems of the 1930s clamored for his urgent attention.[53]

❖   ❖   ❖

In January, two weeks after Curley's inauguration, a man fell over dead in downtown Boston—the Depression's first victim of hunger. Rather than raise the pay of its charwomen from thirty-five to thirty-seven cents an hour to meet the requirements of the state Minimum Wage Commission, Harvard University gave its students a lesson in applied capitalism by firing twenty of them. Striking bakers were shocked to discover members of other unions lining up to take their place. During a February snowstorm, 1,300 men jammed the Municipal Employment Bureau for the chance to shovel snow for $5 a day; Curley hired 1,000 of them, 700 more than usual. In February 1928 the city wood yard on Hawkins Street gave work to 426 people; two years later, the number was 1,031. What the Lynds called the "great knife" of the Depression was coming down on the lives of the men and women of Boston. It would hang over them for the next decade.[54]

Within days of Curley's assumption of power, communist party organizers led a march of the unemployed on City Hall. The mayor had the police drive them away. In March the city saw its first unemployment riot when a communist front group, the Boston Council of the Unemployed, conducted a rally at Parkman bandstand attended by four thousand jobless men and women. To discourage trouble Curley had the Common ringed with police, and when the group began to march on the State House, it was beaten back by charging policemen on horseback. One communist leader referred to the mayor as a "political crooner—crooning lullabies to the people to make them forget their troubles." There was something to this charge, but Curley's generally stern line on radical demonstrations was concordant with local opinion. Boston was not known for its hospitality to radicalism. Groucho Marx put a witty spin on the truth when, speaking to the *Harvard Crimson* in 1929, he remarked that "the Cabots and that crowd are so afraid of a left wing they won't go near one, even if it's on a chicken." Curley was no Cabot, but he was no radical either. He had the Catholic's acute appreciation of order as the primary social good. As an Irishman with more than his share of anarchic impulses, moreover, he was apt to see demonstrations in a drastic light, as harbingers of upheaval. From the first he regarded the Depression as a potentially revolutionary moment in the nation's history. Men could take only so much. "Work and wages" was his formula both for justice and for order.[55]

He refused licenses to apple sellers and pledged there would be no soup kitchens or breadlines in Boston "if I can prevent it." Those seeking relief and unable to find work on one of his construction projects could cut firewood in the wood yard. There would also be no "dole," which he saw as corrosive not only of social discipline but of personal self-respect. "I would rather spend $10 to keep people working," he said, "than give $2.00 in the dole." People did not want handouts. They wanted work.[56]

In a 1930 speech Rooseveltian in flavor, Curley identified the "psychology of fear" as the country's main enemy: "We are living in a state of dread," he said. Positing a company that had to lay off 5 percent of its 3,000 employees, he continued, "While 5 percent of 3,000 persons is but 150 men and women . . . the real injury is not that which comes from cutting off the income of the 5 percent; it is the psychological effect it produces on those who are still working." Afraid they might be fired next, they "husband their income and resources, thereby bringing injury to every industry in the entire land." Employers had an obligation to check this spiral of fear before it destroyed their businesses. "The worker is not responsible for the industrial depression; he is a victim of it and should not be required to shoulder the entire burden of it. The employer should be required to shoulder his part of responsibility. When the day of adversity and depression comes," it was surely the better part not only of fairness but also of self-interest to "reduce the dividend rate" paid to stockholders rather than to fire more workers. Then, with prophetic accuracy, he turned to the Depression's likely political consequences. "I do not know how long this condition will continue in America, but it is the most important proposition today confronting the American people. It will make and unmake in the United States in the next three years, Presidents, Senators, and Governors." Someday the Depression would be his opportunity; for now it was his trial.[57]

Depression without, depression within—wherever he turned in the opening months of his administration, Curley was sorely pressed. Accepting no invitations for evening engagements, and affecting a cheeriness that must have cost him something to achieve, he went straight home from work to calm Mary's pain with his mellow voice. They had shared so much. Now they shared their last hours together. "Mayor Curley's devotion to his wife," the editors of the *Herald* wrote, "made even his enemies admire him."

Mary had never completely regained her health after the almost theological shock of Dorothea's death. Operated on for appendicitis in 1927, she was ominously slow to recover. Cancer of the rectum—euphemized by one newspaper as "an ailment which rarely fails to take its toll"—had weakened her. The next July, at their summer home in Hull, she became acutely ill. Curley took her to New York for surgery; the disease continued to spread. She had radium treatments at the house, "but all they did was delay her death and increase her pain," according to Francis Curley. Several times the Curleys visited the grave of a priest whose spirit was thought to exude healing powers, but the disease still continued to spread. In November she left the house for the last time, to cast her last vote for her husband—a feat those who knew of her pain regarded as heroic and that, in its expression of her love joined to his career, must have moved James to his depths. Thanksgiving, her forty-fifth birthday, was the last time she came downstairs. At Christmas the family put up a tree in her room, where they exchanged gifts. She badly wanted to go to the inauguration, but half an hour before she was to leave she was stricken and had to abandon her plans. Listening to her husband's speech over the radio, she must have been stirred by the testament of his love for her with which he began. At Symphony Hall her daughter Mary cried as she listened to his words. They were so true, and so helpless.

She lingered into the late spring. Off her bedroom was a sun porch, where she would sit for hours holding and talking to five-year-old Francis and watching a rosebush in the garden beneath them for the first hints of new life. How she wanted to see the roses bloom. Privately she was settling her accounts according to the ancient usages of her faith. There was so little to settle. We come across the phrase in nineteenth-century novels: "a blameless life." Wife, mother, constant companion, faithful to every vow of God and man alike, she had led a blameless life. Now, smiling down her pain, struggling against the urge to surrender to comfort her children, she was dying with a courage and grace and consideration for others that transfigured her death into a gift, a final offering, an inspiration to all who witnessed it.

Cardinal O'Connell, who visited her several times, was among those inspired. One day he stopped young Francis Curley on the stairs. "Boy," he said, putting a hand on his shoulder, "there is a lesson I want you to learn and I want you to learn it today. . . . Do not ever let it cross your mind that I came here to give your mother courage to face her day. She is a saint in heaven already, and I come to see her to find the courage to face my day."

The day before she died, a Monday, the cardinal was with her briefly. The warm weather of early June had made her think of the house in Hull: of the happiness the family had known there, of how much she wanted to go there again. But then it had grown unseasonably hot, her remaining strength ebbed, and she took a turn for the worse. James rushed home from City Hall. She rallied briefly; the crisis seemed to have passed. But on Tuesday evening Dr. English summoned the family to her bedside. She was going fast now and she knew it. James carried Francis in to her; and with the sound of little George weeping in her ears, she just had time to give Francis one last kiss. Quickly, James moved to embrace her. She said, "I love you," and died in his arms. .

Over the succeeding days so many floral tributes arrived at the house that they had to be placed out on the lawn, and amidst the profusion of flowers no one bothered to notice if the roses in the garden had bloomed.

The cardinal himself gave the eulogy at the funeral Mass. Many in the audience in the cathedral were in tears as Curley, his face a study in sorrow, walked down the aisle, holding Francis by the hand. Someone noticed that one of the boy's shoelaces was undone, a piercing reminder that his mother would never be there to tie them for him again. "The whole community has been stirred to deepest sympathy in witnessing for two long years the heroic Christian fortitude with which this true wife and mother has borne the unspeakable pain and suffering of a long illness," the cardinal said, his voice echoing over the heads of the five thousand people—governors, senators, ordinary Bostonians. "Again and again in that room of suffering I have been witness to a faith and confidence in God that moved me to depths of admiration." It was difficult for him, given his low opinion of Curley, but from his place on the altar the cardinal turned to him now and said: "To him who now with the great public burden he bears must bow under this great grief the whole community offers with our prayers for her eternal peace in the Lord, our deep, sincere, and affectionate condolence. Under a strain which few could bear without breaking, he has faced his daily task with a breaking heart, but a courageous face and countenance."

"It's God's will," Curley had said when Dr. English told him that Mary was going. But he had been her friend and husband and lover; and over lunch some days later he snatched up a bottle from the table and smashed it to bits on the floor.[58]

A train, slowed to a crawl to cut the noise, was passing on the El outside the cathedral as the plush mauve casket was carried slowly out the door, and a guard between two of the cars was seen to remove his cap out of respect to the memory of Mary Emelda Curley.[59]

❖   ❖   ❖

Curley had a world-historical crisis to distract him from his grief. He could hide in the Depression, a crisis sculpted to the scope of the space he had to fill. Besides battling with the Republican state legislature for authority to borrow outside the city's debt limit to put the unemployed—by April 1930, perhaps a quarter of the labor force—to work; besides suppressing the "Red Roosters" of the communist party according to his own arbitrary calculus, forbidding them the Common to protest the third anniversary of the execution of Sacco and Vanzetti but permitting a demonstration against "imperialist war"; besides inducing the National League Braves and the American League Red Sox to play a game to benefit Boston's poor, and asking the Holy Cross and Boston College football teams to do likewise; besides vainly lobbying the Hoover administration and the Congress to extend federal aid to the cities; besides issuing slightly more liberal rules for the Boston stage—though, in case anyone had any doubts, dances that "contained suggestive or repulsive contortions of the human body" were still out; besides pushing his plan for Greater Boston; besides rewriting Boston's official greeting and by other steps large and small preparing for the Tricentenary—Curley was devising what one newspaper called a "lethally fantastic plan" to elect a new governor.[60]

He faced the same problem as in his second term: the barrier to succeeding himself as mayor. To satisfy the psychic and economic necessity of holding office he had to run for governor. Since he had just been elected mayor of Boston, 1930 was too early to make that particular bold move. The governor of Massachusetts served a two-year term; the next election would be held in 1932, when Curley would still be mayor of Boston and thus able to dragoon the city's work force into getting out the vote.

The current governor, Frank G. Allen, a Republican, had first been elected in 1928; if he won reelection in 1930, he would in all likelihood retire after the expiration of his term, leaving his lieutenant governor, William Youngman, as the Republican candidate for governor in 1932. Since 1932 would also be the year of the next presidential election—held in the midst of an unprecedented economic slump—the expected national tide toward the Democrats could sweep Curley past the nonincumbent Youngman and into the governor's corner office. This scheme required the reelection of Governor Allen in 1930, though a Democrat willing to serve one term and then make way for Curley in 1932 would also do nicely, as would a Democrat who would lose. Curley seemed to have found such a Democrat in John Fitzgerald. Harmony had gone so far as that.[61]

Harmony had also fuddled the brain of the sixty-seven-year-old Fitzgerald. He had intended to run for the Senate in 1930, but lured by Curley's promise to swing the Boston Democracy behind him in the race for governor, he switched offices. He was Curley's Teddy Glynn of 1930—a sure loser to the Republican candidate. Incredibly, he appeared willing to take the fall, until he faced opposition from within his own party. Joseph Buell Ely, a lawyer from western Massachusetts, had declared his candidacy, as had John J. Cummings, who had run for lieutenant governor on the Curley ticket in 1924. Fitzgerald would have had to contest them for the nomination in a party primary. This was decidedly not harmony; Fitzgerald had no stomach for an intraparty fight.[62]

With a week to go before the primary, he succumbed to the political equivalent of the vapors, a timely case of nervous exhaustion, and announced his withdrawal from the race. "Dr. Fitzgerald"—a reference to his honorary doctorate from Notre Dame—"has awakened at the 11th hour to a realization of what everyone has known for months," said Senator Frank Osborne of Lynn,

"—namely that James Michael Curley was leading him on like a lamb to the slaughter so that the gubernatorial field might be clear for Curley in 1932. Curley's 1932 Machiavellian candidacy thus comes to an ignominious end before it was born."[63]

Curley was among the first to visit the ailing ex-candidate in the hospital. "Hello, John," he said, drawing a chair up to the bed. "I'm tremendously sorry to find you a sick man. And I'm doubly sorry, John, because the nomination for Governor is assured you, a fitting reward for your long service to the state and the Democratic party." Fitzgerald, mustering a smile, explained that he had been "carrying on" on nerves alone—just as in 1913, his doctors had told him that to save his health he must withdraw from the race. "John, we're not going to let you withdraw," Curley said, that lethally fantastic plan taking rapid shape. "We're going to nominate you and put you over."[64]

The plan: Curley would be what one observer called "a candidate in the second person," making the race on Fitzgerald's behalf, to cap the sick old warhorse's career with a victory. Once Fitzgerald won the September primary, the Democratic State Committee would choose another candidate—Curley had a list of forty-nine "better" choices than Ely—to run against Governor Allen in the general election in November. "He is proposing that we take away from the people all their rights under the direct primary law," Ely rightly said, for under Curley's plan the primary would not pick the Democratic candidate; the Democratic State Committee would. "The reaction against the Curley dictatorship is tremendous," noted the *Springfield News*. The *Worcester Post* summed up the statewide consensus of opinion in a headline: A PREPOSTEROUS PROPOSAL.[65]

It was screamingly obvious now that Curley's only motive was to keep Joseph Ely (Cummings was not rated a serious contender) from being elected governor. To defeat Ely, a Yankee Democrat, Curley fell back on the "racial issue." At a Fitzgerald rally in Tremont Temple, he declared, "No Irishman worthy of the name can cast a vote for Ely after the facts of his black record of opposition to their race are publicly known." These "facts" were that Ely, at the state Democratic convention in 1919, had opposed a plank calling for reservations favorable to the cause of Irish independence to be made in the League of Nations treaty, and that, disgusted at the demands for the reservations coming from Irish delegates, he had remarked to Daniel T. O'Connell, brother of the ubiquitous Joseph O'Connell, that "if the Irish want to fight, let them go back to Ireland and fight." In view of Ely's "vicious and contemptible hatred for the Irish race," Curley said, "he should take up residence in some peaceful suburb like Piccadilly, just outside of dear old London, and become a candidate for Parliament."

Ely denied having said anything against the Irish, pointed out that in 1919 Curley himself had supported the League of Nations, and denounced Curley's injection of the racial issue as "the last ditch attempt of a traitor to the Democratic party." Speaking over radio station WBZ, he directly addressed the "lovable Irish people quick to appreciate and quick to resent—what do you say of a man who deliberately falsifies every act of my life? Why did I support Gov. Smith if I hated the Irish people? Why have I supported Senator Walsh if I was opposed to the Irish cause? How long must you permit this selfish man to use your noble heritage for his own political ends and to hold you up to the scorn of people who are not your friends?" That was a haunting question: Curley's shamrock politics, his fanning of resentment and bigotry, had been going on for a generation. How long would the Boston Irish permit it?[66]

Invading Curley's home ground, Ely held a rally in the heart of the Tammany ward, at which his every mention of Curley brought jeers and hoots. Nine Irish-American members of the City Council defended Ely and denounced Curley. Witnessing the repetition of the fell tactics Curley had used against him in 1921, John R. Murphy declared that Curley was at it again, "uttering a lie so late in the campaign that a contradiction does not reach many of those who read the original charges." Daniel Coakley, running a quixotic independent campaign for the U.S. Senate, called Curley a "counterfeit Irishman" for raising such a spurious issue against Ely. At the Hendricks Club, in one of his patented "Sunday-befores," Martin Lomasney blasted Curley for scheming with Governor Allen to deliver the state to the Republicans. Quaffing water as the sweat coursed down his face—"Thank God, that's the only stuff I ever drank"—Lomasney passionately admonished the faithful to vote for Joseph Ely. "Did you notice his courage? Ah, there must be Irish blood in him somewhere or he wouldn't be such a fighter."[67]

Later that same Sunday the same destiny that had led James Curley to radio station WNAC on the Sunday night of his explosion at Jennie Loitman Barron once again led him to WNAC. And once again, the station was host to a wild happening.

Dressed in top hat and tails to mark the Tricentenary celebration, which was then under way, Curley had just finished speaking from one of the sound studios and was on his way out the door when over the lobby loudspeaker he heard snatches of a broadcast being delivered in another studio. He stopped to listen. Frank J. Donahue, the chairman of the Democratic State Committee, was denouncing his use of the racial issue, his exploitation of the enfeebled Fitzgerald (saying Curley had privately called his prize candidate a "clown"), and his apparent plot to throw the election to the Republicans. But what froze Curley in his tracks was Donahue's charge that in 1928 Curley had kept thousands of dollars in campaign contributions intended for Al Smith—that he had used his Bull Pen not only to elect himself mayor but to line his own pockets. From the station lobby, Curley, through clenched teeth, shouted "I'm not going to let him get away with THAT!" and started back into the station to get Donahue.

"Head him off!" one of the men with him shouted. Another cried, "Don't let him hit him!" But Curley, snorting, "I'll get him! . . . "I'll get him! He's got away with too much already," brushed past his handlers and closed in on Donahue, who was finishing his speech. Just outside the studio from which Donahue was broadcasting, James Michael Jr. put his arms around his father's shoulders and stopped his charge. "Don't bother him, Dad," he pleaded. Perhaps the hated "Dad" did it; anyway, Curley shook him off: "You keep out of this." He warned another man, "Don't you say a word. Don't you do anything," and flung open the studio door to confront Donahue. "You are the damndest liar I ever knew," Curley swore at the shocked state chairman. "I'll get you if it's the last thing I do"—and he lunged for him. The thousands of people listening over the airwaves, the sound being still on in the studio, must have wondered whether they had tuned in to a crime melodrama. Just as Curley was about to strike, James Jr. flung himself on his father to keep the blow from reaching the bespectacled Donahue, who, outclassed in size and weight, prudently retreated behind the piano. His top hat bobbing giddily, Curley strained in the clutches of his son and two other men to get at Donahue, who now had only one hope of rescue. Twenty-five-year-old Gael Coakley, Daniel's son, was also in the studio. Bravely he stepped between Donahue and Curley; someone hit him, and he went down. The studio door slammed shut. Donahue was trapped.

A quick-witted station employee managed to work his way around the studio and open a rear door, through which Donahue fled, making no attempt to hide his fear. Seeing his quarry escaping, Curley shook off his three holders and went after him.

Designed to let celebrities exit directly onto the street, the rear door led into an alley that ended on Brookline Avenue, just a few steps from the front entrance to the Hotel Buckminster. Anyone passing on the street would have seen the chairman of the state Democratic party run out of the alley as if on fire, with the mayor of Boston in his tall hat a few paces behind him, followed by a welter of panting shouting men in tuxedos. Just as Curley was about to collar Donahue, Gael Coakley again intervened, and again one of Curley's men struck him. Donahue turned and went back to help the boy—in time to witness Curley himself knee Coakley in the groin. Shaken, staggering, gasping for breath, Coakley groaned a plea for mercy. But Curley, by this time firmly in the grip of several of his men, was not merciful. "Give it to him again, Joe," he commanded. At which Joe punched Coakley hard in the face.

To avoid Joe's cosmetic attentions, Donahue retreated to the hotel lobby. Curley and the more hot-blooded of his company made to pursue, but a hotel detective turned them back.

Curley returned to the station some time later to give another scheduled speech. It began with his usual attack on Ely, but then Curley mincingly referred to the brawl. "I had the privilege of addressing the radio audience from this station earlier this evening. I never believed that any man . . . could descend to the depths that the president of the Democratic state committee descended to." If the audience anticipated a refutation of Donahue's charges that he had pocketed at least $15,000 intended for Al Smith, they were in for a surprise. "He stated that in the Smith campaign in 1928 I refused to accept an assignment outside of the city of Boston. There was a very excellent reason for my refusal. A most sad one; it had no place in the political campaign and only one of the smallest character of mind would inject anything of that character into the campaign." Donahue had said that Curley's refusal to speak outside Boston showed he was more interested in electing himself mayor in 1929 than in helping Al Smith carry Massachusetts in 1928. But Curley's was a pretextual indignation. Once again he was

trotting out his now-dead wife, this time to distract attention from
the real source of his ire. He, not Donahue, injected Mary into the
campaign in order to exploit the sympathy nearly all Bostonians
felt for him. He was demagoguing the most intimate and painful
moments of his own life.

"When Mr. Donahue completed his speech," he continued, "I
made it my business to take him to task for what he had said. If he
resembled in any particular what might be termed a man"—a
sneer that would incur Donahue's lasting resentment—"I might be
guilty of asking more harsh measures in bringing him to task than
merely chastising him by the tongue. In this campaign, this being
the tercentenary year, I beg to direct the attention of the radio
audience to my real reason for the position I have taken in advocat-
ing the election of John F. Fitzgerald on the morrow. . . ."

With newspapers across the state bannering the news of Curley's brawl, the voters went to the polls on that morrow and rejected Curley's scheme. Not only did Fitzgerald lose decisively
statewide to Ely—though only narrowly, 43,695 to 42,424, in Boston, where waving the shamrock was still good politics—but Curley's candidate for senator, Joseph O'Connell, lost; his candidate
for lieutenant governor lost; and so did his candidate for secretary
of state. The biggest loser of all, though, appeared to be Curley
himself.[68]

Asked by reporters if he had struck Donahue, the author of
this debacle was cocky and condescending. "No. Donahue wears
glasses. Men who wear glasses don't get hit. I told him that if he
repeated the charges he made against me . . . I would have to
spank him."[69]

Pundits predicted that Curley's broadcast battle royal would
sink the Democratic ticket, but the Depression was making Democrats faster than he could unmake them. To restore harmony Al
Smith had come to town for a monster rally at the Boston Arena,
and everyone had to forget Donahue's charge that Curley had
made a profit off Smith in 1928. John Fitzgerald had to warble out a
chorus of "Sweet Adeline." Curley had to appear on the same
stage as Ely and Donahue, with Dan Coakley, in the front row of
the balcony, cheering heartily. At another venue, Curley had to
present Ely with a $1,000 campaign contribution, for which Ely
warmly thanked him (only to discover later that the check was
made out to the Curley-controlled Boston Democratic committee).

It took prodigious insincerities like these, but Ely, by 1 percent of the vote, managed to unseat Governor Allen in November.[70]

In an editorial entitled "Apologies to Our Guests," the *Transcript* had assured Mayor Salter of Boston, England, and the other dignitaries on hand for the Tricentenary that the Curley melee—this "unfortunate and unexpected addition to the celebration planned in their honor"—was at least unprecedented. "It is not in a boastful but rather a diffident tone that we say to them that in the three hundred years of Boston's history no such happening has ever occurred to mar an anniversary celebration and that we may rightfully be hopeful that another three hundred years will pass before we have another."[71]

For Curley, the Tricentenary was a specific for the Depression. In his inaugural and throughout the year, he reminded Bostonians that their problems were "infinitesimal" next to the privations suffered by the founders of the Bay Colony. The Tricentenary, in addition, was a heaven-sent diversion. If the city could not provide the unemployed with bread, it could at least give them a circus.[72]

Parades, pageants, reenactments, fireworks displays, and banquets, all building to the huge Boston Parade in September, marked that summer. At a "Great Meeting" on the Common, former president Calvin Coolidge was the star attraction. Curley wrung a reluctant smile from Coolidge when, beginning his speech, he addressed Governor Allen and the other assembled dignitaries: "Your Excellency, our President that has been and, if he so desires, may again be; guests of the Commonwealth and fellow citizens." The crowd roared its approval of the idea of Coolidge as president again. As for the parade, a million and a half people watched forty thousand marchers, two hundred floats, and one hundred bands in a marathon of color and noise that began at noon and ended at seven that night. Curley stood on the one-thousand-foot wooden grandstand set up along Tremont Street from start to finish, making speeches, using his tall silk hat to conduct the bands, and giving way to the pleadings of paraders to deliver baritone renditions of "The Sidewalks of New York," the anthem of Al Smith's presidential campaign; "There'll Be a Hot Time in the Old Town Tonight"; and "It Ain't Gonna Rain No More." Long as it was, the parade might have been longer still. In a speech, Curley observed that for the 250th anniversary parade in 1880 the city breweries had entered a spectacular float, and if they could do it this year and if the bootleggers and their customers got in line, "it would take a year round parade."[73]

Held on a hot day, the parade claimed victims. The heat killed one man and sent forty others to the hospital. Riding on Congress Street, James M. Curley, Jr., was nearly injured when his horse, frightened by a shower of confetti, reared and started to topple over. City councilor Clement Norton, who would be a source for and character in *The Last Hurrah*—and who would end his days in a paupers' hospital, banging his tray with his spoon and shouting "I'll tell Jim Curley about this!"—quickly grabbed the bridle and told James to dismount. No sooner had James done so than the horse reared again and fell over heavily into the gutter. All around James were relieved that he had got off in time; the weight of the horse might have crushed him.[74]

The political aspirations of James Michael Curley, Jr., had become an issue in the 1929 mayoral campaign. Sleekly handsome, well educated, well spoken, and gifted with a golden name, James seemed poised to succeed his father. His friends called him "the young Alexander" in sportive acknowledgment of his ambition. Shorter than his father and stockier but with his father's brown eyes, James had received a kind and degree of attention from Curley that he was not able to give to his other children.[75]

Described by many as strikingly like his father in personality, James graduated from the Boston Latin School, where he had been president of the debating society, had captained the debating team, and had won prizes in declamation and history. He had also won a letter in football, though a broken collarbone ended his athletic career. At Boston College he was twice elected president of his class, and his achievements in both debate and declamation brought him special honors. (His mother saw room for improvement; listening to him speak over the radio, she was heard to say, "Oh no, he's never going to be as good as his father.") His subsequent enrollment at the Harvard Law School must have given a certain party fits of ambivalence. Popular with his law school classmates, young Curley was also well liked among his fellow recruits at the Citizens' Military Training Camp held at Fort Devens, where he served in the same company as John Coolidge, the former president's surviving son. The twenty-three-year-old James would graduate from Harvard in June 1931. Immediately after graduation he planned to marry Lauretta Bremner, a college classmate of his sister Mary whom he had been seeing for over a year.

In early January James and Lauretta returned to Boston from a Christmas visit to her family in Chicago to attend the mayor's address to the City Council. ("I am firm in the belief that the year 1931 will be most prosperous," Curley intoned, "and that definite steps will be taken to prevent a recurrence of the industrial depression so much in evidence in 1930.") James's classes were about to resume, and Lauretta had to return home. He saw her off at South Station. Sixty years later she recalled what they said to each other. "It won't be long until June," he assured her. "Just an eternity," she replied.⁷⁶

It was a bad day for Mayor Curley. It had begun with the inauguration of Governor Ely, when Curley must have brooded over the wreck of his plans for 1932. His gall was equal to most occasions, but mounting a primary challenge to a sitting governor of his own party would, as one commentator put it, be "political hari-kari."⁷⁷

At City Hall later in the day he got a disturbing call from his daughter Mary. James Jr. had come home from school complaining of sharp pains in his abdomen. Mary had tried to make him comfortable, but the pains had only worsened and she was worried. Curley, who must have feared death in every nosebleed and stumble of his children, canceled his appointments and rushed home.

He found his son in bed writhing in pain. He and Mary applied ice compresses to James's stomach; the pain abated, only to intensify. He called Dr. English, who consulted with a surgeon, Dr. David Scannell, and a specialist, Dr. Archibald McK. Fraser. They decided that James, who gave every sign of suffering from gall stones, must be operated on immediately. Around midnight Curley and Mary—who insisted that she come with them—drove James to the City Hospital. At 1:00 A.M. on Thursday, January 9, he went under the knife. The surgeons located and removed an unusually large gallstone. The operation completed, they remained with James for over an hour, leaving only when he seemed out of danger. While Mary returned home with Drs. Scannell and Fraser, Curley stayed behind. He wanted to be there when James wakened from the ether. It must have been a nurse who described the following scene to a reporter.

Hunched over his bed, peering at James for any sign of consciousness, Curley saw him stir. "Come on Jimmie, snap out of it," he said.

Awake at last, James blinked back at him. "I'll be all right," he said. "You go along home. You have to go to Washington. Don't let this hold you back."

"All right," Curley replied. "But I want to keep an eye on you. I'll be over in the morning with the children."

"No, never mind, I'll be all right." Quietly, he added, "Put your head down close, pa. I want to whisper something to you."

Curley bent his head down next to his son's.

"Kiss me, pa."

Curley kissed his son. Then he drove home with Dr. English. It was three-thirty in the morning. James dozed for a while. At five he woke long enough to recognize Miss Collier, the nurse who had cared for his mother throughout her long dying. Suddenly Collier noticed that he seemed to be in distress: James was seized with an embolism and died in the seconds she took to reach for the telephone.[78]

Curley had just settled in for what remained of the night when the phone rang. It could only be bad news. He took the call in the library, from which he soon emerged, his family in the hall watching, stunned. "It shouldn't have happened," he said, his voice breaking. "It shouldn't have happened."[79]

At the Harvard Law School, Professor Felix Frankfurter paid tribute to one of his most promising students. "Since last we met," he told his class, "one of our number has gone forever. It is always terrible when death strikes youth and most terrible when there was the high promise of a good life for himself and his community, as was true of young Curley. We must go on with our work, but not without thinking of the father who has been tried by personal affliction as few men ever are. And let us bid farewell to your companion in the words with which his ancient church takes leave of her children 'recquiescat in pace, et lux reterna luceat ei.'" Madame Schumann-Heink, who years before had sung "Boy of Mine" through her grief, sent a one-sentence telegram: "I pray it isn't true."[80]

At James's wake, a woman in the long line of mourners who had come to the Jamaicaway to pay their last respects promised to pray for his soul. Believers of a certain vintage say such things at such times. "Prayers won't bring James back," Curley snapped, and stalked into the kitchen. Love was not enough. Neither was faith.[81]

Six months after laying Mary to rest, he was back at the cathedral again. The same streets, the same people taking off their hats, the same fathomless pain. The cardinal choked up in the midst of his eulogy. Curley's cheeks streamed with tears.

When she was a student at the College of the Sacred Heart in New York, Mary Curley would get unsigned crank letters predicting that her whole family would die tragic deaths. God, the letters said, would punish them; the Curleys were cursed. Looking at his remaining children as he left the cathedral behind his son's coffin, James Michael Curley must have anguished over whether there was such a curse and whether and how long it would spare them.[82]

❖   ❖   ❖

James had wanted him to go to Washington and as soon as the funeral was over he did: to lobby the federal government to turn one of the closer-in harbor islands over to the city, which needed the land to build a first-class airport. Along with the harbor tunnel linking the airport to the city, Curley envisioned the airport expansion as one of the major undertakings of his third term. The cost was high—$25 million for the airport, $10 million for the tunnel—but the farsighted thought it money well spent.

"Is the Boston airport worth all this expenditure?" the Boston Traveler asked. "It is for a number of reasons. Business and the port this year or next year or the year after may not justify the spending of so much money, but just so sure as you are reading these words, it will not be long before Boston will reap huge benefit from having an unexcelled airport. Developing our airport now is an excellent piece of civic judgement."

Curley got the island, he expanded the airport, he built the tunnel. These projects had had lengthy gestations (proposals for a harbor tunnel went back to the 1870s), but they owed a great deal to his energy and vision. Certainly contemporaries saw them in that light. When a newspaper ran a contest to name the tunnel, the leading entries included, the Curley Tunnel, James M. Curley, Jr. Tunnel, James Curley Memorial Tube, James M. Curley Speedway, Curley Traffic Tunnel, Curley Idea Tunnel, Curley's Pass, Curley Motor Meteor, Mary Curley Transit Tunnel, Curley Welfare Tunnel, and Curley's Tube to the Airport.[83]

Curley's vision could also be seen in his proposal for an arterial highway to be built through downtown Boston, to winnow traffic from the city's clogged streets. "There is probably no city in the United States," the City Planning Board found, "where traffic congestion on the streets of the downtown business section is so near the saturation point as . . . in Boston today." The so-called Central Artery connecting to the harbor tunnel had the strong support of local businesses, which recognized the benefits to be derived from a twentieth-century transportation plan to meet twentieth-century transportation needs, but the state legislature would not let Curley borrow the necessary $11 million. The Central Artery would have to wait until after the Second World War, when it would cost many millions more to build. Altogether, the legislature cut Curley's request for a loan of $31 million to $3 million. Funding for the airport was cut from $1.5 million to a pathetic $250,000. Lack of home rule was blighting Boston's future.[84]

The legislature was under Republican control, but Curley got no more help from a governor of his own party. Joseph Ely took his model from the parsimonious stewardship of Governor Calvin Coolidge. "At a time when men with self-inflicted wounds sought admission to the Boston City Hospital in order to get three meals a day and a heated room," Michael Kendall writes, "Ely proclaimed that he did 'not suppose that anyone in the United States will die from starvation.'"[85]

With the state government unwilling to let Boston furnish work to its unemployed in building the city of the future, Curley looked to Washington. Boston was grappling with national problems—the loss of jobs caused by the industrial depression, the transportation crisis brought on by the automobile, the wave of lawlessness unleashed by Prohibition. Yet it was having to meet these national problems with exclusively local resources. Washington must do more: Curley, just elected president of the National Conference of Mayors, could see no other course. Then, as now, forces beyond municipal control impinged on the cities. But today those forces are even more difficult to control. How does a mayor of Los Angeles prevent illegal immigrants from Mexico from taking the entry level jobs in his city away from native-born African-Americans? And how does the major of any city prevent fathers from walking out on the children they bring into the world, the fecund source of infinite social woes?[86]

In September 1930 Curley's 350-member brain trust, which included the president of M.I.T., a roster of local professors, and progressive businessmen and labor leaders, met at the Parker House for the first time to hear Curley unfold his plan for national economic recovery. He called for the establishment of a mandatory five-day workweek to spread work among more workers; for a $1 billion flood control and hydroelectric power project to create an "inland empire" along the Mississippi Valley; for a massive federal commitment to building public works to get the unemployed off the dole and behind the pick and shovel; for the creation of a federal industrial planning board to determine the causes of the Depression and to set up governmental machinery to prevent anything like it from happening again; for old-age pensions to protect the elderly from penury; and for public health insurance to protect the indigent from disease. It was Roosevelt's New Deal and Truman's Fair Deal and Johnson's Great Society in embryo.[87]

Curley met with President Hoover personally to push his ideas, but got nowhere. "President Hoover is very voluminous in his proclamations regarding the emergency," Curley remarked, adding, "If proclamations could settle industrial depressions then we would be the most prosperous of peoples." Hoover's welfare spokesman in Massachusetts, Eliot Wadsworth, expressed the president's attitude when he said, "There's plenty of prosperity now. The automobiles are still running, as you may notice, and the movies are still full. We can handle the problem locally." The administration's ideological reluctance to act tended to slow down the few projects to which it had committed itself. Angry that it should have taken two years to begin construction on a new Boston post office, Curley sarcastically inquired of Postmaster General Walter Brown if he could pasture the "municipal cow" on the empty construction site. "Referring to your desire to pasture your municipal cow on the post-office site," Brown replied, "it is my opinion that the department should not be required to do more than put up with your bull."[88]

Hoover was yesterday's president. Elected to preside over a boom, he was adrift in the bust. As Curley left on a five-week European trip in May, his thoughts turned more and more to the necessity of electing tomorrow's president.

James and Mary Curley had been frequent visitors to Cuba, and they had taken cruises to Bermuda and the West Indies. But Mary was superstitious about making the ocean crossing, so, much as he longed and lobbied for it, they had never visited Ireland together. After her death he had toured the major cities with his family; so this was his second European excursion. The party included his daughter Mary; his near-daughter-in-law, Lauretta Bremner; and his city treasurer, Edmund L. Dolan. Their itinerary called for stops in Ireland, England, France, and Italy. On this trip, as before, he went first-class, staying at the Savoy in London, the Shelburne in Dublin, the Ritz in Paris, the Excelsior in Rome.

How much did all this cost? In 1950, during another of Curley's hegiras to Europe, Francis Curley got a call from the Thomas Cook travel agency that shocked him. His father had started out with $50,000 to last for three months, but had run through that in three weeks and needed a fresh infusion of cash. On the two trips of 1930 and 1931, Francis reckoned, Curley may have spent upward of $100,000. Curley's eagerness to relieve the mounting distress of the unemployed—"If there is no work in three months from this date," someone who signed himself XXX wrote him, "all the city and state buildings will be blown up"—might have seemed more convincing if he had forgone this Grand Tour. But he had the excuse of personal suffering, and few Bostonians seemed to begrudge him the chance to take his mind off his troubles. As for his core constituents, they seemed to regard his flagrant munificence the way the era's moviegoers did Busby Berkeley's musical extravaganzas: as a projection of escapist fantasy immune from criticism.[89]

For years Standish Willcox had made it his habit to write on Curley's behalf what Joseph Dinneen calls "the precisely proper sentiment" on occasions great or small, happy or sad, to important people the world over. Consequently, "there had grown up an impressive number of burghers and lord mayors who might be excused for assuming that Curley ruled America." Thus when their ship landed in Plymouth, England, an invitation to sherry awaited them from the lord mayor. They were about to reap the harvest of Willcox's courtesies.[90]

Curley rose before dawn for his first view of the Irish coast. "I've been waiting fifty years to see Ireland," he told Mary, "and I don't want to miss anything." In three breathless days he covered six hundred miles of the country, meeting with President Cosgrave, with heroes of the Irish war of independence, and with the common people of Ireland, the type of Michael Curley and Sarah Clancy. Riding along a country road, he suddenly ordered the driver to stop their machine. He had noticed an old lady walking by the side of the road carrying a goose to market in her basket, and he wanted to give her a lift. She sat down in the jump seat with her goose. Curley commenced to address her in Gaelic and when she replied in the same tongue, he suddenly laughed out loud. "What did she say to you?" Mary and Lauretta wanted to know. "I asked her, 'Do you have any Irish?' which is how they refer to Gaelic. And she replied, 'A divil of a lot more than you do.'" Spotting an old man smoking his duveen in front of a cottage, Curley gave him a warm greeting. "You know," the old man replied, with charming inconsequence, "I'm ninety years old this day." Just then a woman wearing stout boots against the muck of the fields rounded the corner of the cottage, saw who was there, and burst out with "Glory be to God if it isn't The Curley!" Finding her face familiar, The Curley asked, "Weren't you in Boston once?" "That I was," she replied. Drawn by the prospect of gold in Boston's streets, she told them, she had found only poverty and disappointment. She had gone to Curley and somehow he had helped her get home.[91]

He visited Oughterard in County Galway, his father's village, but no one remembered him—Michael Curley had been a child when he left—or his people. The country roundabout had a melancholy beauty, dotted as it was with the freestanding chimneys marking the abandoned farms of the anonymous thousands who had fled the Famine for America. If he wanted to find an objective symbol of the urge in him for power and money and fame he need look no farther than those gaunt chimneys. There was nothing behind him whether in Ireland or America except these emblems of insecurity.[92]

In Dublin he roused Mary and Lauretta to accompany him on a search for a Rabbi Goldberg, who, he told them, while visiting him in Boston years before, had promised to kill the fatted calf if the mayor should ever call on him in Dublin. The young women, game for a joke, mailed Curley a postcard care of their next stop in Cork signed "Rabbi Goldberg," expressing his regrets that he had not been in Dublin to share the fatted calf with the mayor. "See, I told you there was a Rabbi Goldberg!" he said, delighted.

"Members of my party kissed the Blarney Stone," his autobiography notes, "but I did not think this ritual necessary for myself."[93]

The high point of his visit to England was a reciprocating celebration from Mayor Reuben Salter of Boston, Lincolnshire. Schoolchildren waving Union Jacks and the Stars and Stripes lined the roads leading into Boston as the Curley caravan passed through. Speaking without notes for thirty minutes, Curley addressed the townspeople gathered in the market square from the balcony of the historic Guild Hall. They had never heard the like. "It is the universal opinion," Mayor Salter told the *Boston Globe,* "that he is the finest orator that has visited Boston."[94]

In Paris he and his party were the guests of General John J. Pershing and Ambassador Charles G. Dawes at the French Colonial Exposition. He toured the Louvre wearing a beret and carrying one of the dozens of blackthorn shillelaghs that, with a view to their political utility as gifts back in Boston, he had bought up in Ireland. Paris liberated his puckishness. "Merci Bo-Peep," he would say to waiters and maids, who would sternly correct him: "Oh, no, Monsieur, 'Merci Beaucoup!'" Over tea at the Ritz he startled Mary, Lauretta, and another of their college classmates by directing their attention to a gray-haired gentleman in intimate converse with a woman plainly not his wife. On the back of his card he wrote, "You'd better go home; your wife is in the hotel," and had the waiter deliver it to the couple's table. The young women with Curley could barely contain their laughter as the red-faced gentleman sought the nearest exit.[95]

In Rome he had an audience with the man he called "the Moose," Benito Mussolini, and left an improbably colorful version of what happened.[96]

When Mussolini marched on Rome in 1922, Curley had sent him an official flag of Boston. On a gold plaque attached to the flagstaff were the words PRESENTED TO THE SAVIOUR OF CHRISTIAN CIVILIZATION, BENITO MUSSOLINI, BY THE CITY OF BOSTON, JAMES M. CURLEY, MAYOR. The Moose had delivered Christendom by stopping what Curley called "the mad march of communism." At the time of his visit, Mussolini was in conflict with the church he had saved. To force young men to enlist in the army, he had ordered the disbanding of the Catholic Boy Scouts and other youth organizations run by the church. On learning these facts, from discussions with papal intermediaries, as well as from audiences with Pope Pius XI himself and the duke of Genoa, Curley, a rift-maker at home, sought to heal this rift between church and state.[97]

Four days after he arrived in Rome he was summoned for an interview with Mussolini. A group of *carabinieri* showed up at his rooms in the Excelsior, frisked him, and took him to their leader. Unaccountably, they neglected to part him from his shillelagh. He strode past Mussolini's guards, cudgel in hand, and slammed it down on the desk of a dictator used to monopolizing the theatrics himself, declaring, "I come, sir, to present you with the symbol of authority and chief weapon of my ancestors." Back at the Excelsior he told the rest of his party that he thought he had pretty well persuaded the Moose to stop his harassment of the church. "I had smoothed over a tense situation . . . ," in the words of his autobiography. "And thus was a crisis averted."

From the shillelagh on down the story rings false. Were the people on the scene so incapable of working the problem out for themselves that they had to turn for help to a marvel-mongering American mayor? "That such a story, couched in all seriousness, could make the front pages of a leading Boston newspaper," the *Worcester Telegram* said, "is one more intimation that, for all its learning and splendid attainments, Boston is a disquietingly provincial city." Dismissing Curley's Roman arbitration as a press agent's concoction, the *Springfield Republican* nevertheless savored the meeting between these operatic politicians: "If Mussolini felt he himself was the most bombastic man in the world, he may have his doubts now that he has met the Mayor of Boston."[98]

Curley saw Mussolini in Rome and was effusive in his admiration of him. That much is certain. On boarding the *Leviathan* prior to leaving Europe, he made a remarkable public statement: "Mussolini is a wonderful head of a nation. Hoover is just the opposite type. Mussolini believes in spending public money for the public good, offering advantages and opportunities and thereby providing employment. Hoover's activities are directed by [Treasury Secretary Andrew] Mellon who is still living in the Civil War period." It is as well for Curley's reputation that Boston did not have a large population of German Americans.[99]

❖   ❖   ❖

On June 11, 1931, the *Leviathan* arrived in New York harbor just in time for Curley to catch a providential train to Boston. For he was not the only politician on board; Franklin D. Roosevelt, the governor of New York, was also a passenger. Their meeting would shape Curley's career for years to come.

Roosevelt was on his way to visit his sons at the Groton School and to attend a luncheon being given by Colonel Edward M. House, the enigmatic former adviser to President Wilson, at his summer home on the North Shore. Roosevelt had been quietly preparing to run for president since his election as governor in 1928, but with his reelection in November 1930 by a plurality of more than seven hundred thousand votes, his efforts accelerated and speculation about his availability in 1932 increased. In 1928 Roosevelt had written House, "I would rather have your approval than that of almost any other man I know." This was flattery as strategy—House, who had gained fame as a "president-maker," could serve as Roosevelt's ambassador to the Old Wilsonians in the Democratic party. The flattery worked. Nine days before Curley and Roosevelt shared the same train to Boston, talking to the *New York Herald-Tribune*'s Ernest K. Lindley, House had endorsed FDR's unannounced candidacy, reminding Lindley that he had not done as much for any presidential candidate since 1916—the last time a Democrat had won. House had invited some of the Bay State's leading Democrats and liberal Republicans to meet Roosevelt at his harborside home in Magnolia. The luncheon gave Roosevelt a chance to test the political waters in a key state, one that Al Smith had brought into the Democratic column in 1928 and that would be Smith's for the taking should he choose to contest the nomination with Roosevelt.[100]

Roosevelt and Curley were hardly strangers on that train; while assistant secretary of the navy in the Wilson years, Roosevelt had often felt the Curley persuasion. We can gain some idea of what he thought of Curley from a letter he sent to Andrew Peters two days after Peters's election as mayor of Boston.

Dec. 19, 1917

Dear Andrew:
I had a hunch that you would pull through and the hunch came true, but I am especially glad that your majority was as large as the papers say this morning.

As a personal favor to me, won't you please, as one of your first official acts, give the present Mayor some minor job? I do not want him to come back to Washington; he used to be a most horrible nuisance.

Always sincerely yours,

To which Peters responded:

Dec. 24, 1917

Dear Franklin:
Your favor of the 19th inst. at hand, and I appreciate very much your kind wishes.

I am not so keen about having that man you mention in Boston. Would it not be more satisfactory to get William to give him some diplomatic appointment in a quiet far away corner of the earth?

In tone both notes ("a most horrible nuisance") reek of the clubbable world of well-born old Harvards who judge others on points of style and find nothing so remarkable as a man in bloody earnest. Nevertheless, Curley had since been twice reelected mayor of Boston, and Roosevelt's ambition had since outgrown his tastes. That "most horrible nuisance" might be of some use.[101]

Curley made the first move. Discovering that Roosevelt was on the train, he sent his card to his suite and was invited to come by for a chat. Roosevelt asked for his support, Curley told Joseph Dinneen, saying that he "wanted an Irish Catholic with Curley's persuasive voice to help sell him to the country" and that in return "he would have a place in his cabinet or an appointment of almost equal rank." When Curley said he would like to be secretary of the navy, Roosevelt replied that "he knew of no reason why he couldn't have the post."

Are politicians ever so frontal with each other? It seems massively unlikely. Whatever transpired between them greatly affected Curley, however, for even before the train reached Boston the word was out that Roosevelt was his candidate for president. This struck many observers as a departure, a shifting of shrines. Before leaving for Europe, Curley had spoken glowingly of the putative candidacy of Owen D. Young, the president of General Electric and the eponym of the Young Plan for rescheduling German war reparations payments; he had even invited Young to give Boston's official Fourth of July oration that year.° But as early as November 1930, in introducing Governor Roosevelt to a VFW convention, Curley had said "the time is not far distant when they'll cease calling him 'Governor' and accord to him the title which he merits—President." So Curley was not just boasting when he anointed himself "New England's Original Roosevelt Man."[102]

Arrived at the Back Bay station, Curley stepped from the observation car of the *Yankee Clipper* to a "riotous greeting" from

---

° Young declined; instead Senator David Walsh delivered the speech, which conferred on Curley his favorite title: "His heart has been devoted to helping the poor and I like to think of him as Mayor of the Poor" (*Boston Post*, July 5, 1931).

five thousand demonstrators, many of them city employees, waving placards reading WELCOME HOME, JIM, shaking rattles, blowing horns, and throwing handfuls of confetti. An open car then bore him through streets rimmed with cheering people, some throwing flowers as he passed. The Roosevelt party, including Mrs. Roosevelt, stayed on until the next stop at South Station. Few noticed the man being helped down the train steps to a wheelchair. After a porter pushed him off the platform and onto the concourse, Roosevelt abandoned the wheelchair and walked slowly through the station to a waiting car. Recognizing him, someone said, "That's Governor Roosevelt!" A woman started to applaud; a handful of other travelers in the station joined her. He smiled and waved his hat to them. At the Statler, a smattering of applause from passersby greeted him; but, as one reporter noted, the "tumult of the crowd in the distance welcoming Mayor Curley" drowned the modest welcome out. "The flickering of the torches of the red lights of the mayoralty procession blocks away," he continued, "fell like grotesque shadows as the governor made his way through the hotel entrance." While Roosevelt was barely noticed, Curley was given a clamorous welcome: the relationship between these antipodal personalities would follow a twisted course, but in essential respects it would track the reversal of that image.[103]

When news of Curley's declaration of support for Roosevelt reached him, Colonel House sent the mayor a belated invitation to his luncheon. Present were Senator Walsh and his new Democratic colleague, Marcus A. Coolidge, the former mayor of Fitchburg who was no relation to the former president, though he was like him in one respect—"Mute" Marcus was Curley's cognomen for him; the political columnist and liberal Republican Robert Washburn; Ellery Sedgwick of the *Atlantic Monthly*; and other prominences of the Bay State. The men were as genial as could be considering that all they had to lubricate their talk were "Volstead toasts" of sweet New England cider. But an additional awkwardness hung over the luncheon—the question of Al Smith. House's idea for the luncheon was "to discourage Smith and his followers and to show how hopeless it was to oppose our man." This was hubris: Massachusetts belonged to Smith. Until he officially ruled himself out of the presidential race in 1932, any Massachusetts Democrat backing any other candidate was on thin political ice. That is why Roosevelt, asked about "Colonel House's efforts" on his behalf in recruiting Massachusetts Democrats, was evasive. "I couldn't very well reply to your question," Roosevelt told a reporter after the luncheon, "even if you asked it with a straight face." The reporter hadn't cracked a smile.[104]

Evasion was not Curley's way. On Colonel House's sun-struck lawn, on a bluff overlooking the sea, he locked arms with Roosevelt, faced the newsreel cameras, and said, "Within the next two years we hope that you will come back to us in an even more exalted capacity. We expect to welcome you as President of the United States." At which Colonel House, standing on the other side of Roosevelt, chimed in, "That's the most sensible thing anybody has said at this luncheon." Curley volleyed back, "It's the truest thing too." Sandwiched by admiration, Roosevelt rolled his big upper body from side to side, thrust his head back in that inimitably aristocratic gesture of his, and laughed uncandidly. "We have been making history here today," Curley later told reporters. "Franklin Delano Roosevelt is the hope of the nation." If House anticipated a similar testimonial from Senator Walsh, he must have been disappointed. For after bestowing perfunctory blandishments on FDR, Walsh said, "If Al Smith desires to have the nomination then of course Massachusetts will be for him, and none can prevent such a development."[105]

Next day "Roosevelt and Curley" was the talk of Boston. Curley's traffic commissioner, Joseph Conroy, mounted a "Curley Boom" for vice president. ("It was a very nice luncheon," Washburn reported. "There were twelve of us there, one for President, another for vice-president, and ten for Cabinet places.") Curley deprecated the ROOSEVELT AND CURLEY buttons that began to appear around town, saying he "could conceive of no benefits that would result from a ticket made up entirely of easterners." He was under no delusion that FDR would ask him to be his vice president. His idea was to stay in the public eye waiting for the day when Governor Ely should retire or be defeated by a Republican or run for higher office himself, and the Roosevelt bandwagon was a gaudy vehicle to ride. Besides, if Roosevelt won, Curley could perhaps take a visible federal job for a year or two, wait Ely out, and then return to Massachusetts as a candidate for governor.[106]

For the next eighteen months the fever of presidential politics was upon him. Running Boston—by now he could do the job in his sleep—increasingly took second place to electing "Humanity's

Champion." He had, as well, new family cares: Leo Curley, a six-teen-year-old high school student, driving a car given to him as a present by his father, struck and killed a woman in the Back Bay. (He was charged with manslaughter; but the judge, not finding sufficient evidence to warrant it, ordered the charge dropped.) And new family pleasures: between governing Boston, fighting the Depression, fending off a contentious Democrat-controlled City Council, battling for home rule with a stubborn Republican-controlled state legislature, and striving to deliver Massachusetts to Franklin Roosevelt; Curley found time to enroll in a literature course at the Harvard Extension School alongside his daughter Mary.[107]

On New Year's Day 1932 he sent Roosevelt a public telegram: "I pray you will accept my tribute of greeting and affection. Your nomination and election as the next president of the United States will be our country's richest New Year's gift." Similarly oleaginous messages followed on FDR's birthday ("Kindly accept my best salutation at the 50th milestone you have so happily achieved . . ."); on his victory in the Georgia primary ("Kindly accept my sincere congratulations on your magnificent victory . . ."), and elsewhere ("Kindly accept my sincere and earnest congratulations on your remarkable victories in West Virginia, Arizona, and Wyoming . . ."); on his speeches ("My Dear Roosevelt: Your Columbus address comprises a searching and illuminating and well-defined exposé of the hypocrisy of the Hoover administration . . ."); and on the birth of his grandson ("My Dear Roosevelt: Kindly accept my heartfelt congratulations on the safe arrival of the little stranger who becomes the fourth grandchild of the splendid House of Roosevelt . . ."). In addition Curley sent a telegram in the same vein to Elliott Roosevelt on his wedding ("Kindly accept . . ."); dispatched pots of Boston baked beans to Roosevelt in Albany and crates of lobster to Warm Springs ("Kindly accept . . ."); paid for and distributed five hundred thousand red-white-and-blue buttons saying AMERICA WELCOMES ANOTHER ROOSEVELT—FRANKLIN D. on one side and COMPLIMENTS OF MAYOR CURLEY OF BOSTON on the other (they annoyed Roosevelt, who was ever sensitive to the charge that he was exploiting his great cousin's name); and personally presented Humanity's Champion with a bust of himself by the sculptor Nardini.[108]

On the fateful train ride to Boston, Roosevelt reportedly asked Curley to take his son James, a restive student at Harvard Law

School, under his political wing, which Curley did with alacrity. By December, La Rue Brown, a Boston lawyer who had been at Harvard with FDR, could write him: "Please note that the Mayor's office is now making political capital of Jimmy." The mayor had "Jimmy" in his grip; together, they would head up the Roosevelt campaign in the state. Connecting these two proved a terrible mistake, one that led FDR into a misstep that nearly derailed his drive for the presidential nomination.[109]

In retrospect the drama of the 1932 presidential contest lay not in the November election—almost any Democrat, it seemed, would defeat President Hoover, who was running for reelection under the least auspicious circumstances in U.S. political history. The drama lay in the Democratic primaries and caucuses and in the Democratic national convention in Chicago. Franklin Roosevelt had to win those primaries and caucuses and capture that convention without dividing the party. He had at one and the same time to win and to heal. The one person above all others whose enmity he feared was Al Smith, a symbol of the party's divisions. Smith had felt badly used by Roosevelt since the latter's election as governor. He was cool toward his former political friend. If that coolness turned to anger, Smith might allow his own name to be entered in the party primaries. By corralling enough delegates to keep Roosevelt from surmounting the barrier of the two-thirds rule, Smith could tie up the convention. Though he might not win the resulting scramble himself, he could tip the convention to another candidate. Failing that, he could muddy the waters of Roosevelt's victory by forcing him into a prolonged convention battle that might reopen the party's cultural and religious and sectional wounds over issues like Prohibition. A divided Democracy was President Hoover's only hope of reelection.

On January 23, 1932, Franklin Roosevelt formally declared his candidacy for president. On the same day, at a Democratic convention in Fairbanks, Alaska, he won his first six delegates. Based on the promises of support he had already received, a survey released by his campaign showed him with 678 votes on the first ballot. To be nominated, he needed only 92 more.[110]

A week after Roosevelt's announcement Governor Ely and Senator Walsh pledged their support to Al Smith. "It would be ungrateful," Walsh said, "for the Democracy of Massachusetts to consider any other candidate while Governor Smith was receptive." Smith

soon indicated his receptivity. "If the Democratic National Convention, after careful consideration, should decide it wants me to lead I
will make the fight" he said, "but I will not make a pre-convention
campaign to secure the support of delegates." Would the former
governor, a reporter asked, allow his name to be used in primaries
held in states that did not require his consent to put him on the
ballot? "I don't see how I could stop anyone from doing that," Smith
replied. Of Smith's announcement, Hoover's vice president,
Charles Curtis, remarked, "I view the situation in the Democratic
party with equanimity." George W. Norris, the progressive Republican senator from Nebraska, saw history about to stutter. "The Democratic party has a remarkable record for making a fool of itself at a
crucial time when it has the world by the tail and a downhill pull. It
is expected to repeat its usual performance. This is truly a Democratic year, and the election would truly be a cinch for the Democrats if they could harmonize."'''

Massachusetts law required a candidate's formal consent to
have his name placed on the ballot. The state thus presented a Rubicon for Smith. Cross it, and his passive availability would be
transformed into an active campaign against Roosevelt for the
nomination.

"But as for running for office again—that's finished," Smith
had said the day after his defeat in 1928. What had changed his
mind? To his friends he revealed his hurt over the way he had lost
in 1928—the unfairness of it was something he could not forget; an
American should not be barred from the presidency because of his
religion. He wanted badly to vindicate himself and his faith in what
was indeed shaping up as a Democratic year. But as Oscar Handlin
writes, beyond his own ambitions, Smith sought to stop Roosevelt
because of what he saw as Roosevelt's dangerous radicalism—
Smith had grown increasingly conservative, and Roosevelt's celebrated speech on the plight of the "forgotten man" would strike
him as an incitement to class warfare—and because he loathed and
feared some of the men with whom Roosevelt was allying himself.
A few of these were southern Democrats like Daniel Roper of
South Carolina, who had abandoned Smith in 1928. Others were
from the North, among them James J. Hines, a malodorous New
York politician. Smith feared that "their victory would bring into
power, at the expense of Smith's allies, elements against which he
had long fought." One of these elements was James Michael Cur-

ley, "the prototype of everything Smith"—who stood for bridging ethnic differences, not exploiting them—"had abominated." Fearful that, "In Massachusetts as elsewhere, a Roosevelt victory threatened to defeat those who had been leading the urban machines toward political maturity and to elevate the freebooters like Hines and Curley," Smith decided to cross the Rubicon. Setting a precedent for other states with the same conditions on ballot access, he formally consented to enter his name in the Massachusetts primary.[112]

Curley had been calling on Smith to endorse Roosevelt since Colonel House's luncheon the previous June, when he said of Smith that he "had his chance in 1928"; some observers even speculated that Curley's needling had goaded Smith into his open opposition to Roosevelt. However that might be, Smith's move to block Roosevelt affected Curley's calculations. Back from a cruise to the West Indies and Cuba, reacting to the news of Smith's announcement of his availability, Curley entertained what looked like second thoughts about Humanity's Champion. "I want a long talk with Franklin Roosevelt as soon as I return to see how things are lining up before I commit myself," he said in an interview in West Palm Beach. Asked if he thought the New York governor was the best candidate available, he said he couldn't "comment now."

Much as he had done for Champ Clark in 1912, William Randolph Hearst was booming the newly elected Speaker of the House, John Nance Garner, for president on the front pages of his newspapers. Curley had cordial relations with Hearst—another fruit, according to Joseph Dinneen, of Standish Willcox's epistolary diplomacy. Hearst's *Record-American* was strongly in Curley's corner, and Curley had invited Hearst to be an honored guest at the Tricentenary. These facts were well known, and they led to speculation about a Garner-Curley ticket. Was Curley about to shift his shrines again?[113]

At the opening of the Roosevelt campaign headquarters in Park Square, Curley's claque was noticeably absent. There was also "considerable feeling of disturbance among the Roosevelt men at the new headquarters," the *Post* reported, "because Curley has refrained from continuing his emphatic declarations for Roosevelt ever since the announcement of former Governor Smith's willingness to be drafted." Curley telephoned a Boston reporter to dispel the impression left by his Palm Beach statement. He had been referring to the Massachusetts primary, he said, and the question of whether Roosevelt should run in it against Smith. Clearly though, and understandably, his passion for Roosevelt had flagged when he contemplated what fighting Al Smith in Massachusetts might cost him. "No Democrat in this state," Senator Walsh had prophesied, "can be against Smith and survive."[114]

On March 8, 1932, New Hampshire's Democrats, voting in the nation's first primary, gave Roosevelt a decisive victory over Smith. At the Maine state convention three weeks later, Roosevelt's win was narrower, but it was supposed to be a Smith state, and added to his triumphs in New Hampshire, Washington, Minnesota, North Dakota, Georgia, and Iowa, his Maine win gave Roosevelt the momentum of inevitability.[115]

In the heady days after New Hampshire, Roosevelt made his decision to contest for delegates against Al Smith in the Massachusetts primary on April 26. The Roosevelt strategy had been to steer clear of states like Oklahoma and Maryland with favorite-son candidates on the ballot. Smith was Massachusetts' favorite son by adoption. Why did Roosevelt fail to recognize that? Because, a historian of Roosevelt's quest for the nomination writes, "he was misinformed by his local lieutenant, Mayor Curley of Boston," who, masking his doubts for his own purposes, assured Roosevelt that he could win in a state bedazzled by what the *New York Times* called "Smitholatry." That young James Roosevelt, reflecting Curley's confidence, was eager to make a fight of it in Massachusetts no doubt also influenced him. "Like many another political leader in history," James MacGregor Burns writes, "he may have allowed a family situation to spoil his good judgement."[116]

No sooner had Roosevelt agreed to fight than Curley decided to compromise. Responding to a peace overture from Walsh, Curley said he would agree to run as a Smith delegate—if, after it became apparent in Chicago that Smith could not win, the entire Massachusetts delegation agreed to support Roosevelt. Along with Curley's alternative proposal that he be allowed to name half the Smith delegates, this was a formula for surrender, not compromise; and the Smith people, who had made the sensible counteroffer that their delegates be allowed to vote for any candidate of their choice once Smith was out, "did not even reply to the Mayor's offer."[117]

There was still a chance for a compromise that might win Roosevelt something without having to fight Smith on Smith's own ground. And behind Curley's back, La Rue Brown, who told an astonished Roosevelt that he would not win a single delegate in Massachusetts, sought to achieve it.

Curley meanwhile had gotten himself embroiled in a controversy with Al Smith. It began with a public telegram to Smith requesting that, "for the promotion of harmony," he withdraw the permission he had given Chairman Donahue to place his name on the Massachusetts ballot. Such permission, Curley said, was "inconsistent" with Smith's earlier statement of his availability. When Smith replied that he saw no inconsistency, Curley willfully construed the reply as a statement of withdrawal, and indicated as much in a second telegram. Smith sharply countered, calling Curley "a bit tricky" and saying, "The printing of our telegraphic correspondence indicates to me that you are trying to put me in a false light with my friends in Massachusetts." This telegram reached Curley in Washington, where he was lobbying before the House Rivers and Harbors Committee for improvements to the Port of Boston. He chuckled to himself as he gave reporters this reply, which he also included in a third telegram to Smith: "O what a tangled web we weave, / When first we practice to deceive."[118]

Unfortunately for the Roosevelt cause in the Bay State, Curley's broadside from Sir Walter Scott came just as Roosevelt's agent La Rue Brown, meeting with Ely, Walsh, and Donahue at the Lenox Hotel in Boston, was on the point of arranging a compromise: Roosevelt would not enter the primary if the Smith slate could include several delegates pledged to Roosevelt as a second choice. This was a critical stipulation, for the Roosevelt forces were fearful lest delegates breaking from Smith coalesce behind a third candidate like Garner or Newton D. Baker. "We were making progress," Brown remembered, "when the newspapermen sent in word that Mr. Curley had chosen that particular afternoon to make a bitter assault on Al Smith, charging him with deceit and other improprieties. That 'tore it,' as the English say." Donahue promptly announced that "there will be no one on the Smith slate who is not a loyal Smith supporter."[119]

The next day, with James Roosevelt standing beside him, Curley announced that Governor Roosevelt would enter the Massachusetts primary against Al Smith. Harmony was out the window. Writing to Curley, Mayor Patrick J. Duane of Waltham said, "Apropos your fouling of the Democratic waters, 'Oh what a mess of

306 ❖ THE RASCAL KING

'things we make, / Once we start to bluff and fake.'" Curley's come-back was sharp enough—"There is a great deal covered by a silk hat that is not brains." But his bravado was no shield against the snowballs thrown at him and James Roosevelt a few days later dur-ing the St. Patrick's Day parade in South Boston. Nor could it turn back the poison-pen letter intended for his daughter Mary, which he intercepted and in his grooved way used to win public sympa-thy. He was a pariah in his own party, state, and city.[120]

Cornered, desperate, fighting for his political life, he took to the airwaves to attack Governor Ely, calling his failure to back Roo-sevelt, who was "the one individual who in the opinion of the American people can be elected," "a base and brutal betrayal of the public trust." The upcoming primary would not be Roosevelt versus Smith, but Curley versus the Massachusetts Democratic es-tablishment. "Nothing is heard any more in Massachusetts about 'stopping Roosevelt' or 'stopping Smith,'" the *New York Times* ob-served in an editorial entitled "Curley-Burly." "The question is—and the Boston Anti-Noise Society may have to take it up before long—can anybody or anything 'stop Curley.'"[121]

Over the next forty-five days and nights of campaigning, Cur-ley would, as the *Times* predicted, be "illimitably visible" and "il-limitably audible" as he barnstormed Massachusetts, haranguing sullen audiences to get over their infatuation with Al Smith, face the fact of his unelectability, and vote for Franklin D. Roosevelt. At rallies in Cambridge, Watertown, and Waltham; in Medford, Law-rence, Haverhill, and Newburyport; in Adams, North Adams, Pitts-field, Springfield, and Westfield; in Worcester, Peabody, Salem, Lynn, New Bedford, West Roxbury, and, his voice breaking, in a climactic rally in downtown Boston, Curley made the case for Roo-sevelt. He spoke with wit: "If we have another era of Hoover, Gan-dhi would be the best-dressed man in America"; "At Thanksgiving, instead of eating turkey, we'll be lucky if we are not eating each other." His arguments against Smith were sound and tactfully phrased: "Shall we in Massachusetts, mindful of the suffering of our brethren . . . be revengeful and insist that if the rest of the country will not have our leader or practice our liberalism, we shall be doomed to four more years of shiftless policies and visionless leadership?" And his oratory was an undoubted magnet: "Take Curley out of the Roosevelt rallies and it would be difficult to get half the crowd," the *Worcester Telegram* noted. "The crowds are indicative more of curiosity and interest in Curley than in Roosevelt or Smith." But the "religious issue" was against him. Rumors were being circulated that Mrs. Roosevelt favored birth control. Congressman John J. Douglas, a Smith supporter, asked the Democrats in his district, "Are you going to turn to 'left-handers' now and vote against a man of your own race and religion?" The papal nuncio in Washington heard an odd complaint from a Roosevelt supporter: the Smith campaigners in Massachusetts were urging voters "take your ballot and put the sign of the cross against the name of Alfred E. Smith." A vote for Roosevelt was being depicted as a vote for bigotry. Curley was at war with the very force—ethnic and religious resentment—to which he owed his rise.

Moreover, he was increasingly alone in the ring. "The Mayor has been practically deserted by most of those who started out with him," the *Herald* observed. "Mayor Murphy of Somerville, School Committeeman Maurice Tobin, Mrs. Nellie Sullivan, the National Committee woman, and others of his associates in their frantic endeavors to save themselves have publicly promised to vote for Smith at the convention if they are elected, this in spite of the fact that they are indelibly pledged to Roosevelt." Finally, with Curley so illimitably audible, Ely was able to frame the election in terms devastating to Roosevelt: "It is Smith or Curley. Which do you choose?"

On April 26, statewide, the people chose Smith, by three to one; in Boston, by two to one. Even in Curley's old Tammany ward, the feeling for Smith was so strong that "Roosevelt workers who handed voters slips bearing the names of the Roosevelt candidates saw them torn into bits and stamped on." Roosevelt did not win a single Massachusetts delegate. "Well, I guess that will put a chock under the bandwagon," Smith said, noting with cruel satisfaction that "the delegate at the bottom of the list on my side of the fence up in Massachusetts got more votes than the fellow with the highest number of votes on the other side," one James Michael Curley.[122]

Surveying the wreckage of April 26, which also saw Roosevelt do much worse than expected in Pennsylvania, the *New York Times* concluded, "It is not too much to say that the whole outlook for the Democratic national convention has been changed by what took place in Massachusetts and Pennsylvania." Walter Lippmann was equally portentous: "Mr. Roosevelt's liabilities are great and they will grow greater as the convention approaches. For his defeat on Tuesday has justified the opposition and will increase it." A week later Lippmann's prediction was borne out when Garner defeated Roosevelt in California. "Suddenly," William Leuchtenburg writes, "Roosevelt's nomination was in jeopardy."[123]

"Whoever advised Roosevelt to enter that primary anyway?" Will Rogers wondered.[124]

That hapless adviser appeared to be an even bigger loser than Roosevelt. "Seldom, if ever, in the history of the Commonwealth has a more stinging rebuke been administered to any self-seeking politician than that administered to Mr. Curley at the ballot box on Tuesday," the *Worcester Telegram* pronounced. "James Michael Curley is the most battered political casualty of the Massachusetts primary," the *Cleveland Plain Dealer* observed. "He is still Mayor, but his political prestige is ground into dust and blowing all over the Common."[125]

Slinking away for a rest on Cape Cod with these political obituaries ringing in his ears, Curley was down but not out. For if he had been wrong about Roosevelt's chances in Massachusetts, he had been right about Roosevelt. Al Smith was yesterday's candidate, his victory in Massachusetts a last hurrah for the politics of provincialism. In a prescient column, Robert Washburn called it correctly. "Tuesday last was a great day for James Michael Curley," he wrote. "His was not a rout, neither was it a pyrrhic victory, for it is better to have been right like him, than to have been wrong like the others and to have won. For Smith cannot win and Roosevelt might win. Because of which considerations it might be further asserted that Jim is not politically dead but simply sleeping. And when, after the passing of this blizzard, he has removed the sand and bird seed from his hackle feathers, he will be found again sitting securely on his perch and again serene for the chapter which may come."[126]

Air-conditioned Voice

❖   ❖   ❖   ❖

Curley was born, not with a silver spoon, but with a wooden ladder in his mouth, which he proceeded forthwith to climb.

BOSTON EVENING TRANSCRIPT

❖ ❖ ❖ ❖

Franklin Roosevelt would go to the Democratic national convention in Chicago without the votes to win nomination on the first ballot thanks in determinable part to the "near disaster" that had befallen him in Massachusetts. Yet if he nursed any grudges against its chief perpetrator he kept them hidden. Immediately after the primary he wrote Curley a magnanimous note: "Just a line to express to you my heartiest congratulations and warm appreciation for the magnificent campaign you made despite the obstacles. I realize you had the entire state machine, the two United States Senators and the Governor against you; and that you with Jimmy Roosevelt campaigned the whole state practically single-handed and made a remarkable showing. I want you to know that I personally am more grateful than you will ever know for the wonderful fight you put up in the most extreme conditions."[1]

In Curley's telling, his role at the Chicago convention was critical: everybody was at a loss, the Roosevelt strategists were all at sea, until The Curley arrived and saved the day. In fact his doings at Chicago needed no fabulation.

The band of the Cecil W. Fogg American Legion post was at North Station to serenade Curley and his large party off on the Minute Man. Over and over again it struck up a familiar melody to which the crowd bidding goodbye to the two cars of Roosevelt supporters gave new lyrics:

> *The more we are for Curley*
> *The happier we will be. . . .*
>
> *The more we are for Curley*
> *The happier we will be.*

While the mayor posed for a picture on the rear platform of the train with a various group—his children, his brother John, Mrs. Bremner, her daughters Josephine and Catherine, and sundry city officials—someone in the crowd urged three cheers for "Mayor Curley, the next secretary of state." He smiled and made a deprecating gesture (he was not a complete megalomaniac). Nine-year-old Frank Curley hung suspended by his belly and arms on the rail next to his father. The band played, the crowd waved, clouds of steam frosted the receding platform. Politics was to life as a dream is to a dreary sermon.[2]

Arrived in Chicago, the Curley party posed for news photographers. In one picture the boys and their father are carrying identical straw hats; thirteen-year-old George Curley bears a placard reading, MAYOR CURLEY IS OUR INSPIRATION AND CHICAGO IS OUR DESTINATION. They were at the convention merely as "Roosevelt rooters," Curley having failed to win a delegate's seat in the April primary.

"If it mean but one more vote for Roosevelt, I should be willing to act as a ticket taker at the Democratic Convention . . . ," Curley had said three days after Colonel House's luncheon. He did not have to resort to that expedient. He would be saved by a tropical island.

In the first draft of his unpublished memoirs he told the background to this savory story. He had been trying to see James Farley at the Roosevelt campaign headquarters when a stranger arrived at the suite and demanded to see Farley. "If you don't get that man out of here," one of the people in the room told Curley, "he will kill somebody." The man was now raving "I'm Mohammed the Second!" Curley knew how to handle lunatics. Introducing himself as if to a font of sanity, Curley said he had a question about Islam he badly wanted settled; perhaps they could go to the hotel dining room and discuss it. Grateful for the attention, the man readily agreed and Curley led him out of the room. Among the people on hand to witness this dextrous display was a delegate from Porto Rico (its original Spanish name would not be restored until a year later). She knew of Curley's plight, and when he returned to the room invited him to join her delegation. The chairman had unexpectedly been called home because of illness in his family. New England's Original Roosevelt Man could replace him if he liked. He *did* like. Curley was now and most improbably the chairman of the delegation from Porto Rico.[3]

Reporters sought Curley out at his suite in the Congress Hotel. Could the rumors possibly be true? Could the mayor of Boston be a delegate for the island of Porto Rico? "I am here representing 160,000 Porto Ricans," Curley told them. "I am representing these 160,000 men, women, and children because the depression in the islands—I mean Porto Rico—has particularly affected sugar. The depression has also affected tobacco on the island. And all of this has thrown out of gear the entire economic system of the island." In short, he couldn't find Porto Rico on a map.[4]

Appearing at the convention as a delegate from Porto Rico was one of Curley's mythic coups, the kind of spontaneous stunt that rarely happens in today's premeditated politics. Norman Thomas, visiting Boston, might have disapproved: "It is symbolic of the tough break that the United States has always given Porto Rico," he said. But, led by the *Post*'s Norman, the Boston cartoonists loved it and from that instant began to depict Curley in a sombrero. "Don Jaime" quickly captured the imagination of the public.[5]

To be sure, the delegates from Massachusetts, the butts of Curley's jape, were not amused. Governor Ely called Curley's presence on the floor "insulting to the Commonwealth" and "an undemocratic subversion of the will of the voters," but the Credentials Committee certified him as a bona fide delegate. The Massachusetts delegates booed Curley when he seconded the nomination of FDR from the floor; and they booed and heckled him loudly during his speech from the platform seconding the vice presidential nomination of "that great Texan, John Nance Garner," whose state the Massachusetts delegates couldn't forgive for going back on Al Smith in 1928. But their severest trial came on the fourth and final ballot, when the chair recognized "Alcalde Jaime Miguel Curleo" and the too-familiar figure thus exotically denominated rose and, in a stage Spanish accent, intoned, "Porto Rico casts its six votes for Franklin Delano Roosevelt. . . ." Reveling in their consternation, Curley broke into a mocking jig as he walked past the Massachusetts delegates, who glowered back at him.[6]

Roosevelt, meanwhile, was deep in the trouble into which the slide begun in Massachusetts had mired him. From an abortive effort by some of his supporters to repeal the two-thirds rule to Al Smith's reported agreement with William Gibbs McAdoo, of California, his hated rival from the 1924 convention, to concert a "stop-Roosevelt" strategy, nothing had gone right for Roosevelt in

Chicago. Over three ballots the anticipated bandwagon effect had not materialized. On the first ballot Roosevelt had 666 votes, but he had barely moved by the third, to 682. Together Smith, at 194 votes on the third ballot, and Garner, at 101, could deny Roosevelt the nomination. While the third ballot was being called during the night of June 31, frantic phone calls were being put through to Garner in Washington and to William Randolph Hearst, his chief backer and a close ally of McAdoo's, at his castle-home in California. Everybody knew that California must shift its votes from Garner to Roosevelt to keep the convention from repeating the epic hundred-ballot futility of 1924. And everybody got into the act. "Of the 55,000 Democrats allegedly to have been in Chicago . . . ," Roosevelt's old law partner later remarked, "unquestionably 62,000 of them arranged the . . . shift."[7]

Curley was of this numerous company. James Farley, with Louis M. Howe the chief Roosevelt strategist at the convention, had told his secretary to keep Curley out of the marathon meeting transpiring in Howe's hotel room. Howe, who was from Fall River, was still furious with Curley for his mishandling of the unlamented Massachusetts primary. Unable to rise from his bed because of illness and the sweltering city heat and anxious beyond words that the cause to which he had devoted twenty years of his life was about to founder, there can have been few people in this world Louis Howe wanted to see less than James Curley; yet that was who knocked on his door. Having heard that he was persona non grata, Curley, asked for his name, replied, "Senator Pat Harrison," the Mississippi Democrat. He was shown in; and when Farley went to greet Harrison he was astonished to find Curley.[8]

He had come, Curley said, to offer his services to Roosevelt at this, the critical moment of the convention. Farley and Howe must have blanched at the thought. According to Curley, Howe burst out, "Can't anything be done about that man, Curley?" Over their protests, Curley says, he proceeded to arrange the famous shift by calling Hearst at San Simeon and telling him that Garner was through, but that if he would swing California in behind Roosevelt, Garner would get the vice presidential nomination. Hearst had striven to make Curley's old mentor Champ Clark president; now Curley appealed to his long-frustrated ambition with a pitch aimed squarely at a huge target, Hearst's vanity: "You have the opportunity to name the next President and Vice-President of the United States."[9]

In fact, if a witness without an ax to grind is to be believed, Curley sat in his room for several hours while the operator tried to connect his call, then turned the phone over to an assistant city clerk, John B. Hynes, and retired for the night. Hynes kept at it until 4:00 A.M., when the San Simeon operators told him that Mr. Hearst had gone to bed and probably he should do likewise. Curley's "call to Hearst" never got through.[10]

Joseph P. Kennedy, the son-in-law of John Fitzgerald, did get through to Hearst, warning "W.R." that a deadlocked convention might well nominate Newton Baker, "the great defender of the League of Nations, that ardent internationalist whose policies you despise." His intervention, Kennedy later boasted, persuaded Hearst to order the shift. History records only that, next day, amid jeers and howls from the die-hard Smith followers of Massachusetts, McAdoo, as chairman of the California delegation, dramatically announced that California would shift its votes from Garner to Roosevelt. The last chock finally removed, the bandwagon now began to roll swiftly, carrying Roosevelt to victory on the fourth ballot.[11]

He won without the support of Massachusetts, which stayed with Smith to the end. The Massachusetts delegates sat stony-faced while all around them people danced in the aisles to a tune that would become Roosevelt's anthem, one that Louis Howe, wanting something livelier than "Anchors Aweigh," had casually instructed the band to strike up—"Happy Days Are Here Again." Smith himself remained seated in the gallery, his arms folded, his face "chalky with disappointment." James W. Gerard, the treasurer of the Democratic National Committee, pleaded with Mrs. Charles Dana Gibson, a friend of Smith's, to persuade him to come down to the floor and move that Roosevelt's nomination be made unanimous. She sought Smith out. "I won't do it," he said. "I won't do it. . . . I won't do it. . . . I won't do it."[12]

As Franklin Roosevelt entered the stadium to accept his party's presidential nomination, he stretched out both hands to James Curley, who, a gate-crasher to the last, had positioned himself in the front rank of well-wishers, where he could not be missed. What did Governor Roosevelt say, a reporter inquired? "Just an affectionate greeting; nothing more could have been said," Curley replied. "To hear Franklin Roosevelt express his affection is worth a lifetime of energy." From all over the nation congratulatory telegrams poured in to Curley's suite. The telephone started ringing at 4:00 A.M., when a man from Nevada called to say, "We understand things out here, even if all of Massachusetts wasn't for Roosevelt. Looks like you made a winning fight against great odds."

The Porto Rican Business Men's Club cabled its delight at the attention "Don Jaime" had brought to their island. Messenger boys lined up outside his door. Wanting to shake his hand, friends and strangers alike sought him out. MAYOR CURLEY MADE HERO BY WINNING FIGHT, blared a headline in a Boston paper. And this was only the beginning.[13]

Curley's return to Boston was a triumphal progress: having left a pariah, the prodigal son had come back as the best kind of American hero—a winner. One of the signs in the crowd of twelve thousand that greeted him at North Station captured the prevailing sentiment:

WE LOVE YOU, "AL"

BUT WHAT THE HELL,

WE'RE FOR ROOSEVELT NOW.

The crush at the station was so intense that Curley had to lift Francis up on his shoulders to keep him from being trampled underfoot, and the police had to push the crowd back with main force to make a path for them. "They've got a band wagon, but no band," Governor Ely had said of the Roosevelt forces on arriving in Chicago. Yet here, at Curley's arrival in Boston, were ten bands to welcome New England's Original Roosevelt Man. It was the evening of the Fourth of July—Curley had timed his return with care—and there were thousands in the streets to cheer as his open car, with himself and Francis and Mr. and Mrs. Jimmy Roosevelt perched on the tonneau, passed by, in what was turning into a victory parade to the Common. There a record crowd of over one hundred thousand had gathered—some to see Boston's gift to Porto Rico, others just to watch the fireworks. To judge by Jimmy Roosevelt's speech from the Parkman bandstand, the Roosevelt campaign hoped for a restoration of harmony with the defeated Smith forces. But, his pride swollen by the fulsome introductions ("the greatest Roman of them all"; "the outstanding Democrat of the country"), Curley was in no mood for harmony. Instead he adverted to the booing his fellow Bay Staters had given him at the convention—"It is singular how animals act. Geese cackle; snakes hiss; gentlemen applaud; but only boobs boo"—in a voice heavy with inharmonious emotion.[14]

Yet even while the cheers were ringing in Curley's ears, even while the Boston papers were trumpeting his intimate connections with the Roosevelt family and wondering aloud about the undoubtedly central role he would play in the coming election campaign and which cabinet or high diplomatic post he would receive from a grateful President Roosevelt—even while the laurels of Chicago were still green on Curley's brow, a Boston lawyer friend of Roosevelt's, Harry Bergson, was writing him, "Please! Don't let Curley be the head and front of your campaign here—it means defeat. He is a red rag to the Smith element. . . ." And soon Curley would be getting the word from Roosevelt headquarters that, although his services were appreciated, valued, held in the highest esteem by all concerned, surely he could see that it would be wise for him to stay out of Massachusetts for most of the campaign. Perhaps a speaking tour of the Middle and Far West could be arranged. Something long in duration and distance, something that would keep him out of Governor Ely's way, while that moody-brooder (who could not bring himself to pronounce Roosevelt's name until weeks after the convention) reluctantly, and taking the state organization with him, joined the Roosevelt camp for the fall stretch drive. For Ely would not have him. And Ely had to be wooed for Massachusetts to be won.[15]

So it was that James Michael Curley found himself dispatched for the month of September to the golden West. ("This voluntary and altruistic exile," the *New York Times* sarcastically noted, "may abate the lingering soreness at home.") In a tour of twenty-three states, from Ohio to California and back, he delivered twenty-four major speeches, some from the platform of his railroad car, others before packed houses, some to small clusters at country crossroads, others to mass audiences over the radio. With Herbert Hoover to kick around, he was in top form. Speaking from his train to a crowd near Kansas City, he was interrupted by a crying baby. "That's a Republican baby!" a woman snorted. Curley, laughing, ad-libbed, "It may be a Republican now; it acts like one; but it will be a Democrat when it reaches the age of reason." At the American Legion convention in Portland, Oregon, when some drunken Legionnaires on the street outside his hotel room woke him at 3:00 A.M. with shouts of "We want Hoover!" Curley poured a pitcher of ice water on them. To audience after audience he told this story about Herbert Hoover's arrival at the Pearly Gates. "I am Herbert Hoover, the President of the United States, and this is my Secretary of the Treasury, Andrew Mellon." St. Peter looked them over. "Oh yes, I know you. You also were a great engineer, and you certainly lived up to your reputation there. You ditched and drained the most prosperous nation in the world to the verge of financial ruin. But I don't know your friend. Just a moment. I'll go and check my books on him." When St. Peter returned, Herbert Hoover was gone, Andrew Mellon was gone, and—here Curley would pause—the Pearly Gates were gone![16]

But what he said to these audiences was less impressive than the way he said it, for until the womb of time delivered William F. Buckley, Jr., few Americans would hear a more affected public speaker—one who, like Buckley, loved the big word, the busy sentence, the convoluted paragraph, and one who spoke English in a high-tea accent that owed nothing to the sounds of the American street. To understand why Curley's speeches wowed audiences from coast to coast—more, to appreciate one of the chief sources of his perennial appeal at the ballot box—a short course on his oratory is in order.

❖   ❖   ❖

Contemporary political speech forms a subspecies of English that Philip Roth calls "jerkish," a parched, impoverished, pared-down language consisting of a few banal words used in banal combinations. Here is an example: "Lots of Air Force down there. Lots of planes down there. Lot of knowledge. Hopefully, it will keep Saddam Hussein from doing anything reckless." And yet this terse burst of "jerkish" marks an improvement over "I mean a child that does have a parent to read to that child or that doesn't see that when the child is hurting to have a parent and help out or neither parent there enough to pick the kid up and dust him off and send him back into game at school or whatever, that kid has a disadvantage." That the speaker was a Phi Beta Kappa graduate of Yale University is not something one would guess from anything he ever said as President.[17]

Between the spread of jerkish and the ubiquity of the speech writer, oratory is just not what it used to be. "The fear of every man that heard him was lest he should make an end," Ben Jonson said of Francis Bacon. A dwindlingly few exceptions aside, we fear lest our politicians make a start. One signal difference between Curley's long day and our own is that oratory was formerly a threshold test of office. Poor speakers—verbal slovens, shamblers, stumblers, to say nothing of grinning voids—were weeded out early in the game. Our toleration of jerkish is a reflection of the degradation wrought in our own speech by the plague of television. Curley did not have to fight television. But how did he come to use language so commandingly? How did this man who had so little formal education himself—and who, in the first world of his ward, knew or heard few people who had more—manage to exceed the highest standards of spoken expression in his time?

Curley's transformation from rough-tongued teamster to mellifluous speaker is a Pygmalion story. His Professor Henry Higgins was Delbert Moyer Staley, A.M., Ph.D., L.L.B., Litt.D., the founder and impresario over many decades of the Staley School—and, after Curley became governor—College of the Spoken Word.

The son of an upstate New York farm family, Staley launched his day and evening school in 1901 in a former chapel in Brookline Village, near the Boston line. Shortly thereafter, common councilor James M. Curley enrolled in evening courses at the Staley School; he would be a student there, intermittently, for eight years. "He had the harsh Boston voice," Staley said years later, "and the vocabulary of a fishmonger. But I straightened out his grammar, gave him a vocabulary and trained his voice."[18]

Staley's theorizing had about it a good deal of mumbo jumbo. "Put the soul in the symbol," he told his pupils, by which he meant nothing more than to affect sadness in your voice if your subject was a sad one, gladness if the opposite. In his *Psychology of the Spoken Word* (1951), Staley divides the "grammar of the spoken word" into seven elements: inflection, pitch, pausation, pulsation, colorization, rhythm, and hiatus. Of "pausation," he says this: "It is the process of the mind in the struggle for the birth of a new idea; and in proportion as the mind has recreated a new idea by the laws of association, will the voice show spontaneously this mental change." "Pulsation" he defines as "the rhythmic footfall of the mind upon the central thought word of each successive idea." He set great store by the hiatus or pause for effect in a speech, calling it "the harmonious creation of suspense by a speaker in the minds of the audience, preceding the Central Word Thought." Dr. Staley also wrote *Psycho-Gymnastics and Society Drama*, and one is not surprised to hear it. His books appeared before the age of psycho-credulity, but he wrote in the same vatic key as the shamans of popular psychology who bestride our best-seller lists.[19]

Nor was Staley's pedagogy proof against satire. "As the new semester began last week," *Time* noted in 1951,

> Staley gave the new class his usual thunder. "I want every person in this room to sit up! Get your chests out! Don't wobble like a hog. . . . Breathe deeply. . . . Breathe! Smile! Repeat after me—Ha! Ha!"
> "Ha! Ha!" repeated the class.
> "Hee! Hee!"
> "Hee! Hee!"

This is easy to lampoon, but as a voice coach teaches opera singers the finer points of diction, phrasing, and tone, so Staley taught the mechanics of public speaking not only to Curley, whom he called his "best pupil and the greatest American orator since Daniel Webster," but also to John F. Kennedy, John W. McCormack, Senator David I. Walsh, and Warner Oland—the movies' Charlie Chan.[20]

Curley was the best of the lot not only, to borrow a phrase of Edwin O'Connor's about Skeffington, because of his "air-conditioned Amos 'n' Andy voice," but because of his diligence. "It came after long hard effort, I worked at it," Curley once said when asked how he had become such an accomplished speaker. "I studied books. I read until the early morning hours. My whole life was aimed at understanding the English language." The first homework assignment Staley gave him was to memorize Hamlet's opening soliloquy. By the next evening Curley had mastered all three soliloquies, and was asking for more. The story has its poignancy: the young man is so touchingly eager for culture not as an adornment but as a thing to use, a ladder to scale the ramparts of the world.[21]

Staley also gave his voracious student books about oratory and collections of the great speeches of history. To this Curley added personal observation of the leading orators of the city—including Jesuit priests giving novenas in his parish—as well as of itinerant pipe organs like William Jennings Bryan and Billy Sunday. Staley

Curley's collar sizes increased over the course of a campaign as his speaking parts swelled.

Norman of the Post on Curley as Don Jaime. Curley's coup de theatre at the 1932 Democratic convention in Chicago captured the imagination of the city.

Jim Farley, center, must have been amazed when Curley peeled off $5,000 from his big roll of bills. Curley thought he was making a down payment on a choice foreign post.

Passing out one of his shillelaghs to Oliver Wendell Holmes. This is one of the war clubs Curley would have us believe he rapped on Mussolini's desk.

With Eleanor Roosevelt and Governor Ely at a luncheon in 1933. His feud with Ely was a farcical business, even by Curley's Barnum standards.

The beaming counte- nance on the left belongs to Teddy Glynn. "Hu- manity's Champion" is on Curley's right in the photograph in the background.

*With Gertrude and his two new stepsons, George and Richard Dennis.
Francis Curley stands just beyond his father's protective reach.*

*With Francis Curley in
the mid-1930s. Francis
lived in the shadow of
real, as well as po-
litically convenient,
kidnapers.*

With Father Coughlin in 1935: who betrayed whom?

With FDR in the fall of 1936. To defeat Lodge in the Senate campaign, Curley desperately needed Roosevelt's endorsement. He all but begged for it, but the president did not oblige him.

In deepest Xanadu. He was the only delegate to arrive at the 1936 Democratic national convention with a brass band. Philadelphians thought they were watching a mummer's parade.

Curley timed his leavings and returns like a diva her bows. Collective emotion was his medium, ritual his method.

Paul Curley is at the extreme left, next to George. "No bigger than a pint of peanuts," Paul would fight for his father at the slightest provocation. Leo, extreme right, quit Harvard Law School after a professor insulted "the Boss."

On the staircase at the Jamaicaway with Mary on the day of her wedding. "I beat her," Mary's husband would admit a few years later, and Curley ordered him out of the house.

Profile in dignity. This was Curley's favorite photograph of himself.

taught Curley to "cover his voice," to enhance its resonance and lend it the quality that students of rhetoric call "orotund." Consequently, his speeches were better heard than read. Their ambitions were rhetorical, not discursive. They achieved impressiveness with their cumulative force and their syntactical ingenuity, not their thought or insight. Their matter, characteristically, took a back seat to their manner.

Consider this last sentence from his speech at the Massachusetts Tree-Planting Exercises of 1923 in the grove around the Lincoln Memorial. "Down through the years the breezes will whisper in the leafage of this our offering of trees, the praises of the martyred leader; and their graceful branches swinging and swaying and reaching toward the sun will carry to high heaven our love and affection and gratitude"—if you think a period is coming next, think again—"for that Lincoln whose steadfast courage, unfailing patience and unconquerable charity, have made him the comforter of all who are heavy laden; and the hope and inspiration of them who work and walk in the shadow of oppression." Even read silently, and for all its wind, this sentence is impressive—and not only for how long it stays on the wing. The art of it lies in the paired units—"swinging and swaying," "patience" and "charity," "hope and inspiration," "work and walk"—that make it read shorter than it is. The sentence has no business lasting beyond "gratitude," but with "that Lincoln" it gains altitude and prolongs its flight by involution. Curley understood that the long sentence allowed the speaker to get away with something less than brilliance in his thought. Just bringing the thing safely to rest without a grammatical crash was challenge enough.[22]

He could achieve the mesmeric effect of a prose poem with some of his long sentences—for example, the last paragraph of "Boston's Greeting," prepared for visitors to the Tricentenary. "The murmurous babble of the cradled babe, the wondrous music of the child's innocent prattle and infectious laughter, the sweet and patient presence of one whose love and forbearance could ignore error, forget misdeed, magnify good, and the faith of her who daily brought to the throne of God her prayers for our future safety and success—this is the very soul of 'Home Sweet Home'; the spirit of the mothers of men pulsates in every line of the song; and what the mother is to her child, Boston has been to liberty." Come again? the reader asks. How did we wind up here? The dash after "success" gives this verbal filigree new life and a new direction.[23]

In "Memorial to the Fireman," delivered at Forest Hills Cemetery in 1916 for firemen who had died in the line of duty, Curley
showed a Reaganesque gift for storytelling in bold primary colors. "It
is unfortunate that the public at large who are thrilled and fascinated
at the clang of the gong, the shrill cry of the siren whistle, the gallop-
ing of horses, the breakneck speed of the motor apparatus, could not
open for just a tiny space, the door of the home of he who, after the
evening meal, with a kiss and a caress, has left all whom he held dear
in life to respond to the call of duty." These are the conventions, this
the pathos, of the silent movie, the most technologically advanced
mode of expression of the time. The camera rolls on. "In the discharge of that duty his life was sacrificed that others might live, and
now we see the once manly form, mangled and scorched, tenderly
carried in the arms of his comrade whose turn may come next. . . ."
Next we return to the Home, for an apostrophe to the Widow. "We
see the home, which, a few short hours before, was the center of
happiness, hushed by the presence of death. The wife, companion in
joy and sorrow, suddenly bereft of her husband and happiness, compelled to struggle with sorrow-laden heart, alone. To one who is so
bereft, life is indeed a hardship, not alone the constant struggle to
maintain the flock, but the sorrow ever recalled by the pleading questioning of the young, 'When will father come home?' "[24]

Grand or moving as written oratory, the effect of Curley's
speeches was heightened by his musical voice, by his mastery of
Staley's precepts, above all by his theatrical pronunciation and
studiedly formal turns of phrase. On Curley's tongue labor was
"laybore," provision "proveeshun," obligation "obleegation."
You and I might call the cops; Curley invariably summoned "the
poleeece." Our "last Wednesday" was "Wednesday last," our
nineteen thirty-five "nineteen hundred and thirty-five." World
War II was "World War Number Two," forty-two million dollars
"forty-two millions of dollars." Roosevelt was "Rooosvlt," Boston
was "Bosstun." And Curley was "Cuh-lee"—despite his grandilo-
quent manner, the "peepul's" friend.[25]

Curley had speech writers, public relations men, wordsmiths
of several sorts around him throughout his career who wrote many
of his merely formal speeches. But a man who, on hearing that an
overpass constructed by his administration had just collapsed,
could label the cause an "injudicious mixture of sand and cement"
had no need of phrasemakers. And if we doubt that he wrote the

bulk of his speeches himself, we have only to compare them to his spontaneous talk at press conferences to see the same man speaking in the same way at the different venues.

He mostly ignored the Staley dictum of using "maximum body action" to accompany his speeches, not wanting to compete with his own voice and language. But there was one distinctive Curley gesture. During an oratorical crescendo he would raise his arm above his head, his hand open as if to extend the line of the gesture, and then swing hand and arm down sharply in a pendulum that would scoop beneath his knees. His pompadour would sometimes collapse from the celerity of this motion, bringing a lank of silver-streaked hair down over his temple. The conjoint effect of word, voice, accent, and gesture could overwhelm even cynical reporters used to his speeches. The effect on uninitiated audiences can only be imagined.[26]

Vital to Curley's appeal was the appearance of spontaneity. As Webster said of Edward Everett, another great Massachusetts orator, Curley knew better than to confine himself to "pouring out fervors a week old." Usually he spoke either from notes or without looking at his text, relying on the extraordinary memory Dr. Staley had noted in him as a young man. His memory saw him through a tight spot in 1932, when he arrived at a movie studio without the text of a speech that was to be used in a Roosevelt campaign film. Undaunted, he faced the camera and for eleven minutes delivered his signature oration, "The Forgotten Man," a verbal montage of the unemployed in Hoover's America, without stumble or pause.[27]

President Reagan was an actor, adept at reading a script, but he was "closed for repairs," in Kitty Kelley's painfully evocative phrase, when he had to speak on his own. Curley was a politician of the age of words. And we look back on him from what Kathleen Hall Jamieson calls the age of electronic eloquence, a later but paradoxically more primitive stage in political communications—indeed, in many ways a return to the origins of human history, when pictures, images, and symbols count for more than words.[28]

❖   ❖   ❖

Having traveled ten thousand miles on his campaign trip for Roosevelt, Curley came home to a demonstration of ten thousand people. After receiving tribute from "Billy" Barker, "the yodelling Councilor from East Boston," and Sheila O'Donovan Rossa, "our municipal songbird," and surrounded by baskets of roses and stands of gladioli, the mayor beguiled the throng with tales from the distant hustings. Following Curley's speech in Denver, a local university president asked him if he was a Harvard man—the supreme accolade; anyone, after all, can be mayor of Boston. "I told him that I never went to Harvard, whereupon he expressed the greatest surprise. He said that the speech was the most flawless presentation he had ever heard, and he wanted me to stay over until the next day to address the faculty and the student body." As the *New York Times* wryly commented on this address, "It is Mr. Curley's gift equally to charm the dons and the heelers."[29]

He was looking forward both to a change of administrations in Washington and in the trajectory of his career. He could hardly wait. Reading a list of the names of people retiring from the city, he came to one "Herbert C. Hoover," and then corrected himself: "Pardon me, I'm a bit too hasty." He was booed at the state Democratic convention in Lowell, and booed once more at a Roosevelt rally at the Boston Arena, where Al Smith, who had since grudgingly come around to offer his "unqualified, full, and complete support of Franklin D. Roosevelt," was the featured speaker. Three days later Curley put future booers on notice. "I don't propose to enter into any dissertation about Curley," he told a gathering of Roosevelt campaign workers. "This is the third depression in which I have served as Mayor and the needy people of Boston by the thousands must thank almighty God that Curley is on the job this year. . . . I am 58 years old and weigh 210 pounds stripped down, and I have never met any man regardless of his age or weight, whom I would permit to insult me to my face; and it would be advisable for any individual in the future to refrain from booing so far as I am concerned."[30]

The night after Curley issued this warning, FDR got a cooler reception than Smith had received speaking from the same stage days earlier, but through no fault of Curley's, who, unbooed, urged the audience to cheer for twenty minutes to top the ten given President Hoover earlier that night in New York. Waving one of Curley's shillelaghs, a dusting of confetti on his shoulders, Roosevelt charmed the crowd when by way of launching into a recital of Hoover's failures, he said, "As Governor Smith would say, 'Let's have a look at the record.'" People could sense his victory, and that gave him an aura that Al Smith had never possessed. Leaving the Statler on his way to the Boston Arena that evening, Roosevelt shook hands with a man characterized as of "foreign extraction," who then went through the crowd extending the hand that shook the hand to others. The Roosevelt motorcade left the city via the Jamaicaway. As it passed the house with the shamrock shutters, Curley opened a second-floor window and yelled out a greeting to FDR, who shouted back a response. But in the noise of the traffic, his words were lost.[31]

Election night found Curley at Roosevelt headquarters at the Biltmore Hotel in New York. When Roosevelt carried Massachusetts, Curley must have been relieved, though the victory was a narrow one. Running 6.8 points behind his national average, Roosevelt won with only 50.6 percent of the popular vote, up ever so slightly from Smith's 1928 mark of 50.2 percent. Hoover, with only 39.7 percent of the national vote, got 46.6 percent in Massachusetts. So far had the religious issue, whipped up by Curley's reckless counsel to contest Massachusetts, hurt Roosevelt. Writing in mid-October, Arthur Krock had noted the lingering Catholic resentment over Al Smith's defeat. "Boston women remain indignant. Their attitude appears to be that the party at Chicago notified their sons that they no longer need apply for a Presidential nomination." Smith's emotionally charged speech at the end of the month turned enough votes around to assure Roosevelt his margin of victory. For, identifying the central issue, Smith had said, "There can be no bigotry and there can be no resentment in the Catholic heart." There was plenty of both, but Smith mitigated them sufficiently to put Roosevelt over. The fear-driven get-out-the-vote efforts of Boston's city employees unquestionably helped as well, for Curley had told them that if Hoover won their pay would be cut 10 percent.[32]

"You did a fine piece of work, Jim," the president-elect told him that night. "I want you to give my thanks to the voters of Massachusetts and the boys who helped deliver it."[33]

"Ever so many happy returns!" Roosevelt cabled him on his birthday. "Hope to see you soon." His birthday cake was huge, large enough for fifty-eight candles *and* the words SECRETARY OF THE NAVY OF THE UNITED STATES. He was counting on the job. He felt he had a commitment on it, and a surviving witness bears him out. Lauretta Bremner Sliney says that, along with Mary Curley, she accompanied Curley on a December visit to president-elect Roosevelt at Warm

Springs, Georgia. Its purpose was to "confirm an appointment of Mayor Curley as Secretary of the Navy." At Curley's mention of that post, she recalls Roosevelt replying, "Anything you want, Jim."[34]

His birthday put him in a reflective mood. "I believe that you can't perform a mean, a low or an evil thing without punishment," he said, "and I believe that most of our punishment is received here. You don't have to wait for the hereafter." A revealing remark. Did he believe that in some way the "punishment" he received through the decimation of his family was a harsh repayment for his "mean," "low," or "evil" deeds? We can't know. But clearly the punishment did not fit the crime.[35]

And the punishment was not over. Called to the bedside of the dying Standish Willcox, he arrived two minutes too late to bid his old friend goodbye. He and his brother John entered the room at the same time, and , on seeing Willcox's body, both men wept. "In the death of Standish Willcox I suffer the loss of a faithful, devoted and dependable friend," he said. His eyes filled with tears as he led the honorary pallbearers down the aisle of Trinity Church. The mourners sang "The Strife Is Over."[36]

While these services were unfolding, cannon were being fired on Boston Common to mark the sudden death of Calvin Coolidge. At Coolidge's funeral in Northampton the following day Curley met James Roosevelt, who informed him that he would not be secretary of the navy; that had never been in the cards. (Writing in 1959, Roosevelt said his father "no more would have considered naming the flamboyant Boston brawler to head his beloved Navy Department than he would have appointed the Grand Wizard of the Ku Klux Klan as Ambassador to the Vatican.") But an ambassadorship—Curley says Roosevelt mentioned France or Italy— might be offered, if Curley was interested. Curley was reported to be "grievously disappointed" at the news about the navy job. He fancied giving out contracts to naval shipyards. He also seems to have liked the notion that James Michael Curley of Irish Massachusetts would succeed Hoover's Charles Francis Adams of Yankee Massachusetts as secretary of the navy. He relished the ethnic symmetry of it.[37]

"When I talk to him," Huey Long told a reporter that same January, speaking of Franklin Roosevelt, "he says, 'Fine! Fine! Fine!' But Joe Robinson"—the conservative Senator from Arkansas and an enemy of Long's—"goes to see him the next day and again he says, 'Fine! Fine! Fine!' Maybe he says 'Fine!' to everybody." Curley was learning the same thing about FDR. If Curley had been promised navy, it was now a promise broken. For Roosevelt had also said "Fine!" to the idea of Claude A. Swanson, the senator from Virginia, as his secretary of the navy. Swanson was picked for complex reasons of politics and policy. These, not promises, dictated Roosevelt's actions; he was a supremely successful politician and leader because he always allowed room for maneuver. Curley had jumped aboard the train of the Roosevelt campaign. It would have reached its destination without him—and sooner.[38]

There were rumors current that the president-elect, as part of a deal of Rooseveltian dimensions, would appoint Senator Marcus Coolidge to an ambassadorship and that Joseph Ely, exercising his prerogative as governor, would appoint Mayor Curley to fill Coolidge's Senate seat. According to another rumor he would be appointed assistant secretary of the treasury in charge of public buildings. Porto Rico's Democrats expected him to be named as their next governor. There was speculation he would be made Governor General of the Philippines. The Hearst papers endorsed him for secretary of the navy. The *Boston Globe* reported his imminent appointment as ambassador to Italy. During the Massachusetts primary, James Roosevelt had suggested him as minister to the Irish Free State. The mayor of Seattle, spotting the temperamental affinity, wanted him for secretary of war. "The only man who has any idea of what appointments may be made," Curley told persistent inquirers, "is Franklin D. Roosevelt."[39]

For some weeks Curley had been arranging to place members of his secretarial staff in other city departments. At a luncheon for the City Council at the Parker House he called for the council's cooperation with him "or his successor," according to someone who was there. His friends were convinced that after the inauguration on March 4 he would be on the federal payroll, leaving City Council president Joseph McGrath as the new mayor. One paper ran a photograph of the palatial American Embassy in Rome above the legend CURLEY's "HOME" IN ROME. His well-publicized ties to Mussolini, King Victor Emmanuel, and the pope made his appointment seem inspired.[40]

He left for the inauguration in Washington with a volume on Confucianism under his arm and a Roman holiday in his heart. In the days to come he would need a measure of the sage's equanimity. The strife was not over.[41]

Opposition to Curley in Boston had by this time found a new and more vigorous instrument than the Good Government Association, which, unmourned and unmissed, was about to pass out of existence. This was the Real Estate Owners' Association, whose members had a compelling grievance against "Curleyism": they were paying for it. The major realtors were joined in the anti-Curley ranks by two city councilmen, John F. Dowd of Roxbury and Francis E. Kelly of Dorchester, both die-hard Smith supporters. A young firebrand, Kelly proclaimed himself "viciously against Curley," took out a license for a gun, and declared melodramatically that if he were killed Curley himself would be shot within sixty days of the deed. Together with Mrs. Hannah M. Connors of the Real Estate Owners' Association, Kelly and Dowd filed a petition before the state legislature calling for an investigation into the alleged corruption of Curley and his administration. Mrs. Connors sent a letter to President Roosevelt protesting any appointment for Curley while the legislature was still deciding whether to go ahead with the investigation, and boldly insinuating that "a member of your family is the recipient of the Mayor's largess." Nothing much came of the investigation, but it succeeded in raising an untimely cloud. It embarrassed James Roosevelt, who was called to testify that his insurance agency had not received any city business from the Curley administration; and it came at the worst possible time for Curley, who was all but packing his bags for Washington.[42]

Joseph Dinneen tells a gripping story of how Franklin Roosevelt encouraged Curley to be his ambassador to Italy one day, only to dash his hopes by suggesting Poland as a pale alternative the next. While correct in substance, the account is unbelievable in detail. Dinneen has Curley engaging in extensive conversations with his daughter Mary in Washington when contemporary evidence places Mary in Boston. And this is only the first in a string of improbabilities.[43]

According to one source, Curley received an "informal tender" of the ambassadorship to Italy while still hoping to be named secretary of the navy, that he declined the offer, and that when all the cabinet and "little cabinet" positions were filled, he told Farley, the administration's man in charge of patronage, that he had changed his mind about Italy. But he was too late; the administration had made other plans. Breckinridge Long, an Old Wilsonian, would be ambassador to Italy. After serving for three years, he would then become assistant secretary of state. A man of nativist if not anti-Semitic views, during the Holocaust Long would do his utmost to keep Jewish refugees out of the United States.[44]

The sequence of job offers in this version of events does not square with Curley's recollection that James Roosevelt dangled Italy before him only after he knew he had lost Navy. We can merely note the conflict of stories, not resolve them. Perhaps the "informal tender" of Italy had come earlier from Farley—who knows? At the time, State Department sources reported that the Italian government did not want a Roman Catholic ambassador to Rome in view of the strained relations existing between Mussolini and the Vatican. Perhaps the Savior of Christian Civilization had not appreciated Curley's slamming his desk with his shillelagh. Or perhaps the story told by a writer for the *Saturday Evening Post* in 1941 was true, and Cardinal O'Connell had vetoed Curley's appointment.[45]

In retrospect, the whole Italy idea has an air of unreality about it. The State Department made a practice of not appointing Roman Catholics to Rome to avoid domestic political controversy over their "dual loyalty"; in those days, before the United States sent a separate ambassador to the Vatican, the ambassador to Italy served informally as the American link to the Holy See. As far as the official State Department historian can tell, the first Roman Catholic sent to Italy as ambassador was a James Dunn, who was appointed after the war by President Truman. For multiple reasons, then, Curley was not likely to receive a "formal tender" of Rome.[46]

Dublin was a different story. Friends of Curley's told the *Boston Traveler* that he had been offered the post of minister to the Irish Free State but that, hoping against precedent for the grander portfolio of ambassador to Italy, he had declined. (The State Department had in its gift only a handful of ambassadorships; most countries received ministers.) As ever, Curley wanted to go first class.

His reported rejection of Ireland, which might well have created unfavorable public comment—wasn't Ireland good enough for him?—was lost in his highly publicized declination of Poland. Despite having received a petition signed by ten thousand members and sympathizers of Hannah Connors's group urging him not to appoint Curley to any federal post and threatening to oppose him on the Senate floor—to oppose him, moreover, by invoking the principle the president himself had laid down the year before in the case of New York mayor Jimmy Walker: that a public official must account for his earnings and other income—in other words, despite the certainty that Curley's nomination would be contro- versial, President Roosevelt sent Curley's name to the Senate on April 11 as his nominee for ambassador to Poland. "I want to send you this note to tell you how happy I am that you are to represent the United States in Poland," he wrote Curley. "It makes me very happy to feel that for this post, which is one of the most important of our Embassies, I have someone in whose ability and loyalty I have the greatest confidence."

The president finally went through for Curley because Curley had been, as the saying of the day went, FRBC, "For Roosevelt Before Chicago," and he had to make being for him worth some- thing to get others to be for him in the future. But Roosevelt was under no illusion that he was making a sterling appointment. "When friends went to Franklin D. Roosevelt," one witness re- members, "to say that in Boston all the better people like Andrew J. Peters did not look with favor upon the appointment of James M. Curley as Ambassador to Poland, Roosevelt looked up with the query, 'What is there in Poland that Curley could steal?'" Such was the cynicism of this draft appointment; such was Roosevelt's private opinion of Curley; and such, parenthetically, was the pro- tection that birth and class and breeding still conferred on Andrew Peters two years after the death of Starr Faithfull.[47]

"I've always admired him," Senator Huey Long said of Cur- ley. "I'll vote for his confirmation with pleasure." But there would be no confirmation. In a White House meeting on April 14, 1933, Curley declined the appointment. His reason for not going to War- saw—that "the clear call of duty" made it necessary for him to stay at home "until such time . . . as industrial conditions are materially improved"—would not have stopped him from going to Rome.[48]

In a dramatic scene from that meeting of April 14 Dinneen has Curley responding to Roosevelt's offer this way. "Poland? . . . Po- land? You want me to go to Poland!" (But it was no surprise: his name had already been sent to the Senate.) "If Poland is such a goddam interesting place, why don't you resign the presidency and take it yourself?" Writing in 1949, Dinneen gives no source for this quotation, so it must have come from Curley. In 1951, Curley told a graduate student working on his doctoral dissertation that he looked Roosevelt in the eye and said, "You double-crossing, two-faced, syphilitic son-of-a-bitch!" and that Roosevelt then swore to his aides, "I'll pay him back if it's the last thing I ever do." In 1957, in a chapter of his autobiography entitled "Betrayal," Curley spares us the syphilis but expands on the idea that Roosevelt was out to get him; it was his explanation of why, in the 1940s, he was investigated, indicted, tried, convicted, and ultimately imprisoned for a federal crime. Curley had personally insulted the president, furnishing a motive for Roosevelt's revenge. In the 1957 version he tells Roosevelt off in a letter (of which there is no record) using his favorite tag from Shakespeare to shame the president:

> Had I but served my God with half the zeal
> I served my king, he would not in mine age
> Have left me naked to mine enemies.

His son Leo carries the letter to Washington, manages to sneak it in to the president through his secretaries, and is sitting just outside the president's door when his press secretary, Steve Early, comes out spouting, "Well, that son-of-a-bitch Curley has put it over on the boss again." Leave it to The Curley! In his old age he gave way to this kind of myth-making. The wonder is that a generation of Bostonians has accepted his diaphanous inventions as truth.[49]

To assess Curley's attitude toward these diplomatic appointments, look through the lens of his political needs. He already had the Irish vote. In Massachusetts the Polish vote was not significant. The Italian vote mattered. From Rome he could solidify and expand his support among Italian Americans in the Bay State. Political considerations aside, Poland was a blow to his pride. If he had not been lobbying so publicly for Italy, he might have accepted the appointment. But under the circumstances (which he had largely created), Poland looked like a consolation prize. Curley was always undoing himself, preempting the impersonal fatality that had swept away his father, his wife, and his children from playing any role in his life.

Not getting the Italian appointment was one of the best things that ever happened to Curley. In Rome he might have become what Ambassador Joseph P. Kennedy, a fellow Boston Irishman, became in London: a name synonymous with appeasement. He was already far gone on Mussolini, whom he viewed as nothing more sinister than a New Dealer in a hurry. If at the height of Mussolini's rape of Ethiopia Curley could give the Fascist salute before a crowd of Italian voters in Boston, one cringes to think what he might have done in Rome. With the death of Mary, Curley had lost touch with whole acres of reality. His vanity, his presumption, his self-infatuation, his recklessness now had no check. The daily example of that strutting jackanapes Mussolini might have permanently unhinged him.[50]

Having donated $20,000 plus the expenses of his month-long western road trip to the Roosevelt campaign (he would later tell Roosevelt that he spent $115,000 electing him), he ranked just behind the likes of Bernard Baruch, William Randolph Hearst, and Vincent Astor in the list of Roosevelt's top contributors. (Jim Farley said that after making one radio plea for contributions he returned to Roosevelt headquarters to find Curley waiting for him. "Here's the first answer to your appeal," he said, tossing a fat roll of bills into Farley's lap.) And he had nothing to show for it—except embarrassment, even humiliation, over not getting any of the offices for which he had lobbied. "I've got to take it philosophically. I am not complaining but I am sorry I had to decline the offer. The President was apparently surprised and regretful. I think he felt as badly about it as myself," Curley said in an interview on returning to Boston. "It seemed that everybody I knew contacted me and urged me that I continue as mayor of Boston. I have enjoyed the confidence of the people for a third of a century and I could not treat these requests lightly." In fact there was a "Keep Curley in Boston" drive, dividing the city between one group that wanted him to stay and Mrs. Connors's group that wanted him neither to go nor to stay; but it had an ersatz look, as if Curley, wanting to heighten his popularity for FDR's benefit, was pulling the strings. As soon as he arrived back at the Jamaicaway, he changed clothes and then with George, Leo, Paul, and Mary drove to Calvary Cemetery to place a large Easter wreath on the graves of James Jr. and Mary. "This has been the saddest three years of my life," he said. "I lost Mrs. Curley and lost James during this administration." This was another reason he wanted to put Boston behind him. The city was haunted by his dead.[51]

Shortly before midnight on the day of his return an "unknown tipster" called police to the Boston Common, where a crude wooden cross had been set on fire. In a cigarette tin stuck in the earth nearby they found a note, which ended:

> Mayor Curley refuses to go to Poland but WE HAVE SPOKEN; he must leave Massachusetts. In the sacred unfailing bond,
> Knights of the Ku Klux Klan

Curley was back, and if past was prologue, that burning cross was the opening salvo in his campaign for governor.[52]

❖ ❖ ❖

In December 1931, to call public attention to a private philanthropic effort to succor the unemployed, Curley presided over a waterfront ceremony in which "General D. Pression" was laid to rest. This hated personification was brought to Battery Wharf in a coffin delivered by a garbage truck and lowered into a ferry boat for burial in Boston Harbor. As Curley pushed the boat off from the wharf, he pronounced General D. Pression "well buried for all time."

This act of sympathetic magic signally failed. General Depression had only gotten worse. By the day of Roosevelt's inauguration, thirty-eight of the forty-eight states had had to close their banks to prevent panic runs. In New York the Stock Exchange shut down. The Chicago Board of Trade closed for the first time since 1848. The Kansas City Board of Trade followed suit. In the final days of the Hoover administration, Agnes Meyer noted in her diary, "World literally rocking beneath our feet."[53]

In the commercial city of Boston there was little commerce. A third of the labor force was jobless. Besides its own poor, Boston had four thousand transients—stranded seamen, wandering tramps, runaway children—on its welfare rolls. Seven thousand citizens faced the loss of their homes for nonpayment of taxes. By March 4, 1933, more than a quarter of the householders in Boston had been unable to pay their property taxes for 1932. The employees of many local companies were struggling to get by on two-day workweeks, while police and firemen had payless paydays. The consciousness of need was so acute that it even penetrated the arcanum of the Harvard polo team, which staged an exhibition match to raise money for the unemployed. From his winter retreat in Nassau, Cardinal O'Connell, familiarly known as "Gangplank Bill" for his annual winter-length vacations on the island, wired a charitable donation of $2,000. Governor Ely went door to door in the North End, where the unemployment rate approached 50 percent, begging money from the poor to give to the desperate. Though he had resisted it for three years, plunging revenues forced Curley to cut the salaries of the city's eighteen thousand employees. This was "Hooverism," not "Curleyism." Was he wrong to have passed up Warsaw? "I'll make him sorry he ever came back to Boston," Hannah Connors vowed.[54]

Yet Hoover was gone, Roosevelt was in, and by April, as the first Civilian Conservation Corps (CCC) boys left Boston to clear trails in New Hampshire's White Mountains, relief, if not recovery, seemed at hand. "This nation asks for action," Roosevelt had promised in his inaugural, "and action now." This was the call Curley had been waiting to hear since 1930. This was his hour. Curley should now have bent every effort to cooperate with the New Deal relief authorities to put the unemployed to work. In the remaining months of his term, he should have put his energy and ambition where his mouth had always been—on the side of people in need. That he largely failed them counts more heavily against him than all his graft and his ethnic and religious polarizing. These were, after all, just dubious means to achieve or retain power. By using that power for good—good defined in basic terms: a job for a man down on his luck, a bed in the City Hospital, the building of a neighborhood health clinic, the installation of a solarium on the beach at South Boston, the dollar bill slipped to the wino, with no temperance lecture attached—by such actions, at least partially, he wiped the moral slate clean. "He may have been a crook, but he was our crook"—that claim justified him. But like many politicians, holding office had become an end in itself for Curley; as the following months made clear, he had come to care more about power than about its purpose.[55]

How Curley failed his people is a complicated tale, though the story line is clear enough. He wanted federal relief projects in Boston, but on his own terms. These included spreading work to his pet contractors, who achieved that status by giving him kickbacks—to believe otherwise is to blink his expenses, the high fixed costs of living like a king on the salary of a mayor. In other words, Curley wanted his "cut" from the federal largesse, and his constant feuding with New Deal officials and with the Ely-appointed state administrator of federal aid, Joseph W. Bartlett, slowed the relief effort in Boston. Eligible for 22,800 jobs under the Public Works Administration (PWA), Boston filled only 12,500. Men and women with families to feed did not get jobs because Curley wanted to get his first.[56]

And just when he should have been trying to hustle every possible federal dollar to shore up the dignity of the unemployed while feeding their bellies, just when the work and wages policy he had been demanding for three years was finally being adopted by the federal government, he took lengthy trips abroad. There was an early spring cruise to the West Indies, on which he acted like the owner of the shipping line, tossing books from the ship's library overboard with imperious abandon. The steward explained: "He would take the book and begin to read it. If he didn't like it—and there seemed to be a lot of our books he didn't like—he would throw it over the side. He said to me, 'If any book is so bad that I can't read it then it's too bad for anybody else to read it.' He said as how it was the only effective mode of literary criticism he knew. He advised us to get different books with the money he paid for the ones he threw away." Summer saw him embark on his third European tour in as many years. While Bostonians were erecting cardboard shanties on the mile-long road leading to the Columbia Point dump, the Mayor of the Poor was conducting a lavish six-week peregrination of the Continent.[57]

He was tired of being mayor. Asked by friends to mount a legal challenge to the law barring Boston mayors from succeeding themselves, he refused. "I will not run. I have had enough." His disappointment over the barren results of his courtship of Roosevelt was beginning to take on a tinge of self-pity. Talking to reporters in his second-floor office a few months after the inauguration, he was interrupted by newsboys out on School Street shouting, "Curley for Muscle Shoals Job." "Oh, I had seen that," he replied about the post of director of the Tennessee Valley Authority. "Looks as though they were still making a goat of me." "They" was the Roosevelt administration. In what would become a pattern for him, he alternated criticism of Roosevelt appointees (for example, calling Lewis Douglas, FDR's budget director, "the biggest ass in the

country" for objecting to paying the soldier's bonus) with praise of
the president. FDR would not have appreciated the company he
kept in Curley's idiosyncratic pantheon, though. "The faith of Columbus, of Washington, of Lincoln and of Mussolini is now being
exemplified by Franklin Delano Roosevelt," he said in a Columbus
Day speech, displaying his inveterate regard for Il Duce, one
shared by most Italian-American newspapers, and many prominent
non-Italian Americans as well. Even Mussolini's rougher methods
won his commendation. The bankers resisting the National Recovery Administration (NRA), he told the crowd of ten thousand,
ought to be given educative doses of castor oil; and if that didn't
work, perhaps their arms should be broken. With such treatment,
after all, the "great Italian leader" had "led his people back to
prosperity and equality of opportunity." His calls for dictatorship
to cure the ills of democracy was putting the Bay State on notice as
to what to expect from him when he became governor.[58]

At the funeral of President Wilson's daughter, the Old Wilsonian George Creel was shooed out of the way by someone he did
not recognize. He turned to Curley and asked, "Who is this man?"
Incredulous, Curley said, "Is it possible that you do not know the
former Mayor, John F. Fitzgerald?"

The "former John F. Fitzgerald" would have been more like
it. That once luminous political star had all but faded away. "It is
time for young blood in politics in this city," Curley opined at a
bachelor dinner for thirty-one-year-old Maurice Tobin, a former
state representative from Roxbury who had just been elected to
the School Committee. "John F. Fitzgerald, Martin Lomasney and
the rest of us are getting old. I won't be with you much longer.
There is room and opportunity for young men such as Maurice
Tobin." In words he would regret five years later when he and
Tobin would compete for the office, Curley referred to him as
"perhaps our next Mayor." His remarks created a sensation. For
the first time in decades, Curley was inviting Bostonians to contemplate a future without him. In this context the death of Martin Lomasney in August 1933 seemed a portent. A year earlier, during his
forty-ninth Sunday-before-the-election harangue at the Hendricks
Club, Lomasney's conviction that Roosevelt was a dangerous radical got the better of his desire to endorse the candidate of his beloved Democratic party. He urged his followers to get beyond
their resentment from the Smith campaign and vote for Hoover. "I

mean Roosevelt," he quickly corrected himself. When the laughter subsided, the old man ruefully conceded that, "After listening so much to the radio a fellow doesn't know where he is." With Lomasney gone, the era of the "ward boss," long over in fact, was now over in symbolism. Was Boston politics due for a wholesale changing of the guard?[59]

Not to judge by the candidates in the mayoral election campaign of 1933. The usual suspects—Malcolm Nichols, Frederick Mansfield, Daniel Coakley—were back. Seeking a replay of the 1925 election, Curley endorsed late and campaigned desultorily for a candidate he did not like and may not have wanted to win, District Attorney William J. Foley, whom he once called the "Dumb Dora of Pemberton Square." But this time the outcome was different. Malcolm Nichols, who had proved so congenial a successor to Curley, had opposition from within his own party. Republican state Senator Henry Parkman, Jr., of the Back Bay was in the race to foil any possible Curley-Nichols cabal along the lines of 1925. His counterstrategy worked. He split the Republican vote. Nichols lost. Mansfield won.[60]

Andrew Peters had been the last anti-Curley Democrat to occupy City Hall, and by securing passage of the law on mayoral succession he had tried to end Curley's career. Now Frederick Mansfield would step up the attack. Curley's third term had passed without much trouble from the Finance Commission, because an ally of Curley's had run it. But given possession of the Curley administration's records, the new anti-Curley mayor would furnish a new anti-Curley Finance Commission with evidence indicating payoffs to his predecessor. As Curley had said, we are punished here, not in the afterlife, and for the rest of the decade he would pay for his misdeeds in term three.

The city he was leaving behind him was not just hurting from the cyclical downturn of the Depression. "A society may be embalmed in a can of trusts as a cod may find eternal youth in brine," *Fortune* noted in a depressing survey of the Boston economy in 1933. But in addition to the chronic problem of Boston's inhospitality to financial risk-taking there was the ever-worsening structural problem of underused and overtaxed commercial real estate, one deepened but not created by hard times. In a walking tour of Boston in the fall of 1933, John Bantry noted "a creeping paralysis which is slowly destroying Boston as a business centre." Along Atlantic Avenue, facing Boston Harbor, stood a string of abandoned commercial properties. Block after block between Atlantic Avenue and Milk Street, the heart of the downtown business district, was entirely devoid of tenants. Purchase Street, once thriving, was now empty. On Tremont Street, the commercial thoroughfare bordering the Common, few buildings were occupied above the third floor. TO LET signs lined Boylston Street, in what was supposed to be the new uptown office and shopping area. Along Commonwealth Avenue and Marlborough Street, Bantry gazed on "millions of dollars of dark and shuttered property, once the homes of Boston's largest tax payers, now forlorn, deserted, and unsaleable." Throughout the city large properties were not earning enough in rents to pay their ever-rising taxes. This residual effect of Curleyism was at the same time one of its continuing causes. With such little economic vitality in Boston's private sector, for many in the next generation of Bostonians the only career alternative would be a job "on the Gas Company" or "on the Edison" or "on the city." Vicissitudes later, Curley would return to City Hall because the conditions that gave rise to him and that his tax policies helped to perpetuate had not altered.[61]

For Curley the term ended with his annual Christmas cruise down Boston Harbor to visit the homeless shelter on Long Island. As he stood on the deck of the city institutions boat, his face catching the cold breath of the Atlantic, he must have wondered where the current of the years was taking him. He had never been so alone; had never needed the distraction of politics more. Yet for most of the next year he would be confined to the sidelines—for all he knew, he might never get onto the field again. Escorting his steamer, the city's three fire boats spouted columns of water into the air, and other craft in the harbor rang their bells and blew their whistles. The mayor was coming; all hail the mayor. Stripped of the fanfare, the excitement, the tumult, and the shouting of politics—life was just not enough. George Creel's question "Who is that man?" must have set him to wondering when someone would ask it of him. He would avoid the fate of John Fitzgerald; *he* would not slip back into the anonymous ruck.

Life was just not enough; without Mary, less than it ever had been. The sight of Curley sitting at that big dining room table trying to make conversation with little Frank moved the women who cooked for him and who looked after his—with his daughter grown up and the older boys away at school—rapidly emptying house. Would he ever marry again? He was handsome, charming, powerful, yet all alone, and that seemed a crime to them, a waste of a man.

His availability was so well known that it led to a scam of the affections. A "matchmaker" who was caught and sentenced to jail for the fraud had taken money from widows on the pretext that he could broker a marriage to the mayor. On his ocean cruises women played up to Curley. He liked their attentions; but, perhaps because he was still grieving for Mary, he did not reciprocate them. Once, on an airline flight, a stewardess claimed he stole a kiss from her. She was leaning over to listen to his pleasing voice as he was talking to Frank, when suddenly he kissed her on the cheek. "I didn't mind," she said. "He was such a nice person." Curley denied it. "The lady flatters herself," he ungallantly replied. "I have no recollection of her or of the incident." If he did steal that kiss it might have been the first he had given in three years.[62]

Through Mrs. Bremner, Lauretta's mother, he met Frances Cummings, the daughter of Roger Sullivan, the Irish Democratic machine leader of the Wilson era who had helped defeat Champ Clark at the Baltimore convention twenty years before. Mrs. Cummings was the widow of a dentist who had left her with twelve children and the means to take care of them. When Curley visited Chicago, the Bremners would have Mrs. Cummings over, and with delegations of her children she would make periodic return visits to Boston or to the Curley summer home at Oyster Harbors. Tall, buxom, of vivacious temperament, she was a favorite of the Curley children, who hoped their father would marry her, though Leo quipped it would be more like a "merger than a marriage." Mistaking Curley's gallantries for something more, she reportedly shared the same hope. But perhaps because he felt pressured by their expectations, he held off, and the relationship mellowed into a friendship.[63]

A photograph taken on the boat sailing down Boston Harbor shows him with a group of city officials and entertainers invited to cheer up the cheerless people on Long Island. One of them, somewhat in the background, is a recognizably female person in a fur hat and coat. Exercising the biographer's right of informed surmise—for her back is turned, and the news reports are not much help—she was Gertrude Dennis, a forty-year-old widow with two young boys to support, an accomplished professional singer and pianist, and a glamorous woman in the old-fashioned movie star way. Curley had known her slightly for three years; she had played concerts during political campaigns as well as at municipal facilities like the one on Long Island. But their acquaintance had just taken a new turn at a Christmas party given by Dr. David J. Johnson, Boston's institutions commissioner, when Curley could have invited her on his cruise to Long Island. As the outline of the city receded in the December mist, he must have hoped that he was leaving the three worst years of his life behind, that a new life—a new love— was possible for him. "May the best day that you have had in the past," he told Bostonians in his farewell radio address, "be no better than the worst day you will see in the future." Such was his wish, not only for them.[64]

The
Hit-and-Run
Governor

❖   ❖   ❖   ❖

There is only one political party
in the Commonwealth at the present time—
and that's the Governor.

GOVERNOR JAMES M. CURLEY

When he took office as Governor, he carried with
him the highest hopes of Boston and Massachusetts.

How he maltreated those hopes is one of the
blackest pages in the chronicle of the public life of
any man in the history of the Commonwealth.

BOSTON POST

I would describe a demagogue as a politician
who don't keep his promises.

HUEY LONG

❖   ❖   ❖   ❖

Curley has been called "the last of the bosses," but it would be nearer the mark to call him the first of a new political breed. "American politics has become the realm of individual political entrepreneurs. They are in business for themselves. They survive by creating their own personal followings. Their principal loyalties are to their own careers. And all of this has happened because political parties have lost the ability to organize and còntrol our political life." These words were written in 1991 by the political analyst William Schneider, yet they fit James Michael Curley better than nostalgia-tinged notions drawn from the lexicon of the "bosses." The emergence of the political entrepreneur in the 1980s has changed our map of the past, allowing us to see a figure like Curley as a precursor as much as a throwback.[1]

The strongest party left in the age of the political entrepreneur is the party of "me." That was also Curley's party; his ideology, Curleyism, even bore his own name. Like too many recent politicians, presidents among them, Curley specialized in the politics of division, in using "wedge issues" to split groups apart. Though he delivered the goods to many needy voters, and thus looks like a veritable giant next to our feckless promisers, his symbolic shamrock politics also anticipate our debates over diversions like "family values." "Americans," the journalist E. J. Dionne writes, "are furious at all politicians who would manipulate their worries without solving the problems that caused them." That statement about our politicians applies to Curley. He had a stake in leaving basic problems unsolved, the better to manipulate the frustration that meant votes to him. In short, look past his old-time

343

oratory, consider his crude electioneering the equivalent of our
televisual demagogy, and Curley emerges as a contemporary, a
prince of our disorder.

"The skills that work in American politics at this point in history are those of entrepreneurship," Alan Ehrenhalt writes in *The
United States of Ambition*, a study of today's politics. "At all levels
of the political system, from local boards and councils up to and
including the presidency, it is unusual for parties to nominate people. People nominate themselves." That might be a gloss on James
Michael Curley's campaign for governor in 1934. No machine, no
party bosses, no pudgy men in fedoras nominated him. As he had
done so often before, he nominated himself.[2]

In June 1934, before the state convention of the Democratic
party opened in Worcester, Curley delivered a diktat to the delegates; Norman of the *Post* captured it in a cartoon showing Governor
Ely, Senator Walsh, and other party officials arriving at the convention hall only to find the door closed, a note stuck fast to it by a
dagger. WARNING! the note said. I WILL ABIDE BY THE CHOICE OF THE CONVEN-
TION ONLY IF THE CHOICE IS CURLEY! SIGNED DON JAIME CURLEY. Curley tried to
win nomination at the convention, but under pressure from Ely and
Walsh the delegates chose Ely's hand-picked candidate, General
Charles H. Cole, a brigadier in France during the war who, as the
Democrats' gubernatorial nominee in 1928, had been narrowly defeated by Governor Allen. Having lost the nomination, Curley did
just what you would expect him to do—he denounced the convention as "crooked" and challenged Cole in a primary, masking his
self-seeking ambition in the antiparty cant of the political entrepreneur. "They packed the convention hall," he crowed, "but Governor Curley will have the last laugh."[3]

Curley opened up his old Bull Pen at the still empty (thanks to
Curleyism) former Young's Hotel, where he held forth at the top of
his lungs, calling Governor Ely, Senator Walsh, and Joseph A. Maynard, the chairman of the Democratic State Committee, "the
Hitlers of the Massachusetts Democracy," "political racketeers,"
and "three card monte men," among other piquant appellations. In
a radio address he pickled Cole in condescension, referring to him
as "some person of pleasant appearance and affable manner" and
"a shopworn nonentity."[4]

For Curley the only issue in the race was Franklin D. Roosevelt. "I stand with this man," he declared, charging that Ely and his

"puppet" Cole were less than ardent toward Roosevelt and the New Deal. This was true of Ely, at any rate. His opposition to features of the New Deal injurious to the Massachusetts economy, like the cotton-processing tax levied on New England mill owners, was becoming more prominent and more ideological. Writing in 1944, Ely explained that he had retired from politics ten years earlier because he was convinced that the New Deal was seeking "control of the intricacies of business and agriculture," and he wanted to have the freedom to protest the drift toward statism. With Al Smith and his rich new friends in the Liberty League, Joseph Ely "took a walk" in the 1936 presidential election, away from the Democratic party and its leader.

Curley upheld his region's economic interests against the southern tilt of the New Deal, criticizing the Agricultural Adjustment Act's cotton-processing tax and the National Recovery Administration's minimum wage differential in favor of the South; and he occasionally groused about Washington's emphasis on reform over recovery. But Ely's ideological politics was alien to him. So long as FDR looked like a winner, Curley would stand with (if not on) him.[5]

In the fourth year of the Depression dithyrambs to Roosevelt were enough to guarantee election, but, for insurance, Curley played the racial card. Senator Walsh, who was running for reelection, had voiced the fear that "the ticket will be too green with both Curley and me on it." Walsh had learned the danger of green tickets in 1924, when he and Curley, running together, both lost. General Cole, a Yankee Democrat, provided the senator with ethnic balance. But Cole's convention victory also allowed Curley to play on Irish fears by implying that his "race" had kept him off the ticket. In part it had, though not out of bigotry, but primarily as a way to reelect David Ignatius Walsh, hardly the name of a *Mayflower* descendant.[6]

In a speech at the old Vine Street Church in the Tammany ward, Ely tried to turn Roosevelt's stands against Curley. "Mr. Curley has talked much of his support for the policies and principles of President Roosevelt," he said. "I would like to ask him if he agrees with this Roosevelt policy. That when men holding public office show evidence of wealth not consistent with these offices or the remuneration that goes with such offices, he believed it their responsibilty to tell the people where they get it."

Governor Roosevelt had laid this standard down in the case of New York mayor Jimmy Walker, whose high living had prompted a state inquest into his finances, which led to his resignation. If any governor had had the moxie to apply it to Curley, this standard of public ethics might have driven him out of politics. But only an Irish Catholic governor would have been able to defend such a move against Curley's predictable cry—"I am being persecuted because of my race." Consequently, his use of public office for private gain had an immunity similar to that enjoyed in recent decades by leading black politicians, in cities as diverse as Los Angeles, Washington, and Birmingham—another respect in which Curley appears as a precursor.[7]

"Campaigning is my recreation," Curley said. Tan and rested from a sojourn in exotic parts, tireless as ever on the stump, he acted like a man pursuing his sport. Reminding Ely that he had "contributed" to his gubernatorial campaign in 1930, Curley asked for a reciprocating gesture: "One rubber check deserves another." His jaunty equanimity was momentarily disturbed, however, by a story in the *Herald* that raised anew the issue of corruption.[8]

The Finance Commission had been seeking the files of an out-of-court settlement reached by the city late in the Curley administration; someone had raided the commission's offices and thrown the files out the window. Found some time later in the alley behind the building, they revealed that the city had settled for $85,000 a $129,000 damage claim brought against it, but that only $35,000 of the settlement had found its way to the plaintiff ($30,000 of the missing $50,000 would eventually be traced to Curley's pocket). Curley's former corporation counsel, Sam Silverman, charged that the *Herald* story was a "political plot to assassinate Mayor Curley's candidacy for Governor," and Curley promptly sued the *Herald* for libel. "He knew that if he didn't win the governorship," Ralph Martin writes, "he might find himself in jail." As governor he would have the power to cover up his graft as mayor.[9]

Governor Ely, supplying the fire for General Cole, raked up other aborted Finance Commission investigations into the land takings surrounding the building of the harbor tunnel and the "Prado" Curley had constructed next to the Old North Church in the Italian North End. In a classic example of "honest graft," speculators had obtained inside information about these land takings before they were officially announced, greatly increasing their cost to the taxpayer. There was also the provocatively lucrative business done by the Mohawk Trading Company, which had sold meat to City Hospital at 25 to 35 percent higher than the going price. The evidence suggested, Ely said, that Edmund Dolan, Curley's city treasurer, traveling companion, and fellow mansion dweller on the Jamaicaway, was a principal in Mohawk Trading. But these charges came too late in the campaign; Curley's libel threats silenced the press, and his fervent embrace of Roosevelt and all his works was too convincing for Ely and Cole to prevail against him. On primary day he smashed Cole by 150,000 votes—280,405 to 129,025. The *New York Times* called it "the greatest triumph of his extraordinary political career," but that had been said before and would be said again.[10]

Curley's opponent in the general election, Lieutenant Governor Gaspar Griswold Bacon, bore the stigmata of his party. Blamed for the Depression, the Republicans were still trying to adapt to the new political landscape it had created. Were they for the New Deal or not? If they were, who needed them? If they weren't, they would lose at the polls. In short, with Roosevelt the issue, Bacon was lost.

But just to be sure, Curley flanked him on the ballot with a longtime ally, Frank A. Goodwin, a popular Republican maverick who, having been on the Democratic, Republican, and independent ballots in the primaries, ran as an independent in the general election. Goodwin criticized Curley just enough to be taken seriously as an opposing candidate ("He exploited the taxpayers of Boston through land deals, contracts and the purchase of supplies and if he is elected he will exploit the taxpayers of the state"), but an understanding clearly existed between the two men and had for years. Before leaving office in 1930, Governor Allen had appointed Goodwin to a three-year term as chairman of the Finance Commission. This was an obvious favor to Mayor Curley, who with his farcical campaign in the "second person" for John Fitzgerald had done his worst to sabotage his own party and help Governor Allen's reelection. Goodwin proved an accommodating commission chairman, dutifully sweeping under the rug matters that Curley wanted there and that, under a chairman appointed by Ely, were about to be exposed. According to former governor Alvan T. Fuller, "Curley and Goodwin were in cahoots when Curley was Mayor and Goodwin was chair of Fin Com. That was a set up that made the angels weep." Helpful to Curley in the past, Goodwin, who had won nearly four hundred thousand votes in two previous tries for the Republican nomination for governor, could be supremely helpful now by draining away liberal Republican and independent votes from Bacon."

Bacon made a fight of it. Earlier in the year he had attacked the New Deal in Maine for "Tammanizing" the federal work force; now he endorsed it in Massachusetts. He hit hard at Curley, charging that he was surrounded by "bagmen" and "racketeers" and that he had "shown a greater regard for contractors than he has for those in need of work and wages." He assailed as a reflection on the president Curley's insinuation that he could get more out of the Roosevelt administration than a Republican: was Curley implying that FDR was using federal relief funds in a partisan way? Bacon's sharpest line, "Let us keep Massachusetts honest," looked back to Frederick Mansfield's "Hasn't Curley had enough?" But neither of these nasties was in the class of Daniel Coakley's "nothing Curley is straight."¹²

Curley, in turn, attacked Bacon for his family's links to the firm of J. P. Morgan. In hearings throughout 1933 and 1934, the Senate Banking and Currency Committee exposed some of Wall Street's sharper practices. Under questioning from Ferdinand Pecora, the brilliant Sicilian immigrant who served as counsel to the committee, the financiers of the age answered for the malefactions that had helped bring on the stock market crash and prolong the Depression. J. P. Morgan the younger was obliged to admit that his firm maintained a "preferred list" for "good, sound, straight fellows" who would be sold stock at prices far below market price. Robert Bacon, Gaspar Bacon's father and Theodore Roosevelt's secretary of state, was one of these good, sound, straight fellows. Only a saint could pass up this opening.

Curley pounced on it: "I do not believe that the intelligent electorate of Massachusetts are prepared to reward the beneficiary of the Morgan interests in the November election whose proud boast is that while millions were on the relief roles, he Gaspar Griswold Bacon, was on the Morgan preferred roles." How he loved to sound those words, "Gasss-paar Grees-woled Bay-conn."¹³

Curley went too far, though, in deriding Bacon as an "aristocrat." What about the fellow in the White House? the *Boston Herald* asked. Wasn't he an aristocrat too? Certainly he was maintaining an aristocratic silence on the question of Curley for governor. When Roosevelt came up to Massachusetts for the Groton graduation in June, Curley rushed to get himself photographed with the president and used the photographs in full-page political ads; but no endorsement was forthcoming. Curley was "masquerading as the trusted agent of the President," Bacon truthfully charged, "when in reality the President is ignoring him." Friends of the president's in Massachusetts were disturbed by Curley's usurpation of the Roosevelt name. Professor Frank Taussig of Harvard spoke for many of them when he said that Curley's election would be an affront to "the plainest principles of decent government." James Roosevelt, his days as a Boston insurance man drawing to an end, had come out for Curley before the Democratic state convention. But when that drew what John Bantry called a "sharp admonition" from the White House, he quickly declared himself neutral in the Cole versus Curley runoff. The White House had wanted Cole. It got Curley. It was not happy with the trade.[14]

At a rally in Worcester James Roosevelt declared, "I want to say that the national administration and the President of the United States need and want David I. Walsh in the Senate." But he gave only his personal endorsement of Curley: "I know why I want him for Governor." It was an obvious slight, a hint of trouble to come with the national administration. Still, Curley's unexamined argument that as New England's Original Roosevelt Man he could get more "work and wages" out of the New Deal coffers than could the Republican Bacon carried the day. Goodwin's 94,000 votes gave him his victory margin, allowing him to beat Bacon by 109,000, 736,000 to 627,000, and become the first Democratic mayor of Boston to be elected governor of Massachusetts. Curley had his telephone bank call people past midnight, pretending to be soliciting votes for Bacon. It would not have been a Curley campaign without a dirty trick.[15]

"I recognize that it is not a personal victory for me," Curley said in his speech of triumph, "rather it is a victory for the programs and policies enunciated by our great leader, Franklin D. Roosevelt." The comparative election results, which reveal a striking lack of confidence in Curley, sustain that judgment. Curley ran 2,000 votes behind the Democratic lieutenant governor, Joseph L. Hurley; 15,000 votes behind the Democratic state auditor, Thomas

'H. Buckley; 35,000 votes behind the Democratic state treasurer, Charles F. Hurley; 116,000 votes behind Senator David I. Walsh; and 90,000 votes behind Joseph Ely's total in 1932. Curley would not have won without Roosevelt; the governorship was his Italy, Beacon Hill his Rome.[16]

It shouldn't have happened. For his own sake, Curley should have lost. No amount of scandal had sufficed to dispel his reputation for competence as mayor of Boston: Curley *built* Boston, he got things done. Governor Curley got things done too. But his accomplishments were forgotten, buried in the headlines and obliterated in the common memory by "things that made the government of Massachusetts ludicrous part of the time, shocking most of the time, and tawdry all of the time."

Alvan T. Fuller, no friend of Curley's, was nevertheless speaking from sympathy, not prejudice, when he said that Curley's conduct of the office of governor represented "one of the greatest tragedies of personality and character in the history of our generation."[17]

❖   ❖   ❖

The day after the election, following a wild victory parade led by fifty motorcycle policemen through downtown Boston, the last cheer having been given, the final handshake, Curley slept for twenty-four hours. When he rose, late in the afternoon of the following day, his first act as governor-elect was to visit his dead at Calvary Cemetery. With Francis and Mary kneeling beside him, he bent forward to adjust a new wreath—Mary Emelda had always liked things just so. The wind whistled through the canyons of gray headstones, tousling his silver-streaked hair.[18]

Just before leaving for the inauguration in January, the Curleys had their picture taken gathered around a huge floral arrangement, a "Success Ladder," each rung of which was marked with an office Curley had occupied, from common councilman to representative to alderman to city councilman to congressman to mayor to governor. Beyond GOVERNOR was another rung marked U.S. SENATOR. At a rally in Worcester there had even been cheers for Curley for president in 1940.[19]

Mary Emelda could have told him that hubris was a doubtful vote-getter. But he had yes-men around him now; and on the few occasions when he asked their opinion, they told him what he wanted to hear.

The state constitution called for a new governor to be sworn in before the members of the two branches of the legislature, with the Senate president administering the oath itself. But a Senate filibuster prevented the ceremony from running according to custom, and Curley, saying that the constitutional stipulation was not mandatory, had the secretary of state swear him in before the House alone. His ninety-minute inaugural address was the longest on record. He called for major changes in all three branches of Massachusetts government. The legislature was to be cut by half and to meet biennially. Judges were to be forced to retire by age seventy. And the Executive or Governor's Council, an elected body descended from the days of the Bay Colony that had the power to approve or veto gubernatorial appointments, was to be abolished.[20]

While Curley was making this last proposal, down in the audience in the packed House Chamber, a man rose from his seat and made a mock bow toward the new governor. Seeing who it was, the people seated near him booed. Curley glanced down from the Speaker's rostrum: Daniel Coakley was smiling up at him. In 1932, a decade after his exposure as a blackmailer, Coakley had finally won elected office—to the Executive Council. Curley smiled back and continued with his speech.[21]

Over the next two years none of the progressive measures Curley called for, none of the governmental reforms, would so matter to the citizens of the Commonwealth as that exchange of smiles. The man who had called Curley "a bully, a bravo, a thug, a masquerading mayor, a moral and physical coward, a blackleg and a jailbird" would be his key ally on the Governor's Council. Worse, Curley would govern in Coakley's knavish spirit.[22]

From its exordium ("The depression of the past five years has been so devastating in character as to be more properly characterized as an industrial war") to its call for a $100 million program of joint federal and state public works to provide "work and wages" for the unemployed, Curley's inaugural looked back to Roosevelt's. But whereas Roosevelt wanted to save the country, Curley seemed bent on saving himself. Too many of his proposals were shaped more with a view toward enhancing the powers of his once and future office as mayor of Boston than with those he was to exercise as governor. These included the abolition of the State

Board of Tax Appeals, the only recourse for commercial property owners seeking relief from the killing valuations of Curleyism, the repeal of the act under which the governor and not the mayor named the Boston police commissioner; and the abolition of the Finance Commission.

Curley was in a race with the Finance Commission. He had to remove the commissioners appointed by Ely before they got to the bottom of his graft in term three. And he did not have much time. The commission was on the point of requesting that legal proceedings be instituted against Edmund Dolan, whose doctor had conveniently ordered him to Florida for his health. Among other things, Dolan was suspected of having been a secret partner in a securities firm that had done most of its business with the city of which he was chief financial officer. To quote from a Finance Commission report, Dolan "bought a large amount of securities from himself as a bond broker by the device of setting up a dummy corporation to handle the transactions." Curley's third term, it was beginning to appear, had resembled his first. The names had changed, not the practices.[23]

Looking back, people who lived through the next few weeks could not believe it had really happened in Massachusetts. The epithets hurled at Curley within days of his inauguration have a desperate air. By the end of Curley's first month in office, Henry Parkman was saying, "Curley's reign of terror has converted Massachusetts into another Louisiana." After Curley's election Robert Washburn was hopeful that "if he will only develop those qualities which, in the opinion of many, are subjugated and give the Commonwealth the high kind of government of which he is capable, he will take a high place among the great Americans of the country, few if any more so." But soon after the Curley administration began, Washburn was describing a hearing led by Curley as a "lynching bee." The "Huey Long of the Bay State," the "Barbarian of School Street," a demagogue aiming to "Hitlerize" the state: no Massachusetts governor before Curley had ever been spoken of in such a damning key. These withering estimates were the price Curley had to pay to derail the Finance Commission's investigations. He paid it willingly. He would rather be called a dictator than proved a thief.

His text was straight out of Machiavelli: commit your killings openly and early, to sow salutary fear. Within twenty-four hours of taking office, he had given one member of the Finance Commission, Joseph A. Sheehan, a Superior Court judgeship and replaced him with a faithful ally. On January 9 he asked the Governor's Council for permission to remove two other Finance Commission members, Joseph J. Donahue, a distinguished lawyer, and Charles M. Storey, son of Moorfield Storey of the *Birth of a Nation* controversy. (Curley feuds reached through the generations, kept alive by his defiance of political gravity.) But by a five-to-four vote, the Republican majority on the Governor's Council turned him down.

Stymied, Curley announced that he would hold a public "trial" before the Governor's Council to remove the targeted Finance Commission members "for cause." With armed state troopers standing behind him to add to the atmosphere of fear, Curley led the Governor's Council in an inquisition. When Storey's lawyer asked if he would be able to cross-examine witnesses and produce evidence, John P. Feeney, a noted criminal lawyer whom Curley had hired as a sort of special prosecutor, told him, "Like hell you will." When Donahue's lawyer protested that his client's rights were being denied because Curley would not divulge the charges against him, Curley snapped, "You sit down or I'll throw you out." Storey was put on the stand for four days and grilled for eight hours at a stretch without being permitted to break for lunch or go to the toilet. At one point he actually started to faint. His attorney appealed to Curley to show mercy, but, in a whispered conference, Curley demanded Storey's resignation. "He has done no wrong, and he won't resign," the attorney replied. So Storey stayed on the stand, with Feeney and Daniel H. Coakley alternating as his inquisitors. Coakley shamelessly bore down on Storey's alleged violations of ethics—Storey had sat on the Finance Commission while it was investigating a client of his firm.

"What will it be, war or peace?" Coakley had asked his old enemy the new governor the first time he entered his office. "Have I the choice?" Curley asked. Coakley nodded. "Then it will be peace," Curley said, and the two men shook hands. Extensive powers of patronage in the Department of Public Works in exchange for Coakley's vote on the council would cement their alliance. In the Storey inquest Coakley came through royally for Curley, going so far as to claim that unnamed denizens of State Street, the center of Boston's legal establishment, had offered to reinstate his license to practice law if he would vote for Storey. Coakley threatened to tell the governor who they were if they dared to approach again. "The spectacle of Daniel H. Coakley posing as an authority on ethics," the *Herald* noted, "has caused sardonic laughter throughout the state."[24]

By a five-to-four vote along party lines, the councilors refused for the second time to remove Storey.[25]

Infuriated at this display of independence from an independently elected body, Curley threatened to resort to his version of the fireside chat: to use the radio to destroy the reputation and business of an obdurate Republican councilor. The threat was credible because an aide of Curley's, a former newspaperman named Richard Grant, had been broadcasting attacks on Storey during his inquisition. But the stick didn't work, so Curley tried a carrot: an offer to appoint yet another Republican councilor to a $5,000-a-year job on the Fall River Finance Commission. In a third balloting that brought a public outcry, this councilor switched his vote and Storey was dismissed from the Finance Commission. Along with his replacement, Curley could now also appoint a Democrat to substitute for the Republican member. Thus for the first time in Massachusetts history, the council had a Democratic majority.[26]

To replace Storey, Curley named attorney Edward P. Hassan. But Curley had to withdraw the appointment when it came out that Hassan had once served as legal counsel to Edmund Dolan, whose alleged wrongdoings were the chief business before the Finance Commission. "Naturally I did not know," Curley said when told of Hassan's link to Dolan. The brazenness of naming Dolan's former lawyer to investigate Dolan's former crimes left Alvan T. Fuller speechless: "My vocabulary is too limited to describe the depths of infamy to which the affairs of Massachusetts have sunk."[27]

More and worse followed. Donahue was removed. The chairman of the Finance Commission, Judge Jacob J. Kaplan, was forced to relinquish his position to a Curley appointee. The very morning the chief investigator of the commission, George R. Farnum, was to appear before the Supreme Court to compel Dolan's return from Florida, the now Curleyized Finance Commission ordered him to stop all proceedings against Dolan. Saying that the new commission clearly intended "to render my position untenable and to destroy the effectiveness of my investigation," Farnum resigned. In Florida Edmund Dolan, restored to health, made plans to return to Boston.[28]

Curley now controlled the Finance Commission. Several months later, with the naming of yet another Republican member of the Governor's Council to a judgeship and the appointment of a Democrat in his place, he consolidated his hold over the council. "The whole episode is not a happy one," the *Post* editorialized. During the campaign Curley had dubbed the council "a glorified hockshop." It isn't often that a man gets to demonstrate the felicity of his own phrases.

He could now fire and hire virtually at will. The purge of Ely's appointees began his third week in office, when he threatened to discharge William F. Callahan, the powerful commissioner of public works, unless he fired the registrar of motor vehicles, Morgan T. Ryan, and installed Frank Goodwin in his place. Callahan did as he was told. Goodwin had been registrar for eight years in the 1920s, so his appointment was not completely political. Besides, Ryan had incurred Curley's displeasure by suspending the license of his son Paul, who had been arrested for drunken driving.

When a mobster was killed in a Boston nightclub, Curley used the occasion to charge another Ely-appointed police commissioner, Joseph J. Leonard, with incompetence, to attack his department as corrupt, and to send in State Police detectives to take over the investigation of the shooting. Leonard wrote him that if he was interested in police reform he should use his influence to achieve one of the goals enunciated in his inaugural speech—allowing the mayor of Boston to pick his own police commissioner. "This action would be evidence of your good faith," Leonard said, "and if your effort were successful would result in my removal by force of law." Curley found this call for home rule "unwarranted, gratuitous, and impertinent" and promised to start removal proceedings against Leonard the next day, without granting him the chance to testify in his own defense. "No hearing will be given," Curley, at his brutalitarian worst, told reporters. Leonard did not wait for Curley's Star Chamber. Citing the ruinous effect that his dispute with the governor would have on police morale, he resigned.[29]

Home rule had been one of Curley's causes for a generation, but the last thing he wanted was to allow Mayor Frederick Mansfield to choose his own police commissioner. So that principle had to go overboard. It soon had company. Far from abolishing the Finance Commission, as he had promised to do in his inaugural, Curley used it to harass Mansfield. Far from abolishing the State Tax Appeal Board, he stuffed it with patronage appointees, including two former governor's councilors and his brother John.[30]

Bullying Leonard out of office was bad enough, but Curley went further. Complaining that the Boston Police could not enter nightclubs like the one where the gangster was killed without first getting a cumbersome warrant, Curley filed a bill that would allow them to enter "any place or building, other than a private dwelling, at which or in which people are congregated for the purpose of entertainment, amusement, or any other purpose, whether licensed or not, with the exception of religious assembly," to see if the people inside were obeying the law. He was giddy with excess.[31]

No sooner was Leonard out than Richard Grant, Curley's propagandist, launched a radio attack against the reputation of another Ely appointee, Eugene C. Hultman, chairman of the Metropolitan District Commission. This campaign of vilification lasted for months, with outrageous charges of "moral turpitude" being thrown at Hultman in public hearings before the Executive Council. But these new depths of calumny yielded nothing more than public laughter, which brought the proceedings to a close. For Hultman's alleged "turpitude" turned out to be trivial: while Boston police commissioner under Governor Ely, he had taken some Police Department horse manure for the flower beds in his summer home! At stake in Curley's fight with Hultman was patronage: the District Commission was in charge of a $25 million reservoir and water supply construction project in central Massachusetts, and Curley wanted its head under his thumb so that he could control who got the work and wages.[32]

Surveying the Leonard defenestration, the call for curbing the right of free assembly, and the Hultman witch trial, the *Springfield Union* found Curley's comment in a speech before the Insurance Society of Massachusetts alarmingly indicative: "There is only one political party in the Commonwealth at the present time—and that's the Governor." In an opinion echoed on editorial pages throughout the state, the *Union* concluded that "Governor Curley appears to be suffering now from delusions of grandeur and sees himself becoming dictator of this Commonwealth à la Huey Long."[33]

Firing qualified people, Curley appointed "the smallest and cheapest political heelers," according to the longtime *Globe* political reporter Louis M. Lyons, "that ever shined their trousers in the seats of public office in Massachusetts." As medical examiner he named a doctor whose license to practice medicine had once been suspended for drunken driving. The man he appointed as director of the division of dairying and husbandry, whose responsibility it was to monitor the purity of milk sold in the state, had once been fined for selling adulterated milk. Curley hired a longtime favorite, "Countess" Elektra Rosanska, who probably hailed from the duchy of Michigan, to teach folk songs to the female inmates at the women's reformatory at Sherborn. He appointed his gardener to serve as an inspector at the local race track and his chauffeur to a post in the Department of Public Works. The chauffeur quickly awarded over $100,000 in contracts to an auto body firm that must have been one of Curley's favorites. A law professor who had made a campaign speech for Curley and who Curley believed could carry the Masonic vote for him landed a $9,000 part-time job, his son and daughter also got jobs, his law partner a judgeship, and one of his clients a license to operate a dog track. As an auditor in the Department of Agriculture, Curley appointed a man who had done three years at hard labor for forging U.S. Treasury checks. When one of his subordinates wondered at the qualifications of a man Curley wanted given a job at the Grafton State Hospital, Curley sought to ease his mind. "Don't worry about Joe," he said. "He's an excellent man. Why, he hasn't had a drink or lost a day's work in twenty years." Told of Curley's endorsement of his character, Joe replied, "You know, the Governor was right about my not drinking or loafing in twenty years. Like I told him, I just finished a twenty year sentence at Dannemora prison."[34]

Arthur T. Lyman, the commissioner of corrections, got the word that Curley was cashiering him from an emissary who was— droll touch—an ex-convict. Amid resounding controversy Curley fired education commissioner Dr. Payson Smith, a distinguished educator, and replaced him with the school superintendent of the small city of North Adams. This man's sole qualification for the job, aside from his Irish Catholicism, was his enthusiastic backing of Curley's main educational initiative—a mandatory loyalty oath to the state and national constitutions to weed out "reds" and their cousins along the spectrum of sedition, "pinkos," in the public *and*

private schools. The *Herald* termed Smith's firing "a new low in
the administration of the affairs of the state." Beneath the visible
firings and hirings, there were unheralded purges in the insurance
and banking departments; the new commissioner of public welfare
fired twenty-three of his employees; the education commissioner
forced out five of his best people. On and on it went, an unprecedented trashing of the public service.

The new men sponsored new policies, some of them lunatic.
Within months of Curley's inauguration, his Parole Board released
seven murderers serving life sentences, five men serving twenty
years each for manslaughter, and five gunmen serving long terms
for armed robbery, not one of whom had completed so much as
half of the minimum sentence imposed by the courts. Over Christmas 1935 Curley issued 254 pardons and paroles. Notoriously, pris-
óners thus favored paid large fees not only to the attorneys
representing them but *through* those attorneys to the officials who
had the last word on pardons, members of the Governor's Council
and the governor, which is to say, Coakley and Curley. When riots
broke out at the state prisons in Concord and Charlestown, Curley
claimed the Parole Board's delay in granting pardons and paroles
was the cause and called for the ousting of members of the board.
"Is it not possible," the *Post* objected, "that the wholesale pardon-
ing of murderers, bandits, and hold-up men by consent of the
Council is far more responsible for unrest than any Parole Board
ruling?" The convicts who could not buy their way out of prison
were understandably angry.[35]

The governor himself was making controversial innovations in
policy. In a move that struck at the ancient barriers between
church and state, he threatened to revoke the license of any justice
of the peace who officiated at a civil marriage. As in the days of the
Puritan theocracy, clergymen would henceforth perform all weddings in Massachusetts. A nationwide radio show poked fun at Curley for this one, but within the state his attempted usurpation of
power was no laughing matter. "The atheist who espouses no religion has the right under our liberal constitution to be wedded by
civil authority, if he so desires," the *Lowell Telegram* wrote. "This
is not Germany and our people are not keen on Hitlerism."[36]

Curley kept a photograph of Mary Emelda on his big mahogany desk in the governor's corner office. "Governor Curley greets
the memory of the late Mrs. Curley," an observant reporter noted,

"every time he sits down or moves away from his gubernatorial desk, by gently and ever so slightly changing the position of her cabinet portrait under the bowl of flowers in front of him." Touchingly dear to him, her memory no longer influenced his conduct. The spirit of his administration seemed better expressed not by the other photograph on his desk, that of President Roosevelt, but by the desk set with the emblem of a snarling tiger on it, a memento of his Tammany years, and above all by yet another symbolic prop—a chair sent by Benito Mussolini.

Weary from purges, pardons, and paroles, Curley left Massachusetts for a two-week vacation in Florida and Cuba in February following a stopover in Washington for some lobbying. He was accompanied by the semimilitary retinue of guards who formed a kind of visual punctuation around him now; with their navy blue capes, their gold trimmed caps, gold-striped trousers, gold sleeve braids, and gold epaulets they caused Washingtonians to wonder what princeling was in town. In Florida he golfed, using Massachusetts state policemen as his caddies; he also swam, rode, boated, partied, and tried his luck at Hialeah. He was chauffeured from place to place in his state limousine, number S-1, which had been sent over the road from Massachusetts with two police sergeants garbed in electric blue uniforms to convey him whither he would go and with such swank as would make him the admired object of every eye.[37]

His $10,000 salary as governor was only half of what he had earned as mayor. Still, a poor boy at heart with his nose forever pressed up against the restaurant window, he took his idea of the good life neither from his church nor from the example of his parents—the Sunday afternoon ride on the swan boats, the telling of Irish fairy tales, the sharing in what Dr. Johnson called the "bread and tea" of existence—but from the kind of people who adorned J. P. Morgan's "preferred list" and who owned the bread industry and who could buy enough tea to brew the oceans.

❖   ❖   ❖

Working with a Republican-controlled state legislature, Curley had impressive success in getting his work and wages bills passed. His budget message of January 24 called for total expenditures of $61 million and a 10 percent surtax to run for two years on income, corporation, and inheritance taxes. The legislature embraced the budget and swallowed the taxes. His first "work and wages" bill, a proposal to cut the hours of employees at state institutions from sixty to forty-eight hours a week, also passed, thanks to what one scholar calls "skillful lobbying" by the governor. In an effort to establish state relief projects separate from those run by Washington, Curley asked for a $35 million bond issue to be financed by the state tax on gasoline. The legislature split the proposal in two and lowered the amount, passing (by one vote) a $13 million bond issue for construction. The Republican Speaker of the House, Leverett Saltonstall, balked passage of the second bond issue.

The legislature also rejected Curley's call for a graduated state income tax, a retail sales tax, and a new tax on intangible wealth. But it passed a host of bills backed by Curley favorable to labor, including a law patterned after the federal Norris–La Guardia Act, which limited the use of injunctions in labor disputes; another guaranteeing the prevailing wage on all state construction projects; and a third broadening the protections offered under the state's Workmen's Compensation Act. Payments to incapacitated workers would not be ended after five years, as previously, but would extend for the lifetime of the worker. And the rate of payment would be pegged at the average weekly wage, a humane advance over the prevailing standard, which had left many disabled workers unable to provide for their families.

Curley got these and other progressive measures through a conservative legislature by Curleyesque means. Speaker Saltonstall charged that Curley's operatives promised to steer state legal work to the law office of one state legislator if he went along with the governor. Another was threatened with the loss of state business given his family's firm. The governor's office searched civil service lists for legislators' friends and relatives, who did not get state jobs unless their sponsoring legislators voted with the governor. Representative Christian A. Herter, a Back Bay Republican who would one day be President Eisenhower's secretary of state, claimed that any legislator voting against Curley's work and wages bills "found that the unemployed of his district had no chance of getting a state job." By contrast, Republicans who voted right got patronage on state construction projects. In any case, with many Republican legislators looking for state sinecures themselves, Curley did "not need to offer jobs for votes," as one paper observed. "He [was] bombarded with offers of votes for jobs."[38]

In his autobiography, Curley quotes William Green, president of the American Federation of Labor, as saying, "More progressive, constructive, liberal laws were enacted under Curley in two years than under all previous administrations in any ten-year period in the history of the state." A modern historian assesses Curley's record this way: "All in all, during Curley's two years in office the General Court . . . abandoned a good deal of its one time conservative aversion to large scale government spending—in response to the proddings of an aggressive governor and the whip of a persistent economic crisis." Obviously, such liberalism reflected the temper of the times. The Depression lasted so long and cut so deep, Robert S. McElvaine writes, that a "far larger segment of the middle class was directly affected" than had been touched by economic slumps in the past, "and hence came to identify its interests with those of the poor." The 1930s were the "time in which the values of compassion, sharing, and social justice became the most dominant that they have ever been in American history." Still, Joseph Ely had not seized this progressive moment as Curley did or as his successors, Democrat and Republican alike, would, and for doing so Curley deserves the gratitude of posterity.[39]

❖   ❖   ❖

The seasonal rigors of Florida behind him, Governor Curley prepared for the wedding of his daughter Mary. It was to be the high point of an administration of which the multiplicity of contenders make it too difficult to pick out the low. The bridegroom was Edward Calvin Donnelly, a graduate of the Canterbury School in Connecticut and a member of the Harvard class of 1930. Donnelly was a lieutenant colonel on Curley's National Guard military staff and the chief executive officer of John Donnelly and Sons, a major Boston outdoor advertising agency: as every sentient citizen of the Commonwealth would soon know, Donnelly was the state's billboard king. His father was dead but his mother, Julia, a woman ever on her dignity, was conscious of her family's social position among the city's Irish elite—they lived in the Back Bay, on Commonwealth Avenue—and she was reportedly unhappy that, in Governor Curley's daughter, her son was marrying beneath him.[40]

The June wedding in Holy Cross Cathedral, where so many of the sorrows of the Curley family had been played out, was a huge public event. Once again the trains passing on the Elevated slowed to a noiseless crawl. Once again there were thousands of onlookers on the streets outside—so many that several women fainted in the crush. But this time the mood was celebratory. When the bride arrived in her gray chantilly lace gown (the rumor was that her trousseau cost $10,000, and that the downtown stores had marked the bills "NC"), mounted police had to turn back a surge of people who wanted to get a closer look.

That morning Curley presented Mary with a string of pearls he had given her mother when he was a congressman. From the pearls around his daughter's graceful neck to his early morning visit to Mary Emelda's grave to the presence of Lauretta Bremner as one of the bridesmaids, the day was full of memento mori.

Sun lay on the red velvet carpet with the white runner. At its end William O'Connell, resplendent in the crimson robes of a car-dinal, waited to perform the marriage before the thirty-five hundred guests. Mary had wanted to be married by her own priest in her own parish, Our Lady of Lourdes in Jamaica Plain, but the cardinal had other ideas. He phoned her and announced that it was "fitting" for him to join "two such prominent Irish Catholic families." Mary demurred, but he insisted.

Later she was in tears over allowing him to take over her wedding. She had a presentiment about it. The cardinal had married his two nieces; she knew them, and knew they had had terrible marriages, and didn't want that to happen to her.

A company of mounted National Guardsmen carrying lances led the motorcade of limousines from the cathedral to the Copley-Plaza Hotel for the second reception of the day, a sumptuous wedding breakfast having gone before. It took two thousand pounds of lobster, two thousand of potatoes, one hundred pounds of table butter, forty-five baskets of fresh garden peas, four thousand rolls, fifty gallons of coffee, enough wine to fill six thousand glasses, and thousands of tiny finger sandwiches tied with red silk ribbons served on eight thousand separate plates and in six thousand cups and glasses, to feed and water the guests. The hotel's pastry chef spent ten days building the five-foot-high wedding cake, which Mary used Colonel Donnelly's saber to cut.[41]

Like an emperor of old, wherever Curley went in the reception hall he was accompanied by a State Police sergeant holding the flag of the Commonwealth over him.

Immediately after the reception, the Donnellys left for an around-the-world cruise. A Morgan honeymoon: this was the measure Curley wanted for his daughter.

While they were away, Curley dragged their marriage into a controversy by filing a bill before the legislature removing the power to veto the erection and placement of billboards from the Commonwealth's cities and towns and vesting it in a director of advertising appointed by the commissioner of public works, whom he appointed. Alvan T. Fuller denounced the bill as the "pay envelope" to Donnelly Advertising for the CURLEY FOR GOVERNOR billboards that had covered the state in the fall campaign. "Shouldn't the proper title of this bill be, 'An act making a grant to the royal family of Massachusetts'?" Christian Herter asked. Despite heavy pressure from the Curley administration, the House narrowly rejected the billboard law. The Senate at first also rejected it, then, with two Republican senators obligingly gazing out the window as the vote was taken, it reconsidered. One paper termed this Curley's "greatest victory on Beacon Hill." But by then the public outcry against his wedding gift to the Donnellys had given Curley rare pause. The day after the vote to reconsider he sent a special message to the Senate urging that the bill he had worked so hard to pass be rejected, thereby enraging the senators who had backed the bill because he wanted it. Nothing Curley, they had discovered, was straight.[42]

The arrant royalism of the billboard law was not an isolated piece of arrogance. Curley was exhausting the governor's $100,000 contingency fund for expenses incurred in running his office. Fresh flowers daily, expensive cigars, $800 hotel bills, $280 vases—such expenditures were clearly for personal items, not for the public purposes the legislature had envisioned in establishing the fund. When a Republican representative from Brookline, Philip G. Bowker, attacked Curley's profligacy, the governor ordered an investigation of Brookline's finances.[43]

Then there were the tragic adventures of the governor's new twelve-cylinder Lincoln, the limousine with the license plate S-1. In May a forty-year-old motorcycle policeman, a wounded veteran of the World War and a bridegroom of only five months, was killed while escorting the governor along the Jamaicaway, a four-lane undivided road. With S-1 behind him, the officer was rounding a curve when he had to swerve to avoid hitting a car in the oncoming lane.

His bike hit the soft shoulder on the side of the road, catapulting him twenty-five feet through the air toward the tree that split his head open. "We were not going fast at the time," the governor was careful to say, though he conceded that the officer's siren—the royal coming had to be announced—might have "rattled" the driver whose sudden weave had triggered the crash.[44]

The Fourth of July saw an even stranger incident in Newton Highlands. Leading S-1 down the Worcester Turnpike toward Boston, another motorcycle escort suffered life-threatening injuries when he cut sharply to the right to avoid a slow-moving car, spun completely around, was thrown from his machine, and landed, head first, on the highway. To avoid running over him, the chauffeur of S-1, Charles Mannion, cut across the median strip of the highway. S-1 careened through the traffic until it came to rest against a tree.

The speedometer on the trooper's motorcycle had stopped at ninety miles an hour. The speed limit for that stretch of road, a steep hill on which there had been many serious accidents, was forty-five miles an hour. Curley had been due at an engagement in Boston at noon; the accident occurred at 12:37. It was clear why S-1 had been speeding.

Seeing the governor standing by the side of the road surveying his wrecked limousine, a passing motorist offered him a ride home. Curley accepted. Eight other witnesses placed him at the scene; one said he shook hands with him. At the hospital to which the injured trooper was taken, Curley's "adjutant general," William Rose, listed Curley as one of the occupants of S-1. So did the official report filed by the first Newton police officer to arrive at the crash site.[45]

Nevertheless, Curley denied being there. He claimed he was in a second car that, returning from a distant holiday celebration, had turned off the turnpike in Framingham, fifteen miles to the west.[46]

This was too much for the Republican mayor of Newton, Sinclair Weeks. Pointing to the testimony of the nine witnesses who saw the governor, he said that "the only logical conclusion that can be drawn from Curley's denial, and in his sudden slipping away from the scene, must be that he was conscience stricken."[47]

In an official report that outraged decent opinion, the registrar of motor vehicles, the pliant Frank Goodwin, blamed the driver of the slow-moving car, a woman, for the accident. Such "road mopes," he wrote, were a hazard. The "woman driver" in question, Mrs. Caroline A. Wrightson of Natick, responded heatedly. "Registrar Goodwin is merely trying to cover up Gov. Curley by this report. He knows I was not responsible for that accident. Why does he lie? They came tearing down the hill behind me, tooting horns and blowing whistles, trying to drive me out of the traffic lane." But she was in that lane to make a left turn at the light at the crest of the hill. "How could I get out of it and make my left turn safely?"[48]

Mayor Weeks branded Goodwin's "whitewash" of Curley as "too despicable for words." Mayor Mansfield christened Curley the "first hit-and-run Governor."[49]

The extended Curley family, official and personal, was going through a bad patch with its means of conveyance. On official business, a Curley chauffeur collided with another car while going over sixty miles an hour. An Executive Department driver, booked for speeding one day, was hauled in for reckless driving the next—he had rammed S-1 into a car containing five passengers. Two of the governor's aides were taken to police headquarters after driving through downtown Boston's twisting streets as though on a race track. Letters-to-the-editor columns of the Boston papers featured communications from people like Francis Stickland of Brookline, who reported seeing S-1 shoot through a red light at high speed. Flags flying, horns blaring, cutting in and out of traffic, ignoring red lights, S-1 was a public menace. "As part of the safety-first campaign on the highways," the *Herald* asked, "would it not be possible to publish well in advance a map of the roads over which Gov. Curley intends to travel day by day in the juggernaut of. S-1?"[50]

And S-1 was not alone. Returning from "Governor's Day" at the Suffolk Downs racetrack in East Boston, Miss Mary A. Donnelly, Edward's sister, struck a six-year-old boy. With her in the car was Leo Curley. Two days later, a car driven by another Donnelly sister, Catherine, while "traveling at terrific speed," was wrecked against a stone wall in rural Dover. A month later, someone who gave his name as Paul Curley was arrested for speeding in Connecticut. Curley denied it was his son—"My son has not been away for some time, and I am certain he was not in Connecticut last week"—but he had also denied being in S-1 at the time of the accident in Newton.[51]

Nothing was safe with a member of the "royal family" aboard, not even the 'Maicaway, the ninety-three-foot yacht Curley shared with Edmund Dolan, which ran aground in Nantasket Harbor. The people of Massachusetts were lucky that the royal family included no amateur aviators.[52]

The sentimental goo in which Curley has long been brined locally has made him the model of a "man of the people." The Curley legend and the Curley life run together, run apart, run speciously together at various points in his career. But nowhere is the gap between man and myth greater than in his gubernatorial years, as these Bourbon instances attest.

Curley had planned to journey to Hawaii to meet the honeymooners on the last lap of their three-month world-girdling trip. But he was tempted to advance his plans after receiving a cable from Donnelly informing him that Mary had been stricken with appendicitis at Shanghai. Several hours of torment later, a second telegram arrived saying that Mary had been operated on and was rapidly recovering. Her appendix had burst while on an ocean liner somewhere between Calcutta and Shanghai. With a temperature of 104°, she had been in critical condition, though only briefly.[53]

Anxious to see his daughter, the governor prepared to leave the state for a vacation in Hawaii, followed by a stay at San Simeon with William Randolph Hearst.

There were 180,000 unemployed in Massachusetts. Beyond the cyclical unemployment, if one can speak of the Great Depression in such terms, the state's industrial base, the textile and shoe industries, was vanishing, migrating to the South or succumbing to foreign competition, meaning that even when recovery came the Massachusetts economy would employ many fewer people and at lower wages than in the past. The downward trend was inexorable. In 1923 Massachusetts had employed 113,000 textile workers; in 1935, perhaps as few as 35,000. Wages paid by the textile industry in 1923 totaled $115 million; in 1935, $25 million. In the North Shore city of Lynn, in 1924, ninety-five shoe factories employed 7,258 workers at a payroll of $8 million; in 1934, fifty-three shoe factories employed 3,800 workers at a payroll of $3 million. Total wages in Fitchburg had fallen in the decade from $48 million to $22 million; in Taunton from $8 million to $3 million; in Holyoke from $18 million to $8 million. The distress in industrial cities like Lowell, Fall River, Lawrence, Brockton, Haverhill, and Chicopee had only one precedent in Bay State history—the time of the coming of the Famine Irish.[54]

In 1935 an unemployed Boston seamstress of French-Canadian descent poured out her desperation in a letter to Eleanor Roosevelt:

> Pleading, asking you to help a single girl, good moral character. Pretending any longer I cannot do. They must be some one some where to help me. Where could we find abandoned farm, good enough to live in and do farming. With allowance from E.R.A. I could be self support and it would be a place to call home. Happiness to enjoy the beautiful sun, nature all so interesting.
> Handy at most everything.
> Good little fixer.[55]

Hers was the voice of tens of thousands in Massachusetts in that terrible year. The great knife of the Depression was slicing down on the hopes, the lives, of a generation. Yet Governor Curley was taking a month-long Hawaiian holiday.[56]

A four-piece Hawaiian string band was at the station to see him off in style. After his twenty-two pieces of luggage had been put aboard the train, Curley reflected on the uncertainties of life in a brief speech to well-wishers: one never knew what might come on the great journey between the framing darknesses. Then he added: "But I have labored long and hard to put over in Massachusetts my program of work and wages. I am glad to say that as I leave, the program is complete, and will be in full swing next week. I may be gone four weeks or five weeks. But whether I return or not, I rest secure in the knowledge that the program will be carried out. And on my return I know that it will already have brought happiness and prosperity to those in want."[57]

George Reedy, the former adviser to President Lyndon B. Johnson, has contributed a useful concept to political science, one that is worth using to elucidate Curley's remarks. The concept is the "Xanadu effect," after Coleridge's famous poem beginning, "In Xanadu did Kubla Khan a stately pleasure dome decree . . ." The Xanadu effect is a peculiar kind of nemesis, to mix mythologies, laid up for politicians who lose touch with reality and come to inhabit their own semiprivate worlds. Surrounded by courtiers and yes-men, sustained by an often abject because "objective" press, they easily mistake their words for deeds, their wishes for realities.[58]

So with Curley. No doubt he believed what he said about the imminent deliverance of "those in want" by his work and wages "program." The Xanadu effect had him in its grip. But to the hard-pressed citizens of the Commonwealth who had elected him to provide real work and wages, not the incantatory variety, Curley's "Aloha" must have brought bitter laughter. For work and wages was his greatest failure, a figment of autosuggestion, a hoax. He shouldn't have been governor, and the saga of work and wages shows why with pitiless clarity.

❖   ❖   ❖

It began with the campaign pretense that his well-known close personal ties to President Roosevelt meant he could get more for Massachusetts from Washington than his Republican opponent. These ties did not exist. We have seen what Roosevelt thought of him privately, though hiding his real feelings was a honed instinct with him. But Louis M. Howe, the gateway to the president, was openly contemptuous of Curley. According to a report published early in 1935, Howe had "knocked off" Curley as secretary of the navy, ambassador to Italy, and governor general of the Philippines and had put out the word to Postmaster General Farley that all federal appointments for his native state of Massachusetts must come in over his desk. "This is my patronage," he was quoted as saying. Howe's enmity was no secret to Curley, but the voters knew nothing of it, and so they elected him on a promise he had no means of fulfilling.[59]

A skeletal account of the grand fiasco of work and wages is all that this pen can endure. With his gold-braided entourage, Curley first descended on Washington on February 1, 1935, asking for relief assistance totaling $160 million. Five days later he upped his request to $236 million. The relief authorities, Harry Hopkins, soon to be administrator of the Works Progress Administration (WPA), and Harold Ickes, the secretary of the interior and head of the Public Works Administration (PWA), ignored him. A few weeks later he claimed he had federal backing for the construction of a $40 million sewer system along the Merrimack River Valley that would employ eight thousand. Washington said it knew nothing of such a plan. In April, stopping in Washington on his return from another trip to Florida, he floated a $400 million plan of which $140 million was for the Merrimack Valley. Next day, leaving Washington, he upped the total amount to $600 million (why stint on imaginary money?) and the number of jobs to thirty thousand. "Our projects are in such complete harmony with the President's purpose," he told reporters, "that I expect a speedy approval of at least the majority of our projects." On May 7, back from Washington, he talked up a $35 million program to eliminate grade crossings and construct seven hundred miles of sidewalks alongside state highways. A *Boston Globe* headline—GOV CURLEY COULD NOT SEE HOPKINS OR ICKES—told a different story. On May 9 he proposed hiring, with federal money, five hundred engineers, architects, and accountants, to investigate the phone and electric light companies with a view to forcing a cut in rates. Price: a piddling $1 million. No, said the relief authorities; projects of that character were not eligible for consideration.[60]

Finally, on June 27, criticizing Washington for being too slow and balky, he announced his plan for a $35 million bond issue: if the federal government would not give him control over the spending of its money, Massachusetts would provide its own work and wages. Months later that $35 million got whittled down to $13 million for the whole state, a figure just $3 million more than the amount for work and wages he had initially promised to the small western Massachusetts town of Lenox.[61]

In August he swooped down on Washington again, this time emerging with the claim that the federal government had promised $30 million to tear down the rickety El that ran in front of the cathedral. Fifty years would pass before it was dismantled. That same month of August 1935, after another descent on Washington, Curley's new figure was $72 million, half of which was to go toward the building of two heavy cruisers at the Boston Navy Yard. There was at least a wisp of truth in this claim: the navy said it had committed to two destroyers, but the credit for procuring them should go to Congressman John W. McCormack and Senator David I. Walsh. TWO CURLEY CRUISERS AT $32,000,000 SHRINK TO $2,500,000 DESTROYERS, ran one headline. "Navy Yard officials were astonished at the prediction," the story reported, "saying that it was physically impossible to build cruisers with the present facilities at the Yard." As for the rest of his plan, another headline makes clear that it too came straight from deepest Xanadu: DENY PROMISE TO CURLEY; CAPITAL OFFICIALS SAY $72,000,000 PLAN HAS NOT BEEN APPROVED. Claiming that the $72 million was "practically assured," Curley stuck by his fantasy: "I certainly was far more successful in my mission than I had in any way anticipated."

On September 3, Curley's El plan having been rejected, he asked Washington for $5 million to plant trees along state highways and $25 million to construct farm-to-market roads. On September 12, after a private meeting with the president at Hyde Park, he assured those who could still credit his promises that $25 million was on the way for sidewalks and trees. Back from five weeks in Hawaii, he now spoke of $10 million soon to arrive from Washington to purchase and plant lilac bushes along the Boston-Providence highway. Evidently the abundant flora of the tropics had made an impression on him.

On December 14, Harry Hopkins announced that federal funds to reimburse Massachusetts for Curley's sidewalk-building campaign would be withheld because the governor, in his panic to provide a simulacrum of work and wages, had gone ahead on his own. In other words, while Curley was grandstanding for one imaginary project after another, he was failing to follow through on the one project that had a chance of completing the hard journey to reality. As a result, Massachusetts taxpayers stood to forfeit millions in federal aid.

He could not stop himself. In January 1936, he claimed that the president had just promised him federal support in the amount of $1.8 million for the construction of the $5 million Suffolk County Courthouse in Boston. So here, at last, was the promised work and wages—$1.8 million worth. Alas, even this nubbin appeared to be a mirage, according to Mayor Mansfield. On checking with Washington, he said that no federal funds would be available for building the courthouse.

To be sure, federal relief efforts went forward in Massachusetts. Between 1934 and late 1935, the Federal Emergency Relief Administration (FERA), the first edition of the WPA, spent $70 million in the state, employing an average of 115,000 people on eighty-four hundred projects. But they went forward under federal, not state, control. Their funding was based on formulas worked out in the federal bureaucracy and approved by Congress, not by Curley. They concentrated on small jobs that could be completed within a year, not on the kind of massive multiyear undertakings Curley wanted, and that were so rewarding to his pet contractors. These projects mostly employed people already on welfare, as a way of clearing the lists, not those Curley wanted to hire—workers represented by the powerful unions he was eager to reward for their support. He hoped the federal treasury would substitute for the Boston property holders in executing the painless formula of Curleyism.[62]

Looking back on a year of rhetorical work and wages, the *Boston Post* observed, "Governor Curley did not actually promise 'work and wages for all' in his campaign, but a good many persons assumed he did and that was a fair inference. No doubt he has struggled hard to keep the work and wages promise, but that is impossible. He may have failed to get the necessary financial cooperation from the Federal Government, but he promised he could."

Later that same week, Curley all but conceded the failure of work and wages. "If it were humanly possible to effect any material benefit for these thousands of unemployed, it would, of course, be a source of gratification. But as a matter of fact, the problem is one which is much too large to be accomplished through merely state legislation and activity." The job was certainly beyond him. "While I might go on and continue to be governor for the next 18 months if I accepted all the invitations to speak and attended all the meetings to which I am invited, I could not stand the strain. . . . No man could live four years on this job under present circumstances," he said, by way of explaining why he would not seek a second term. "I could not have stood it up to date, if it were not for the fact that I have regulated my living carefully during the past year. Four or five times a week I have to get a thorough physical rubdown. All this is stimulating but it amounts to working on borrowed time." Thus, "I have made up my mind to go to the United States Senate."[63]

These comments could not have been more revealing. Their narcissism—the emphasis on his "gratification," the "strain" of those dreary meetings, his precious "rubdowns"—is alarming. This is the way people talk in *People*. Of course, the job was bigger than anything that could be handled at the state level. But why had he promised to handle it? Had he imagined that Roosevelt really was his friend? Or had the promise, and the subsequent command performances in Washington, been an exercise in Barnumism? In the one case he was a fool, a victim of the Xanadu effect; in the other, a demagogue.

The growing band of his articulate opponents in Massachusetts inclined decisively to the latter view. If Curley had simply failed to deliver on work and wages, the opposition to him would not have been so toxic. But Curley's dictatorial manner—Curley as Nero, Lord Jim, King James I—envenomed criticism of his policy failures. The purges, the Louis XIV asides ("There is only one political party in Massachusetts . . ."), the eagerness to criminalize political differences, S-1, the royal family, Edmund Dolan, the packing of the Finance Commission and the Governor's Council, the suspected sale of pardons and paroles, the Dogpatch appointees—such actions proclaimed a contempt for democratic norms that made Curley look more like a menace than a bungler.

So long as opposition to him was centered in the Republican party, Curley could depict attacks on him as attacks on the New Deal, or he could play the racial card against the Saltonstalls and Herters and Parkmans who led the Republican resistance to him. What he had to avoid was any quickening of anti-Curley sentiment from within his own party. That would tend to legitimize the Republicans' case and to neutralize his political and racial counterpunches. Democrats could not be accused of being anti–New Deal; Irish Democrats could hardly be branded anti-Irish or anti-Catholic. If they began to say the same things about Curley as the Republican politicians and editorial boards, then he would effectively be, to paraphrase one of his favorite tags, naked to his enemies.

In late August he ignited the intraparty opposition that would help undo him. Fearful that the Mansfield administration would press ahead with its own investigations of the Dolan and other cases left over from his third term as mayor, he made a bold move: he appointed a special commission to investigate the Mansfield administration. The thundering cynicism of this appointment galvanized a dangerous and indefatigable opponent. In a vituperative radio address, Mayor Mansfield struck back. "I am calling upon every citizen of Massachusetts, regardless of party or political creed, to get behind me in this campaign to drive Governor Curley out of political life forever." He characterized Curley as "a man who is not only vindictively cruel and absolutely ruthless but wholly unreliable and unscrupulous." Nothing less than the "Commonwealth and its fair name" was at stake. "Massachusetts is now held up as a spectacle to the entire nation. Years ago Daniel Webster said of Massachusetts, 'There she stands.' . . . Where is she now? Disgraced, her proud traditions trailed in the dust and her sons and daughters compelled to apologize for the kind of man we have in the Governor's chair. . . .

The fight to terminate misrule in Massachusetts has just begun. I shall continue it unceasingly until the people have retired this man who would outdo Hitler to private life."[64]

In the fall election the people gave their verdict on the events of the past year, and their view of Curley seemed to accord with Mansfield's. In a special election in Essex County, a Curley-backed candidate for the state Senate lost a vital Democratic seat to a Republican who had made Curley the issue, charging that "the Governor had established a personal despotism which was plundering the people." A Curley-backed mayoral candidate with a huge Donnelly Advertising billboard in the city center lost in Worcester in an upset that saw a swing of 9,300 votes from the winning Democratic total of two years before. Curley supporters lost in municipal elections in Lowell, Somerville, and Everett. To put his candidate over in Chelsea, Curley dispatched a fleet of luxury motor buses to transport 1,500 unemployed men across county lines to a Curley sidewalk construction project. Denounced by the *Post* as "an attempt to buy the Chelsea election," this move backfired spectacularly, impelling Chelsea voters, outraged at this exploitation of their distress, into electing Curley's opponent by a 4,400-vote plurality. "The recent elections in Worcester and in Essex County, in Lowell, Chelsea, and elsewhere," the *Transcript* concluded, "prove that the voters of the State are being alienated from Governor Curley, not attracted to him, by the use of dictatorial methods in the Commonwealth's affairs."[65]

Reflecting on the elections to a group of Democratic women, Curley sounded as if he had at least temporarily emerged from Xanadu: "If mistakes are to be corrected, there is ample opportunity. If organization is necessary, there is time to effect organization." Yet he was soon at it again, publicly vowing to fire Democratic appointees if they did not make electing him senator their chief preoccupation, ordering five thousand of the state's forty thousand teachers who refused the loyalty oath to "take the oath or get out," threatening to withhold state aid from public schools and to withdraw the state charters of private institutions harboring such recalcitrants, forcing a Donnelly billboard on the town of Athol, and installing a Donnelly electric sign in front of the State House that extended SEASON'S GREETINGS AND HAPPY NEW YEAR TO ALL. Thus ended what one paper termed "the most amazing year in the political history of the Commonwealth."[66]

In his January State of the State address to the legislature, he strove to put the best face on things, but the galleries were noticeably bare of spectators, and he was interrupted for applause only twice in the twelve-thousand-word speech. One of his sons even fell asleep in the middle of what Senator Parkman termed a "welter of vague generalities." As Curley was ticking off the labor bills passed by the legislature, a thirty-three-year-old lawmaker in the House chamber smiled broadly. Henry Cabot Lodge, Jr., had reason to be pleased. As chairman of the Committee on Labor and Industries, he had steered the legislation through the House. In recognition of his services, he had been invited to address the fiftieth convention of the Massachusetts State Federation of Labor, the first Republican to receive that honor within memory. Tall, trim, handsome, suave, superbly well educated (at the Middlesex Preparatory School, Harvard, and the Sorbonne), this grandson and namesake of Curley's old rival from the struggle of a generation before over immigration restriction was to be Curley's opponent in the upcoming Senate race.[67]

Curley's political prospects were dolorous indeed. He had alienated most of the Democratic state legislators by his repeated appointments of Republicans to high posts. The failure of "work and wages" was manifest in the long lines of the unemployed whom he saw outside his home the first thing every morning and extending down the corridors outside his State House office the last thing every night—forty-six hundred people on one record day. The cloud of scandal was inexorably drifting over him now that Mayor Mansfield had retained the former investigator for the Finance Commission, George Farnum, to get to the bottom of Edmund Dolan's creative accounting. Finally, he had lost favor with the public: the fall election left no doubt of that. Facing a liberal Republican opponent with a famous unmottled name, he badly needed to redeem and renew himself for the fight of his life. The year 1936 would bring him one last chance for political redemption. It would also bring him personal renewal.

❖ ❖ ❖

He called at her apartment for the first time on Christmas Eve. She was at midnight Mass, and a strange man answered the door. Flustered, Curley refused to come in; he just stood there awkwardly with his gift—an exquisite little brocade purse with a jade clasp—in his hand. He thought he had a rival; she hadn't told him she lived with her brother.[68]

Their courtship was fitful: long periods would elapse before Gertrude Dennis heard from him. He was ardent and lonely enough, and he liked her company, but he was also in conflict over his attraction to her. There was the memory of Mary Emelda to restrain him. How could he fall in love with Gertrude and still be faithful to Mary? There was the disparity in their ages: he in his early sixties, she twenty years younger. There was the difficulty of acknowledging romantic interest, to say nothing of physical passion, at his time of life. Finally, there was the lack of privacy attaching to his position as governor. He would have to reconcile his conflicts, navigate his compunctions, surmount his ambivalence in public.

With her help, he managed it. They met downtown for midday movies, when fewer people were in the theater. Afterward, they had ice cream sodas in a high wooden booth at a nearby drugstore. In the early evenings they would drive up Corey Hill on the Brookline-Boston line and walk hand in hand through the park, enjoying the view of the great city beneath them. "He was sweet and wholesome," she told an interviewer years later. "He was courtly and handsome and gallant. He always came with flowers. I had no fear of him whatsoever. And suddenly I had no fear for my sons' future from such a gentle, kind man."[69]

Born, raised, and educated in Boston, Gertrude Casey early displayed a musical precosity. After high school, about the time Congressman Curley was leaving for Washington, she got an ideal job in the music department of a Tremont Street department store, playing the piano in sales demonstrations. The store manager was George Dennis of South Boston. They fell in love, George went away to fight in the World War, and when he came back they got married. In the 1920s they started a family: their first son, George, was born in 1923; their second, Richard, two years later. George Dennis's time with his family, however, was cut short by a brain tumor. At thirty-four Gertrude, like Sarah Curley, was left a widow with two boys to support.

With her mother, Ellen M. Casey, her brother Richard, and the boys she took up her now truncated life in a second-floor walk-up apartment on Beacon Street in Brookline. She had talents that allowed her to meet her responsibilities to her family, and spiritual resources to help her cope with her grief and loneliness. Her religious faith was sincere, devout, and sustaining. She became a member of the Third Order of St. Francis (she would later talk Curley into joining too), which the holy man of Assisi had established for lay Catholics who could not enter the monastic life but in whom burned a spark of his pure flame. She played the piano and sang in her rich soprano voice at radio stations, parties, and political gatherings. And then she met Mayor Curley; and her life took a turn for the better. "No woman could have helped falling in love with him," she said. "He just swept me off my feet. We were both in our teens again."[70]

His fame, his magnetism, his charm and manly bearing all attracted her. But she was equally drawn to his Franciscan dimension. "His generosity is undiscriminating," she said of him. After his death she echoed Francis Curley's judgment that James Michael Curley cared "even for people who really didn't deserve it," in remarkably similar language. "He had a tremendous big heart. He wanted to take care of everybody in trouble. You didn't have to be a Democrat. You didn't have to be sober. You didn't even have to be clean." That last bit, "You didn't even have to be clean," won for Curley the lasting spiritual admiration of this follower of St. Francis.[71]

Faith, alas, is not probative of morality. Believers are not reliably kinder, more caring, more tolerant than the rest of us (in the most famous election ever held in Louisiana, the neo-Nazi David Duke captured the vote of 69 percent of white Protestants who claimed to be "born again"). And phariseeism, the devil's ninth-inning snare, is always a temptation. So we can't reason from the piety of their faith to the goodness of the two women who loved James Curley. There may be a connection, but not a necessary one. Still, whatever its source, the goodness, the personal virtue of both these women is impressive. Something in Curley that escaped the headlines (and probably escapes this narrative as well) attracted them. Marriage is not probative of morality either—scoundrels married to saints keep their nature—so we can't reason from their goodness to his. But they knew a side of him that is forever closed. All one can do is point to it, a suggestive vacancy at the edge of the page.[72]

❖   ❖   ❖

He asked Gertrude to marry him just before he left to see Mary—they could make the Hawaiian trip their honeymoon. But she demurred. She wanted Mary to be firmly established in her own life as Mrs. Edward Donnelly: she had been Curley's "first lady," and that distinction must not be taken away from her. She sensed that her relationship with Mary would be troubled, and time proved her right. One can't be sure when their engagement was set, but Mrs. Dennis was seen more and more often with him in 1936, notably at the annual Tammany Club grand ball to which, thirty years before, he had escorted Mae Herlihy. Just as that special date heralded his coming marriage, so did Gertrude's presence at the ball. In the closing weeks of his term, Curley announced that he and Mrs. Gertrude Casey Dennis would be married on his last day as governor.[73]

So Curley, courting Mrs. Dennis, was lucky in his personal life in 1936. He had found a woman who by reason of her character, capacity, beauty, and faith would do all that any spouse could do to make him happy. He couldn't have known it, but as the heavy snows of that winter accumulated on the peaks of New Hampshire's White Mountains, as the ice ramified in the ponds and lakes and gorged the streams of Vermont, as the upland ground froze to iron, nature was about to provide him with another chance.

When March brought temperatures like those of May, boys dropped their hockey sticks for baseball bats and people sunned themselves next to piles of browning snow. It was that rarity in New England—a real spring.

Sudden heavy rains in midmonth transformed the melt into a flood. The snow on one side of Moat Mountain in New Hampshire let go all at once, burying one house with its inhabitants in the valley below and splitting another in two, leaving its owner alive in the unburied half. The frozen upland ground could accept no water, absorb no snow, so a great flow set in to the streams and rivers. On the Passumpsic River above St. Johnsbury, Vermont, a nine-mile ice jam gave way, burying highways and railroads, sweeping homes and telegraph poles and cattle into a macabre floating stew. At White River Junction, the rising water in the Connecticut River was within two feet of the main bridge linking Vermont to New Hampshire. The New England Power Company predicted that the peak height of the devastating flood of 1927 would be reached on the Connecticut and Deerfield rivers within twenty-four hours. Riverine Massachusetts was about to be inundated.[74]

Three hundred fifty men, women, and children were marooned on rooftops in Hatfield Center as the Connecticut poured through the town. Others were not so lucky. A sixty-year-old Hadley man was swept into the flood just as three rescuers tried to pull him off his roof. The three then spent the rain-lashed night clinging to the branches of an apple tree. Northampton, where Calvin Coolidge had begun his patient climb, was cut off from the outside world, its business district flooded, its sewers overflowing into submerged streets. Hundreds sought refuge in the state armory, where young women volunteers from Smith College along with young men from Amherst helped care for them. Along the Connecticut, the Swift, the Deerfield, the Nashua, and farther east along the Merrimack, thousands of men and women, their faces white with strain and fear, piled sandbags in back of the dams and along the rapidly filling riverbanks that separated their sleeping children from certain death.[75]

Governor Curley had been giving a speech in Scranton, Pennsylvania, when the torrents of spring began. With S-1 breasting flooded roads, he set off for Boston, calling out the National Guard en route and ordering the immediate dispatch of cots and blankets to state armories in the stricken cities and towns of western Massachusetts. Arrived in Boston, he empaneled key public safety and public works officials to plan the relief effort, and he communicated with the Red Cross, the state administrator of the WPA, and the Boston police commissioner, urging the last to send elements of his force west at once. After making other arrangements, he again set off in S-1 to see what he and his state were up against.[76]

National Guardsmen with fixed bayonets had to force residents and tradesmen to evacuate downtown Springfield just ahead of the rushing waters. The collapse of a wall of the local power station plunged the city into darkness. Twenty thousand were homeless; one hundred thousand others had to seek refuge with friends or relatives. Residents of the Tatnuck section of Worcester felt panic in their bones in the wake of reports that cracks were showing on the huge Holden reservoir just above them. In Leominster a man and his two children were killed when a bridge they had been standing on gave way. There was a ptomaine outbreak in flooded Lowell. All funerals were suspended in Haverhill and Lawrence, the cemeteries being awash. The towns of Hadley and South Hadley were now wholly under water. A herd of pigs squealed for their lives atop the roof of Hadley's most outspoken opponent of piggeries. Fearful of the spread of disease, workers wearing sterile masks quickly set about burying five hundred drowned cows in

Northfield. On the Connecticut River south of Hartford, seventy people swept down from Massachusetts were plucked off floating rooftops. From a floating gate on the fast-moving flood, a lonely dog howled into the night.[77]

There was wild talk of lynching looters in Lowell and of vigilante groups forming in Greenfield and the isolated towns along Millers River. The receding floodwaters sucked the plate glass windows out of stores and businesses in downtown Haverhill. There were food shortages in Northampton, and panic was spreading in the Pioneer Valley from news that the Vernon Dam was about to burst. Tens of thousands of people were thrown out of work across the state and thousands more were homeless—and the forecast predicted more rain and more snow-melting fog. With Massachusetts in one of the great crises of its history, state government had to act fast, and it had to lead.

It took S-1 four hours to cover the eighty miles to Springfield. Surveying damage, estimating need, and showing concern to people huddled in armories from town to town along the way, Curley made several stops in the city and pushed on through the night to Pittsfield, in westernmost Massachusetts. Then he cut across the Berkshires to Northampton and the other cities and towns of the Connecticut Valley. Somewhere on this loop of the trip, S-1 was overtaken by the flood, and boats had to be sent out to rescue the governor and his party. At the armory in Northampton, women clung to his hands and tugged forlornly at his sleeves, pleading with him to find their missing husbands and children. He promised to do everything in the power of man to locate them. Issuing orders on the fly—to dispatch floodlights from Boston to find people huddled on rooftops or in trees; to scour the waterfronts of Salem and Gloucester for dorries and send them west; to round up all available state public works vehicles and pool them at a central point, whence they could be sent to emergency sites—inspecting dams, testing bridges with S-1, ordering the reallocation of resources, Curley was in command. His shoes muddy, his tall silk hat exchanged for a beat-up fedora, he had left Xanadu behind and was once more in touch with rude actualities.[78]

"Thousands slept better that night because the Governor eased their worries," one reporter noted. "Here was a voice carrying the roar of conviction and the sure note of friendship and sympathy not only, but action as well." His promises of jobs on flood reconstruction projects—O admonitory shades of work and wages!—brought cheers from the five hundred refugees gathered in the Springfield Armory. "This work must go through," he told them, "and it will go through at once and its accomplishment will provide work for you men during the period which is bound to elapse before private industrial plants in this vicinity can repair the damage done to them and reopen." After pulling a blanket up over one sleeping child and hiding a few silver dollars under the pillow of another, the governor left the building to heartfelt applause. Just as he was going out the door, a woman nearby burst out with a sincerely inaccurate effusion: "O-o-o-h, there goes Governor Ely—isn't he grand!"[79]

Having seen what was needed in the west, Curley turned S-1 back to Boston, where he exhorted the legislature to provide emergency relief funds—and to be generous about it. Then he toured the Merrimack Valley. "What do you figure your greatest need of the moment?" he asked the mayor of Lowell. "Governor, what we need most of all is adequate protection. We could use twice as many National Guardsmen as we have now." Curley picked up the telephone, dialed his military adjutant, and said, "I want four or five hundred men. Get in touch with the commandant of the Marine Corps and call out the Marines." When General Rose questioned some instruction, Curley was wonderfully himself. "Never mind the expense," he responded. "This is an emergency." That had ever been his watchword, but for once he was right. He was more than that. Up for forty-eight hours straight, the urgency of his nature matching the urgency of the situation, he was just what the state needed.[80]

When the legislature dithered over passing a sufficiently robust relief appropriation, "Governor Curley—in a move as dramatic and unprecedented as it was surprising—yesterday turned to military strategy and nominated himself . . . the dictator—the supreme power—in the tremendous task of bringing immediate aid, comfort, and normalcy to the thousands of Massachusetts flood sufferers." The Boston Globe was not describing a coup d'état. During the World War the legislature had conferred extraordinary powers on the governor in the event of a public disaster, which this unquestionably was. "I hope it will not be necessary to commandeer food, fuel, shelter and other supplies," he told reporters, "but I have exercised my powers under the law as a precautionary measure because of the reprehensible and indefensible action of the Republicans in the Legislature in playing politics with this situation. . . ." To be sure, he was playing politics with the situation too. But he had also seen the material ruin and social hopelessness in the west, and he knew that the $750,000 the legislature wanted to spend on flood relief was not nearly enough—he had asked for an $8 million bond issue—to repair damaged infrastructure or revive dangerously low morale.[81]

The *Lowell Sun* placed Curley first in its "Flood Honor Roll." The *Lowell Leader*, expressing the consensus of editorial opinion across the state, assayed the political consequences of the catastrophe: "One thing is positively certain, the events of the past few days in Massachusetts have conspired to place Governor Curley in an impregnable position in so far as his aspirations are concerned, whether those aspirations point to the governorship or point to a senatorial seat in Washington." By rising to the emergency, Curley "demonstrated unequivocally that he is a leader fit to lead."[82]

The flood was the peripeteia of Curley's term: his one chance to change course. "Take physick, pomp," Lear discovers on the stormy heath. Learlike, Curley had taken his medicine. He had come down off Beacon Hill (and off Palm Beach) to give food to the hungry, shelter to the homeless, hope to the despairing. He had briefly recovered the human measure he had lost: safety, food for the family, a roof over one's head—that and love had been all Michael and Sarah Curley had been able to give him, and yet it had been enough. These were the basic values the flood had put at risk. The people he saw on his tour of the armories during his wild night's ride through the Berkshires did not want a Morgan life. They wanted what his own parents had wanted: the things that make a real life. He had only to show them that he had learned from their distress—that, like Lear, he was willing to shake off the superflux and to act like a democrat, not a dictator—to maintain his new hold on their regard.

The chance was there. He did not take it.

Within days he was back to the "work and wages" flummery, claiming that his $8 million bond issue was needed because the federal WPA, which had pledged Massachusetts $5 million in flood relief, would not pay to reconstruct bridges. Harry Hopkins corrected him: Federal money *could* be used for that purpose. It was the same old story: Curley wanted to spend state money so he could put his

·fingerprints over all the patronage to contractors, politicians, and laborers who, following the Tammany template, would show their gratitude at the ballot box. Instead of securing all the federal aid he could to help the communities and families who were counting on him—whose suffering he had seen with his own eyes—a month after the flood Curley had still not applied for WPA aid. When Christian Herter charged as much, Curley termed his statement "a deliberate falsehood . . . without foundation." Yet the WPA administrator in Massachusetts, Paul Edwards, backed Herter, saying "as things stand now, the state has filed no requests for funds with me in the proper form. . . ." Just as he had with work relief, Curley was playing the worst sort of politics with flood relief.[83]

He was also back to his gilded habits. By April, he had spent $85,000 of the people's money for personal expenses, including $2,900 for flowers, $8,700 for out-of-town trips, and nearly $6,000 for taxis. In one seven-week period, he spent $13,000, $2,000 more than what his predecessors over the last decade had spent, on average, in a year. Routinely his aides were using cabs to travel to weddings, hotels, even burlesque shows. Some had taken cabs to Springfield, New Bedford, and Pittsfield, 130 miles away; others, equally censurable dollar rides from the State House to the Parker House, a distance of three hundred yards. Always heavy, Curley had swollen to a porcine 240 pounds, as if he was eating his position.[84]

And the royal family was back too. George Curley, seventeen, a student at the exclusive Andover Preparatory School, signed up to take polo lessons in New Hampshire for the summer. Driving through Roxbury at 5:00 A.M., Paul Curley, a senior at Georgetown University, smashed S-2, a twelve-cylinder Cadillac registered to his sister Mary, into a sedan carrying two people. Later in the summer, driving with Curley and his chauffeur in East Boston, Paul leaped out of S-1 at a traffic light to pummel a motorist who had made a disrespectful gesture toward the governor, who remained in S-1, watching his son and his chauffeur beat up a citizen. One of Curley's secretaries was also a friend of Registrar Goodwin's, through whom he procured a low number license plate. "Whose car is that?" Mary Donnelly demanded to know when she saw the Ford Phaeton with the special plate parked under the rear archway of the State House. Informed, she said, "I want that plate. Get it transferred to me immediately. I want to give it to Leo as a present." Over the objections of the town's selectmen, a Donnelly billboard went up in Brookline and thirty-one billboards sprouted elsewhere in the state urging motorists to SLOW DOWN—YOU'RE NOT ALONE ON THE ROAD!—signed by a governor notorious for ignoring that advice. Charging that Republican employees of state institutions had been keeping his official portraits in closets and putting them on the walls only when he was visiting, Curley ordered that large photographic likenesses of him be bolted to the walls of every state institution. "Now . . . the pictures are going to be put up so they will stay up," he said. Pomp had not only failed to take enough physick, it had come down with a royal case of paranoia.[85]

His course was set now: it was downhill all the way.

In May he committed what the *Post* called "the major blunder of his career": his declaration that, on reaching the age of seventy, every state judge would have to appear before competent medical and psychiatric authorities, in the presence of the governor and the Executive Council, to be tested for signs of senility. Those deemed unfit would be retired. There were thirty-six judges in the state courts that age or older, among them one in the Suffolk Superior Court who was about to hear the Dolan case. Curley wanted them out so he could fill their places with stooges who would take Dolan off the hook, reinstate Daniel Coakley to the bar, and give himself both the legal impunity he had long sought and life-tenure patronage jobs to buy more votes from governor's councilors and key legislators. Curley's purge thus had the same object as FDR's 1937 attempt to pack the Supreme Court: to get his program through. But the Massachusetts courts were not nullifying his social and economic legislation as the U.S. Supreme Court was nullifying the New Deal.[86]

Fearing humiliation, one Springfield judge resigned. To prove his vigor, another offered to fight Curley. "I still have the two mitts I left Ireland with 72 years ago this month," he said. The idea of physicians and psychiatrists and politicians botanizing on old men seemed a "wicked proposal" to the *Transcript.* At long last the "limit in Curleyism" had been reached. In the Hitler-like effort to control the judiciary, the *Holyoke Transcript* saw new evidence of Curley the dictator. "Please will the people of Massachusetts read Sinclair Lewis' 'It Can't Happen Here.' It can happen—it is happening." The *Baltimore Sun* pronounced him "the Codfish

Fuehrer." The *New York Times* kept its comparison on native grounds: "How Long, O Curley, how Huey Long?"[87]

In the face of such criticism, Curley backed off, saying he would file a bill permitting judges to retire voluntarily at seventy at three quarters' salary; if the legislature did not go along he would put an initiative petition on the ballot, asking the voters to decide whether judges, like all other state employees, should be required to retire at seventy. His earlier statement about examinations, along with the questionnaire inquiring as to their age and health that he had sent to all Massachusetts judges, had simply been an educative joke—a way of calling attention to the need for better judicial pensions. "The only ones deceived by the message were the press, the petty leaders of the Republican party, and their Democratic allies." In the meantime, he had bullied one judge off the bench and could make a substitute appointment.[88]

June saw him shoulder Senator Marcus Coolidge out of renomination to his seat in just the kind of "boss-run" state party convention that candidate Curley had decried two years before. Only now he was the boss, self-nominated to the Senate. "I consider Marcus Coolidge a dear sweet old man," he unctuously confided to one reporter. "As a member of the U.S. Senate, I shall be delighted to confirm his appointment as Minister to Albania." The mood of the convention was sour. "On all sides, there came the comment, 'Curley's licked.'" The delegates were doing something shameful—denying renomination to a U.S. senator who had done nothing to deserve the back of the hand—and they were sullenly angry at Curley for turning them into cowards. In a fiery convention speech that Curley had to sit through, Coolidge's son-in-law, Robert Greenwood, mayor of Fitchburg, lit into him for his arrogance and condescension. When the senator declined to fight Curley for his seat in the primary, Greenwood declared his own candidacy. Playing off Curley's alliterative dismissal of his relative as Mute Marcus, Greenwood struck back in kind, calling Curley the "passionate pledger of pathetic but persuasive, perfumed but petrified, promises of plunder; the promiscuous and priceless, preposterous and prattling pledger of polluted prevarications; the pontificate of piffling potency; the pernicious procrastinator of plenteous personal profits, of pompous political progress—the deliverer of perishable plums that turn to prunes."[89]

For over a year, Curley had publicly encouraged Lieutenant Governor Hurley to succeed him as governor. But at the convention

Curley abandoned him, with John Curley, a delegate from Suffolk County, not even remaining in the hall to vote for him. Another Hurley, Charles F., the state treasurer, got the nomination, leaving Joseph L. Hurley a victim of Curley's piffling promises.[90]

As Curley prepared to leave for the 1936 Democratic national convention in Philadelphia, he gave every sign of being back in Xanadu. GOV. CURLEY O.K.'S BOOM FOR VICE-PRESIDENT POST read the headline in the *Boston American*, which was owned by his friend William Randolph Hearst. "I have no idea if it will be tendered," he said, "but if it is, of course I will accept. And it would be tantamount to election." He claimed to know nothing about the reported "boom" for him among delegates from the West to replace John Nance Garner on the ticket; still, there were those "Curley-for-President-in-1940 clubs" on the West Coast. "Seven of them are in California and some of them correspond with me occasionally," he said, willing the boom into being. At Philadelphia he was met by James Roosevelt and a seventy-piece band and, escorted by this motley retinue, began to march to the convention hall past thousands of bemused Philadelphians who had turned out to see the Mummers parade, though he must have thought they came to see him. He deprecated any talk of the vice presidency now: "Let there be no mistake about it, I am for Garner." He had something bigger in mind. MAN OF DESTINY, the placards carried in his parade read; WATCH 1940. He entered the hall amid great fanfare from his band and his claque and great puzzlement among the delegates. "Who is Governor Curley?" delegates asked. "What state?" The entry, loyal Massachusetts delegates conceded, was "something of a flop."[91]

While the platform was being read, he and his gold-braided, armed military aides shuttled up and down the aisles, shaking hands, fanning the ultimate Curley boom. "It looks mighty good for 1940," Curley commented after sampling the mounting enthusiasm for him.[92]

After returning to Massachusetts (he would not return to reality for some time), he created a stir with his proposed appointment of a seventy-one-year-old general practitioner from New Bedford as state commissioner of mental diseases, replacing a nationally known psychiatrist. Asked if he would take the job, Dr. John V. Thout was depressingly frank: "Would I? Would a duck take to water? Of course I'd take it. It's a nice plum, $10,000 a year. That's pretty good money, especially these days." Reacting to the opposition to his appointment from psychiatrists, who cited his lack of any relevant experience and his not being a member of any state or national medical societies, he gave an answer that extended Curley-style populism to the field of mental health: "I don't give a damn for those societies. What good are they? What good are they doing for the man in the mill?"[93]

Clearly it would take more than a flood to change the course of the Man of Destiny. He meant to go out as he had come in.

❖   ❖   ❖

Throughout his career, Curley had to contend with rough editorial comment, but the sort of people who read editorials were already lost to him anyway. He did not have to contend with popular columnists who could reach a wider audience because Boston journalism had none. For most of his career, John Bantry and Robert Washburn were the only writers on the Boston papers who could be considered columnists, but Bantry was more an analyst than a purveyor of opinion, much less satire, and Washburn was both an old-school gentleman and an active (Republican) politician, which tended to temper his views and his tone. But the phenomenon of Curley had roused the interest of magazine editors outside Massachusetts, and in 1936 three articles appeared in national publications that gave him something like the treatment he would receive today from Boston's free-swinging columnists.

The first article, "Jim Curley, Boss of Massachusetts," appeared in H. L. Mencken's *American Mercury*. The author, Ray Kierman, surveyed Curley's career in a fairly even-handed way, but also referred to him as "the late Louisiana dictator's twin" (Huey Long had been assassinated a few months before) and spoke of the "virtual dictatorship . . . established in the Commonwealth of Massachusetts by James Michael Curley."[94]

The second article, "Jim Curley and His Gang," appeared in *The Nation*. The author, Louis M. Lyons, approached Curley with a bite of phrase and an evaluative liberty that he kept out of his work as a "straight" reporter for the *Globe*. Announced in the subtitle, "The Irish Revolt in Massachusetts," Lyons's theme was that Curleyism represented the revenge of the Irish against the old Yankee Protestant order in Massachusetts; having persecuted them in the Know-Nothing years, it still denied the Irish "social recognition" and kept them out of "the commercial leadership of the most class-bound city in America." Noting the campaign against civil marriage, the decisive defeat of a bill banning child labor because the cardinal was against it, and the loyalty oath for teachers, Lyons wrote, "What has happened is that one set of intolerances has been replaced by another." Lyons characterized Curley's regime as "frankly racial beyond anything known elsewhere in America. . . . Such names as Dana, Conant, and Payson Smith, which stood for the kind of departmental administration Massachusetts had boasted, have given way to Reardon, McCarthy, Murphy, which suggest the only qualification required of their bearers." Then there was the emblematic role of Curley's "most formidable ally," governor's councilor Daniel H. Coakley. "Coakley and Curley were long enemies. But they have joined forces to undo the painful progress that penal reform has made in Massachusetts and to put pardons once more at the disposal of politics." After running through the bestiary of Curley's appointments ("A politician who had served a sentence for perjury became the employment secretary of the administration"), Lyons concluded that "the record of the Curley administration is the great liability that the New Deal carries into the 1936 campaign in Massachusetts."[95]

The first sentence of the third article, which appeared in *Harper's* in September, made this point more pungently. "The greatest embarrassment to the President of the United States," Joseph Dinneen wrote, "is the Governor of Massachusetts. . . ." Dinneen's title, "The Kingfish of Massachusetts," prepared readers for a tour of a bizarre polity, the "magnificent ward" Curley had made of Massachusetts. The governor, flanked by his military escorts, carried a gun. "Infernal devices" (which invariably proved to be hoaxes) regularly showed up in his mail, as did kidnaping threats against his youngest son—though some people had trouble taking them seriously, since they rarely seemed to deter the governor from Palm Beach. "His office is the center of as much intrigue as Saint Petersburg in the days of the Tzar. Spies, according to his own report, lurk behind the huge marble pillars outside his office. . . ." The atmosphere of suspicion, the purges, the loyalty oath, the adventures of S-1—it all added up to a picture of a state "in the grip of a dictator." Dinneen concluded, "It can't happen here, thought Massachusetts. It has happened here."[96]

Of course, it hadn't really happened there. Curley was a musical comedy dictator, not the real thing. Dinneen was trying to scare his readers. The Kingfish of Louisiana, who used National Guard troops to silence his opponents, presided over "the nearest approach to a totalitarian state the American republic had ever seen," Arthur Schlesinger, Jr., writes. The Kingfish of Massachusetts couldn't resist a Fascist salute before a crowd of Italians—it always got a big hand— but he was himself no fascist. Dinneen wrote before the most sinister event of Curley's administration, however, and if he had had the details of the third major accident in which S-1 was involved before him, he would have seized on them as proof of his thesis.[97]

In late September, having defeated Mayor Greenwood in the primary, Curley was in the stretch drive of his Senate campaign against Henry Cabot Lodge, Jr. On the night of September 23, after speaking at a Fall River rally, he boarded S-1 for the return trip to Boston. At 1:30 A.M. in Dighton, just outside Fall River, S-1 collided with and demolished a sedan driven by a nineteen-year-old boy. Miraculously—for S-1 was traveling at sixty miles per hour—aside from bruises, neither the boy, Luis Ferreira, nor his companion, John Perry, eighteen, both of Fall River, was hurt. Curley was shaken up; otherwise, he and the other occupants of S-1 escaped unscathed.[98]

When reporters reached the scene, state senator Joseph L. Langone, a Curley henchman, and an inspector of the Registry of Motor Vehicles both denied that the governor had been in S-1. They were following the model laid down the year before at the time of the accident in Newton. But back at 350 the Jamaicaway, their mercurial boss was singing out of a different hymnal. "We were driving back from Fall River," he explained to reporters, "when, in Dighton, we noticed this other machine zigzagging along the road, coming in the opposite direction. Joe Coppenrath was driving my car. . . . [He] tried in every way possible to avoid an accident, but the driver of the other car continued to come right for us." At his noontime rally in the Bull Pen, Curley "expressed . . . profound sympathy" to the "lad" and said how fortunate it had been for all concerned that Coppenrath had swerved to avoid a head-on collision.[99]

The two boys remembered another accident. They said they had been going at about forty miles an hour, passing a slow-moving truck in the legal passing lane of the three-lane highway, when the governor's car shot out of a line of cars going in the opposite direction, crossed the white line dividing the highway, and headed straight for them. Unable to cut right—the slow-moving truck was in that lane— Ferreira darted left, taking S-1's hit across the right front fender.

After the crash, Ferreira went over to S-1 and demanded to know who was in the car. "Shut up," Senator Langone told him, and threatened him with the loss of his driver's license for ten years if he dared to talk, hinting that silence could land him a state job. Surely the youth had heard of work and wages.[100]

When a newspaper photographer tried to photograph S-1 outside a restaurant in nearby Taunton, a Curley man grabbed him, saying, "I'll break your God-damned neck if you try to make a picture." Langone, intervening, told the man to return to his car. "Keep your mouth shut," he warned the photographer.

Two other witnesses substantiated the boys' claim that S-1 had been on the wrong side of the highway. But that did not impress registrar of motor vehicles Goodwin. "The entire blame for this incident rests with the boy," Goodwin said, suspending Ferreira's driver's license.[101]

Earlier in the month Curley had sued *Harper's* for $500,000; now he sued the *Herald-Traveler* for printing the boy's version of the accident.[102]

On their face the facts of the accident were troubling to anyone who believed in the primacy of laws over men in American government. S-1 had been driving on the wrong side of the road, and the governor had gotten away with it. Operating S-1 recklessly to meet his schedule, his chauffeur had nearly killed two boys, and had gotten away with it. His registrar of motor vehicles had covered up his responsibility for the accident, and had gotten away with it. Curley's toughs had intimidated a news photographer and Curley himself had sued a newspaper that tried to get at the truth. He was a law unto himself. It *had* happened here.

More amused than frightened by Curley's litigious bluster, the *Herald* forecast S-1's last accident. "There will be a head-on collision of political machines in November. The Democratic limousine S-1, transporting his excellency, will meet a Republican sedan occupied by Henry Cabot Lodge, Jr. All the indications are that there will be a major casualty and that it will be suffered by the person in S-1."[103]

❖ ❖ ❖

Lodge was not an ideal candidate. He could never get the vote of people like my parents, for example. My father in these years was working for the WPA (often sleeping in the back of his car if the job was far from home). My mother, with two baby girls to feed, was running a tiny subsistence farm in New Hampshire, canning her own vegetables and fruit, killing her own chickens, baking her own bread—and happily making pies for the Civilian Conservation Corps (CCC) boys working in the nearby forests. "Those boys loved my pies," she once said. "We didn't have much, but it was such a pleasure to see them larrup up my pies." They didn't have much? They had practically nothing, and they shared it because that is the kind of people they were. Probably for months on end, they dropped out of the money economy altogether. To them Henry Cabot Lodge, Jr., who had married Emily Sears (David Sears, her grandfather, "owned half the West Coast and all of Alaska," said one descendant) at her father's sixty-acre North Shore estate, was of a different species. As for Curley, they gave him credit for trying to provide work and wages; they did not see what was wrong with replacing people named Smith in the state executive departments with people named Murphy—and they would have resented Louis Lyons's insinuation that the Irishmen Curley appointed were all hacks. The royal family was sometimes hard to swallow, but it at least offered vicarious entertainment; so long as you stayed out of the path of S-1, you could sit back and enjoy the show. And in a way that all his Morganism could not efface, Curley was one of them; he made state government, long an alien entity, seem like their government. Since there were tens of thousands like them, Lodge could not win in a walk. Still, he had a rare target in Curley's record. He had the Sears money. He also had his prematurely distinguished self.

"Of all the men with whom I have been intimately thrown," Theodore Roosevelt wrote of Lodge's father, "he was the only man I have ever met who, I feel, was a genius." George ("Bay") Lodge was a poet who served as secretary to his father, "the Old Senator," as he was remembered in the family. "I sincerely thank God I shall never be a rich man," George wrote after a stay among the vulgar cottages of Newport. A sensitive poet of the marshes and the tides, he felt out of place in both the commercial ethos of Boston and the political ethos of Washington. Edith Wharton, his friend, said this about him: "Abundance—that is the word which comes to me whenever I try to describe him. . . . There was an exceptional delicacy in his abundance and an extraordinary volume in his delicacy." In 1900 he married Elizabeth Davis, a belle of Washington society, whose grandfather had been President Arthur's secretary of state. The volume of his delicacy increased, however, under the strain of his late poetic work, and in August 1909, while staying at the family camp on Tuckanuck Island off the Massachusetts coast, he suffered a heart attack and died in his father's arms. "You will not know the agony of that moment for me," the Old Senator later wrote to a friend. "I cannot write of it without wanting to cry out as I did then." Bay Lodge was thirty-five, and like Michael Curley, dead at thirty-four, he left a widow and two sons, John Davis Lodge, age four, and Henry Cabot Lodge, Jr., seven.

Elizabeth ("Bessie") Lodge raised her children in their father's image, as scholars and gentlemen. Evenings she read aloud to them, and in this way over the years got through all of Dickens, Thackeray, and Sir Walter Scott. The literacy James Curley had to wrest from labor came to Cabot Lodge as a gift of love.

The Old Senator replaced his son as father to his grandsons. His namesake was his special favorite. "An austere man," a witness remembers, "he thawed completely with his grandson . . . treating him as an equal in knowledge and experience and talking with him, man to man, about national and international affairs." He also took a proprietary interest in his formal education, expressing his shock to the headmaster of Middlesex School on discovering a grave lack in the curriculum: "I am unwilling to have my grandsons deprived of the opportunity, if they desire it, of reading Homer in the original." Frequent travel to interesting places full of interesting people—he stayed with Edith Wharton in France, and plucked mulberries in Henry James's garden in Rye while his mother and the novelist chatted about old times—rounded out the education of Cabot Lodge.

Cabot rowed at Harvard. He also rode; later, with his North Shore neighbor George Patton, he would gallop across the seagirt fields of Hamilton and Beverly Farms. He became a reporter, first with the *Boston Evening Transcript* and later with the *New York Herald-Tribune*, among whose bookkeepers he was famous for not cashing his paychecks. After a stay at Edith Wharton's graceful house at Hyères, Cabot and Emily Lodge decided to build one like it in Beverly Cove. An L-shaped brick structure, its great front rooms opened on the ocean. Floor-to-ceiling bookcases, containing the Old Senator's library, lined the walls, and Sargent's portrait of the Old Senator hung in the small sitting room. As visitors ascended the grand staircase they beheld George Cabot's parchment commission from President John Adams as the nation's first secretary of the navy, as well as Trumbull's portrait of Alexander Hamilton, which Hamilton had given to his great friend Cabot. There were also portraits of John Davis, U.S. senator from Massachusetts and governor of Massachusetts, Cabot's great-great-grandfather; Hasbrouck Davis, brigadier general in the Civil War, his great-grandfather on his father's side; and of Theodore Frelinghuysen, U.S. senator from New Jersey, and his son Frederick Theodore Frelinghuysen, also a New Jersey senator and a secretary of state, his great-great- and great-grandfathers on his mother's side. Among the obscure faces a photograph of President Theodore Roosevelt inscribed to Cabot's grandmother ("A.C.M.L. from T.R., X-mass 1908") leaped out. Giant conch shells, "big as baskets," stood in the hallway. Brought back from China by John Lodge as ballast on his clipper ships, they served to remind the family that its culture and learning and tradition of public service stood on a deep-sunk foundation of mercantile wealth.[104]

As the Old Senator had done before him, Cabot had to learn the common touch to win votes among the fishermen and factory workers of his district. Elected to the Massachusetts House in 1932, he was appointed chairman of the Committee on Labor and Industry by Speaker Saltonstall with a vague mission to liberalize the Republican party. This he accomplished. "As everyone knows," he was saying on the campaign trail that fall, "I am a liberal and a friend of labor. Everyone also knows that I will not permit either predilection to override the dictates of my own conscience." William V. Shannon's gloss on that statement is worth quoting: "He did not explain why there should be any conflict between one's liberalism and one's conscience." The conflict was between the conservatism he had inherited from the Old Senator and his own liberal times. Fed by conviction and informed by intelligence, Cabot's liberalism was also politically expedient.[105]

The Republican sedan occupied by Lodge picked up speed with the addition of Tom White, a former Coolidge strategist, who advised the too-natty candidate to wear the oldest suit he had, never to press it, and to throw it on the floor at night. Lodge spoke perfect French to French-Canadian mill workers in Lowell. Before Italian audiences he displayed his brother's beautiful wife, the Florentine-born Francesca, daughter of a prominent musical family, who would sing Italian songs. Most important, he had the Old

Senator's knack for occasionally relaxing his political conscience. Meeting with supporters of the Townsend Plan, a crackpot redistribute-the-wealth scheme that would give $200 a month to every person over sixty on the condition that he or she not work and agree to spend the money within thirty days—he said he backed it "to the extent considerations of prudent finance permit," a delphic formulation that allowed him to win the Townsend vote with no obligation to further the Townsend Plan. "Afterward," his biographer, William J. Miller writes, "he regarded this demagogy as one of the less creditable performances of his career."[106]

"When my youthful rival was still wearing diapers I was serving the Commonwealth of Massachusetts in the halls of Congress," Curley was saying on the stump. If a contest for the best reply Lodge could make to that thrust were held, this offering of Michael Hennesey, a political writer for the *Globe*, would probably be the winner: "When I was still wearing diapers, my opponent was serving a six-month sentence in Charles St. Jail." Lodge never mentioned Curley. He didn't have to.

But Curley never stopped mentioning Lodge, referring to him now as "a young man who parts both his name and his hair in the middle," now as "a very handsome child," as "bright young Mr. Lodge," as "Puny Henry," "Little Henry," "the little lad running against me, or rather after me," and, famously, as "Little Boy Blue." The *Falmouth Enterprise* gave its verdict on that epithet in verse:

> *Little Boy Blue*
> *Come Blow Your Horn*
> *Lodge Will be in the Senate*
> *When Curley is Gone*[107]

Unable to draw any major differences with Lodge over issues—both men were prolabor and pro-Social Security, and both were equally for and against the New Deal—Curley tried to muscle Lodge out of the race. Claiming that Henry Cabot Lodge, Jr., was not Lodge's real name—for "Jr." implied that he was the Old Senator's son, not his grandson—he brought legal action before the state Ballot Commission to have the impostor purged from the ballot. "Curley claimed Cabot was posing as his grandfather," as one former Lodge aide put it. Since the chairman of the Ballot

Commission, Charles McGlue, was a Curley appointee, another former aide says, "We were frightened." "For all we knew, McGlue might rule Cabot off the ballot, and we might never get him back on in time." But in court proceedings Lodge's attorneys produced a birth certificate showing he had been "Jr." from birth; and Curley's reputation was spared the scar of having subverted an election on transparently technical grounds.[108]

Curley was "slipping, slipping, slipping," Robert Washburn wrote. His campaign was a series of blunders relieved by stumbles. When Curley said that Washington had promised him a $20 million or $30 million WPA grant, fifteen hundred jobless men converged on his State House office. "I never told him such a thing," Harry Hopkins said of Curley's claim. The men had come for nothing. Theirs had been "a futile ordeal," said Paul Edwards, the state WPA administrator. While James Roosevelt was inside a ballroom at the Copley-Plaza extolling the "harmony" of the Massachusetts Democracy, Curley was outside in the lobby engaged in a shouting match with Joseph A. Maynard, who, as collector of the Port of Boston, was the highest-ranking Roosevelt appointee in the state. In the speech he had just concluded, Curley deliberately praised one of his henchmen in a Roosevelt for President fund-raising venture that Maynard had launched. "Why don't you give credit where credit is due?" Maynard asked him. "I'll give you a punch in the nose," Curley replied, and wound up to swing. Mary Donnelly grabbed his arm before the blow landed, and a burly Boston policeman stepped between the men. But the headlines revived unsenatorial memories of Curley the brawler. When Curley announced that he would spend $10,000 of the Commonwealth's money celebrating President Roosevelt's visit to the state on October 23, the president sent a public telegram through James Roosevelt urging Curley not to do so since the trip would be a political one. Curley, appearing foolish, pretended that the celebration fund was "another one of those little jokes that we have to play on such serious people as Bob Choate of the *Boston Herald*," referring to the paper's managing editor. The joke was not only little; it was private—understood only in Xanadu.[109]

Roosevelt was Curley's only hope. When the president came up to Massachusetts as part of his reelection campaign, Curley had to get his endorsement. The only issue in his race, once again, was Roosevelt. "I'm not here to talk about Curley," he said in Northampton. "I'm here to talk about Roosevelt." Calling himself an expert on Social Security, Curley said, "Roosevelt is entitled to finish out the plan he has formulated, and I would like to go down there and help him." (This emphasis on Social Security showed how out of touch Curley had grown: the program had been enacted in 1935, and no longer had serious Republican opposition.) "Most of the time," one paper observed, "he talks like a stump speaker for the New Deal who has no personal stake in any office." His strategy was to throw himself at the president's feet in the hopes that the president would save him. Absent Roosevelt's endorsement, Curley would forfeit the vote of New Deal liberals, already offended by an ever-lengthening list of his actions—from his giving of the Fascist salute before an Italian-American rally at Faneuil Hall to his loyalty oath to his benighted call to "militarize" the CCC and his characterization of those who opposed the idea as "pinks." For embracing Roosevelt, meanwhile, Curley would lose the slice of his Catholic base that followed the lead of the "radio priest," Father Charles E. Coughlin.[110]

That fiery cleric was in his own Xanadu. "We have no Lincoln today to plead our cause," he said in a speech at Braves Field. "But we have a Lemke." This was perhaps the most hilarious pairing of names in American political history. William Lemke, the obscure North Dakota congressman, was the presidential nominee of a third party founded by Coughlin that summer—the Union Party. Coughlin saw the election of 1936 in world-historical terms. "Democracy is doomed. This is our last election. . . . It is fascism or communism. We are at the crossroads." Asked which road he would take, he replied: "I take the road of fascism."[111]

The politics of ethnic and religious resentment we have been tracing in this narrative combined with the social cataclysm of the Depression to make Boston, in the opinion of James Michael Curley, "the strongest Coughlin city in the world." With his passionate attacks on the perfidies of "international bankers," Coughlin gave the Boston Irish someone to blame for the Depression—a faceless, nameless, uncaring, un-Christian power. "Father Coughlin provided Irish Catholics during the crisis of the Depression with a religious justification for their strongly felt but intellectually undefined impulses toward radicalism and rebellion," William V. Shannon, the historian of the American Irish, writes. This was Curley's own psycho-political terrain. Curley tried to stay close to

Father Coughlin, making much of the Michigan priest on his occasional visits to Boston. But their differing opinions of the man Coughlin called "Franklin Double-Crossing Roosevelt" drove them apart. In his autobiography, Curley claims that Coughlin offered to put his influential voice (his increasingly anti-Semitic radio broadcasts had a national audience of over forty million) behind him if he ran for the Senate. "This was one of the reasons that prompted me to run against Henry Cabot Lodge, Jr., in 1936, instead of seeking re-election as Governor," he says. Father Coughlin may have promised Curley his support, but as we have seen, Curley had the Senate in mind even before his term as governor began. As Father Coughlin drifted further away from the New Deal—"Roosevelt or Ruin" had been his slogan in 1932—such commitments as he had made to New England's Original Roosevelt Man were, in effect, rescinded. Moreover, he had a personal score to settle with Curley. By the fall of 1936, he had entered a candidate against Curley in the Senate race, Thomas C. O'Brien, a former Suffolk County district attorney who, in a political efficiency, also doubled as Lemke's running mate.[112]

O'Brien was Lodge's Frank Goodwin. And Curley was cast in the role of Gaspar Bacon. Curley says he offered O'Brien $10,000 to quit the race, but that the Republicans gave him $25,000 to stay in. At least half of that story is believable.[113]

❖   ❖   ❖

The presidential train was on time at the Providence railroad station. Recognizing him in the crowd of welcoming dignitaries, the president invited Rhode Island governor Theodore F. Green up on the train platform to share in the applause of the crowd. But in a slight canceling the golden moment when FDR had clasped Curley's hands upon arriving at the Chicago stadium four years before, he ignored Curley, who was standing right behind Green—and who, as the only one in sight wearing a tall silk hat, was hard to miss. For the next fourteen hours Curley sat by the president's side in S-1, traveling from rally to rally throughout eastern Massachusetts accompanied by a cavalcade of more than two dozen carloads of Curley rooters and by a sound truck bedecked with CURLEY AND ROOSEVELT signs and at times by a plane trailing a streamer reading ROOSEVELT AND CURLEY—PERMANENT RECOVERY. He introduced the president several times, held the microphone for him, led the cheering for him. Photographs taken of Roosevelt during that campaign swing also show Curley. He does not look happy. For the president did not endorse him. Other than thanking him for his introductions, he did not mention him.[114]

"I'll beat this little lad by more than 150,000 votes, yes, nearer 200,000 votes," Curley shouted from the Bull Pen in the closing days of the campaign. Curley had the right margin, but the wrong result. Lodge beat him by over 140,000 votes. He was described as "stunned" by the fact, the scope, and the context of his defeat—for 1936 was a Democratic year in which FDR won every state in the union save Vermont and Maine, in which the Democrats achieved their greatest partisan majority in the Senate in history, in which even small-fry Francis E. Kelly, the former city councilor and opponent of Curley's, was elected lieutenant governor of Massachusetts solely by dint of the "D" after his name on the ballot. The returns leave little doubt that Father Coughlin plus Roosevelt's cold shoulder made the difference. Lodge got 875,000 votes to Curley's 732,000 and O'Brien's 131,000. Without O'Brien in the race, Curley would have been within 10,000 votes of Lodge, a number small enough to be responsive to a presidential endorsement.

"May I congratulate you on your successful victory in Massachusetts," Frank Kane, one of Curley's secretaries, wired Father Coughlin. "You have deprived this State and this nation of real representation in the Senate of the United States. As Christ had his Judas and Caesar his Brutus and Washington his Arnold, so has Governor Curley his Father Coughlin." In fact Curley played Judas first. When Father Coughlin was establishing his movement in the state, he asked Curley to recommend someone to handle its organization. Curley touted Frank Kane. "He carefully concealed from Fr. Coughlin that Kane was his henchman. Father Coughlin thought the Governor free from any sort of guile in recommending Kane and appointed him," John Bantry reported in his election postmortem. A trusted emissary told the priest that Curley had "put something over" on him. Curley wanted to turn the Massachusetts chapter of Coughlin's National Union for Social Justice into his own instrument. Instead, Coughlin, discovering Curley's betrayal, betrayed Curley. Months before, Curley had boasted to Roosevelt that he "couldn't even lick myself" for the Senate seat. He was wrong.[115]

In the last week of the campaign, Curley came down with a heavy cold, leaving the whole family, from Mary Donnelly to Francis Curley, to pinch-hit for him on the hustings. As he stepped from his car in the driveway of the house on the Jamaicaway the day after his defeat, reporters waiting to question him thought he looked like a sick man. His coat collar was turned up, his head was hunched down, his step was heavy and slow. "The Governor will see no one today," his chauffeur told them. "There will be no callers. That's final." The next day he left for Florida. Yet even as his train was pulling out of South Station, even as editorial writers across the state and country were searching for synonyms for "finished" in describing the point his vertiginous career had reached, Senator Joseph Langone was strolling the streets of Boston with a button the size of a sunflower pinned to his chest. FOR MAYOR, it said, BOSTON'S BEST AND BOSTON'S NEXT.[116]

❖　　　❖　　　❖　　　❖

Himself Again

❖   ❖   ❖   ❖

Nobody is through with politics
who has ever tasted it.

JAMES M. CURLEY

❖   ❖   ❖   ❖

Toward the close of his administrations Curley tended to lose all subtlety in his graft. He had never been able to secure what he had boasted of in the 1914 campaign, "a sufficient income to render me independent of political office." And, as he faced the looming austerity of life in the private sector, he began to panic. To ensure his comfort in his retirement he had to fill the two safes he kept in the house on the Jamaicaway with cash, and do it fast. In the fall of 1936 he was instrumental in the granting of "sweetheart" contracts to two firms for work on the Quabbin Reservoir project in central Massachusetts. The contract had originally been awarded to the Benjamin Foster Company. But at a secret meeting of the three-member Metropolitan District Water Supply Commission, one Curley appointee joined with a member appointed by Ely who was under Curley's influence to redirect the work to two other firms, Two Companies, Inc. of Boston and the Cendella Company of Milford, Massachusetts. They were to receive $450,000, far more than what they had estimated in their bids, and $300,000 more than what Foster had bid for the same job.

The chairman of the Metropolitan District Commission, Eugene Hultman, whom Curley had tried to purge from office the year before, was absent when his fellow commissioners held this secret meeting. At a hearing before the attorney general of Massachusetts, Paul A. Dever, who was investigating the contracts, Hultman revealed that Governor Curley had privately urged him to grant excavation work to Two Companies (a merger of the C. J. Maney and B. Perini construction companies) at the Quabbin. He described Curley as "anxious" and "insistent" that the contracts be let, even though, in refusing, Hultman told the governor they

401

were "outrageous." Complaining that it wasn't very "gentle-manly" of Hultman—a man he had accused of "moral turpitude" for taking municipal manure—to divulge their private conversations, Curley admitted that he "might have said something to Mr. Hultman" about giving work to Maney and Perini.[1]

Acting on the facts brought out at his hearing, Attorney General Dever canceled the controversial contracts. Shortly after he and Dever were first sworn in, Curley had dropped by his office, parked his foot on Dever's radiator, and established instant rapport with the younger politician by perkily inquiring, "Listen, you little pisspot, what do you want?" Publicly decrying the award of the contracts as a "serious breach of the public trust" in the thick of Curley's election campaign against Lodge, the little pisspot had got his own back.[2]

In his book *The Tax Dodgers,* Elmer Irey, a longtime federal tax agent, says that in looking into other Quabbin contracts federal investigators found that Two Companies' award of a $1 million contract for a dam included an $80,000 to $100,000 kickback for a leading politician. Four officers of Two Companies were convicted and fined for offering the bribe. But the politician, by then out of office, was not prosecuted for taking it. At his trial for tax evasion, the president of Two Companies was asked to name the politician, but he refused. "If I talk," he said, "I'll never make another dime so long as I live." The link between Curley and Two Companies already on the public record casts more than a shadow of suspicion on the identity of the politician.[3]

The Quabbin contracts were let before the election; after it, free of political constraints, Curley let her rip. He paid an extra $135,000 to a contractor who had finished and been paid for the work for which he was receiving this bonus eighteen months earlier; he sought to settle damage claims against the state in connection with the Quabbin land takings for $1 million—four years before the damage would take place; he fired the Boston police commissioner, according to one of his secretaries, for daring to close down his personal bookie, one Paddy Conlin; and he rushed through a batch of paroles and pardons in time for Christmas. "Two pardons of atrocious murderers," John Bantry reported, "one a man who is, by reason of insane actions in the past, a menace to the community, the other a desperate and notorious gangster, looked suspiciously like favors granted by the Governor under pressure" to Daniel Coakley, whom Curley had to pay off for favors and who held the pardon franchise on the council. It had happened here.[4]

Amidst these and other present scandals came reminders of scandals past: Edmund Dolan was found to owe the City of Boston $171,000, the amount of the "unusual profits" he had awarded himself—and surely his neighbor on the Jamaicaway as well—in funneling city business through one of his dummy corporations.[5]

While appointing his brother, his adjutant general, another military aide, his secretary and other well-connected souls to well-paid sinecures "on the state," Curley discharged two thousand Boston men who had been clearing brush at the Quabbin site. The election over, their votes were no longer needed. When word of their firing reached the laborers, they rioted, smashing tool boxes and tearing down small buildings, causing the governor to extend their appointments for another two months. "Say, Governor," a man asked Curley as he was leaving the State House in his final days, "can you do anything about getting me a job?" Curley replied, "Sorry, mister, I'm looking for one myself."[6]

The term ended with two weddings in the family. Just before Christmas, twenty-two-year-old Paul Curley married Marie Phillips, also known as Lillian Duval, a dancer in a New York cabaret and an almond-eyed southern beauty. The wedding took place in New York; afterward, the couple flew to Boston for a holiday dinner at the Jamaicaway. Then, on his last day as governor ("I decided that my bride should have the honor of being the First Lady of the Commonwealth, even for a brief period"), Curley married Gertrude Dennis in a modest ceremony held in a Brighton chapel.[7]

The night before making his wedding plans public, Curley had asked the entire family to dress up for dinner with an "important guest." He was "nervous as a colt," as his son remembered it, before the guest arrived. Mary Donnelly was there for the occasion, and Francis recalled his father asking her to yield her usual place at the far end of the table to the guest—Mrs. Dennis, dressed in a Russian sable coat and a sweeping blood-red evening gown and wearing a twelve-carat emerald cut engagement ring. The family had met her before; she had been at Curley's sixty-first birthday celebration a year earlier. But now she had come for a special announcement.

"Mrs. Dennis is going to become Mrs. Curley," Curley told them, "on the last day of my term." He said this with Mary Emelda's portrait looking down at him from the living room wall. Gertrude showed she was conscious of their mother's place in their hearts in the little speech she made them. "I don't want any of you to ever think of calling me 'Mother.' I know you are still in mourning, but your father and I have fallen in love, and I hope you'll accept me as his wife."

After Mrs. Dennis left, Mary Donnelly confronted her father. "Why did you do this to us? Why did you wait to spring it on us so close to the wedding?" He replied that he didn't want to allow any time for animosity to build up. "It's a fait accompli," he said. "You will not see Mrs. Dennis again before the wedding." The Curley children had nothing against Gertrude Dennis; it was the idea of their father marrying anyone that was difficult to accept. Their mother had become an icon to them, and when her picture was taken down the day before the wedding, "It marked the end of a world for us," in the words of Francis Curley.[8]

With his military aides, General William Rose and Major Joseph Timilty, along with the faithful Dr. English acting as ushers and his brother John as best man, Curley and Mrs. Dennis were pronounced man and wife on the morning of January 7, 1937, by Francis J. Spellman, then an auxiliary bishop in the archdiocese of Boston, who in years to come would consecrate the marriage of the American Catholic church to the cold war. Outside, a crowd of one thousand milled around the gubernatorial automobile, standing on the fenders and the bumpers to get a better look at the newlyweds as they left the chapel. In the crush, someone made off with license plate S-1.[9]

En route to his honeymoon, Curley stopped by the State House to hand the reins of power over to his successor, Democrat Charles F. Hurley. Breaking with the tradition calling for the retiring governor to walk alone down the State House steps and then across the Common, Curley rejoined his bride, radiant in a lynx coat and white orchid corsage, at the foot of the steps and drove away in a new Lincoln limousine, a gift from his staff. On their way to Nassau, the first stop in a seven-week tour of South America, the Curleys passed through Grand Central Station, where Curley told reporters about the surprise gift. Laughingly, he added: "As a rule when a man goes out of public office in my State they present him with a brick house, one brick at a time."[10]

John F. Fitzgerald had dominated the first quarter of Curley's career; he and Curley were bound together by chains of ambivalence. Franklin Roosevelt took Fitzgerald's place as Curley's politically and emotionally charged other in the second quarter. Though Curley was older than FDR, their disparate power cast Curley in the subservient role. In the quarter of his career just beginning, Curley could for the first time play the father as Maurice Joseph Tobin, young enough to be his son, enters Curley's story.

❖   ❖   ❖

Tyrone Power is not what he used to be. For one thing, he is dead, having departed the day after Curley himself; for another, he is largely forgotten. But those who remember his looks have the image of Maurice Tobin, the matinee idol as politician. Handsome in the suave double-breasted way of movie actors in the thirties, with thick dark hair parted in the middle, a long thin face, and a tall trim frame, Tobin would elicit the complaint from Curley that their tilts were not elections but beauty contests.

Tobin was born in the Mission Hill section of Roxbury in 1901. His parents were Irish immigrants—James Tobin from Clougheenafishogue in County Tipperary, Margaret Daly from Garryleigh in County Cork. Maurice was their firstborn; two other boys, Timothy and James, and a girl, Margaret, completed the family. James Tobin was a carpenter and a founding member of the local carpenters' union, a fitting thing for the father of a future secretary of labor. Maurice attended the Mission School attached to the Mission Church in Roxbury; he had the Sisters of Notre Dame as teachers, and the Redemptorist Fathers as priests. Even while at the Mission School, Maurice had to work to help the family. His day began at 4:30 A.M., when he would catch the "owl car" to Newspaper Row to pick up the dailies he and his brother hawked to motorists and pedestrians at busy Roxbury Crossing. After school they would peddle the evening papers, selling as many as five hundred copies a day.

Maurice got to meet God's plenty of people on his job, which by its nature forced him to keep current with city politics. "I used to turn from the sporting page to the political stories," he told an interviewer years later, "and I thought it would be good to have something to do with public service." In his mid-teens he confided to his cousin that someday he wanted to be mayor of Boston.

Maurice went on from the Mission School to the High School of Commerce in Roxbury, but quit school at sixteen to fulfill the economic obligations of the oldest son in a poor family. His dreams of a life in politics had come up hard against realities that had changed little since James Curley had faced them thirty years before. One generation of the Boston Irish after another was being forced by present need to sacrifice future promise. ("As compared with the Jews," Robert A. Woods noted of them early in the century, "they seem like a people without ancestry. Each generation stands in its own strength.") This social immobility was, of course, Curley's continuing political opportunity.

From 1917 to 1922, when he was laid off in the postwar slump, Maurice worked, probably as a shipping clerk, for a leather goods firm near South Station. Evenings he sought to better himself by taking classes at Jesuit-taught Boston College High School. He kept at night school for twelve years, ultimately attending Boston College Law School and then Suffolk Law School, from which he obtained a degree. He also found time (life was longer before television) to join social clubs on Mission Hill and to become a member of the debating team of the Roxbury Council of the Knights of Columbus. Active as a volunteer in the congressional campaign of a local jazz musician, Maurice was eager to make his own political debut.

But 1922 was a bad year for the Tobins. Maurice not only lost his job, but the senior James Tobin was hit by a streetcar and permanently incapacitated. Once again Maurice's dreams had to be pushed aside for the sake of his family. And once again we see the father of an Irish-American politician felled in his prime. The pattern is arresting. Were the sons of such fathers liberated to experience ambition without guilt for surpassing their fathers? Did necessity spare them the debilitation of identifying with men who may have been good and loving and strong but who by no dilution of the word could be considered successful? Or was paternal exhaustion so common in the immigrant generation that this pattern explains nothing? Probably the last. The immigrant is too important as a symbol of national renewal to allow the facts of immigrant life to mar the allegorical perfection of our view of the peopling of America.

Through a friend, Tobin obtained a job as a cable splicer for the New England Telegraph and Telephone Company. He would remain an employee of the utility for over a decade, rising from the ranks to a position in middle management. In 1926, with his brother James as his campaign manager, Maurice Tobin declared his candidacy for a seat in the Massachusetts House. Local pols dismissed him a cheeky pup. But he had visited every family in Ward 10, leaving behind an impression of earnestness and conviction and good looks, and in the primary he placed first in a field of five and won the general election against a Republican in November (one of Maurice Tobin's background could only be a Democrat) by six thousand votes.

In the House, by then himself a member of a labor union, Tobin championed legislation to provide workmen's compensation payments to those, like his own father, whom accident or illness had left unable to work. And he showed political courage by voting for an investigation of New England Tel and Tel. Not pleased, the monopoly ordered him and another phone repairman-legislator who had also voted for the investigation to take leaves of absence from their jobs during their time on Beacon Hill.

In 1928 Tobin gave up his seat in the Massachusetts House to run for the U.S. House of Representatives against a local institution, a red-bearded, lion-hunting Republican congressman named George Holden Tinkham. His Eleventh Congressional District ran out from the Back Bay to parts of Roxbury and Jamaica Plain—he was Curley's representative. Thanks to Gertrude Ryan, his secretary, Tinkham was able to service the needs of his Irish constituents well enough to prolong what was an anomalous career in the era of ethnic politics.

Along with William Arthur Reilly, Curley's chief opponent in his 1945 comeback race for mayor, Tobin had become friendly with James Michael Curley, Jr. They were both members of the Bostonia Court of the Massachusetts Order of Foresters, a chapter of the Catholic youth group founded by Curley to widen the circle of his eldest son's political acquaintance. Given these social connections, and since both he and Curley had been elected as Smith delegates to the Democratic national convention in 1928, Tobin appealed to Curley to help him defeat the formidable Tinkham. "I recall vividly that when I . . . went to him, the wealthiest Democrat in the city, for a small campaign contribution, he stated that he did not make a practice of giving such contributions—that's the man who gave me my start in political life," he related, his bitterness by then (the mayoral race of 1937) politically enhanced. Tobin lost his fight against Tinkham. But in doing so, he won his own and the adjoining ward by comfortable margins. He had established a political base.

Tobin and Curley had begun as they would end; but in between came a period of close personal relations. Vincent Lapomarda, S.J., Tobin's biographer, writes, "When James Michael Curley Jr. died in 1931, Maurice Tobin filled the vacuum in the Curley family and was regarded as another son and protégé being groomed to succeed James Michael Curley in politics." Francis Curley said of Tobin, "He practically lived at the house on the Jamaicaway," where he received "on-the-job-training" in politics. Because Tobin had been privy to some of the master's secrets, Curley regarded his decision to run against him as "an absolute stab in the back." Curley loved to cast himself in the role of the man betrayed, but unquestionably he had helped Tobin, hiring his brother, James, as one of his secretaries during his third term, and ranging his organization behind Tobin when he ran for a seat on the Boston School Committee in 1931. With the mayor's help, Tobin topped the twelve-candidate field with sixty-five thousand votes.[11]

Curley enlisted the wavering Tobin in his drive to win the Massachusetts primary for Roosevelt, and Tobin rendered FDR important service in the fall campaign against Hoover. "Mr. Tobin assisted in no small measure in making possible the election of Franklin D. Roosevelt," Curley later said. Shortly afterward, Curley made the speech at Tobin's bachelor party in which he referred to Tobin as "perhaps the next Mayor of Boston."[12]

In 1934 both Tobins worked the convention hall floor in Worcester for Curley, whom they addressed as "Boss," and they enlisted in his primary fight against General Cole—Maurice slamming Governor Ely for trying to incite a riot by decrying Curley's personal extravagance in a speech in the Tammany ward. Curley's manner of life was not extravagant, Tobin insisted; Ely was just trying to avoid the main issue of the primary campaign, "namely the support of the policies of President Franklin D. Roosevelt in order to make possible work and wages for the people of the United States." While Curley, with Tobin managing his campaign in Boston, was beating Gaspar Bacon, Tobin himself was being elected chairman of the Boston School Committee.[13]

Somewhere in this period it must have occurred to Curley that Tobin was a potential rival. He had no idea of handing on his political inheritance to the next generation. He was in politics for life, which he construed generously. "His concept of being dead was that he wouldn't be," according to his stepson Richard Dennis. "He saw himself as living forever. He was going to live to be 125 years old and bury his enemies." Perhaps he would have stepped aside for James Michael Jr. But there was no blood tie between him and James Michael Jr.'s contemporary Maurice Tobin.

He first tried to buy Tobin off with work and wages, offering to appoint him police commissioner and taking him to Washington to see if he could get the job of collector of internal revenue in Boston (he couldn't; David Walsh held that patronage). Unable to sidetrack Tobin, Curley decided to destroy him.

When Curley appointed that hunk of mud Teddy Glynn as first clerk of the Roxbury District Court instead of Maurice's brother James Tobin, who had expected the job, relations between the political father and his son cooled rapidly. Running for reelection in November 1935, Maurice Tobin won eighty-five thousand votes in a field of twenty-nine candidates. Now Curley moved openly against him by trying to deny him a place as a delegate to the 1936 Democratic national convention. Tobin fought back, urging primary voters to "repudiate bossism" by electing him as a delegate over Curley's candidate. By a three-to-one margin, they did. Tobin had found a winning theme.

He made a radio speech for Curley in the Lodge fight, but strictly out of party loyalty. On St. Patrick's Day 1937, Tobin announced his candidacy for mayor, the incumbent mayor, Frederick Mansfield, being barred from succeeding himself. With an unmistakable target in mind, Tobin said, "Age does not always bring wisdom, and the quality of sincerity in an individual who would entice or attract voters by glittering promises incapable of fulfillment is much open to question." Curley, already a candidate, turned the age issue around: "The people of Boston won't elect a schoolboy Mayor." Thus the stage was set for the first of Curley's three Oedipal election campaigns.[14]

Despite the mess he had made of being governor and the ignominy of being the only Democratic senatorial candidate in the country to lose in 1936, Curley still had some of the old magic, the zest for political theater that his followers loved. It was on unforgettable display at the Bunker Hill Day parade in Charlestown on a bright June day in 1937.

Maurice and Helen Tobin were there and they made a handsome couple. Governor Hurley was in the line of march and the lancers accompanying him were something to see. But Curley stole the show. Wearing a white "ice cream suit," he sat in the back seat of his big green Lincoln beside his new wife, chic in a blue suit and a white hat. The parade route was lined with ice cream vendors, and as Curley's machine approached them Teddy Glynn and other Curley aides would shoo the vendors toward Curley's car, where "the Governor," peeling bills off his bankroll, bought out their stock, filling the boot of the convertible knee-deep with chocolate-covered ice cream sticks, ice cream sandwiches, ice cream pies, Popsicles, creamsicles—the works. When he had accumulated enough to cause a riot, he caused a riot by tossing a block of ice cream to one youngster; at which others "dashed from under ropes, between coppers' legs, over parked cars and fell out of baby carriages to get at the Curley car and the free ice-cream." Curley slung ice cream at the firehouses as he passed by, and the firemen rewarded him by blowing their sirens and tooting their horns. For the adults, Glynn and his cohorts had distributed kegs of beer to the various social clubs along the line of march. While the band Curley had hired to lead his car in the parade ran through chorus after chorus of "The Isle of Capri"—which, as part of his effort to woo the Italian vote, he had made his signature song during his gubernatorial term—men drank Curley's health with Curley's beer; children ate from his hand; and the boot of the big car dripped a rainbow of ice cream. The spectacle overwhelmed Senator Joseph Langone—the Boss had really pulled one off! "It was the best reception that I have ever received in Charlestown," Curley said, knowing that the children who saw the parade would tell their children, who would tell theirs, bearing the moment into the Boston future. Pericles had it right: finally, men enter politics for the immortality.[15]

Show business had always been part of Curley's way in politics; by now he had it down to a system. He always had a campaign song, for example. The one for 1937 was called "Curley's Coming Back," and he brought Morton Downey to Boston to sing it before a crowd of nineteen thousand at the arena.

'Tis Curley again for Mayor, my boys
'Twas lonesome while he was away
But he'll be back four years more

So chase those blues away
The old town has not been the same since those good old Curley days.

To hold his crowds until he arrived, a troupe of entertainers would perform until the moment when "Up-Up" Kelly would come racing down the aisle, shouting, "Up, up for the Governor!" The star of this sideshow was usually Louis Brems, an old Keith Circuit vaudevillian. His specialty was "Uncle Dinny" stories, like this one about Dinny McGonicle of Charlestown:

> While working as a longshoreman, Dinny, drunk as usual, fell off the dock and drowned. The union man went to his wake to see Mrs. McGonicle, who was sitting with her friend Celia Brady.
> "I know Dinny has given you a lot of trouble, Mrs. McGonicle," the union man said, "him being a drinking man and all. But we all liked him on the docks, and we've taken up a collection for him. Here's a check for $5,000."
> "Glory be to God, Celia," Mrs. McGonicle said. "Can you imagine that? Why, he never had two nickels to rub together. He couldn't hold a job. Couldn't write. Couldn't read."
> "Thank God," Celia rejoined, "he couldn't swim."[16]

Brems had a trunkful of such stories. The hope was that the laugh would prove father to the vote.

Curley was so sure of victory that he bet $25,000 on himself, giving odds of ten to eight. It's "the softest touch I ever had," he boasted. He seemed to be counting on the crowded field—District Attorney Foley, former mayor Nichols, Tobin, and a minor candidate—to split the anti-Curley vote. He even sought to turn this vote against Tobin. Approaching one of Tobin's closest friends in the lobby of one of Boston's busiest hotels, he confided in a "whisper" audible on the upper floors, "Keep the young man in there, and if he needs any money let me know." To nullify the effect of this "whispering campaign," Tobin had to make a radio broadcast denying that he was Curley's "stalking horse" or "assistant candidate."[17]

Tobin was not above some campaign tricks of his own. Grouped around him were young men who had labored in the barren vineyards of Curley's shade—men like William Arthur Reilly, whom Curley had appointed to the Boston Finance Commission in

1935; John B. Hynes, Tobin's campaign strategist; and former Roxbury state senator Michael J. Ward, a longtime Curley apparatchik, who is reputed to have said of Curley that he would have been president if he had been honest. These men had learned politics from Curley, and now they taught their mentor a few lessons. According to one story, Mike Ward hired a stenographer to hide on the fire escape outside the room in the Parker House where Curley was dictating a speech. With Curley listening in astonishment, Tobin gave the speech over the radio that night. Ward also spooked Curley by filling the first two rows at one of his rallies with hecklers. Before a subsequent rally, to foil Ward's trick, Curley ordered the first two rows in the hall to leave. Unhappily, the people in them were not Tobin plants but loyal Curley backers—until he gave them the bum's rush.[18]

At sixty-three, Curley had inevitably lost something off his fastball. In one campaign appearance, building a portrait of Tobin as an "ingrate," he listed all the favors he had done for him and added, "Why, I even obtained a position—and a very good one indeed—for Maurice Tobin's sister." This was too much for an informed heckler, who shot back, "You're a liar, Curley. Tobin doesn't even have a sister." Which was true: Margaret Tobin had died at age six. The story quickly got around the city, and did Curley no good.[19]

Curley's stumbles, and indeed his campaign theme, that Boston could not afford to "experiment with inexperience," reinforced Tobin's overarching case—that it was time for a change, for "new faces, the new method, and the new spirit from which will come a New Deal in the political and civic life of our city." The Young Boston Movement, representing one hundred thousand Bostonians between the ages of twenty-one and thirty-one, rallied around his candidacy. The election split families between memory and hope, with the parents for Curley, the children for Tobin. In the *Post*, which ignored Curley's campaign, Norman depicted Curley as "Old Runitis," an owlish gray head, in front-page above-the-fold cartoons, while front-page editorials heaped garlands on Tobin as full of the "vigor and promise of youth." On Curley's "experience," the *Post* was decisive: "Experience in what? Experience in political fakery; experience in confusing and deluding the voters; experience in concealing the operations of grafting friends; experience in making lavish promises with neither the ability nor the intention of keeping them? Mr. Tobin has not that kind of experience."[20]

Curley's "record," in both senses of the word, was Tobin's torch issue. Two months before the election, Curley and a former associate, Dr. Joseph Santosuosso, were ordered to stand trial on the charge of absconding with $50,000 due the city in the General Equipment Company's damage claim settlement back in 1933. A few weeks later Edmund Dolan was indicted for fraud; when he tried to bribe one of the jurors, he was held in contempt of court and sentenced to jail for two years. Then there was flap over the nomination papers of Alonzo B. Cook. Curley had inserted the former Republican state auditor into the contest to draw votes from Malcolm Nichols, whom he mistakenly saw as his main rival. But two thousand people whose names were on Cook's nomination papers denied having signed them. In a triumph of boldness over common sense, among the phony signatures was that of Tobin's father. "Take Cook out of the contest, Mr. Curley," Tobin declared.[21]

"Every voter in Boston knows Mr. Curley's public record," Tobin said in a paint-peeling speech reviewing Curley's gubernatorial term that concluded with this grim warning: "Mr. Curley, why don't you retire while you still have remaining a shred of your self respect? If you do not, you will face a more detailed description of your public record, not as a faithful public servant—but as you really have been, a faithless public servant, and if you do not retire from the contest, you will live to sup again the bitter cup of ignominious defeat."[22]

Even though Nichols, a Republican, was in the race, Tobin was a true "fusion" candidate. The Democratic City Committee, the city's New Deal liberals, John F. Fitzgerald, Republican grandees like former city councilman Henry L. Shattuck and Senator Henry Parkman, Jr., were all in his corner. "Maurice Tobin is the candidate of the forces which offer the one chance of redemption of the city," the *Post* loftily summed up the fusion cause.[23]

The addition of Shattuck, Parkman, and others like them to the Tobin camp gave Curley a pretext to wave the shamrock. In the last weekend of the campaign, belatedly realizing the mortal threat from Tobin, he and his campaigners made direct appeals for votes on the religious issue, intimating that Curley was being opposed because of his faith and that Tobin had sold out his "own" by accepting the endorsement of these leading Republicans and—saints forbid!—Protestants. "One Curley speaker, Joseph Scolponeti, even insinuated that the angels in heaven were weeping at the thought of Curley's defeat," John Bantry wrote, adding that this radio invocation of the cherubim and seraphim probably cost Curley a thousand votes.[24]

Curley's last-minute descent into religion licensed the *Boston Post* to use religion against him in the most flagrant piece of propaganda in the history of Boston journalism.

The *Post* was settling old scores. In 1920, knowing that the paper would throw the weight of its influence as Boston's largest daily against him in his comeback election in 1921, Curley gave a St. Patrick's Day speech in which he accused Edwin A. Grozier, the *Post's* editor and publisher, of being a paid agent of the British government. The timing made the charge combustible: British irregulars, the infamous Black and Tans, had just been sent to Ireland to stamp out the Irish rebellion against British rule. Grozier replied with a long front-page invitation to Curley to "prove his interesting charges." If Curley could offer "a scintilla of evidence," Grozier promised, he would turn over his controlling interest in the paper to him. There was no evidence; the charge was a baseless slander. But Curley diverted public attention by offering to debate Grozier on the question of whether or not he was an agent of British imperialism. This Grozier was not foolish enough to do.[25]

There the matter stood until 1937, when, under Grozier's son Richard, the *Post* had its revenge. Clifton Carberry, alias John Bantry, the *Post's* managing editor, was by this time so deaf that there were only two people whose voices he could hear. One of them was the cab driver who took him home every night. Carberry would question this fellow about politics and from that sampling of public opinion go on in his column to limn the mood of the Boston electorate. The other person Carberry could hear was Maurice Tobin.[26]

The 1937 Boston municipal election fell on All Souls' Day, when thousands of Catholics would be attending Mass to pray for their dead. As they filed out of churches across the city that morning they were met by hundreds of Tobin volunteers who pressed free copies of the *Post* into their hands. Across the top of the front page in a "banner box" the paper usually carried a famous quotation or bromidic sentiment a line or two long. This day it carried a considerable text in bold type running the full eight-column width of the paper. "Voters of Boston," it read:

> Cardinal O'Connell, in speaking to the Catholic Alumni Association, said, "The walls are raised against honest men in civic life." You can break down those walls by voting for an honest, clean, competent young man, Maurice J. Tobin, today. He will redeem the city and take it out of the hands of those who have been responsible for graft and corruption. Maurice Tobin can win with the help of those who have had enough of these selfish old-timers. Too long they have been supported by the taxpayers. They have had more than enough.[27]

The cardinal had made this comment, but in some versions months, in others years earlier, and not in connection with the Boston election or Maurice Tobin or James Michael Curley. But the *Post* did not point any of this out, and many of its 360,000 readers, overlooking the closed quote after "life," took the statement as the cardinal's endorsement of Tobin. According to one story, a Curley worker called his mother to say that he would send a car to transport her and her three daughters to the polls. "Don't bother," she said. "Coming home from Mass this morning the girls bought a *Post* and there, big as life, His Eminence comes out for young Mr. Tobin. We've already voted for the lad." Curley reportedly sent an emissary to the cardinal's residence in Brighton to beg him to disavow the "endorsement" in a radio broadcast; but the cardinal had for years been waiting to settle his own scores with Curley—who privately referred to His Eminence as "that old S.O.B."—and was too busy to see him.[28]

Tobin won the election, 105,000 to 80,000, and Carberry's typographical trick was thought by many to have made the difference.[29]

Arthur Inman, the Back Bay Proust whose sixteen-hundred-page (abridged) diary offers an idiosyncratic social history of Boston in these years, noted three days after Curley's defeat: "Some of the Irish have turned against him for killing policemen with his car. . . . One of his partners in pilfering has been indicted. He has obtained no Federal sinecure from Roosevelt. And now he is at last out. He sounded both angry and amazed on the radio. Another young Irishman was elected Mayor in his stead. Wonder what Curley will do now. It cannot be possible that his gay days of political racketeering are over and done with. We passed his home this morning. I wondered if he were there and if so what were his thoughts."[30]

He was planning his next race; he ran for office as the rich play polo, in season. Addressing the James M. Curley Club (the former Tammany Club) six months later, he made it official: "The state needs leadership, and I am going to do all I can to give it." In short, he was running for governor again.[31]

"Nobody is through with politics who has ever tasted it," he said after losing to Henry Cabot Lodge. Now he had lost to Maurice Tobin. "The bitter cup of ignominious defeat" was not his preferred drink, but he knew that to win you had to risk losing. And there was little self-pity in him, no Nixon-like whimpering over his "crises." His people expected him to get off the mat and return, dukes up, to the ring—and in this at any rate he never let them down.[32]

Branding Charles F. Hurley a "do-nothing Governor," "the most incompetent chief executive in the history of the state," and an "excelsior-stuffed moron with the mentality of a three year old child," he set out to make history by denying him renomination to office. No Democratic governor had ever been ousted by his own party in Massachusetts before. But the Massachusetts Democracy, after the harmony of the Al Smith years, had entered on the era of its civil wars. Lacking ideological definition—church influence kept it from being a New Deal or liberal party—it was and is no more than a collection of careerists, unable or unwilling to subordinate their personal ambitions for the "good of the party," much less of the state. Thus in the decades to come, his intraparty feud with Curley would make Maurice Tobin a one-term governor, Endicott Peabody would be ousted in a primary, and so would Michael Dukakis, and so, four years later, would the man who beat him, Edward King, who would lose in a primary to the same Michael Dukakis. In short, Curley's challenge to a sitting governor of his own party marked the start of a bad habit that would regularly turn one of the most Democratic states in the nation over to Republican governors.[33]

There were two other candidates in the race against Hurley—Richard Russell, a former congressman from Cambridge, and Francis Kelly, Hurley's own lieutenant governor. In trying to steer a course between the reactionary cardinal and the liberal New Deal, Charles Hurley had drifted too far toward the cardinal, strongly

(Above) Richard Dennis, George Dennis, and Catherine and Leo Curley round out this wartime Christmas photograph. At his trial, Curley would trade on his sons' military service.

(Right) The grayer Curley got the more he looked the role of a chief executive—a role he played well.

The fedora's choice. Even after his second felony conviction, one poll found that over sixty percent of Bostonians still thought Curley was doing a good job as mayor.

"Curley gets things done": such was the hope of these returning veterans in 1945.

With George Curley in a postwar parade. "Missus didn't approve of his way of living" one former housekeeper said, referring to the tension between Gertrude and George.

The St. Patrick's Day parade, South Boston, 1946. George Curley is driving. The fellow under the tam-o'-shanter is "Knocko" McCormack, whose feelings Curley would never hurt.

He liked golf for the conviviality and the status, an effect heightened by having state troopers caddy for him.

With John F. Kennedy and John F. Fitzgerald. JFK was the only member of the Massachusetts Delegation to refuse to sign the petition sent to President Truman asking that Curley be released from jail.

Charlestown gets a pool. Few who saw the Bunker Hill Day parade of 1937 could forget the sight of Curley being mobbed by boys wanting free ice cream.

Breaking ground for the D Street housing project in 1948. Grateful contractors made sure to stick $2,000 into the Christmas baskets they sent to City Hall.

With Gertrude at play.

Curley had a pioneering affinity for Florida. Here, pictured with Gertrude.

With Paul Dever ("You little pisspot," Curley once called him), a president he wanted General MacArthur to replace, and Maurice Tobin. Curley's feelings toward Truman were decidedly mixed—but in the end, Harry came through for him.

A term too far. The 1951 mayoral campaign was over by the September primary, though Curley stayed on the ballot, hoping for a miracle. "If they love me so much," he remarked as a crowd cheered him, "why won't the sons-of-bitches vote for me?"

opposing the Roosevelt administration's drive to prohibit child labor, for example. In endorsing Richard Russell, James M. Landis, dean of the Harvard Law School and the Roosevelt-appointed former chairman of the Securities and Exchange Commission, made clear the administration's displeasure with Hurley. "To President Roosevelt's efforts to alleviate our national evils," Landis said, "to his broad and sympathetic social program, Governor Hurley has not only lent a deaf ear, but has been outspoken in his opposition and antagonism." So Curley could once more run as Roosevelt's friend, condemning Hurley as the president's "most caustic critic and betrayer."[34]

Promising to put more men on the state payroll than the incumbent, and wooing the elderly with pledges to lower the minimum age for old-age assistance from sixty-five to sixty, Curley barnstormed the cities and filled the airwaves with "blasts" at Hurley. "Except for the President," the New York Times observed, "it is doubtful if the country has a more persuasive radio personality." It was enough to put him over. Buoyed by a 50,000-vote lead over Hurley in Boston, Curley won easily, 169,000 to Hurley's 130,000, with the two other candidates trailing far behind. What one critic termed Curley's "verbal dynamite" had connected to something in the lives of the state's hard-core Democrats. "There was a reciprocal relationship between Curley and his audiences," William Shannon explains; "an audience would have to be conditioned by history and circumstances to have such an avid taste for invective and verbal violence, and Curley, by consistently pandering to that taste, helped confirm it and establish a norm."[35]

His victory parade from the James M. Curley Club in Roxbury to a radio station downtown was a wild affair. With a band playing "The Isle of Capri" leading the way, the motorcade moved slowly through the Roxbury streets where Curley had made his start. As it passed by, windows opened, crowds emerged from the cafés and taverns, and Curley's people—some staggering, others sober—joined the parade. One reporter nicely pictured Gertrude Curley, sitting in the open Lincoln, "extending a hand with ruby-tinted nails to her husband's strangely varied supporters." At the Hotel Brunswick, "frantic partisans tore Curley away from his wife," and beefy police sergeants had to rescue him. For four years his supporters had had no occasion to cheer, and they meant to make the most of it.[36]

In a "victory statement" delivered over the radio, Curley said that his candidacy had been "actuated only by the desire to prevent the election of a reactionary Republican." That would be former Speaker of the House Leverett Saltonstall. But in his statement on winning his primary that night, Saltonstall did not sound like one of those, much less like the "bovinistic reactionary" Curley had earlier labeled him. "I shall be elected Governor of Massachusetts on next Nov. 8," the lanky former Harvard hockey star said, "because I stand for an honest state budget ever recognizing the fact that until such time as private business is ready to take care of the unemployed it is the duty of the government to provide jobs for those who want work but are unable to get work." And ominously, Saltonstall had captured nearly a hundred thousand more votes than Curley, beating his nearest competitor by a majority of two hundred thousand.[37]

"The party has never had a more likable, a more wholesome, or a more deserving candidate," the *Herald* gushed. "A dear, dumb man," is the way a former aide remembers "Salty," like Henry Cabot Lodge a liberal Republican with roots extending back to the founding of New England. "When Leverett Saltonstall was having campaign photographs taken on his Needham farm," Cleveland Amory notes of a later stage in his career, "the pictures of the Senator doing some off-hours work in his garden were regarded as the first evidence of shirtsleeves in the Saltonstall family in not three, but nine generations."[38]

Against so acceptably liberal and appealing an opponent, and with a divided party behind him, Curley needed all the help he could get. "Tonight is a big night in Boston politics," John F. Kennedy, twenty-one, a Harvard junior, wrote to his father in England, "as the Honorable John F. Fitzgerald is making a speech for his good friend James Michael Curley. Politics makes strange bedfellows." Hoping he would prove to be another Frank Goodwin, Curley inserted one of his stalwart lieutenants of many years, William H. McMasters, on the Republican ticket as a Townsend Plan candidate.

Curley had trouble, though, with another of his lieutenants. Senator Langone's unbuttoned candor was disconcerting. "I've made Judges in North Adams under Curley as Governor," he breezily confided to reporters. "I want to see Curley go back to the hill because I know I'll get a few more appointments."[39]

Worse, day after day the papers were full of revelations damaging to Curley stemming from the perjury trial of a lawyer for the insurance company representing the General Equipment Company. On the witness stand Frederick H. Graves said that he approached Mayor Curley in the lobby of the Mayflower Hotel in Washington in late 1933 and inquired if his company could reach a settlement with the city. "How much is in it for me?" Curley asked him. Forty thousand dollars, Graves said. "All right," Curley replied, "see Santosuosso and have him put it through."[40]

Earlier in the year Curley and Dr. Joseph Santosuosso, his factotum, had been convicted, to quote from Suffolk Superior Court Judge Frederick W. Fosdick's ruling, of "corruptly" receiving $50,000 of the $85,000 the city had paid to settle General Equipment's damage claims. Thus ended the long "suit in equity" brought by the city against its former mayor. The Mansfield administration had mounted a civil rather than a criminal case, "to keep me from having a jury trial," Curley says in his autobiography. Thus he was not liable for criminal penalties; instead he was ordered to repay his part of the swag, $37,575 plus interest, to the municipal treasury. Curley's appeal of the ruling was still pending, but in case any voters had forgotten that he was the first—and only—mayor in Boston's history to be found guilty of illegally profiting from conducting the city's business, Graves's testimony refreshed their recollection.[41]

For Curley, the campaign had one brief moment of nobility. When former governor Alvan Fuller attacked him in a much-cited speech, calling him a leopard who could not change his spots, Curley rose to the occasion with some of the old-time eloquence. "I am the same Jim Curley today that I have been for forty years. . . . Where I found a muddy lane, I left a broad highway; where I found a barren waste, I left a hospital; where I found a disease-breeding row of tenement houses, I left a health center; where I found a vacant lot, I left a magnificent temple of learning; where I found a weed-grown field, I left a playground: throughout life, wherever I have found a thistle, I endeavored to replace it with a rose. No, this leopard has no desire to change his spots. If to keep faith with the people and lead the fight for liberal legislation, to give jobs to the jobless, food to the hungry, and to rescue children and mothers from malnutrition and exploitation and bring comfort and security to the aged constitutes leopard spots, then I submit that I am covered with them."[42]

The same man who could express such oceanic compassion for the common man very nearly killed two of them while driving through Westfield in western Massachusetts. One oncoming car was forced into a ditch; the other ran up against a fence to avoid the hurtling ghost of S-1 going sixty eastbound in the westbound lane of a state highway. Heckled at a New Bedford rally, Curley threatened to put the offenders in the hospital if they didn't shut up. At East Boston High School auditorium, a witness remembers, "All eyes turned as Curley strode in, surrounded by flunkies and glancing right and left, a benign emperor. Suddenly he stopped and said a word to a young guy wearing the Republican candidate's button and slapped the guy hard in the face. And moved on to give his set speech, which drew . . . tumultuous applause. He was our man, 'The Mayor of the Poor,' and he could do no wrong, even if he did wrong."43

Bitter over his defeats, frustrated at the sparse turnout at his rallies, nettled by the constant questioning about the General Equipment case, he could not hold himself in check. Some years earlier, Robert Washburn, the columnist for the *Boston Evening Transcript,* had quipped that Saltonstall had a Back Bay name and a South Boston face. Curley incautiously revived this line in his campaign. "The only reason Saltonstall advances for why he should be elected Governor," he said, launching a political boomerang, "is that he has a South Boston face. This is a colossal stupidity. If he ever walked down the streets of South Boston with that face, he would be put in the hospital within a hundred yards."44

Acting on the advice of one of his aides, Jacob Spiegel, Saltonstall riposted over the radio. "I have many friends in South Boston," he said, "and I have always found the people of South Boston to be warm-hearted, decent, law-abiding citizens. What right has my loose-talking opponent to even intimate that the citizens of South Boston would inflict bodily harm on anyone?" A few days later, embracing the link Curley had made for him between his craggy countenance and Boston's toughest Irish neighborhood, he said, "I am proud of that South Boston face. It's not a double face. It's the only one I have and it will be the same face after the election." It is a local legend that Saltonstall, whose father had been a founder of the Immigration Restriction League, then spent a day walking the streets of South Boston, greeting one and all with his winning homespun Yankee charm.45

Of course Curley lost the election, 733,000 to 641,000, dragging most of the Democratic ticket down with him. Hoping to carry Boston by 100,000, he fell 40,000 votes short. Saltonstall, Thomas O'Connor writes, had "captured an impressive number of Irish-Catholic votes by capitalizing on . . . his South Boston face." Through his verbal incontinence, Curley had defeated himself.[46]

❖   ❖   ❖

A compulsive candidate, Curley did not plot his political moves; he ran for whatever office was open in the year he was unemployed. After the arrangement with Hibernia Savings came to an end, campaign funds were his only source of income when out of office. Proof is lacking, but the suspicion that he did not spend all the money he raised on his campaigns is eminently warrantable. There was nothing he could run for in 1939, so he set his sights on 1940, when the Senate seat held by David Walsh would be up for election.

Nineteen forty, of course, was to have been the year when the Man of Destiny would make his boldest political move. But that had been a Xanadu projection. Three straight elections and three straight defeats had disabused Curley of presidential illusions. "I always had an appreciation and trust that I shall continue to appreciate that crowns of roses fade," he said at the conclusion of his "leopard spots" radio speech; "crowns of thorns endure— Calvarys and Crucifixions are remembered longest." Never mind president, he wanted to be Jesus! He was turning his personal losses, of which there were more to come, and his political reverses into character references. Through ethnically calibrated spin control—the Irish are suckers for suffering—he was transmuting his defeats into victories. Curley had created himself; now he was laying the foundation of his legend.

❖   ❖   ❖

In a speech before ten thousand supporters at a Boston armory, he lashed Walsh as "David Ignorus"—a senator who had left no mark on the laws of state or nation—and hinted that he might challenge him in the primary. There had long been strained relations between these two Irish-American totems. From a small central Massachusetts town, Walsh attracted the kind of independent and even Republican vote that Curley never had a hope of capturing. As the international horizon darkened toward war, however, Walsh, who had since 1936 been chairman of the Senate Naval Affairs Committee, played to a different constituency: Irish Americans who detested Britain and who wanted the United States to stay out of "foreign"—that is, British—wars.[47]

He took the same line on the European war that began in September 1939 as Cardinal O'Connell, *The Pilot*, and much of the Irish Catholic flock. Battered by the Depression, frustrated at their lack of economic progress, seeing with their own eyes how much better Boston's Jews were doing than they were, in the war years the Boston Irish would apply the politics of provincialism to the world. O'Connell said that it was hard for him to understand "why some of the propagandists are allowed to cry down the normal wish of the American people for peace. What is their purpose? They cannot be real Americans, because real Americans think of their country first. They are CERTAIN EXPATRIATES, I think you know what I mean—who are raising their voices in LOUD accents." This was a nudge in the ribs of anti-Semitism, and these words preluded actions in the streets of Dorchester and Mattapan as gangs of Irish Catholic boys set upon and beat up Jewish boys. Just as in the 1850s *The Pilot* had been blind to the moral issue posed by slavery, so in the late 1930s and early 1940s it displayed an equal blindness to the transcendent moral issue posed by Hitlerism. It hit out instead at communists, anglophiles, New Dealers, atheists, and liberals—often, code for Jews—who were dragging the country toward war. It was these views Walsh reflected when he threatened to resign his Senate seat rather than vote to send the United States into another war, and when, in June 1940, with German panzers surging across France, he asked, "When have the German government or the German people ever done anything to us as a nation, that should cause us to go to war?"[48]

Yet Walsh was also consistent in his belief that the United States should adhere to a strict policy of neutrality and non-intervention. As governor of Massachusetts in 1915, he had backed Secretary of State Bryan in the controversy over the U.S. response to the sinking of the *Lusitania*. Fearing it would lead to war, Bryan resigned when President Wilson insisted on sending a tough note of protest to Germany. At the time Curley had derided Bryan as "the ex-tinguished Secretary of State." Of this difference of opinion between the state's two leading Democrats, one newspaper editor wrote: "Jim Curley has as much use for the Governor as a maiden lady for a shaving mug." That remained true, and the comment had other grounds than politics.

David Walsh, the "bachelor governor" of 1915, was a homosexual. He may have been the mysterious Senator X who in 1942 was accused of patronizing a male brothel in New York frequented by sailors and what the New York tabloids hyped as Nazi spies. Curley knew of Walsh's sexual preference and disapproved of it, both on moral grounds and as a matter of pragmatic politics—if widely known, it might hurt the party. In turn, Walsh regarded Curley as his personal cross. When Curley was running against Lodge for the Senate, Walsh was said by Robert Washburn to be about as happy at the prospect of serving with Curley "as a naked baby in the lap of a porcupine."[49]

In the event, Curley thought better of taking on Walsh. Without politics to preoccupy him, he was at the mercy of the speculative mania that would sweep into his life when he was idle. Thus it was that James Michael Curley became co-owner of a Nevada gold mine.

❖   ❖   ❖

Gertrude was against it, Mary Donnelly pleaded with him not to do it, but neither could avail against his obsession. Moreover, he had those two safes full of cash—this banker used no bank and wrote no checks.° What was he to do with them? He could either spend the pile down in hopes of being returned to office before it ran out or he could invest it in hopes that it would provide him with a sufficient income to render him independent of political office. He was an ideal mark for speculators who had schemes to finance. They could take his money, secure in the knowledge that if the deal soured Curley would not sue them in court. The question he could never get away from—where did he get it?—would stop him.[50]

According to his son and people who worked for him, that is what happened with the Nevada mine. He was fleeced.

Mary Donnelly possessed some of her mother's "discernment of spirits," a phrase of St. Ignatius Loyola's that Frank Curley used

---

° "Never open a checking account," he advised his son Francis. "I'm not going to explain it to you. Just do not open a checking account."

to describe Mary Curley's ability to spot a phony a mile away. She tried to warn him off Nevada. "Father, that man is a riverboat gambler," she said of the operator who visited the Jamaicaway and played on Curley's cupidity with stories of rich ore in the distant hills waiting for a visionary financier to mine it. "If you play poker with him, we're through." But Curley wouldn't listen. As a politician he was used to conjuring realities with words; that the bottom line was not amenable to the same magic was something he never learned. "I've seen the pictures, Mary. There's gold all through it."[51]

He had seen the pictures, and on a trip to extreme northwestern Humboldt County in Nevada, he even saw the gold. But according to Frank Curley, the mines had been "peppered"—the walls blasted with scatter guns filled with gold fragments. The people who sold him the mine showed him the gold flecks embedded in the rock walls, and he was a goner.

This verdict on the gold mine jibes with a report that Robert Cutler, Tobin's corporation counsel and later President Eisenhower's special assistant for national security affairs, received on a quicksilver deposit Curley bought at the same time. Wanting to know if Curley's properties could cover the General Equipment judgment against him, Cutler asked the president of a mining company to cast his professional eye over them. Returned from Nevada, the man told Cutler that there was quicksilver in one of the mines. Cutler's eyes lit up: the city could attach it. "But you haven't asked the important question," the mining executive added. "All right," Cutler said, "what is the important question?" He replied: "How long has the quicksilver been there?" The deposits were all on the surface. Farther down the shaft there was no quicksilver.[52]

"He gambled away his future—and ours—on that mine," Frank Curley said, estimating that Curley may have poured as much as two million untaxed dollars into what was known in Nevada as the Curley Luck Mine.

The record shows that, in February 1939, with two co-investors, James A. Smoot, the postmaster of Salt Lake City, and O. C. T. Thurber, a mining engineer, Curley bought the Ashdown mine 105 miles northwest of the town of Winnemucca for $300,000 and, in a separate transaction, obtained the nearby Vicksburg, Navajo, and Dry Gulch claims for $200,000. To these properties Curley soon added quicksilver fields described in the mining pages of the Humboldt County newspaper as "one of the most promising quicksilver areas in this section." Curley was identified as "president of the Hibernia Savings Bank of Boston," a position he was to hold for only a few more months, and, with poignant imprecision, as "a prominent Eastern financier." The stories rang with hope. "Extension of the wide business interests of Ex-Governor James M. Curley of Massachusetts to Nevada gold and quicksilver mining fields," one story began, "is failing to darken what Eastern financiers term 'ceaseless Curley luck.' . . . "[53]

With Gertrude, Curley now became a frequent visitor to his remote underground dominion. They stayed at the mining camp twelve miles south of the Oregon-Nevada border. The mine employed forty-five workers, and Curley paid for the erection of a two-hundred-ton mill to refine the ore, as well as for housing and tents and machinery. The Yankees could keep their clipper ships—he had his gold mine. Thoughts of retiring to Palm Beach must have danced in his head.[54]

What went wrong is hard to say. The Ashdown mine, one of the oldest in the state, was considered a potentially large producer of gold. However, a lawsuit was filed against the Curley Luck Gold Corporation over the rights to claims adjoining the Ashdown. Perhaps Curley bailed out of the mine to avoid a long draining siege of litigation over the rights to Cherry Gulch One. Or perhaps he was taken from the outset, as his daughter Mary feared and as Francis Curley remembered. More likely and more consistent with the Ashdown's reputation, Curley and his partners could not sustain the stream of capital investment needed to reclaim a mine that had not been seriously worked since the Bannoch Indians attacked it and burned down its mill in 1864. This interpretation accords with the memories of both Frank Curley and Helen McDonough, one of the Curleys' maids and a trusted family friend, who both recall telegrams from Nevada streaming into the house, all asking for big sums of money. Whatever the cause, by 1941 Curley had sunk his two safesful of cash in the mining business and was getting little or nothing in return.[55]

Luckily, 1941 was an election year.

❖   ❖   ❖

Early in the year, Curley was haled into the West Roxbury District Court on a plea filed by the City of Boston, which, the state Supreme Court having refused Curley's appeal, wanted him

.to pay the $42,735 he owed. "So far as my ability to pay is concerned," Curley, dapper in a dark blue suit, white shirt, and blue tie, told the lawyer for the city, "there is not a chance in the world." Asked what property he owned, he listed his house, on which he claimed to have a $30,000 mortgage; 165 shares worth $100 in a New Hampshire brewery; a number of insurance policies in his own name and those of his children, on which he had borrowed to the limit to finance the mine; and an art collection that might bring $30,000 to $40,000. He denied having interests in a local radio station, racetrack, and construction company and said that, notwithstanding rumors that "I have $3,000,000 buried in Canada," his savings totaled no more than $1,500. He did admit an interest "in a quicksilver mine 20 miles beyond Midas in the County of Ivanhoe in Nevada representing an investment of $125,000. I have a reasonable prospect of selling it in the next ten days at a profit, provided there is not too much publicity given it." He admitted to quicksilver, passing over the gold. The judge gave him two weeks to sell the mine. Shortly thereafter, his marathon of appeals and delays at an end, he was ordered to pay the city $500 a week for eighty-six weeks to settle its claim against him.⁵⁶

Lewis H. Weinstein, the city's attorney in the case, writes that "the next morning's newspapers carried notices that Curley would be on the radio that evening with an 'urgent message.'" In his most richly upholstered voice, Weinstein remembers, Curley urged all who heard and cared to "bring whatever you can: nickels, quarters, half-dollars, dollars, two-dollar bills, fives, tens, whatever your heart tells you; bring them to my white house with the green shamrock shutters on the Jamaicaway, or come in. I'll be there. Or throw them on the lawn. I can't thank you enough. And you, my friends, know me and what I've done for you." Here his voice flooded with emotion: "You know me!"

"Curley," Joseph Dinneen writes, "had to pay or go to jail. The newspapers headlined his predicament; and almost everybody in Boston knew now that Curley was broke—he could not pay." How a man with an art collection worth $40,000 and an *admitted* interest of $125,000 in a silver mine "beyond Midas in the County of Ivanhoe" could be considered broke in an era when women's dresses cost $10 and men's shirts $1.35 may escape us; but this fabulation enables Dinneen to tell a touching story of lines forming outside the Jamaicaway, an "unorganized army of the grateful coming to his rescue" with contributions of dimes and dollars. Lewis Weinstein remembers a similar scene: "Cars were lined up in a traffic jam. People came with their hands full of bills and coins, which they left on the Curley lawn or the entrance floor."

No doubt devoted followers did drive by and throw coins on Curley's lawn. But to give probability equal time, these stories of Curley being bailed out by the nickels and dimes of Boston's little people clearly also belong to what William Allen White, in his biography of Calvin Coolidge, calls "the apocrypha of politics." To quote White: "The apocrypha of politics is, of course, the gossip of politics; but a little more than that. It is the folk tales . . . somewhat based upon truth, the stories that ought to be true, that grow out of men's estimates of their minor gods." The vision of "trucks, limousines, pushcarts, delivery wagons, automobiles of all sizes, shapes, makes and models" pulling up to Curley's door *ought* to be true. They fitted Curley's idea of his career as a trust held by the little people, of his house and his car and his flagrant trappings as somehow also theirs. And the legend of these anonymous benefactors would certainly have helped Curley with the IRS, which had begun to look over his shoulder in these years.[57]

Whether really or just theatrically "broke," Curley had to lay off members of his domestic staff. Helen McDonough, who had come straight from her Irish village to the Jamaicaway, sought employment where her sister Nora worked, the Back Bay home of Mrs. Frederick L. Ames. Nearly thirty years before, in the course of denouncing John Farwell Moors—who in a speech at the Ames mansion had given a politically incorrect version of how the Irish had come to Boston—Curley had characterized Mrs. Ames and her sister members of the New England Woman's Department of the National Civic Association as "gabbing spinsters" and "dog raising matrons." When Mrs. Ames asked Helen to name her last employer and Helen replied Curley, Mrs. Ames said that she would not accept a reference from him. "What's the matter with Curley?" Helen asked. "Oh, we all know he's a crook," Mrs. Ames replied. Helen McDonough stood up and put on her coat. "He's no crook, Mrs. Ames," she said. "I don't like what you're saying about the Governor. I wouldn't work for you if I never worked again."

All the way back to her Dorchester home on the subway, Helen felt terrible guilt—not for losing her chance at the job but for jeopardizing her sister Nora's job with her impetuous display.

When she got home, Nora was on the phone; Mrs. Ames was calling. Far from being angry, Mrs. Ames was so impressed with Helen's loyalty to her former employer that she wanted to give her the job. "No, Nora," Helen said, refusing to take the phone. "Tell her to stick it."[58]

That Curley could inspire such loyalty from people of Helen McDonough's caliber says something good about him, something that belongs to the hidden history at the edge of the page. Bullying subordinates, especially women, seems to be one of the accepted ways Important Men establish their identity. "You grovel, therefore I am" might be the maxim of their conduct. Curley knew who he was. ("He was a loquacious lion," a man who first met him in these years says.) And he remembered where he came from. The picture people who worked for him paint is of a generous, thoughtful man.[59]

The picture is also of a man under great stress. Losing elections and court cases and a fortune in mining, with his friend Dolan in jail, the IRS looking over his returns, and death claiming more and more of his voters, Curley had also lost the Place of Rest. Gertrude did all she could to re-create the old enveloping security, but his children were grown now, and they could be neither controlled nor protected.

Mary's marriage was a nightmare. Donnelly hit her; one witness saw him burn her hand with a lighted cigarette. He had other women in her bed, forcing her to watch. Curley knew something of what was going on between them—if he had known the whole truth, he would have taken one of his shillelaghs to Donnelly—and one night during a family dinner he came out with it. Mary refused to yield on a point Curley was pressing in a political argument. "What can you do with a woman like that, Eddie?" he said, laughingly. "I beat her," Eddie replied. The smile fell off Curley's face. "Yes, I know. Now get out of this house before I throw you out." Hoping against the evidence that Eddie would change, fearing the effect a divorce would have on her father's political career, Mary resolved to stick her marriage out.[60]

Paul Curley's marriage had also failed. "Paul didn't think he was good enough for her," according to Helen McDonough. He and Lillian lived for a while in a house behind the Jamaicaway, where Paul would sit in the sun room, staring at the house with the shamrock shutters, and drinking.

It started when he was a teenager and would smuggle a pint into his locker at Boston Latin and raid the thick tangy bourbon his father kept in the cellar. He showed up at the New Hampshire summer training camp for the Boston College varsity squad in a roadster with a rumble seat full of beer. Knowing nothing of football, he took a battering in practice. His "old man" had arranged for the tryout, he told a teammate, so he could quit his drinking and prove himself. At law school he answered an exam question on crops and mortgages this way: "To hell with mortgages and the new mown hay / I'm off to Minsky's and old Broadway." That ended his law school career. He had a succession of jobs—road secretary for the Boston Braves, radio announcer—but the demon rum always tripped him up, and his father had to pay his bills. "He loved his father," a friend says, "and though he was no bigger than a pint of peanuts, he would fight anyone who insulted him at the drop of a hat." Chasing show girls, quoting verse, lifting the jar, he recalls Eugene O'Neill's Jamie Tyrone, another son who desperately missed his mother.[61]

After his divorce he moved back to the Jamaicaway, where he became a trial to Gertrude. Amiably drunk, he once staggered into one of her dinner parties spouting doggerel—"I shot an arrow in the air / It fell to earth I know not where / I lose more god-damned arrows that way"—which hugely amused him but humiliated Gertrude. On another occasion, her son Richard was entertaining himself by dropping lighted sheets of toilet paper out the window of an upstairs bathroom. In the butler's pantry fixing a drink, Paul saw one of these lighted puffs float by. Furious, he charged upstairs to get the teenager. George Curley barred his way and a fight broke out between the two brothers on the landing.[62]

George was the peacemaker. He reached out to Gertrude and tried to make her feel part of the family. But George was also a homosexual, and Gertrude could not abide the parade of boyfriends he would smuggle into his room at night, especially in their summer house at Scituate. "George loved Missus," Helen McDonough says, "but she was against his way of living." The only time she saw Curley lose his temper with Gertrude was once when she tried to raise the question of George's "strays" with Curley over breakfast in Scituate. He was so angry that he got up and left the house without finishing his breakfast. "Helen, I blew it. What could I do?" Gertrude said to her. "She was thinking of us," Helen says, meaning Gertrude was afraid that George's friends might sneak into the rooms of the Irish girls who worked for them and whose safety and morals were her first concern.

Not everything was bleak. Young Francis was showing the brilliance that would gain him two advanced degrees from the Jesuits. George and Richard Dennis were flourishing at boarding school. On weekends and during school vacations, Francis, George, the Dennis boys, and their friends would stay at Ard Rye, the Donnellys' Dover estate where they kept their horses and had a swimming pool, bowling alley, and private movie theater. The childless Mary liked having the boys around. She felt a special responsibility to act as a substitute mother to Francis. As for Leo Curley, the warmest and most beloved member of the family had quit Harvard Law School in protest when a professor insulted his father, pleasing the old man no end. After completing his law degree at Boston University, he seemed on the verge of a successful legal—and perhaps political—career. And most of all there was Gertrude.[63]

To speed her up in the confessional, Curley would toss quarters in at her feet—a sign of the intimacy between them that perhaps only Catholics of the pre-ecumenical church can fully appreciate. "You don't tell him everything, do you?" he would ask when she came out. Curley had no finer pleasure than to sit in the living room after dinner and listen to Gertrude play the piano. After a while she would stop and come over to him on the couch, where they would sip their nightcaps together and hold hands. Here was the reason he rarely gave way to self-pity. He could lose elections, money, friends, even children because married love had happened to him twice in a lifetime. This was the real "ceaseless Curley luck," and Curley was man enough to know it.[64]

❖   ❖   ❖

Like his contemporary Fiorello La Guardia, Maurice Tobin was a fusion mayor, backed by a coalition of both Republicans and Democrats. Curley called him a "Democratic-Republican" and vowed to drive him from office in the city election of 1941. He nearly did the trick.

In 1938 the Republican-controlled state legislature, thinking Curley dead for all time, rescinded its 1918 ban on Boston's mayors succeeding themselves; and though Curley opposed it, in a referendum in 1939 the voters gave their approval. Tobin was the first mayor in twenty-three years who was eligible to run for reelection. Patrick Collins, in 1905, had been the last incumbent to run and win.[65]

"College professors and philosophers who go up in a balloon to think are always discussin' the question: 'Why Reform Administrations Never Succeed Themselves!'" Thus the Tammany sage George Washington Plunkitt, who goes on to liken reform administrations to "mornin' glories" that "looked lovely in the mornin' and withered up in a short time, while the regular machines went on flourishin' forever, like fine old oaks."[66]

The professors could land their balloons. The answer to the question was that reform means austerity, austerity means reduced services and laid-off city employees, and these mean angry voters. Tobin's moderate austerities had won him praise from patrician Republicans like Henry Parkman, whom he appointed his first corporation counsel; Christian Herter, the Republican Speaker of the Massachusetts House, who endorsed Tobin for reelection; and Henry Shattuck, his close adviser who was retiring from the City Council that year (twenty-two-year-old McGeorge Bundy, a wellborn Republican, was running for his Back Bay–South End seat). Tobin's reform administration was also popular with the bankers and businessmen of the Back Bay, Beacon Hill, and the nicer Boston suburbs—sound men who knew all about municipal bond credit ratings and such. But the cuts did Tobin no good in the city's neighborhoods, whose people paid the price for soundness, and where the cry was once more going up for Curley.[67]

Still, the irony of his running for mayor of a city he had so recently been found guilty of defrauding was glaring. Claiming to have been "the victim of the most horrible frame-up ever attempted in American politics," Curley acted as if he had done nothing wrong. At one rally, referring to the General Equipment case, he declared, "I had no more to do with settling that case than that man"—pointing to a drunk in the audience—"has to do with sarsaparilla."[68]

Events far away from Boston, though, were working in Curley's favor. The 1941 election took place a month before Pearl Harbor, but Bostonians already sensed the worst was coming. In a Labor Day speech to the nation made against the background of Hitler's conquest of Europe and invasion of Russia, President Roosevelt laid it starkly on the line. "We cannot hesitate, we cannot equivocate in the great task before us," he said, that task being "defeating Hitler."

432 ❖ THE RASCAL KING

The *Herald* glossed his remarks with equal bluntness: "He left little doubt that the country was virtually at war." Exploiting the sense of impending crisis, Curley stirred memories of his first term. "Do you want as Mayor, Curley, who had no bread lines or soup kitchens in the last war, nor would again?" And he urged Bostonians to look ahead to the time after the war, when there would be layoffs, hardships, possibly even riots, unless they voted for the man who had guided them through the last postwar period, "a man of heart, a man of character, uncontrolled by the bankers." Curley's sound trucks, placarded with scarlet hearts, cruised the city blaring out, "You gotta have heart, you gotta have heart."[69]

Curley wanted the voters to remember his compassion, but the headlines about Daniel Coakley were annulling that association. At seventy-six the old reprobate had finally reached the end of the line. In the last days of the Hurley administration he had rushed through the pardon of a Providence, Rhode Island, gunman, Raymond Patriarca, who would go on to become the leader of the New England underworld. Investigation revealed that Coakley had prepared letters signed by a fictitious "Father Fagin" extolling Patriarca's character. Governor Hurley later said he would not have signed the pardon if he had known the priest was a fake. For these and other violations of his public trust as a member of the Executive Council—including accepting $1,000 from a pardoned convicted murderer on the last day of Governor Curley's term—Coakley had been impeached that spring by the House of Representatives. That fall, defended by his son, attorney Gael Coakley, he was being tried by the state Senate. He delivered an eloquent, tearful speech from the well of the Senate in his own behalf. But finding him guilty of ten of the fourteen articles of impeachment brought against him, the Senate removed him from office by a vote of twenty-eight to ten, with the latter being nearly all Irish Catholics from the cities. He had the distinction of being the first man to be impeached in 321 years of royal and state government, barred forever from running for "any office of honor or trust or profit in the Commonwealth."[70]

For over thirty years Coakley had been Curley's alter ego, his shadow self, his evil twin. The Coakley who had placed $1 million in cash in two hotel safes after being disbarred in 1922 had shown Curley the way. The parallels between their careers, with Coakley always on the far side of legality and Curley closer to the near, were so obvious that Maurice Tobin did not need to point them out.[71]

Another candidate in the race, school committeeman Joseph Lee, made the sharpest attacks on Curley. "It is a tragedy that he should have wrecked a great career," he said. "It is a deeper tragedy that he does not recognize the wreckage and retire from public life." And again: "Curley has not had enough of Boston, but Boston, recognizing the wreckage of a great career by Curley's own hand, has had enough of Honest Jim."[72]

In addition, although he was making few public appearances, this campaign was Mal Nichols's last hurrah. But everyone knew that the real contest was between Curley and Tobin.

Curley was famous among politicians for coming into a hall in time to step on someone else's speech. On the last night of the campaign he made a "Curley entrance" to a Beacon Hill community meeting as Maurice Tobin was listing the city improvements "we have built." Curley had just sat down after distracting the audience from Tobin long enough to fracture its attention, but now he stood up and strode to the front of the hall. "What do you mean 'we have built'?" he shouted. "The P.W.A. built those projects." Tobin, facing him, the one man forty, the other sixty-six, heatedly replied, "By 'we' I mean the citizens of Boston."[73]

"It was a tough, bitter, violent campaign," in the recollection of Robert Cutler. There was even an attempt on Tobin's life.

It happened one night in the North End under the Boston Elevated tracks. Tobin and Cutler were riding in a fast-moving limousine from one rally to another when a small car sped out of a side street and headed straight toward them. To Cutler it looked as if they would be crushed between the Elevated uprights and the oncoming car. But at the last second Tobin's driver swerved, missing the iron wall by inches. The car raced away, but its license plate was visible: the car was registered in the name of a known Curley supporter. Tobin's people debated making the story public but decided the publicity might backfire. "It was the nearest I ever came to being killed," Cutler writes.[74]

Straw polls predicted a 50,000-vote Tobin win. Tobin himself boasted that he would sweep every ward. "It is not a close election," the *Post* pronounced. They were wrong.[75]

Curley's attacks on Tobin's Republican appointees and alliance with the city's "financial overlords"; his shameless exploitation of Tobin's cuts in city services—at one rally, he produced a crippled girl who he claimed had been deprived of vital city aid; and the rhetorical vigor with which he made these charges·

narrowed the gap in the closing days. Curley the underdog was connecting with the underdogs in the city electorate. "I have suffered temporary defeat," he declaimed, knowing he was not alone in that, "in campaigns to make this city and this Commonwealth a healthier place for the flowering of democratic ideals. I, too, have suffered from wounds inflicted by political 'traitors' and 'renegade' Democrats. But I am up! I am standing on my feet again! I am fighting for the people and for the Democratic party! I am fighting for the lost ideals that have been surrendered to the 'money changers.' I am going to win! Or rather, it is you, the people, who are going to win!" The slip in syntax, "I, too, have suffered" rather than "I have also suffered," reveals the speech's unconscious agenda. Curley was sketching a similitude between his defeats and theirs, inviting them to identify with his adversities and with his fierce defiance of final defeat: "But I am up!"[76]

The gap was narrowed, not closed. Curley got 116,000 votes, more than he had received in any of his five earlier mayoral races, more than Tobin had received in 1937; but Tobin got 125,000. Losing East Boston, South Boston, and the North and West ends, Tobin held Curley off in Dorchester and West Roxbury and swept the Back Bay by three to one. "I shall refrain from congratulating the winner," Curley said of the results. "I thoroughly believe that there are serious doubts of the honesty of the returns."[77]

A few weeks later two allies of Curley's, Francis E. Kelly, the former lieutenant governor and city councilman, and Emil Fuchs, a former part-time judge and sometime owner of the Boston Braves, sought to void the election by charging that Tobin had violated the Corrupt Practices Act in the financing of his campaign. The suit dragged on for months, seriously upsetting Maurice Tobin ("The young man was much broken up by this guerrilla action," according to Robert Cutler) and staining his victory. Ultimately a three-judge panel appointed by the chief justice of the state Supreme Court threw the charges out. Vengeful in victory, Curley was vindictive in defeat.[78]

❖   ❖   ❖

Nineteen forty two: what offices were up for election then? Going down the list, Curley must have been tempted to declare for the Senate against Henry Cabot Lodge, but a popular young congressman, Joseph Casey, a New Dealer, would be coming out against him (after Casey disposed of his primary challenger, the seventy-nine-year-old John F. Fitzgerald, making his last race at the instigation of his anti–New Deal son-in-law, Joseph P. Kennedy). Leverett Saltonstall was up for reelection as governor; no, that would be too tough. The House of Representatives? It would be a step down, but he needed a win.[79]

Thomas Hopkinson Eliot was his chosen victim.

Eliot was a Democrat, an idealist, a reformer, a devoted New Dealer, a well-educated, high-minded young man. He was also a Harvard graduate, the grandson of the famous Harvard president, and, most damning of all, the son of a Unitarian minister. Curley must have beamed when he discovered that. For Eliot was the congressman representing such longtime Curley bastions as Irish Catholic Charlestown and the Italian Catholic North End and East Boston, neighborhoods Tobin had lost to Curley and where he could poke fun at what he called Eliot's "unfortunate denomination" in the serene certainty that no one who lived there belonged to it. Bring on "the young man of Harvard"![80]

Every American is in Thomas Eliot's debt. In the first year of the New Deal, just out of law school, Eliot went to Washington to serve in the Roosevelt administration, in time becoming a friend of both the president and Mrs. Roosevelt. As counsel to the Committee on Economic Security, he was the principal drafter of the Social Security Act, which he also shepherded through Congress. He then served as general counsel to the first Social Security Board. He might have been content to spend the rest of his career in government as a high-level lawyer but for Robert Luce, the longtime Republican congressman from the Ninth Congressional District of Massachusetts. In a speech at the Harvard Club in Washington, Luce ventured the benighted opinion that "we" should not look down on the poor and unemployed, because "God made them lazy." Listening in the audience, Eliot felt his blood rise. "Lois, start packing," he said to his wife when he got home. "We're going to run for Congress."

The Ninth District nipped a part of Boston, a shard of Cambridge, and then moved out in an arc encompassing a string of suburbs to the west of Boston. Eliot managed to win his primary in this marginally Republican district against a brace of candidates with Irish names, then ran hard against Luce in the general election. It was 1938, the year of Curley's ill-fated run against Saltonstall. To win, Eliot needed to attract independent and even some Republican votes in the suburbs. These would be difficult to get, however, without disavowing Curley, who was a red flag to these swing voters. But if he cut Curley, he would lose votes in the Irish wards of Boston and Cambridge. In the event, he lost by less than 1 percent. Curley cost him the election. "Curley was my nemesis all the way through," he said years later.

He tried again in 1940 and won. It was a presidential election year, and while FDR lost the Ninth District by eight thousand votes, Eliot won it by eight thousand.

In the 1940 census Massachusetts lost population, so the Republican governor and the Republican state legislature redrew the congressional districts. Eliot found himself in a new district, the Eleventh, made up mostly of heavily Irish and Italian Boston wards. When Curley announced that he would run in the Eleventh in 1942, Eliot got one phone call after another from his Italian-American friends, immigrants or the children of immigrants, delivering variants of the same message: "Sorry, I gotta be with Curley. He gotta my old man a job."[81]

Like James Gallivan in 1918, Eliot made much of Curley's living outside the district. That was the only issue in the campaign, a flavorsome Curley production.

In a civil defense parade through downtown Boston, Curley rode with a skid row bum perched beside him in the back seat of his convertible. "Who's that guy?" the crowd yelled to him along the way. When he reached the reviewing stand on Tremont Street, the dignitaries already there asked the same question. "Oh," he said in a voice that carried out to the audience, "that man is an opponent of mine for Congress. He had no invitation to participate in this fine parade."[82]

Curley had delicious sport with Eliot's religion in Irish Charlestown. "My young opponent is a Unitarian. Do you know what a Unitarian is?" he asked, his voice lathered with incredulity. "A Unitarian is a person who believes that our Lord and Savior is a funny little man with a beard who runs around in his underclothes." Also in Charlestown, Curley gave Eliot a lesson in Urban Political Technique 101.

In the Bunker Hill Day parade, Eliot's car was right behind Curley's open limousine. Suddenly the parade stopped, and a little old lady emerged from the crowd, walked over to Curley, and presented him with a bouquet of flowers. The crowd cheered. Up the hill, around the corner, and out she came again, with a second bouquet. The parade continued, the little old lady keeping pace with it.

The speech Curley delivered that day must have been a rouser because Eliot, seated beside him on the platform, was transported. "He was absolutely magnificent," Eliot recalled. "I began applauding wildly until I noticed my wife in the audience gesturing me to stop." After the speeches, Bishop John Wright shook hands with Eliot but snubbed Curley. It was an editorial gesture. The Catholic hierarchy preferred the Unitarian candidate.

On the Sunday before the primary, Eliot's campaign manager came to see him in a state of high excitement. A woman who had worked for Curley for years had just come into Eliot's headquarters with a tantalizing proposition. She claimed·that Curley had let her down, and that she had in hand a list of all the registered voters in the district who were away in the service—it was the middle of World War II—which she would give to Eliot. He had only to find people to impersonate the missing voters on election day. Knowing a put-up job when he saw one, Eliot declined the offer. If he had taken the bait, the papers would have the story the next morning—of that he was sure.

Come primary day, Eliot traveled to every precinct in his district. In Charlestown, in East Boston, in the North End, and finally, to his increasing exasperation, in Brighton, he saw the same six men get out of the same car and go into the different polling places. "My God," he said, confronting them, "how many people are you voting?" They were impersonating missing servicemen, voting early and often for Curley.[83]

Curley won going away. The Republicans conceded the general election. So, after twenty-eight years, he would be returning to Congress. And, as Thomas Eliot wryly noted, he would take with him the woman who had represented herself as a defector from his camp.[84]

Francis Curley, having joined the Jesuit order, was at Shadowbrook, the Jesuit seminary in western Massachusetts. In the monastic furlong of his training, he was forbidden to have contact with anyone in the outside world. But Curley, who had raised him on Shakespeare, sent him a one-sentence telegram announcing his first victory in five trys in a code that Frank cracked at once: "Richard is himself again."[85]

❖   ❖   ❖   ❖

Fedora

❖   ❖   ❖   ❖

Curley today represents Boston as no other
individual can claim to do. . . .

LOUIS LYONS

It would perhaps be a little regretful that a city
of 770,816 should be run from a jail.

BOSTON HERALD

❖   ❖   ❖   ❖

I n the Taft era, when Curley first went to Washington, tourists could visit the president's office while he was out and test his capacious chair. Even as late as the thirties, according to David Brinkley, a man driving a convertible down Pennsylvania Avenue, caught in a sudden downpour, pulled under the White House portico to raise his top. In the early forties, traces of the sleepy southern town still survived in Washington; attending the Christmas tree-lighting ceremony in 1941, shoppers left their presents on the grass outside the White House, confident of finding them there when they returned. But the pressures of war were inexorably creating the modern capital of the Free World. John Dos Passos, asking his cab driver to hurry, got this revealing reply: "Hurry. Nobody ever used to be in a hurry in Washington."[1]

The quickening pace of life, the sense of contributing to the transcendent enterprise of victory that made time itself seem a scarce war material, had not reached Congress. A glance through the *Congressional Record* for the war years confirms that there was no remission of toxically boring speeches. In an era of action, the nation's laboratory of loquacity could not be still. Brinkley estimates that about 90 percent of the members were, like Curley, "figures from the Victorian past," old men in a young man's war, given to talk and idiosyncracy. Thus Senator McKellar of Tennessee would periodically wander off the Senate floor to urinate against the marble columns in the reception room. Thus a congressional page could tell the exact moment when David Walsh, slumped at his desk, would surrender to sleep: His tongue would cease resisting his dental plate, which, free at last, would slide to the front of his mouth.[2]

"The Congress," Richard Strout, *The New Republic*'s TRB wrote in 1942, "is almost wholly negative; it has shown no leadership for constructive planning in the world crisis." Its Republican members, however, had led in developing an issue that would make careers once the war against fascism was over: the bacillus of domestic communism. By 1944 the Republicans would deploy it for the first time in a presidential campaign, with Thomas E. Dewey charging that those who favored a fourth term for President Roosevelt were communists.[3]

The hive of anticommunism in the House was the newly created Committee on Un-American Activities, a title that would have seemed un-American to Thomas Jefferson. Its chairman, Martin Dies of Lufkin, Texas, was a Democrat; yet intraparty deference did not stop that regular party man, James Curley, from voting against the reauthorization of the Dies committee. For taking this surprisingly liberal position Curley received a congratulatory telegram from Thomas Eliot. ("When Curley did Tom Eliot out of a seat in Congress," an unidentified Harvard professor told *Public Opinion Quarterly*, "every liberal in Massachusetts was in mourning. But when Curley started voting, the surprises began. I don't think Curley failed to support with his vote any single liberal issue of the sort that Tom Eliot would have supported. The fact of the matter is that Curley's record in Congress has been that of a liberal.") Yet two years later, Curley fought a primary campaign against Eliot under the banner of a Dies-like slogan: "Curley or Communism." Curley was a "pragmatist" of Bushian dimension—he would do whatever it took to win.[4]

Anticommunism was not the only feature of the postwar era gestating in wartime Washington. Spending on the war, so critical to so many postwar industries and fortunes, was transforming the federal budget. "The hand that signs the contract is the hand that shapes the future," a Senate report concluded. Huge sums were at stake. By Pearl Harbor, before the United States entered the war, military spending was running at $2 billion a month. "In the first six months of 1942," John Morton Blum writes, "federal procurement officers placed orders for $100 billion of equipment—more than the American economy had ever produced in a single year." By the end of 1943 federal spending exceeded the total output of the entire U.S. economy in 1933.[5]

"If you are going to . . . go to war . . . in a capitalist economy," Roosevelt's secretary of war Henry L. Stimson observed, "you have to let business make money out of the process or business won't work." Most of the money being made out of the war was being made by big business. In 1940, when the surge in defense spending began, 175,000 companies turned out 70 percent of manufacturing output while 100 giant companies produced the remaining 30 percent. By 1943, this ratio had been reversed. "The great bulk of federal funds expended on new industrial construction," Blum writes, "had gone to the privileged one hundred companies." Alarmed at this trend, in early 1942 the Senate voted 82–0 and the House 244–0 to require the Roosevelt administration to appoint a special deputy to help small business get a fairer share of the largesse.[6]

This was the emerging context in which James Curley, seeking the elusive grail of financial security, lent his name to a shady firm involved in procuring contracts for small businesses. Charged with being part of a "front" to defraud contractors, he would be hounded by the Justice Department of the man he had helped to elect, dragged out of a sickbed to be sentenced by a judge deaf to the testimony of his doctors that his multiple ailments were life-threatening, and forty-two years after his first sentence, jailed for the second time in his life. Editorialists would hold him up to public scorn. John Gunther, in his best-selling *Inside the U.S.A.*, would label him "that grotesque old man." Yet at the very time the powers of the land were turning against him, the voters of Boston, as if knowing that holding his old office was the only salve for the shame of his disgrace, would award him his greatest victory.[7]

It all began in the lobby of Washington's Mayflower Hotel, a purlieu that seemed to liberate Curley's avarice—for it was the place where, in 1933, he had asked Frederick Graves, the insurance claims man, "What's in it for me?" The time was June 1941, shortly after the courts had ordered him to pay the City of Boston $500 a week to compensate for the money he had taken from Graves. Curley had stopped to light a cigar when a former Massachusetts political operative with whom he was acquainted, Marshall J. Fitzgerald, approached with another man in tow. This was James G. Fuller, a short, sharp-nosed, balding former encyclopedia salesman. Fitzgerald knew but did not tell Curley that Fuller had a long criminal record—indeed, he had just been bailed out of the District of Columbia jail, where passing bad checks had landed him. This "fast talker," as Curley would call him in testimony before the Special Committee to Investigate the National Defense Program (better known as the Truman committee, after its chairman), persuaded

Curley into becoming president of a firm he was founding, Engineers' Group Inc., which only needed a big-name figurehead like Curley at its helm to boom. "He never talked less than a million, usually one hundred million," Curley told the committee. It's a wonder he didn't swallow his cigar.[8]

Curley testified that he agreed to head Engineers' Group only because he understood it to be a syndicate formed to develop kalunite deposits in Utah, a mineral used in making aluminum, so vital to the war effort. Fuller might conjure with millions, but Curley joined "for patriotic purposes"; he had "no idea" of making a profit; he was acting only "nominally" for the company. "I think there are very few people who could resist an appeal by him"— meaning the magnetic Fuller—"supplemented by the imposing array of outstanding men he claimed were going to be associated with him." These included Donald Wakefield Smith, a former member of the National Labor Relations Board. Curley said he resigned from Engineers' Group in December 1941 on learning that it had nothing to do with kalunite and was in fact advertising itself as a brokerage firm for small businesses seeking to land government contracts.[9]

After a group of New York contractors had paid Engineers' Group a $20,000 retainer without receiving a single contract in return, they took their complaints to the Truman committee, which was how, in hearings held in April 1942, the story came out.

Curley had a tense few hours before the committee. Kalunite was the reason he had joined Engineers' Group, he said, but the committee counsel quoted from a letter on Engineers' Group stationery that Curley had sent to a shoe manufacturer hoping to sell trench shoes to the government. "Mr. Fuller was very skillful with the pen and perhaps I am identifying signatures of mine that were never made," he said when asked to identify his signature. More damning was a letter from "J. F." headed "Dear Governor" and dated October 16, 1941, in the midst of second Tobin. It said that a member of the group had been instrumental in procuring a $67,000 paint contract for a Boston contractor, and that "therefore it is suggested that they contribute something to the campaign in view of the business." Fuller had fled to Mexico and was unavailable to explain what paint had to do with kalunite. Curley said he knew nothing about any paint contract, and agreed with a senator that the group member mentioned in the letter, probably Fitzgerald, was trading on the contractor's "innocence" by pretending to have procured the contract. "It happens every day in the week, Senator," Curley complacently allowed. Yet he was enough embarrassed by his incriminating testimony to promise to resign as the member of the Democratic National Committee from Massachusetts.[10]

After the hearing, Curley later said, Senator Truman told him he had a clean slate and should forget about the investigation. Perhaps; but Truman also assured the press that the committee's inquiry would continue. Not long after, Curley said he heard rumors that the Justice Department had asked the FBI to look into his role in Engineers' Group. The case now went to the attorney general, Francis Biddle. In his memoirs, Biddle says that even though Curley's "profit had been trifling, his activities hardly more than lending his name to promote a fraud," there was sufficient evidence to ask for a grand jury indictment. When Biddle told the president, Roosevelt seemed "a little startled." Curley, he said, had always been loyal to him; and remained a politically important figure in Massachusetts. "I'd like to give him a break, if it were possible," he said. Biddle asked what he had in mind. Roosevelt paused for thought, then said, "Would he be permitted to appear before the grand jury on his own behalf? He's very persuasive."[11]

Though he considered the request "unusual," Biddle could see no objection to it. "Curley appeared before the grand jury shortly afterward," he writes. "He did not testify, but made a speech about himself for an hour. The jury promptly indicted him."[12]

About two weeks before the indictment came down John McCormack, by then House majority leader, wired Roosevelt to ask him to see Curley, who doubtless wanted to make an eleventh-hour personal appeal. The White House copy of this telegram bears an interesting notation across the bottom: "Atty General advises strongly that President see Curley." But Roosevelt rejected Biddle's advice. It was one thing to allow Curley to make a personal appearance before the grand jury, but before the president? That was quite another. Instead his secretary, General Edwin M. Watson, wired back that "it is impossible for him to see Congressman James M. Curley under present circumstances."[13]

Unable to see the president, Curley sent him a "for your eyes only" letter, which he passed along through Biddle. "I have hesitated to write to you about my problem," Curley said, "which is meaningless as contrasted with your major ones, but to me personally it is monumental. . . . Four of my sons are in the armed services and one a novice in the Jesuit Order, and you, a father like myself, can well appreciate the seriousness of the infamous charges leveled against me. . . . A dear friend, outraged by the false and cruel charge, recalled to me the words of Shakespeare in the address of Cardinal Wolsey to Cromwell— 'Had I but served my God with one-half the fervor that I served my King, he would not leave me in my old age naked before my enemies.'" Curley added that he was sure these words could never apply to their thirty-year friendship. They are of course the very lines Curley's autobiography claims he used to tell FDR off for not appointing him ambassador to Italy in 1933. That source also depicts FDR as "behind" Curley's prosecution. Biddle, of course, paints a different picture of a president who gave Curley a potentially saving chance.[14]

On September 17, 1943, Curley, Fuller, and the other officers of Engineers' Group were indicted by a federal grand jury for using the mails to defraud. Would it have made any difference if Curley had appeared before Roosevelt? The scene would have been highly pathetic, a florid replay of Curley's painful importunity during Roosevelt's campaign swing through Massachusetts in 1936. Besides, the Truman committee revelations had cast such a public cloud over Curley that it was probably too late for the president to intervene behind the scenes. Curley had had his chance to talk his way out of the indictment before the grand jury, and in its supreme test, his eloquence had failed him. The disgrace Curley's letter to the president makes clear he would do anything to avoid could not be avoided.

The twenty-one-count indictment charged Engineers' Group with making thirty-two "false and fraudulent" statements about itself to prospective clients. These ranged from the claim that the firm had been in business for twenty-five years, whereas it had just been established, to the claim that it could obtain bank credit for $1 million, whereas it had no assets on which to base any credit, to the claim that it held Federal Housing Administration construction awards totaling $4 million in several states and the District of Columbia, whereas it held no such awards. Engineers' Group mailed these false representations to would-be customers, from whom it received "retainers," its sole capital. To his intimates, Curley later summed up the mistake he had made in lending his name to this dubious business: "The lesson for you boys here is this: 'The spoken word is a word to the wind, and the written word is a political sin.'"

"I have pursued an independent course and refused to be a rubber stamp while serving as a member of Congress," Curley said in his statement to the press, "and shall continue to follow such a course. Indictments, threats or pressure of any character shall not deter me from doing what in my judgement is the best for the American people." Assimilating the third indictment in his career to the insular fears and prejudices of the Boston Irish, he told *Time*, "It's just a political move. I'm being persecuted." "They" were after him—the New Dealers, the reformers, the people who had gotten the country into the war. What Richard Hofstadter once called "the paranoid style in American politics" works best when it is least explicit—when communication between leader and led approximates the efficiency of silence.[15]

Curley was more voluble four years later in an interview for the *Globe* with Joseph Dinneen. "I wasn't indicted for this trumped up offense. I was indicted because I stood athwart the path, a nuisance to the Communists and radical reformers who surrounded [Roosevelt]. I was indicted because I wouldn't go the full distance on the New Deal, and they couldn't get rid of me the way they got rid of Al Smith, Jim Farley, Joe Ely, Joe Kennedy and the company of men who launched Roosevelt. There are none left. They were all forced to walk the plank by that strange crew of starry-eyed, long-haired political sophomores, the liberals and fellow travelers who came aboard with Roosevelt and took over to man the ship. They disguised Communism as Americanism and tried to force it down the throats of experienced political veterans." Curley had been in Washington long enough to pick up and exploit the major theme of Republican attacks on the New Deal and liberalism for the next generation. He would not be the last scoundrel to seek refuge in anticommunism, but it is sad to see one of "the company of men who launched Roosevelt" in the company of Richard M. Nixon and Senator Joseph R. McCarthy.[16]

The indictment was soon voided on technical grounds, but the Justice Department sought—and obtained—a new one. The case would not come to trial for two years.[17]

Meanwhile, Curley served out his term in Congress, gathering his waning energies for his last bold move.

He made news within a month of taking office with a speech urging the administration to earmark 10 percent of all lend-lease funds for China, the idea being that China should do the bulk of the fighting against Japan in Asia, saving "the lives of more than 500,000 Americans." The advice might be geographically whimsical—Japan being an island, and China having no navy to speak of—but it had a certain racial logic. Curley thought that U.S. sailors and marines could not withstand Asian germs. Asia was not "a white man's country," he would say in 1945, after the war; the boys should be brought home fast, before they came down with dreadfully immoral diseases. There was also an anti-Soviet and, the reader will not be surprised to learn, anti-British twist to the advice, since any enlargement of China's share of aid would almost certainly come at the expense of the two leading recipients.[18]

In a bantering letter addressed "Dear Shamus" and partially in Irish dialect, Roosevelt remonstrated with Curley that while the "intintion" of his strategic advice was good, "the ixecution is bum," and asked how in the world he would ever get such vast quantities of supplies into Japanese-occupied China. Curley replied:

My Dear Mr. President:—

It was a source of joy to receive your comforting letter of recent date with reference to forwarding supplies to China and I have, other than by the "Mr. Dooley route," checked up with different groups who are familiar with the terrain and this is the concensus [sic] of their opening which I am enclosing herein.

I do not feel, however, that it is necessary that I should do it for the reason that we are living in the age of miracles and I consider you as the Miracleman of the age. First, when you broke the precedent relative to a Third Term for President with a fourth term shortly if you again drafted; and I, likewise, sometimes believe that I am a miracle-worker myself, having arisen from the dead after being interred four times and returning to the scenes of my youth as part of the most interesting adventure in which America ever engaged.

It is most pleasing, I assure you, to be a party to helping America win the war and later win the peace and to that end, I am doing my full part; three of my sons, like your own, are in the service and I closed up the mansion on the Jamaicaway, Boston, and have taken a modest little house in Washington to camp here until you win the war.[19]

Roosevelt's use of the Irish dialect, meant in good fun (this was some months before Curley's indictment) and taken that way, is also revealing. The year before Roosevelt had expressed what Geoffrey

C. Ward carefully calls "something of his underlying view of the real position of Jews and Catholics in the United States" in a conversation at the White House with Leo T. Crowley, an economist who had just been appointed to a government post and who was a Catholic, and Henry Morgenthau, Jr., his treasury secretary, a Jew. "Leo, you know this is a Protestant country," he said, "and the Catholics and Jews are here under sufferance. It is up to you"—meaning both Crowley and Morgenthau—"to go along with anything that I want. . . ." The statement is not attractive; the president was only too conscious of his power as a member of the Protestant ascendancy. Other groups lived in the United States only "under sufferance": endured, put up with, at best tolerated. Subordinate peoples, they were expected to do what they were told. Had something of this seigneurial attitude always been at work in Roosevelt's dealings with Curley, Al Smith, Joseph P. Kennedy, and other Irish-American figures with whom he had fallen out over the years? We begin to see that Curley's decade-long feeling that Roosevelt had used him to get elected and then summarily dropped him as if he did not matter had some basis, if not in the facts of the 1932 campaign then in the antecedent fact of the president's attitude toward people like Curley. In this regard at any rate, Roosevelt had not transcended the prejudices of the class he was often accused of betraying. He expected the kind of deference from members of subordinate groups that Curley had refused to give to the Boston Brahmins, and that he had shown the Boston Irish in the great positive lesson of his career, that they did not have to give either.[20]

This exchange of letters between Curley and Roosevelt—the last between them—thus sums up a latent strain in their whole relation.

Catholics and Jews may have appeared to FDR as sharing outsider status in Protestant America, but in Catholic Boston only the Jews were outsiders. As far back as 1902 Robert Woods, the sociologist of the "zone of emergence," noted the religious cleavage: "The Irish have made great efforts to win the Italians to the Democratic party. They are co-religionists, and they can love each other for their common enmity to the Jew." Father Coughlin still remained popular in Boston. Lack of money forced the radio priest off the airwaves in 1940, but the Christian Front, a quasi-military profascist organization he had set up in 1938, flourished in certain Boston neighborhoods. Christian Fronters denounced the "Jew

Deal" and at their military camp in upstate New York took rifle practice using a likeness of FDR as a target. If they had been privy to his private views, they might have picked a different one.[21]

Before Pearl Harbor, Francis P. Moran, the leader of the Christian Front in New England, conducted Nazi propaganda meetings at Hibernian Hall, in Curley's old Tammany ward, at which he showed the Nazi film *Victory in the West*, praised the America Firster Charles Lindbergh, scalded President "Rosenfelt," and pelted scurrilities on "the Jews." Ordered by police commissioner Joseph F. Timilty (a Curley appointee) to suspend meetings after Pearl Harbor, Moran confined himself to boosting the circulation of Father Coughlin's paper, *Social Justice*, which, wrote a correspondent reporting on "Coughlin's new capital" in *The Nation*, "continues to be the inspiration of all the little Fuhrers in America." Moran had great success selling a newspaper that printed the "Protocols of the Elders of Zion," a vintage anti-Semitic document, and named Mussolini its Man of the Year for 1940. Until suppressed as seditious by Attorney General Biddle, *Social Justice* was sold outside every Catholic church in the Boston diocese.° When Father Edward L. Curran, a Coughlin ally, spoke in Boston in early 1942, he drew an audience of twelve hundred to cheer his acidulous comments about Britain and the Soviet Union along with his barely disguised defeatism, especially his insistence that the country's shores were going undefended while the fleet was across the seas.[22]

As Donald Grant pointed out in *The Nation*, Curran's visit had "an interesting sequel." To build its circulation among the South Boston and Charlestown Irish, the *Boston Herald* had hired away the star sports columnist of the *Boston Post*, Bill Cunningham, installing him as a front-page pundit on the war. Cunningham soon began to push Father Curran's line about the New England coast being defenseless. Two days after one of these Sunday articles— which Cunningham introduced with "I heard a naval story con-

---

° And not only in Irish neighborhoods, but in Italian ones as well. Rendered politically powerless by the gerrymandering of Irish politicians (of 110 City Council members elected between 1924 and 1949, only four were Italian, and as late as 1930, only one Italian had been elected to the state legislature)—living in one of the worst slums in the Western world, and holding some of the worst jobs in the city, until Pearl Harbor made them "100 percent Americans"—Boston's eighty thousand Italians looked on "Il Duce" as a military leader whose conquest of Ethiopia brought them what they could not get from their fellow Bostonians, a measure of respect.

FEDORA ❖ 451

cerning Boston harbor that would literally curl your hair"—David
Walsh took to the Senate floor to echo (and augment) the panic the
article had sown among many of his constituents. "The day may
come," he said, "when we may have to bring back from the four
corners of the world our depleted navy to be a source of defence
for our own shores." This was just what the Axis powers wanted to
hear: defending America, the navy could not be used to press the
war against them. The next week their radio propagandists "repeated Walsh's remarks with glee."[23]

"One of the most outspoken isolationists, Coughlinites, and anti-
Semites in America," to quote a recent historian, Father Curran was
invited to appear in Boston several more times—most sensationally,
as the official city speaker at the joint Evacuation Day–St. Patrick's
Day proceedings at South Boston High School in 1942. Two thousand
people filled the auditorium and a thousand more listened through
loudspeakers in the gym. Mayor Tobin, conveniently, was in Florida;
Governor Saltonstall had another commitment; but Cardinal
O'Connell gave Curran his official approval. Irish Catholic men and
women whose sons would soon be giving their lives to defeat fascism
in the Battle of the Atlantic, at Guadalcanal, and on Omaha Beach
heard him out with a respect they would never have given a secular
figure with the same views. After all, he was a priest. "And whatever
else you may say about him, the average Irish American is loyal to the
Catholic Church," Donald Grant wrote. "If he is sorry for himself and
repeats Social Justice nonsense, it is because he has been given his
cue by Catholic priests." The Boston Irish had broken with deference
democracy long since, but their civic consciences were still in thrall
to the fallible representatives of a church that expected unquestion-
ing deference to its priests. "When I ask you to do anything," Cardinal O'Connell had told them, "trust me and do it." Who were they
distinguish one priest from another? They had been taught to obey,
not to make distinctions among religious authorities. "The fact is that
the Boston Catholic laity are in leading strings to the clergy and are
impotent," Katherine Loughlin wrote in *Commonweal*. "In an excess
of goodness, docility, almost infantilism, they respond to every dictum of the clergy as to their individual lives and their homes and the
support of every authorized ecclesiastical activity."[24]

The unexampled moral authority enjoyed by Catholic priests
in Boston makes their failure to denounce anti-Semitism in the city
a lasting shame. People would have listened if they had spoken out;

but they kept silent. The press kept silent. Mayor Tobin and Governor Saltonstall, fearing to offend the Irish vote, kept silent, while gangs of Irish boys beat Jewish boys in the time of the Holocaust.

The outrages began in earnest as early as 1939, when Jews in Dorchester, a district roughly split between Irish and Jewish Americans, were shouldered off the sidewalk by Irish gangs. After Pearl Harbor the streets were blacked out at night, and in the darkness the incidents increased. Irish boys would lie in wait for Jewish boys as they left the Hecht Neighborhood House off Blue Hill Avenue—also known as "Jew Hill Ave"—and beat them bloody. There were eight such incidents in July 1943 and eleven in September. These were not "fair" fights. Always there were more Irish boys; always they were bigger than the Jewish boys. Sometimes the Irish toughs would miscalculate; three of them once jumped an amateur Jewish boxer, who laid them out. But the fear was mostly on one side, the disgrace all on the other.

October brought the worst incident of all. Jacob Hodas and Harvey Blaustein, both seventeen, were being severely beaten by an Irish gang when the police arrived. Instead of arresting the gang members, the police dispersed them and arrested the two Jews for protesting their decision to release the Irish boys. Held overnight at Police Station 11, Hodas and Blaustein were beaten with rubber hoses by ranking officers of the Boston Police Department who called them "yellow Jews." Shortly thereafter, an Irish Catholic judge found Hodas and Blaustein guilty of taking part in an "affray" and fined them $10 each.

This was too much for decent Catholic opinion to bear. Frances Sweeney, a courageous liberal Catholic, put the blame where it belonged. "These attacks on Jewish children are the complete responsibility of Governor Saltonstall, Mayor Tobin, the church and the clergy—all of whom have for three years buck-passed and ignored the tragedy." (When a reporter from *P.M.*, the liberal New York paper, had asked Saltonstall to comment on the reports of anti-Semitic outrages, the governor "shouted him down and had him physically ejected from his office.") In a radio address denouncing the judge's decision, the *Globe*'s Joseph Dinneen identified anti-Semitism as "the cornerstone of Fascism" and warned the Boston Irish that "every time you listen to stories about Jews, and I mean unfavorable stories, critical stories, you're listening to Nazi propaganda, and, if you repeat those stories yourself, you're spreading Nazi propaganda, enemy propaganda. . . . No matter what anyone tells you, there are

Jewish boys, hundreds of thousands of them fighting and dying in the U.S. Army, the Navy, the Marine Corps and the Air Force, so you can grow up in the kind of free world your fathers knew." This was splendid, and this very point of Jewish participation in the war was the heart of a profoundly important speech given by Dinneen's future subject, James Michael Curley.[25]

Curley spoke on the House floor, but his real audience was the Boston Irish. In the taverns and war plants of Boston, members of the Christian Front were circulating vile squibs like this one, called "The First American":

> First American killed in Pearl Harbor—John J. Hennessy
> First American to sink a Jap ship—Colin P. Kelly
> First American to sink a Jap ship with torpedo—John P. Buckley
> Greatest American air hero—"Butch" O'Hare
> First American killed at Guadalcanal—John J. O'Brien
> First American to get four new tires—Abraham Lipshitz[26]

Using some of the same statistics and anecdotes from his immigration speech of a generation before, Curley gave his constituents a history lesson on Jewish valor, from the three thousand Jews who fought in the Revolutionary War to the two hundred thousand who served in World War I—constituting 4 percent of all U.S. troops, though Jews were only 3 percent of the population. Fifteen thousand Jews were wounded in the World War, he pointed out, "and some twenty-eight hundred made the supreme sacrifice that free government might continue to be the heritage of America."

"The record of achievement by the people of Jewish faith in the present war," he continued, "is now being written in their blood." And for the next twenty minutes he read an incomplete list of Jews who had been awarded Purple Hearts, Silver Stars, and Distinguished Service decorations. They ranged from "Pvt. (1st Class) Leslie Aaron, 23, of Oak Grove, L.I., Purple Heart. Wounded in action in the South Pacific" to "Lt. Arthur M. Zuckerman, 25, Army Air Force, of Los Angeles, Ca. Purple Heart. Killed in action in the South Pacific" by way of "Corp. Jacob Lifschitz, 23, of Brooklyn, New York. Wounded in action in North Africa." And they included the first American who really blew up a "Jap ship," "Sgt. Meyer Levin, 25, Army Air Forces, of Brooklyn: Distinguished Flying Cross, Silver Star, 2 Oak Leaf Clusters, and Purple Heart." "As Captain Colin Kelly's bombardier," Curley read, "he

launched bombs which sank the Japanese battleship Haruna off the
Philippines, later sank an enemy cargo ship at Coral Sea, took part
in more than 60 combat missions; died in the act of saving his crew
mates when a Flying Fortress on a reconnaissance flight crashed in
a storm off New Guinea." Together, and with men of other nation-
alities and other creeds, an American named Kelly and an American named Levin had sunk that enemy battleship. This was the
America of Al Smith's dream, a country beyond bigotry, invincible
in its patchwork fraternity.

Curley's list fills sixteen pages of the *Congressional Record*. He
called it "worthy of study by every citizen who still harbors the
illusion that men of Jewish faith are lacking in courage, loyalty, or
full sense of patriotic duty for a common country." And after hearing it, no one could doubt the truth of the speech's title "Service
and Sacrifice of the Jewish People Entitle Them to the Respect of
Their Fellow Americans and an End of Jewish Persecution Here
and Abroad."[27]

When Curley finished reading his list of Jewish war heroes,
majority leader McCormack asked for the attention of the chair.
"The gentleman from Massachusetts has always been a leader in
progressive thought and action," he said. "Above all he has exemplified and inspired others to follow the noblest traditions for which
our country stands, first and foremost being tolerance on the part of
all for the other; he is a man who has always condemned intoler-
ance and bigotry in any form." Yet this was only one face of the
truth. For if Curley denounced bigotry, he also encouraged it by
pandering to the conspiratorial worldview the Know-Nothing per-
secutions had engendered among the Boston Irish. He had made his
political (and personal) fortune by encouraging them to blame others for their troubles. True, he had never encouraged them to
blame the Jews. The Brahmins, the Yankees, the "State-Street
wrecking crew," the "bankers"—these were his targets. But he
had imbued his people with the habit of suspicion. They needed
scapegoats, and he had fed the appetite of their need. That a small
minority of them (Lemke, Father Coughlin's presidential candidate
in 1936, got 11 percent of the vote in Boston Irish working-class
neighborhoods compared to 2 percent nationwide) had picked the
wrong scapegoats does not exculpate Curley.[28]

A month later Curley made another speech denouncing Hitler's
policy of "extermination and murder." A Jewish group had given

him a book documenting the destruction of Polish Jewry, which he cited movingly. "I could read you passages from this book," he said, "that would bring tears to your eyes: passages describing starvation, torture, and deliberate massacre; stories telling of the deliberate violation of families: stories so grim as to make a decent individual sick and accompanied by photographs of dead starved children more horrifying than the stories themselves." He urged the State Department to make every effort to admit Jewish refugees to the United States. Instead, the man Roosevelt had appointed ambassador to Italy over Curley, Assistant Secretary of State Breckinridge Long, was actively denying sanctuary to the Jews, blocking a plan advanced by the American Jewish Committee to bribe Romanian authorities to evacuate seventy thousand Jews, and ordering the American minister at Bern to stop revealing details of the Holocaust.[29]

The same man who praised the "service and sacrifice of the Jewish people," eloquently evoking his moral nausea on reading of Hitler's atrocities, could also stoop to the despicable stunt described in this diary entry of Jonathan Daniels, a Roosevelt aide who was the son of FDR's old boss from the Wilson administration, and was a close friend of Congressman Joseph Casey, a frequent visitor to the White House:

> Casey told some amusing stories about ex-Governor James Michael Curley. One that he and some friends, who share his anti-Semitism, spent the other evening in the bar and dining rooms of the Mayflower Hotel, getting bellhops to continually page Colonel Finkelstein, Major Cohen; they even paged an admiral with a Jewish name.

The incident occurred in late 1942 or early 1943, against a background of charges that Jews were avoiding the draft or serving only in above-the-battle positions as high officers. Curley was promoting the very stereotype he later denounced. He was a hero to break your heart.[30]

❖   ❖   ❖

"**D**ear Lem," reads the letter from Kirk Le Moyne Billings's twenty-eight-year-old friend, who had lately been given a medical discharge from the navy. "As I may have told you, I am returning to Law School at Harvard (not Johns Hopkins) in the Fall—and then if something good turns up while I am there I will run for it. I have my eye on something pretty good now if it comes through." The "something pretty good" John F. Kennedy was referring to in this letter of February 26, 1945, to his Choate classmate was almost certainly the congressional seat held by James Curley. On the night of his reelection to Congress in November 1944, Curley announced that he would be a candidate for the office of mayor of Boston in the city election to be held a year later. Yet he was deeply in debt. "My finances were so depleted when I ran for reelection against Eliot," he says in his autobiography, "that I kept down campaign expenses by sending postcards to households in the district." Nevada had long since emptied his safes; the General Equipment judgment had cost him $50,000; legal fees for his Engineers' Group defense loomed inexorably. He needed somewhere in the neighborhood of $100,000 to make the run. He got it from Joseph P. Kennedy; negotiations between Kennedy and Curley were going forward even as Jack Kennedy was writing to Billings. Kennedy's father was about to buy him a seat in Congress.³¹

Such is the conclusion reached by Nigel Hamilton in his meticulously researched multivolume life of John F. Kennedy. Hamilton says that sometime in late 1944 Joseph Kennedy approached Curley with an offer to fund his inclinations: Kennedy would pay off Curley's debts, finance his campaign, and subsidize the salary of the former police commissioner Joseph Timilty (whom Saltonstall, in the wake of the scandal surrounding the police beating of the two Jewish boys, had not reappointed) as his campaign manager. All Curley had to do was run for mayor—and resign his congressional seat if he won.³²

The elder Kennedy had hoped to launch his namesake, Joseph P. Kennedy, Jr., into politics. Young Joe was willing enough. Writing to his father from England, where he served as a navy pilot during World War II, he said he was sorry to hear that his grandfather, John F. Fitzgerald, had been beaten by Congressman Casey in the 1942 Senate primary, adding "Maybe I'll get a shot at Casey when this thing is over." In August 1944, however, he was killed in a heroic aerial exploit over the English Channel.³³

If not Joe, then Jack: Kennedy would found his dynasty, and in so doing, extend Curley's rejection of deference democracy from the city to the nation. The example of Al Smith did not deter him. His son's immersion in Harvard would garb his Catholicism in tweed, and inherited wealth would shield him from Tammany stereotypes. So different in so many ways—if only Curley had pos-

sessed a trace of Kennedy's financial genius!—Curley and Joseph
P. Kennedy were alike in their drive for vindication, Curley for
himself, Kennedy for his sons. But both men also achieved it for
their tribe, their people. Isaiah Berlin uses the image of the bent
twig to convey the reactive energy of nationalism: bend a twig, and
it snaps back. Boston had bent the twig of Irish resentment in the
1850s as it was not bent elsewhere in America. In the twentieth
century it snapped back, producing a Curley for the city, a Kennedy for the country.

If not Joe, then Jack: Kennedy sent his second son to Joe Kane,
his cousin and a sage of Boston politics, for an appraisal of his potential. Kane saw in the sickly young man the makings of a politician. "He has poise, a fine Celtic map. A most engaging smile," he
reported back. Kennedy should "buy him in."[34]

Kennedy's money enabled Curley to mount a radio campaign—his only alternative, since he would get no help from the
newspapers, which, having lost all pretense of objectivity as far as
Curley was concerned, would promote his opponents and ignore
him. Moreover, fewer and fewer people went to rallies by this
time. Radio was the only way to get his message out. He would win
this one on his voice or not at all.

❖   ❖   ❖

To the student of Boston's mayoral campaigns, the pattern is
unmistakable. Commanding the front page in the 1890s and
early 1900s, by the beginning of the Curley era local political news
had lost space to national news. By its end, news of the world and
of the U.S. role in the world had largely pushed Boston news of any
kind to the inside pages. An alienation of interest, a clash between
the reader's life and the life described by the newspaper, had set
in. The politics of daily needs practiced by Mary Parker Follett at
the Highland Union and by James Michael Curley at the Tammany
Club seemed a distant memory in the post–New Deal Leviathan
state at the dawn of the atomic age. This loss of scale, this displacement of the local by the global, was accompanied by a dispersion of
tribal identity. In the world, whether they liked it or not, the Boston Irish lost some of what made them a people apart—the bad
with the good, the prejudice with the pride. But just at the moment when the forces making for the dissolution were in the ascendancy, just when the word "suburbia" was about to come into

'common use, they made one last grab for the old solidarity. James Michael Curley would be the candidate of their nostalgia for a past from which they were being rapidly swept away.

Maurice Tobin had been elected governor in 1944, with one year to go in his second mayoral term. Briefly there was talk of holding a special election to fill his seat, but to save costs in wartime, John E. Kerrigan of South Boston, thirty-eight, president of the City Council, was elected by his colleagues to serve as acting mayor until January 1946. He was in office only a few months, however, when he mysteriously disappeared. For weeks no one at City Hall knew where he was. Finally he turned up at the Hotel St. Charles in New Orleans. His office put out a story that he was there to study "municipal procedure and recreational facilities," but the truth slowly filtered out: he had fallen for a show girl whom he had first seen in Boston and then pursued to New Orleans. This untimely infatuation considerably lessened the advantages of his incumbency in the mayoral race.

Quitting Kerrigan's camp in disgust, Kerrigan's campaign manager tartly remarked that New Orleans was hardly known as a model of civic government worthy of such prolonged study. William Arthur Reilly, another mayoral candidate, flayed Kerrigan on his disappearance: "On what days were you in New Orleans, Mr. Kerrigan, and what were you doing there? What recreational activities or municipal procedures did you investigate there? What public officials in New Orleans did you consult? Name three—name two—name one!"[35]

Reilly, Curley's chief rival in the race, had baggage of his own. He was the sort of young, well-educated, well-spoken, reform-minded candidate that Maurice Tobin had been—indeed, Tobin and his brother James had put him in the race—and that was one of his troubles. Tobin had proved a better candidate than mayor. Not only did his budget cuts cost him votes in the neighborhoods in 1941, but his failure to significantly reduce the city's tax burden had in addition weakened support for him and for candidates like him among key figures in the city elite. In a surprisingly pro-Curley column, William Mullins, the voice of the Yankee Protestants in the *Herald*, wrote that "events of the past eight years have distinctly discredited the fashion plate type of mayor." Like Tobin, Reilly was of that type.[36]

Reilly's other trouble was that he had been Tobin's fire commissioner during the worst disaster in Boston's history, the fire at

the Cocoanut Grove nightclub in November 1942 that killed 490
people. The inquest into the calamity stained many reputations—
rumors were widespread that only the vote of a single grand juror
had kept Maurice Tobin himself from being indicted on the charge
of accepting bribes from the nightclub's owner—and though
Reilly had not been indicted, a fire inspector under him was, and in
the campaign "the issue of the Cocoanut Grove Fire kept on crop-
ping up to the embarrassment of Reilly and Tobin. . . ."[37]

Reilly nevertheless had the endorsement of the people who
mattered. "To elect anyone except Mr. Reilly . . . ," the *Post* stiffly
noted, "would be to 'let down' various groups of able citizens, who
have got together for the first time in a quarter of a century to plan
for the postwar future of the city." On that day the *Post* ran three
pro-Reilly stories headlined VETERANS FOR REILLY, ASK WOMEN TO RALLY
TO REILLY, and LASHES OUT AT CURLEY RECORD, without a single story reporting what Curley had been saying in his fifteen-minute radio
addresses. Reilly spoke effectively against Curley: "Whether by
reason of his record, his age, or his pending indictment, Mr. Curley
does not fit in with Boston's plans for its future." Reilly even raised
the question about him: "Mr. Curley's public career was practically coincident with the period of Boston's decline, and I doubt
whether that is just a coincidence." But just when these arguments
had been repeated often enough to cross the threshold of public
attention, a sudden tragedy supervened.[38]

Paul Curley, thirty-two, died.

Helen McDonough, up early for Sunday Mass, found his body
in the living room. Paul called her "Nell," as did his father, who
called all his women servants that, Helen and Mary and Agnes
alike. "I know you'll always take care of me, Nell," Paul once confided in her. "I'll never die alone." But he had.

Helen could hear Curley stirring upstairs. Looking in at Paul's
door, he shouted to Gertrude, "His Nibs didn't come home last
night." While Curley was in the bathroom, Helen rushed up to
Gertrude in the bedroom. "Missus, get up quick," she said. "Paul
is dead!" Gertrude broke the news to Curley.

Paul had been a cross to bear. Repeatedly Curley had had to
choose between his oldest living son and Gertrude, whose innate
refinement got the better of her Franciscan charity when it came to
dealing with drunken men. At one Thanksgiving dinner, Curley
ordered Paul to leave the table for drunkenness, an action which

must have been deeply disturbing to his domestic ideal, his Every-man's longing for a normal, happy family. Paul, who had had scar-let fever as a child, had been under treatment for years for a heart condition; the army had turned him down when he tried to enlist. Knowing his son was sickly, knowing he drank to oblivion, Curley was haunted by the thought of Paul's someday being found dead in the gutter. This dread of disgrace will seem discreditable only to those who have never had to fight negative stereotypes for "re-spectability." Irish-American children were raised with the bur-den of maintaining their family's reputation. A standard argument for being "good" was that being "bad" would reflect poorly on one's parents. Paul, who loved his father, hurt his father in just that way. And that must have tormented him.[39]

With Paul dead in his own house, Curley no longer had to fear that he would die in the gutter. With Paul dead, family tensions would be relieved. With Paul dead, public sympathy would flow his way. That is why, when Gertrude told him about Paul, the first thing he said was, "That takes care of the election." She was shocked and so are we.[40]

"Too long a sacrifice turns the heart to stone"—Yeats's line applies here. Death and grief had made Curley hard. The measure of our disappointment in him for his callous and calculating reac-tion is the measure of what he had suffered.

As Curley's remaining children streamed home for the fu-neral—Lieutenant George Curley from the battleship USS *Caro-lina*, Corporal Richard Dennis from Guam, Lieutenant Leo Curley from Moffet Field in California, Machinist's Mate George Dennis from his naval air squadron, Francis Curley from the Jesuit novi-tiate—the electorate turned in sympathy to the grief-stricken old man.[41]

After a decent interval Reilly resumed the attack: "You and your children are paying—and will be paying for the next 40 years—for Curley's debts, Curley's waste, and Curley's folly," he said. Speaking plainest truth, he added, "what Curley has always lacked is any concept of public office as a public trust." The head-lines portended one result: JEWISH LEADERS SUPPORT REILLY, K OF C HEAD FOR REILLY, NOTED JURIST FOR REILLY, MORE VETERANS FOR REILLY, TRIUMPH FOR REILLY SEEN, LOOK FOR HUGE REILLY VICTORY TODAY.[42]

But in a saturation radio campaign, Curley's golden voice sounded a message plausible to thousands of returning servicemen

and other Bostonians fearful of what the postwar period might
bring: "Curley gets things done!"

When the results were in—Curley, 112,000; Kerrigan, 60,000;
Reilly, 45,000—the *Post* could only wonder at "the amazing Mr.
Curley." He had won nineteen of twenty-two wards, carrying his
own ward in Jamaica Plain and by four votes even capturing Ward 5
in the Back Bay. It was not only his biggest victory margin; it was
the biggest any mayoral candidate had ever received. Curley was
back on top, and he meant to stay there. The day after the election
he sported a new license plate on his car, number 5, to signify his
intention of seeking his fifth term even before he had started his
fourth. "He is the personal hero of a substantial and loyal segment
of the city's population," the *Post* reluctantly concluded. Sympathy played a part in his victory, but that alone doesn't account for
its magnitude. More was involved: his message, his reputation for
effectiveness, the appeal of his personality in an age of bureaucracy, nostalgia for tribal solidarity.[43]

The morning after the election he had breakfast in bed. Coming downstairs with a batch of telegrams in his hands, he lost his
footing, let go of the telegrams, and slid down the banister, landing
on his feet. "It wouldn't do to have a dead Mayor on your hands so
early," he quipped as the red-and-yellow envelopes streamed
down to the hall floor around him.[44]

❖ ❖ ❖

Entering politics when Queen Victoria still sat on her throne,
Curley had lived on into the age of social science. The psychol-
ogist Jerome Bruner, along with a colleague from the Laboratory of
Social Relations at Harvard, Sheldon Korchin, conducted an intensive preelection survey of voter attitudes in the Boston mayoral
campaign of 1945. Published in *Public Opinion Quarterly*, the case
study "The Boss and the Vote" is full of interesting bits. During the
campaign Bruner and Korchin remarked to Curley that he could
not have designed a better field to run in with two major Irish candidates and three other minor candidates splitting the anti-Curley
vote. If he had had "one good Irishman" against him, they said, he
wouldn't have had a chance. "Curley, who is nothing if not a real-
ist, agreed readily." They documented Curley's usual skill in electioneering: "When Kerrigan appeared to be getting too strong,

several known members of the Curley entourage went out and talked publicly about placing bets on Reilly to make it seem as if he were the man most feared"—and vice versa if Reilly's chances looked to be improving. Just as he had mailed copies of his immigration speeches to households in Jewish neighborhoods in 1914, they noted, so Curley mailed copies of his paean to the Jewish fighting man to those same neighborhoods in 1945. They found, unsurprisingly, that Curley won 66 percent of voters with below-average incomes; 59 percent of the Irish vote, 59 percent of the Italian vote, and 37 percent of the Jewish vote (14 points above the amount received by his nearest rival). He had also won 33 percent of the Yankee Protestant vote; *that* was a surprise. So was Curley's winning 58 percent of the vote of those between ages twenty-one and twenty-nine, compared to only 43 percent of those age fifty and older. Glossing this last finding, the authors wrote, "Many of the young supporters of Curley do not know at first hand his transgressions but have only 'heard about them.'" They had been born into the Curley legend. The Curley of history was already on his way to the absolution of *The Last Hurrah.*

The researchers calculated that Curley may have known personally or at least met fully eleven thousand of the people who voted for him, and found that he had given money to three people they randomly interviewed "in the darkest days of the Depression when they were completely broke." Even his core voters knew Curley was dishonest; "He's a lousy crook," one said. "You can never be sure of his motives," said another. But they thought no better of the other candidates. "Oh they're all the same. That's what politics is." One "intelligent voter" put it this way: "In Boston, as elsewhere, politicians will get their percentage. But with Curley, politics is like R. H. Macy: big turnover and a small cut on everything. The others do nothing and take a big slice anyway." Such cynical realism had sustained Curley's career.[45]

❖   ❖   ❖

Curley did not take a big slice of the retainers Engineers' Group had mulcted from contractors—a "trifling" profit, according to Attorney General Biddle. In the roughly six months of its existence, Engineers' Group had hauled in $60,000, but it had "dissipated" most of this on hotel bills and entertainment expenses aimed at luring new customers. Lack of profit, however, was no defense against the charge of mail fraud; "the offense was complete when a scheme to defraud has been devised," in the words of the indictment.[46]

Franklin Roosevelt had died in April 1945 ("Well, the son-of-a-bitch is dead," Curley told Francis over the telephone. "Maybe I won't go to jail after all"); Harry Truman was now president. Just before Curley's trial was to begin, on the heels of the Boston election, Speaker Sam Rayburn and majority leader John McCormack asked Truman's new attorney general, Tom Clark, to drop the case. Speaking for Truman, Clark turned them down. Truman had chaired the hearing in 1942 at which Curley's professions of kalunite had come into conflict with evidence touching on shoe manufacturing and painting contractors, and he may have formed his own opinion of Curley's guilt.[47]

Moreover, as a Missouri politician who owed his career to Tom Pendergast, the head of the Kansas City political machine, Truman could not afford to be lenient to yet another tainted pol. Until his conviction for tax evasion in 1939, "Boss" Pendergast had been the real thing; not for nothing was the Capitol Building in Jefferson City, Missouri, known as Uncle Tom's Cabin. Vice President Truman had flown to Kansas City in an army bomber to attend Pendergast's funeral, and President Truman continued to pay dues to the Jackson Democratic Club run by Pendergast's nephew James, and to pull the strings of the machine in congressional elections. The "Truman gang" he had brought to Washington was already notorious for its sleaziness. "The composite impression," I. F. Stone writes, "was of big-bellied, good-natured guys who knew a lot of dirty jokes, spent as little time in their offices as possible, saw Washington as a chance to make useful 'contacts,' and were anxious to get what they could for themselves out of the experience. . . . The Truman era was the era of the moocher. The place was full of Wimpys who could be had for a hamburger." If the Justice Department dropped the case against Curley, it would only reinforce this politically damaging impression of Truman's presidency.[48]

A week after Curley's seventy-first birthday, the three chief officers of Engineers' Group, Curley, Fuller, and Smith, went on trial in the federal district court in Washington. Curley's lawyers depicted him as a dupe, a victim of the smooth-talking Fuller. But at least some of the evidence could not be squared with that portrait. The special assistant to the attorney general John M. Kelley, Jr., one of two prosecutors handling the case, pointed in particular to a conversation a sworn witness reported having had with Curley. The witness, a Chicago contractor, had come to Washington to discuss signing up with Engineers' Group. He met Curley in the anteroom of the firm's office on Seventeenth Street. Curley said he was waiting for a telephone call to go through to a young man who had developed a new method of making high-octane gas. He had just secured a contract from the Air Corps to build a plant to refine this gasoline, Curley claimed, and was about to break the good news to the inventor. "Do you see the significance of that?" Kelley asked the jury. "There was the president saying, 'We have just got a contract from the Air Force to build a new trial plant.' The president of the concern." The air force contract, the young inventor, and the high-octane gas were all inventions—sucker bait.⁴⁹

The trial lasted into early January, with the prosecution calling over a score of witnesses, and the defense calling only a character witness for Smith, and none of the defendants taking the stand. Through most of it Curley was accompanied by George and Leo, both in their navy uniforms. Curley himself wore four service stars in his lapel for each of his children and stepchildren who had served in the war. In his summation to the jury Curley's lawyer, William E. Leahy, who was selective service director for the District of Columbia, made the point of this martial display explicit: "And he wouldn't at this time of his life, and at this time in his country's need, with his right hand shake the hand of his sons and bid them to the service of their country, and then turn and join in the violation of one of its laws."⁵⁰

Leahy appealed to the judge in the case, James M. Proctor, a Hoover appointee, to direct the jury to find Curley not guilty, arguing that the government had not furnished enough evidence against him. But prosecutor Kelley cited testimony from other witnesses who said that Curley was present when they signed their contracts with Engineers' Group. "Must we entertain the presumption that Curley was peeling an apple or looking out the window?" he asked Judge Proctor, who rejected Leahy's appeal. Curley's name must go to the jury with those of the others.⁵¹

Before the verdict came the inauguration: Curley was sworn in as mayor in ceremonies held before an overflow crowd at Symphony Hall. When Judge Field, the chief justice of the Massachusetts Supreme Court, halted over some words in the oath of office, Curley, "who has some acquaintance with the oath," the *Globe* wryly noted, "quietly supplied them."

Curley began his long speech with himself. "God willing, I shall have been Chief Executive for sixteen years at the end of my term"—a Boston record. "Could any Bostonian ask for more?" He then turned to the city, pronouncing its condition "most drab" and outlining an ambitious program of public works to spark its postwar revival, including razing the El, constructing a new bridge across the Charles River, sinking a major highway, and building a parking garage under the Boston Common. He promised to do all this and more by borrowing $10 million from the state legislature on the "assurance" that he would attract $150 million in new construction to the city within a few months' time. He would also ask the legislature to declare a moratorium on appeals to the appellate tax board. That way he could fulfill his campaign promise to cut taxes on householders in the neighborhoods by raising taxes on downtown businesses. "In other words," the *Herald* wrote, "he proposes to make the property owners in downtown Boston pay for his program by closing to them any legal recourse to the present excessive valuations or even add to them." This was Curleyism in its classic economy-killing form.[52]

Curley could not long bask in the glow of what he called "the happiest day of my life," however. He had unfinished business in Washington.

The jurors in the mail fraud case, nine white men, one "colored" man, and three white women, deliberated a day and a half, not reaching their verdict until nearly 11:30 P.M. on January 18. Curley intended to fly back to Boston that evening, but had to cancel his reservations to await their decision. The Eastern Airlines flight he would have taken had the jury been quicker crashed in Connecticut, killing all seventeen passengers aboard.[53]

He was found guilty of ten of the fourteen counts of the indictment against him. His possible sentence was not so severe as Fuller's, who was already serving time in federal prison for another fraud conviction: sixty-seven years and a $23,000 fine. But at forty-seven years and $19,000, it was severe enough. He stared hard at the jurors as they were polled for their verdict, which he received standing up. Then he sat down with a sigh.[54]

"Three Cheers for James Michael Curley," an old-timer shouted in a quavering voice, "the greatest man alive!" The crowd of one thousand waiting in the cold outside Back Bay station the evening after the trial gave out with the cheers. "God bless you, Governor!" someone yelled. "We don't care what Washington thinks of you," yelled another, "Boston loves you!" With a wave of her slim gloved hand, Mary Donnelly stilled the crowd so her father could be heard.[55]

He would not resign from Congress, he said. He would not give up being mayor. He would not accept the court's verdict as final; his attorney was even now preparing his next legal move. "Curley has been reported dead many, many times," he reminded them. Indeed, on one of those occasions, in 1918, having seen the good Andrew Peters safely ensconced in City Hall, the state legislature had repealed the law allowing for the recall of Boston's mayors. The law was no longer necessary: Curley was dead. It was beginning to appear as if that would be the only way he would leave office—as a dead man. "It is quite possible that Mr. Curley will not resign, either as Mayor or as Congressman," the *Herald* commented, adding sourly: "He is not famous for placing the public interest above his own."[56]

Sentencing came in February. Thumping the banister in front of Judge Proctor's high desk, Curley made a final passionate plea. "Four of my sons were in the service," he said, as Gertrude, by his side, teared up. "Do you think I would do anything to jeopardize the lives of my children?" The relevance of this comment was not apparent. Nothing he had been accused of doing was hurtful to the war effort. He was groping for the lever of Proctor's sympathy. Quoting Emerson on the value of friendship, he said that his constituents "knew all about the indictment" and yet had given him his biggest victory ever. If his alleged fraud didn't bother them, he seemed to be suggesting, why should it bother the judge?[57]

Proctor was not swayed by that desperate argument. He sentenced Curley to six to eighteen months in federal prison and levied a $1,000 fine on him. Fuller was given sixteen months to four years; Donald Smith, four months to a year. Measured against the worst punishment possible under the law, Curley had gotten off lightly.

He stepped from the train at South Station into a sea of white fedoras. Under them, visible above their cigars, were his liegemen—Joe Langone, Edso Carroll, Kid Zissel, Teddy Glynn, Mal Nichols, and a festive throng come to buck up their leader, boss, friend, and champion at the low point of his life. As a band played "Hail the Conquering Hero," Curley and Gertrude were engulfed by a smiling, cheering mob. It took them thirty minutes to cross the hundred yards to their waiting car. With thousands of rush-hour commuters blocked by hundreds of the fedoras, trains had to be delayed. Twenty-two police sergeants were helpless to clear the jam. It was one of Curley's great "returns," right up there with his Fourth of July return from the 1932 Democratic national convention in Chicago. "These things exhilarate you," he said after reaching City Hall. "They cheer you up."[58]

Appeals would delay the day of reckoning for Curley for another year and a half. In the meantime he had a city to run.

❖   ❖   ❖

The inquirer into the "record" of the fourth Curley administration soon realizes that he is missing the point. The witnesses to those years don't tell of sewers or streets. They tell of a man etching in the lights and darks of an outsized self-portrait: the "Boss" as American original.

They describe Curley regaling theater people in the lobby of the old Clarendon Hotel with the story of how he gave John Barrymore permission to stage the American premiere of *The Rape of Lucrece* in Boston. "I told him, 'Do what the old Greeks did. Be suggestive. You'll get the permit.'" Then he began to imitate Barrymore playing the key scene. "'Lucrece, Lucrece,'" he said, then, looking at his retinue, cut in, "Now, boys don't interrupt me if I flub a line"—and went on to recite portions of the dramatic poem from memory. The aside was a throwaway joke; the fedoras wouldn't know Shakespeare from Dangerous Dan McGrew. Next he told how, just as Barrymore was reaching for his sword—"'For in thy bed I purpose to destroy thee'"—Ruth Chatterton, "the most beautiful woman in Hollywood," surrounded by her entourage, made a late entrance, stepping all over Barrymore's big moment. After his final scene, "Jack, being a gentleman of the theater," made a little speech of acknowledgment from the stage. "'And I thank the Mayor of the Athens of America,'" Curley playing Barrymore-paying-tribute-to-Curley said, "'for permitting us to mount this production of a play that I am certain you will now see all over America. I thank you, Mr. Mayor, from the bottom of a grateful heart.'" Then, with a freezing look at Chatterton, "'And I thank and salute Ruth Chatterton for co-starring with me.'"

They picture Curley rushing to City Hospital just in time to confront a dying contractor to whom he had steered much city business and from whom he expected reciprocity. "Where's that $50,000 you owe me, you son-of-a-bitch!" he shouted, slapping the old man out of his last sleep.

They tell the one about Curley coming into his office ("Good morning, boys") only to find city councilor Julius Ansell at his desk. Ansell was famous for walking behind the snowplow as it cleared his Dorchester district, tipping his top hat to his constituents in a Curleyesque piece of political theater. Described by recent writers as "obsessed with Curley," Ansell could imitate Curley's voice over the telephone—which he was doing that morning, probably ordering various city departments to hire more Jews. "Get out of that chair before I throw you out the window!" Curley boomed at him, and chased him out of the office.

They insist they remember the wooden phone booth Curley installed in that office—his private line to his bookie.

They picture Curley looking out his second-floor office at a crowd of people gathered on the plaza outside. "What the hell are those people doing out there?" he asked one of his aides. "They're waiting for you, Governor," the man replied. It was Benjamin Franklin's birthday and Curley was scheduled to give a speech honoring the eminent Bostonian émigré. "Oh," he said, then went out to give the talk. He had been reading about Leonardo da Vinci the night before; apparently forgetting the occasion, he went on for fifteen minutes extolling Leonardo's achievements. Finally, looking up at the statue of Franklin, reality intruded on his reverie and he ended by saying, "and such a man was Benjamin Franklin."

They tell the one about John F. Fitzgerald walking down School Street with young Edward M. Kennedy. Teddy wanted an ice cream cone, so he handed his school bag to his grandfather while he went into Thomson's Spa to get one. Fitzgerald was standing outside on the sidewalk holding the school bag when Curley, rounding the corner from Washington Street in his limousine, spied him and asked his driver to slow down. Curley stuck his head out the window and in his best "Oxford undertaker's accent" said, "I see that you are still carrying your burglar tools, John."

They describe Curley visiting a building in the Back Bay in which his son George wanted to rent an apartment. Curley knew the whole history of the place. "Don't touch that!" he said when the owner remarked that he was thinking of removing the staircase. Curley went on to rhapsodize over the features of this Boston architectural treasure. The owner beamed. "What's the rent?" Curley, noticing, suddenly asked. "I should be asking $400," says the owner. "I know, but you're going to take $150, aren't you?" Curley said, and of course the owner agreed. The Curley charm was irresistible.

They tell of the room near City Hall where contractors would leave off their "Christmas baskets": fruit, candy, nuts, and $2,000 in cash.

They tell of Curley's admiring a historical painting in a local gallery, *The Retreat from Breed's Hill* by Dennis Malone Carter. "That's a good Irish name," Curley says to the proprietor. "Maybe the city will buy it, provided there's something in it for me."

They throw light on the patented Curley modus operandi. A young contractor came in to see Curley. "Roofing?" Curley said. "Why, roofing is essential. Life would be intolerable if one were exposed to the inclemencies of the climate. I congratulate you, young man, for choosing such a profession. And I think we in the city can help you get your business going. Come over here by the window with me." The young man complied. "See that gentleman over there?" Curley said, pointing across School Street to a fedora making the high sign from a room in a facing office building. "Well, I want you to go over there and talk to him about getting a contract. He will handle all the details. There is, I believe, a school in Hyde Park that needs a new roof. Well, it's been a pleasure to meet you. Roof the world, young man, roof the world." The young man went across the street. On this side all was straight talk. The fedora told him that the city would pay $25,000 for the job; the young man would then do it for $20,000 and kick back $5,000 to him. He readily agreed. He went out to the school eager to get started, only to find that the roof was practically brand new. "Oh, yes," the principal said, "we had a new roof put on about three months ago." Back to the fedora. "Don't worry about a thing. Just put your ladders up there and look busy," he said. "Tell them you're repairing the first job. Nobody will climb up on that roof to check."

They recount the story of how Charlie Ianello, a tough guy from the tough South End, went in to see Curley after the election and said he had been "with him" in the campaign and expected a job for it. "Fine," he said, "go to see Bob Curley," the head of the

Public Works Department (and no relation to James). "The Governor has sent me over here for work," Ianello said to Bob Curley. "Yes, yes, come back next week," Curley replied. Ianello came back a few weeks later and got the same brush-off. "Goddamn it," he shouted, pulling the public works chief out of his chair by his necktie. "I'm here for work. Get me work now!" At which Bob Curley, a small man, cried out, "Put me down! Put me down! You've been on the payroll for a month!"

They speak with admiration of Curley's adherence to the code of the political boss. Henry Selvitella, a former City Council member, had been the penal commissioner for the city under Tobin. After Curley's election he heard that another man, Colonel Maxwell Grossman, was about to be appointed to his job. He went to see Curley, who led him by the elbow into a corner of his office. "Sorry I have to do this, but the Colonel is growing anxious to get started in your job," Curley said, adding those talismanic words: "You know he was with me." Selvitella appealed to Curley's memory. "But Your Honor, for twenty years I was the chairman of your committees and worked for you in campaign after campaign." Curley grinned, and held out his hand. "But you bet on the wrong horse in the last election."

They lovingly evoke his winks. They savor his stylish recognitions, his subtle gestures of preferment. A "you did a fine job, young man" is a treasured memory. They create a vanished world with its own special raffish virtue, where a man handed a large stack of bills might say, "I don't have to count that, do I?" And where one fedora could describe another this way: "He was no mug. A very elegant guy."[59]

❖   ❖   ❖

Aside from entertaining "the boys" ("It was like B. F. Keith's all day long," says one) and catching the attention of the voters—for example, by announcing, apropos of nothing, that he sported a tattoo of a schooner in full sail across his back—Curley's chief business in the time remaining before his appeals were exhausted was to ensure that he would still be mayor of Boston when he got out of prison. The surest way to do that was to elect the next governor of Massachusetts. Boston still did not enjoy home rule; Curley would have to be in his grave before that could even be consid-

ered. The governor and the state legislature continued to have ple-
nary power over the city. In 1946, an election year, the governor
was Maurice Tobin. Supporting him would get Curley nothing because it would give Tobin nothing he did not already have—in
1944, running against Saltonstall's lieutenant governor, Horace T.
Cahill, Tobin had carried eighteen of Boston's twenty-two wards,
winning the city by more than fifty thousand votes. Supporting
Tobin's Republican rival, however, might yield fruit. Curley had
thousands of Boston votes to trade with the Republican nominee,
Tobin's lieutenant governor, Robert Fiske Bradford. In one of the
minor ironies of his career, the great Brahmin-baiter set out to
make this *Mayflower* descendant governor of Massachusetts.[60]

Although he had strongly endorsed Tobin two years before
("With Tobin in the State House and Curley as Mayor of Boston the
government will be restored to the people"), he blamed Tobin for
not calling a special session of the legislature to expedite his request for the $10 million loan to the city. And he deeply resented
Tobin's twice having pressed the "bitter cup of ignominious defeat" to his lips. Defeating Tobin mattered as much to him as electing Bradford.[61]

At the Democratic state convention held at the Copley-Plaza
Hotel six weeks before the election, Curley gave a dramatic display
of calculated bitterness in the midst of a "unity" talk over the radio. With Tobin sitting six feet behind him, he said, "I question that
there is any man in the Democratic party that would have more
reason for opposing the ticket, were he to be governed by envy,
hatred, personal disappointment or personal grievances, than myself. I have been twice defeated by the man who is the candidate
for Governor," he said, putting aside his manuscript. "It would be
easy for me to take a walk. I don't think any man could be more
vicious or cruel than he has been to me." The fifteen hundred delegates and spectators were stunned; the leading Democrats on the
platform behind Curley wore looks of panic. Was he trying to
wreck the party? Curley went on in his best Marc Antony vein to
endorse the "Democratic ticket in its entirety," but the damage
had been done, the phial of poison already poured into the radio
audience's ear.

The crowd erupted in applause as Curley finished his speech.
He shook hands with four or five men as he worked his way to
the rear of the platform, finally stopping as he came to the seated

Maurice Tobin. Placing his left hand on Tobin's shoulder, he gave him what in Tremont Temple thirty-two years before he had given John F. Fitzgerald, "a cold grasp of the hand."[62]

Bradford was quick to placard Boston with posters quoting Curley's words about Tobin, "vicious" and "cruel." The fedoras quietly put out the word that Curley wanted Tobin knifed. Publicly, Curley predicted a Republican victory and, to help his prediction come true, launched an attack on Tobin over the air the night before the election.[63]

Running in a year in which his party captured both houses of Congress and a majority of the state governorships, Bradford got 134,000 votes in Boston to Tobin's 142,000, a loss of 38,000 votes from Tobin's showing in 1944. The Boston vote had put Bradford over. Curley hailed the Republican's win as "a great victory for America and the American way of life." But it was a greater victory for James M. Curley, who now had a friend in the State House, one who owed him an answering favor.[64]

❖   ❖   ❖

He could control much, but not his health. The stress of the four-year passion play surrounding his indictment, trial, conviction, and pending incarceration had taken a heavy toll. Also, his domestic life was unquiet. Having finally divorced Donnelly, Mary was now frequently around the house on the Jamaicaway, and she was often drinking. A gentle woman when sober, she turned nasty when drunk. Once, before the war, she set out after Gertrude's sons, who, as teenagers will, had left a mess in the house. The Curleys were at their summer place in Scituate (Curley never went back to Hull after Mary Emelda died) and the boys were sleeping on the sun porch. Quickly Gertrude went to the porch, locked the door, and put her arms around them while Mary raged outside. Gertrude calmly told her to go away. That was just the trouble: Mary did not want to go away. She saw Gertrude as a usurper who had come between her and her beloved father.[65]

Her resentment reached such a pitch that one evening when Gertrude went into the library to look for something, there was Mary, pointing a gun at her. Accounts differ as to what happened next, with some witnesses claiming she actually blasted a hole through the wall.[66]

Curley had not bargained on this in his old age. And yet he had never needed the Place of Rest more.

In 1945 he had come down with what the Joslin Clinic diagnosed as a severe case of diabetes. He kept the illness secret during the election campaign, when the news would hurt him—only to reveal it at his trial, when it might help. Until he learned to administer them himself, a nurse gave him insulin shots several times a day. He was supposed to change his diet, but the lure of lobster Newburg, curried chicken with chutney, and bernaise sauce on nearly anything consistently overmastered his resolve.[67]

In January 1947, by a vote of two to one, the U.S. Court of Appeals upheld Curley's conviction. In his dissent, Judge Wilbur K. Miller wrote that he believed Curley to be guilty of no wrongdoing since he "had made no representations to anybody." The court refused to hear a second appeal, and the case went to the Supreme Court, which in early June, by a vote of eight to one, refused to review the appellate court's findings. Frank Murphy, the former mayor of Detroit, was the lone dissenter. (Murphy owed Curley; in the early thirties, as president of the National Conference of Mayors, Curley had successfully appealed to President Hoover to provide Detroit with emergency financial aid.) Curley's lawyers asked the Court to reconsider. While that final appeal was pending, Curley was rushed to the hospital near his summer home. His blood pressure had risen with each legal reverse, and his doctors feared he would have a cerebral hemorrhage.[68]

Finally, on June 18, 1947, all legal options ended when, by a vote of seven to one, the Court refused to reconsider its earlier decision. (In a gesture to the father of his former student James Michael Curley, Jr., Justice Felix Frankfurter abstained.) Curley's condition now worsened so dramatically that he requested, and received, the last rites of the Catholic church.[69]

Coming out of the hospital the night the family broke the final piece of bad news to him, Gertrude collapsed on the stairs. Her husband was dying and Judge Proctor was ordering him to Washington for sentencing—to certain death. It all seemed so unfair.[70]

A letter to Proctor from a man whose sister had worked at the Jamaicaway described the James M. Curley Gertrude knew. "Never once did he leave his home without first kneeling by a chair on the dining room floor to say his morning prayers," the man wrote, pleading for clemency. "Your Honor, between you and me, there aren't many of us that do that!" Surely the hundreds of letters and telegrams the judge received on Curley's behalf would soften his heart.[71]

Accompanied by a doctor and a nurse, the Curleys took the train to Washington to face the music. A reporter described the mayor as looking "nervous and troubled, worn and tired" as he was pushed through Union Station in a wheelchair. He wore dark glasses and a shirt whose collar was too big, to enhance the pathos of his appearance. "Mr. Curley is planning to make a plea on his own behalf tomorrow," the reporter wrote. "If he does, it will probably be one of the most impassioned of his career."[72]

The next day before Judge Proctor, William Leahy played the health card for all it was worth. How could the Judge sentence to prison someone suffering from "cystitis, gall bladder trouble, arteriosclerosis, diabetes, cerebral thrombosis, hemorrhage of the eye, hypertension, trouble with the prostate gland and impending cerebral hemorrhage"? Such a harvest of illnesses in a seventy-two-year-old man indicated "an approaching fatal termination." Proctor replied that appeals for clemency on the grounds of health should be directed to the executive branch, not the judicial. During this brief exchange Gertrude began to cry, giving Mary's tears permission; the noise of their sobbing added to the pathetic tone of the proceedings. Proctor said he would provide a memorandum containing his ruling. "There is nothing further to say. My conclusion is that this motion should be denied." Leahy requested a stay in the sentence: Curley and Governor Bradford needed to have an important meeting about the future of Boston. Proctor replied that Curley could take such matters up "with his keepers." He continued, "I think he should be sentenced today. I regard this case as ended."[73]

Leahy quickly asked if Curley could address the Court, but Proctor said no. And with that, the old man grabbed the railing in front of him and stood up: *he would be heard.* At this sign of insubordination Proctor cleared the Court.

Curley stood there, alone and defiant, while the spectators filed out. He reached down to comfort Gertrude, then began his statement to Proctor. "With the medical record in front of you, and for the infraction here involved, you are imposing a death sentence upon me. . . ." Hearing her great fear put into words, Gertrude wept the louder. In a firm and manly voice, as if to add his strength to hers, Curley continued, "But I shall return to my people—" But saying only, "This is a distressing situation," Proctor abruptly left the courtroom while Curley was still reading. Curley could not even finish his speech, which built up to a quotation from Shakespeare, his big gun: "The quality of mercy is not strained, / It droppeth like the gentle rain from heaven. . . ." He was left standing there—alone and ignored.[74]

After a further tearful interval the guards came and took him away.

Gertrude and the Curley children had come with Curley, but they had to leave without him. George and Mary held their composure as they left the courthouse, but when the door opened before her and she started to walk away from the building without her husband, Gertrude put both hands to her face and sobbed with such forlorn passion that she lost her balance and had to be helped the rest of the way to the car. Curley had already been taken to Union Station, the first leg of a seven-hour journey to the federal prison at Danbury, Connecticut.[75]

Escorted by two federal marshals, he quit the train at Bridgeport for the sixty-mile drive to Danbury. And on the platform of the station he displayed some of his old jauntiness. When a reporter asked one of the marshals if his name was Hennessey, Curley broke in with a faint smile. "He's of the Dorchester Hennessey's"—a king of Tara, knowing the lay of his great families. "That's right," said Hennessey of Dorchester. Curley's doctor, who had ridden up in a separate compartment, asked him how he was doing. "Pretty well," he said, though he complained of numbness in his leg. The doctor gave him some medication and a new supply of insulin. He was as sick as Leahy had claimed. Moved by his frailty, the two marshals apparently wanted to help him by the arm down the dimly lit stairway to the street. But in what one reporter watching the scene called "a compelling gesture of personality," he said something to them, they walked out ahead of him, and he proceeded at his own pace and under his own power. They might take away his freedom; he would keep his dignity.[76]

A short while later, K. E. Thieman, the acting warden of the Danbury Correctional Facility, made this entry in the prison register: "James M. Curley arrived here at 11:15 P.M." He was sent to a private room at the prison infirmary. "Today was the bitterest day," the *Post* noted of June 26, 1947, "and tonight the bitterest night in the life of James M. Curley."[77]

The quality of Proctor's mercy had been strained by law. This was Curley's second felony offense, and the law explicitly ruled out any probation of sentence for second offenders. Curley's impersonation of the would-be letter carrier Bartholomew Fahey forty-four years earlier had come back to haunt him. In his memorandum giving his reasons for sentencing Curley, Judge Proctor wrote: "It is a paramount concern that public confidence be maintained in the fair and impartial administration of justice to all alike: to the high and the low; the rich and the poor." Curley could hardly argue with the standard of equality, the premise of his career. Trapped by his past, sentenced in the name of his prime value, he was caught up in his own Shakespearean drama of fate.[78]

While the train carrying Curley to federal prison was nearing Bridgeport, a Republican governor and a Republican legislature were preparing a pleasant surprise for the Democratic mayor. Curley had elected Robert Bradford, and now Bradford came through for Curley. In a bill that passed the legislature in ninety minutes, he deposed the acting mayor of Boston, City Council president John B. Kelly, appointing city clerk John B. Hynes in his place as temporary mayor; and he not only guaranteed that Curley would take over from Hynes when his sentence expired, but also provided Curley with his full $20,000 salary while he was rusticating in Danbury. Hynes was sworn in by Bradford minutes before Warden Thieman recorded Curley's arrival.[*][79]

The choice of Hynes had not been a casual one, and the way it was made foreshadows the nascent power relations of post-Curley Boston. Andy Dazzi, the classified advertising manager of the *Boston Globe*, had campaigned for Maurice Tobin and was a close friend of John Hynes. Dazzi was also friendly with *Globe* executive John I. Taylor, who had also come to know and like Hynes. Both Taylor and Dazzi, in turn, were close to Charles Moore, the *Globe*'s promotion manager. Moore had been Robert Bradford's campaign

---

[*] Bradford told Tip O'Neill, then minority leader of the Massachusetts House of Representatives, that he went to these lengths to help Curley retain his job, to avoid the charge of bigotry: "If I go the first route and strip him of the office, the Irish in this state will say that Bob Bradford is a no-good, bigoted bastard." This sort of political fear had kept more governors than Bradford from confronting Curley. It was surely why Curley was able to get away with so much for so long. (See Thomas P. O'Neill with William Novak, *Man of the House: The Life and Political Memoirs of Speaker Tip O'Neill* [New York, 1987], pp. 50-51.)

manager in the 1946 race, and after the election the governor appointed Moore as his chief secretary. It was Moore who suggested
Hynes's name to Bradford. A nexus of friendships among powerful
and influential men—Bradford to Moore to Taylor to Dazzi to
Hynes—had made the city clerk mayor.[80]

For all the haste with which it passed, Bradford's bill was controversial. Citing City Council president Kelly's recent acquittal
on a charge of soliciting bribes, a rural legislator objected that the
governor was removing an acting mayor who had been found not
guilty in favor of saving the job of a mayor who had been found
guilty. Kelly was removed for political reasons, not legal ones: he
might be a potential political rival to Curley, whereas Hynes, a
Boston civil servant for twenty-seven years, was assumed to harbor
no political ambitions. Saying that Bradford should have unseated
Curley on the basis of the law banning felons from holding public
office, then appointed a special commission of leading citizens to
manage Boston's affairs and root out every vestige of Curleyism,
the *Herald* denounced what it saw as a "conspiracy to put municipal affairs into the hands of a convicted felon. Boston stands condemned in the eyes of the nation. Why put gold on the State House
dome to crown a city so disgraced?"[81]

A VACATION FOR CURLEY read the headline over the *Herald* editorial.
It was far from being that. Built between 1938 and 1940, set in the
midst of 150 acres of open fields, Danbury had no outer walls to confine the short-term, tractable offenders for whom it was designed. In
1947 most of its 260 inmates were GI's who had gone AWOL during
the war. Many had their own cells; they had access to an excellent
library, and enjoyed other amenities. But Danbury was still a prison,
and it had its own rituals of degradation. Clement Norton, the longtime Boston pol who later filled Edwin O'Connor's ear with Curley
stories, claimed that Curley's cigars were taken from him and broken
up before his eyes when he arrived. Curley himself said that the
guards tried to steal some of the money he turned over to them.
Inmates were allowed to write and receive only three letters and to
see only one visitor for one hour a month. The food was tolerable,
but an infantilizing regulation required inmates to eat everything on
their plates. They had no numbers, but all wore the same khaki
uniforms; and the guards called them by their last names. For decades addressed as "Your Honor," "Mr. Mayor," "Congressman,"
and "Governor," he was now just "Curley."[82]

He had been at Danbury for a month when he was told that his son George was in the Cohasset Hospital. Pneumonia had led to a blood clot in one of George's lungs that required an emergency operation. His condition was critical.

Granted a ten-hour pass, Curley had an anxious four-hour ride from Danbury. On arriving in Cohasset, a community neighboring Scituate, Curley looked wan and thin in his baggy white summer suit. The two prison guards who had escorted him wanted to hustle him through the hospital doors, but he had other ideas. Spying a clutch of photographers, he paused with theatrical weariness on the first step to give them a good shot, and while the guards waved their arms at the photographers, he gave them a long slow wink. He was concerned about George (who soon recovered), but plainly he was also happy once again to have the narcotic of an audience.[83]

His letters from Danbury to members of his family show an admirable firmness of mind. "I have discovered that God has placed certain creatures in the world . . . . roaches who greeted me upon my arrival and whom I found most companionable—in fact my affection for them exceeds that for some two legged creatures I have met in exalted positions." His fellow inmates had taught him to play new card games. Otherwise, "I am communing daily with Hugo, Shakespeare, and Ralph Waldo Emerson so I am in good company as well as bad."

"The guests at this hotel are grand and cannot do enough for me. They give me cigars, oranges, and razor blades and talcum powder, all of which are most welcome as I cannot get any of these things until I have been a guest for ten days so that I am fortunate to have friends everywhere I go." He paid the other inmates back by "writing letters to wives and endeavoring to straighten out marital tangles." Getting cigars regularly was difficult, and for the first time in his life he had to make do with cigarettes, which he treated like small white cigars, wetting the paper with his tongue and swallowing a mouthful of tobacco every time he lit up. "How do you smoke these goddamned things?" he once asked Francis, there visiting. "I can't even get them to hold together!"

Writing to George, he expressed his delight at hearing the "cheering news" of his recovery, then invoked a familiar line.

As Bill Shakespeare said in Wolsey's address to Cromwell, "Had I but served my God with half the fervor that I have served the Democratic party, they would not leave me thus in mine old age naked before mine enemies."

However my son every cloud has a silver lining and I shall return from here better mentally and physically than when I entered prepared to repay those responsible for my being here.

He continued to blame Roosevelt for his persecution, which he now saw as having ethnic and religious motives. "Am enclosing a clipping about another victim of F. D. R. whose only crime was that he refused to make a football out of the Supreme Court, Senator Lonergan, a friend from Connecticut with whom I served in Congress. The list of victims of his sadistic tendencies continues to *grow*, and strange to relate all are Irish Catholics, Smith, Farley, Kennedy, Kelly, Nash, Hague, Walker, Walsh, Curley and others . . ."

And he alluded to conversations with Truman and Clark, which (if they really occurred) must have filled many hours with bitter reflection. Speculating on a pardon he hoped was in the offing, he wrote, "If favorable action takes place this week I shall send a letter to [Truman] . . . directing his mind to what he said, that an indictment—a verdict of guilt in my case was outrageous as I was innocent of wrongdoing and reminding him of what was said by Attorney General Clark that there never should have been an indictment. . . ."

Above all he felt justified; his conscience was clear, unlike Truman's, Clark's, Judge Proctor's, and those of "the powers who insist on keeping me here . . . the Communists and the New Dealers." In one letter he remarked, "I had the satisfaction to attend confession again today and for the seventh time to have not even a swear word to tell."[84]

This benign self-portrait is hard to reconcile with the one offered by Mary Curley in a newspaper interview in 1948 in which she described her father as having "suffered terrible anguish" at Danbury. Once on seeing a man being maltreated in the hospital ward, "He protested to the guard and was told to mind his own business. My father lost his temper. He was restricted as a punishment for that one." She smuggled cigars in to him in her shoe and told how on their way back to Boston after his release they stopped for lunch in Hartford. Curley seemed distant. She asked if he wanted a second cup of coffee, and when he answered with a plaintive "May I?" she was shocked: "The prison had taken so much out of him that he was afraid to ask for a second cup of coffee." The story is affecting, but not true—Mary did not make the return trip to Boston with her father. She was working the old sympathy racket her father exploited so well, blunting his constituents' envy by making them feel sorry for him.[85]

Still, it would be like Curley to keep his real feelings and his actual experience of prison out of his letters so as not to alarm the family. The letters reveal a tender paternal warmth toward his children that doesn't fit with our picture of the man who reacted in so crassly political a way to Paul's death. It is the same man, however, whom many people remember kissing his grown children goodnight.

By midsummer 1947 over one hundred thousand Bostonians had signed a petition asking President Truman to grant "executive clemency" to Curley. Stalwart John McCormack, who had come over to the courthouse to be with Curley on the day of his conviction, led the effort. Over a hundred members of the House signed the petition, including some Republicans, and every Democrat in the Massachusetts congressional delegation except one, the newly elected congressman from the Eleventh District, John Fitzgerald Kennedy. His uncritical admirers have tried to paint this decision as an early profile in courage rather than as an exercise in résumé sanitation by an ambitious politician already looking beyond Boston to the White House, one who wanted to keep his reputation free of the tar attached to "the last of the bosses." And, true, at the time it was seen as a major political mistake. His staff urged him to sign; so did his father, arguing that Curley had kept his part of the bargain with them by vacating his congressional seat. But the cool young man refused, giving various technical reasons for withholding his signature; he even claimed to have checked with the surgeon general to see if Curley could be feigning one or another of his illnesses. Kennedy's most extensive biographer, however, thinks the real reason was a desire to strike back at Curley for what Curley had done to his beloved grandfather, John F. Fitzgerald, long before. "Don't get mad, get even" would be Kennedy's motto in politics as it had been Curley's.[86]

A week after his seventy-third birthday on November 20, Curley was in the prison hospital ward when a fellow inmate brought him the eagerly awaited word. "Hey Jim, did you hear the news? You're going home tommorrow. I just heard it on the radio." Curley, who had known something was in the works, said "Thanks, dear God."[87]

On receiving the report of the prison physician that Curley had "an acute heart condition and diabetes," President Truman had commuted his sentence. "I did it for you, John," he told McCormack. It was not much of a favor. Truman had let Curley stay in prison five of the six months of his minimum sentence, and the conditions cited as the reason for the commutation had been present all along. Truman had not acted sooner because he could not afford to be seen as being soft on a city boss. He had to balance the political damage he might suffer in Boston for keeping Curley in jail against what he would suffer elsewhere for releasing him. Even after waiting five months, and timing the release for the sentimental occasion of Thanksgiving, Truman was attacked for commuting the sentence on predictable grounds by Republicans like William E. Jenner, the Indiana senator who professed himself "astounded by the brazen action. . . . The President's action, however, cannot be said to be unexpected. It is in line with the activities of one who boasts of his close social and political relationship with the infamous Pendergast machine in his home state of Missouri."[88]

Truman had issued a commutation of sentence, not a pardon, which would have been too controversial. Curley's record had not been cleared. That would take something extraordinary.

Arriving home in Boston, Curley was met by a brass band outside his house on the Jamaicaway. On the short walk from the car to the door, his head lowered in fatigue, he needed support from two policemen on either side of him. The fedoras were there in force to welcome him home, but twenty pounds lighter than when he entered prison and disoriented by the commotion around him, the boss was clearly not his old self.

In a brief speech from the landing of the great staircase, Curley promised to work for the release of the hundred thousand GI's still in federal prison. He "felt ten years younger" and with his wife and children beside him, he did look better than he had outdoors. As for his crime: "I was the victim of a professional confidence man." The next day was Thanksgiving, but the day after that he would be back on the job.[89]

"I am teetering on the brink of obscurity if the reports that Mayor Curley is to be pardoned are true," said the man who had been holding down Curley's job for the past five months when he heard the news. But destiny had another end than obscurity in view for John B. Hynes. Destiny's agent was the hubris of James M. Curley.[90]

After a combination Thanksgiving dinner and birthday party at home (HAPPY BIRTHDAY TO OUR BELOVED BOSS, read the lettering on his cake), Curley returned to City Hall two days after leaving prison. Shortly after Curley's sentencing, Hynes had met with Mary Donnelly and assured her that, in so far as it was possible, he would let all important decisions wait for Curley's return. Since many of those decisions had to do with contracts, and since grateful contractors furnished Curley with his real living, Hynes's promise meant something to Curley. When he got back to City Hall contracts worth $39 million were waiting on his desk for his approval; in addition, Hynes had not fired a single Curley appointee. "Good morning, Johnny, I'll see you later," Curley said on first seeing him that morning. Hynes dutifully retreated to the city clerk's office, and Curley spent the balance of the day signing contracts and other important papers.

After finishing he held a press conference that began in awkwardness and ended in disaster. The reporters didn't know what to ask him at first. Finally one of them broke the ice: "Well, how was it Governor?" Curley smiled. "Well, they gave us spaghetti in the morning for breakfast, and we had spaghetti in the afternoon for lunch, and we had spaghetti at night for dinner." Pause. "You'd think I was a goddamned guinea." That not-for-attribution aside got a big laugh. The old winking charm was still there. Then, speaking on the record on his first day back on the job, he made the comment that would end his career: "I have accomplished more in one day than has been done in the. five months of my absence."[91]

❖   ❖   ❖

John Bernard Hynes was an unassuming man. The day he was appointed temporary mayor, Curley's chauffeur came by to take him to his summer home on the South Shore. "I'll be going in my own car, George," he said. "Thanks just the same." Then, realizing that he had left his car for a grease job at a Dorchester garage, he asked George for a lift. A reporter went with them.

Hynes asked George to stop at a meat market en route so he could pick up a roast for Sunday dinner. "I'll go in George," he said when the driver started to get out. "They know me here." Between errands, he told the reporter, "I think the municipal government ought to be run for the people." Short (five-six), trim (145 pounds), with wavy brown hair and plain rimmed glasses, John Hynes looked more like a man of the people than the regal Curley. His parents had been born in Ireland, but, in a departure from the pattern of immigrant mortality in the families of Irish-American politicians, it was his mother, not his father, who died when he was a youngster. Raised in Roxbury, he left school at thirteen to take a job as an office boy at the American Telegraph Company's offices downtown, where he cleaned inkwells and changed pen points. "They were grand people to work for," he said. Hynes tried to enlist in the marines after President Wilson declared war in 1917, but he was rejected and joined the army instead. The great adventure passed him by, however. He spent the brief time of his enlistment guarding Bolling Field outside Washington, D.C.

In 1920 he entered the Boston city service, working his way up through the health and auditing departments until "Mr. Curley" appointed him assistant city clerk. His boss, Wilfred Doyle, a legend in his time, gave Hynes an example of pride in professionalism that helped him keep straight while working for crooked mayors. Hynes had seen them all, from Peters to Tobin, crooked and otherwise. He had even been Curley's own secretary. He married in 1928 and raised five children, joining the army after Roosevelt declared war at the end of 1941. He was given an officer's appointment because of his managerial experience. Once again he did not get overseas. And a severe ear infection soon brought his discharge. "But I tried," he told the reporter. "Enlisted both times."

Through night classes Hynes finished high school and then law school. Good with both numbers and words, he had written *That Man Curley*, a campaign biography for Curley's 1936 fight against Lodge, as well as speeches for Curley and Tobin. He liked a quiet game of cards; he was an avid Notre Dame football fan; he belonged to the Holy Name Society. Reaching Red's Garage in Dorchester, he told the reporter, "Well, I guess I'm not much of a story."[92]

Yet like Grant lolling in the general store in Galena, waiting for his moment to come, this man who had sought and missed the chance to fight for his country in two world wars was about to be cast in the role of giant killer. For if John Hynes was modest and unassuming, he was also tough and proud. CURLEY TAKES SLAP AT HYNES read the headline in the evening papers when he came out of City Hall the day of Curley's return. Meeting a friend on School Street, he was "shaking mad," in the words of an eyewitness. "He couldn't let the day go by without taking a shot at me," he said, with bitter intensity. "I had never seen my father like that before—it was entirely out of character," his son Jack recalls of the scene he witnessed later that night. "When Dad came home he was positively livid with rage, and I had no idea what had happened or what it was all about. His face was all flushed, and he stamped from room to room shouting: 'I'll kill him! I'll bury him! I'll get that no-good son-of-a-bitch!'" Throughout his life John Hynes had played by the rules and done the jobs that fell to him, from cleaning the inkwells at the telegraph company to running a major city, without fuss or fanfare; and all he had to show for it was a small wood frame house *and* a respected name. He would not stand for it. That night he talked on the phone to his friends and to other people who could help him do the thing he now started to plan.[93]

❖   ❖   ❖

Just before Curley went to jail, a *Globe* poll found that 62 percent of Bostonians approved his performance in office. The poll concentrated the minds of Curley's opponents in the city's business community and among elements of the bipartisan reform coalition that had rallied to Maurice Tobin. The man was on his way to jail, yet a majority of the people still thought he was doing a good job. Worse, the popular jailbird mayor could run for reelection, thanks to the tragically premature anti-Curley reform of 1939, which rescinded the anti-Curley reform of 1918 barring Boston's mayors from succeeding themselves. Neither reform, a generation apart, had killed off Curley. He had subverted them both. There was a radical lesson in this sorry record, and his opponents now drew it.[94]

The job of mayor of Boston must be abolished. The City Charter must be changed. Boston must have a professional, nonpolitical city manager with an elected City Council. The neighboring city of Cambridge had adopted a government on this model just before the war, and taxes had fallen for six consecutive years. This Plan E form of government, as the state legislature labeled it in 1938 when it gave the cities and towns of Massachusetts permission to adopt it, was the answer to Boston's chief ill, Curley's seeming immunity from political mortality.[95]

Plan E would not only put an end to Curley; it would also replace the twenty-two-member ward-based City Council adopted in 1924 with a council of nine members elected at large, which would be less responsive to the needs of the neighborhoods and more responsive to downtown financial interests. The present council was doing everything it could to hasten its own demise. In early 1947 it brought disgrace on itself when councilman Isadore Muchnick of Mattapan charged that an application to grant a license for a water-taxi service was being held up "pending a payoff" to other council members. James Coffey, the councilman from East Boston, leaped to his feet. "Who the hell does Muchnick think he's kidding?" he shouted. "Especially me. I will take a buck and who the hell does not know it, and I am probably the only one who has guts enough to say I will take a buck. I would like to see the guy who does not take a buck, let me know the guy who does not take a buck." The *Herald* promptly thanked Coffey for providing the "one sure-fire unanswerable argument for the scrapping of Boston's present system of government. . . ."[96]

With its mayor in jail and its City Council sodden with corruption, Boston cried out for reform, and throughout 1947 and 1948 a movement to put the Plan E option before the voters gathered momentum. Curley would have to fight off opposing mayoral candidates with one hand and a referendum aimed at abolishing his office with the other. An opponent could defeat him in 1949, or the referendum could end his career in 1952, when the city would implement Plan E government if the voters approved it in 1949. Of course, Curley would be seventy-eight years old in 1952. But since apparently nothing he could do, short of becoming an Episcopalian, would cost him the support of a decisive slice of the Boston electorate, he meant to keep running and winning and governing until he died.

To meet the twin challenges against his rule Curley built up what the *New York Times* adjudged "the most powerful machine in his forty years of political life." By 1948, according to the Municipal Research Bureau, the number of city employees on Boston's payroll was 45 percent higher than the average for the eight largest cities in the country. One of every fourteen residents—some fifty-five thousand people—lived in public housing, a proportion higher than that in any other major city. (During the campaign, charges were leveled that Curley threatened public housing tenants with eviction if they did not support him.) Per capita expenditures for welfare, health, and hospitals were the nation's highest, as were per capita expenditures for police and fire departments, which Curley had turned into virtual employment bureaus. Funding this political juggernaut pushed real estate taxes to the highest level in the nation.[97]

To help him survive locally, Curley also dabbled briefly in national politics. Although he was slated to be a delegate at large to the 1948 Democratic national convention in Philadelphia, which would be called on to nominate Harry Truman, he publicly boomed General Douglas MacArthur for president. Curley was described as "furious" at Truman for letting him stay in jail so long. At the time of Governor Bradford's eleventh-hour deliverance, it was widely conjectured that one reason the Republican Bradford had saved Curley was to embarrass Truman. The idea was that Curley, getting even for Danbury, would work to prevent Truman from taking Massachusetts. Shifting his shrines from Truman to MacArthur, Curley gave an early indication that he just might fulfill Republican hopes. In the potlatch of favors, his newfound Republican friends might even be willing to help him beat back Plan E.[98]

Curley's salute to MacArthur brought an angry response from ex-governor (thanks to Curley) Maurice Tobin: "Presumably General MacArthur is but the first of a number of Presidential candidates that from time to time will be proposed by the Mayor for nomination to the Presidency." Charging that Curley's "personal feelings" prejudiced his views of Truman, Tobin went on to say, "The cause of the party in the Commonwealth has been sacrificed before by the Mayor when he has given vent to his personal animosity, placing it above the welfare of his own party, the most recent occasion occurring in the 1946 election—I remember that well." Tobin flatly refused to be a member of any slate of delegates to the Democratic national convention headed by Curley, who as the national committeeman from Massachusetts was the nominal leader of the state party.[99]

Given his coolness toward Truman, Curley was a somewhat lonely figure at the Philadelphia convention. Waiting several hours on the platform for Speaker Rayburn to introduce him to make a brief speech, he sat on a chair placed well back from the rostrum, and for most of the time he was ignored and for part of the time he had to listen to Tobin deliver a fiery speech on civil rights ("We are all Americans and under the law we are all entitled to equal rights") that drew boos and cheers from, respectively, southern and northern delegates. When Curley was finally recognized, his speech was not about civil rights, the issue that wracked the convention, or any of the other political and social issues facing mid-twentieth-century America. It was instead a provincial appeal for the convention to call for the unification of Ireland and for President Truman "to use his best efforts to make possible the absolute and complete independence of Ireland."[100]

He had to get up early to catch a ride to the airport the next day, disrupting his old-man's morning routine. "You know, boys," he said to the younger men with him in the car, "when you reach my age you'll find that a good shit beats a good fuck any day." He had not lost his capacity for surprise, for saying and doing the unexpected. He was relying on it to frustrate Plan E.[101]

To weaken resistance from Democratic state legislators, the Plan E for Boston Committee changed its strategy to gain support to get the plan on the ballot in 1949. The committee drew up new legislation giving citizens a choice of three plans, each of which would establish a different governmental configuration. Plan A would maintain the structure adopted in 1909 of a strong mayor and a nine-member council, but would allow for a primary election in September before the two-man runoff in November. Multicandidate fields had been a key to Curley's successes (and to one of his failures, the Peters race), so Plan A would undermine his hold on Boston politics, though it was far less threatening than Plan E. Plan D was Plan E with minor variations. Whichever letter of the alphabet they chose, therefore, voters would either wound or administer the coup de grace to Curley. Or so the advocates of charter reform hoped.

But stationing two of his lobbyists outside the doors of the Massachusetts House and Senate while the ADE bill was being debated, Curley was able to insert an amendment at the last minute that allowed only one charter reform question to be put before the voters in any single election. The first plan to gain 41,068 signatures in a petition would go on the ballot in 1949. Curley had decided to use Plan A to kill Plan E.

"The Plan A Committee made its appearance in January, 1949," William P. Marchione writes. "Though Mayor Curley professed to have no link to the group, his son, Leo Curley, addressed its first public meeting. The younger Curley informed his audience that Plan E would 'result in a wholesale discharge of city employees.'"¹⁰²

The ADE law required any group supporting each charter reform to obtain petition blanks for voters' signatures from the Boston Election Commission on February 2, 1949. Groups would then have ten days to gather the necessary signatures. Partisans of Plan E showed up at the commission's offices at City Hall just before 9:00 A.M. on the appointed day, but supporters of Plan A had been waiting in line since 6:45. Curley was playing his career backward, repairing to the devices of his Tammany days. The Plan A people got most of their official petition forms, but just as the Plan E advocates appeared in line the presses mysteriously broke down at the City Printing Department—the very machinery balked at the idea of retiring Curley—and they had to wait a week to get theirs. In two days they gathered over fifty thousand signatures, but they were too late. Plan A, its supporters having already gotten their forty-one thousand signatures in, would be the only restructuring scheme on the ballot.¹⁰³

"I'm positive that Curley bought off leaders of the Plan E group," said a reporter who covered City Hall in those days for the *Christian Science Monitor*. It was no coincidence that the Plan E people showed up late at City Hall. However that might be, bribes were becoming a regular part of the Curley way. Low-paid reporters were special targets. George Oakes, the Republican running against Curley in 1949, came to the *Monitor* reporter with a sensational story. "Curley is passing money to my campaign," he said. "He's doing it through Billy Mullins," the *Herald* columnist. "Mullins is passing me $500 a week." The *Monitor* reporter replied, "Well, that's not a surprise." "Yes, but that's not the worst of it," Oakes said. "Curley is giving *him* $1,000."¹⁰⁴

The same reporter was once offered a bribe himself. Acting in Curley's name, a fellow journalist sought him out in the press room at City Hall and promised him $50,000 to stop writing exposés on the parking meter scandal (Boston's five thousand parking meters cost $64 each to install, whereas Cambridge paid $12 each for its one thousand), the tax abatement racket, and the printing, paint-

ing, milk, and paving contract scandals. "There wasn't a department you could go in without finding corruption," he says. He got
some stories from reporters for other newspapers, who were unable to get them into their own papers because Curley used his
power over real estate assessments to keep the publishers in line,
just as he used bribes to keep reporters in line. As the publication
of a religious institution, the *Christian Science Monitor* was exempt
from taxes and so was beyond Curley's reach. The reporter's
mother, however, was not. She called her son to complain that he
was being too rough on the mayor. "Don't you forget that Curley
saved your life," she said, reminding him of how, when their Dorchester neighborhood had been flooded years before, Curley ordered the gas company to restore service without delay. Such old
loyalties were Curley's trump card. For many Bostonians, his good
works would ever stay their dudgeon at his bad deeds.[105]

A corrupt mayor, a corrupt City Council, a corrupt press, a
swollen city payroll, a dying city economy, and the highest taxes
beneath the wandering moon: such was the Boston scene as the
1949 election campaign began. In the twentieth century three Boston mayoral elections deserve the epithet "historic." That of 1910,
when John F. Fitzgerald defeated James Jackson Storrow and the
era of ethnic politics began in earnest; that of 1967, when Kevin
White, a racial liberal, defeated Louise Day Hicks, a School Committee woman who had risen to prominence by exploiting white
resentment of blacks; and that of 1949, when Boston would have to
choose between its heart or its head, its past or its future, an ambig-
uously great man and a merely good one.

Competition from the dramatic American League pennant
race between the Red Sox and the Yankees served to muffle the
mayoral campaign until early October, but after that the city came
alive. There was a premonitory chill in the fall air. City bosses had
recently been turned out, their political machines smashed, in Chicago, Memphis, and Jersey City. Would a stubborn irrational affection for one old man make Boston immune from this trend?[106]

"My re-election is so assured," Curley announced, "that I
have planned no active campaigning." He ostentatiously returned
a campaign contribution of $500, saying, "I will not need it." He
had three main opponents: they were the Republican, George B.
Oakes, who was strongly backed by Bill Mullins of the *Herald;*
Patrick J. ("Sonny") McDonough, thirty-eight, a member of the

Governor's Council (in Dan Coakley's old seat) from South Boston; and John B. Hynes, fifty-two. Curley was financing Oakes's campaign in the hope that he would drain votes away from Hynes. "Sonny is running for Mayor of Boystown," he said of McDonough, who had hastened to have his nickname printed on the ballot in quotation marks after hearing that Curley intended to precipitate another Patrick J. McDonough into the race. Running into him at a crowded rally in South Boston, Curley said, "I understand you've changed your name." McDonough glared at him. "Yes," he replied, speaking in a loud voice, "but I didn't change it to a number." Curley was furious. Hynes Curley dismissed as "a little city clerk who has never been out of the city except to attend a convention," a "supine creature" who would do the bidding of the "faded handful" of Boston Brahmins. In a City Hall toast, he joked, "Johnny can have my job anytime. Whenever I quit." These were not opponents worthy of his steel.[107]

With the same broad coalition that had elected Tobin behind Hynes and city workers behind Curley, the campaign quickly became a two-man race. Sonny McDonough, frustrated at being ignored, issued a challenge to both men to "swap words" with him outside City Hall. "I want Curley to meet me," he said, "and I suggest he take his City Clerk by the hand and bring him along too." Next day he parked his sound truck in front of City Hall and, standing on the rooftop, shouted before the old Victorian structure, "Come down, come down wherever you are and face the issues!" But up in their adjoining offices Curley and Hynes—who could not be fired because Bradford had given him life tenure to protect him from political reprisal—ignored him.[108]

"The city today is nearing its doom," Hynes said in one speech. "It's all the usual," said a man who had just heard Curley. "Been listening to it man and boy for all them forty years, and it's still a darling of a speech."[109]

Without ever mentioning his name, Hynes made Curley the issue, linking him to the winds of change. "The day of that kind of man is gone forever. We can't afford the city bosses anymore."[110]

In his radio speeches Curley stressed his experience. "Do you want the most proov-en"—the syllables lengthened out under his tongue—"experienced man, with a proov-en record of accompleesh-ment, or do you want someone to take over the pi-lot's job who does not know his nav-ee-gation?"

Hynes shot back: "I did it for five months as your Mayor in 1947. I will do it again starting in January of next year." Under pressure from Sonny McDonough, who called him "a man who has worn the carpet thin to Mayor Curley's office," and George Oakes, who tasked him with being a former protégé of Curley's, Hynes admitted in a debate that he had "loved, admired, and respected" Curley for a number of years; but he had broken with him in 1937, and since then the carpet had seen little wear.[111]

In the first television ads Bostonians had ever witnessed in a mayoral campaign, Curley displayed what he called "my monuments": the bathhouses, branch libraries, beaches, schools, clinics, hospitals, roads, municipal buildings, parks, gymnasiums, playgrounds, and swimming pools he had built in his four terms. At some of the tonier watering holes in the city, the appearance of that ad on the screen brought shouts to change the channel at once.

Deriding his opponents as "puny economists," Curley claimed that "they want to reduce the tax assessments on extremely profitable downtown business property"—his voice rising in disbelief—"and to increase the assessment on homes throughout Boston." That was not Curleyism.

"It is possible to have better government in Boston," Hynes countered. "It is possible to look forward to a better city. It is possible to preserve and protect the interests of the homeowner, the rent payer, and the business man."[112]

In a speech at the Michelangelo School in the Italian North End, Curley summed up the vision the Irish of his day—he first among them—had given to American government. "Republicans don't want someone to care for babies, the aged, and to pay a living wage. They want someone who will sit on the lid, will not spend and will cut down debt. Government was not created to save money and to cut debt," he shouted, his voice full of the one conviction no one ever doubted he possessed, "but to take care of people. That's my theory of government."[113]

But a growing number of people resented the paternalistic, semimonarchical tenor of that theory. They didn't want government to "take care of" them; they could do that for themselves. Government should instead get out of the way of progress by lowering its predacious taxes on the private local economy. Boston did not have to be a civil service city. Wanting something better than a future of being taken care of by a gamy old mayor, the young men and women in Boston's many colleges and universities flocked to a group called Students for Hynes. It was the kids versus the fedoras.[14]

The biggest fedora, in size at any rate, wore a tam-o'-shanter. His name was Edward McCormack, but everybody called him "Knocko." Round, florid-faced, always with a cigar dangling from the side of his mouth, Knocko was a combat veteran of the First World War, the owner of a tavern in South Boston, the brother of Congressman McCormack ("the Congy," as Knocko referred to him), a devoted Curley follower, and a man Curley loved for his loyalty and his affection and his Falstaffian fullness. "What do you have to report, Knocko?" Curley would ask at meetings of his campaign strategy board, and Knocko, brightening under the benignant gaze of the boss, would vent his wrath upon the latest offense of the ingrate Hynes or the wretched McDonough. In Curley's headquarters on Bromfield Street, which was decorated with over three hundred photographs of Curley at different times in his career, Knocko cut a commanding figure, but his cigars, his open-shirted big-bellied presence, and his often profane enthusiasm for the boss caused problems. Curley had a devoted following of old ladies from Beacon Hill who appreciated his efforts to preserve Boston's historic monuments. They would drop by the headquarters to make their donation to the campaign, only to confront the daunting Knocko, whose desk was close to the door and whose essential kindness and decency were well hidden behind his belly and his cigar. Something had to be done about Knocko. Several of his aides wanted Curley to tell him to lie low for the rest of the campaign, but Curley would have none of that; Knocko's feelings must not be hurt. "Here's what we'll do with Knocko," he said, and outlined a plan to make the campaign office safe for refined Boston ladies while also saving Knocko's face. Dressed in his Yankee Division uniform—and yes, wearing his tam-o'-shanter—Knocko was to head up a new group, Veterans for Curley. His desk would be moved to the back of the office under a big sign that said, VETERANS: SIGN UP HERE WITH KNOCKO. The plan worked. Knocko was delighted at the chance to appear in his old uniform, and Curley's money man, a Princeton graduate named Peter Allen, posted at the front desk, made the ladies feel comfortable.[15]

When the Hynes campaign put up posters throughout the city urging Bostonians to GET RID OF CURLEY GANGSTERS! VOTE HYNES! Knocko was incensed. And when Hynes referred to himself over the air as a "veteran," Knocko, who had charged German machine guns in the Argonne, could not be contained. "That phony son-of-a-bitch!" he exploded at his friend Peter Caparell, another of Curley's strategists, who had triggered Hynes's broadcast with an earlier broadcast of his own, in which he attacked Hynes for intimating that well-known veterans who worked for Curley were "gangsters." Knocko now took to the airwaves himself to arraign Hynes. "I want to say to you, Johnny Hynes," he said in his tavern-keeper's voice, "that the closest you ever came to a foxhole was in the back of a movie house, watching John Wayne win the war. You Johnny Hynes served 29 days in World War I, and 60 days in World War II. Now, federal law says that a guy must serve 90 days to be classified a bonafide veteran. . . . You marched into the Army a private, and marched out as a captain. Now, Mister Johnny without a Gun, who was the political gangster that bribed Santa Claus and got you your commission? Think about that one, voters, when you go to vote next Tuesday!"[116]

The papers headlined KNOCKO'S SOCKO BLAST, much to the delight of hard-core Curley voters, who saw Knocko as Curley's fiercest and most colorful knight. But to young first-time voters especially, Knocko and his "blast" were dated reminders of the politics of a vanishing era.

"Your uncle was operating in a diminishing market," a reporter tells Adam Caulfield, Mayor Skeffington's nephew, in *The Last Hurrah*. "You couldn't pry his old supporters away from him with a crowbar, but their trouble was that they *were* old; they were dying off, sport, and they were being replaced by the kids." Curley had carried the vote of the "kids" in 1945, but wartime rent controls had since been lifted, and with rents increasing by 8 percent one year and 13 percent the next as landlords struggled to keep up with real estate tax bills that had risen 43 percent in the decade, young married couples were feeling the pinch.[117]

They were not the only ones who were hurting. The Finance Commission found that 65 percent of the premature babies born in Curley's beloved City Hospital died soon after. Overall, the death rate at City had risen 27 percent since 1943. Nursing care was "skimpy," and the hospital's nursing school so bad that the State of New York refused to recognize its graduates as competent professionals. Since 1946, twenty-two nursing schools had withdrawn their affiliations with the hospital, which Curley had turned into a patronage haven, starting with the chairman of its board of directors, his family physician for decades, Martin J. English. Paid to put three coats of paint on the walls of the hospital, contractors put on only one—and painted right around the pictures. Paid to dig out the cement base of streets being fixed, contractors left it alone and paved two inches of blacktop over it. Roofs were repaired that didn't need repairing; sidewalks replaced that didn't need replacing. In the coin of higher rents, poorer services, and abridged economic hopes, the "little people" were finally paying the overhead of Curleyism. The Robin Hood formula had broken down.[118]

With the end approaching, one of Curley's old friends became an enemy, but an old enemy also became a friend. Joseph Dinneen, whom Curley had sued in 1936 over his article about Curley in *Harper's*, had just published a biography of Curley ("A readable, journalistic account of a fortunately unique career," in the opinion of *The Nation*). At first, though he had cooperated with Dinneen, Curley attacked the book; there were even wholly believable hints of an impending libel suit. Thus Dinneen was surprised to be summoned to City Hall and then shocked when he got there to find Curley sitting before a blown-up poster of THE PURPLE SHAMROCK, the title of his biography. "I've decided to embrace your book," Curley told him. "That will kill it with the people who will vote against me, and the people who will vote for me don't read." Curley called it right: the book started out strong, but sales died after his killing embrace.[119]

Dinneen's publisher gave a big dinner for Curley at the Copley-Plaza. Speaking in a humorous vein, Dinneen related the denouement of Curley's libel suit. "Lawyers were expensive. Curley was broke at the time and the suit never went to trial. However, I have since been highly honored that I was even remotely associated with $500,000." Curley laughed heartily. "And don't think Curley agrees with all I've written, either," Dinneen added. Curley shook his head. Dinneen then launched into an emotional tribute to the old man, saying he had made most of the improvements in Boston for the last fifty years; without him Boston would have been a tenth-rate city. "Yes, it is a Roman toga of purple that drapes our shamrock," he concluded. Curley beamed.[120]

He was increasingly borne back to the past: there was so much more behind him than ahead of him, and the stories, the anecdotes, the memories streamed from him, his last monuments. To one reporter he related a parable about his Tammany days. The scene was the Vine Street Church; the time, long ago. An opponent stood up at a public meeting and predicted, as so many errant prophets had done so often over the years, that "the bark Tammany" would sink at the next election, taking Curley down with it. In a speech that he claimed lasted half an hour, Curley made the most of the sentimental associations latent in that nautical image. "I asked what would become of the sick and needy, the widows and the orphans, the friendless and the homeless and the poor without Curley and the bark Tammany. Old Charlie Bannon sitting in the front row was so affected he pulled out his bandana handkerchief and sobbed. He stood up and . . . said 'Good old bark Tammany!' And Curley," said Curley, "was elected."[121]

But the old bark was now sinking fast, and one notable member of the crew jumped ship. Curley's most faithful fedora, his election commissioner, Joseph Langone, broke with what everybody in it called "the organization." Curley had unaccountably failed to endorse Langone's son, Fred, who was running for the City Council—perhaps that was why just days before the election Joe leaped up on the Scollay Square subway kiosk near City Hall and denounced "the forces of evil" that had taken over the city. Bellowing fiercely, he vowed to send Curley to Alcatraz, adding, "I might go too. But I'll take a lot of them with me!" The kiosk was in the middle of the street, and with the sound trucks of the mayoral candidates passing him right and left, Langone's tirade died away and all that the crowd of people who had gathered on the sidewalks could see was a frantic little man in a gray fedora making mute inscrutable gestures.[122]

Election day brought the highest recorded turnout in Boston's history. Curley got 126,000 votes, nearly ten thousand more than he had ever received before, but with neither McDonough nor Oakes doing much of anything, John Hynes got 138,000, giving him a 12,000-vote victory. Hynes carried the streetcar suburbs of Boston: the outer wards of Dorchester, Roslindale, West Roxbury, Brighton, Allston, and Hyde Park. Curley took the inner wards of Charlestown, South Boston, East Boston, the North and West ends, and lower Roxbury, with the old Tammany ward coming through for him by two to one. Each man won eleven wards; Curley's just had fewer people in them. John Hynes later told his son that if

Curley had only called him into his office when he returned from prison and said, "John, you've done a wonderful job. I really appreciate it. Let's have lunch someday"—if Curley had only said something like that, "That would have been the end of it. I probably would have worked for him at the next election. It's funny how things turn out."[123]

Bill Shakespeare would have made the sky grow dark in day, and the stars to cease their courses. But we must report that November 7, 1949, was fair and bright.

Pardoned

❖   ❖   ❖   ❖

The oldest hath borne most; we that are young
Shall never see so much nor live so long.

EDGAR,
SPEAKING THE LAST LINES OF *KING LEAR*

This is the West, sir. When the legend
becomes fact, print the legend.

THE EDITOR OF THE *SHINBONE STAR*
IN *THE MAN WHO SHOT LIBERTY VALANCE*

Curley would be a candidate in two more mayoral elections, but he never held office again. When he left City Hall days before Hynes's inauguration it was thus the first in a string of lasts. John Fitzgerald had whistled as he stepped off the pages of Boston's official history. James Curley made a less seemly exit.

Of Curley's final month in power, one city councilor said, "We are seeing the rape of Boston in the dying days of the Administration." Another charged that Curley's attitude seemed to be "To hell with everybody." When the council presented Curley with a medal in recognition of "fifty years of meritorious service," some members walked out in protest. They were angry at a series of odoriferous deals Curley had cut: his decision to award a garbage and ash removal contract to a New York firm whose bid was two times ($14,200 a month to $6,585) the amount submitted by the next highest bidder, his granting of $2.5 million in tax abatements to big property owners, and above all, his breaking of a campaign promise not to grant licenses to two drive-in theaters. One of these was on Gallivan Boulevard (named after the spoiler in the Peters race) in Dorchester, the other in West Roxbury. When Curley indicated that he would let the theaters open despite his promise, residents of these neighborhoods appealed to the City Council to stop him. A councilman obtained a temporary restraining order forbidding the mayor to grant the licenses. A judge gave the order to Deputy Sheriff Margaret C. Lang to serve on Curley, setting the stage for the crowning indignity of fifty meritorious years.[1]

Curley was at City Hall clearing out his office when he heard the sheriff was coming. He locked the door and posted a fedora outside it. Sheriff Lang arrived just as Curley was leaving. She tried to hand him the restraining order as he started down the stairs, but he kept his arms rigidly by his sides while a phalanx of fedoras formed around him. She tried again on the first floor as he was going out the door, but a fedora grabbed her and when she started to break loose knocked her down. Meanwhile, walking faster than anyone had seen him move in years, Curley made for his car, which was parked on School Street. Lang got up and dashed after him, giving it one more try as he started to get in. "I don't want that God-damned thing!" he shouted as the fedoras pushed her away. The car drove off, leaving George Curley alone on the sidewalk, forgotten in the moil of his father's going.[2]

The passing from the scene of the Irish city bosses has occasioned much comment, scholarly and otherwise. Until recently Edwin O'Connor's analysis was undisputed. "All you have to remember is one name: Roosevelt," the wiseguy Jack Mangan tells Adam Caulfield in *The Last Hurrah*. They are discussing the reasons why Mayor Skeffington, Adam's uncle, lost the election chronicled in the novel. Adam, a quondam sports writer, is a bit slow on the political trigger. "I don't get *that* at all," he says. "Why Roosevelt?"

> "Because," Jack said patiently, "he destroyed the old-time boss. He destroyed him by taking away his source of power. He made the kind of politician your uncle was an anachronism, sport. All over the country the bosses have been dying for the last twenty years, thanks to Roosevelt. . . .
> . . . "What Roosevelt did was to take the handouts out of the local hands. A few little things like Social Security, Unemployment Insurance, and the like—that's what shifted the gears, sport. No need now to depend on the boss for everything; the Federal Government was getting into the act. Otherwise known as a social revolution."

Jack goes on considerably, as most everybody does in the novel; O'Connor loved to do windy talk. But we get—and grant—the point.[3]

Steven P. Erie, a political scientist, does not. In *Rainbow's End*, a major revisionist work on the Irish political machines, he shows how old political machines were "revitalized" (as in Jersey City) and new ones "incubated" (in Pittsburgh and Chicago) by the resources the New Deal pumped through their coffers. Combined

with a demographic change as profound in its consequences as the
Irish immigration—the black internal migration—the growth of
social programs under Roosevelt did not cause the Irish machines
to fall; the cutbacks in social programs under Reagan did. "The
black revolt in the 1980s against the last of the machines," he
writes, "was in large part fueled by welfare state retrenchment."⁴
    Thus the debate. It has only tenuous applicability to Boston. It
never had a machine. It had a charismatic leader instead. William V.
Shannon is right when he says that "Curley's political significance
can only be apprehended in cultural terms." Shannon again: "Curley was less powerful than a party boss and more significant than a
conventionally successful party leader. He was the idol of a cult,
arbiter of a social clique, and spokesman for a state of mind." Curley's grip on his voters had less to do with the favors he dispensed—
though by the end, there were so many that, to quote Erie, Boston
had "the ethos of a civil service city"—and more to do with the
communal resentments he articulated and the vicariously involving
drama of his life. Many Bostonians were worse off in 1950 than they
or their families had been in 1914, and Curley was a major reason
why. Speaking of the Irish takeover of "big-city political machines
in the nineteenth century" in his study of the trend toward downward mobility among the Boston Irish, Stephan Thernstrom adds,
"But what is too often overlooked is that such a victory—winning
control of 3,000 jobs in the Public Works Department, let us say—
may involve seizing one kind of opportunity *at the expense of other
opportunities.* The success of the Irish in the political sphere was not
matched by comparable gains in the private economy." But what on
earth were they to do in Boston's meager "private economy," the
126,000 Bostonians who voted for Curley in 1949 might have asked
Thernstrom—become Harvard professors? More than jobs, Curley
had given them something of value. Asked why he remained devoted to Argentine president Juan Peron even though Peron had
done little to improve his material existence, a Peronist replied in
words that light up Curley's gift as no others can do: "Before Peron I
was poor and I was nobody; now I am only poor."⁵
    Curley had been out of office just over a month when the
drama of his life took a tragic turn. The years had hardened him,
but steel would break under what he was to suffer next.
    After working feverishly on her father's election campaign,
Mary Curley Donnelly first caught a cold and then had a bad

reaction to a smallpox inoculation. Alarmed, Curley sent a nurse to look after her in her penthouse apartment in the Back Bay.

In the years since her divorce from Ed Donnelly in 1943 ("No more!" the judge finally burst out at the trial as she listed the incidents of abuse she had suffered at his hands), Mary opened a dress shop on Beacon Street. But her heart was in politics, not business, and she had recently closed the shop down. At forty-one, her face was fuller, rounder than it had been formerly, which made her look more attractive, more womanly. She accepted the church's one-marriage-to-a-customer edict and did not contemplate marrying ever again.

It was a Saturday morning. Mary was supposed to have gone to the Jamaicaway for dinner the night before, but begged off, pleading her lingering illness. She felt better this morning, or so the nurse who had spent the night at her apartment later said. She was looking forward to a vacation in the West Indies; she had even had a white silk party gown made for the cruise, which was to begin on Tuesday. Just before eight o'clock she went into her bedroom to place a telephone call to her friend Lauretta Bremner Sliney, her brother James's one-time fiancée. Years before, Lauretta had married a naval officer, James Sliney ("Hope you make Mrs. Dionne look like a piker," Curley said in his wedding note to her, which contained five $100 bills), and she and her husband lived in Chicago. "It's Boston calling long-distance," the operator told Lauretta, "but apparently they've hung up." At the other end of the line, Mary had abruptly cradled the phone, crying out, "I have a terrific pain in my neck," and placing her hand there as a look of agony convulsed her face. Her nurse, Moniker Reimer, did what she could to comfort her, then called a doctor, a priest, and her father. "Mr. Curley," she said, "please come at once. Mary has had a shock." He arrived just as the priest was giving her the last rites. The matching luggage containing her cruise clothes stood neatly in a row near her body.

When Curley came out of the apartment some time later he held his hand out to the photographers who had gathered on the sidewalk and asked them not to take any pictures. His eyes were raw but through an effort of will he had stopped his tears. "I'm going, now, to pick out her casket," he said, as Gertrude took him by the elbow to their waiting car. George Curley, leaving the apartment after his father, could only say, "I don't understand it.

She was feeling fine. She was going out today, you know. . . ." His voice trembling, Leo Curley said he was shocked by his sister's death.

In 1940, just graduated from law school, Leo had done what his brother James had planned to do in similar circumstances nine years before: he got married, the bride being his childhood sweetheart, Catherine Sweeney, an exceptionally pretty young woman. Described as "a big Teddy bear" by his friends, Leo was warm, friendly, companionable. He opened a downtown law office, which was soon full of hard cases. "Christ," one friend recalls, "no one thought of paying him anything. He was too nice a guy to practice law." After the war, like George and like Gertrude's brother Richard Casey, Leo took a job (as traffic commissioner) with the Curley administration. He and Mary had been very close. Once when Donnelly was particularly violent, Mary had called Leo for help. "Leo! Kill him!" she shrieked, her self-control surrendering to her rage.

Throughout that bitter Saturday Leo had been wracked by fits of sobbing. "He wept constantly," one friend remembered, "and many times cried out, 'She was like a mother to me!'" Though he was only thirty-four, Leo's health was not robust; he had been released from the hospital just a few days before. It is unclear why he was there, but as both Mary and Paul had done, he drank more than was good for him. That night he and Catherine went through Mary's things at her apartment. Around nine-thirty he was talking to his brother Francis, who had come home for Mary's funeral, on the same phone Mary had used that morning to dial Lauretta Sliney. "He started to talk about Mary," Francis later said. "His voice was breaking and he was in a rather bad way emotionally. All of a sudden I heard the telephone fall on the floor and various thumping sounds. . . ." Leo had been stricken by a massive cerebral hemorrhage; minutes later, he was dead of the same cause that had killed his sister.

After making the arrangements for Mary's funeral, Curley had retired to his library. The floor was littered with copies of the afternoon and evening editions of the newspapers, Mary's face or name visible on all of them. He had years since installed Mary Emelda's portrait in his sanctum and for long stretches that evening he stared at it, as if beseeching her image for a clue to their family's harrowing history. "I believe that we are punished here," he had once said; we do not have to wait for the next life to answer for our sins. Was this laceration part of his punishment? The thought that the death of his children was the harvest of his sins was unsupportable, yet Curley, alone in his library, may have been tormented by it. His Catholicism was fatalistic, Jansenist, fed by the mists and moors of pre-Christian Ireland, land of curses and cursed kings. "It's God's will," he said repeatedly that day, banishing all such dread reckonings from his mind.

After receiving Leo's strangled call, Francis Curley rushed to Mary's apartment. Gertrude kept the news from Curley. She was stalling for time, waiting for a doctor to arrive. Her son Richard remembers that his mind was haunted by the image of a chain of death pulling first one and then another of the family away: Mary's death had killed Leo, the news of Leo's death would kill James, and James's death would kill Gertrude. Finally a doctor arrived, and with him a priest, perhaps from Curley's parish in Jamaica Plain, perhaps from Mary's in the Back Bay; no one is sure which. Gertrude met them in the hall and asked them to stand by, then went back into the living room, where she and Curley had been sitting. To raise his blood pressure to keep him from going into shock, she deliberately provoked him, saying that, after all, whole families perished in fires in Maine farmhouses every year; compared to that, their sufferings were bearable. He responded, grew animated, grew hot. Now the priest, who had stayed out of Curley's sight in the hall, stepped forward.

"Governor," he said. "I have some more terrible news for you."

"Francis?" Curley asked.

"No, Leo."

Curley took the news in stunned silence. Sonless, Lear was lucky. Some time later, with the resignation that would mark his conduct throughout the next few days, he said, "The Lord giveth and the Lord taketh away. I'm very tired now. Help me upstairs to bed."

His religious fatalism was not indifference. Psychologically, it was a defense against the unappeasable ache of loss. "Whatever is, is right": that anxious affirmation will seem strange only to those whose lives have not been touched by death.

The next day, Sunday, he insisted on going to Mass at Our Lady of Lourdes. After Mass, as if by signal, the entire congregation formed a line from the church doors to the street. When Curley and Gertrude came out no one spoke a word, no one made to shake hands with him, but the women wept openly and the men bit their lips as they extended their hearts in their glances.

Boston had never seen anything like what happened later that day. The bodies of Mary and Leo were laid out in the hallway of 350 the Jamaicaway, Leo in his naval officer's uniform, Mary in the white silk party dress she had bought for her cruise. And Curley held a wake for them and invited his city to come.

And, from 1:00 P.M. to after midnight, at the rate of twenty-four hundred people an hour, the city came. Curley stood near the feet of the caskets for hours at a time, receiving the condolences of high and low alike. Thirty schoolchildren from the nearby Mary E. Curley School were among the first in line. Mayor and Mrs. John Hynes soon followed, joined by the sister of Governor Paul Dever, Archbishop Richard J. Cushing, Congressman John F. Kennedy, Arthur Fiedler of the Boston Pops, and groups of fedoras, some of whom got in line twice, just to be sure the boss saw them. President and Mrs. Truman had sent a heartfelt letter of condolence along with dozens of red roses. (Curley had come around strongly behind Truman in the 1948 campaign, and the Trumans had visited with the Curleys during a stopover in Boston.) Maurice Tobin, now Truman's secretary of labor, flew up from Washington to represent the president. In a dramatic radio address on election day, Tobin had endorsed Hynes, and for that among other trespasses against him, Curley received the secretary coldly. Under the provocation of seeing Tobin, and even in the presence of his dead children, Curley was briefly his mischievous self. Speaking to Francis, in an unctuous voice, he said, "I think such a distinguished visitor as this, especially since he was"—gesturing to the caskets—"their friend in former times, I think he should be given a few moments to sit down in quiet reflection. Why don't you show him to that private room opposite the Moraine Street entrance?" Francis blushed; the "private room" was a bathroom. Familiar with the house, Tobin understood. "I know where it is," he said to Gertrude as he shook her hand. "And I know what he meant."

Toward evening Edward Donnelly, who had since remarried, came by and stood silently looking into Mary's coffin.

Later, as a snowstorm whipped the last of the estimated fifty thousand mourners remaining in line, Curley bent low over Mary's form and kissed her lovingly on the forehead. He was weeping openly now, for the first time that day, and to the people still in line and the newspapermen in the room it was a wrenching moment. He looked with pride at his son's uniform and then kissed him for the last time. Shaking from the effort of suppressing his sobs, he retired to bed, walking slowly up the staircase of his aspirations where he had posed with Mary on her wedding day. It was eleven-thirty. He had stood over their bodies for ten hours. At 1:30 A.M., snow clotting their eyes, a delegation of cleaning women who worked the night shift arrived to pay their respects. Curley had waited for them as long as he could.

It must have been numbingly familiar to him: the long (seventy-five-car) funeral cortege through streets lined with sad-faced people, the trains on the El overhead slowed to a crawl, the sudden hush that came over the bulging crowd in the cathedral as he began to walk down the aisle. "A tragedy such as that which has befallen James Michael Curley transcends any political or other private considerations," Archbishop Cushing, Cardinal O'Connell's successor as head of the archdiocese of Boston, said in his eulogy from the altar. "It immediately becomes a community sorrow and the hearts of all, without any possible exception, go out to the devoted father of a family so suddenly, so overwhelmingly visited by the angel of death. . . . I want him to know that we are all grateful for his demonstration, under difficult circumstances, of the truth that the Christian, confronted with tragedy, must not languish in fruitless and unavailing grief, nor sorrow as those who have no hope."[6]

Inevitably there were rumors of suicide by both Mary and Leo. The Curleys were strongly religious people, and those who are not strongly religious find it hard to credit religious motives, or to understand how religious conviction can determine personal conduct. That Mary was deeply unhappy, that Leo was inconsolable in his grief over Mary's death: we can stipulate these facts without finding in them motives for suicide, a heaven-barring sin to a Catholic.

Coming out of the house on the Jamaicaway, moved by the sight of the old man standing up under the cracking burden of his grief, John Kennedy remarked to his friend David Powers, "No matter what you say of him, you have to admire him for his great courage." Later that evening he described the scene to his aging grandfather, John Fitzgerald, who was too infirm to come to the

Jamaicaway himself. Fitzgerald was stirred by the sufferings of his rival of yesteryear. Doris Kearns Goodwin writes: "'In times like this,' he told his grandson, 'you realize how fleeting our small political battles are compared with the enduring legacy of family.' For now Curley had no successor to carry on his name. Only two sons remained, one a Jesuit and the other temperamentally unsuited to politics. There would be no one to keep the political tradition alive." Kennedy later told Lem Billings that the love he had seen displayed toward Curley at his children's wake, along with the similiar feeling displayed toward John F. Fitzgerald at his funeral later that year, was a revelation to him. "It was as if he were seeing for the first time that he really might be able to touch people as a politician," Billings said, "and that if he could, then they could give him something back. . . ." It is grimly fitting that John F. Kennedy, whose own funeral would fix the drifting continents in sorrow, should have gotten the heart to press on with his career from what he had seen of political affection at the Fitzgerald funeral and the Curley wake.[7]

The pardon was announced two months later, just as the Curleys were leaving for a Holy Year pilgrimage to Rome. "Full and unconditional," it wiped the slate clean not only of the Engineers' Group conviction but also of the conviction in 1904. Harry Truman had come through at last.[8]

❖   ❖   ❖

The normal mayoral term in Boston was four years, but as part of the Plan A scheme adopted in 1949 the term of the mayor elected in that year would be up in 1951. John Hynes would have to face James Curley again.

Curley, now seventy-six, could not give it up. In the past he had lived to run, but now, confiding to his son that he needed the money raised by his campaign, he ran to live. His key issue was the $12 increase in the property tax since 1949, which he denounced as "exorbitant" and promised to lower with a wave of the wand of Curleyism.

Paradoxically, that tax rate was a sign of returning fiscal health. Curley had kept commercial assessments artificially high so as to keep residential property tax rates artificially low. But every year he had to pay out millions of dollars in abatements to commercial property owners who appealed the high assessments, and every year the city had to borrow to make up for the resulting shortfall in revenue. During Curley's last two years in office, Boston returned $20 million in abatements. During two years of Hynes it returned only $6 million, borrowed proportionately less, and was paying less in interest charges on its borrowing. The city had begun the arduous road back from Curleyism. The finance of decline had ended. The economics of decline would take longer to arrest, but at least government was no longer its agent. And the pattern that had obtained for the first five decades of the century was now reversed: Boston would rise as Curley fell.[9]

In radio and television appearances Curley took up his ancient cry: "There is no substitute for experience." Hynes had an answer for that one: "You have had the experience of me in office the past two years, and you have had experience with my predecessor for many years. I agree, as my opponent has said, that there is no substitute for experience."[10]

Any hope Curley had of winning ended with the entry into the race of his former campaign manager and political protégé, Joseph Timilty. Curley charged that Timilty had secretly sold him out in the 1949 campaign, saying, "I was the victim of a conspiracy the details of which are being unfolded in the present campaign." No Curley election would be complete without a Judas—or a revenant from the past: "like a nightmare from an ancient time," Thomas O'Brien, Father Coughlin's candidate against Curley in the 1936 Senate campaign, also declared his candidacy. Curley claimed to be a better friend of Joseph R. McCarthy's than was O'Brien, the Boston Irish having found a new hero in the Wisconsin senator and a new target for their resentment. The Puritan had passed, but the communist remained.[11]

Plan A called for a September primary to select two candidates to face off in November. Hynes won this easily, 108,000 to 77,000 for Curley, and 16,000 for Timilty. Even if Curley captured every Timilty vote and all 1,500 O'Brien votes, he would still lose in November. "James Michael Curley . . . is through politically," the *Herald* exulted. "Dame Boston may soon again lift her head with pride among American municipalities."[12]

A few days later Curley called the press to the Jamaicaway for a historic announcement. Looking like a winner in his best blue pin-striped suit and with Gertrude, wearing a pink satin gown with a burgundy jacket, beside him, Curley said he was suspending his campaign for mayor to save Boston from the New Boston Committee, a nonpartisan reform group that had evolved out of Students for Hynes, and its "leftist" candidates for the School Committee and the City Council. He would direct his shot and shell at this latest insidious manifestation of the reform virus. Would he take his name off the ballot? reporters asked him. No, he said, pleading nebulous legal technicalities. As he later confided to a graduate student preparing a thesis on his oratory, his stratagem might just lull the Hynes campaign to sleep, allowing him to win by default on the big sympathy vote he expected in November. If not, he told the student, "I will have the luxurious leisure to return to Plato, Plutarch, and the almost inexhaustible reservoir of the wisdom of the ages, always waiting to be tapped by anybody who has the time or inclination."[13]

The vote Curley hoped for did not materialize. ("If they love me," he remarked to a friend as a crowd cheered him during the primary campaign, "why won't the sons-of-bitches vote for me?") Hynes won the general election, 154,000 to Curley's 75,000. Only two wards went for Curley, foremost among them the old Tammany ward, which "stood out like a beacon in a vast sea of Hynes strength." When Curley got the news at the Jamaicaway, he made preparations to go downtown to the Hotel Brunswick to meet with friends and supporters. "I always go down there," he told a reporter, "win or lose." But just as he was walking out the door an aide, telephoning the hotel, discovered that no one was there. They had all gone home. Curley took this dampening intelligence in stride, saying, "I'll spend a quiet night in the library."[14]

He was philosophical in defeat. "There would be no hope for future generations if I went on forever," he said. "It's got to end sometime." Asked if he would do it all again, he replied without hesitating, "Yes. I have had an interesting life. It has had success and defeat and I wouldn't do it differently." Ed O'Connor would have the dying Frank Skeffington put that very avowal into the vernacular. And borrowing from O'Connor borrowing from Curley, John Henry Cutler, the ghostwriter of Curley's autobiography, would use a variant for the title of that book, *I'd Do It Again*. From life into art and back again to something more like Life: Curley would follow the same path as his thought.[15]

Each campaigning season saw Curley return to the arena: if he could not run himself (the Plan A changes in the City Charter having been effected, Hynes's new term ran for the regular four years), as national committeeman from Massachusetts he could play a role at Democratic conventions and could lend his voice to other candidates. Thus in 1952 he agreed to speak for Adlai Stevenson on the "Irish Hour," a Boston radio program. Dwight Eisenhower, Stevenson's Republican opponent, had summoned the Western world to a "Cromwellian crusade" against communism. Curley was all for the crusade, but the epithet made him see green. "General Eisenhower has shown his unfitness to be President of the United States," he said over the airwaves, "by invoking the name of the infamous Oliver Cromwell." As Stevenson campaign workers smiled at him from outside the booth, he then expanded on the horrors of Cromwell's subjugation of Ireland, including his policy of scattering the Irish rebels to distant places across the seas. "Why, to this day," he said, "you can visit the West Indies and find people with proud Irish names like Murphy and Kelly and O'Brien who are *black as the ace of spades!* Oh, the shame of it! Black Kellys and Murphys and O'Briens!" The smiles had vanished from the faces of the Stevenson handlers.[16]

Curley himself briefly became an issue in the 1952 campaign, through the ministrations of Thomas P. ("Tip") O'Neill. In 1948 the Massachusetts Democracy had taken control of the lower house of the state legislature for the first time in history. O'Neill, who had been elected to the House in 1936, was the Speaker. One day he got a sad letter from Malcolm Nichols: the former mayor had no pension and was having trouble making ends meet. Could O'Neill help him? Moved by Nichols's plea, O'Neill put through a pension for him. In 1952 Curley came to see O'Neill. "Tip, you took care of Nichols," Curley said. "Now I'm broke too, and I'd appreciate it if you'd take care of my wife and me the same way." (This being "broke" was a relative condition: he was just back from a long European vacation during which he had spent over $100,000.) O'Neill arranged to have a bill written tailored to Curley's specifications as to length of service and tenure in office. Slipped in at the end of a forty-three-hour marathon session of the House, it passed with many legislators unaware that they had voted James M. Curley an annual pension of $12,000.

When word leaked out of this favor, O'Neill found himself in the middle of a controversy, one that Republican politicians were quick to exploit. Visiting East Boston on a campaign swing, the Republican vice presidential nominee, Senator Richard M. Nixon of California, drew a big hand from a partisan crowd when he declared that Republicans stood for social security "but for the greater masses of the people and not for just a few favored politicians," adding with Nixonian insinuation, "and you know who I mean in Massachusetts." When Republican calls for a special session of the legislature to repeal O'Neill's gift grew in volume, Curley declared that "under no conditions" would he accept the pension he had privately sought and publicly welcomed. He wanted no part of "a scheme upon the part of the Republican machine to gain control of the Legislature."[17]

Later that fall, though, Curley gave aid and comfort to a leading Republican, Henry Cabot Lodge. Having resigned his Senate seat to fight in the war, Lodge resumed his political career in 1946 by challenging and defeating the aging, scandal-scarred isolationist David I. Walsh. Thus, in the span of a decade, Lodge had beaten the two leading first-generation Irish-American politicians in Massachusetts. In 1952 he was himself being challenged by a second-generation Irish-American politician, Congressman John F. Kennedy. With his father's money behind him, Kennedy was a formidable candidate. A $500,000 "loan" from Joseph Kennedy to the publisher of the failing *Boston Post* had not only changed that paper from pro-Lodge to pro-Kennedy but also had gotten Kennedy a front-page editorial endorsement. The *Post* still had great influence among the Boston Irish, and knowing of Curley's feud with Kennedy, Lodge went to the Jamaicaway to ask Curley to help him garner some of that vote. Accounts differ on whether Curley did or did not publicly endorse Lodge, but he did not endorse Kennedy. In any case, the two men struck up a friendship. After Lodge's defeat, President Eisenhower appointed the former senator U.S. ambassador to the United Nations. When Lodge refused to shake the hand of the Soviet representative after the latter attacked the United States on the floor of the U.N., Curley sent him a congratulatory letter in which he predicted that Lodge would someday be president. Lodge had a reciprocal affection for Curley and would visit him from time to time during the fifties to drink the wine of his company. When, in 1980, Boston honored Curley statues and a park bench (Fitzgerald got an expressway named after him; Tobin a bridge; Hynes a convention hall), old Henry Cabot Lodge came down from Beverly for the occasion.[18]

In 1953, at age seventy-nine, Curley declared his candidacy for the U.S. Senate seat held by Leverett Saltonstall. A few months later he announced he would run for governor instead. The old man was refighting the battles of his middle age. His name was placed in nomination for governor at the 1954 Democratic state convention, but he got only one vote in the balloting. Wisely, he had stayed home, sparing himself gratuitous humiliation.[19]

In 1955, in his eighty-first year, he ran for mayor of Boston for the tenth time. He hired a plane to buzz the city, trailing a banner that read CURLY. When scores of people called to alert him to the misspelling, he was overjoyed. Keep that peccant banner flying! He summoned "the suffering public" to a big open-air rally at Pemberton Square, and over two thousand people showed up. "There is no substitution for experience," he told them. But the electorate felt he had had enough; in a four-man field, he placed third, with the votes of twenty-four thousand people who would be "with Curley" for as long as Curley was. He was not so much King Lear now, bending over the body of his daughter, as Cuchulain, the warrior king of Irish myth[20]:

> *Cuchulain stirred,*
> *Stared on the horses of the sea, and heard*
> *The cars of battle and his own name cried;*
> *And fought with the invulnerable tide.*[21]

On a hot Sunday morning at his Scituate summer house, after calling the rectory of the parish church to check the schedule of Masses, as well as to settle the vexed question of whether his wife's taking two aspirin the night before meant that she could not receive Holy Communion at Mass—after finishing this last business of his life, Maurice Tobin suffered a heart attack in bed and died at the age of fifty-two. He was the third governor from the Curley era to die in 1953, Joseph Ely, and Paul Dever having preceded him. "Well, that only leaves Mansfield," Curley said when he heard the news.[22]

His own health was shaky: the diabetes was filing his body down, he suffered several bone-breaking falls, his circulation was failing. And it had been years since he had been able to restock those two safes. Tip O'Neill tells a story of how Curley, "on his 'uppers,' which meant that he didn't have enough money to fix the heels of his shoes," approached him one day with an offer to raise money for the Speaker's congressional reelection campaign. O'Neill readily agreed. Shortly afterward, Curley came to him with an envelope. "I raised $500 for you," he said. Yet O'Neill found only $450 in the envelope. This went on for several days, the sums, less Curley's 10 percent, rising. After the election, O'Neill got a call from a man claiming to be a big contributor who wanted a favor. O'Neill checked the list of his contributors: the name was not on it. Would the man refresh his memory? "Jim Curley came to me and said he was raising money to put Tip O'Neill on television," he said. "And I'm the one who paid for your TV time the night you went on. Didn't he give you my name?" O'Neill had a good laugh: no, Curley had refused to share his list of contributors, probably because he had taken 10 percent off the top. "Now I understand why you've never heard of me," the man said, laughing. "But I remember how much money I gave to Curley to pay for those ads, and let me tell you something, Jim Curley made out fine. I'm afraid *you* were the one who was working for ten percent!"²³

There were only so many times he could put the touch on his old contributors, however, and to make a little cash on the side he became a kind of shill at conventions held in Boston. He would stand in a five-by-eight-foot booth wearing his black alpaca wool coat with the velvet collar and his gray wide-brimmed Borsalino and act as a draw for the refrigeration equipment or construction implement salesmen of the firms that hired him. The man in the booth was the former governor of the Commonwealth. "It was a pathetic scene," one witness recalled. Once while visiting Boston from St. Louis, where he worked as president of Washington University, Thomas Eliot saw Curley in a corridor of the State House. "He was all alone, just leaning against the wall, staring at nothing." He brightened when "the young man of Harvard," deferentially addressing him as "Governor," greeted him, but the impression he left with Eliot was a sad one. "He looked beaten, forgotten. Finished."²⁴

Edwin O'Connor was about to come to rescue him from the politician's hell—the realm of the forgotten. Most biographies of writers seem designed to show how wrong Malcolm Cowley was when he said, "No complete S.O.B. ever wrote a good sentence." But O'Connor, who died in 1968 at age forty-nine, proved Cowley right; he was a writer you could take home to your mother. He lives in the recollections of his friends as warm, generous, witty, and self-effacing. It will mean something to some readers to know that he went to Mass and received Holy Communion seven mornings a week.

O'Connor was third-generation Irish. His father, John V. O'Connor, was a physician with advanced training in internal medicine at both Johns Hopkins and Harvard medical schools. His mother, Mary, was a teacher in the public schools of the city where Ed grew up, Woonsocket, Rhode Island, a declining textile center just across the Blackstone River from Massachusetts. Rhode Islanders live in relation to Massachusetts as Canadians do to the United States: with their noses pressed to the glass watching the fabulous goings-on in their larger and vastly more interesting neighbor. Thus, after taking a degree (cum laude) in English at Notre Dame, and after wartime service in the Coast Guard on Cape Cod and in Boston, O'Connor was following the prevailing currents of local desire by taking a job as a writer-announcer for a Boston radio station. He would have been at WNAC when James Michael Curley conducted his Kennedy-financed radio campaign for mayor, would have seen the leonine candidate at the station, and heard more honeyed words than can have been good for his health.

After a year in broadcasting, O'Connor quit to devote himself to developing his now-insistent gift for prose. He wrote radio reviews for the *Boston Herald* and facetious skits for the *Atlantic Monthly* while working on his first novel, *The Oracle*, a send-up of a pompous radio commentator. Like *The Last Hurrah*, the novel is mostly talk, some of it funny, some tedious, all of it stylishly dished out. Published in 1951, it was poorly received critically and did even worse commercially, netting the young writer $720, which he used to help finance a trip to Ireland.

There is not, O'Connor's friend Arthur Schlesinger, Jr., has observed, a single Irish character in *The Oracle*; but an Irish character of Homeric dimensions was playing out the last act of his political career in Boston, and from his rented room in the Back Bay O'Connor would have seen something of James Michael Curley in the mayoral campaigns of 1949 and 1951. Sometime in the latter year he stopped work on a novel he was calling "A Young Man of Promise" to begin a very different project.

"I would like to do for the Irish in America what Faulkner did for the South," he confided to a friend. "I wanted to do a novel on the whole Irish-American business," he later said. "What the Irish got in America, they got through politics; so, of course, I had to use a political framework." Woonsocket had been a mostly Yankee town, with an exotic fringe of French Canadians; but Boston was by way of being the capital of Irish America. These were the people of his blood, and in telling their story he would find his voice as an Irish-American storyteller.

He spent four years working on the novel, tentatively called "Not Moisten an Eye." Ted Weeks, Ellery Sedgwick's successor as editor of the *Atlantic Monthly*, had rejected *The Oracle*, but he continued to publish O'Connor's work in the magazine and, with his colleague Charles Morton, who was also a friend of O'Connor's, to encourage Ed's novel writing. The Atlantic Monthly Press offered a $5,000 prize for the best novel they received each year. Ed got his manuscript in just before the deadline in January 1955. Its first two readers were unimpressed, but a third, Esther Yntema, saw its gold. "I think the two main things to be said about the book," she wrote in her advisory to Weeks, "are: that it is profoundly moving, and that its scope is very great." O'Connor won the prize. He sent the press a memo urging the editors to "go easy on this business of the *political* novel" in promoting the book and changing its title to "The Last Hurrah."[25]

"The whole novel, form and content, is an extended Irish wake," writes the literary historian Shaun O'Connell. How apt for a novel about the "whole Irish-American business." At the center of the wake is seventy-two-year-old Frank Skeffington, twice governor of his state and incumbent mayor of a municipality identified only as "the red-brick city." The title "Mayor," however, does not do justice to Skeffington's public role. "You see," he explains to his nephew, the young newspaper reporter,

> "my position is slightly complicated because I'm not just an elected official of the city; I'm a tribal chieftain as well. It's a necessary kind of dual officeholding, you might say; without the second, I wouldn't be the first."
> "The tribe," said Adam, "being the Irish?"
> "Exactly. . . . I think you realize that the body of my support does not come from the American Indian."[26]

That this funny line is buried sentences deep in Skeffington's answer shows the one great problem of the novel—Adam's dimness.

Here as elsewhere, Skeffington and the other equally garrulous old parties Adam encounters are too deferential to his pardonable (born in Boston, he has been raised in the Middle West) but implausibly elementary ignorance.

The tribal chieftain is engaged in his final campaign, a "last hurrah," and he invites his nephew to watch it over his shoulder. The mayor's son, Francis Jr., is "unsuitable" for a career in politics, as George Curley was. A widower, the mayor daily puts fresh flowers in a vase by his late wife's portrait. His grand house, his retinue of fedoras, his taste for poetry, his oratorical genius, his glad-handing generosity, his wit, his piety, his shady reputation—to say nothing of the fact that he loses the election to a fair imitation of Maurice Tobin: these are just a few of the parallels between Skeffington and Curley.

Reviewers were in no doubt as to the novel's character as a roman à clef. Writing in the *Saturday Review*, Howard Mumford Jones commended *The Last Hurrah* to "anybody who wants to read large generous-minded fiction, and to anybody else who wants to know how American politics really operated in the generation of J-m-s M. C-r-y." Reviewing the book in *The New Republic*, Thomas Eliot, having been smeared as a communist by the man who was Skeffington's model ("I want you to know . . . ," Curley said at a rally in Pemberton Square, "that there (is) more Americanism in one-half of Jim Curley's ahss than in that pink body of Tom Eliot!"), offered a more measured judgment on the relation of art to life, Skeffington to Curley. "Nobody like Skeffington could be quite as consistently delightful, warm-hearted, learned, and generous. . . . The big boss of a big city is likely to brush up against unmitigated evil more often than this book indicates. The utterly ruthless politician is sure to be, at least occasionally, a brutal human being. Insofar as Mr. O'Connor has failed to portray evil and brutality in all their darkness, he has painted too happy a picture." Anthony West, in *The New Yorker*, didn't mention Curley, but in what was at once a touching display of political innocence and a sharp literary criticism, he called the novel "genuinely subversive" for "persuasively pretending" that Skeffington's "mean vices" (he steals some food from the City Hospital to provide for the widow of Knocko Minihan) are "virtues."[27]

It was this quality of *The Last Hurrah*—the sentimental machinery by which it transmuted the dab of bad in Skeffington into a lump of good—that was to mean the most in refashioning the reputation of James Michael Curley.

❖   ❖   ❖

An Atlantic prize novel, a main selection of the Book-of-the-Month Club, excerpted in the *Reader's Digest*, and the subject of an ecstatic review on the front page of the *New York Times Book Review*, *The Last Hurrah* quickly became a best-seller. Reacting characteristically to the book's publication, one of the major literary events of 1956, Curley at first wanted to sue O'Connor. He was especially angry at him for making "my mother" a thief: a kitchen mechanic for a Beacon Hill family, Mrs. Skeffington lifts a banana from the Yankee prunes who employ her to take home to her children. Sarah Curley would sooner have starved than steal a morsel, Curley maintained, taking the novel as his life story. Francis and George persuaded him to cool his temper. People all over America had fallen in love with Skeffington, they told him. That argument seems to have changed his mind. He decided to do with *The Last Hurrah* what he had done with Joseph Dinneen's *The Purple Shamrock*: embrace it, appropriate it, use the book to secure and set the terms of his own fame.[28]

Skeffington began to possess him. In their meeting outside the Parker House, after Curley told O'Connor how much he liked "the part where I die," O'Connor sought to get this tangle between Curley's life and his legend straightened out. "Isn't it strange, Governor," he said, "how so many people confuse fact with fiction? Skeffington with yourself, for instance? I know and you know, the difference between the two, that the one isn't like the other. . . ." But Curley was carried away with his new identity. "Yes," he said, as if talking to himself. "Yes, there I am in my bedroom, dying. Breathing my last. I'm lying flat on my back with my eyes closed when suddenly into the room comes . . ."—and he re-created the scene. When Curley/Skeffington had breathed his last, he and O'Connor shook hands and promised to have lunch one day soon. "The governor and I never did have that lunch," O'Connor wrote three years after Curley's death, "and that is something I regret. I don't know why we didn't, but I rather suspect it was because we both had become too preoccupied with our own activities: I with my book, he with my book."[29]

For Curley had "taken on *The Last Hurrah* as a full-time occupation," accepting offers to give talks on it and his own life from many different quarters. Thus the man Thomas Eliot had seen staring forlornly at the State House walls was once more in demand. And again and again he returned to the part where he died. In a laughter-filled lecture he gave at the University of New Hampshire, for example (*Life* magazine later printed it as a review of *The Last Hurrah*), with Ed O'Connor smiling up at him from the audience, he said:

> I feel that the last paragraph of that book contains everything that is worthwhile in that book. I am supposed to have received the last rites of the Catholic Church and I'd been in a state of coma for about 12 hours when the owner of the Boston Herald comes in and looks at me in that sad state, and he said, "I suppose, Skeffington, if you had to do it all over again, you'd do different." And I replied to him . . . , "The hell I would."

In fact the character who repeats the question a reporter asked Curley after his defeat in the 1951 primary is not the publisher of the *Herald* but a wealthy Irish businessman, the father of Adam Caulfield's wife. But no matter, Curley was making Skeffington and the book his own.[30]

He went further. Since 1953 he had been working on his memoirs, and had accumulated a substantial manuscript. Several publishers had turned it down, but that was before his rebirth as Skeffington. Now Prentice-Hall offered to publish his autobiography and to hire a ghostwriter to whip it into shape. He agreed: Ed O'Connor was making a fortune off his life. Why shouldn't he get into the act? There was more than enough of Curley to go around.

Through the late summer and fall of 1956, John Henry Cutler, a Harvard graduate, a former English professor at Dartmouth, and the publisher and editor of a remarkable small-town Massachusetts newspaper, the *Duxbury Clipper*, talked to Curley, rode about town with him, pored over the six hundred volumes of clippings Curley had collected in his basement, and sifted through the meandering pages of Curley's unpublished (and unpublishable) memoirs seeking to capture the man and his times. Written in a few months, *I'd Do It Again* was published in the spring of 1957 in the still-white wake of *The Last Hurrah*.[31]

Some reviewers found they liked Curley much better as Skef-fington than as the voice of this autobiography. Rushing to meet his deadline, Cutler gave his invention a braggart's tone that might be palatable in a (brief) conversation with an eighty-two-year-old man, but that, along with his haughty use of the third person in sentences like "Curley could not be deterred by threats," make the narrator insufferable. Other reviewers, though, saw the book in just the way Curley wanted. "Nature often imitates art," Arthur Schlesinger, Jr., wrote in the *Saturday Review*. "Reading James M. Curley's book . . . one cannot help wondering what the Curley autobiography might have been like had Edwin O'Connor never written last year's best-selling 'The Last Hurrah.'" Noting Curley's initial threats of a libel suit, Schlesinger said that "Curley has now contrived a subtler revenge. He has appropriated Skeffington for his own purposes, rebaptized him Curley, and done his best to transform art into nature."[32]

Together, both books gave the "rebaptized" Curley a new public face. They took him out of the history we have been trying to return him to and made him available to myth. Along with the mounting infirmities of his old age and the deaths of his children, they won him a pardon.

❖   ❖   ❖

He spent his final years dying in the glow of his own fame as a funny, lovable, forgivably roguish last-of-a-kind. Having lived a politician, he died a celebrity.

It was a season of final, heightened pleasures. Interviewed by Edward R. Murrow for "Person to Person," he looked delighted to be in the national eye. His old foghorn of a voice had lost some of its timbre, but it was still redolent of a rich personal culture. Gertrude and his son George seated on either side of him, along with Murrow back in the studio, treated his every word like a victory wrung from mortality, a trophy to be cherished, like himself. He had the singular satisfaction of seeing his son Francis ordained, after years of demanding training in theology and church doctrine, as a Jesuit priest. The prestige of having a *Jesuit* in an Irish-American family of Curley's generation cannot be exaggerated. "This is not a day for me or grand oratory," Curley said in a speech that meant everything to Francis. "It is my son's day and I will only speak a moment. Senator David I. Walsh gave me years ago what I thought was the greatest accolade that any man ever had. He called me 'the Mayor of the Poor.' My son Francis gave me a prouder title, 'Father of a Priest.'" He could even claim a final political victory when he defeated John Hynes in a contest to pick delegates at large to the 1956 Democratic national convention. The top vote-getter was John McCormack, with 17,856; Senator John F. Kennedy came next with 16,426, followed by Curley, with 16,347. There were also 160 ballots cast for "Skeffington"—which led Curley to observe: "It's too damn bad for McCormack and Kennedy that they didn't count the vote for that fellow from 'The Last Hurrah.' What's his name? Skeffington? I'm supposed to be Skeffington and he got 160 votes. Add those to my votes and I would have topped the ticket." Not quite; but he would have topped Kennedy, who was angling to get Curley to retire as national committeeman so he could install a Kennedy loyalist as state party chairman and move the current chairman, William ("Onions") Burke, to Curley's post. "He hasn't got enough money to buy me," Curley said of Kennedy, refusing to quit. Beating Kennedy, with Skeffington's help, was Curley's last political victory.[33]

True, his health broke down: he suffered a "circulatory collapse" followed by severe hemorrhaging and had to be placed in an oxygen tent and have most of his stomach removed to stop the bleeding. But he rallied, recovered, lived nearly two more years, and the cards, letters, spiritual bouquets, telegrams of sympathy, and testimonials he received to the wonderful man he had been and the wonderful things he had done gave him the rare satisfaction of attending his own wake.[34]

Leaving the house with the shamrock shutters was hard, but he and Gertrude could no longer afford to keep it up, and some of its memories were too bitter to live with in these, his ambrosial days. He sold it to an order of priests who used it as a rectory for the next thirty years. In 1988 the order sold it to the City of Boston for $1.2 million. "Only the churlish would point out the city had by then paid for the house *twice*," Shaun O'Connell writes, and oh, how Curley would have enjoyed the joke of that![35]

The subject of a novel by a great Irish-American novelist, Curley/Skeffington became in his last year the subject of a film by a great Irish-American director and starring a great Irish-American actor. The filmmaker, born John Martin Feeney, was raised up the

Atlantic coast from Boston in Portland, Maine, in a house where Gaelic was often spoken. Following his brother Francis, an actor, to Hollywood, John also took Francis's less obtrusively ethnic stage name, becoming John Ford. In a career that stretched from the silent era to the sixties, Ford made beautiful and moving and important films such as *The Informer, The Grapes of Wrath, Stagecoach, The Searchers,* and *The Man Who Shot Liberty Valance.* Though it has some fine Fordian moments and Spencer Tracy as Skeffington is irresistible, *The Last Hurrah* is not of this company. Asked what he thought of it after seeing the premiere in Boston, Ed O'Connor was caustic: "The back of the seats at Loew's Orpheum ought to have the same kind of equipment they have on airplanes." He had hoped the novel would be made into a Broadway musical; if it had to be a movie, he would have preferred that Claude Rains rather than Spencer Tracy play Skeffington. There is no accounting for taste.[36]

At any rate, the critics loved it. "Now that the key districts have all been heard from, including Hollywood," Bosley Crowther wrote in the *New York Times,* "it is safe to expect that Edwin O'Connor's highly touted political character, Skeffington, will repeat in an overwhelmingly landslide as the People's Choice this year." If O'Connor had idealized Skeffington, Ford approached him, Crowther noted, with "an affection amounting to sheer idolatry"; Ford was so "kind to him in this film that one searches in vain for a reason why anyone should think him a rogue." Instead of holding Columbia Pictures up for a few thousand, Curley should have paid the studio for the hagiography.[37]

By Hollywood standards *The Last Hurrah* did not do well at the box office, but even a poorly performing film reaches a much larger audience than a best-selling novel. People came away from *The Last Hurrah* loving Skeffington and mourning his death as the end of an era. Curley may not have gone to heaven, but in his last months he attained something like the secular equivalent of eternal life.

Pardoned himself, he could now pardon others. A little short of a year before his death he received a letter from a Mr. Seneca B. Anderson, a Miami attorney, informing him that "John M. Kelley, Jr., the attorney who represented the government in its case against you is in the terminal stages of cancer of the liver. His prosecution of the case against you was the big event of his professional life and he speaks of it as such. I am sure he fought you as hard as he could, but . . . never have I heard him speak unkindly of you or attempt to criticize your character or motives." Anderson concluded with a special plea. "It occurs to me that you might find it in your heart to write this dying man and assure him that you hold no ill will toward him."

The letter was dated April 18, 1958. Ten days later Curley sent this letter to Kelley:

Dear Friend,

You probably will be surprised to hear from me but a mutual friend informed me of your present illness and I hasten to extend my sincere and best wishes for a speedy recovery.

I would like you to know that I hold no ill will toward you in the performance of your duties in the past. I am quite sure that no one could have dealt more fairly with me than you did, under the circumstances of that particular time. I hope and pray that you will recover shortly from your serious illness and that the Lord will shower you with every blessing. Keep your chin up and place your faith in Our Blessed Mother Who has befriended me upon many occasions over the years.

With every good wish for a speedy recovery, I remain

JAMES M. CURLEY

A subsequent letter from Anderson thanked Curley for giving Kelley "more pleasure than anything which has happened to him in months." A third letter, this time addressed to Curley's secretary, Frank Howland, said that Kelley had died "several months ago." This letter was dated March 15, 1959, by which time Curley himself was four months dead.[38]

❖   ❖   ❖

"The part where I die . . ."
The details of Curley's physical deterioration needn't detain us; let us cut to the final scene. He is in the City Hospital, ending where he began, close as memory to the walk-up on Northampton Street where Michael and Sarah Curley had taught him all he ever needed to know about kindness, generosity, and the love of God. He learned other lessons too, not from them but from their circumstances; and these lessons—about poverty, and power, and money—were often in conflict with his parents' values. The "bread

and tea of life" was never the dish for him. Michael, that "grand man," had not lived to see what he made of himself but Sarah had, and she was in his delirious thoughts in his last hours—her sacrifice, the punishment taken by her flesh, her knees, on rough strange floors to keep him and his brother alive, it moved him still.[39]

Coming off the elevator after a five-hour operation for stomach cancer, jouncing into momentary consciousness on the stretcher as it encounters a bump in the floor, he glimpses the reporters and photographers waiting for him down the hall, and in a voice nearly as strong as of old, looks up at his son and says, "Franno, I wish to announce the first plank in my campaign for reelection."

"What's that, Governor?"

"We're going to have the floors in this goddamned hospital smoothed out," he says, with a wink and a laugh. Leave it to James Michael Curley to have his last words be a campaign promise.

Notes

❖   ❖   ❖   ❖

Prologue

1. My account of the last days, wake, and funeral of James Michael Curley is based on readings of the *Boston Globe, Boston Herald, Boston Traveler,* the *Christian Science Monitor,* the *New York Times, Boston Daily Record,* and *Boston American,* issues for Nov. 1–18, 1958. Notes can be found in my file on Curley's funeral.

2. Private interview with Robert Healy.

3. Anecdotes are from a harvest published by the *Boston Traveler* in daily installments between Nov. 17 and 20, 1958, as well as from private interviews with Francis X. Curley, John E. Powers, Robert Bergenheim, and Peter Caparell.

4. Arthur M. Schlesinger, Jr., ed., *The Best and the Last of Edwin O'Connor* (Boston, 1970), 15.

5. *Boston Globe,* Nov. 11, 1958; *New York Times,* Nov. 13, 1958.

6. John T. Galvin, "Patrick J. Maguire: Boston's Last Democratic Boss," *New England Quarterly* (Sept. 1982), 392–419. I am grateful to Mr. Galvin for making Curley's unpublished memoirs available to me.

7. For Collins see John T. Galvin, "Boston's Eminent Patrick from Ireland," *Boston Globe,* Mar. 17, 1988.

8. *Boston Globe,* Nov. 4, 1958. The quotation from Nat Hentoff is from his memoir *Boston Boy* (New York, 1986), 81.

9. Private interview with John Henry Cutler, to whom Curley expressed his view of the electorate.

10. William Dean Howells, *The Rise of Silas Lapham* (Boston, 1885); Shaun O'Connell, *Imagining Boston: A Literary Landscape* (Boston, 1990), 120. For "sifted few" see Gerald H. Gamm, *The Making of New Deal Democrats: Voting Behavior and Realignment in Boston, 1920–1940* (Chicago, 1989), 111.

11. My thanks to Martin F. Nolan of the *Boston Globe* for bringing the quotation from Adams to my attention. It can be found in *The Education of Henry Adams: An Autobiography* (Boston, 1961), 7.

12. Richard Hofstadter, *The Age of Reform: From Bryan to F.D.R.* (New York, 1955), 182; Thomas H. O'Connor, *South Boston: My Home Town* (Boston, 1988), 84.

13. O'Connor, *South Boston,* 85.

14. For Up-Up Kelly see Thomas P. O'Neill, Jr., with William Novak, *Man of the House: The Life and Political Memoirs of Speaker Tip O'Neill* (New York, 1987), 33–34.

Chapter 1. The Shin of a Sparrow

1. Charles H. Trout, "Curley of Boston: The Search for Irish Legitimacy," in *Boston 1700–1980: The Evolution of Urban Politics,* ed. Ronald P. Formisano and Constance K. Burns (Westport, Conn., 1984), 170.

2. R. F. Foster, *Modern Ireland, 1600–1972* (New York, 1988), 324, 319.

3. Foster, *Modern Ireland*, 326.

4. Ibid., 318, 351.

5. Joseph F. Dinneen, *The Purple Shamrock: The Hon. James Michael Curley of Boston* (New York, 1949), 13–15; James Michael Curley, *I'd Do It Again: A Record of All My Uproarious Years* (Englewood Cliffs, N.J., 1957), 17.

6. Trout, "Curley of Boston," 167.

7. Oscar Handlin, *Boston's Immigrants* (Cambridge, Mass., 1979), 55, 132.

8. Thomas H. O'Connor, *Fitzpatrick's Boston, 1846–1866* (Boston, 1984), 82; Handlin, *Boston's Immigrants*, 36; John F. Stack, Jr., *International Conflict in an American City: Boston's Irish, Italians, and Jews, 1935–1944* (Westport, Conn., 1979), 21.

9. Handlin, *Boston's Immigrants*, 49.

10. Cecil Woodham-Smith, *The Great Hunger* (New York, 1970), 205.

11. Handlin, *Boston's Immigrants*, 59, 114–15.

12. Samuel Eliot Morison, *One Boy's Boston* (Boston, 1983), 15; Allan Nevins, *The Emergence of Modern America, 1865–1878* (New York, 1927), 230; Handlin, *Boston's Immigrants*, 22; Ronald Story, *The Forging of an Aristocracy: Harvard and the Boston Upper Class, 1800–1870* (Middleton, Conn., 1980), 96, 133.

13. Handlin, *Boston's Immigrants*, 133.

14. O'Connor, *Fitzpatrick's Boston*, 79, 51.

15. Handlin, *Boston's Immigrants*, 121.

16. John R. Mulkern, *The Know-Nothing Party in Massachusetts: The Rise and Fall of a People's Movement* (Boston, 1990), 63.

17. Ibid., 68, 69, 76, 94.

18. Ibid., 103.

19. Ibid., 103, 117.

20. See Proceedings, Boston City Council, 1910.

21. O'Connor, *Fitzpatrick's Boston*, 159, 150.

22. Ibid., 188.

23. Thomas H. O'Connor, *South Boston: My Home Town* (Boston, 1988), 57; Handlin, *Boston's Immigrants*, 208–11.

24. Trout, "Curley of Boston," 170, 168.

25. Ibid., 171.

26. Ibid., 191.

27. Dinneen, *The Purple Shamrock*, 10, 21; private interview with Francis X. Curley.

Chapter 2. The Boy from Home

1. Robert A. Woods and Albert J. Kennedy, *The Zone of Emergence*, ed. Sam Bass Warner (Cambridge, Mass., 1962), 136; Samuel Cobb, Inaugural Address, 1874, Bostonian Society Library, Boston; Charles H. Trout, "Curley of Boston: The Search for Irish Legitimacy," in *Boston 1700–1980: The Evolution of Urban Politics*, ed. Ronald P. Formisano and Constance K. Burns (Westport, Conn., 1984), 190. See also the biographical article by J. R. Milne (the first in a series of five) in the *Boston Sunday Post*, Sept. 21, 1930.

2. Herbert Marshall Zolot, "The Issue of Good Government and James Michael Curley: Curley and the Boston Scene from 1897–1918" (Ph.D. diss., State University of New York, Stony Brook, 1975), 149; Woods and Kennedy, *The Zone of Emergence*, 142. See also Joan Tonn, *The Life and Work of Mary Parker Follett* (forthcoming from Oxford University Press), MS 245.

3. Trout, "Curley of Boston," 169; *Boston Daily Record*, Nov. 14, 1958.

4. James Michael Curley, *I'd Do It Again: A Record of All My Uproarious Years* (Englewood Cliffs, N.J., 1957), 34. See also Trout, "Curley of Boston," 173; *Boston Sunday Post*, Sept. 21, 1930; Curley, *I'd Do It Again*, 35; private interview with Richard Dennis.

5. *Boston Sunday Post*, Sept. 21, 1930.

6. William V. Shannon, *The American Irish* (New York, 1963), 38. For photograph of Sarah Curley see the *Boston Sunday Post*, Sept. 21, 1930. The stories about her are from a private interview with members of John Curley's family.

7. *Boston Sunday Post*, Sept. 21, 1930.

8. Trout, "Curley of Boston," 172.

9. Private interview with Francis X. Curley.

10. *Boston Sunday Post*, Sept. 21, 1930.

11. Private interview with William Morrissey, former employee of the City of Boston.

12. See Boston City Directory for the years 1874–85; Trout, "Curley of Boston," 190; *Boston Globe*, Dec. 11, 1934.

13. *Boston Globe*, Dec. 11, 1934.

14. Curley, *I'd Do It Again*, 38, 39; *Boston Sunday Post*, Sept. 21, 1930.

15. See Boston City Directory, 1900–1908; private interview with John Curley's three daughters; *Boston Sunday Post*, Sept. 21, 1930.

16. *Boston Sunday Post*, Sept. 21, 1930; Joseph F. Dinneen, *The Purple Shamrock: The Hon. James Michael Curley of Boston* (New York, 1949), 22; Curley, *I'd Do It Again*, 39, 40.

17. "Memoirs of James M. Curley" (n.d.), 2, author's files. See also Zolot, "The Issue of Good Government," 2.

18. James M. Curley, "Life-Story of Mayor-Elect Curley As Told by Himself," *Boston Sunday Globe*, Jan. 18, 1914; *Boston Sunday Post*, Sept. 21, 1930.

19. Shannon, *The American Irish*, 24.

20. *Boston Sunday Post*, Sept. 21, 1930.

21. See review of John Milton Cooper, Jr., *Pivotal Decades: The United States, 1900–1920* (1990), in the *New York Times Book Review*; private interview with John Henry Cutler.

22. Curley, *I'd Do It Again*, 40.

23. Ibid.; *Boston Sunday Post*, Sept. 21, 1930; Dinneen, *The Purple Shamrock*, 23; Curley, *I'd Do It Again*, 41.

24. *Boston Sunday Post*, Sept. 21, 1930; Curley, *I'd Do It Again*, 41–42; Dinneen, *The Purple Shamrock*, 24.

25. *Boston Sunday Post*, Sept. 21, 1930.

26. Curley, "Life-Story."

27. Curley, *I'd Do It Again*, 42.

28. Peter K. Eisinger, "Ethnic Political Transition in Boston, 1884–1933: Some Lessons for Contemporary Cities," *Political Science Quarterly* 93 (Summer 1978); George J. Lankevich, ed., *Boston: A Chronological and Documentary History, 1602–1970* (Dobbs Ferry, N.Y., 1974), 50; Robert H. Wiebe, *The Search for Order, 1877–1920* (New York, 1967), 50.

29. Wiebe, *The Search for Order*, 54, 62; John F. Stack, Jr., *International Conflict in an American City: Boston's Irish, Italians, and Jews, 1935–1944* (Westport, Conn., 1979), 26. See also chronology appended to J. Joseph Huthmacher, *A Nation of Newcomers* (New York, 1967); Barbara Miller Solomon, *Ancestors and Immigrants: A Changing New England Tradition* (Boston, 1989), 102–104. For Paine's Roxbury holdings see Boston City Directory, 1890.

30. Curley, *I'd Do It Again*, 44; *King's Guide Book*, 1881.

31. Michael E. McGerr, *The Decline of Popular Politics: The American North, 1865–1928* (New York, 1986), 40.

32. Ibid., 188.

33. The journalist was J. R. Milne; see *Boston Sunday Post*, Sept. 28, 1930.

34. Dinneen, *The Purple Shamrock*, 31; see also 30.

35. *Boston Sunday Post*, Sept. 28, 1930.

36. Ibid.

37. Zolot, "The Issue of Good Government," 146–47. See also Woods and Kennedy, *The Zone of Emergence*, 138.

38. Zolot, "The Issue of Good Government," 154; Robert E. Sullivan and James M. O'Toole, eds., *Catholic Boston: Studies in Religion and Community, 1870–1970* (Boston, 1985), 236.

39. Woods and Kennedy, *The Zone of Emergence*, 138. See also Tonn, *The Life and Work of Mary Parker Follett*, MS 245–47. *Boston Globe*, Nov. 30, 1991.

40. Woods and Kennedy, *The Zone of Emergence*, 139. See also Gerald H. Gamm, *The Making of New Deal Democrats: Voting Behavior and Realignment in Boston, 1920–1940* (Chicago, 1989), 140.

41. William Schneider, "The Decline and Fall of American Politics," public lecture delivered at Boston College, Chestnut Hill, Mass., Dec. 1990.

42. Curley, *I'd Do It Again*, 44–45; Dinneen, *The Purple Shamrock*, 29. The quotation is from a private interview with John Henry Cutler, the ghostwriter of *I'd Do It Again*.

43. Curley, *I'd Do It Again*, 45–48; Dinneen, *The Purple Shamrock*, 32. See also the photograph between pages 214 and 215 in Curley, *I'd Do It Again*.

44. Zolot, "The Issue of Good Government," 160–61; Dinneen, *The Purple Shamrock*, 32.

45. Ibid.

46. William Jay Foley, "Public Speaking in the Political Career of James Michael Curley" (Ph.D. diss., University of Wisconsin, 1952), iii; Curley, *I'd Do It Again*, 30; *New York Times*, Mar. 26, 1922. Elliot Norton's observation is from a private interview.

47. Francis Curley interview. See also the fragment "Richard III" (n.d.), in the notes for "Memoirs of James M. Curley," author's files.

48. Curley, "Life-Story"; Owen Galvin obituary, *Boston Globe*, Dec. 18, 1897; Francis Curley interview.

49. Francis Curley interview. See also Reinhard H. Luthin, *American Demagogues: Twentieth Century* (Boston, 1954), 12.

50. "Memoirs of James Michael Curley," chap. 2, p. 2; *Boston Sunday Post*, Sept. 28, 1930.

51. Dinneen, *The Purple Shamrock*, 33; Curley, *I'd Do It Again*, 43.

52. Curley, *I'd Do It Again*, 43; private interview with Lauretta Bremner Sliney.

53. *Boston Sunday Post*, Sept. 28, 1930; Curley, *I'd Do It Again*, 47; Dinneen, *The Purple Shamrock*, 36; Zolot, "The Issue of Good Government," 161.

54. *Boston Globe*, Sept. 16, 1899; Zolot, "The Issue of Good Government," 161; *Boston Globe*, Nov. 16, Dec. 22, 1899; Curley, "Life-Story."

Chapter 3. The Crouching Tiger

1. *Boston Sunday Post*, Sept. 21, 1930; Proceedings, Boston City Council, 1900; Brennan to Curley, author's files, marked 1903; original is in James Michael Curley Collection, College of the Holy Cross, Worcester, Mass.

2. Curley quotation is from an article in the biographical series by J. R. Milne, *Boston Sunday Post*, Sept. 28, 1930.

3. *Boston Sunday Post*, Oct. 19, 1930.

4. Proceedings, Boston City Council, Mar. 28, 1901.

5. Joseph F. Dinneen, *The Purple Shamrock: The Hon. James Michael Curley of Boston* (New York, 1949), 51. See also James M. Curley, "Life-Story of Mayor-Elect Curley As Told by Himself," *Boston Globe*, Jan. 18, 1914; Milne, *Boston Sunday Post*, Sept. 28, 1930; Herbert Marshall Zolot, "The Issue of Good Government and James Michael Curley: Curley and the Boston Scene from 1897–1918" (Ph.D. diss., State University of New York, Stony Brook, 1975), 163.

6. *Boston Sunday Post*, Sept. 28, 1930.

7. William V. Shannon, *The American Irish* (New York, 1963), 79–83.

8. Curley, "Life-Story"; *Boston Globe*, Jan. 18, 1914; *Boston Sunday Post*, Oct. 5, 1930.

9. *Boston Sunday Post*, Oct. 5, 1930. See also Zolot, "The Issue of Good Government," 164.

10. *Boston Sunday Post*, Oct. 5, 1930.

11. Ibid. See also James Michael Curley, *I'd Do It Again: A Record of All My Uproarious Years* (Englewood Cliffs, N.J., 1957), 54. The comparison with Bob Hope is from Herbert Warren Wind, "On the Veranda with James Michael Curley," in idem., *The Gilded Age of Sport* (New York, 1961), 467–78.

12. *Boston Sunday Post*, Oct. 5, 1930.

13. Curley, *I'd Do It Again*, 55–56. See also *Boston Sunday Post*, Oct. 12, 1930.

14. Joan Tonn, *The Life and Work of Mary Parker Follett* (forthcoming from Oxford University Press), MS 264.

15. Ibid., MS 266; *Boston Post*, Dec. 6, 1903. Riesman is quoted in Eric L. McKitrick, "The Study of Corruption," *Political Science Quarterly* 72 (Dec. 1957): 503.

16. Tonn, *The Life and Work of Mary Parker Follett*, MS 267; *Boston Sunday Post*, Oct. 5, 1930; *Boston Traveler*, Nov. 28, 1905.

17. Quotations from testimony in the case are from records of U.S. Circuit Court proceedings; U.S. District Court proceedings, file 82410, Federal Records Center, Waltham, Mass. See also Charles H. Trout, "Boston During the Great Depression 1929–1940" (Ph.D. diss., Columbia University, 1972), 96. For Hughes's address see undated newspaper clipping (1903), author's files; originals of these clippings are in Curley Scrapbooks, Curley Collection, Holy Cross.

18. Zolot, "The Issue of Good Government," 172; Charles H. Trout, "Curley of Boston: The Search for Irish Legitimacy," in *Boston 1700–1980: The Evolution of Urban Politics*, ed. Ronald P. Formisano and Constance K. Burns (Westport, Conn., 1984), 175. See also *Boston Journal*, Sept. 25, 1903.

19. Tonn, *The Life and Work of Mary Parker Follett*, MS 260.

20. *Boston Sunday Post*, Oct. 12, 1930; Zolot, "The Issue of Good Government," 167–68.

21. Tonn, *The Life and Work of Mary Parker Follett*, MS 262.

22. Ibid.; Curley to McCarthy, Jan. 1, 1903, author's files; original is in Curley Collection, Holy Cross. See also Zolot, "The Issue of Good Government," 168.

23. *Boston Globe*, Feb. 26, 1903; *Boston Post*, Feb. 25, 1903.

24. See trial proceedings, U.S. District Court, file 82410, Federal Records Center, Waltham, Mass.; *Boston Journal*, Sept. 25, 1903; *New York Times*, Mar. 26, 1922. See also notes on undated newspaper clippings (1903), author's files.

25. Curley, *I'd Do It Again*, 69. A playbill listing the names of the singers who performed at the benefit is in Curley Collection, Holy Cross. See also *Boston Post*, Sept. 25, 1903.

26. Private interview with John Henry Cutler.

27. *Boston Globe*, Apr. 5, 1904; *Boston Post*, Nov. 23, Dec. 10, 1903.

28. Trout, "Curley of Boston," 176.

29. Ray Ginger, *Age of Excess: the United States from 1877 to 1914* (New York, 1965), 100–102.

30. Robert H. Wiebe, *The Search for Order, 1877-1920* (New York, 1967), 6.
31. Gordon Wood, "The Massachusetts Mugwumps," *New England Quarterly* (Dec. 1966).
32. William L. Riordon, *Plunkitt of Tammany Hall* (New York, 1963), 14.
33. Wood, "The Massachusetts Mugwumps."
34. Tonn, *The Life and Work of Mary Parker Follett*, MS 264-65. For "repeaters" see Zolot, "The Issue of Good Government," 212.
35. *Boston Post*, Dec. 6, 1903.
36. Records of Circuit Court proceedings, file 82410, Federal Records Center, Waltham, Mass. See also Trout, "Curley of Boston," 175.
37. *Boston Globe*, Nov. 8, 1904; *Boston Journal*, Nov. 7, 1904. See also Trout, "Curley of Boston," 177; *New York Times*, Nov. 8, 1904.
38. *Boston Herald*, Nov. 8, 25, 1904. See also Zolot, "The Issue of Good Government," 175; Trout, "Curley of Boston," 173; *Boston Evening Transcript*, Nov. 8, 1904; *New York Times*, Mar. 26, 1922.
39. *Boston Post*, Jan. 7, 9, 1905; *Boston Herald*, Jan. 7, 1905; Trout, "Curley of Boston," 177. For statistics on the number of Irish Americans taking the exam see Zolot, "The Issue of Good Government," 179.
40. Proceedings, Boston City Council, Jan. 30, 1904. For Linehan see Zolot, "The Issue of Good Government," 74.
41. Proceedings, Boston City Council, Aug. 7, Sept. 25, 1905. See also *Boston Post*, Aug. 27, 1905; *Boston Herald*, Aug. 22, 23, 1905.
42. *Boston Traveler*, Nov. 5, 38, 1905.
43. *Boston Globe*, Nov. 12, 1905. See also Zolot, "The Issue of Good Government," 207.
44. *Boston Herald*, Nov. 12, 1906; *Boston Globe*, Nov. 11, 1906.
45. *Boston Post*, Oct. 29, 1930. See also Zolot, "The Issue of Good Government," 212-14.
46. Zolot, "The Issue of Good Government," 216. See also Curley, *I'd Do It Again*, 52; Angus Wilson, *The Strange Ride of Rudyard Kipling* (New York, 1978), 193; David M. Kennedy, *Over Here: The First World War and American Society* (New York, 1980), 15. For Big Bill Kelliher see Zolot, "The Issue of Good Government," 247-48.
47. Tonn, *The Life and Work of Mary Parker Follett*, MS 274. See also Trout, "Curley of Boston," 17. For the arrest of boys for throwing stones see Proceedings, Boston City Council, Sept. 25, 1905.
48. *Boston American*, Oct. 1, 1907; *Boston Post*, Oct. 29, 30, 1907. For Daniel Coakley see Leon Harris, *Only to God: The Extraordinary Life of Godfrey Lowell Cabot* (New York, 1967), 240-41.
49. Proceedings, Boston City Council, Dec. 26, 1906. The editorial is from the *Boston Traveler*, Nov. 28, 1905. For the ad see *Boston Traveler*, Dec. 17, 1906.
50. Proceedings, Boston City Council, July 12, 1909.
51. Doris Kearns Goodwin, *The Fitzgeralds and the Kennedys: An American Saga* (New York, 1987), 190-93; Francis Russell, *The Great Interlude: Neglected Events and Persons from the First World War to the Depression* (New York, 1964), 178-80; Thomas Byrne Edsall with Mary D. Edsall, "Race," *Atlantic Monthly*, May 1991, 58.
52. Robert Aidan O'Leary, "William Henry Cardinal O'Connell: A Social and Intellectual Biography" (Ph.D. diss., Tufts University, 1980), 61, 180; James M. O'Toole, "Prelates and Politicos: Catholics and Politics in Massachusetts, 1900-1970," in *Catholic Boston: Studies in Religion and Community, 1870-1970*, ed. Robert E. Sullivan and James M. O'Toole (Boston, 1985), 125-33.
53. O'Toole, "Prelates and Politicos," 127-57. See also O'Leary, "William Henry Cardinal O'Connell," 142, 156; Thomas C. Reeves, *A Question of Character* (New York, 1991), 165.

54. James W. Sanders, "Catholics and the School Question in Boston: The Cardinal O'Connell Years," in *Catholic Boston*, ed. Sullivan and O'Toole, 145, 162–64. See also *Boston Sunday Post*, Sept. 28, 1930. For O'Connell's conservatism see O'Leary, "William Henry Cardinal O'Connell," 194–226.

55. *Boston Sunday Post*, Oct. 5, 1930.

56. Zolot, "The Issue of Good Government," 201; T. Harry Williams, *Huey Long* (New York, 1969).

57. *Boston Sunday Post*, Oct. 5, 1930.

58. See undated fragment of newspaper clipping (1903), author's files.

59. See note in the hand of Curley's secretary Frank Howland, from an interview with Curley, author's files; original is in 1903 notebook.

60. *Boston Post*, June 28, 1906; *Boston Traveler*, June 28, 1906; *Boston Sunday Post*, Oct. 5, 1930.

Chapter 4. To Washington and Back

1. *Boston Sunday Post*, Oct. 19, 1930. See also "Memoirs of James M. Curley" (n.d.), chap. 3, pp. 3–4, author's files; James Michael Curley, *I'd Do It Again: A Record of All My Uproarious Years* (Englewood Cliffs, N.J., 1957), 76–79.

2. *Boston Sunday Post*, Oct. 19, 1930.

3. Curley, *I'd Do It Again*, 86; "Memoirs of James Michael Curley," chap. 2, p. 7.

4. *Boston Herald*, Mar. 1, Apr. 26, Sept. 17, 1910. See also Judith Icke Anderson, *William Howard Taft: An Intimate History* (New York, 1981), 139, 189; *Congressional Record*, Mar. 19, 1910, 3427; John Milton Cooper, Jr., *Pivotal Decades: The United States, 1900–1920* (New York, 1990), 122–23.

5. Joseph F. Dinneen, *The Purple Shamrock: The Hon. James Michael Curley of Boston* (New York, 1949), 74–75. See also Alfred Steinberg, *The Bosses* (New York, 1972), 145; Curley, *I'd Do It Again*, 91.

6. *Boston Herald*, Sept. 10, 18, 1910.

7. *Boston Herald*, Sept. 17, 24, 28, 1910. See also *Boston Post*, Sept. 13, 1910; Herbert Marshall Zolot, "The Issue of Good Government and James Michael Curley: Curley and the Boston Scene from 1897–1918" (Ph.D. diss., State University of New York, Stony Brook, 1975), 283–84. For Galway story see *Boston Traveler*, Nov. 17, 1958.

8. Curley, *I'd Do It Again*, 98–99. See also Richard B. Morris, ed., *Encyclopedia of American History* (New York, 1953), 253; Dinneen, *The Purple Shamrock*, 83–84. For McNary's efforts see Steinberg, *The Bosses*, 146.

9. Arthur S. Link, *Woodrow Wilson: The Road to the White House* (Princeton, N.J., 1947), 337–98; idem, *Woodrow Wilson and the Progressive Era* (New York, 1964), 337; Frank Parker Stockbridge, "Champ Clark, of Pike County," *The World's Work*, Mar. 1912, 27–36; Barbara Tuchman, *The Proud Tower* (New York, 1966), 155–56.

10. Proceedings, Boston City Council, 1911; *Boston Sunday Post*, Oct. 19, 1930. I am indebted to Robert F. Hannan, chief of research for the Boston City Council, for information on Curley's attendance in 1911.

11. Standish Willcox obituary, *Boston Globe*, Jan. 7, 1933; notes for "Memoirs of James Michael Curley" (n.d.), Congress 1 folder, author's files; Dinneen, *The Purple Shamrock*, 74–79.

12. For Curley's Washington house see *Practical Politics*, Feb. 22, 1913, papers of John Henry Cutler, the ghostwriter of *I'd Do It Again*. I am indebted to Mr. Cutler. See also *Boston Sunday Post*, Oct. 12, 1930. For the anonymous man who knew the Curleys in Washington see article accompanying Mary Curley's obituary in the *Boston Herald*, June 15, 1930. For the society reporter see undated clipping "Woman of Many Sides."

Boston Daily Record, author's files; originals of clippings are in Curley Scrapbooks, Curley Collection, Holy Cross.

13. Robert H. Wiebe, *The Search for Order, 1877–1920* (New York, 1967), 225.

14. *Congressional Record*, May 3, 1911, 916; Dec. 13, 1911, 338. For Curley's speech on American Jews unable to enter Russia see Howland notebook, author's files; original is in Frank Howland Collection, Boston Public Library. See also Charles H. Trout, "Curley of Boston: The Search for Irish Legitimacy," in *Boston 1700–1980: The Evolution of Urban Politics*, ed. Ronald P. Formisano and Constance K. Burns (Westport, Conn., 1984); *Boston American*, Apr. 25, 1913.

15. Link, *Woodrow Wilson: The Road to the White House*, 381–98. See also David Sarasohn, *The Party of Reform: Democrats in the Progressive Era* (Jackson, Miss., 1989), 61–62.

16. Link, *Woodrow Wilson: The Road to the White House*, 398.

17. Curley, *I'd Do It Again*, 108.

18. Sarasohn, *The Party of Reform*, 137, 135; Link, *Woodrow Wilson: The Road to the White House*, 422; Anderson, *William Howard Taft*, 240.

19. Link, *Woodrow Wilson: The Road to the White House*, 440–49; Sarasohn, *The Party of Reform*, 138; Arthur M. Schlesinger, Jr., *The Age of Roosevelt*, vol. 3: *The Politics of Upheaval* (Boston, 1960), 581.

20. Sarasohn, *The Party of Reform*, 138–40. See also "Memoirs of James Michael Curley," chap. 5, p. 7.

21. Curley, *I'd Do It Again*, 99; E. Digby Baltzell, *The Protestant Establishment: Aristocracy and Caste in America* (New York, 1964), 79. See also Burner, *The Politics of Provincialism: The Democratic Party in Transition, 1918–1932* (New York, 1967), 182, 211, 203; for analysis of the 1960 vote see 220–21.

22. John Higham, *Strangers in the Land: Patterns of American Nativism 1860–1925* (New York, 1978), 21, 159. See also J. Joseph Huthmacher, *A Nation of Newcomers* (New York, 1967), especially the appendix, which gives a chronology of federal laws and regulations relating to immigration; David M. Kennedy, *Over Here: The First World War and American Society* (New York, 1980), 63.

23. John A. Garraty, *Henry Cabot Lodge* (New York, 1953), especially 1–107. See also Wallace Stegner, "Who Persecutes Boston?" *Atlantic Monthly*, July 1944, 48; Peter K. Eisinger, *The Politics of Displacement: Racial and Ethnic Transition in Three American Cities* (New York, 1980), 43.

24. Higham, *Strangers in the Land*, 101–105; *Jewish Advocate*, Feb. 14, 1913; Curley, *I'd Do It Again*, 103–104; "Memoirs of James M. Curley," chap. 11, p. 2.

25. *Congressional Record*, Dec. 12, 1912, 675–77. See also Curley, *I'd Do It Again*, 104.

26. For Taft's pen see Curley to Rudolph Forster, White House executive clerk, Feb. 15, 1913; Forster to Curley, Feb. 15, 1913, William Howard Taft MSS (microfilm), series 6, item 3686, reel 446; series 8, item 200, reel 516.

27. *Washington Post*, Feb. 15, 1913. See also *New York American*, Feb. 15, 1913; *Boston Daily Record*, Feb. 19, 1913; *Boston Journal*, Feb. 20, 1913; *Boston Globe*, Feb. 20, 1913; *Boston Advertiser*, Feb. 20, 1913; *Congressional Record*, Feb. 19, 1913, 3424.

28. Higham, *Strangers in the Land*, 203, 318–24; Huthmacher, *A Nation of Newcomers*, especially chronology in the appendix. For exclusion of Jews see Baltzell, *The Protestant Establishment*, 204.

29. *Boston Herald*, Dec. 16, 1913; Doris Kearns Goodwin, *The Fitzgeralds and the Kennedys: An American Saga* (New York, 1987), 244–52.

30. *Boston Herald*, Dec. 16, 1913; John Henry Cutler, *Honey-Fitz: Three Steps to the White House; The Colorful Life and Times of John F. ("Honey-Fitz") Fitzgerald* (Indianapolis, 1962), 194.

31. *Boston Evening Transcript*, Dec. 19, 1913; Francis Russell, *The Great Interlude: Neglected Events and Persons from the First World War to the Depression* (New York, 1964), 182. See also Goodwin, *The Fitzgeralds and the Kennedys*, 251, 252.

32. Goodwin, *The Fitzgeralds and the Kennedys*, 251, 252.

33. *Boston Herald*, Nov. 29, Dec. 1, 1913; Goodwin, *The Fitzgeralds and the Kennedys*, 245; Zolot, "The Issue of Good Government," 317, 319. For Lodge and Douglas see Richard A. Abrams, *Conservatism in a Progressive Era* (Cambridge, Mass., 1964), 110–23; for McLaughlin see Cutler, *Honey-Fitz*, 195.

34. See the campaign biography of Kenny by his City Council colleague Walter Ballantyne, "Why Thomas J. Kenny Arrived," Term 1, author's files; original is in Curley Collection, Holy Cross; George Read Nutter diary, vol. 5 (1914), Massachusetts Historical Society, Boston; Curley, *I'd Do It Again*, 116.

35. Copy of Kenny's platform, Term 1 (1913), author's files; Zolot, "The Issue of Good Government," 335.

36. Zolot, "The Issue of Good Government," 327–29. See also Abrams, *Conservatism in a Progressive Era*, 293; R. W. Apple, "Fierce Fight Pits Old Against New," *New York Times*, Oct. 30, 1990.

37. *Boston Herald*, Dec. 19, 1913. See also Zolot, "The Issue of Good Government," 344–45; *Boston Herald*, Jan. 6, 1914; John T. Galvin, "Curley's Big Win," *Boston College Magazine*, Spring 1989, 37.

38. *Boston Herald*, Jan. 6, 1914.

39. For Curley's platform see Zolot, "The Issue of Good Government," 338–40; *Boston Herald*, Dec. 20, 1913; Jan. 6, 1914. For banks and railroads see Reinhard H. Luthin, *American Demagogues: Twentieth Century* (Boston, 1954), 22.

40. *Boston Herald*, Jan. 11, 1914; *Boston Evening Transcript*, Jan. 14, 1914. Information on endorsements of Curley by Boston newspapers comes from William Joseph Grattan, "David I. Walsh and His Associates: A Study in Political Theory" (Ph.D. diss., Harvard University, 1957); Michael Kendall, "Mayor of the Poor: James Michael Curley as an Urban Populist" (senior honors thesis, Harvard University, 1979), 31.

41. *Boston Herald*, Jan. 4, 1914; Zolot, "The Issue of Good Government," 346. For Curley's use of sexual blackmail see undated newspaper clipping "Vicious Campaign Expected," Term 1, Notebook 4, author's files. For Curley's version of the coat story see *I'd Do It Again*, 121. See also Thomas H. O'Connor, *South Boston: My Home Town* (Boston, 1988), 100–101.

42. *Boston Evening Transcript*, Jan. 1, 1914; Nutter diary, vol. 5 (1914); Zolot, "The Issue of Good Government," 475; Galvin, "Curley's Big Win," 37; *Boston Herald*, Jan. 13, 1914.

Chapter 5. The Metamorphistical Mayor

1. See the various accounts of Curley's inauguration in the *Boston Herald, Boston Globe, Boston Evening Transcript, Boston Post, Boston American,* and *Boston Journal* for Feb. 2 and 3, 1914. All subsequent descriptions of that day are based on these accounts.

2. Doris Kearns Goodwin, *The Fitzgeralds and the Kennedys: An American Saga* (New York, 1987), 252; David M. Kennedy, *Over Here: The First World War and American Society* (New York, 1980), 237.

3. Charles H. Trout, "Curley of Boston: The Search for Irish Legitimacy," in *Boston 1700–1980: The Evolution of Urban Politics*, ed. Ronald P. Formisano and Constance K. Burns (Westport, Conn., 1984), 168.

4. Shannon is quoted in ibid. For "municipal monarch" see William P. Marchione, Jr., "The 1949 Boston Charter Reform," *New England Quarterly* (Sept. 1976): 374. For

Sarah Curley see James Michael Curley, *I'd Do It Again: A Record of All My Uproarious Years* (Englewood Cliffs, N.J., 1957), 122.

5. Alpheus Thomas Mason, *Brandeis: A Free Man's Life* (New York, 1946), 372. See also Herbert Marshall Zolot, "The Issue of Good Government and James Michael Curley: Curley and the Boston Scene from 1897–1918" (Ph.D. diss., State University of New York, Stony Brook, 1975); Philippa Strum, *Louis D. Brandeis: Justice for the People* (New York, 1984), 258–59. The quotation from Brandeis's speech is taken from Hillel Levine and Lawrence Harmon, *The Death of an American Jewish Community: A Tragedy of Good Intentions* (New York, 1992), 48: The motto is that of the Anti-Imperialist League, which was founded in Boston to protest U.S. annexation of the Philippines.

6. *Boston Post*, Mar. 7, 1914; *Boston Herald*, Mar. 19, 1914.

7. *Boston Post*, Mar. 29, 1914.

8. Ibid. See also Zolot, "The Issue of Good Government," 376. The epithet "Metamorphistical Mayor" comes from former state representative Gordon of Ward 9, as quoted in an undated newspaper clipping, Term 1, Notebook 1, author's files. Many of the dates of these clippings—and in some cases, even the newspapers they came from—are hard to identify; originals are in Curley Scrapbooks, James Michael Curley Collection, College of the Holy Cross, Worcester, Mass.

9. For Toodles Ryan see Mike Ryan, "That Man Curley!" *Irish America*, Oct. 1989, 39; Zolot, "The Issue of Good Government," 367–71.

10. *Boston Post*, Feb. 3, 1914. See also *The Republic*, Mar. 21, 1914.

11. *Boston Post*, Mar. 27, 1914.

12. *Boston Post*, Mar. 29, 1914.

13. Zolot, "The Issue of Good Government," 369.

14. *National Journal*, Jan. 21, 1989, 129. The typology of how mayors can go wrong politically is borrowed from Steven P. Erie, *Rainbow's End: Irish-Americans and the Dilemmas of Urban Politics, 1840–1983* (Berkeley, Calif., 1988).

15. *Boston Herald*, Mar. 19, 1914.

16. Zolot, "The Issue of Good Government," 387–95; Trout, "Curley of Boston," 181; Melvin G. Holli, *Reform in Detroit: Hazen S. Pingree and Urban Politics* (New York, 1969), 166–67.

17. Zolot, "The Issue of Good Government," 370–83.

18. *Boston Journal*, Apr. 2, 1915; Ralph G. Martin, *The Bosses* (New York, 1964), 225–27.

19. *Boston Post*, Mar. 4, 1914; Zolot, "The Issue of Good Government," 403–408.

20. Zolot, "The Issue of Good Government," 578–81.

21. *Boston Post*, Jan. 21, 1918; Zolot, "The Issue of Good Government," 596–97.

22. Trout, "Curley of Boston," 182; Zolot, "The Issue of Good Government," 599; Erie, *Rainbow's End*, 80 (table).

23. *Boston Post*, Dec. 10, 1915. See also Zolot, "The Issue of Good Government," 387; *Boston Herald*, Apr. 3, 1914.

24. Zolot, "The Issue of Good Government," 385. For details of Curley's workday see also undated newspaper clippings, Term 1, Notebook 1–5, author's files.

25. Thomas Kessner, *Fiorello H. La Guardia and the Making of Modern New York* (New York, 1989), 271.

26. Zolot, "The Issue of Good Government," 517–21; *Boston Herald*, Jan. 23, 1914.

27. Undated newspaper clippings, Term 1, Notebook 1–5, author's files.

28. Barbara Miller Solomon, *Ancestors and Immigrants: A Changing New England Tradition* (Boston, 1989), 104; *Boston Post*, Jan. 31, 1916. See also Zolot, "The Issue of Good Government," 533–36.

29. Zolot, "The Issue of Good Government," 541.

30. Cleveland Amory, *The Proper Bostonians* (New York, 1947), 329–31.

31. H. G. Wells, *Travels in America* (New York, 1905), 230.

32. Amory, *Proper Bostonians*, 328. See also *Boston Herald*, Feb. 7, 1914.

33. Amory, *Proper Bostonians*, 265. See also *Boston Herald*, Feb. 7, 1914.

34. Private interview with Francis X. Curley; *Boston Post*, Jan. 5, Apr. 2, 1915; Zolot, "The Issue of Good Government," 545.

35. *Boston American*, Sept. 18, 1916; *Boston Traveler*, Sept. 19, 1916; Zolot, "The Issue of Good Government," 548–49.

36. *Boston Journal*, Sept. 19, 1916; *Boston American*, Sept. 18, 1916; Zolot, "The Issue of Good Government," 548.

37. Thomas Cripps, *Slow Fade to Black: The Negro in American Film, 1900–1942* (New York, 1977), 64. See also Stephen R. Fox, *The Guardian of Boston* (New York, 1970), 206; Zolot, "The Issue of Good Government," 546.

38. Fox, *The Guardian of Boston*, 2–30.

39. Ibid., 20, 33, 51, 53.

40. Ibid., 170. See also undated newspaper clippings, Term 1, Notebook 1, author's files; Ronald Schaeffer, *America in the Great War: The Rise of the War Welfare State* (New York, 1991), 76.

41. Fox, *The Guardian of Boston*, 179–82.

42. Cripps, *Slow Fade to Black*, 52; Richard Schickel, *D. W. Griffith: An American Life* (New York, 1984), 269–70; Wyn Craig Wade, *The Fiery Cross: The Ku Klux Klan in America* (New York, 1987), 126; Fox, *The Guardian of Boston*, 190.

43. *Boston Post*, Apr. 2, 1915; John Milton Cooper, Jr., *Pivotal Decades: The United States, 1900–1920* (New York, 1990), 73; Wade, *The Fiery Cross*, 138, 146.

44. Peter K. Eisinger, "Ethnic Political Transition in Boston, 1884–1933: Some Lessons for Contemporary Cities," *Political Science Quarterly* 93 (Summer 1978): 228; *Boston Journal*, Apr. 13, 1915. See also Zolot, "The Issue of Good Government," 556; Cripps, *Slow Fade to Black*, 58–59; Wade, *The Fiery Cross*, 136.

45. Schickel, *D. W. Griffith*, 293–96, 232. See also Cripps, *Slow Fade to Black*, 59; Fox, *The Guardian of Boston*, 192–94.

46. *Boston Post*, Apr. 19, 1915; *Boston Journal*, Apr. 20, 1915.

47. Schickel, *D. W. Griffith*, 296.

48. Zolot, "The Issue of Good Government," 560; *Boston Globe*, Apr. 14, 1915. See also Michael Kendall, "Mayor of the Poor: James Michael Curley as an Urban Populist" (senior honors thesis, Harvard University, 1979), 85; *Boston Sunday Globe*, Jan. 5, 1992.

49. *Boston Post*, Apr. 19, 1915; Schickel, *D. W. Griffith*, 274.

50. *National Journal*, Jan. 12, 1991; press release, Federal Election Commission, Feb. 22, 1991; Brooks Jackson, *Honest Graft: Big Money and the American Political Process* (New York, 1988), 109; Tom Wicker, "An Alienated Public," *New York Times*, Oct. 13, 1991.

51. *Wall Street Journal*, Aug. 18, 1989; *New York Times*, Aug. 22, 1989; *Boston Globe*, June 3, 1989; *Wall Street Journal*, Mar. 5, 1991; Carol Matlack, "Connected Couples," *National Journal*, July 20, 1991, 1793–98; Arthur M. Schlesinger, Jr., "A Bad Idea Whose Time Has Come," *Wall Street Journal*, Oct. 29, 1991.

52. Alexander von Hoffman, "Local Attachments: The Making of the American Urban Neighborhood, Jamaica Plain, Massachusetts" (draft of thesis for Graduate School of Design, Harvard University), 110ff.

53. Alfred Steinberg, *The Bosses* (New York, 1972), 151; Martin, *The Bosses*, 226; Finance Commission to Curley, Aug. 7, 1917, in *Journal of the House*, May 11, 1922; Jack Thomas, "History for Sale," *Boston Sunday Globe*, n.d., author's files; *Boston Globe*, Apr. 17, 1988; auctioneer's prospectus issued prior to the sale of the house, author's files; original is in Curley Collection, Holy Cross.

54. Zolot, "The Issue of Good Government," 454–55.

55. Ibid., 453, 430, 214, 215.

56. Ibid., 436.

57. Private interview with the grandson of a contractor who worked on the house; Peter F. Volante letter, *Boston Globe*, May 24, 1988; Ray Kierman, "Jim Curley, Boss of Massachusetts," *American Mercury*, Feb. 1936, 140; private interview with John Henry Cutler. See also Mike Ryan, "John Cutler—Chronicler of Boston's Irish," *Boston Irish Echo*, June 30, 1984.

58. *Boston Globe*, Sept. 28, 1917. See also *Boston Evening Transcript*, Sept. 28, 1917.

59. Zolot, "The Issue of Good Government," 436–52; *Boston Journal*, July 5, 1916.

60. Zolot, "The Issue of Good Government," 436–52; Finance Commission report, Nov. 17, 1917, 151.

61. Steinberg, *The Bosses*, 154.

62. Zolot, "The Issue of Good Government," 440.

63. David Yallop, *The Day the Laughter Stopped* (New York, 1976), 68–69; *New York Times*, July 12, 1921.

64. Yallop, *The Day the Laughter Stopped*, 68–69.

65. Francis Russell, *The Knave of Boston* (Boston, 1987), 6–7.

66. Leon Harris, *Only to God: The Extraordinary Life of Godfrey Lowell Cabot* (New York, 1967), 229–47.

67. *Boston Post*, Jan. 1, 1917; Zolot, "The Issue of Good Government," 600–603; undated newspaper clipping, Term 1, Notebook 3, author's files; Francis Curley interview.

68. James J. Kenneally, "Catholicism and Woman Suffrage in Massachusetts," *Catholic Historical Review* (April 1967): 43–57.

69. Ibid.

70. John D. Buenker, *Urban Liberalism and Progressive Reform* (New York, 1973), 160; *Boston Post*, Nov. 3, 1915.

71. *Boston Post*, Nov. 2, 3, 1915; Zolot, "The Issue of Good Government," 602. Curley lost South Boston's Ward 15.

72. Undated newspaper clippings, Term 1, Notebook 4, 5, author's files. See also William M. Leary, Jr., "Woodrow Wilson, Irish Americans, and the Election of 1916," *Journal of American History* (June 1967): 68. For Curley's attack on the war see editorial in the *New York Times*, June 8, 1917.

73. Kennedy, *Over Here*, 68, 79, 88; Schaeffer, *America in the Great War*, 22; *Boston Herald*, July 6, 1917. Various speeches made by Curley in this period can be found in a separate volume of the Curley Scrapbooks covering his first term; Curley Collection, Holy Cross. For Karl Muck see George J. Lankevich, ed., *Boston: A Chronological and Documentary History, 1602–1970* (Dobbs Ferry, N.Y., 1974), 59.

74. Undated newspaper clippings, Term 1, Notebook 3, 4, author's files. The Madame Schumann-Heink story is from Francis Curley interview.

75. Francis Curley interview.

76. *Boston Evening Transcript*, Nov. 3, Mar. 10, May 1, 1917.

77. *Boston Daily Record*, Dec. 10, 1917.

78. Undated newspaper clippings, Term 1, Notebook 4, author's files.

79. Undated newspaper clipping, *Boston Journal*, Term 1, Notebook 4, author's files.

80. *Boston Herald*, July 6, 7, 1917; *Boston Journal*, July 7, 1917.

81. Francis Curley interview. For note on Curley's desk see Term 3, Notebook 2, p. 131, author's files; original is in Curley Collection, Holy Cross.

82. Undated newspaper clipping, Term 1, Notebook 4, author's files. See also Zolot, "The Issue of Good Government," 604.

83. Russell, *The Knave of Boston*, 78; for details on Peters see "The Mayor and the Nymphet," 68–84.

84. Ibid., 68–84. See also Morris Markey, "The Mysterious Death of Starr Faithfull," in *The Aspirin Age, 1919–1941*, ed. Isabel Leighton (New York, 1949), 258–74.

85. Markey, "The Mysterious Death of Starr Faithfull"; *Boston Evening Transcript*, Dec. 3, 1917.

86. *Boston Herald*, Oct. 17, 1917.

87. Zolot, "The Issue of Good Government," 609; Leslie G. Ainley, *Boston Mahatma: The Public Career of Martin M. Lomasney* (Boston, 1949), 126.

88. Undated newspaper clippings, Term 1, Notebook 5, author's files.

89. Zolot, "The Issue of Good Government," 604; Francis Curley interview; undated clipping, *Boston Journal*, Term 1, Notebook 5, author's files.

90. *Boston Herald*, Nov. 28, 1917.

91. *Boston Post*, Dec. 2, 1917; *Boston Herald*, Dec. 2, 1917; undated newspaper clipping, Term 1, Notebook 5, author's files.

92. Undated newspaper clippings, Term 1, Notebook 5, author's files.

93. *Boston Evening Transcript*, Dec. 13, 1917; Zolot, "The Issue of Good Government," 614.

94. *Boston Daily Record*, Dec. 18, 1917.

Chapter 6. Builder and Demagogue

1. Ralph G. Martin, *The Bosses* (New York, 1964), 229.

2. *Boston Post*, Dec. 21, 1921. For "Plutarch's Lives" see undated newspaper clipping, Term 1, Notebook 5, author's files; originals of all clippings cited are in Curley Scrapbooks, James Michael Curley Collection, College of the Holy Cross, Worcester, Mass.

3. Newspaper clipping, Dec. 28, 1918, Term 2, Notebook 1, author's files.

4. *Boston Post*, Oct. 10, 1921. For Coolidge's pickle see William E. Leuchtenburg, *The Perils of Prosperity, 1914–1932* (Chicago, 1958), 95.

5. Private interview with Francis X. Curley; *Boston Post*, Oct. 20, 1921.

6. John D. Hicks, *Republican Ascendancy, 1921–1933* (New York, 1960), 81; Martin, *The Bosses*, 230.

7. John Milton Cooper, Jr., *Pivotal Decades: The United States, 1900–1920* (New York, 1990), 364–65; Hicks, *Republican Ascendancy*, 25.

8. *Boston Post*, Dec. 5, 1921. For the number of striking policemen see George J. Lankevich, ed., *Boston: A Chronological and Documentary History, 1602–1970* (Dobbs Ferry, N.Y., 1974), 59; police memorial day speech (n.d.), Term 3, Notebook 3, p. 11, author's files; original is in Curley Scrapbooks, Curley Collection, Holy Cross.

9. Francis Russell, *A City in Terror: The Boston Police Strike, 1919* (New York, 1975).

10. "The Hibernia Savings Bank: 75 Years" (annual report, 1987), pp. 8–11.

11. Michael Kendall, "Mayor of the Poor: James Michael Curley as an Urban Populist" (senior honors thesis, Harvard University, 1979), 40–42; Joseph F. Dinneen, *The Purple Shamrock: The Hon. James Michael Curley of Boston* (New York, 1949), 127. For O'Connor's lunatic pile see Shaun O'Connell, *Imagining Boston: A Literary Landscape* (Boston, 1990), 130.

12. *Boston Post*, Sept. 21, 1921.

13. *Boston Post*, Dec. 6, 1921.

14. *Boston Post*, Oct. 2, 1921.

15. *Boston Post*, Dec. 6, 1921.

16. *Boston Post*, Dec. 1, 2, 6, 1921.

17. *Boston Post*, Dec. 3–6, 1921.

18. *Boston Post*, Dec. 7, 1921.

19. *Boston Post*, Oct. 20, 1921.

20. *Boston Post*, Oct. 17, 1921.

21. Kendall, "Mayor of the Poor," 44; John Henry Cutler, *Honey-Fitz: Three Steps to the White House; The Life and Colorful Times of John F. ("Honey-Fitz") Fitzgerald* (Indianapolis, 1962), 232–34.

22. Francis Curley interview.

23. James Michael Curley, *I'd Do It Again: A Record of All My Uproarious Years* (Englewood Cliffs, N.J., 1957), 158. For McLaughlin see Cutler, *Honey-Fitz*, 233.

24. Richard Hofstadter, *The Age of Reform: From Bryan to F.D.R.* (New York, 1955), 289.

25. *Boston Post*, Dec. 4, 1921.

26. *Boston Post*, Dec. 12, 1921.

27. Ibid.; Francis Curley interview; Curley, *I'd Do It Again*, 16; private interview with members of John Curley's family; *Boston Evening Transcript*, May 3, 1921.

28. *Boston Post*, Dec. 14, 1921.

29. Ray Kierman, "Jim Curley, Boss of Massachusetts," *American Mercury*, Feb. 1936, 141; *Boston Post*, Dec. 14, 1921.

30. For renters see Charles H. Trout, *Boston, the Great Depression, and the New Deal* (New York, 1977), 14. See also *Boston Globe*, Sept. 12, 1991; *New York Times*, July 19, 1991; Harold Gorvine, "The New Deal in Massachusetts" (Ph.D. diss., Harvard University, 1962), 313.

31. *Boston Post*, Feb. 1, 5, 1922.

32. Undated newspaper clipping, Term 2, Notebook 1, author's files.

33. Kendall, "Mayor of the Poor," 46.

34. Ibid., 45–52; undated newspaper clippings, Term 2, Notebook 1, 2, author's files; Hicks, *Republican Ascendancy*, 50.

35. Kendall, "Mayor of the Poor," 51; private interviews with Joseph Slavet, director of the Urban Observatory at the McCormack Center, University of Massachustts, Boston, and Robert Bergenheim, formerly a reporter with the *Christian Science Monitor*, which exposed the abatement racket. See also Bergenheim's series on abatements in the *Christian Science Monitor*, July 1, Aug. 5, 10–12, 1954. For Bantry on Young's Hotel see *Boston Sunday Post*, Oct. 1, 1933.

36. Francis Curley interview.

37. *National Journal*, July 20, 1991.

38. Herbert Warren Wind, "On the Veranda with James Michael Curley," in idem, *The Gilded Age of Sport* (New York, 1961), 467–78.

39. Hicks, *Republican Ascendancy*, 80–81; *Boston Post*, Oct. 7, 1924; *Boston Herald*, Oct. 5, 1924; *Boston Post*, Sept. 10, 1924.

40. John A. Garraty, *Henry Cabot Lodge* (New York, 1953), 418.

41. For "newer races" see *Gloucester Times*, Sept. 23, 1936. The campaign song is in Martin, *The Bosses*, 236.

42. James M. O'Toole, "Prelates and Politicos: Catholics and Politics in Massachusetts, 1900–1970," in *Catholic Boston: Studies in Religion and Community, 1870–1970*, ed. Robert E. Sullivan and James M. O'Toole (Boston, 1985), 27–29; William V. Shannon, *The American Irish* (New York, 1963), 192; Trout, *Boston and the New Deal*, 22.

43. *Boston Traveler*, Aug. 13, 1924; *Boston Post*, Oct. 7, 1924; *Boston Herald*, Oct. 8, 1924.

44. O'Toole, "Prelates and Politicos," 31.

45. Wyn Craig Wade, *The Fiery Cross: The Ku Klux Klan in America* (New York, 1987), 180, 173; Leuchtenburg, *The Perils of Prosperity*, 211.

46. Leuchtenburg, *The Perils of Prosperity*, 210–11; Craig, *The Fiery Cross*, 198–99; Hicks, *Republican Ascendancy*, 96.

47. J. Joseph Huthmacher, *A Nation of Newcomers* (New York, 1987), 88; *Boston Evening Transcript*, Apr. 21, 1924; *Boston American*, May 17, 1924.

48. Undated newspaper clipping (1923), Term 2, Notebook 2, author's files; *Boston Post*, Oct. 16, 1924.

49. Martin, *The Bosses*, 236.

50. *Boston Post*, Oct. 29, 1924; undated newspaper clipping, Term 2, Notebook 2, author's files; *Boston Post*, Oct. 1, 21, 1924; *Boston Herald*, Oct. 26, 1924; *Boston Evening Transcript*, Sept. 2, 1924. For Athol speech see *Worcester Telegram*, Aug. 8, 1983.

51. Curley, *I'd Do It Again*, 183.

52. *Boston Post*, Oct. 18, 1924; Alfred Steinberg, *The Bosses* (New York, 1972), 162. For "I'll never be Governor" see *Collier's*, Feb. 25, 1935.

53. Private interview with Dorothy MaGowan; *Boston Post*, Jan. 30, 1925; *Boston Globe*, Jan. 29, 1925.

54. *Boston Globe*, Sept. 6, 1925; *Boston Telegram*, Sept. 18, 1925.

55. *Boston Post*, Oct. 25, 1925; Sept. 19, 1934.

56. *Boston Post*, Oct. 18, 1925.

57. Curley, *I'd Do It Again*, 190; *Boston Post*, Nov. 5, 1925.

58. *Boston Post*, Nov. 5, 1925; Steinberg, *The Bosses*, 164; *Boston Herald*, Nov. 4, 1925.

Chapter 7. Depression Mayor

1. *Boston Globe*, Oct. 4, 1926.

2. Ibid.; *Boston Post, Boston Evening Transcript, Boston American*, issues for Oct. 4–6, 1926; *New York Times*, Oct. 5, 1926.

3. *Boston Telegraph*, Oct. 5, 1926; *Boston Evening Transcript*, Oct. 8, 1926; Ralph G. Martin, *The Bosses* (New York, 1964), 236–37; *Boston Daily Record*, Nov. 10, 1934.

4. For President Lowell's comment on Curley see undated fragment, Term 1, Notebook 1, author's files; originals of unidentified newspaper clippings are in Curley Scrapbooks, James Michael Curley Collection, College of the Holy Cross, Worcester, Mass. See also Herbert A. Kenny, *Newspaper Row: Journalism in the Pre-Television Era* (Boston, 1987), 170.

5. William V. Shannon, *The American Irish* (New York, 1963), 151.

6. Oscar Handlin, *Al Smith and His America* (Boston, 1958), 9; Richard O'Connor, *The First Hurrah: A Biography of Alfred E. Smith* (New York, 1970), 16, 23.

7. O'Connor, *The First Hurrah*, 24.

8. Ibid., 26.

9. Shannon, *The American Irish*, 157, 155; O'Connor, *The First Hurrah*, 10, 22, 26, 27.

10. Shannon, *The American Irish*, 157.

11. O'Connor, *The First Hurrah*, 71; Shannon, *The American Irish*, 163–75.

12. *Boston Post*, Nov. 6, 1928; Shannon, *The American Irish*, 164.

13. Handlin, *Al Smith*, 168; Joseph F. Dinneen, "The Kingfish of Massachusetts," *Harper's Monthly*, Sept. 1936, 347; John F. Stack, Jr., *International Conflict in an American City: Boston's Irish, Italians, and Jews, 1935–1944* (Westport, Conn., 1979), 31; *Boston Post*, Oct. 9, 12, 1928.

14. *Boston Post*, Oct. 14, 17, 1928.

15. *Boston Post*, Oct. 25, 1928.

16. *Boston Post*, Nov. 5, 1928.

17. Andrew Sinclair, *Prohibition: The Era of Excess* (Boston, 1962), 303; John D. Hicks, *Republican Ascendancy, 1921–1933* (New York, 1960), 211; *Boston Post*, Nov. 6, 1928.

18. J. Joseph Huthmacher, *Massachusetts People and Politics* (Cambridge, Mass., 1959), 180–83; *Boston Post*, Nov. 3, 1929.

19. Huthmacher, *Massachusetts People and Politics*, 190.

20. *Boston Post*, Oct. 25, 1928.

21. Private interviews with Mary Angus Theresa MacDonald Lemmon and Francis X. Curley.

22. Elmer Davis, "Boston: Notes on a Barbarian Invasion," *Harper's Monthly*, Jan. 1928.

23. *Boston Globe*, Mar. 17, 1929.

24. *Boston Globe*, Aug. 17, 1929; *New York Times*, Aug. 17, 1929; undated newspaper clippings, Term 3, Notebook 1, author's files.

25. *Boston Post*, Oct. 3, 5, 10, 17, 1929.

26. *Boston Post*, Oct. 15, 29, 1929.

27. *Boston Post*, Oct. 2, 1929; Charles H. Trout, *Boston, the Great Depression, and the New Deal* (New York, 1977), 43; undated newspaper clipping, Term 3, Notebook 2, author's files.

28. Alfred Steinberg, *The Bosses* (New York, 1972), 165; Trout, *Boston and the New Deal*, 21.

29. Martin, *The Bosses*, 237.

30. *Boston Post*, Oct. 6, 1929; Trout, *Boston and the New Deal*, 43.

31. Trout, *Boston and the New Deal*, 28.

32. *Boston Post*, Oct. 6, 1929.

33. Ibid.; undated newspaper clipping, Term 3, Notebook 2, author's files.

34. *Boston Post*, Oct. 6, Nov. 1, 1929.

35. *Boston Post*, Nov. 2, 1929; *Boston Globe*, Oct. 30, 1929.

36. *Boston Post*, Oct. 28, 1929.

37. *Boston Post*, Nov. 4, 3, 1929.

38. Undated newspaper clipping, Term 3, Notebook 1, author's files.

39. *Boston Globe*, Nov. 5, 1929; *Boston Post*, Nov. 5, 1929.

40. *Boston Post*, Nov. 5, 1929.

41. Ibid.

42. *Boston Globe*, Nov. 5, 1929; *Boston Post*, Nov. 5, 1929.

43. *Boston American*, Jan. 6, 1930; *Boston Evening Transcript*, Jan. 6, 1930.

44. *New York Times*, Jan. 7, 1930; undated newspaper clipping, Term 3, Notebook 2, p. 73, author's files.

45. Trout, *Boston and the New Deal*, 53.

46. For desegregation see J. Anthony Lukas, *Common Ground: A Turbulent Decade in the Lives of Three American Families* (New York, 1985), a classic account of what Lukas calls "the realities of urban America." For "cities without suburbs" see Neal R. Peirce, "The Economic Drag of Discrimination," *National Journal*, Mar. 28, 1992.

47. *Concord Journal*, Sept. 27, 1991.

48. James Michael Curley, Inaugural Address, Boston City Council, 1930; George J. Lankevich, ed., *Boston: A Chronological and Documentary History, 1602–1970* (Dobbs Ferry, N.Y., 1974), 49; *Boston Herald*, Jan. 13, 1931.

49. Undated newspaper clipping, Term 3, Notebook 2, author's files; private interview with John E. Powers.

50. Walter Liggett, "Bawdy Boston," *Plain Talk*, Jan. 29, 1930; Trout, *Boston and the New Deal*, 70.

51. Liggett, "Bawdy Boston."

52. Davis, "Boston: Notes on a Barbarian Invasion."

53. *Boston American*, May 16, 1930; undated newspaper clipping, Term 3, Notebook 3, p. 51; *Boston Daily Record*, Mar. 28, 1931; *Los Angeles Herald-Examiner*, Nov. 2, 1932; *Boston American*, May 5, 1932.

54. Trout, *Boston and the New Deal*, 54, 55.

55. Ibid., 25, 55; *Boston American*, May 5, 1932; undated newspaper clipping, Term 3, Notebook 2, author's files.

56. *Brockton Times*, Nov. 15, 1930; *Boston Advertiser*, Jan. 24, 1931.

57. *Boston Globe*, Sept. 5, 1930.

58. Lemmon interview.

59. *Boston Globe, Boston Herald, Boston Evening Transcript, Boston Post*, issues for June 10–12, 1930; Francis Curley, Lemmon interviews; private interview with Lauretta Bremner Sliney.

60. Trout, *Boston and the New Deal*, 54; *Boston Advertiser*, Sept. 27, 1930; *Boston Globe*, Nov. 12, 1931; *Springfield News*, Sept. 10, 1930; undated newspaper clipping, Term 3, Notebook 2, p. 83, author's files.

61. For an analysis of Curley's thinking see *Worcester Gazette*, July 30, 1930.

62. John Henry Cutler, *Honey-Fitz: Three Steps to the White House; The Life and Colorful Times of John F. ("Honey-Fitz") Fitzgerald* (Indianapolis, 1962), 257.

63. *Boston Herald*, Sept. 10, 1930.

64. *Boston American*, Sept. 9. 1930.

65. *Springfield News*, Sept. 10, 1930; *Worcester Post*, Sept. 11, 1930.

66. *Boston Evening Transcript*, Sept. 13, 1930; *Boston Herald*, Sept. 14, 1930.

67. *Boston Evening Transcript*, Sept. 15, 1930; Trout, *Boston and the New Deal*, 69; *Boston Herald*, Sept. 15, 1930.

68. *Boston Herald*, Sept. 15, 1930; *Boston Evening Transcript*, Sept. 16, 1930; *Boston Daily Record*, Sept. 16, 1930; *New York Times*, Sept. 15, 1930.

69. *Boston Post*, Sept. 16, 1930.

70. Undated newspaper clipping, Term 3, Notebook 2, p. 3, author's files.

71. *Boston Evening Transcript*, Sept. 16, 1930.

72. Trout, *Boston and the New Deal*, 51.

73. *Boston Post*, July 20, 1930; *Boston Daily Record*, Sept. 18, 1930; *Boston Post*, Aug. 26, 1930.

74. *Boston Evening Transcript*, Sept. 18, 1930.

75. Sliney interview; private interview with John Evans-Harrington.

76. Lemmon, Sliney interviews.

77. *Worcester Telegram*, May 3, 1931; Sliney interview.

78. *Boston Post, Boston Herald, Boston Traveler, Boston Evening Transcript*, issues for Jan. 10–14, 1931.

79. Lemmon interview.

80. Undated newspaper clipping, *Boston Evening Transcript* (Jan. 1931), Term 3, Notebook 2, author's files; Sliney interview.

81. Lemmon interview.

82. Sliney interview.

83. Undated newspaper clipping, *Boston Evening Transcript* (Jan. 1931), Term 3, Notebook 2, author's files; *Boston American*, Feb. 3, 1931.

84. Lawrence J. Kennedy, *Planning the City Upon a Hill: Boston Since 1630* (forthcoming from the University of Massachusetts Press); undated clipping, *Boston Post* (1931), Term 3, Notebook 2, author's files.

85. Michael Kendall, "Mayor of the Poor: James Michael Curley as an Urban Populist" (senior honors thesis, Harvard University, 1979), 69.

86. Private interview with Ray Dooley, former aide to Mayor Raymond L. Flynn of Boston.

87. Trout, *Boston and the New Deal*, 63; Kendall, "Mayor of the Poor," 70.

88. *Boston Herald*, Mar. 22, 1931; Kendall, "Mayor of the Poor," 69; *Waterbury Republican*, May 5, 1931.

89. Sliney, Francis Curley interviews; undated newspaper clipping, Term 3, Notebook 2, p. 54, author's files.

90. Joseph F. Dinneen, *The Purple Shamrock: The Hon. James Michael Curley of Boston* (New York, 1949), 169–70.

91. James Michael Curley, *I'd Do It Again: A Record of All My Uproarious Years* (Englewood Cliffs, N.J., 1957), 212.

92. Sliney interview.

93. Ibid.; Curley, *I'd Do It Again*, 214.

94. Curley, *I'd Do It Again*, 212.

95. Dinneen, *The Purple Shamrock*, 171; Sliney interview.

96. Sliney interview.

97. Curley, *I'd Do It Again*, 216, 218.

98. Ibid., 217, 219; *Worcester Telegram*, June 6, 1931; *Springfield Republican*, June 13, 1931; undated newspaper clipping, Term 3, Notebook 2, p. 51, author's files.

99. United Press dispatch, June 6, 1931.

100. Kenneth S. Davis, *F.D.R.: The New York Years, 1928–1933* (New York, 1985), 212.

101. Roosevelt to Peters, Dec. 19, 1917; Peters to Roosevelt, Dec. 24, 1917, file C-5, Franklin D. Roosevelt Library, Hyde Park, N.Y.

102. Dinneen, *The Purple Shamrock*, 179; *Boston Post*, Apr. 2, 1931; *Boston Evening Transcript*, Nov. 12, 1930; Curley, *I'd Do It Again*, 231.

103. *Worcester Telegram*, Dec. 18, 1932 (one of a series of articles by James P. Guilfoyle).

104. Undated newspaper clipping, Term 3, Notebook 2, p. 58, author's files.

105. Dinneen, *The Purple Shamrock*, 182; Ralph G. Martin, *Ballots and Bandwagons* (Chicago, 1964), 298.

106. Undated newspaper clippings, Term 3, Notebook 2, pp. 56, 57, author's files; *Worcester Telegram*, June 14, 1931; *Springfield Union*, June 14, 1931.

107. Undated fragment (Dec. 1931), Term 3, Notebook 2, p. 91, author's files; *New York Times*, Jan 12, 1932; undated newspaper clipping, Term 3, Notebook 2, p. 88, author's files; *Boston American*, Oct. 4, 1932.

108. *Boston Post*, Jan. 1, 1932; *Boston Herald*, Jan. 31, 1932; *Worcester Telegram*, Mar. 26, 1932; *Boston Evening Transcript*, May 11, Jan 29, 1932; newspaper clipping (Aug. 23, 1932), Term 3, Notebook 3, p. 24, author's files; *Boston Post*, Nov. 19, 1932.

109. Davis, *F.D.R.*, 216; Brown to Roosevelt, Dec. 6, 1931, file C-7, Roosevelt Library.

110. Earland Irving Carlson, "Franklin D. Roosevelt's Fight for the Presidential Nomination, 1928–1932" (Ph.D. diss., University of Illinois, 1955), 221–23.

111. Ibid., 227–29.

112. *Boston Post*, Nov. 7, 1928; Carlson, "Franklin D. Roosevelt's Fight," 231, 387; Handlin, *Al Smith*, 162.

113. *New York Times*, June 20, 1931; *Hartford Courant*, Aug. 21, 1931; *Boston Herald*, Apr. 15, 1932; *Boston Evening Transcript*, Feb. 19, 1932; Carlson, "Franklin D. Roosevelt's Fight," 237; Dinneen, *The Purple Shamrock*, 190.

114. *Boston Post*, Feb. 20, 1932; *Boston Herald*, Feb. 20, 1932; Carlson, "Franklin D. Roosevelt's Fight," 387.

115. Carlson, "Franklin D. Roosevelt's Fight," 380–82.

116. Ibid., 235, 387; *Boston Herald*, Jan. 30, 1932; Trout, *Boston and the New Deal*, 102; James MacGregor Burns, *Roosevelt: The Lion and the Fox* (New York, 1956), 132.

117. Carlson, "Franklin D. Roosevelt's Fight," 388.

118. For Roosevelt's reaction to Brown's bad news see Trout, *Boston and the New Deal*, 105. See also *New York Times*, Mar. 11, 1932.

119. Carlson, "Franklin D. Roosevelt's Fight," 389; *Boston Post*, Mar. 12, 13, 1932; *Boston Herald*, Mar. 12, 13, 1932; Martin, *Ballots and Bandwagons*, 298.

120. *New York Times*, Mar. 13, 1932; *Boston Evening Transcript*, Mar. 17, 1932; undated newspaper clipping, Term 3, Notebook 3, p. 5, author's files; *Boston Daily Record*, Mar. 18, 19, 1932.
121. *Boston Post*, Mar. 17, 1932; *New York Times*, Mar. 19, 1932.
122. *Worcester Telegram*, Apr. 17, 1932; Robert K. Massey, Jr., "The Democratic Laggard: Massachusetts in 1932," *New England Quarterly* (Dec. 1971): 562; *Boston Herald*, Apr. 24, 1932; *Boston Traveler*, Apr. 27, 1932.
123. *New York Times*, Apr. 28, 1932; *Los Angeles Times*, Apr. 28, 1932; William E. Leuchtenburg, *Franklin D. Roosevelt and the New Deal, 1932–1940* (New York, 1963), 7.
124. Carlson, "Franklin D. Roosevelt's Fight," 389.
125. *Worcester Telegram*, Apr. 27, 1932; *Cleveland Plain Dealer*, Apr. 29, 1932.
126. *Springfield Republican*, Apr. 29, 1932.

Chapter 8. Air-conditioned Voice

1. Lyle W. Dorsett, *Franklin D. Roosevelt and the City Bosses* (Port Washington, N.Y., 1977), 21.
2. *Boston Globe*, June 26, 1932.
3. *Worcester Gazette*, June 28, 1932; Charles H. Trout, *Boston, the Great Depression, and the New Deal* (New York, 1977), 104; Richard Oulahan, *The Man Who . . . : The Story of the 1932 Democratic National Convention* (New York, 1971), 47; *Boston Post*, June 28, 1932; James Michael Curley, *I'd Do It Again: A Record of All My Uproarious Years* (Englewood Cliffs, N.J., 1957), 234; "Memoirs of James Michael Curley" (draft, n.d.), Howland notebook, 105–108, author's files; original is in Frank Howland Collection, Boston Public Library.
4. *Springfield Republican*, June 28, 1932.
5. *Boston Globe*, June 28, 1932.
6. Trout, *Boston and the New Deal*, 107; Ralph G. Martin, *Ballots and Bandwagons* (New York, 1964), 358.
7. Kenneth S. Davis, *F.D.R.: The New York Years, 1928–1933* (New York, 1985), 324; William E. Leuchtenburg, *Franklin D. Roosevelt and the New Deal, 1832–1940* (New York, 1963), 8.
8. Draw Pearson's column in Jersey City, N.J., *Observer*, Mar. 28, 1933. For Howe's attitude toward Curley see James MacGregor Burns, *Roosevelt: The Lion and the Fox* (New York, 1956), 132.
9. Curley, *I'd Do It Again*, 237.
10. Richard J. Whalen, *The Founding Father: The Story of Joseph P. Kennedy* (New York, 1964), 125.
11. Doris Kearns Goodwin, *The Fitzgeralds and the Kennedys: An American Saga* (New York, 1987), 429.
12. Davis, *F.D.R.*, 322; Richard O'Connor, *The First Hurrah: A Biography of Alfred E. Smith* (New York, 1970), 263.
13. *Boston Advertiser*, July 3, 1932.
14. *New York Times*, July 9, 1932; *Boston Post*, June 28, 1932; *Boston Herald*, July 5, 1932.
15. Bergson to Roosevelt, July 4, 1932, file C-8, Franklin D. Roosevelt Library, Hyde Park, N.Y.
16. *Boston Post*, Aug. 24, 1932; Michael Kendall, "Mayor of the Poor: James Michael Curley as an Urban Populist" (senior honors thesis, Harvard University, 1979), 135; William Jay Foley, "Public Speaking in the Political Career of James Michael Curley" (Ph.D. diss., University of Wisconsin, 1952), 78.

17. *New York Times*, Fall 1990; *The New Republic*, Jan. 27, 1992.

18. *Time*, Feb. 12, 1951; *Brookline Chronicle-Citizen*, Aug. 10, 1961.

19. Foley, "Public Speaking of James Michael Curley," 57.

20. *Time*, Feb. 12, 1951; Foley, "Public Speaking of James Michael Curley," 68.

21. Foley, "Public Speaking of James Michael Curley," 54; *Boston Traveler*, Nov. 19, 1958; Edwin O'Connor, *The Last Hurrah* (Boston, 1956), 283.

22. Foley, "Public Speaking of James Michael Curley," 73.

23. Ibid., 74.

24. "Memorial to the Fireman" (1916), Term 1, Notebook 5, author's files; original can be found in bound volume of Curley's speeches for his first term in Curley Scrapbooks, James Michael Curley Collection, College of the Holy Cross, Worcester, Mass.

25. My thanks to Ken Gloss, owner of the Brattle Book Shop, a Boston institution, for providing me with over ten hours of tapes of Curley's speeches from the 1945 mayoral campaign and his last term.

26. Herbert Marshall Zolot, "The Issue of Good Government and James Michael Curley: Curley and the Boston Scene from 1897–1918" (Ph.D. diss., State University of New York, Stony Brook, 1975), 233; private interview with Elliot Norton on his early days as a reporter for the *Boston Post*; private interview with Francis X. Curley.

27. Ralph G. Martin, *The Bosses* (New York, 1964), 241.

28. Kitty Kelley, address to the National Press Club, Washington, 1991 (C-Span broadcast); Kathleen Hall Jamieson, *Eloquence in an Electronic Age: The Transformation of Political Speechmaking* (New York, 1988). See also Christopher Buckley's review of Jamieson in the *Manchester Guardian*, Aug. 21, 1988.

29. *New York Times*, Oct. 3, 1932.

30. *Boston American*, Oct. 10, 1932; *Boston Herald*, Oct. 28, 1932; *Boston Post*, Oct. 31, 1932; *Boston Globe*, Oct. 31, 1932.

31. *Boston Evening Transcript*, Nov. 1, 1932; *Boston Globe*, Nov. 1, 1932; undated newspaper clipping, Term 3, Notebook 3, p. 31, author's files; originals of unidentified clippings are in Curley Scrapbooks, Curley Collection, Holy Cross.

32. Robert K. Massey, Jr., "The Democratic Laggard: Massachusetts in 1932," *New England Quarterly* (Dec. 1971): 569, 571–74.

33. *Boston Daily Record*, Nov. 7, 1932; undated newspaper clipping, Term 3, Notebook 3, p. 31, author's files.

34. Roosevelt to Curley (telegram), Nov. 20, 1932, Term 3, Notebook 3, p. 37, author's files; *Boston Globe*, Nov. 21, 1932; Lauretta Bremner Sliney affidavit, Aug. 15, 1973.

35. *Boston Post*, Nov. 21, 1932; *Boston Globe*, Nov. 21, 1932.

36. Joseph F. Dinneen, *The Purple Shamrock: The Hon. James Michael Curley of Boston* (New York, 1949), 204; *Boston American*, Jan. 2, 1933.

37. Undated newspaper clipping, Term 3, Notebook 3, p. 46, author's files; Dinneen, *The Purple Shamrock*, p. 204; *Boston Globe*, Jan. 1, 1933; Sidney Shalett and James Roosevelt, *Affectionately F.D.R.* (New York, 1959), 184.

38. Davis, *F.D.R.*, 407; Burns, *Roosevelt: The Lion and the Fox*, 149.

39. *Boston Globe*, Nov. 17, 1932; *New York Times*, Nov. 17, 1932; undated newspaper clipping, Term 3, Notebook 3, p. 46, author's files; *Worcester Telegram*, Apr. 10, 1932; *Boston Globe*, Mar. 3, 1933.

40. *Boston Evening Transcript*, Feb. 25, 1933; *Boston American*, Feb. 28, 1933.

41. Undated newspaper clipping, Term 3, Notebook 3, p. 46, author's files.

42. Undated newspaper clipping, Term 3, Notebook 3, pp. 61–62, author's files; *Boston American*, Feb. 9, 1933; *Lawrence Eagle-Tribune*, Feb. 11, 1933; *Boston Post*, Jan. 11, 1933.

43. Dinneen, *The Purple Shamrock*, 206–10; *Boston Evening Transcript*, Apr. 14, 15, 1933; *Boston American*, Apr. 14, 1933.

44. *Worcester Telegram*, Mar. 4, 1933; David S. Wyman, *The Abandonment of the Jews: America and the Holocaust, 1941–1945* (New York, 1984), 191.

45. *Boston Herald*, Mar. 22, 1933.

46. Private interview with William Z. Slany, State Department historian, Oct. 16, 1991.

47. *New York Times*, Apr. 15, 1933; Roosevelt to Senate, Apr. 11, 1933, Howland notebook, 36–37, author's files; Trout, *Boston and the New Deal*, 342.

48. *Boston Post*, Apr. 14, 1933; *New York Times*, Apr. 15, 1933.

49. Dinneen, *The Purple Shamrock*, 210; Foley, "Public Speaking of James Michael Curley," 147; Curley, *I'd Do It Again*, 250.

50. For Fascist salute see *Italian News* (Boston), Oct. 23, 1936; *Boston Post*, Sept. 12, 1936. This view of Curley without Mary Emelda is based on Francis Curley interviews.

51. *Boston Herald*, Jan. 5, 1933; *New York Times*, Feb. 25, 1936; *Boston Globe*, Aug. 14, 1938; *Boston American*, Apr. 15, 16, 1933.

52. *Boston Evening Transcript*, Apr. 15, 1933.

53. Trout, *Boston and the New Deal*, 54; Leuchtenburg, *Franklin D. Roosevelt and the New Deal*, 39.

54. Trout, *Boston and the New Deal*, 119–22; *Boston Evening Transcript*, Jan. 19, 1932; *Boston Post*, Mar. 28, 1933; undated newspaper clipping, Term 3, Notebook 3, p. 72, author's files.

55. Trout, *Boston and the New Deal*, 127, 123.

56. Ibid., 156, 157.

57. *Boston Globe*, Apr. 6, 1933; *Springfield Republican*, July 27, 1933.

58. *Boston Post*, Sept. 17, 1933; *Springfield News*, Oct. 13, 1933.

59. Undated newspaper clippings, Term 3, Notebook 3, pp. 55, 38, author's files; *Boston American*, Aug. 12, 1933; Trout, *Boston and the New Deal*, 114.

60. *Boston Post*, Oct. 1, 1933; Sept. 19, 1934.

61. *Boston Post*, Oct. 1, 1933; *Fortune*, 1933. For substantiation of the claim about taxes see *Boston Evening Transcript*, Aug. 7, 1932.

62. Private interview with Dorothy MaGowan; *Boston Globe*, Dec. 23, 1933; Francis Curley interview; undated newspaper clipping, Term 3, Notebook 3, p. 62, author's files; *Boston Post*, Aug. 13, 1933; *Boston Globe*, Aug. 13, 1933.

63. Francis Curley interview; confidential interview; William V. Shannon, *The American Irish* (New York, 1963), 328.

64. *Boston Globe*, Dec. 23, 1933; *Boston Post*, Dec. 31, 1936; Dec. 28, 1933.

Chapter 9. The Hit-and-Run Governor

1. William Schneider, "When Ambition Replaces Party Ties," *National Journal*, June 22, 1991.

2. Alan Ehrenhalt, *The United States of Ambition: Politicians, Power, and the Pursuit of Office* (New York, 1991), 18, 23.

3. *Boston Post*, June 7, 13, 1934; *New York Times*, June 22, Aug. 26, 1934.

4. *New York Times*, Aug. 26, June 24, Nov. 1, 1934.

5. Undated newspaper clippings, State House Notebook 2, pp. 4, 3, author's files; originals of clippings are in Curley Scrapbooks, James Michael Curley Collection, College of the Holy Cross, Worcester, Mass.; *New York Times*, Mar. 3, 1935; June 28, 1936; Harold Gorvine, "The New Deal in Massachusetts" (Ph.D. diss., Harvard University, 1962), 5, 8, 9, 31.

6. *Worcester Sunday Times*, July 1, 1934.

7. *Boston Post*, Sept. 8, 1934.

8. *Worcester Telegram*, Aug. 15, 1934; *Boston Daily Record*, July 2, 1934.

9. *Boston Post*, Sept. 16, 1934; undated clipping, *Boston Herald*, State House notebooks, author's files; *Boston Daily Record*, Oct. 4, 1934; Ralph G. Martin, *The Bosses* (New York, 1964), 242; Lewis H. Weinstein, "The Night Curley Appealed for Nickels," *Boston Globe*, July 23, 1988.

10. *New York Times*, Sept. 30, 1934.

11. *Boston Post*, Oct. 3, 1934; *New York Times*, Aug. 26, 1934.

12. *Boston Post*, Nov. 1, Oct. 2, 1934; *Boston Herald*, Oct. 25, 1934.

13. Arthur M. Schlesinger, Jr., *The Age of Roosevelt*, vol. 2: *The Coming of the New Deal* (Boston, 1959), 434–36; *Boston Post*, Nov. 2, June 25, 1934.

14. *Boston Herald*, Nov. 11, 1934; *New York Times*, June 2, 1934; *Boston Herald*, Oct. 3, 1934; *New York Times*, Oct. 8, 1934.

15. *Boston Globe*, Oct. 15, 1934; *Boston Evening Transcript*, Nov. 7, 1934. For Curley's dirty trick see Martin, *The Bosses*, 243.

16. *New York Times*, Nov. 7, 1934; Wendell D. Howie, *The Reign of James I: A Historical Record of the Administration of James Michael Curley as Governor of Massachusetts* (Cambridge, Mass., 1936), 7.

17. *Boston Herald*, Nov. 3, 1938.

18. *Boston Post*, Nov. 9, 1934.

19. *Boston Post*, Jan. 3, 1935; Dec. 4, 1934.

20. *New York Times*, Jan. 6, 1935.

21. *Boston Herald*, Sept. 22, 1932; *Worcester Telegram*, Jan. 4, 1935; *Boston Post*, Jan. 4, 3, 1935.

22. Ray Kierman, "Jim Curley, Boss of Massachusetts," *American Mercury*, Feb. 1936, 143.

23. *Worcester Telegram*, Mar. 19, 1935.

24. *New York Times*, Feb. 3, 1935; undated newspaper clipping, State House Notebook 2, p. 55, author's files; *Boston Traveler*, Dec. 16, 1942; private interview with Robert Gallagher.

25. *Boston Traveler*, Jan. 16, 1935.

26. Joseph F. Dinneen, *The Purple Shamrock: The Hon. James Michael Curley of Boston* (New York, 1949), 238; Howie, *The Reign of James I*.

27. *Worcester Telegram*, Jan. 20, 1935.

28. *Boston Evening Transcript*, Jan. 25, 1935.

29. *Boston Globe*, Jan. 26, 1935; Howie, *The Reign of James I*, 36; *Boston Evening Transcript*, Feb. 1, 1935; *Christian Science Monitor*, Feb. 12, 1935; *Boston Herald*, Feb. 9, 1935.

30. Howie, *The Reign of James I*, 36; *Boston Post*, Dec. 27, 1941.

31. *Hyannis Patriot*, Feb. 21, 1935.

32. *Boston Evening Transcript*, Mar. 26, 1935; *New York Times*, Apr. 7, 1935; Kierman, "Jim Curley," 147; *Springfield Republican*, Mar. 1, 1935.

33. *Springfield Union*, Feb. 22, 1935.

34. Gorvine, "The New Deal in Massachusetts," 22; *Boston Traveler*, June 26, 1935; *Boston Evening Transcript*, Apr. 15, 1935; *Christian Science Monitor*, Dec. 15, 1935; *Framingham News*, Dec. 10, 1935; *Boston Traveler*, Jan. 14, 1936; *Boston Post*, Jan. 3, 1937; *Boston Traveler*, Nov. 12, 1942; June 13, 1957.

35. *Boston Post*, Dec. 8, 1935; Howie, *The Reign of James I*, 35; *Boston Herald*, Nov. 28, 1935; confidential interview.

36. *Boston Post*, Mar. 1, 1935; *Boston Evening Transcript*, Jan. 25, 1935; *Boston Globe*, Feb. 17, 1935; *Lowell Telegram*, Feb. 3, 1935.

37. *Springfield Republican*, Mar. 13, 1935; *Boston Globe*, Sept. 29, 1935; Gorvine, "The New Deal in Massachusetts," 18; *Taunton Gazette*, May 10, 1935.

38. *Boston Post*, Nov. 3, 1935; Gorvine, "The New Deal in Massachusetts," 18–21.

39. Robert S. McElvaine, *The Great Depression: America, 1929–1941* (New York, 1984), 7; Gorvine, "The New Deal in Massachusetts," 498.

40. Confidential interview; *Boston Globe*, June 9, 1935.

41. Private interview with Dorothy MaGowan; *Boston Globe, Boston Herald, Boston Daily Record, Boston Evening Transcript*, issues for June 9–11, 1935; *Boston Traveler*, June 17, 1935.

42. *Brockton Enterprise*, July 11, 1935; *Pittsfield Eagle*, Aug. 5, 1935; *Worcester Telegram*, July 16, 1935; *Springfield Union*, Aug. 3, 1935; *Chelsea Record*, Aug. 6, 1935.

43. *Worcester Telegram*, July 20, 1935.

44. *Boston Globe*, May 18, 1935.

45. *Boston Herald*, July 19, 1935; *New York Times*, July 7, 1935.

46. *Boston Evening Transcript*, July 5, 1935; *New York Times*, July 5, 1935.

47. *Boston Globe*, July 18, 1935.

48. *Worcester Post*, July 15, 1935.

49. *Boston Herald*, July 10, 1935; *Worcester Telegram*, Sept. 18, 1935.

50. Howie, *The Reign of James I*, 40–43; undated editorial, *Boston Herald*, State House notebooks, author's files.

51. *New Bedford Mercury*, Aug. 8, 1935; *Boston Traveler*, Aug. 10, 1935; *Christian Science Monitor*, Sept. 18, 1935.

52. *Springfield Union*, May 27, 1935; undated clipping, *Boston Post*, State House notebooks, author's files.

53. *Boston Post*, Sept. 8, 1935; *Boston Globe*, Oct. 17, 1935.

54. *New York Times*, Mar. 3, 1935; *Boston Post*, Oct. 20, 1935.

55. Charles H. Trout, *Boston, the Great Depression, and the New Deal* (New York, 1977), 173.

56. *Boston Herald*, Sept. 30, 1935.

57. Undated newspaper clipping, State House Notebook 2, p. 96, author's files; *Boston Herald*, Sept. 30, 1935.

58. This is the theme of George Reedy's *Twilight of the Presidency: An Examination of Power and Isolation in the White House* (New York, 1970).

59. *Boston Post*, Mar. 24, 1935.

60. *Boston Evening Transcript*, Feb. 21, 1935; *Boston Traveler*, Feb. 21, 1935; *Boston American*, May 8, 1935; *Boston Globe*, May 7, 1935.

61. Howie, *The Reign of James I*.

62. Ibid., chap. 7; *Boston Traveler*, May 17, 1935; *Boston Herald*, May 20, 1935; *New Bedford Standard-Times*, June 12, 1935; *Worcester Telegram*, June 22, 1935; *Boston Evening Transcript*, June 27, 1935; *Boston Herald*, Aug. 22, 1935.

63. Gorvine, "The New Deal in Massachusetts," 28; Howie, *The Reign of James I*, 44; William V. Shannon, *The American Irish* (New York, 1963), 223; *Holyoke Transcript*, Dec. 4, 1935; *Fitchburg Sentinel*, Dec. 5, 1935.

64. *Boston Evening Transcript*, Aug. 21, 1935; *Worcester Telegram*, Sept. 18, 1935.

65. *New York Times*, Oct. 20, 1935; undated newspaper clipping, State House Notebook 2, p. 99, author's files; Howie, *The Reign of James I*, 100; *Boston Evening Transcript*, Nov. 15, 1935; *New York Times*, Dec. 3, 1935.

66. *Greenfield Recorder*, Jan. 11, 1936; *Fall River Herald-News*, Nov. 7, 1935; *Boston Evening Transcript*, Nov. 15, 1935; undated newspaper clipping, State House Notebook 2, p. 114; also undated clipping, *Braintree Observer*, State House notebooks, author's files.

67. Undated clipping, *Christian Science Monitor*; also State House Notebook 2, p. 124, author's files; *Boston Post*, Jan. 2, 1936.

68. Interview with Mary Cremens, *Boston Globe*, June 13, 1957.

69. Ibid.; confidential interview.

70. *Boston Post*, Dec. 31, 1936; *Boston Globe*, Jan 13, 1937; June 13, 1957; private interview with Richard Dennis.

71. Recording of Gertrude Dennis Curley provided to me by her son Richard Dennis, to whom I am grateful.

72. *New York Times*, Nov. 20, 1991.

73. *Boston Globe*, June 13, 1957; Jan. 28, 1936.

74. *Boston Globe*, Mar. 22, 1936; *Worcester Post*, Mar. 18, 1936.

75. *Boston Traveler*, Mar. 20, 1936; *Boston American*, Mar. 18, 1936; *Boston Post*, Mar. 22, 1936.

76. *Boston Herald*, Mar. 18, 1936.

77. County Recorder (Dedham), Mar. 20, 1936.

78. *Boston American*, Mar. 19, 1936; *Boston Herald*, Mar. 19, 1936.

79. *Boston Post*, Mar. 24, 1936.

80. *Boston Herald*, Mar. 22, 1936; *Lowell Sun*, Mar. 21, 1936.

81. *Boston Globe*, Mar. 23, 1936; *Boston Post*, Mar. 22, 1936.

82. *Lowell Leader*, Mar. 24, 1936.

83. *Boston Traveler*, Mar. 23, Apr. 3, 1936.

84. *New York Times*, May 4, 1936; Joseph F. Dinneen, "The Kingfish of Massachusetts," *Harper's Monthly*, Sept. 1936, 344.

85. *Laconia* (N.H.) *News*, June 3, 1936; *Lawrence Tribune*, June 17, 1936; *Salem News*, June 25, 1936; *Brockton Enterprise*, Aug. 5, 1936; Gallagher interview; *Boston Herald*, Sept. 26, 1936; *Boston Globe*, June 29, 1936.

86. *New York Times*, May 15, 24, 1936; *Attleboro Sun*, May 15, 1936.

87. *Holyoke Transcript*, May 4, 1936; *Baltimore Sun*, May 18, 1936; *New York Times*, May 18, 1936.

88. *Worcester Telegram*, June 11, 1936; undated newspaper clipping, State House Notebook 2, p. 51, author's files; *New York Times*, May 16, 24, 1936.

89. *Fitchburg Sentinel*, May 29, 1936; *Worcester Telegram*, June 6, 1936; *Boston Post*, Sept. 14, 1936.

90. *Boston Herald*, June 7, 1936.

91. *Boston American*, June 23, 1936; *Holyoke Transcript*, June 26, 1936; *Springfield Union*, June 26, 1936.

92. *Boston Traveler*, June 26, 1936.

93. *North Adams Transcript*, July 13, 1936; *New Bedford Mercury*, July 13, 1936.

94. Kierman, "Jim Curley."

95. *The Nation*, Apr. 29, 1936.

96. Dinneen, "The Kingfish of Massachusetts."

97. Arthur M. Schlesinger, Jr., *The Age of Roosevelt*, vol. 3: *The Politics of Upheaval* (Boston, 1960), 62.

98. *Southbridge News*, Sept. 24, 1936.

99. *Boston Traveler*, Sept. 24, 1936.

100. Ibid.

101. *Fall River Herald-News*, Sept. 30, 1936.

102. *New York Times*, Sept. 12, 1936; *Fall River Herald-News*, Sept. 25, 1936.

103. Undated editorial, *Boston Herald*, State House notebooks, author's files.

104. William J. Miller, *Henry Cabot Lodge* (New York, 1967), 1–150; see especially 41, 118, 131–32.

105. Shannon, *The American Irish*, 358.

106. Miller, *Henry Cabot Lodge*, 133.

107. *Worcester Telegram*, Sept. 30, 1936; undated newspaper clipping, State House Notebook 2, author's files.

108. Miller, *Henry Cabot Lodge*, 130.

109. *Worcester Telegram*, Oct. 3, 1936; *Springfield Republican*, Oct. 25, 1936; *Chicago Tribune*, Oct. 25, 1936; *Attleboro Sun*, Oct. 9, 1936.

110. Undated newspaper clipping, State House Notebook 2, pp. 126, author's files; *Boston Post*, Sept. 12, 1936.

111. *Boston Traveler*, June 15, 1936; *Boston Globe*, Oct. 12, 1936; Schlesinger, *The Politics of Upheaval*, 629.

112. Nat Hentoff, *Boston Boy* (New York, 1986), 18; Shannon, *The American Irish*, 304; James Michael Curley, *I'd Do It Again: A Record of All My Uproarious Years* (Englewood Cliffs, N.J., 1957), 297.

113. Curley, *I'd Do It Again*, 298.

114. Undated newspaper clipping, State House Notebook 2, p. 135, author's files.

115. *Augusta* (Maine) *Journal*, Nov. 5, 1936; *Springfield News*, Nov. 4, 1936; *Bridgeport* (Conn.) *Times-Star*, Nov. 5, 1936; *Boston Post*, Nov. 8, 1936.

116. *Springfield Republican*, Nov. 5, 1936; *Boston Post*, Nov. 5, 1936; undated newspaper clipping, State House Notebook 2, p. 98, author's files.

Chapter 10. Himself Again

1. *Boston Globe*, Sept. 16, 1936; *Worcester Telegram*, Sept. 18, 1936.

2. Private interview with John Henry Cutler; *Boston Globe*, Sept. 23, 1936.

3. Elmer Irey, *The Tax Dodgers* (New York, 1948), 204–209.

4. *New Bedford Mercury*, Jan. 1, 1937; *Worcester Telegram*, Dec. 22, 1936; *Boston Post*, Nov. 25, 1936; *Fall River Herald-News*, Dec. 24, 1936; private interview with Robert Gallagher, former secretary to Governor Curley; *Boston Post*, Dec. 13, 1936.

5. *Boston Post*, Sept. 11, 1936.

6. *Boston Traveler*, Nov. 9, 1936; *Nashua Telegram*, Dec. 9, 1936.

7. "Memoirs of James M. Curley" (n.d.), 352, author's files.

8. Private interview with Francis X. Curley.

9. *New York Times*, Jan. 8, 1937.

10. *Boston Globe*, Jan. 1, 1937; *New York Times*, Jan. 18, 1937; *Pawtucket* (R.I.) *Times*, Dec. 2, 1936.

11. *Boston Globe*, Oct. 7, 1987. For quotation from Robert Woods see Gerald H. Gamm, *The Making of New Deal Democrats: Voting Behavior and Realignment in Boston, 1920–1940*(Chicago, 1989), 142. For details on Tobin see Vincent Anthony Lapomarda, "Maurice Joseph Tobin, 1901–1953: A Political Profile" (Ph.D. diss., Boston University, 1968); the quotation is on p. 16.

12. Vincent Lapomarda, "Maurice Joseph Tobin: The Decline of Bossism in Boston," *New England Quarterly* (Sept. 1970): 358.

13. Ibid., 359; Gallagher interview.

14. Mike Ryan, "That Man Curley!" *Irish America*, Oct. 1989, 40; Lapomarda, "Maurice Joseph Tobin: The Decline of Bossism," 363.

15. *Boston Globe*, June 18, 1937.

16. Private interview with John Quigley, son of the former mayor of Chelsea. For Morton Downey and Curley's song see Howland notebook, 14, author's files; original is in Frank Howland Collection, Boston Public Library.

17. *Boston Post*, Nov. 7, 1937; *Boston Globe*, May 25, 1937.

18. *Boston Globe*, Oct. 18, 1987.

19. *Boston Globe*, Oct. 7, 1937; Lapomarda, "Maurice Joseph Tobin, 1901–1953," 6.

20. *Boston Post*, Oct. 19, 1937; Lapomarda, "Maurice Joseph Tobin, 1901–1953," 32; idem, "Maurice Joseph Tobin: The Decline of Bossism," 366; *Boston Post*, Oct. 28, 1941; private interview with Dave Powers.

21. *Boston Post*, Sept. 23, Oct. 16, 1937; Joseph Dinneen, *The Purple Shamrock: The Hon. James Michael Curley of Boston* (New York, 1949), 257; *Boston Post*, Oct. 17, 1937.

22. *Boston Post*, Oct. 8, 1937.

23. *Boston Post*, Oct. 30, 1937.

24. *Boston Post*, Nov. 7, 1937.

25. Herbert A. Kenny, *Newspaper Row: Journalism in the Pre-Television Era* (Chester, Conn., 1987), 168–69.

26. Ibid.; private interview with Elliot Norton.

27. *Boston Post*, Nov. 2, 1937; Kenny, *Newspaper Row*, 172.

28. *Boston Herald*, Nov. 2, 1937; *Boston Globe*, Oct. 7, 1987. For Curley's opinion of O'Connell see Jonathan Daniels, *White House Witness* (New York, 1975), 140.

29. *Boston Post*, Nov. 3, 1937.

30. Arthur Inman, *The Inman Diary: A Public and Private Confession*, ed. Daniel Aaron (Cambridge, Mass., 1985), 800.

31. *Boston Globe*, July 1, 1938,

32. *New York Times*, Jan. 9, 1937.

33. *Boston Post*, Sept. 11, 1938.

34. Harold Gorvine, "The New Deal in Massachusetts" (Ph.D. diss., Harvard University, 1962), 34–35; *Boston Herald*, Sept. 19, 1938; *Springfield Union*, July 28, 1938.

35. *New York Times*, Sept. 21, 25, 1938; *Boston Herald*, Sept. 19, 1938; *Boston Post*, Nov. 2, 1938; William V. Shannon, *The American Irish* (New York, 1963), 215.

36. *Boston Herald*, Sept. 2, 1938.

37. *New York Times*, Sept. 21, 1938; *Springfield Union*, July 28, 1938; *Boston Herald*, Sept. 19, 1938.

38. *Boston Herald*, Sept. 21, 1938; confidential interview; Cleveland Amory, *The Proper Bostonians* (New York, 1947), 34.

39. John Henry Cutler, *Honey-Fitz: Three Steps to the White House; The Colorful Life and Times of John F. ("Honey-Fitz") Fitzgerald* (Indianapolis, 1962), 275; *Boston Post*, Sept. 18, Oct. 2, 1938.

40. *Boston Post*, Oct. 8, 1938.

41. James Michael Curley, *I'd Do It Again: A Record of All My Uproarious Years* (Englewood Cliffs, N.J., 1957), 309; *Boston Globe*, Feb. 17, 1938.

42. *Boston Post*, Nov. 6, 1938.

43. *Springfield Union*, Aug. 5, 1938; *Boston Post*, Oct. 31, 1938; Bernard Adelman, Winthrop, Mass., to author.

44. Cutler, *Honey-Fitz*, 275; *Boston Post*, Oct. 31, 1938.

45. *Boston Post*, Nov. 2, 1938; Leverett Saltonstall with Edward Weeks, *Salty: Recollections of a Yankee in Politics* (Boston, 1976), 63; *Boston Post*, Nov. 4, 1938; Cutler, *Honey-Fitz*, 275; Barbara Miller Solomon, *Ancestors and Immigrants: A Changing New England Tradition* (Boston, 1989), 104.

46. *Boston Post*, Nov. 9, 1938; Thomas O'Connor, work in progress on the mayoralties of John Hynes, John Collins, and Kevin White, chap. 1, p. 37.

47. *Boston Post*, Jan. 27, 1939.

48. John F. Stack, Jr., *International Conflict in an American City: Boston's Irish, Italians, and Jews, 1935–1944* (Westport, Conn., 1979), 117–25.

49. *New York Times*, Dec. 7, 1935. For David I. Walsh see Dorothy Wayman, *David I. Walsh, Citizen Patriot* (Milwaukee, 1952), 80–83, 309–14. Wayman denies that Walsh was Senator X.

50. Francis Curley interview.

51. Ibid.

52. Robert Cutler, *No Time to Rest* (Boston, 1965), 141–42.

53. *Humboldt* (Nev.) *Star*, Feb. 22, 1939. See also undated clipping from the same paper, author's files; originals of clippings are in Curley Collection, Holy Cross.

54. *Humboldt Star*, May 5, 1940.

55. Undated clipping, *Humboldt Star*, author's files; Francis Curley interview; private interview with Helen McDonough.

56. *Christian Science Monitor*, Nov. 22, 1940; Alfred Steinberg, *The Bosses* (New York, 1972), 178; *Christian Science Monitor*, June 2, 1941.

57. Lewis H. Weinstein, "The Night Curley Appealed for Nickels," *Boston Globe*, July 23, 1988; Dinneen, *The Purple Shamrock*, 280; advertisements in the *Boston Post*, Sept. 6, 1941; William Allen White, *A Puritan in Babylon* (New York, 1938), xv.

58. McDonough interview.

59. Private interview with Martin Hanley.

60. Private interview with Lauretta Bremner Sliney; Francis Curley interview.

61. Confidential interview; letter dated Feb. 8, 1993, from Maurice Whalen.

62. Private interview with Richard Dennis; McDonough interview.

63. Dennis, McDonough interviews.

64. Dennis, McDonough interviews.

65. Lapomarda, "Maurice Joseph Tobin: The Decline of Bossism," 370.

66. William L. Riordan, *Plunkitt of Tammany Hall* (New York, 1963), 17.

67. *Boston Post*, Oct. 12, 5, 1941.

68. *Boston Post*, Nov. 1, 1941.

69. *Boston Herald*, Sept. 3, 1941; *Boston Post*, Oct. 30, 1941; Cutler, *No Time to Rest*, 143.

70. *Boston Post*, Sept. 17, 4, 3, Oct. 3, 1941.

71. *Boston Post*, Oct. 3, 1941.

72. *Boston Post*, Oct. 25, 29, 1941.

73. *Boston Globe*, Nov. 3, 1941.

74. Cutler, *No Time to Rest*, 143.

75. *Boston Post*, Nov. 1, 1941.

76. *Boston Post*, Oct. 31, 1941.

77. *Boston Post*, Nov. 7, 1941.

78. Cutler, *No Time to Rest*, 146; *Boston Globe*, Dec. 24, 1941.

79. Doris Kearns Goodwin, *The Kennedys and the Fitzgeralds: An American Saga* (New York, 1987), 625.

80. Norton interview.

81. Private interview with the late Thomas H. Eliot.

82. *Boston Traveler*, Nov. 13, 1942.

83. Eliot interview.

84. *Boston Post*, Oct. 27, 1942.

85. Francis Curley interview.

Chapter 11. Fedora

1. David Brinkley, *Washington Goes to War* (New York, 1988), 83, 102; John Morton Blum, *V Was for Victory* (New York, 1976), 93.

2. Brinkley, *Washington Goes to War*, 115; private interview with Peter Davison.

3. Brinkley, *Washington Goes to War*, 197.

4. Ralph G. Martin, *The Bosses* (New York, 1964), 253–54; private interview with Thomas H. Eliot.

5. Blum, *V Was for Victory*, 90–91.

6. Ibid., 123, 126.

7. John Gunther, *Inside the U.S.A.* (New York, 1947), 478.

8. *Boston Herald*, Apr. 23, 1942.

9. Ibid.

10. *Boston Herald*, Sept. 17, 1943.

11. Alfred Steinberg, *The Bosses* (New York, 1972), 189; *Boston Globe*, Apr. 23, 1942; Francis Biddle, *In Brief Authority* (New York, 1962), 267–69.

12. Biddle, *In Brief Authority*, 267–69.

13. McCormack to Roosevelt (telegram), doc. PP2 1154, Franklin D. Roosevelt Library, Hyde Park, N.Y.

14. Biddle, *In Brief Authority*, 267–69.

15. *New York Times*, Sept. 17, 1943; private interview with Peter Caparell; *Washington Evening Star*, Dec. 30, 1945; Steinberg, *The Bosses*, 193; transcript, Engineers' Group trial, Federal Records Center, Suitland, Md.; *Time*, Sept. 27, 1943.

16. *Springfield Free Press*, June 14, 1947.

17. *New York Times*, Feb. 9, 1943; radio broadcasts from 1945 campaign courtesy of Ken Gloss of the Brattle Book Shop, Boston.

18. *New York Times*, Nov. 1, 1943.

19. Curley to Roosevelt, doc. X-150, Roosevelt Library.

20. Geoffrey C. Ward, *A First-Class Temperament: The Emergence of Franklin Roosevelt* (New York, 1989), 254.

21. William V. Shannon, *The American Irish* (New York, 1963), 318; Gerald H. Gamm, *The Making of New Deal Democrats: Voting Behavior and Realignment in Boston, 1920–1940* (Chicago, 1989), 81; William E. Leuchtenburg, *Franklin D. Roosevelt and the New Deal* (New York, 1963), 277.

22. Donald Grant, "Coughlin's New Capital," *The Nation*, Mar. 21, 1942; John F. Stack, Jr., *International Conflict in an American City: Boston's Irish, Italians, and Jews, 1935–1944* (Westport, Conn., 1979), 33, 231–33.

23. Grant, "Coughlin's New Capital."

24. Stack, *International Conflict*, 131–35; Grant, "Coughlin's New Capital"; Katherine Loughlin, "Boston's Political Morals," *Commonweal*, Mar. 15, 1946, 545.

25. Stack, *International Conflict*, 131–35; Wallace Stegner, "Who Persecutes Boston?" *Atlantic Monthly*, July 1944, 45–52.

26. Stegner, "Who Persecutes Boston?" 50.

27. *Congressional Record*, Mar. 30, 1944, 3327–45.

28. Ibid., 3345; Stack, *International Conflict*, 55.

29. *Congressional Record*, Mar. 30, 1944, 3345; *Congressional Record*, Apr. 26, 1944, 3709; Blum, *V Was for Victory*, 174–80.

30. Jonathan Daniels, *White House Witness* (New York, 1975), 118–19.

31. My thanks to Nigel Hamilton, author of *J.F.K.: Reckless Youth*, for the letter from Kennedy to Billings; James Michael Curley, *I'd Do It Again: A Record of All My Uproarious Years* (Englewood Cliffs, N.J., 1957), 314.

32. Private interview with Nigel Hamilton.

33. Doris Kearns Goodwin, *The Fitzgeralds and the Kennedys: An American Saga* (New York, 1987), 627.

34. Ibid., 700; Hamilton interview.

35. *Boston Post*, Oct. 22, 24, 1945; private interview with William Morrissey.

36. *Boston Herald*, Jan. 7, 1946; Thomas O'Connor, from his work in progress on the mayoralties of Hynes, Collins, and White, chap. 2, p. 8.

37. Paul Benzaquoin, *Holocaust* (Boston, 1959), 20; Vincent Anthony Lapomarda, "Maurice Joseph Tobin, 1901–1953: A Political Profile" (Ph.D. diss., Boston University, 1968), 96.

38. *Boston Post*, Nov. 1, Oct. 24, 1945.

39. Private interview with Helen McDonough.

40. Private interview with Francis X. Curley.

41. *Boston Post*, Oct. 15, 1945.

42. *Boston Post*, Oct. 27, 30, Nov. 3, 6, 1945.

43. *Boston Post*, Nov. 7, 1945.

44. Ibid.

45. Jerome S. Bruner and Sheldon J. Korchin, "The Boss and the Vote: A Case Study in City Politics," *Public Opinion Quarterly* (Spring 1946): 1–23.

46. Biddle, *In Brief Authority*, 267; *Boston Post*, Jan. 18, 1946.

47. Francis Curley interview; *Boston Post*, Jan. 19, 1946.

48. Maurice M. Milligan, *Missouri Waltz: The Inside Story of the Pendergast Machine by the Man Who Smashed It* (New York, 1948), 98, 218–41; William E. Leuchtenburg, *In the Shadow of FDR* (Ithaca, N.Y., 1983), 21. I am indebted to Joseph Webber of St. Louis for lending me a copy of *Missouri Waltz*.

49. Transcript, Engineers' Group trial, 3402, Federal Records Center.

50. Transcript, Engineers' Group trial, 3648, Federal Records Center; *Sunday Star*, Dec. 30, 1945.

51. *Boston Globe*, Jan. 5, 1946.

52. Ibid.; *Boston Herald*, Jan. 8, 1946.

53. *Boston Post*, Jan. 8, 1946; *New York Times*, Jan. 9, 20, 1949.

54. *New York Times*, Jan. 19, 1946.

55. *Boston Herald*, Jan. 20, 1946.

56. *Boston Post*, Jan. 20, 1946; *Boston Herald*, Feb. 19, 1946.

57. *New York Times*, Feb. 19, 1946; *Boston Globe*, Feb. 19, 1946; *Boston Herald*, Feb. 19, 1946.

58. *Boston Herald*, Feb. 22, 1946; *Time*, Feb. 22, 1946.

59. Private interviews with Charles Murphy, Robert Bergenheim, William Morrissey, Peter Caparell, Robert Healy, Robert Vose, and Jack Hynes. See also article by Peter Caparell in *The Real Paper* (Boston), Dec. 19, 1973; Hillel Levine and Lawrence Harmon, *The Death of an American Jewish Community: A Tragedy of Good Intentions* (New York, 1992), 14; *Boston Traveler*, Nov. 14, 1945.

60. Private interview with Martin Hanley; *New York Times*, Sept. 27, 1946; Lapomarda, "Maurice Joseph Tobin," 78.

61. *Boston Globe*, July 21, 1944; Lapomarda, "Maurice Joseph Tobin," 100.

62. *Boston Herald*, Sept. 22, 1946.

63. *New York Times*, Nov. 24, 1946; Lapomarda, "Maurice Joseph Tobin," 101.

64. Lapomarda, "Maurice Joseph Tobin," 104; *New York Times*, Nov. 8, 1946.

65. Private interview with Richard Dennis.

66. Dennis, McDonough, Francis Curley interviews.

67. Francis Curley interview.

68. *New York Times*, Jan. 14, June 5, 1947; *Time*, Feb. 5, 1947.

69. *New York Times*, June 19, 1947.

70. *Boston Post*, June 17–19, 1947.

71. Undated newspaper clipping (1947), Term 4, author's files; originals of unidentified clippings are in Curley Scrapbooks, James Michael Curley Collection, College of the Holy Cross, Worcester, Mass.; *Boston Post*, June 17, 1945.

72. *Boston Post*, June 25, 1947.

73. *New York Times*, May 27, 1947.

74. *Boston Herald*, June 25–27, 1947.

75. *Boston Post*, June 27, 1947.

76. *Boston Post*, June 22–29, 1947.

77. *Boston Post*, June 27, 1947.

78. See Judge Proctor's decision, Term 4, author's files; original is in transcript, Engineers' Group trial, Federal Records Center.

79. *Boston Herald*, June 27, 1947; *Boston Post*, June 27, 1947; *Boston Globe*, June 27, 1947.

80. O'Connor, work in progress, chap. 2, p. 9.

81. *Boston Globe*, June 27, 28, 1947; *Boston Herald*, June 27, 1947.

82. Undated newspaper clipping, Term 4, author's files; *Boston Herald*, June 27, 1947; *Boston Post*, June 27, 1947; *Boston Globe*, June 27, 1947.

83. *Boston Traveler*, July 27, 1947.

84. My thanks to Ken Gloss of the Brattle Book Shop for making Curley's letters from this period available to me; see also Caparell article cited in note 59 above.

85. *Boston Herald*, Nov. 13, 1948.

86. Hamilton interview; *Time*, July 3, 1947; Herbert S. Parmet, *Jack: The Struggles of John F. Kennedy* (New York, 1980), 183–84; James MacGregor Burns, *John Kennedy: A Political Profile* (New York, 1959), 92.

87. *Boston Post*, Nov. 26, 1947.

88. *Boston Globe*, Nov. 26, 1947.

89. *Boston Globe*, Nov. 27, 1947.

90. *Boston Post*, Nov. 26, 1947.

91. *Boston Globe*, Nov. 28, 1947; Bergenheim interview.

92. *Boston Post*, June 29, 1947.

93. *Boston Globe*, Nov. 29, 1947; O'Connor, work in progress, chap. 2, pp. 11–12; Morrissey interview.

94. William P. Marchione, Jr., "The 1949 Boston Charter Reform," *New England Quarterly* (Sept. 1976): 381.

95. Ibid., 385.

96. Ibid., 382.

97. *New York Times*, May 16, 1948; Marchione, "The 1949 Boston Charter Reform," 391; Steven P. Erie, *Rainbow's End: Irish-Americans and the Dilemmas of Urban Machine Politics, 1840–1985* (Berkeley, Calif., 1988), 177.

98. *New York Times*, May 16, 1948; Marchione, "The 1949 Boston Charter Reform," 387.

99. *Boston Post*, Feb. 17, 1948.

100. *Boston Post*, July 15, 1948; Charles Angoff, "Curley and the Boston Irish," *American Mercury*, Nov. 1948, 619.

101. Confidential interview.

102. Marchione, "The 1949 Boston Charter Reform," 391.

103. Ibid., 391–92.

104. Confidential interview.

105. Ibid.; *Boston Herald*, Sept. 4, 1949.

106. *New York Times*, May 30, 1949.

107. *Boston Herald*, Oct. 7, 1949; Mar. 15, 1964; O'Connor, work in progress, chap. 2, pp. 17–23; *Boston Herald*, Nov. 3, 1949.

108. O'Connor, work in progress, chap. 2, p. 25.

109. *Boston Herald*, Sept. 14, 15, 1949.

110. *Boston Herald*, Oct. 20, 1949.

111. *Boston Herald*, Oct. 18, Sept. 14, 1949.

112. *Boston Herald*, Oct. 27, 1949.

113. *Boston Herald*, Nov. 2, 1949.

114. Private interview with Jerome Rappaport.

115. Caparell interview.

116. O'Connor, work in progress, chap. 2, p. 21.

117. *Boston Herald*, Sept. 20, 1949; Edwin O'Connor, *The Last Hurrah* (Boston, 1956), 375.

118. *Boston Herald*, Sept. 18, 1949; Bergenheim interview; *Boston Herald*, Sept. 20, 1949.

119. Private interview with George Brockway.

120. *Boston Herald*, Sept. 15, 1949.

121. *Boston Herald*, Oct. 18, 1949.

122. *Boston Herald*, Nov. 5, 1949.

123. *Boston Herald*, Nov. 8, 1949; Jack Hynes interview.

Epilogue

1. *Boston Herald*, Dec. 30, 1949.

2. *Boston Herald*, Dec. 31, 1949.

3. Edwin O'Connor, *The Last Hurrah* (Boston, 1956), 374.

4. Steven P. Erie, *Rainbow's End: Irish-Americans and the Dilemmas of Urban Machine Politics, 1840–1985* (Berkeley, Calif., 1988), 133, 17.

5. William V. Shannon, *The American Irish* (New York, 1963), 228, 203; Stephen Thernstrom, *The Other Bostonians: Poverty and Progress in the American Metropolis, 1880–1970* (Cambridge, Mass., 1973), 167 (emphasis in original); Douglas Madsen and Peter G. Snow, *The Charismatic Bond: Political Behavior in Time of Crisis* (Cambridge, Mass., 1991), 150.

6. Details of this tragic day are taken from the *Boston Herald, Boston Post, Boston Globe, Boston Traveler, Boston Daily Record, Boston American*, and the *New York Times*, issues for Feb. 12–15, 1950, as well as from private interviews with Lauretta Bremner Sliney, John Evans-Harrington, Richard Dennis, Peter Caparell, and Francis X. Curley; see also *Boston Globe Sunday Magazine*, July 25, 1971.

7. Doris Kearns Goodwin, *The Fitzgeralds and the Kennedys: An American Saga* (New York, 1987), 746, 748.

8. *New York Times*, Apr. 15, 1950.

9. *Boston Herald*, Sept. 16, 1951.

10. *Boston Herald*, Sept. 24, 1951.

11. Alfred Steinberg, *The Bosses* (New York, 1972), 196.

12. *Boston Herald*, Sept. 27, 1951.

13. *Boston Herald*, Sept. 3, 1951; William Jay Foley, "Public Speaking in the Political Career of James Michael Curley" (Ph.D. diss., University of Wisconsin, 1952), 77.

14. Private interview with Edward J. McCormack; *Boston Post*, Nov. 7, 1951.

15. *Boston Post*, Nov. 8, 1951.

16. McCormack interview.

17. Thomas P. O'Neill, Jr., with William Novak, *Man of the House: The Life and Political Memoirs of Speaker Tip O'Neill* (New York, 1987), 70–71; *New York Times*, Aug. 31, Sept. 18, 7, 1952.

18. Herbert S. Parmet, *Jack: The Struggles of John F. Kennedy* (New York, 1980), 242; Francis Curley interview; private interview with George Cabot Lodge, Jr. Peter Allen, an assistant of Curley's, denied that Curley had endorsed Lodge; see Allen letter, Frank Howland Collection, Boston Public Library.

19. *New York Times*, Nov. 24, 1953; May 4, 1954; *Boston Globe*, June 6, 1954.

20. *Boston Globe*, Sept. 22, 1955.

21. William Butler Yeats, "Cuchulain's Fight with the Sea," in *The Collected Poems of William Butler Yeats* (New York, 1966), 36.

22. *Boston Globe*, July 20, 1953; Francis Curley interview.

23. O'Neill with Novak, *Man of the House*, 71–73.

24. Private interviews with John Quigley and Thomas Eliot.

25. For biographical details on Edwin O'Connor see the introduction by Arthur M. Schlesinger, Jr., to *The Best and Last of Edwin O'Connor* (Boston, 1970), 3–35.

26. Shaun O'Connell, *Imagining Boston: A Literary Landscape* (Boston, 1990), 129; O'Connor, *The Last Hurrah*, 216.

27. *Saturday Review*, Feb. 4, 1956; *The New Republic*, Mar. 12, 1956; *The New Yorker*, Feb. 16, 1956. For Curley's "ahss" see O'Neill with Novak, *Man of the House*, 32.

28. *The New Yorker*, Feb. 16, 1956; Francis Curley interview; *New York Times*, Feb. 25, 1956.

29. Edwin O'Connor, "James Michael Curley and the Last Hurrah," *Atlantic Monthly*, Sept. 1961.

30. James Michael Curley, "Hurrah for Curley by Curley," *Life*, Sept. 10, 1956, 41; Schlesinger introduction, *The Best and Last of Edwin O'Connor*, 15.

31. Private interview with John Henry Cutler; *New York Times*, Aug. 27, 1956.

32. *Saturday Review*, May 27, 1957.

33. A transcript of the interview is in Howland Collection; Francis Curley interview; *Boston Globe*, May 6, 1956; Steinberg, *The Bosses*, 197. For "Person to Person" see clips in the extraordinary documentary film *Scandalous Mayor* by Thomas Lennon Productions for the PBS television series "The American Experience."

34. *New York Times*, Dec. 29, 1956.

35. O'Connell, *Imagining Boston*, 125.

36. Tag Gallagher, *John Ford: The Man and His Films* (Berkeley, Calif., 1986), 2, 8; private interview with Elliot Norton. See also Schlesinger introduction, *The Best and Last of Edwin O'Connor*, 16.

37. *New York Times*, Oct. 24, 1958.

38. Anderson to Curley, Apr. 18, 1958; Curley to Kelley, Apr. 28, 1958; Anderson to Howland, Mar. 15, 1959, Howland Collection.

39. Francis Curley interview.

Index

❖   ❖   ❖   ❖

Springfield News, 280
Springfield Republican, 295
Springfield Union, 356
St. Denis, Ruth, 174
St. Louis Post-Dispatch, 177
Staley, Delbert Moyer, 14, 319–323
State Board of Tax Appeals, 351–352, 356
Stebbins, (U.S. Civil Service) Commissioner, 78, 81
Stevens, George M., 193
Stevenson, Adlai, 510
Stickland, Francis, 365
Stimson, Henry L., 442
Stone, Elihu, 244
Stone, I. F., 463
Storey, Charles M., 353–354
Storey, Moorfield, 181–182
Storrow, James Jackson, 103, 119, 138, 166, 489
Strandway, 164, 230
Strange Interlude (O'Neill), 273
Strong, Josiah, 49
Strout, Richard, 442
Students for Hynes, 492
Sullivan, Daniel P., 192
Sullivan, John A., 156, 161, 173, 194
Sullivan, John L., 75, 98
Sullivan, Nellie, 307
Sullivan, Roger, 339
Sullivan & Daly (plumbing supply company), 192
Sumner, Charles, 84
Swanson, Claude A., 327
Sweeney, Catherine, 503
Sweeney, Frances, 452

Taft, Nellie, 121–122
Taft, William Howard, 115, 121, 125, 132–134
Tague, Peter F., 208–211, 262
Tammany Club, 74–80, 108, 377, 416.
    See also Pro Bono Publico Club
  election successes/losses, 87, 190
  founding of, 71–72
  hiring of repeaters by, 87
  pressure on city employees to support, 160
  removal of Thomas F. Curley from, 96–97
  social services of, 87
  support of Curley in civil service case, 82, 88–89
  violent behavior of members, 95–98
  work in Curley's first mayoral election, 144
Tammany Hall, 71, 126, 188–189, 255, 256

Taussig, Frank, 349
Tax Dodgers, The (Irey), 402
Taylor, Gene, 187
Taylor, John I., 476–477
Tech House, 87
That Man Curley (Hynes), 483
Thayer, W. R., 83
Thernstrom, Stephan, 22n, 501
Thieman, K. E., 475
Third Order of St. Francis, 376
Thomas, Norman, 313
Thorpe, Jim, 237
Thout, John V., 385
350 The Jamaicaway house. *See* Jamaicaway house
Thurber, O. C. T., 424
Time, 320, 447
Timilty, Diamond Jim, 157, 163
Timilty, Joseph F., 404, 450, 456, 508
Tinkham, George Holden, 407–408
Tobin, James (brother), 407, 408, 409, 458
Tobin, James (father), 405, 406
Tobin, Maurice J., 336, 405–416, 476–477, 483, 484, 486, 505, 511
  anti-Semitism and, 451, 452
  civil rights speech by, 487
  Cocoanut Grove fire and, 459
  Curley's support for Bradford against, 471–472
  death, 512
  as governor, 458
  as mayor, 430–431
  mayoral campaign of, 1940, 431, 433–434
  as Al Smith supporter, 307
Tonn, Joan, 87
Townsend Plan, 418
Tracy, Spencer, 6, 521
Tremont Temple, 149, 151
Trevelyan, Charles, 20
Trilling, Lionel, 102
Trotter, James, 176
Trotter, William Monroe, 176–184, 211, 262
Trout, Charles, 33, 41, 84, 151, 164–165
Truman, Harry, 463, 479, 480–481, 486, 505, 507
Truman committee, 443–445, 446
Tuchman, Barbara, 119
Tufts, Nathan, 196–198, 221
Two Companies, 401–402

Union Club, 221
Union party, 395
Unitarianism, 24, 435, 436
Uzcudun, Paulino, 237